DESIGNS IN DIPLOMACY

DESIGNS IN DIPLOMACY

Pages from European Diplomatic History
in the Twentieth Century

by MARIO TOSCANO

Translated and edited by George A. Carbone

The Johns Hopkins Press
Baltimore and London

Earlier versions of Chapters I, IV, V, and VII were published in *Pagine di storia diplomatica contemporanea*, Vol. II: *Origini e vicende della seconda guerra mondiale* by A. Giuffrè, Milan, 1963; © 1963 by Mario Toscano. An earlier version of Chapter II was published as *L'Italia e gli accordi Tedesco-Sovietici dell'agosto 1939* by G. C. Sansoni, Florence, 1955; © 1955 by Mario Toscano. An earlier version of Chapter III was published as *Una mancata intesa Italo-Sovietica nel 1940 e 1941* by G. C. Sansoni, Florence, 1955; © 1955 by Mario Toscano. An earlier version of Chapter VI was published as "Sondaggi italiani per uscire dal conflitto prima della caduta di Mussolini" in *Clio* for April, 1965.

To My Daughter Fabrizia

PREFACE

With the exception of Chapter VI, "Italian Soundings to Abandon the Conflict Prior to Mussolini's Fall," the essays and articles appearing herein were first published prior to 1963 in various professional journals. Access to the documents preserved in the Historical Archives of the Ministry of Foreign Affairs of the Italian government made it possible to undertake a serious revision of these inquiries, which added clarifying detail without, however, fundamentally altering the basic conclusions reached previously. In 1963 these articles and essays, as revised and enlarged, were published in my *Pagine di storia diplomatica contemporanea*, Vol II: *Origini e vicende della seconda guerra mondiale* (Milan: A. Giuffrè, 1963).

In the five years that have elapsed since publication of the revised edition of the studies comprising this volume, a number of excellent interpretative works and some new documentary materials have appeared on all of the subjects treated in these studies. Therefore, in the preparation of this translation the time seemed propitious to make certain indicated revisions, largely in the interest of further clarifying specific points and updating bibliographical materials.

I am greatly indebted to Professors Pietro Pastorelli and Gian Luca Andrè of the University of Rome: to the former for his labors in revising the article "Italian Soundings to Abandon the Conflict Prior to Mussolini's Fall," and to the latter for handling the tedious work involved in revising the other studies contained in this American edition.

MARIO TOSCANO

Rome
September 4, 1968

CONTENTS

DESIGNS IN DIPLOMACY

I.

FAILURE OF THE HUNGARIAN-RUMANIAN RAPPROCHEMENT OF 1920

*Summary: 1. Premise. 2. Eastern Europe immediately after the Peace Confer-
ence. 3. Positive and negative forces in Hungarian-Rumanian relations. 4. The
first references to the advisability of a collaboration between Budapest and
Bucharest. 5. The initial reserve of the two governments when presented with
the prospects of a rapprochement. 6. Italy's mediatory efforts and the first steps
taken toward a renewal of relations between the two countries. 7. The problem
of a Hungarian-Rumanian entente within the framework of the Franco-Magyar
accords. 8. The Hungarian action in Warsaw paralleling the Quai d'Orsay
mediation. 9. The Magyar diplomatic efforts in Paris to launch negotiations
with Rumania promptly on the basis of a moderate territorial revision of the
Treaty of Trianon. 10. Growing obstacles to the realization of the initial program based on French mediation. 11. The negative evolution of the general
situation accentuated by the efforts of Prague to draw Rumania into the Little
Entente and the tenacious attempts by Budapest to continue the attempts at
rapprochement with Bucharest even on a reduced basis. 12. Paléologue's fall
and the reversal of French policy with respect to the Little Entente; its negative
repercussions. 13. The frustration of further efforts to move against the current
by the opposition of Take Jonescu. 14. The resolute prosecution of Magyar
diplomatic action in the face of stiffening resistance by the Rumanian foreign
ministers. 15. Conclusion.*

1

The material contained in the first volume of the Hungarian collection
of diplomatic documents relating to the period immediately following the
end of World War I[1] has already made it possible to investigate several
important episodes in Danubian-Balkan policy for those years.[2] This brief
article will reconstruct, on the bases of the above-mentioned material,[3] a
particularly interesting page of diplomatic history relating to the efforts
made in 1920 to realize a Hungarian-Rumanian rapprochement. This

---

* An earlier version of this chapter appeared as "Un Mancato riavvicinamento
Ungaro-romeno del 1920," *Rivista di studi politici,* III (1941).
[1] Francis Deak and Dezsó Ujváry, eds., *Papers and Documents Relating to the
Foreign Relations of Hungary 1919–1920* (Budapest: Royal Hungarian Ministry
for Foreign Affairs, 1939), I. Hereafter these are cited as *H.D.*
[2] Mario Toscano, "L'accordo revisionista franco-ungherese del 1920," *Politica*
(1941), pp. 142–45.
[3] I have also made use of a number of documents, largely unclassified and unpublished, located in the Historical Archives of the Italian Foreign Ministry. Hereafter these are cited as *I.D.* (Italian Documents).

episode, closely linked to the negotiations for the creation of the Little Entente and to the Franco-Magyar accord of 1920, will help to clarify the complex diplomatic panorama then developing in eastern Europe.

2

Toward the end of 1919 at the close of the great war, the political and diplomatic situation in eastern Europe and the Danube Basin was, at best, extremely confused. A number of the peace treaties (Versailles, St. Germain) were ready for practical application; others (Neuilly, Trianon), already substantively defined by the various commissions at the Peace Conference, were nearing completion in the legal sense, while a number of land areas remained to be precisely defined (Italo-Yugoslav, Russo-Rumanian, Polish-Russian, Polish-Lithuanian, Polish-Czechoslovak frontiers), and the entire eastern question had been reopened for discussion by the armed resistance of the Turkish National Assembly. The cycle of provisional military occupations was drawing to a close, but the souls of men, severely tried by long anguish, were still filled with rancor and were often moved by a desire for revenge rather than a desire to collaborate. The new territorial alignment of Europe was clearly developing, but the work of reconstruction yet to be accomplished remained immense. The sudden demise of three great empires had left a deep void which had to be filled by new diplomatic structures, while the Bolshevik unknown remained a serious menace. Everywhere the economic crisis, precipitated by the devastations of war, civil conflict, and the breakup of previously existing large units, was assuming extremely serious proportions. Everyone recognized that it was impossible to delay further attempts to move toward a better solution for this huge complex of problems, but the choice of ways and means to resolve them was a delicate and difficult one. Europe stood at an important crossroads but, perhaps, was not yet fully aware of it. Yet the decisions taken at that time were to decide the future destinies of the countries, either favoring a real collaboration between the powers or condemning them to a sterile and fatal antagonism. It was in that period, after a great deal of uncertainty and vacillation, that the new diplomatic system for eastern Europe was to take shape gradually and from which World War II was to emerge. It is in this setting and in that period that the attempted Magyar-Rumanian rapprochement is to be placed.

3

The political forces that urged the diplomats of the governments involved to arrange a fruitful collaboration between Budapest and Bucharest were varied and complex, direct and indirect, internal and external.

Hungary, emerging from the conflict terribly mutilated, realized the absolute necessity of putting an end to the isolation that threatened her. Moreover, it was also imperative that the open hostility of her neighbors be prevented from creating a formal and general alliance which would make her encirclement total and final. Among the new states created at Versailles, only Poland nurtured sentiments of traditional and abiding friendship toward Hungary and had nothing to fear from Magyar territorial claims. Thus, Warsaw appeared to offer the best prospects. But Poland, despite her sentimental inclination to seek more intimate relations with Hungary and her desire to share a common frontier with the latter in the Carpathians,[4] in addition to being involved at that very time in a bloody and uncertain conflict with Russia, was limited in her diplomatic activity by her anti-Soviet ties with Rumania and also by the fact that she was apparently very sensitive to the will of the Quai d'Orsay. Thus, a long-lasting clarification of relations between Budapest and Bucharest remained indispensable to the formal understanding between Poland and Hungary championed by the Hungarian volunteers on the battlefields.[5] Warsaw also apparently supported the idea of a three-power pact but, since it could not be realized, settled for the bilateral alliance with Rumania. Moreover, Hungary was convinced that a rapprochement with Rumania would be very advantageous for its nationals residing within the borders of the now enlarged Rumania, as well as for the prompt economic recovery of the country. And, of course, the idea that it might eventually lead to Rumania's returning a portion of the lands assigned to her by the Entente had never been abandoned.

A number of significant factors were simultaneously at work in Rumania to the same end. The first was the Soviet unknown. This made the question of Slavic predominance in the Balkans acute. The problem had been foreseen by Italian diplomats as early as October, 1914, in prophetic terms, and it was obvious that this threat would only be countered successfully by the creation of a non-Slavic bloc in the area.[6] Second, there

---

[4] H.D., I, Docs. 94, 96, 126, 194, 321, 322, 739, 765.

[5] Ibid., Docs. 554, 595, 621, 665, 712.

[6] On October 7, 1914, the Italian Ambassador to Petrograd, Carlotti, told the Rumanian Minister in that capital, Diamandi, that he considered it necessary to go beyond the first Italo-Rumanian accord of September 23 but that "once these territories have been acquired, it is to our interest to prevent the reduction of Austria-Hungary and the total collapse of the balance with Slavism and the creation of the Duchies of Bohemia and Croatia. It is of interest to block Balkan Slavism by a counter-balance consisting of Greece, Rumania, Albania, and Turkey under our leadership." Diamandi, "Ma mission en Russie," Revue des deux mondes, November 15, 1930; L. Aldrovandi Marescotti, Nuovi ricordi (Milan: Mondadori, 1938), pp. 194–95. See also H.D., I, Doc. 415.

was nothing more satisfactory than a direct rapprochement with Hungary, which would favor consolidation of recent gains, renewal of economic life in the new provinces, and elimination of the spiritual and material disaffection of minority groups. The vicissitudes of war had sorely tried the fabric of the young state, which now had also to face the enormous problems of reconstruction. Moreover, Rumania was in urgent need of a long period of peace so that she could profitably devote all of her energies to these problems. Any extremist position could very soon have involved Rumania in new hazards, and this involvement would, above all, have meant the elimination of those sound premises for loyal internal and external collaboration (especially by the minorities) so essential for political activity seeking to produce sound foundations for the state.

The moderate forces for peace prevalent in Budapest and represented by the clearest-thinking statesmen in Bucharest encountered emergent opposition of equal strength in both countries.

Ultraconservative extremists, uncompromising in their insistence on Hungary's acquisition of all the ancient domains under the crown of St. Stephen, continued to survive in Hungary and rejected every compromise. However, because of the circumstances, their influence was still very modest. The natural reaction to the recent territorial mutilations and the bitter humiliations, the rising spirit of revenge, though certainly comprehensible, had to be put aside in favor of the more immediate problems of life. A prompt acceptance of the first overtures for collaboration would undoubtedly have reduced the drive of the traditional forces and, above all, would have eliminated a not indifferent part of the most firmly based Magyar claims. The problem of revision would have been confined to a few well-defined sectors without being complicated and exasperated by the economic and spiritual tensions of the minorities.

The situation was entirely different in Rumania. In the first place, the choice between the two policies, to the extent that it was not conditioned by the imperative necessities of life, seemed to be an entirely free one. The intransigent nationalist forces were at the peak of their power: the psychological reaction foreseen by Lloyd George was thus allowed to take place the moment the military clauses were introduced.[7] External pressures and the bad example set by other nations strengthened the hand of the less well-advised and the less mature elements. The dangers associated with this political course were understood only by a select, farsighted minority. It is the privilege of very few and, in any event, a very dis-

---

[7] Meeting of the Supreme Council, May 15, 1919. For the minutes of this meeting, see L. Aldrovandi Marescotti, *Guerra diplomatica* (Milan: Mondadori, 1936), p. 351.

agreeable task, to run counter to the general current and to oppose the least noble of human instincts. The diplomatic activity under investigation here took place within the framework of the two alternative courses.

4

The occasion for clarification of Hungarian-Rumanian relations paralleling a close Polish-Rumanian collaboration as a premise for the creation of a bloc of these three powers is clearly mentioned for the first time in an interesting dispatch by the Hungarian representative in Warsaw, Count Csekonics, on December 11, 1919.[8] In this report, the Magyar diplomat pointed out that the Polish government was well disposed toward Budapest,[9] but his primary attention appeared to be focused on the evolution of Rumanian-Polish relations. The fact that Count Csekonics, in his colloquy with the Polish Secretary of State, Skrzynski, referred directly to the repercussions produced by the Rumanian "atrocities" as obstacles to the immediate creation of a common bloc which would include Rumania and Hungary suggests that the proposal had been discussed previously by the two governments. This political tendency of the Hungarian cabinet seems to be confirmed by an allusion to it, accompanied by unfavorable comments, by the chief of the political section of the French mission to Kassa, Doctor Eck, who, a few days later, in a colloquy with Count Semsey, affirmed that "according to his information there survived in Hungary a rather influential group advocating an alliance with Rumania."[10]

Equally significant references to the question were also made on the Rumanian side. On January 3, 1920, the Rumanian Minister to Vienna, Isopescu-Grecul, had an important meeting with his Hungarian colleague, Gratz, on the matter.[11] The Rumanian diplomat expressed the opinion that "the non-Slavic peoples in Central and Eastern Europe are threatened by many dangers which they can only resist by eliminating conflicts and establishing friendly relations. He himself is in favour of such policy and he knows that Prime Minister Vaida-Voevod is of the same opinion."

His Magyar counterpart expressed his complete agreement with this premise and recalled the tragic consequences of the Rumanian military occupation during the summer of 1919 and of the treatment inflicted on

---

[8] *H.D.*, I, Doc. 51.

[9] "Neither I nor anyone else who may succeed me will be able to carry out a foreign policy that does not take into account a close collaboration with Hungary," stated the Polish Secretary of State for Foreign Affairs, Skrzynski.

[10] *H.D.*, I, Doc. 61.

[11] *Ibid.*, Doc. 67.

the Magyar minorities in Transylvania.[12] These events notwithstanding, he believed that the good will of both parties should be employed in seeking an understanding. The same Isopescu, on January 23, 1920, informed the Secretary of the Hungarian Legation in Vienna of his government's refusal to adhere to an Austrian-Czechoslovak accord directed against Hungary.[13] Rumania preferred a conservative power to a Communist one as a neighbor, and for this reason she would never oppose the restoration of the Hapsburgs in Budapest. From Vienna, one week later, the Hungarian government was informed of the possibility of exploiting the eventual reactivation of the arms plant at Cespel in order to replenish the supply of Polish munitions in the struggle against the Soviet Union, as a point of departure for a rapprochement with Rumania and the participation in a common anti-Bolshevik front.[14]

5

These positions represented nothing more than the views of individuals, and while they are interesting, they did not commit the respective governments in any way. They were a useful first step, a significant premise, but the road was a long one. No decision had been made by one side or the other regarding the policy to adopt. Before this phase could be reached, a more detailed development of the ideas involved and a clarification of positions was required.

An important dispatch from the Hungarian Foreign Minister, Sommsich, to the Magyar Minister in Vienna on February 6, 1920, revealed the first reaction of the Hungarian Cabinet to these future prospects.[15] After approving Gratz's position in the latter's colloquies with Isopescu, the Magyar Foreign Minister added:

Guided by practical considerations, I am also in favour of a policy which,

[12] In a colloquy which took place on December 29, 1919, with Anmbrò, an official in the Hungarian Foreign Ministry, the Italian High Commissioner in Budapest, Cerruti, declared that he too had warned Diamandi of the unfortunate consequence of the conduct of the Rumanians in the occupied territories and that he had expressed his disapproval of such a myopic policy. On that occasion, Diamandi had affirmed that only the military authorities were responsible for that error because they ignored the instructions of the Rumanian Foreign Ministry, which hoped to effect a conciliation with the Hungarians. Moreover, the Italian diplomat told Anmbrò that he believed that Hungary would have to acquire friends and that a friendly agreement with Rumania, out of consideration for the cordial relations that existed between Italy and the latter, would save Hungary from isolation. Unfortunately, the differences between Rumania and Hungary were so great that he could not see how they could be bridged. *H.D.*, I, Doc. 65.

[13] *Ibid.*, Doc. 98.

[14] *Ibid.*, Doc. 106.

[15] *Ibid.*, Doc. 119.

without abandoning the ultimate objective of regaining a substantial part of our lost territories, recognizes the immediate necessities arising from our present situation and seeks to find a *modus vivendi* through friendlier relations with our neighbors. The basis of rapprochement already exists in the undeniable economic interdependence of all Danubian states. Therefore I believe that, for the time being at least, rapprochement should be sought in the economic field. In following this road, we can demonstrate our specific intentions without in any way prejudicing our future policies. Nevertheless we must be careful not to take the initiative because our neighbours, still drunk from victory, would doubtless regard any such step on our part as a sign of weakness. . . . It would be desirable to ascertain whether Mr. Isopescu-Grecul acts and speaks on his own initiative or pursuant to instructions from his Government. In any event, considering the nervousness of Rumania threatened by the Bolsheviks and plagued by internal difficulties, it seems more opportune to await proposals from Rumania. In your subsequent conversations with the Rumanian Minister you can suggest to him the idea that the Hungarian Government would certainly not decline to negotiate concerning certain concrete issues. You should also emphasize that it is not the fault of Hungary that relations between the two countries are not better. Finally you should make clear that in your opinion territorial questions ought not to form part of such negotiations as a matter of diplomatic courtesy toward the Peace Conference.

As is evident, Count Sommsich inclined toward a policy of watchful waiting before deciding on a definite course of action. In addition to the reasons given in his dispatch, two other considerations guided him in his views. In the first place, the work of the Paris Peace Conference toward the conclusion of a peace treaty had not yet completely clarified the situation. Second, Budapest still had great faith in the beneficial results to be derived from the direct negotiations going on with France for a rapprochement between the two countries and the effects these might have on the ultimate nature of that understanding. Yet, despite the above-mentioned reticence, they had traveled a long way from the heated tension of six months earlier. It was not so much a matter of the principle of collaboration that was being questioned as the means of arriving at a more fruitful rapport between the two countries. The positive premises for a rapprochement were not being challenged—far from it. It is understandable, therefore, that under the simultaneous pressure of other factors, such as the efforts toward peace of a number of powers, along with the understanding in principle reached with the Quai d'Orsay on the bases for a moderate revision of the territorial arrangements, Magyar policy assumed a clear and precise character.

The Hungarian diplomatic documents do not, of course, permit us to observe from so close a vantage point the contemporaneous and parallel orientation of the Rumanian statesmen. However, the precise position taken by the Rumanian government vis-à-vis the above-mentioned Czech

initiatives and the preliminary steps in preparing the groundwork for the
Little Entente suggest that Rumania, too, in the early phases adopted a
prudent, temporizing position. The internal political situation, the Bolshevik threat, and the still undetermined territorial settlement undoubtedly
worked to produce this attitude.

6

Meanwhile, in Hungary, the necessity for prompt restoration of diplomatic relations with Rumania was rapidly gaining acceptance. Obviously,
this restoration was an essential premise to a rapprochement between the
two countries. In this initial phase, the mediating and moderating activity
of Italy was important[16] but gradually declined in importance as the
direct Franco-Magyar negotiations under Paléologue's leadership moved
toward a positive conclusion. The spirit of moderation of Italian foreign
policy and the Rumanian government's comprehension of the Hungarian
problems were as well known to Budapest as the ties of friendship between Italy and Rumania. Thus, it was logical that Budapest should turn
to Italy not only as a useful channel through which to achieve the first
steps toward a rapprochement with Rumania, but also because the Italian
government—in contrast with France's later action—had no intention of
binding Hungary to accords that limited her freedom of action.[17] In
February, 1920, Count Sommsich approached the Political Commissioner
to Budapest, Cerruti, asking that it be suggested to the Rumanian government as soon as possible that the latter send a representative to Budapest
in order to establish a direct contact between the two countries.[18]

The request—which the Hungarian representative to Rome, Count
Nemes, delivered on March 2[19]—was promptly accepted by the *Consulta*.[20] The Italian Minister to Bucharest, Alberto Martin Franklin,
undertook colloquies with Rumanian political leaders and officials on the

---

[16] It should be noted that in this same period an analogous action, albeit far less
than the Italian one, was undertaken by the British government. (Cf. *Documents
on British Foreign Policy 1919–1939* [London: Her Majesty's Stationery Office,
1962], 1st series, XII, Doc. 114, and *ibid.*, note 5. Hereafter cited as *B.D.*)

[17] *H.D.*, I, Doc. 155.

[18] Cerruti to Scialoja, telegram, February 16, 1920, *I.D.* On that occasion Count
Sommsich declared that Hungary had no aggressive intentions toward Rumania but
desired that the latter assure her that she would not attack her if Hungary were
fighting on another front. Count Sommsich alluded to a possible action in Slovakia
aimed at reacquiring lost territory and creating a common frontier with Poland. The
Hungarians hoped that this action would be tolerated by the victorious powers in
view of the necessity of strengthening the anti-Bolshevik front.

[19] *H.D.*, I, Doc. 155.

[20] Bonin to Martin Franklin, telegram, February 28, 1920, *I.D.*

matter,[21] and on March 5 he was able to announce that, according to the assurances received, a diplomatic representative would be sent soon.[22] However, his contacts had also confirmed Rumania's complete lack of confidence in Hungary's real aims and its decision to avoid important concessions, so that whatever accord was reached was so precarious as to be of no real value.[23] This situation not only limited Italy's moderating activities but also alerted the *Consulta* to proceed with greater caution on the question in order to avoid endangering Italo-Rumanian relations in an attempt to achieve an objective whose realization appeared to be very uncertain.[24]

[21] Martin Franklin telegraphed as follows:

I lose no occasion to counsel the Rumanian government to act with maximum prudence toward the Hungarian government. That government always replies that it is motivated by the friendliest of sentiments but that it is preoccupied by the statements made by Hungarian politicians, by the tone of the Budapest press, and by irredentist organizations of Magyar minorities in Transylvania, which demonstrate that Hungary has not yet abandoned all ideas of revenge. I am convinced that if the Hungarian attitude changed, Rumanians would liberalize their policy in Transylvania and become more friendly toward Hungary. In any event, there is no idea here of attacking Hungary because the Rumanians are too much concerned about the hostility of all of their neighbors.

Telegram to Scialoja, March 2, 1920, *I.D.*
[22] Martin Franklin to Scialoja, telegram, March 5, 1920, *I.D.*
[23] Auriti, the Italian Chargé d'Affaires in Bucharest, reported as follows:

The major stumbling block to an understanding, insofar as the Rumanians are concerned, is to be found in the conviction that for a long time to come the Hungarians will not forgive the loss of Transylvania and will not resign themselves to it. Now, from what Cav. Cerruti reports in his telegram of February 16, that is, that while the Hungarian government seeks assurance that the Rumanians will not attack them in the event of their own attack against the Czechoslovaks, Budapest proposes in due time to make war against Rumania as well and, if this proves the pugnacious character and the love of country of the Magyars, it also proves that Rumanian suspicions are well founded. As long as there are manifestations of this nature, either prompted by declarations of the Budapest government or by the plots of private citizens in Transylvania, there is no reason to believe that Rumania's attitude toward Hungary will change. The Magyars should consider whether the advantages to be gained from their present attitude are greater than what could be obtained by adopting a different approach toward the Rumanians and then decide upon a course of action according to their own ideals and interests. However, they cannot request the aid of this Royal Legation to obtain both benefits, since this Royal Legation would encounter impossible obstacles producing no advantages to them and rebounding to our own disadvantage.

Auriti to Scialoja, telegram, March 30, 1920, *I.D.*
[24] This aspect was particularly stressed by Martin Franklin, who revealed that Bucharest grew increasingly suspicious of Italy following the pro-Hungarian and pro-Bulgarian manifestations in Italian policy. He added, "In this situation it is my judgment that a discussion with the present government aimed at inducing it to

On March 23 the Secretary-General of the Hungarian Foreign Ministry again instructed the Hungarian representative, Count Nemes, to call the attention of the Italian government to the fact that "the Rumanians have not yet sent a diplomatic mission to Budapest, although it would seem to be in the interests of both countries to reduce the tension at present characterizing their relations."[25] The Italian Minister, then present in Rome, informed the Hungarian diplomat that the instructions he had received ordered him "to urge in Bucharest the establishment of a Rumanian mission at Budapest and, in general, to work for rapprochement between Hungary and Rumania and thus to forestall an agreement between Rumania and Yugoslavia." However, he also made it clear that good relations between Hungary and Rumania depended, first of all, on the attitude of Budapest. Martin Franklin added that in responsible Rumanian circles a real desire to arrive at a modus vivendi existed and that Italian mediation had been sympathetically received by King Ferdinand, on the understanding that Hungary abandon all actions indicating an intention to reacquire lost territories. Rome clearly understood how impossible it was for Hungary to forever renounce her claims to Transylvania. However, for the moment, a Rumanian-Hungarian accord was of interest to Italy as well as to Hungary. The realization of this goal required great tact and careful diplomacy, and Martin Franklin believed that it would facilitate matters if Hungary, rather than appeal to the Allied Powers, would negotiate a solution of existing problems directly with Rumania.[26]

While this information was colored by Martin Franklin's own opinion (he was seriously concerned over the repercussions provoked in Bucharest by the Italian initiative undertaken in favor of the Magyars), it did indicate clearly the course of action the *Consulta* intended to follow. The Italian diplomat's reference to the Rumanians being disposed to negotiate did not accurately reflect the views he had, up to that moment, expressed in his dispatches or, at the very least, would have required further clarification in order to reflect the situation realistically. In any event, his statements confirmed Rome's real desire to pave the way to Hungarian-Rumanian collaboration, to be achieved via direct negotiations and, there-

---

adopt a less rigid policy toward Hungary, while it certainly would produce no advantages to Europe or to Rumania, would probably work to Italy's disadvantage. It would increase the suspicions against us which have been reawakened in recent days, and our actions would appear as astute double dealing and not as an effort by a disinterested party to contribute to the peace of Europe and to ensure the future of Rumania herself." Martin Franklin to Scialoja, telegram, March 20, 1920, *I.D.*

[25] *H.D.*, I, Doc. 197.
[26] *Ibid.*, Doc. 214.

fore, without the intervention of third parties, an intervention which was not always selfless and well-meaning. However, the plan presupposed reciprocal goodwill, prompting Martin Franklin's appeal to the Magyars not to limit their willingness to eliminate the difficulties existing vis-à-vis the Rumanians to statements alone but to demonstrate their moderation and goodwill in order to achieve the desired goal.

The appeal seemed to have had some effect: on April 11 the Hungarian envoy to Rome personally confirmed to the Italian Foreign Minister the desire of his government to arrive at a modus vivendi with Rumania. He assured him of Budapest's gratitude for Italy's supporting action, and he renewed his appeal that Italy continue to work toward the establishment of a Rumanian mission in Budapest.[27] The selfless, conciliatory position of the Italian government undoubtedly influenced the comportment of the Hungarian envoy, and it certainly had some effect on the gradual positive evolution of Rumanian-Hungarian relations. On April 21 Count Nemes told the Italian Foreign Minister that "in view of Italy's interest I felt that I could not take an *openly* hostile attitude toward Rumania,"[28] and on May 3 the new Hungarian Foreign Minister, Count Teleki, informed Rome of his position on the crucial question in the following terms: "search for a *modus vivendi* is a serious and urgent necessity for both Hungary and Rumania, partly because of our common friends and, even more, because of the danger of bolshevism which threatens us both."[29]

7

With Count Teleki in the Magyar Foreign Ministry, Hungarian diplomacy moved more resolutely toward Magyar-Rumanian collaboration.[30]

[27] *Ibid.*, Doc. 215.
[28] *Ibid.*, Doc. 238.
[29] *Ibid.*, Doc. 251.
[30] The Italian representative in Budapest reported as follows:

Yesterday, the new Foreign Minister told me it was his intention to seek an understanding with Rumania and to this end he counted heavily on Italian support. Among the states surrounding Hungary, Rumania, because of its monarchical form of government and ancient traditions, was the only state with which Hungary could achieve a rapid rapprochement despite the deplorable conduct of the Rumanian army in Hungary. He attributed these excesses to the troops rather than to the Rumanian government. However, it would be necessary that Rumania demonstrate its favorable intention to reopen relations with Hungary by sending a representative to Budapest. I explained to Teleki how much the Italian government had done in the matter and informed him that Rumania had indicated its intention to send to Budapest the former deputy from Transylvania, Mihaly. Teleki, who is also a Transylvanian, noted that, aside from the fact that under the circumstances the Hungarian government would prefer to negotiate with a Rumanian from Rumania proper, he had to admit that Mihaly was, with the exception of

Now, at last, the temporizing phase seemed to have passed, and Budapest began issuing concrete instructions leading toward the establishment of better relations with Rumania. Teleki's point of view on the complex problem has already been noted, and the renewal of relations was pursued with determination through Italy's good offices. In a parallel fashion, Hungary was to undertake similar action in Paris as well as in Warsaw.

During that period Magyar diplomats were extremely active in the French capital: Budapest was banking heavily on the help of the Quai d'Orsay to reduce the territorial demands of the Entente. This goal led to a series of lengthy discussions with Paléologue (then Secretary-General of the French Foreign Ministry and supporter of a pro-Hungarian French policy) aimed at concluding a formal accord between the two governments. These negotiations will be examined in greater detail elsewhere.[31] Here it is primarily necessary to note the way in which, within the framework of those negotiations, the problems separating Budapest and Bucharest were approached. On April 15, in a preliminary note, Paléologue summarized the conversations undertaken by the two parties apropos of the matter in the following terms:

> The questions to be resolved, which at this moment divide Hungary and Rumania, are the most difficult and delicate of all those facing us to resolve. Hungary will offer proof of her evident good will in agreeing to begin conversations with that state with the aim, above all, to resolve the question of her relations with Rumania. It is understood, of course, that in the event it appears useful to proceed along different lines, Hungary will offer no opposition.
>
> The Hungarians declare their firm intention of reestablishing completely satisfactory relations and to arrive at a durable *modus vivendi* between the Hungarian and Rumanian peoples. Given the fact that it is the Magyars of Transylvania who must live together with the Rumanians of Transylvania, it is obvious that the stability of the peace to be achieved will depend entirely on the good relations between those two Transylvanian peoples. Therefore, it is of the greatest importance that before these conversations get underway, the known and

---

Maniu, the former Rumanian deputy from Transylvania, the most moderate in the Rumanian Parliament. Let Mihaly come, providing he comes quickly. Teleki spoke to me of the internal situation in Rumania, pointing out that it was critical and that the Transylvanians, intolerant of the Bucharest government, were agitating for an autonomous administration. He added that the Transylvanians, even under the old Hungarian regime, had always had a strong sense of independence, in part deriving from historical recollections of their independent existence as a Transylvanian principality, so that it is natural that under new domination these feelings should become acute.

Cerruti to Scialoja, telegram, April 30, 1920, I.D.

[31] On these, see Mario Toscano, "L'accordo revisionista franco-magiaro del 1920," *Pagine di storia diplomatica contemporanea*, 2 vols. (Milan: A. Giuffré, 1963), Vol. I, pp. 303–438.

fully qualified representatives of the Hungarians of Transylvania and of the Rumanians of Transylvania be heard.

The following are the bases for a direct accord between Rumania and Hungary.

I. From the national and political viewpoint:

a. Modifications of the common frontiers in such a way as to insure that the territories clearly Magyar in character and forming a united bloc with the bulk of the Magyar race are not taken from Hungary. Authorization to the Swabian peoples living on the edge of the Magyar blocs in territories which are Magyar and Swabian in the majority to decide on their own destiny via plebiscite. Hungary will provide all proofs of her good will in this situation in matters of communications and others which might arise from this new delineation of the frontiers.

b. Regional autonomy for the territories inhabited in the majority by Magyars, Széklers, and Saxons under Rumanian domination. The extent, details, and the guarantees of this autonomy to be arranged by joint decision.

c. Linguistic and religious freedom and material security guaranteed to the Magyar minorities living in an area where Rumanians are in the majority. Effective guarantees are to be incorporated in the text of the peace treaty.

d. Equitable solution to the problem of the old Hungarian state employees along with that of the Hungarian state employees in state-controlled industries.

e. General amnesty for all under political accusation.

II. From the economic viewpoint:

a. Prompt restitution to the extent possible of all rolling stock, industrial and agricultural tools, in addition to the primary materials removed by Rumanian occupation troops and carried off to Rumania beyond the requisition limits determined by the armistice treaty.

b. Conclusion of agreements concerning the following questions: Reciprocal freedom of trade for the greatest possible number of products and particularly raw materials. Fullest possible freedom of rail, postal, and telegraphic communication. Complete freedom and facilitation for depositing funds in both countries. Identical accord and agreement on the questions concerning both regimes.

c. Proportional assumption of the financial obligations contracted by Hungary before and during the war.

d. Unqualified guarantee to Hungary of the right to exploit the salt resources and salt products of Màramaros.[32]

The specific importance of this document is that it is possible to acquire from it a reasonably good idea of the extent of the concessions desired by the Magyars as a basis on which to conclude a lasting agreement with Rumania under French patronage. Keeping in mind the fact that these requests were formulated prior to the conclusion of the Treaty of Trianon, and that the Hungarian government itself recognized that "an agreement or even a *modus vivendi* with our neighbors, to be reached through French mediation, would also entail a heavy moral sacrifice since such an agreement would be interpreted as an implied renunciation of our claim

[32] *H.D.*, I, Doc. 226.

for territorial concession,"[33] it must be agreed that the statement of the problem was reasonable. During the course of the negotiations with Paléologue, the formulation of this question generally remained within the terms outlined above.[34] Yet in the final draft of the Franco-Magyar accord of June 21, these terms were referred to in a note presented by the French High Commissioner to Budapest in language that was extremely vague.[35]

8

In considering the problem of Hungarian-Rumanian relations within the much wider context of political negotiations with the French, it was natural that the general postulation of the question would undergo some modification because of the difficulties involved in achieving the desired objective. The first change was a lessening of Italian interest in the matter,[36] since the Italians openly disapproved of the Franco-Magyar entente.[37] Naturally, Paris had become the focal point of Hungarian diplomatic action. However, before all Magyar illusions regarding the effective-

[33] *Ibid.*, Doc. 242.

[34] *Ibid.*, Docs. 242 (a), 255 (b), 285.

[35] *Ibid.*, Doc. 393.

[36] The first information regarding a possible shift in French policy toward Hungary was transmitted to the *Consulta* by the Legation in Berne. Accame to Scialoja, report, March, 1920, *I.D.* Some time later, the same legation was able to furnish reasonably exact details on the French plan for the economic penetration of Hungary. Orsini to Scialoja, May 20, 1920, *I.D.* This information was also confirmed by Cerruti, the Italian High Commissioner in Budapest, who reported as follows:

Upon my return to Budapest I found the situation completely changed. Hungary is throwing herself into the arms of France. The local press is regularly reprinting articles favorable to Hungary which have appeared in French newspapers and is making every effort to demonstrate that French hostility toward Hungary had been based on inaccurate information on the Hungarian problem and that now this hostility had been replaced by a cordial rapport. The Minister for Foreign Affairs, with whom I spoke yesterday expressing Italy's friendly disposition toward Hungary, according to instructions given to me by Your Excellency and the Prime Minister, told me that in France, too, the same tendencies were evident and that the present attitude of the Quai d'Orsay was far different from that displayed during the Peace Conference. From a long conversation I had yesterday with the Prime Minister I was able to ascertain that negotiations have been under way for a number of weeks with the French aimed at concluding a political accord. The Prime Minister also admitted to me that Hungary was not averse to concluding a binding alliance with France. He added that France had realized the absurdity of its original plan to create a group she would lead composed of Czechoslovakia, Hungary [Rumania?], and Yugoslavia and now, instead, aimed at gathering Poland, Hungary, Rumania, and Bulgaria around her. From what I was able to understand, negotiations are very far along.

Cerruti to Scialoja, telegram, June 1, 1920, *I.D.*

[37] The information transmitted by Cerruti prompted Nitti to telegraph to Scialoja that it was imperative to make every effort to block the formation of a Franco-Hun-

ness of French support were destroyed, Budapest continued to use the good offices of Poland to arrive at an improvement in her own relations with Rumania. This fact confirms the impression gained from reading the documents relative to the so-called Paléologue negotiation that the reaching of a modus vivendi with Bucharest was of major concern to Hungarian statesmen. When it is recalled that, once all hope for a rapid revision of the Treaty of Trianon disappeared, Magyar diplomats continued to seek an accord with Rumania without altering the terms of the peace treaty,[38] this focus on a modus vivendi appears fully justified.

On May 5 Count Teleki instructed his representative in Warsaw, Count Csekonics, to take the initiative in leading the Polish government, giving substance to Pilsudski's vague verbal promises to obtain from Rumania a guarantee of neutrality in the event that Czechoslovakia should attack Hungary.[39] However, this interesting undertaking did not bring immediate results because, shortly thereafter, the Polish Foreign Minister undertook an extended mission outside the country. The Hungarian government took advantage of this delay to set the problem of Magyar-Rumanian relations within the broader framework of negotiations with Poland, which were designed to lead to an entente with Warsaw similar to that being hammered out with Paris.[40]

On June 6 the Regent, Horthy, addressed a letter to the President of Poland, Marshal Pilsudski, the significant portions of which are as follows:

On the other hand, the diversity of relations upon which the lives of people depends obliges us to respect the special interest of our friends.

It is no secret to me that in the numerous questions regarding eastern

---

garian accord. Nitti to Scialoja, telegram, June 8, 1920, *I.D.* For the action taken by Cerruti in the matter, see *H.D.,* I, Docs. 415, 420, 433, 563, 581, 617.

[38] *H.D.,* I, Doc. 803.

[39] *Ibid.,* Doc. 257.

[40] The action by the Budapest government was certainly taken after giving due consideration to the information transmitted by Count Csekonics on May 16 that the Rumanians were applying great pressure on Warsaw to conclude a pact with Bucharest without delay. Rumors were that Take Jonescu was about to visit Warsaw for this purpose. *H.D.,* I, Doc. 290. Apparently the Rumanian pressure was directly related to the growing Soviet threat against Bucharest. On the other hand, there were indications that other factors were affecting the growing rigidity of the Rumanian position. In that period the Italian Minister to Bucharest reported as follows:

I spoke to His Majesty relative to the need to improve relations with Hungary. He told me that he was extremely well disposed to make all possible concessions to the Magyars in Transylvania. However, Hungary must first sign the entire peace treaty and cease all irredentist intrigues. The Rumanian King hopes that the Allied Powers will demonstrate by their signatures affixed to the treaty the same energetic action toward the ex-enemy, Hungary, as they do toward their Rumanian ally. The Minister for Foreign Affairs expressed the same views.

Martin Franklin to Scialoja, telegram, May 8, 1920, No. 131, *I.D.*

Europe, the interests of Poland and Rumania present a certain analogy. In order to facilitate the collaboration between Poland and Hungary in the domain of general policy, the Hungarian government is ready to seek satisfactory solutions to the many difficulties which presently divide Rumania and Hungary.

I will be particularly grateful to Your Excellency if your friendly and certainly effective intervention in Bucharest would serve to convince that power to adopt toward its own subjects of Hungarian nationality as well as toward Hungary herself a more friendly policy.[41]

In the instructions sent to Count Csekonics at the same time, the Hungarian Foreign Minister explained Magyar policy as follows:

You should refrain from raising, on your own initiative, the question of Rumania's disinterestedness. Should President Pilsudski himself raise this issue, you are instructed to declare that while we attribute great importance to accomplishing our objective, nevertheless we would prefer to deal concretely with this issue after we have had opportunity to ascertain the attitude of Rumania toward Hungary in the course of the Hungaro-Rumanian negotiations which will be shortly initiated. You are authorized to inform President Pilsudski that Hungary is willing to establish friendlier relations with Rumania on the following basis: 1. The return to Hungary of territories contiguous to the demarcation line which are inhabited by overwhelmingly Magyar or Swab population; in the adjustment of matters of communications and railway transit Hungary would show generous consideration to Rumanian interests. 2. The grant of broad territorial autonomy to Transylvanian districts where the majority of the population is Hungarian, Székler, or Saxon. The details of this autonomy would be worked out by agreement in the negotiation in which the Magyar leaders of Transylvania ought to participate. 3. In the districts to which no autonomy is granted, the rights of the Hungarian and Saxon minorities should be broadened by agreement to fully safeguard their national existence. 4. General political amnesty; the equitable adjustment of the question of former Hungarian civil servants. 5. Agreement concerning the reestablishment of railway communications, post and telegraph service; the resumption of commercial intercourse on the basis of free trade as far as possible. 6. The proportionate assumption by Rumania of Hungary's war debts. 7. Exploitation of the salt mines of Máramaros by the Hungarian state. 8. Return to Hungary of the railway, industrial, and agricultural equipment requisitioned in Hungary or payment of its value.

Concerning the 9 billion crowns damages which President Pilsudski believes Rumania is bound to pay to Hungary, we have received no official information. If such an obligation was in fact imposed on Rumania, you are empowered to authorize the Polish Government to utilize this sum for compensation in proportion to the willingness of Rumania to agree to the conditions above set forth. However, I reserve the final decision concerning the amounts to be remitted to Rumania in each concrete instance.[42]

Obviously, the Hungarian political program was at the time closely

[41] H.D., I, Doc. 321.
[42] Ibid., Doc. 322.

akin to the proposals advanced simultaneously in Paris. The doubts it raised did not so much concern its compass, which did not seem to be unreasonable, as the means chosen for its realization. Once the Entente confirmed the requests regarding the peace treaty, in order to render the famous accompanying Millerand letter operable, it was necessary that the mediation efforts, if such efforts were to be regarded as preferable to direct negotiations between the states of Central Europe, be entrusted to the three great powers and not to one power alone. This was all the more true since, as was admitted by one of the Hungarian negotiators, it was impossible to see how France would fulfill the promises she made,[43] and the suspicion raised by British diplomats seemed to be entirely legitimate,[44] that is, that the Quai d'Orsay was promising to support Hungary in order to conclude an important economic agreement involving French control of the Hungarian railways. In any event, the primary fact of interest here is that, in this phase, while recognizing the need for a rapprochement with Rumania, Budapest believed that it should be achieved via a moderate revision of the territorial clauses of the peace treaties. In fact, this conception appeared to be inspired by a desire to arrive at a general, total, and long-lasting agreement between the two countries without upsetting, indeed by preserving, the general structure of the treaty.[45] Only later would Budapest, realizing that the prospects for an immediate overall agreement were reduced, modify her position on the problem by first seeking an accord with Rumania on the basis of the status quo,[46] undoubtedly as a preliminary step to a later arrangement to be concluded in an atmosphere of mutual faith.

[43] On May 5, Count Emeric Csáky noted: "According to my instructions, I endeavoured to obtain information from Mr. Paléologue concerning the means whereby France could induce our neighbors to recognize Hungary's claims. I regret to report that my endeavours in this direction were unsuccessful since Mr. Paléologue cautiously avoided a direct reply. My impression is that *at present* neither Paléologue nor the French Government disposes of means whereby they could compel our neighbours to recognize and comply with our claims." H.D., I, Doc. 259.

[44] In a memorial on the Franco-Hungarian accord transmitted to Budapest on June 30, the British government, according to the British Foreign Minister, Lord Curzon, noted that "if the French statesmen have made any promises of a political nature to the Hungarians, particularly promises concerning territorial concessions, such promises cannot be in conformity with the real intentions of the French government and, in his view, the French have played a shady game with the Hungarians." Cf. H.D., I, Doc. 409. Early in July, Cerruti sought to obtain the collaboration of the British High Commissioner in Budapest, Athelstan-Johnson, in order to act with greater efficacy to block the accord with France. However, the offer was ignored because London feared Hungarian pressures against British companies which had acquired important positions in the shipping companies on the Danube. Cf. B.D., 1st series, XII, Doc. 114, and *ibid.*, note 5.

[45] H.D., I, Docs. 259, 378, 755 (b).

[46] *Ibid.*, Doc. 803.

Because of a Polish cabinet crisis, the audience with President Pilsudski for the presentation of Admiral Horthy's letter was postponed for a time.[47] On June 21 Count Csekonics reported to Budapest on his colloquy with the Marshal as follows:

He said that he was particularly gratified to learn that Hungary realizes the implications of Poland's relations with Rumania because under such circumstances he will be able to intervene in Bucharest in Hungary's favour much more effectively. President Pilsudski was also much pleased to hear that negotiations between Hungary and Rumania may be initiated in the near future. Concerning the subject of these negotiations, I informed the President pursuant to my instructions. After hearing our conditions he stated emphatically that in his opinion they are very reasonable. I remarked that it is in consideration of Poland only that our claims are so moderate. This explanation which I concluded with the sentence "la Hongrie est prête à sacrifier ses rancunes envers la Roumanie sur l'autel de l'amitié polonaise," pleased the President very much. Incidentally, Mr. Pilsudski talked about the Rumanians during our whole conversation in a rather uncomplimentary way, especially in connection with the question of the 9 billion crowns damages, which he himself mentioned. I frankly admitted that we have knowledge of this matter only from the information conveyed to me by Mr. Patek[48] just before I left Budapest and that we have no knowledge whatever of the circumstances under which this obligation has been imposed on Rumania. Thereupon Mr. Pilsudski told me that when General Rozwadowski was sent to Bucharest a few weeks ago, the chief purpose of his mission was to intervene in Pilsudski's name with the King of Rumania in Hungary's interest. It was [on] this occasion that the 9 billion crowns was mentioned; the King told Rozwadowski that the Allied Powers imposed this

[47] Meanwhile, the Italian Minister to Bucharest reported to Rome on the views of the new Rumanian Foreign Minister:

Today, I had my first official conversation with Take Jonescu, newly appointed Foreign Minister. He renewed his assurances of his friendship for Italy, but he also confirmed that he had not abandoned the idea of Rumania's alliance with Greece, Yugoslavia, and Czechoslovakia. He did not know if this idea would win the approval of the King and Cabinet. I, of course, explained all of the valid arguments against such an alliance, but he rejected them all and affirmed that only such an alliance could prevent Hungary and Bulgaria from attacking Rumania, perhaps even sooner than one might think. However, he assured me that an eventual alliance with Yugoslavia would be extremely precise so as to exclude every possibility, no matter how remote, of encouraging hostile Yugoslav action against Italy. I noted that this information would produce only disappointment in Italy. Take Jonescu has promised to keep me fully informed. I confirm the information in my previous telegrams, and I call Your Excellency's attention to the fact that neither the King of Rumania nor General Averesco favor any formal alliance at this particular time. Public opinion is opposed to a Yugoslav alliance because of the latter's annexation of part of the Banat. At present, Take Jonescu lacks support in Parliament and therefore cannot impose his views on the government. However, in any case, the situation will bear careful watching.

Martin Franklin to Sforza, telegram, June 15, 1920, No. 179, *I.D.*
[48] Polish Foreign Minister.

amount on Rumania for the damage caused to Hungary by requisitions during the occupation. The reason why the Allied Powers kept Hungary in ignorance about this decision is that they never intended to have this money paid to Hungary, but to have it turned over to the Reparation Commission. The Rumanians succeeded in Paris to have the date of payment indefinitely postponed. Nevertheless, the theoretical obligation to pay this debt remains and the Rumanians would like to free themselves from the unpleasant prospect of paying this money if Hungary would be willing to abandon her claim. Pursuant to my instructions, I informed President Pilsudski that while we are not willing to renounce our claim in the course of direct negotiations with Rumania, we are prepared to leave it to Pilsudski's discretion to relinquish part or all of our claim in proportion to the success which he expects from his mediation in Bucharest. The President was much pleased with this suggestion but remarked with a smile that in his opinion we are not making much of a sacrifice because he doubts that we would ever see a cent from these famous nine billion crowns. . . . Immediately following my audience with President Pilsudski I gave a copy of the letter of his Serene Highness to Mr. Okecki[49] in the Ministry for Foreign Affairs, with the request that he show it to Mr. Dabrowski.[50] Okecki was very much pleased with the letter, especially with the passage relating to Rumania.[51]

The Polish Chief of State replied directly to the Hungarian Regent on July 1 in a letter in which he said:

I am fully aware of the great importance to be ascribed to Your Serene Highness's words which are dedicated to a very sound appreciation of the political necessities which led the Hungarian Government to the decision to seek a solution to the difficulties which divide Rumania and Hungary at the present time.
As for myself, I hasten to assure Your Serene Highness in the name of the Polish Government as well as my own that, on our part, we will do everything in our power to contribute to the smoothing out of these difficulties since we are absolutely convinced that the rapprochement of the three states: Hungary, Poland, and Rumania will be such as to serve their mutual interests in peace in this part of Europe. I am convinced that the Western Powers will also fully appreciate the importance of the good news and will want to give their support to the realization of this idea.[52]

There was no doubt about Poland being well disposed toward helping Hungary and Rumania realize a permanent rapprochement on the basis of the moderate revision plan suggested by Hungary. Magyar diplomats were counting heavily on Warsaw's support, not only revealing their entire plan to Marshal Pilsudski but also, in a way, suggesting that the entente with Poland could be realized only after a clarification of the

---

[49] Chief of the Political Section of the Polish Foreign Ministry.
[50] Secretary-General of the Polish Foreign Ministry.
[51] *H.D.*, I, Doc. 383.
[52] *Ibid.*, Doc. 440.

August 15, Count Teleki was already informing Paris of his satisfaction with Bucharest's proposal to nominate Starcea, and he in turn nominated Count Emeric Csáky and Baron Lang as Hungarian negotiators for this matter.[59] Two days later, from Paris, Praznovszky warned against any delay in seeking a rapprochement with Rumania in order to break through the isolation barrier. In his dispatch the Hungarian diplomat, after recalling the determined efforts to create an Austro-Czech-Rumanian-Yugoslav bloc made by the Bohemians, noted that

> looking at the situation from here, the breaking of this ring of isolation would seem to be our most important task. This could best be done by reaching an agreement with the Rumanians, since Take Jonescu is perhaps more amenable to compromise than any other statesman of neighboring states. Also, the present confused international situation appears to be suitable for an active foreign policy: in this general instability, every State seeks backing or support in every direction. While I do not know the status of Hungarian public opinion, I believe that we should try even the impossible in order to reach an agreement with the Rumanians. The position of the Czechs here is not very good at present and we ought to make use of this opportunity.[60]

Similar hopes were expressed by Paléologue in a colloquy with Count Csáky on August 18. According to the Secretary-General of the Quai d'Orsay, the recent step taken by Bucharest opened the door to unexpected possibilities. He was of the opinion that Bucharest's conciliatory approach had been prompted by the imminence of the Soviet threat. On the other hand, he believed that the Rumanian government, having concluded that no help was to be expected from a Great Britain which had declared its lack of interest in eastern Europe, was now forced to follow the line suggested by the French government for a solution to the Hungarian question. Furthermore, Paléologue was of the opinion that Rumania was also seeking a rapprochement with Budapest: her government could not or would not join without reservations a bloc whose primary objective was the isolation of Hungary, for this isolation would not give Rumania sufficient protection against the Russian peril. Therefore, he strongly recommended that Budapest take advantage of the situation while the atmosphere in Bucharest was favorable to Hungary and gain the approval, and possibly the aid, of Rumania in return for help in strengthening itself against the Soviet threat. In addition to pointing out how all of this worked to the advantage of Hungary, Paléologue asserted that an agreement between Hungary and Rumania would also greatly strengthen the French position on the rearmament of Hungary. As soon as he had re-

[59] *Ibid.*, Doc. 572.
[60] *Ibid.*, Doc. 582.

ceived a reply to his message to the Rumanian government informing it of Budapest's satisfaction with the nomination of Starcea, he would seek to arrange a meeting in Paris between Count Csáky and the Rumanian Minister to France. In addition, he added, General Joffre was in Bucharest at that very moment and had been instructed to ascertain the attitude of the Rumanian government toward the Hungarian-Rumanian defensive action against the Soviet Union.[61]

Undoubtedly the diagnosis offered by Paléologue was unduly optimistic and overestimated the importance of the Rumanian overture. It appears that up to that moment the substance of the Magyar proposals had not been communicated to Bucharest. However, there was some truth in what the French diplomat had to say, particularly concerning the Soviet aspect of the question. Of course, Paris had been deeply impressed by the successes of the Red Army,[62] and the French desired, above all, the rearmament of Hungary,[63] misreading the extent of the opposition of Hungary's neighbors.[64] The French press was told to direct its warnings to Beneš and to the Yugoslavs, who were now accused of aiming at the encirclement of Hungary.[65] Meanwhile, the number of contacts between the representatives of the French General Staff and the Magyar envoys increased, arousing hope for a prompt solution to the Hungarian rearmament problem. On August 19, Colonel Lang reported as follows from Budapest:

From conferences with General Desticker and Lieutenant Colonel Courtin I gained the impression that both the French government and the General Staff regard the danger of bolshevism as serious a threat as we do. Although France is unable to send an army to Russia, she will use every available means to fight bolshevism in Russia before she is compelled to fight it at the Rhine. France considers it most important that we should establish friendly relations with Rumania. This alone would render it possible for her to supply us quickly with armament since war supplies could only be sent over sea and then through Rumania on account of the attitude of the States bordering Hungary on the north, west, and south.[66]

[61] *Ibid.,* Doc. 590.
[62] *Ibid.,* Doc. 443.
[63] *Ibid.,* Docs. 591, 596.
[64] *Ibid.,* Doc. 594.
[65] *Ibid.,* Doc. 597.
[66] *Ibid.,* Doc. 596. A day earlier Baron Lang had transmitted a summary account of a colloquy he had had with General Desticker, who was in practice performing most of the functions of the Chief of the General Staff, in very nearly the same terms. The General suddenly asked what the status of relations with Rumania were and whether the Magyars regarded cooperation with Bucharest as possible. He was visibly relieved by the reply he received which affirmed that, in the face of the common threat, cooperation would be possible with demonstrable goodwill despite serious difficulties.

In the midst of so much enthusiasm the first realistic note arrived from
Budapest on August 21. It contained Count Teleki's request to be informed whether Paléologue had told the Rumanians of the conditions
Budapest advanced as a basis for discussions, or whether the Rumanians
sought a rapprochement without conditions.[67] Two days later Count
Teleki instructed Count Csáky to request an explanation from Paléologue
regarding the significance of the Rumanian-Czechoslovak accord announced by the Prague press information bureau.[68]

10

A more realistic estimate of the difficulties involved was gradually replacing the euphoric atmosphere of the first weeks of the attempt to apply
the Paléologue accord. Although Budapest did not slacken in its efforts to
seek an arrangement with Rumania, it became evident that the obstacles
were serious. Numerous factors were responsible for this adverse turn of
events. Among these should be mentioned the continuing Czechoslovak
pressure on Bucharest, the growing local hostility to Paléologue's policies,
the weakening of Soviet military pressure, the indecision of the Rumanian
government regarding its final foreign policy guidelines, and the conclusion of the Yugoslav-Czechoslovak alliance of August 14. The action
undertaken in Paris a few weeks earlier with so much enthusiasm continued for a time but less feverishly, and the documents reveal the gradual
disappearance of the original optimism.

Count Csáky replied to Teleki's query of August 21 three days later.
He reported that the French government had not yet communicated the
Hungarian claims to Bucharest in the form agreed upon in the negotiations with Paléologue, although it had informed the Rumanians that
France considered a number of the Magyar requests as useful bases for
discussion.[69] On August 25, Csáky telegraphed to Budapest that he had
been assured at the Quai d'Orsay by more than one source not only that
Rumania had not adhered to the Yugoslav-Czechoslovak alliance but also
that this accord had not yet been formally concluded.[70] Peretti,[71] however,

[67] *Ibid.*, Doc. 598.

[68] *Ibid.*, Doc. 602.

[69] *Ibid.*, Doc. 604.

[70] As noted, the accord was reached eleven days earlier. This incorrect information
tends to confirm the Quai d'Orsay's initial abstention, in response to the political
directives issued by Paléologue, from the negotiations which preceded the signing of
the Little Entente and the hostile position toward this agreement taken by France
during the early stages of the negotiations. This is one of the most interesting of all
of the revelations contained in the published Hungarian documentary collection.
Ibid., Doc. 695.

[71] Substituting for the Chief of the Political and Commercial Section of the Quai
d'Orsay.

had informed Csáky that the Czechs were doing everything possible to create a Yugoslav-Rumanian-Czechoslovak alliance against Hungary, an alliance which would include Greece, Bulgaria, and Poland at a later date. Meanwhile, he recommended that Budapest establish contact with the Rumanians without delay before the latter succumbed to the pressures of the Czechs. In Csáky's judgment, Rumania was attempting to guarantee her position on both fronts, hoping to have Hungary by her side against the Soviet peril while, at the same time, seeking the protection of an alliance with Hungary's neighbors against a possible attack from Budapest. It is worth noting that Rumania was keeping secret an accord with the Czechs and the Yugoslavs, (if it really existed—Prague widely publicized it, perhaps for the purpose of embarrassing the Rumanian government and preventing any possible rapprochement with Hungary).[72]

As is evident, the tone of this dispatch differed considerably from that used in the earlier ones from Paris. On August 26 Count Teleki noted that the only possible way to open negotiations with Bucharest was to accept Paléologue's promise to arrange a meeting between Count Csáky and the Rumanian Minister to Paris, Prince Ghika.[73] However, other discouraging news arrived from Paris. On August 27 Praznovszky telegraphed to Budapest the essence of his conversation with Paléologue that day on the question of Hungarian rearmament. The attitude of the French diplomat had

changed noticeably due to the Polish victory. According to him the danger of bolshevism no longer exists and he does not believe that it will recur. Consequently, he does not consider the question of our rearmament pressing. He counselled caution on account of our neighbors. He gave no positive answers to military questions but emphasized some commonplace phrases about slow and patient work, economic rapprochement with Serbia, Rumania, and Bulgaria (without mentioning, however, Czechoslovakia), etc.[74]

The following day Paléologue informed Praznovszky that the Czechs and Yugoslavs had, in fact, concluded an alliance against Hungary. Praznovszky reported the conversation as follows:

Paléologue, however, does not attach much importance to this in view of the fact that the Serbs are immobilized, being economically dependent on France and threatened on three sides by the Bulgarians, Albanians and Italians. He denied that Rumania could have acceded to this agreement, since that would be contrary to her policy inaugurated toward Hungary. According to him, Beneš received a non-committal reply in Bucharest to the effect that the project is interesting but would be of real value only if Bulgaria, Greece and Poland

[72] H.D., I, Doc. 607.
[73] Ibid., Doc. 609.
[74] Ibid., Doc. 613.

would also join. Mr. Paléologue told me that he mentioned to Pasic, when he recently visited Paris, the Rumanian rapprochement with us. Pasic was much interested and declared that the Serbian government would also welcome a rapprochement with Hungary.[75]

Paléologue's attitude was somewhat singular. While the about-face on the rearmament question was to some extent comprehensible, his minimizing of the importance of the Yugoslav-Czechoslovak alliance and praise of attitudes that corresponded little with the facts must have given Hungarian statesmen much to reflect upon. (In effect, Rumania had limited her action to accepting the renewal of diplomatic relations and to postponing to a later date her decision regarding adherence to the Little Entente, while Paléologue spoke of nothing less than a new orientation of Rumanian foreign policy. Added to this were the convenient phrases uttered by Pasic, which had to be weighed against Yugoslavia's adherence to the system of anti-Magyar encirclement sponsored by Prague.) French support, upon which so many hopes had been placed and for which so many sacrifices had been made, began to appear of very limited value. Nor did De Montille's reassuring statements, transmitted by Praznovszky to Teleki on September 2, 1920, alleviate Budapest's growing anxiety.

The Magyar diplomat had gone to the Quai d'Orsay the previous day to seek further information of Beneš' encirclement plan and on the Hungarian-Rumanian rapprochement. He reported as follows:

According to De Montille, the Rumanians did not join the Little Entente: there were conversations of a general nature to consider the case of Hungary attacking one of her neighbors. Mr. Beneš failed to clothe the little Entente with the aggressive character he had intended. There is no ground for anxiety; moreover, if Hungary had been threatened in any manner, France would have been the first to advise us accordingly. Rumania, supported by France, declined to enter into Beneš's combination by pointing to the necessity of having Poland and Greece included in the alliance. In addition to deferring the date of the conclusion of the alliance, this proposal also broadens the combination so as to take away its definitely anti-Hungarian character.

During the course of the same conversation, Praznovszky also brought up the Hungarian situation and pointed out the urgent need for France to employ all of her authority and influence to improve conditions. De Montille, who, after Paléologue, was probably the most sincere defender of the Hungarian cause at the Quai d'Orsay, listened with comprehension to these observations but warned in strong terms against undertaking any venture. He believed that if Budapest attempted to reacquire her lost territories by a military attack or a surprise action of

[75] *Ibid.*, Doc. 618.

some kind, she would have to face a coalition of her neighbors. He did not believe that these states would attack without provocation but said that France would prevent them from doing so no matter what the circumstances. De Montille had no further information on the Hungarian-Rumanian rapprochement. Here, too, he counseled patience and warned against any attempt to apply pressure on the Rumanians which could be misinterpreted. A few days later, after a visit to Peretti, spokesman for the Political Section of the Quai d'Orsay, Praznovszky was able to learn something more.[76]

The embarrassment of French diplomats in seeking to perform the political acrobatics demanded by Paléologue's policy orientation was reasonably clear. The failure of the action taken in Bucharest was insufficiently masked by De Montille's calming phrases. In effect, Rumania had not rejected Beneš' offers outright, as the Hungarians earlier had been led to believe, but had supported a combination which, excluding Hungary, would have been at the very most also anti-Bulgarian. The evolution of the situation was becoming increasingly clear. Two days later, the colloquy between Praznovszky and Peretti revealed further adverse developments.

According to the information reaching Peretti, there was a growing suspicion of Hungary among her neighbors. Praznovszky reported this colloquy as follows: "Beneš has not yet succeeded in Bucharest but since both the Czechs and the Yugoslavs are cultivating the Rumanians, Peretti advised that we also show accommodation to the Rumanians. He believes we should first establish friendly relations; this can be attained only by staying within the treaty structure. It is only later that we can expect, on the basis of direct negotiations, the carrying into effect of the *lettre d'envoi*."[77]

Peretti had asked when Hungary would ratify the treaty of peace. According to his instructions, Praznovszky pointed out the difficulties involved in arriving at ratification, along with Hungary's disastrous position brought about by the treaty. Peretti admitted the difficulties but insisted that prompt ratification and a rapid accord with the Rumanians would be in the Magyar interest. Praznovszky then pointed out that it had been precisely for this reason that Hungary had sought a meeting between Count Csáky and Prince Ghika, which Paléologue had more or less

---

[76] *Ibid.*, Doc. 629.
[77] This is the well-known letter sent by Millerand as President of the Peace Conference accompanying the final terms stipulated by the Entente, in which vague promises were made for improvement in the terms of the Treaty of Trianon. For the text, see *ibid.*, Doc. 265.

promised to arrange. Peretti's reply was evasive, but he added that the Quai d'Orsay also considered a prompt meeting to be desirable and that he would seek to bring Praznovszky and Ghika together. The French diplomat then went on to describe the grave difficulties encountered by his government because of its pro-Hungarian policy. He mentioned that the visit of Count Csáky and Baron Lang had not remained a secret and that the governments of the neighboring states had protested these meetings to France violently and bitterly. Praznovszky did not conceal his surprise and pointed out that Hungary could offer no better proof of her peaceful intentions and of her loyalty than by reorganizing her army according to the French system and equipping it with French arms. The adoption of the French system seemed to be the best guarantee she could offer to her neighbors and to France. Peretti fully agreed with this thesis and later in the conversation vigorously defended the Hungarian position. However, he did conclude by counseling the greatest caution in order to avoid the collapse of the entire action. He suggested that Hungary move to defend her own interests with greater diplomacy than in the past. Moreover, he observed, the Little Entente could almost be considered to be directed against France, and this fact alone clearly indicated the extent of the political caution Hungary would have to observe in order to immobilize her enemies. This goal could be realized only through able diplomacy and not through a challenge to overwhelming power.[78]

This important colloquy can be regarded as concluding one phase of Hungary's diplomatic activity. The indications from French sources put an end to the hope of simultaneously arriving at a rapprochement with Rumania and a moderate revision of the frontiers between the two countries. Budapest quickly adapted to this new situation without abandoning, for a time, the hope of realizing the other portion of its plan. At the same time the counsels of caution and delay advanced by the Quai d'Orsay revealed the uncertainty and the hesitation in Paris regarding the wisdom of tying France too firmly to a pro-Hungarian policy. The threat of seeing the instruments forged at the Peace Conference turned against her was too serious not to give French statesmen pause. Sooner or later Paris would have to make a choice between the two policies, and it was clear that it would be extremely difficult for France to detach herself from the forces and interests that had determined her policy only a few months before and which had fertilized the political ground during the course of the Conference. This ominous development did not pass by the attentive Magyar diplomats unobserved, and Budapest sought to learn from the new experience while attempting to salvage in Paris what little remained.

[78] *Ibid.*, Doc. 631.

11

The disconcerting news reaching Budapest from Paris was certainly not unconnected with Count Teleki's sudden decision to ask for Bucharest's approval, through the Rumanian Legation in Vienna, of the nomination of Legation Counsellor Maisirevich as Hungary's Chargé d'Affaires in the Rumanian capital.[79] In taking this step directly without intermediaries, Hungary indicated that her goal was something more than prompt action:[80] she wished greater autonomy for Magyar foreign policy and offered, at the same time, a veiled hint that she lacked faith in French mediation. In transmitting his decision to Paris, the Hungarian Foreign Minister informed Praznovszky that, for the moment, Hungary was only interested in establishing a contact; negotiations would come later. However, he was forced to include as a precondition to any rapprochement a tangible improvement in the treatment of the Magyar minority residing in territories assigned to Rumania. Moreover, Teleki observed, insofar as the difficulties encountered by the Quai d'Orsay in implementing its pro-Hungarian policy were concerned, the difficulties he encountered because of his French orientation were even greater, particularly with Italy, and he agreed with Peretti that the Little Entente was anti-French.[81]

Unquestionably, the most important element contained in that dispatch was the decision to reduce the principal condition for the conclusion of an accord with Rumania to the issue of the treatment of minorities. Budapest was adjusting rapidly to the new situation, sensing its urgency. The declaredly anti-French nature of the Little Entente merits particular attention. This could be a convenient hook on which the Quai d'Orsay could hang its theoretically pro-Magyar policy, and Teleki perhaps erred in following Peretti's lead without hesitation. In Budapest, on the basis of information from Austrian sources, diplomats had reached the point of accusing Italy of having favored the creation of the Little Entente, but Cerruti,[82] in a heated colloquy with Horthy on September 12, categorically denied the insinuation and explained in lucid terms the significance of the new alliance.[83] The facts later revealed exactly confirmed Cerruti's interpretation; among other things, he also announced the Rumanian government's decision to adhere to the Yugoslav-Czechoslovak accord.

The threat posed by the emergence of a new alliance system raised

[79] *Ibid.*, Docs. 632, 634, 637.
[80] *Ibid.*, Docs. 645, 647.
[81] *Ibid.*, Doc. 658.
[82] Italian High Commissioner in Budapest.
[83] H.D., I, Doc. 649.

profound concern in Budapest despite the assurances coming from all sides. On September 7 the Hungarian Chargé d'Affaires in Prague reported that Beneš, when questioned as to the significance of the negotiations under way between Prague and Bucharest, had denied that the Little Entente was anti-Magyar, affirming that the purpose of the alliance was to preserve the peace and to strengthen the political and economic relations between the succession states bound together by mutual interests.[84] The implicit confirmation of Rumanian-Czechoslovak negotiations presaged little advantage for Budapest. On September 13 Praznovszky telegraphed further interesting information to Teleki. He reported that France, having failed to prevent the consummation of the Yugoslav-Czechoslovak alliance and to convince Rumania to reject outright demands for a similar alliance, was working to eliminate its specific anti-Magyar character by urging the enlargement of the alliance so that the position of Hungary in regard to the Little Entente would be less isolated. From the evidence available it does appear that Rumania, on the basis of Take Jonescu's recent declarations, accepted the idea of enlarging the base of the Little Entente as a guideline for Rumanian foreign policy. At that time the Rumanian statesman was at Aix-le-Bains, and during the four days preceding he made significant statements to a number of important newspapers concerning Rumanian foreign policy in general and his attitude toward the Little Entente in particular. In effect, Jonescu stated that Rumania had no need of written treaties to protect the gains made with the Treaty of Trianon or other similar gains. Moreover, albeit very cautiously, he hinted that he did not see the need for an open alliance for offensive and defensive purposes with Czechoslovakia and Yugoslavia. Because of these statements, the Czechoslovak government, when faced with official communiqués from Prague indicating that Rumania had already joined the Yugoslav-Czechoslovak alliance, was finally forced to take a clear stand. It was clear that Rumania was continuing to pursue the policy she had adopted during the war, proceeding cautiously and, at a propitious moment, doing only what appeared to be in her best interests. If it had been to their advantage, the Rumanians would have abandoned the Czechs and the Serbs with the same lack of concern with which they had deserted the Hungarians, notwithstanding the fact that they may have had an alliance. In his statements, Take Jonescu had indicated the desirability of including Poland, Greece, and even Austria in the Little Entente. He had referred to Austria as the only defeated state which had accepted its fate. Finally, he added that, at a later time, even Hungary and Bulgaria could also be included. These revelations clearly proved that

[84] *Ibid.*, Doc. 643.

Paris and Bucharest understood each other very well. It was hoped that Hungary could profit from these circumstances. The Magyar diplomat continued his report as follows:

These far-reaching plans bear close resemblance, *mutatis mutandis*, to the plan of a "Great Austria" conceived by Archduke Francis Ferdinand. That the French are very sympathetic to this plan is unquestionable; that they will try to promote it can be assumed; that we may find the place due to us in such a combination, enabling us to achieve our national aspirations, may also be assumed; but it will doubtless require more time than the more impatient elements in Hungary believe. Just what induced Rumania to push the idea of such a confederation will probably appear from the reports of the Hungarian representative who will be sent shortly to Bucharest. Looking at it from Paris, it seems that the internal troubles of Rumania are more serious than they may appear to the public. A distinguished French diplomat a few days ago expressed a very pessimistic view about internal conditions in Rumania and grave doubts as to the possibility of her overcoming them. The statements of Take Jonescu above referred to do not contain in general unfavourable remarks concerning Hungary but the distinction between various states is very specific. He speaks with a certain amount of good will and condescension about Austria; he doesn't seem to pay much attention to Bulgaria but is very cautious in regard to Hungary. He referred to the desirability of good neighbourly relations and economic rapprochement but it is obvious that he considers Hungary alone as a dangerous adversary. So far as the attitude of the French press toward the Little Entente is concerned, the strong opposition manifested at the outset has dwindled away in consequence of the Czech press campaign, continued with tremendous expenditure of money. Today there are voices which endeavour to show that existence of the Little Entente is in the interests of France.

The report indicated that the chief of the Press Bureau of the French Foreign Ministry, Corbin, in a colloquy with Praznovszky on the press campaign, revealed that, unfortunately, there were a number of eminent Frenchmen who did not realize that they were fighting for Czech or Rumanian interests and not for those of France. In conclusion, the Magyar diplomat believed that for the moment the leaders of French foreign policy were generally opposed to the Little Entente. If they failed, the reasons for this failure would have to be looked for not only in the general international situation, but also in the power of the opposition recruited from among Clemenceau's friends, a force sufficiently powerful to advance the interests of Hungary's neighbors at Hungary's expense. However, a portion of the press and some statesmen continued to attack the Little Entente, and the Czechs in particular.[85]

The information and the emphasis contained in this noteworthy dispatch provided a complete picture of the situation. The direction in which

[85] *Ibid.*, Doc. 650.

Rumanian foreign policy was moving was becoming clear. Of course, the
last word had not yet been said in Bucharest. The majority of Rumanian
statesmen were still hesitant, but, in effect, it did appear that once the
Bolshevik menace seemed to have abated, the idea of a total rapprochement with Hungary seems also to have given way in the face of other
pressing problems. As a matter of fact, the Rumanian government had
never compromised itself to any great extent but, in any event, the
thermometer in Paris did register a noticeable change in temperature, and
not without reason. Take Jonescu had referred to the uselessness of a
written treaty.[86] The expression did not have much reassurance value
because a common interest did bind Czechoslovakia, Yugoslavia, and Rumania together against Hungary. The situation would have been different
if the Rumanian Foreign Minister had spoken of a specific understanding
with Hungary, but he had been very careful to avoid doing so. As for
the vast project for enlarging the Little Entente, its realization for the
moment presented too many grave difficulties for it to be given serious
consideration. In any event, Hungary might have been asked to participate
only after her isolation was complete. Evidently, in Bucharest those same
negative forces which had closed the brief Paléologue parenthesis were
assuming control of foreign policy. The rather pessimistic note with which
Praznovszky closed his report made the destiny of France's efforts to give
the Little Entente a new direction fairly clear. Hungary played no role
in the unfavorable evolution of the general situation. Unfortunately, the
outcome of her efforts to improve her relations with Rumania was conditioned by factors beyond her direct control. Despite the intensification of
the negative aspects of this political drama, Budapest pursued its policy
until the last hope was gone; that is, until April 23, 1921, immediately
after the first attempt to restore former Emperor Karl, when Rumania
formally signed the anti-Magyar pact.

The direct efforts made to neutralize Prague's political action did continue without a break. On September 24, 1920, Praznovszky informed the

---

[86] According to a statement made by Giolitti during the course of a colloquy held
in mid-September, Take Jonescu was opposed to Rumanian participation in a
Yugoslav-Czechoslovak alliance. He believed that to implement the Treaty of
Trianon written treaties were unnecessary "because Rumania would have attacked
Hungary without hesitation in the event that the latter had attacked Yugoslavia, but
that he would not consider any alliance in which Greece and Poland were excluded,
an alliance which, to date, is not easy to realize." Giolitti to Sforza, telegram, n.d.,
I.D. Some time later the Rumanian Minister of the Interior, Argetoianu, also ex-
pressed an extremely strong opposition to assuming any obligations with Czecho-
slovakia and Yugoslavia. Moreover, he indicated that both the King and General
Averescu were "absolutely opposed to any ideas of this nature." Martin Franklin to
Sforza, telegram, October 2, 1920, *I.D.*

new Hungarian Foreign Minister, Count Csáky, that he had learned at the Polish Legation in Paris that Pilsudski and Sapieha were working to create a Hungarian-Polish-Rumanian alliance to offset the Little Entente but that the Rumanians were opposed to it. Poland had sounded out the French and found the idea favorably received.[87] Undoubtedly, Warsaw was a factor of primary importance in countering Beneš' policy, but it was clear that its efficacy appeared to be subordinated to the Quai d'Orsay's final orientation.[88]

The following day Count Csekonics, after reporting the growing efforts by the Czechs to induce Poland to join the anti-Magyar front and noting that such an event would not only increase the prestige of the Little Entente but would also bring to an end Poland's policy of supporting Hungary, commented:

From our point of view, it is important to note that the Polish Government must choose between two possible foreign policies, a choice which involves an alliance either with or against us. The first alternative is a Polish-Hungarian-Rumanian alliance; the other, adherence to the Little Entente. The latter already exists between Czechoslovakia and Yugoslavia; Rumania is sympathetic but will probably make a decision in the light of the position which Poland eventually takes. Here everybody including even Prince Sapieha, but with the exception of the extreme National Democrats (whose chief representative in the foreign service is Piltz),[89] is anti-Czech and is inclined toward a Hungaro-

[87] H.D., I, Doc. 667.

[88] The Italian Minister to Warsaw, Tommasini, reported on the matter as follows:

Completely absorbed in the struggle against Bolshevik Russia, the Polish public has paid scant attention to the so-called Little Entente which Mr. Beneš has sought to create. However, it is undeniable that, in these quarters, this alliance arouses little sympathy and no trust. Prince Sapieha, Minister for Foreign Affairs, told me that "The Little Entente is devised to force Hungarian observance of the Treaty of Trianon: this has nothing to do with Poland, which has not annexed any Hungarian territory; therefore, we are not concerned with it." However, this is an evasive view. The mere fact that Czechoslovakia took the initiative for the creation of the Little Entente would suffice to cause the entire combination to be hated here rather than simply distrusted. It would be illusory to believe that the Solomon-like judgment of the Supreme Council in the Teschen question had appreciably reduced the hostility existing between the two countries contesting that region. . . . Moreover, the fact that France does not particularly favor the idea of the Little Entente is not forgotten here. France's influence has increased since the contribution made by General Weygand and his colleagues to the Polish victory, and it is known that Paris would like to counter the effect of the Little Entente with a Rumanian-Hungarian accord which Poland would be very tempted to join, hoping, in a division of Czechoslovakia, to acquire all of eastern Silesia along with the Spiz and Orawa regions which were denied to her by the Supreme Council.

Tommasini to Sforza, September 14, 1920, I.D.

[89] Secretary-General of the Polish Foreign Ministry.

phil policy. But Sapieha and others who have some reservations toward a Hungarophil policy (they condition this on agreement with Rumania and the approval of the French), are unwilling without further consideration to discard the advantages which may be derived from participation in the Little Entente. Sapieha requested Count Skrzynski and Count Szembek, the Ministers of Poland in Bucharest and Budapest respectively, to return to Warsaw. They have both arrived and conversations have already begun which may have a great influence on the future tendency of Polish foreign policy. I have not yet had an opportunity to see either Skrzynski or Szembek but I called yesterday on Okecki; my conversation with him strengthened the impression outlined above. I also learned that France does not look with complete satisfaction on these efforts to strengthen the Little Entente which might easily lead to its emancipation from the Great Entente.[90]

As is evident, the situation in Warsaw was far from reassuring, and the disagreeable surprises were not yet over. On September 26, 1920, Paléologue was dismissed from his post as Secretary-General of the Quai d'Orsay; Millerand, called to succeed the ailing Deschanel at the Elysée Palace only two days before, had been replaced by Leygues, and France reversed her policy vis-à-vis the Little Entente.

12

The first rumors of a probable replacement of Paléologue, based on his recognition of Wrangel and his pro-Hungarian policy, which had provoked the creation of a Little Entente with anti-French overtones, were persistent in Parisian diplomatic circles as early as September 24, 1920, the day of Millerand's election to the presidency of the republic.[91] The following day Paléologue signed another collective note to Budapest drafted by the Entente requesting that the Treaty of Trianon be ratified promptly.[92] This act, not entirely in harmony with his views, was the last of his diplomatic career, which ended a few hours later. The Quai d'Orsay immediately replaced Paléologue with Berthelot and promptly stated that this shift did not indicate any change in French policy.[93] For a time, even Paléologue seemed to believe this statement.[94] The facts were soon to destroy this illusion.

On October 2 Count Csekonics reported from Warsaw that the French Minister in that city, carrying out instructions received by him from Paris, had told the Polish Foreign Minister that France, "contrary to the attitude heretofore adopted, is now sympathetic to the Little Entente; moreover it

[90] H.D., I, Doc. 668.
[91] Ibid., Doc. 666.
[92] Ibid., Doc. 669.
[93] Ibid., Docs. 674, 695.
[94] Ibid., Doc. 683.

would be glad to see the establishment of friendly relations between Poland and Czechoslovakia."[95] In immediately communicating this information to the Hungarian diplomat, Prince Sapieha did not hide his astonishment at this new turn in French foreign policy, which he, on the basis of Panafieu's statements,[96] attributed to Take Jonescu's influence on Millerand. The Polish Foreign Minister, when questioned as to the future attitude of his country, emphatically stated that he would ignore the Little Entente and continue a policy of friendship toward Hungary, but that he would be happy to conduct this policy within the framework of a Hungarian-Polish-Rumanian bloc. In his judgment, the new French policy would not last long, but, for the moment, he could say nothing more since the news from Paris had caught him unprepared. Prince Sapieha considered completion of the announced visit of Take Jonescu to Warsaw as improbable because Jonescu knew that his proposals concerning the Little Entente would be rejected.

The upheaval could not have been more serious. How long would Poland be able to maintain her friendly attitude toward Hungary once French support was withdrawn or reduced? Two days later Count Csáky asked for supplementary information from Paris and demonstrated that he did not believe that Rumanian policy could be as negative as described in Warsaw. Thus he implicitly confirmed his desire to proceed toward a rapprochement with Bucharest.[97] The Magyar Foreign Minister explained the reasons for his continued optimism in the following dispatch to Count Csekonics, dated October 5:

I was able to ascertain during my last visit in Paris which was before the conclusion of the Belgrade treaty, that Messrs. Beneš and Pasic laid their plans concerning the formation of the Little Entente before the French Ministry for Foreign Affairs and that they asked the French Government to help them to induce the Rumanian Government to join this alliance. Not only did the French Government decline to give any promises in this respect, but Mr. Paléologue declared that the French Government does not approve of this alliance and will use its influence in Bucharest against Rumania's adherence thereto. He intimated to Messrs. Pasic and Beneš that France has great economic and, therefore, political interests in Hungary and that consequently they should refrain from forming an alliance directed primarily against Hungary. It is true that Mr. Paléologue, who was the initiator and the leader of Hungarophil French foreign policy, left his post as Secretary General of the Ministry for Foreign Affairs a few days ago and was compelled to surrender it to his personal enemy, Mr. Berthelot who is decidedly friendly to the Czechs. It is equally true, however, that Mr. Paléologue embarked on and pursued a Hungarophil policy

[95] *Ibid.*, Doc. 689.
[96] French Minister to Poland.
[97] H.D., I, Doc. 692.

which, according to his own words, constituted the foundation stone of France's future policy in Central and Southeastern Europe, with the full approval of Millerand. This seems to be supported by Praznovszky's impression during the last days that the leading French statesmen continue the attitude of friendliness adopted toward us in the last few months.[98] Further evidence is supplied by the unequivocal assurances given by the French High Commissioner in Budapest[99] that the change of personnel in leading positions in the French Ministry for Foreign Affairs will in no way affect the direction of French foreign policy. Mr. Fouchet, in giving these assurances, referred to express instructions received from the new Minister for Foreign Affairs.[100] It is interesting to note, in connection with your code telegram No. 168,[101] that I was confidentially sounded out during the last days on the role of Take Jonescu in the possibilities of rapprochement. It was even intimated that Rumania would be willing to exclude Czechoslovakia from the Little Entente and to substitute Poland and Hungary. All this is communicated for your own information; you also may communicate this confidentially and in appropriate form to the Polish Minister for Foreign Affairs in the course of a future conversation. I personally believe that Rumania is playing a double game; she seeks protection against Hungary through the Little Entente and seeks a rear guard against Russia in Hungary. This should not, however, prevent us from seeking a basis of agreement with Rumania; therefore, you should continue urging the Polish Government to support wholeheartedly our efforts in this direction.[102]

Evidently Count Csáky, as one of the architects of the Franco-Magyar understanding, obstinately closed his eyes to harsh reality, attributing an excessive importance to purely formal and courteous statements which were, in any case, nullified by events. However, the most interesting portion of the report concerned Rumania. The interpretation advanced by Prince Sapieha regarding the origins of the reversal in French policy vis-à-vis the Little Entente is very likely erroneous, since these were attributed largely to the work of the Czechs[103] and to internal French op-

---

[98] On September 27, in referring to the assurances given by De Montille, Praznovszky telegraphed, "I cannot fully subscribe to this optimistic outlook until we know the changes in the Quai d'Orsay." *H.D.*, I, Doc. 674. On October 2, in transmitting a summary of his colloquy with Cambon, President of the Ambassadors' Conference, Praznovszky noted, "I gathered from some of his remarks that the French are constantly attacked because of their Hungarophil policy and they have much difficulty in accomplishing their objectives." *Ibid.*, Doc. 690.

[99] Fouchet.

[100] Leygues.

[101] October 2, 1920; cited above.

[102] *H.D.*, I, Doc. 695.

[103] Cf. the particulars on the matter transmitted by Praznovszky to Budapest on October 8, 1920, *ibid.*, Doc. 703. It should be noted that the Polish Foreign Minister mentioned Millerand as being under the influence of the Rumanian statesman while he, Millerand, after his election as President of the Republic, had ceased to exert any influence whatsoever on foreign policy which, prior to his election to the Elysée Palace, had been Hungarophil. The impotence of Millerand as President

position to the revisionists, rather than to the personal influence of a Take Jonescu who, for unknown reasons, took so long to reveal himself. Moreover, it does not appear that the confidential soundings attributed to the Rumanian Foreign Minister were particularly serious, although, as will be noted below, Csáky was to focus on them again. For a number of months Rumania had been aware, through Italian as well as French interventions, of Hungary's desire for a rapprochement. To ask what role Jonescu could play in implementing such a policy was at once a waste of time and of no significance. As for attributing to him the intention of eliminating Czechoslovakia from the Little Entente and replacing her with Poland and Hungary, it would require a considerable degree of naïveté to give serious consideration to a plan which Jonescu had opposed publicly and privately and which, moreover, had absolutely no chance of success. On the other hand, it was fundamentally important to note Csáky's resolve to continue to pursue a policy directed toward the realization of a Rumanian-Hungarian understanding.

On October 9 Count Csekonics confirmed for Budapest the impression that the Polish government did not intend to join the Little Entente despite French pressure. The Magyar diplomat continued his report as follows:

However, two questions remain to be answered. First, what was the object of the French Government in raising its voice in the interest of the Little Entente to which it had not heretofore been sympathetic? Second, what steps will the Little Entente now take to persuade Poland to abandon the dreaded idea of alliance with Hungary? A reply to the first question can perhaps be best obtained directly from our Paris representative. In my opinion, based on observation alone, France would have liked to bring Poland into the Little Entente in the hope that she could thereby exert greater influence over the Entente and that Poland's adherence would take away its predominantly anti-Hungarian character. Mr. Panafieu has endeavoured to convince Sapieha that the Little Entente is not directed against Hungary but he gave no proof in support of this contention. Sapieha apparently does not know what is behind the French representations and expressed the view that this change of French policy was brought about by Millerand's change of heart who in turn was perhaps influenced by the clever machinations of Take Jonescu. This is quite possible; but if Take Jonescu has not now succeeded in diverting Poland's friendship from Hungary, he will try to do it in some other way. This brings me to the second question raised above. Even though Poland is not a member of the Little Entente, there are some Polish supporters of that alliance, primarily among the National Democrats, many of whom are in the Foreign Office. One of their leaders,

---

of the Republic was not unlike that of his predecessors in that office and was borne out by Paléologue's dismissal from the Quai d'Orsay and Millerand's inability even to arrange to have him appointed to the Ambassadors' Conference, an appointment which he strongly advocated. *H.D.*, I, Doc. 755.

Piltz, recently took over the post of Okecki whose dismissal Sapieha was unable to prevent since the National Democrats control the Foreign Affairs Committee. I have not yet called on Piltz who took over his office only in this week; but I shall soon have an opportunity to talk with him and shall report to Your Excellency the impressions gained in my conversation.[104]

It requires no particular insight to recognize that Count Csekonics' observations raised the question of how long Poland's resistance would last. In the meantime, while news arrived from Prague that the Rumanian diplomatic mission would be sent to Budapest only after Hungary ratified the Treaty of Trianon,[105] on October 17 Count Csáky instructed Praznovszky to see Berthelot in order to assure him of Hungary's peaceful intentions and to inform him that she continued to count on French support in order to realize her principal objective of establishing good relations with all of her neighbors.[106] As is evident, the Magyar Foreign Minister had chosen to pursue a narrowly restricted program and, for the moment, had abandoned any idea of even a moderate revision of the treaty.

Reports from Paris continued to be discouraging. On October 17 the Magyar representative in Paris telegraphed as follows:

There can no longer be any doubt that the policy adopted by the personnel of the Quai d'Orsay is the support of the Little Entente. Every effort is being made to bring together the Czechs and the Poles. It is conceivable that at a later stage this development could be harmonized with Paléologue's Hungarophil policy by turning the Little Entente into a confederation of all states in Southeastern Europe. At present, however, the aim is to set this combination of powers against Hungary's irredentist aspirations and thus to compel her to acquiesce. This policy of Berthelot could best be neutralized by frustrating conciliation between Poland and Czechoslovakia and by our concluding a separate agreement with Rumania.[107]

Budapest's last illusions of support from Paris were about to collapse. However, it is interesting to note the evident insistence on achieving a direct arrangement with Rumania.

On October 23, 1920, Praznovszky reported that he had not yet been able to see Berthelot and that France would intervene in favor of the Hungarian minorities only after the issue had been formally presented to the Ambassadors' Conference.[108] On the same day, Count Csekonics reported from Warsaw on his long colloquy with Piltz.[109] The latter was

[104] *Ibid.*, Doc. 708.
[105] *Ibid.*, Doc. 792.
[106] *Ibid.*, Doc. 723.
[107] *Ibid.*, Doc. 725.
[108] *Ibid.*, Doc. 738.
[109] *Ibid.*, Doc. 739.

not yet in possession of special information concerning the new course in French foreign policy, but he believed that Berthelot, while not anti-Magyar as such, being Paléologue's bitter enemy, would probably pursue a policy diametrically opposed to that of the former Secretary-General of the Foreign Ministry. However, the matter had not yet been definitely settled, and this led the Hungarian diplomat to conclude that Piltz would maintain a policy of procrastination regarding Polish-Hungarian relations until French intentions became clear. All of this could be deduced from the fact that the Secretary to the Polish Foreign Ministry had pointed out that he was aware that every Pole desired a rapprochement with Hungary, but that, for the moment, he could not express an opinion on the matter since he was not yet familiar with the details of the question, having only recently assumed his office. From the point of view of general policy, Piltz supported the need for a new Central Europe. He had been a fervent believer in Pan-Slavism, but now considered the idea to be outdated. In his opinion, the new Central Europe should consist of Poland, Czecho-slovakia, Yugoslavia, Rumania, Hungary, Greece, and Bulgaria. He pointedly noted that he had listed the countries in the order of their importance as he saw them. France, and in a less intimate way the United States, should participate in the new alliance of nations. Permanent peace in Europe could be maintained only by such an alliance of the Central European states, and not by the Little Entente. Piltz stated that his objective was the realization of this proposal and that he would seek to win over Take Jonescu to his view, Jonescu being expected in Warsaw on an official visit toward the end of the month. In his view, a strong Hungary would be important to Poland only if they shared a common frontier. Ruthenia should be returned to Hungary. Csekonics was not familiar with Prince Sapieha's views on these plans, but he did know that he was seeking allies among the non-Slavic states. The Polish Foreign Minister championed a Hungarian-Polish-Rumanian bloc and was interested in the Baltic States, proposals and areas in which Piltz had no interest. In conclusion, it was foreseeable that during Take Jonescu's visit, in all likelihood, means of improving the rapport between Poland and Rumania would be discussed. The plans in contention were: (1) the Little Entente suggested by Jonescu; (2) Piltz's Central European plan; and (3) the transversal bloc, supported by Prince Sapieha, which included Finland, the Baltic States, Poland, Hungary, and Rumania. The number of solutions to be considered made it highly unlikely that any one would be adopted during the visit of the foreign statesman. However, in the event that this did come to pass, the Hungarian diplomat was convinced that such a solution would not be in favor of the Little Entente.

Evidently the earlier positive attitude expressed by Count Csáky must have had a negative influence on Csekonics' powers of observation, leading him to adopt an optimistic position unwarranted by the facts in his report. What were, in fact, the differences between Piltz's views and those of Take Jonescu? Since the Ruthenian question had been resolved to Hungary's disadvantage, Poland's interest in strengthening Hungary had been reduced proportionately as the Soviet menace subsided. It was now clear that Poland was about to adopt a policy of watchful waiting, and the key to the situation remained in Paris.

13

Notwithstanding its drastically reduced prospects of success, Magyar policy continued to be directed toward achieving its immutable goal. On October 27, 1920, Praznovszky, whom Berthelot had not yet agreed to receive, announced in Budapest that Halmos[110] had delivered two memorials to the new head of the government and Minister for Foreign Affairs, Leygues. In the first of these, which concerned the aims of the Franco-Hungarian rapprochement, it was noted that the pre-eminent aim was "to find the elements for a reconciliation between Hungary and her neighbors and the bases for mutual collaboration between those countries created out of the ashes of the ancient monarchy,"[111] emphasizing, moreover, that the "conversations undertaken were always contained within the limits of the Treaty of Trianon and they strictly observed the outlines traced by the *Lettre d'Envoi* annexed to this treaty." Leygues pointed out the enormous opposition raised by the Hungarian military program and noted the serious difficulties encountered by the French government because of the attitude of Hungary's neighbors. However, he assured his listener that there were no changes in French policy,[112] although information reaching Praznovszky indicated that Berthelot remained unchanged in his irreconcilable enmity to Hungary and that Paléologue had, at least for the moment, lost every influence.[113]

Budapest still hoped for a rapprochement with Rumania based on the Treaty of Trianon as interpreted by the accompanying letter from Millerand. Yet, even within these more modest limits, the plan did not succeed in making any progress. On October 31, while Take Jonescu was making some rather cold observations to the Magyar representative in Prague,[114]

[110] A Hungarian jurist on special mission to Paris to negotiate the conclusion and application of a Franco-Magyar accord.

[111] H.D., I, Doc. 755(a).

[112] Ibid., Doc. 755. See also Docs. 757, 763.

[113] Ibid.

[114] When queried on the matter of a diplomatic mission being sent to Budapest from Bucharest, the Foreign Minister replied, "I have been away for two months

the Polish envoy to Budapest, in a colloquy with Count Csáky on November 1, also confirmed the difficulties of the situation. Prince Sapieha remained favorable to a Polish-Hungarian-Rumanian bloc to be strengthened by a Polish-Baltic States agreement. Up to that moment the Polish Foreign Minister had no indication that Rumania might be interested in entering into such an agreement, but he hoped to be able to persuade Bucharest of the wisdom of his proposal. This hope was based on information that the King and Chief of State, Averescu, favored this political orientation, although it was said that the Foreign Minister was opposed to it. Prince Sapieha believed that Take Jonescu wanted to create a kind of United States of Central Europe composed of Poland, Czechoslovakia, Rumania, Yugoslavia, Bulgaria, and Greece. Hungary and Turkey could be admitted to the union at a later date. In such an arrangement, Rumania would assume leadership because of her centralized geographic location, if for no other reason. In the judgment of the Polish Foreign Minister, the plan was entirely unrealistic because of the number of states involved and their conflicting interests. The Polish Foreign Minister had adopted an attitude of caution toward the Little Entente, and he would not have joined it even had he been forced to do so. During Jonescu's forthcoming visit to Warsaw, Prince Sapieha would make every effort to win him over to the idea of the Hungarian-Polish-Rumanian bloc.

Up to this point the colloquy had revealed nothing new except for details on the internal conflict in Rumania on policy and the possibility of Polish adherence to the Little Entente if circumstances warranted it. The second part of Count Csáky's notes were of greater interest and read as follows:

In the course of our conversation Count Szembek told me that his Government authorized him to assure me that the Polish Government continues to regard the establishment of a common Polish-Hungarian border a matter of vital interest for Poland. The Polish Government is of the opinion that the best way to attain this objective would be the solution of the Ruthenian question according to Hungary's desire, a solution for which a legal basis could be found in the relevant passage of the *Lettre d'envoi*. In this matter, we can always count on the full support of Poland and the Polish Government deems it desirable that the two governments agree upon a uniform policy in this respect. Count Szembek also told me that the Polish Foreign Office follows with much interest the development of Franco-Hungarian relations. He remarked that the observations of the Polish Legation at Paris and the attitude of the French

from Bucharest and I am not informed on the matter. After my return some five days hence, I will take the necessary measures. The postponement of Colonel Starcea's departure may have been caused by the incident affecting our military attaché in Budapest. Our intentions toward Hungary are peaceful. As long as the Hungarians remain calm, we have no intention of annoying them. Yet, it appears that we should continue to expect a number of incidents." *H.D.*, I, Doc. 762.

Legation at Warsaw seem to indicate that the Quai d'Orsay did not abandon its Hungarophil policy despite the recent changes in the personnel. At the end of his call, Count Szembek once more mentioned Hungaro-Rumanian relations and expressed his anxiety that Rumania may oppose the solution of the question of Ruthenia according to Hungary's desire. He suggested that this opposition could perhaps be overcome if Poland could guarantee the present Hungaro-Rumanian frontier in exchange for support or, at least, the neutrality of Rumania for such a solution of the question of Ruthenia. I gave a non-committal reply to this suggestion.[115]

This report indicates that Poland was extremely interested in obtaining a common frontier with Hungary in the Carpathians. The issue evidently was the key factor in Poland's Hungarophil policy. The failure to achieve this aim would undoubtedly have resulted, as might have been deduced from Piltz's earlier observations, in an adverse effect on Poland's entire Magyar policy. In addition, the observations made by Szembek make it possible to acquire a reasonably good idea of the Rumanian resistance to Prince Sapieha's plans. Obviously, Warsaw realized far more clearly than did Budapest that Rumania would not entertain the idea of ceding lands to Hungary. In any event, it became clear with the proposal to guarantee the Hungarian-Rumanian frontier created by the Treaty of Trianon that the Ruthenian question was of much greater interest to Poland than were any of the other Magyar claims, and that the realization of a Hungarian-Polish-Rumanian bloc was based on acquiring a common Polish-Hungarian frontier and on Hungary's abandonment of immediate plans for a revision of the treaty at Rumania's expense. Apparently, many things had changed since Pilsudski had judged the Hungarian requests to be just and reason-able. Count Csáky's nonbinding reply revealed not only Budapest's re-luctance to confirm all of Rumania's acquisitions but also an unsatisfactory evaluation of the role of future Hungarian-Polish relations in the overall economic picture.

Take Jonescu's long-awaited visit to Warsaw substantially confirmed the negative cast given to Rumanian policy by the Foreign Minister. On No-vember 3 Count Csekonics reported the substance of his colloquy with the Rumanian Foreign Minister during the latter's sojourn in the Polish capital as follows:

I told the Minister for Foreign Affairs that in Hungary there is an increasing appreciation of the desirability of better relations with Rumania, dictated by geography, economic interests and the necessity of cooperation between two non-slavic peoples. The Minister assured me that he is anxious to reestablish economic intercourse between the two countries as soon as possible and to create an atmosphere in which inevitable frictions along the new frontiers will

[115] *Ibid.*, Doc. 765.

be adjusted in a friendly spirit; he already gave instructions to this effect to Baron Starcea. Mr. Take Jonescu said that he fully understands the feelings of the Hungarians whom he sincerely admires: and that he appreciates the difficult position of the Hungarian government. He also assured me that he would never have allowed Rumanian troops to remain in Budapest more than 24 hours. However, when I suggested that better economic relations could pave the way for political rapprochement, Take Jonescu interrupted me and insisted that in his conception of foreign policy friendlier relations between Hungary and Rumania are possible only in the economic field, for there cannot be any question about revision of the Paris peace treaties and, particularly, of the territorial settlements. He declared with pride that "there was for a while a Hungarophil movement in France but I put an end to it." But, he said, he assured both London and Paris that, with this reservation, he will seek to improve relations with Hungary and that he is prepared to cooperate in her economic reconstruction. Without my asking, Mr. Take Jonescu enlightened me about his conception of foreign policy which is of course his plan for a little entente, consisting of Rumania, Poland, Czechoslovakia, Yugoslavia and Greece. He even referred to Hungary's possible inclusion in this bloc saying that he does not expect Hungary to join. When this question was raised in Paris, he replied that Hungary is an honest country which always honoured her signature and she can hardly be expected to become a party to a treaty whose preamble indicates the primary objective of guaranteeing and preserving the stipulations of the treaties of Versailles, St. Germain, Trianon and Neuilly. The Minister here again digressed to praise the virtues of the Hungarian people and to assure me of his great sympathies for Hungary. At the same time he declared that he always hated the Germans and will always hate them. Mr. Take Jonescu is quite confident of the power of his country and of his own greatness. He believes that he will succeed in winning Poland for his plans. On the other hand, he considers Hungary very weak; but, being a shrewd politician, he wants to create a semblance of fairly tolerable atmosphere so that in case of need he could swap horses and turn to us.[116]

In effect, behind the façade of courteous expressions and diplomatic language, the Rumanian Foreign Minister made it clear that he proposed to pursue a course in which a Hungarian-Rumanian rapprochement had no place. Taking Jonescu at his word, the impression is clear that the trend of Rumanian policy was not the result of external pressures but, rather, as he had made clear to Prince Sapieha earlier, the result of his not indifferent role in bringing about the reversal of policy at the Quai d'Orsay. In this situation it was also clear that Warsaw's efforts were to be unsuccessful. On November 15 the Polish Foreign Minister informed Count Csekonics that his Rumanian counterpart had told him categorically that the crown of St. Stephen had been offered to King Ferdinand through Jonescu's good offices by powerful Magyar leaders. Prince Sapieha, in the light of such an offer, found it logical that the Magyar requests

[116] *Ibid.*, Doc. 770.

regarding Transylvanian autonomy and the cession of lands occupied by wholly Magyar populations were ignored. Take Jonescu told him that he was opposed to a personal union because it was disadvantageous to Rumania, and, for this reason, he had rejected the offer of the crown to King Ferdinand without even taking the time to consult with Bucharest. Count Csekonics expressed his surprise at this account of the Foreign Minister's statements, assuring Prince Sapieha that he had never heard of such an offer. Moreover, he had been informed by Budapest of Take Jonescu's recent sounding out of Count Csáky regarding a rapprochement with Rumania. This, in turn, astonished the Polish Foreign Minister, who said that, in view of the statements made by Jonescu, such an overture seemed to him to be inconceivable.[117]

Obviously, the Rumanian Foreign Minister had discovered an effective technique for puzzling his Polish colleague. If, in fact, an offer to unite the two states in a personal union through the crown had been seriously proposed, it would be impossible to comprehend how Jonescu could take it upon himself to refuse it without first consulting Bucharest and, moreover, why he had not mentioned such a development to Csekonics in his talk with the Magyar diplomat, particularly when the latter had mentioned the subject of a Hungarian-Rumanian rapprochement as being of interest and desirable to the Magyars. On November 23 Csáky informed his representative in Warsaw that the story that authoritative persons had offered the crown of St. Stephen to King Ferdinand was absolutely false. It was true, however, that radical elements close to Count Karolyi had made such an overture secretly and without the knowledge of official circles. The Hungarian government had become aware of the offer after the fact and was in no way involved. Moreover, the Hungarian Foreign Minister confirmed that Jonescu had made some confidential soundings in Budapest in view of a possible Hungarian-Rumanian accord, but that the government had no way of confirming or denying their sincerity.[118]

14

Notwithstanding the increasingly evident Rumanian resistance, Magyar diplomacy did not cease its efforts either in Paris or Warsaw. On November 1 Praznovszky had an interesting conversation with Cambon on the matter,[119] and the following week Berthelot told Halmos that he was

[117] *Ibid.*, Doc. 799.

[118] *Ibid.*, Doc. 820.

[119] *Ibid.*, Doc. 767. To the question raised by the French Ambassador, "Was not Mr. Paléologue a great friend of Hungary and did he not make you serious promises?" Praznovszky replied that he knew nothing of any particular friendship Mr. Paléologue might have had for Hungary since he had always believed that the

not opposed to Paléologue's policy but, rather, that he disapproved of a number of the details and particularly of the proposed methods of application.[120] As a matter of fact, while adopting a much more restricted program, the Quai d'Orsay continued for some time to support a number of the Magyar requests, particularly in the area of protection for minorities.[121]

On November 15, 1920, Count Csáky informed Count Csekonics of the Hungarian foreign policy directives regarding the problems of Hungarian-Rumanian rapprochement in terms which merit reporting in their entirety:

> Your interesting conversation with Take Jonescu seems to indicate that he hesitates to engage in a policy of rapprochement chiefly for fear that we would conceive this to be a revision of the Trianon treaty and, above all, revision of the territorial clauses. You may express to the Polish Government my desire that this erroneous belief of the Rumanian Minister for Foreign Affairs be corrected. With this end in view, we would appreciate it if Prince Sapieha would discreetly inform Mr. Take Jonescu that we realize fully that at present we could negotiate with the Rumanian Government only on the basis of the Trianon treaty.[122]

Apparently, the negative information reaching him from every quarter had not yet discouraged the Hungarian Foreign Minister, who intended to pursue his goal, adjusting his program to the needs of the moment. Not even this adaptation of Hungarian foreign policy moved Bucharest from its intransigent position. On November 29, 1920, Praznovszky telegraphed from Paris:

> I was confidentially informed today in the Foreign Office that following one of our recent representations, the French Government made a *démarche* in Bucharest suggesting that it would be time to do something about the long-contemplated Hungaro-Rumanian rapprochement. It was pointed out that in view of Hungary's conciliatory attitude and of France's willingness to mediate, success depends on Rumania. Rumania replied that until three Rumanians kidnapped in Hungary [?] are returned, she will not only refuse to even consider negotiations, but rather is contemplating reprisals.[123]

---

latter worked exclusively in the interest of France and judged that his interests could be best served by a lasting peace. As a cautious diplomat he sought a guarantee for such a long-lasting peace in accords between Hungary and her neighbors. He was disposed to assist Hungary whenever she was ready to pursue a peaceful policy. His sole objective was to stimulate friendly understanding between Hungary and her neighbors through French mediation. Paléologue's promises referred only to this purpose, and his friendship for Hungary did not go beyond this. During the course of this conversation the Magyar diplomat outlined in detail the significance of Millerand's *lettre d'envoi* regarding frontier adjustments.

[120] *Ibid.*, Doc. 783.

[121] *Ibid.*, Docs. 785, 814, 822, 832, 878. The question of Hungarian rearmament was discussed at length without any definite conclusion on the issue.

[122] *Ibid.*, Doc. 803.

[123] *Ibid.*, Doc. 831.

In effect, it was made clear that Take Jonescu had no intention of accepting French mediation and that he proposed, instead, putting off any contact with Hungary.[124] It was not surprising that, given these conditions, the general situation was developing in precisely the reverse of the way originally planned. In a colloquy held on December 29 between the Vatican's Cardinal Secretary of State, Gasparri, and the Hungarian Minister to the Holy See, Count Sommsich, reference was again made to the possibility of a rapprochement between the two countries in the face of the Bolshevik menace,[125] but, evidently, the intercession of the Vatican requested by the Magyars was not able to change the course of events. And Poland, too, according to the report from Csekonics on December 30, while declaring that it was still determined to pursue its objective of creating the famous Hungarian-Polish-Rumanian bloc in both Bucharest and Paris, finally decided to conclude an alliance with Rumania immediately and separately. Economic necessity far more than Bolshevik threats had forced Prince Sapieha to renounce his plan of insisting upon Hungarian participation in this alliance as the *conditio sine qua non* for the accord.[126] The door which might have led to the desired accord had closed in Paris, and the same was now happening in Warsaw.

15

In concluding this inquiry and summarizing the principal factors revealed by the documentation referred to above, it is clear that the Hungarian desire to achieve an accord with Rumania prior to the formation of the Little Entente was intense and serious. From the beginning Budapest understood that the key to peace in the Danube lay in Bucharest. From the Rumanian side, during the first phase a certain comprehension was displayed and action was taken to avoid commitment to the blandishments from Prague. The Soviet menace, French, Italian, and Polish pressures, the sense of responsibility, and the foresight of several eminent Rumanian statesmen simultaneously contributed to opening the way toward an understanding between the two countries. At a given moment this understanding appeared to be on the verge of consummation. It was at this precise point that Budapest, in concert with France and with Polish approval, laid down the essential lines of what was perhaps too excessive a program for territorial revision to serve as the basis for a general accord. However, shortly thereafter it was possible to note a change in the general political picture. The Bolshevik danger began to diminish; Czechoslovakia

---

[124] See Count Csáky's comments on the Rumanian declarations in *ibid.*, Doc. 846.
[125] *Ibid.*, Doc. 888.
[126] *Ibid.*, Docs. 891, 892.

energetically championed an antirevisionist policy and took the initiative in creating the Little Entente, which was largely anti-Magyar; Paris, fearing that the results of the Peace Conference might be compromised, severely reduced or eliminated entirely its support for the Hungarian program by dismissing from the scene those men who were committed to the Hungarian cause; Poland, closely tied to the Quai d'Orsay and frustrated in her dream of having a common frontier with Hungary, acted with constantly decreasing conviction. At this point, the Hungarian statesmen reexamined the position they had originally taken in seeking an arrangement with Rumania and modified it to make it more acceptable; in other words, they redefined their position to fit within the framework of the Treaty of Trianon. Unfortunately, Take Jonescu's policy gradually became more closely identified with Prague's and neutralized the cautious French efforts to change the ultimate aims of the Little Entente. The evolution of the situation took place gradually, but the tenacious efforts to prevent the inevitable developments were in vain. The weak moderate forces in Rumania were overcome. The conclusion of the Polish-Rumanian alliance and Rumania's adherence to the Little Entente, decided immediately following the first attempt at restoring Charles IV of Hapsburg to power, were to complete the encirclement and the isolation of Hungary. At the same time, tempers were brought to the boiling point, and the entire revision problem was placed on a much more vast and complex plane. The decision taken in these two solemn acts was to close the door definitively to attempts to realize a fruitful Hungarian-Rumanian rapprochement on an equitable basis and was to have a negative influence on future events in Danubian Central Europe. Thus, a favorable opportunity was lost because of the efforts of those same negative forces which had already contributed to the failure of the Peace Conference and which were working to sabotage the further attempts at conciliation in Europe.

II.

ITALY AND THE NAZI-SOVIET ACCORDS
OF AUGUST, 1939

Summary: 1. *Premise, objectives, and limits of the investigation.* 2. *Stalin's speech of March 10, 1939, and several probable explanations of its origins. The confidential statements by Litvinov and Potemkin on Soviet reactions to Chamberlain's conversations in Rome. Moscow's conviction of the existence of a British plan to direct German expansionism toward the Ukraine. The U.S.S.R.'s overture to Italy. The Italian reaction and the opinion of Ambassador Rosso.* 3. *Mussolini's suggestions to Goering for a rapprochement with the Soviet Union and their effect. The Duce's instructions to Ciano of May 4, 1939, and the Italo-German understanding reached in Milan on the nature of proposed Axis policy toward Moscow. Litvinov's resignation and the penetrating observations made by Ambassador Rosso. Von Schulenburg's confidential statements to the Italian Minister to Teheran prior to the former's departure for Munich.* 4. *Initial complete Italo-German collaboration in Moscow. The influence of Von Ribbentrop's consultations with Attolico on the directives issued by the Wilhelmstrasse. Consequences of the negative position of the Italian Ambassador to Berlin on Mussolini and Ciano. Progress in the Nazi-Soviet trade nego-*

---

* An earlier version of this chapter appeared as "L'Italia e gli accordi Tedesco-Sovietici dell'agosto 1939" in *Rivista di studi politici internazionali*, IV (1951). In 1955 it appeared in book form, published by Sansoni of Florence under the same title. The following is the foreword to the text of the Italian edition.

 Much has been written from the most disparate points of view and for a multitude of different reasons—and probably much more will be written—on the Nazi-Soviet accords of August 23, 1939, one of the crucial international developments that preceded the outbreak of World War II.

 The publication of the German diplomatic documents, the memoirs of a number of high Nazi officials, and the materials emerging from the Nuremburg trials has permitted a closer examination of the intentions of the Nazi leaders, although a number of issues concerning Germany remain to be treated definitively.

 On the other hand, there is no published Soviet documentation. It is not likely that this lacuna can be filled, and, therefore, every attempt at scientific reconstruction must be a unilateral one.

 This study, which also utilizes the documents contained in the Historical Archives of the Italian Foreign Ministry, does not pretend to examine the entire problem of the Nazi-Soviet negotiations but seeks, instead, to reconstruct that part—far greater than what has been generally supposed—played in them by the Fascist government, the Italo-German talks on the subject, and the extent to which Mussolini and Ciano had prior information of the preparations for the event.

 Only if these clearly defined limits are kept in mind will this inquiry be considered to have contributed to the understanding of an interesting aspect of the overall negotiations, an aspect which, to date, has hardly been touched.

tiations and the first German projects for a political understanding with Moscow. Goering's confidential observations to the Italian Consul General in Berlin. Ambassador Rosso's skepticism regarding the Anglo-Soviet negotiations then under way. 5. Ciano's and Rosso's approaches to the Soviet Chargé d'Affaires in Rome and to Vice Commissar Potemkin in Moscow on behalf of Germany in late June and early July, 1939. Von Schulenburg continues to keep his Italian colleague informed of developments in the Nazi-Soviet negotiations. 6. Effect of the first Italo-German differences of opinion over the possibility of localizing an eventual German-Polish conflict on Von Ribbentrop's attitude toward Moscow. The Attolico-Von Ribbentrop meeting of July 7, 1939, and further precise information from the Italian Embassy in Moscow. Rejection by Berlin of Mussolini's proposal to Hitler for the convocation of an international conference without the participation of the Soviet Union prompts Von Ribbentrop to intensify his activity in Moscow. 7. The situation on the eve of the Salzburg meeting. The Italian Embassy in the U.S.S.R. informs Palazzo Chigi in great detail about Von Schulenburg's activity, while the Wilhelmstrasse is more reticent with Attolico. Berlin makes no attempt to dissipate the growing conviction that the Anglo-Soviet negotiations will probably fail and carefully avoids encouraging the Japanese to hasten their decision to join the Italo-German alliance. 8. Von Ribbentrop's and Hilter's declaration to Ciano on August 11 and 12, 1939. The purpose of these declarations. The effect of the dissension between the two Axis governments over the Polish problem on subsequent German action in Moscow. 9. Further confidential comments by Von Ribbentrop to Attolico on August 18 and new information gathered by Rosso on the progress of the Nazi-Soviet negotiations on the eve of the coup de scène of August 21, 1939. The Fascist government persists in its skeptical attitude and loses the opportunity to induce the Germans to evaluate the significance of the Soviet gambit more carefully. 10. Ciano's and Mussolini's surprise at the announcement of Von Ribbentrop's departure for Moscow. The information gathered by Rosso and by Attolico on the activity of the Nazi Foreign Minister in the Soviet capital. 11. Conclusion.

1

Not the least interesting of all of the historical questions raised by the conclusion of the Nazi-Soviet accords of August 23, 1939, is that regarding the actual position the Fascist government took during the course of the entire negotiation. The existing uncertainty derives from the existence of two sources, apparently contradictory and generally well known. Mussolini, on August 25, wrote to Hitler, "Concerning the agreement with Russia, I approve of it completely. His Excellency Goering will tell you that in the discussions which I had with him last April, I affirmed that a rapprochement between Germany and Russia was necessary to prevent encirclement by the democracies."[1] On the other hand, Ciano's diary

---

[1] Mussolini to Hitler, letter, August 25, 1939, *Italian Diplomatic Documents* (Rome: La Libreria dello Stato, 1952—), 8th series, XIII, Doc. 250, hereafter cited as *I.D.; Documents on German Foreign Policy 1918–1945* (London: Her Majesty's

records the surprise and confusion provoked in Rome on the evening of August 21 by the announcement of the coup achieved by the Germans.[2]

What is the real significance of these two documents? If, in fact, the Fascist government was not only fully aware of the negotiations between Moscow and Berlin but had, moreover, recommended them, how did it happen that at the announcement of their conclusion it was taken by surprise to the extent that, for a moment, Rome's view of the general European diplomatic situation was completely confused?

The purpose of this investigation is to examine the documents of Palazzo Chigi[3] in order to provide answers to these questions and to dis-

---

Stationery Office, 1949—), Series D, VII, Doc. 271, hereafter cited as *G.D.* Italian documents cited without reference to number, series, or volume are from the Historical Archives of the Italian Foreign Ministry and have not yet been or are in the process of being classified for publication.

In seeking to evaluate this step it should not be forgotten that Mussolini's judgment was based only on the text of the Nazi-Soviet accord which had appeared in the press and not on the secret adjunct to the treaty, the exact terms of which became known only after the end of the war and which had never been transmitted to Mussolini, although he was aware of its existence.

[2] Galeazzo Ciano, *The Ciano Diaries, 1939–1943* (New York: Doubleday & Co., 1946), p. 126:

Last night at ten-thirty a new act opened. Von Ribbentrop telephoned that he would prefer to see me at Innsbruck rather than at the frontier, because he was to leave later for Moscow to sign a political pact with the Soviet Government. I suspended all decisions and reported to the Duce. He agreed with me in feeling that my trip to Germany would no longer be timely. I spoke again with Von Ribbentrop to tell him that our projected meeting would be postponed until his return from Moscow.

A long telephone conversation with the Duce. There is no doubt the Germans have struck a master stroke. The European situation is upset. Can France and Great Britain, who have based all other anti-Axis policy on an alliance with the Soviets, count upon the unconditional support of the extremist masses? And will the system of encirclement by means of the small states continue to prevail now that the Moscow balance has collapsed? Nevertheless, we must make no hasty decisions. We must wait, and, if possible, be ready ourselves to gain something in Croatia or Dalmatia. The Duce has set up an *ad hoc* army commanded by Graziani; I have established contacts with our Croatian friends in Italy and in their own country.

[3] During the course of my research, insofar as the problem in question is concerned, I discovered no lacunae. Therefore, I must conclude that I have consulted all of the existing material. As noted above, the numbering system used on the envelopes and on the bundles of documents is entirely provisional in anticipation of their proper classification and publication. Therefore, in this study no attempt will be made to classify a document, and identification will be made to the extent that the document itself permits. The italics used in the documentary texts cited here appear in the originals.

When this study was first published in 1951 the publication of the collection of Italian diplomatic documents had not yet begun, a fact which induced me to

close how the Fascist government, undoubtedly familiar with the details of most of the Nazi-Soviet negotiations up to the very last moment and in fact participating in them, could be stunned by their conclusion.

2

Scholars have generally focused their attention on Stalin's speech of March 10, 1939, before the Eighteenth Congress of the Bolshevik Party as the external manifestation of the Soviet Union's shift in foreign policy that led to its rapprochement with Germany. The significance of the occasion was not lost on Italian diplomats. However, before considering the reactions to this shift, it is pertinent to recall that as early as January 13, 1939, the Italian Ambassador to Moscow, Rosso, had transmitted confidential information given to him by his Polish colleague. Litvinov, in speaking of the Ukraine, had observed to the latter: "London and Paris are going to great lengths to persuade Berlin that its destiny lies toward the east. However, Hitler is less convinced of this than are either the French or the English."[4]

The exact reasons for this statement are not precisely known, but they are probably related both to the long conversation which took place between Hitler and the Soviet Ambassador during the reception for the diplomatic corps at the Reichschancellory the previous day and which had created something of a sensation among those present[5] and to certain information reaching Moscow on the eve of the Chamberlain talks with the Italians in Rome, the details of which will be discussed below.[6] In any event, in a detailed account of Stalin's speech, Ambassador Rosso also

---

reproduce here in great detail the archival materials on which this study is based. In preparing this edition, I could have summarized those documents which now have been published in the Italian documentary collection. I have chosen not to do so in order to facilitate the work of those scholars whose knowledge of the Italian language is limited.

[4] Rosso to Ciano, telexpress, January 13, 1939, No. 163/75. See also the earlier notations in the diary of the Italian Ambassador to Moscow, Augusto Rosso, "Obiettivi e metodi della politica estera sovietica," *Rivista di studi politici internazionali* (1946), I, pp. 9–10.

[5] Rosso, "Obiettivi e metodi," p. 17.

[6] The Chamberlain-Halifax visit to Rome lasted from January 11 to 14, but the interesting colloquies in Moscow took place on January 12. The Italian minutes of these colloquies are published in Galeazzo Ciano, *L'Europa verso la catastrofe* (Milan: Mondadori, 1948), pp. 394–404. The English minutes, with the exception of certain specific points to be examined below, substantially correspond to the Italian version and may be found in *Documents on British Foreign Policy 1919–1939* (London: Her Majesty's Stationery Office, 1949—), 3rd series, III, Doc. 500, hereafter cited as *B.D.*

referred to an episode which had taken place in January and which had been mentioned to him by Grzybowski. Rosso observed:

The suspicions nurtured at that time by Litvinov regarding the policies of London and Paris were surfaced today clearly and explicitly by Stalin in an accusatory statement delivered in the tone of one who was absolutely sure of his ground. For some time the Soviet press has been conducting a continuous and violent campaign against the Anglo-French policy of nonintervention but, up to the present, it has done so with the air of deploring the naïveté and blindness of the statesmen of the two western powers, who refuse to recognize that their overly permissive policies indirectly encourage the aggressiveness of the totalitarian powers and, therefore, can provoke a conflict. Now, instead, Stalin's statement attributes an unconfessed objective to the Anglo-French policy, i.e., that of encouraging Germany to look toward the east and to involve the U.S.S.R. in a war. Symptomatic of this reasoning is Stalin's statement referring to the clamor created by the English, French, and American press as being obviously stimulated "to aggravate the Soviet Union's ire against Germany, to poison the atmosphere of Russo-German relations and to provoke, *without plausible motives*, a conflict between Germany and the U.S.S.R."[7]

In the same report, the Italian Ambassador added:

Of course, I am in no position to identify the information or the evidence upon which Stalin based his accusations, but I do believe it interesting to refer Your Excellency to a very confidential statement made to me by my Polish colleague here, Ambassador Grzybowski, on this theme in which he told me that, a short time after Chamberlain's visit to Rome, he had occasion to talk with Litvinov and that the latter had affirmed that the Soviet government had learned *from an unimpeachable source* that, during his Rome talks, Chamberlain sought to raise the Ukrainian question and left the impression that England tended to support German aspirations in that area. However, the Duce is supposed to have promptly cut off any further comment of this nature by firmly stating that Italy was not directly concerned with this problem. According to Grzybowski, Stalin and Litvinov were evidently highly gratified by this "lesson" imparted to the English Prime Minister by the Duce. I have no way of evaluating the credibility of the Soviet version of this episode, but I thought it to be of interest to Your Excellency if for no other reason but that it demonstrates that Moscow's suspicions toward London are deeply rooted.[8]

Without overestimating the significance of the two episodes referred to by Grzybowski (the second of which Rosso had confirmed by Potemkin, as will be noted later), they apparently cast new light on the genesis of the Kremlin's policy, which, in the accords of August 23, 1939, was also designed to subvert a hypothetical British plan to direct Hitler's aggres-

---

[7] Rosso to Ciano, report, March 12, 1939, No. 1045/412.
[8] *Ibid.*

sion toward the east. In any event, these episodes are important for a further examination of the problem.

The Italian Ambassador continued:

The overall impression to be drawn from a study of Stalin's statement on the international situation is that the keynote is moderation in both tone and substance. It contains no direct attacks against Japan, Italy, or Germany and, as a matter of fact, the totalitarian powers are treated with greater courtesy than are the democratic states. The affirmation of the Soviet Union's peaceful intentions recurs again and again in Stalin's speech, and the Soviet desire to improve commercial relations with all countries without distinction is clearly emphasized. . . . Worth noting among the directives given to the Communist Party is Stalin's recommendation that the party *act prudently and not allow* those war provocateurs accustomed to having their chestnuts pulled out of the fire by third parties to involve the U.S.S.R. in international conflicts. . . . Moreover, it is also symptomatic that Stalin has put aside all reference to world revolution.[9]

A few days after these first well-reasoned comments reached Rome from the Italian Embassy in Moscow, Rosso dispatched a telegram to Palazzo Chigi in which he summarized the substance of his conversation with Potemkin. Among other statements, Potemkin observed: "I am convinced that before long your great leader will recognize that common political interests existing between Italy and the Soviet Union are such that differences between our two systems of government should not preclude a repetition of that collaboration between our two countries which I had the good fortune of initiating when I had the honor of representing my government in Rome."[10]

The Peoples' Vice Commissar for Foreign Affairs then concluded by "observing that the U.S.S.R. found herself in so strong a position as to fear attacks from no quarter, while many powers (he had named France, England, Poland, and even Germany) are making every effort to win the sympathies of the men of Moscow."[11]

Both of Potemkin's statements should have caused serious reflection. In his comment on the general political situation in the U.S.S.R., the reference to Moscow's freedom of action and to the approaches also being made from Berlin, placed on the same plane with those from Paris and London and Warsaw, was clearly a symptom of change insofar as Moscow was concerned. At the same time, the reference to the German offers acquired a special significance in that it was preceded by remarks designed to de-emphasize the importance of ideological differences and served as a clear overture to Rome for a rapprochement.

[9] *Ibid.*
[10] Rosso to Ciano, telegram, March 18, 1939, No. 26.
[11] *Ibid.*

To be sure, the invitation extended for a greater Italo-Soviet collaboration was the product of very recent developments, but this time the initiative was taken entirely by the Soviets and formulated in terms of unusual warmth. In fact, on January 23, 1939, Potemkin, in an academic discussion with Rosso on the relations between the two countries, referred to a statement made only a few days previously by Ciano to Ambassador Stein in which the Fascist Foreign Minister expressed "the hope for an amelioration of relations between the two countries, at least in the economic field,"[12] but the matter remained no more than a friendly comment.

Rosso's telegram of March 18 arrived in Rome at a time in which the surprise and confusion in the Italian capital was at its height after the receipt of the news of the German coup against Prague.[13] Despite the situation, Count Ciano did not ignore the Moscow overture, and, while he repeated his statements made earlier in January to the Soviet Chargé d'Affaires, he immediately instructed Rosso to discuss the matter further with Potemkin.[14]

At very nearly the same time, in a note addressed to Attolico, the Italian Consul General in Berlin, Renzetti, included the following:

I have been asked for information on what agreements have been reached between Minister Ciano and the Polish leaders. Impressions drawn from conversations reported here during the last few days indicate a growing resentment against the Poles, and there is talk again, without clearly defined threats or precisely stated plans, of the need for Germany to regain Memel and the Polish Corridor. Some recognize that it is necessary to compensate Poland, to give her an outlet to the sea; others, albeit in the vaguest of terms, refer to the "Polish mosaic" and to the possibility of reducing it in size. The latter view is advanced particularly by those who would seek a Nazi-Soviet entente.

These are no more than ideas and desires which have not yet been clearly or realistically defined; they are desires and thoughts mentioned only in whispers and very cautiously. However, in my modest opinion, we should take note of these developments because if it were true that Hitler, up until very recently, had made it crystal clear that he was opposed to coming to terms with Russia, it is equally true that with the disappearance of Czechoslovakia, with its forty divisions (figures given to me by the Germans), and with the marked reduction and improvement in her frontiers, Germany now no longer fears Russian or pro-Russian bases on her flanks and is, therefore, in a situation that is entirely different from that existing a few months ago. It could be this fact that might induce Hitler to modify his views toward Russia. I repeat, these are no more than ideas and thoughts which, however, acquire greater substance as the tempo of the deterioration in Anglo-German relations noticeably increases.[15]

[12] Rosso to Ciano, courier telegram, January 24, 1939, No. 318/130.

[13] See Mario Toscano, *The Origins of the Pact of Steel* (Baltimore: The Johns Hopkins Press, 1967), pp. 168–98.

[14] Ciano to Rosso, telegrams, March 19 and 22, 1939, Nos. 206/22 and 208/24R.

[15] Renzetti to Attolico, note, March 19, 1939, re-transmitted by Attolico to Ciano in summary form via telexpress, March 20, 1939, No. 02223/659.

Despite the fact that these impressions and indications were vague, they were important when related to the overtures coming from Moscow and, therefore, were matters of vital concern.

Two weeks later, the Italian Embassy in Moscow renewed its reporting on the Kremlin directives in a series of communications designed to emphasize and clarify the preceding developments. On April 3, taking as his starting point a Tass communiqué in which the Soviet government denied that it had agreed to furnish Poland with war materiel in the event of German aggression, Ambassador Rosso telegraphed that, in his judgment, this move demonstrated that

Moscow was not disposed to accepting partial agreements, but that it intended to take advantage of the present international situation to force England and France to openly champion the system of collective security. . . . It is reasonable to ask whether, by employing this tactic, the U.S.S.R. is in reality seeking to avoid assuming too precise and definitive obligations and thus to remain out of a European conflict. . . . It remains my conviction (as it was during the September crisis of last year) that the Kremlin leaders see a European war as an instrument for a possible proletarian revolution in the bourgeois countries and are pushing Europe toward conflict while, at the same time, seeking to maintain their own freedom of action in order to be able to exploit the situation at a given time for the triumph of their own ideology.[16]

These theories were repeated by Rosso the following day in a telegram to Rome on the subject of the just concluded Russo-Japanese agreement on the question of fishing rights in Siberian waters:

The circumstances in which these long negotiations were concluded demonstrate that the Soviet government, despite its apparent intransigence, did not dare face the prospect of an armed conflict.

However, I do not believe that this should be attributed exclusively to its lack of faith in its own military strength.

In my judgment Moscow's policy is, at this time, dominated by the conviction that, in the present international situation, the U.S.S.R. should avoid becoming involved on any front until the crisis between the totalitarian and democratic powers has exploded into a world war.[17]

On April 6 Rosso, prompted by an editorial appearing in the *Journal de Moscou* on April 5,[18] again voiced his views on the general foreign policy of the Soviet Union in a personal letter to Count Ciano, as follows:

Permit me to make use of this personal letter to give you my impressions and views on Soviet policy, which would not be easy for me to do in an official report.

Yesterday I went to see Vice Commissar Potemkin to discuss the matter of

16 Rosso to Ciano, telegram, April 3, 1939, No. 37.
17 Rosso to Ciano, telegram, April 4, 1939, No. 38.
18 Rosso to Ciano, telegram, April 5, 1939, No. 39.

exchanging Italians arrested in the U.S.S.R. for Soviet sailors interned in Spain, and I took advantage of the occasion to sound him out on the Soviet attitude concerning the current state of international affairs.

I was particularly interested in learning precisely what Moscow's intentions were in the light of the Chamberlain initiative.

Potemkin was very cautious in his replies to my questions, and, naturally, he indicated that he was expressing only his personal views. He explained the official view on the matter of collective security and repeated the arguments which have appeared in the Soviet press. However, he did dwell at length and very firmly on the point made by Stalin in his speech to the Party Congress: the accusation that England was working to drive Germany into an attack on the U.S.S.R.

On this point Potemkin repeated, in tones of absolute certainty, that Chamberlain, during his visit to Rome, had sought to engage the Duce in a discussion on the Ukraine as a natural area for German expansion, but that he abandoned the approach after the Duce refused to discuss the matter. I then sought to learn how the Soviets regarded the Polish attitude, and I seemed to grasp that on this matter too Moscow is extremely suspicious of England: that is, there is the suspicion that London is applying pressure on Warsaw to prevent the latter—or perhaps to dissuade the latter—from tying herself too closely to the Soviet Union against Germany.

In conclusion, it is my impression that in the depths of their souls these gentlemen continue to believe that England is continually working "to channel the German torrent toward the east."

At the most propitious time during the conversation I imparted the communication you instructed me to give in response to his statement regarding a renewal of Italo-Soviet collaboration; that is, I told him that the Fascist government also was considering the possibility of a gradual improvement in the relations between the U.S.S.R. and Italy. Potemkin then told me that Helfand, the Soviet Chargé d'Affaires in Rome, had talked with you and that you had made a similar statement to him which was noted here "with great satisfaction."

Potemkin dwelled on this theme at length recalling the "very interesting" period of his tour of duty in Rome when he had the good fortune to work in harmony with the views of the Italian Chief of State. He again spoke of "common interests" in the political as well as in the economic fields. This time he made no further mention of raising a barrier against German expansionism but only of "taking a common equilibrating action, particularly in southeastern Europe."

If you were to ask me how I evaluate and what significance I attribute to statements of this kind, I would reply that they are made in complete sincerity. It is obvious that it would be advantageous to the U.S.S.R. to have a friendly Italy that does not hamper the traffic and movement of the Soviet navy in the Mediterranean. It is even more obvious that Moscow would like to have a friendly Italy disposed to cooperate with the U.S.S.R. in applying the brakes to German penetration of the Balkans. This is the reason why, despite the violent Soviet attacks against our regime and against Axis policy (attacks, we must recognize, which are the exact counterparts of the no less violent attacks against the Soviets appearing in our press), the U.S.S.R. has avoided a definite break in relations with Italy but, instead, has continued to leave the door open to a possible amelioration of relations.

If, however, you desired to probe my innermost thoughts on the matter, I would have to add that this improvement in relations with us is purely a matter of contingency and is designed to achieve tactical ends which primarily interest Litvinov and his collaborators in the Narkomindiel, who must maneuver according to the needs of the moment. The fundamental and ultimate goal of the Kremlin, the one which determines the general directives of the Politbureau, remains the proletarian revolution which will destroy the "capitalist encirclement" often referred to by Stalin. From these fundamentals stems my view that the Soviet leaders desire and indirectly encourage a world war that will force the antagonistic elements in the capitalist world to clash and to destroy themselves. The U.S.S.R. will make every effort to remain out of the conflict until the moment arrives which will permit her to facilitate the creation of the largest possible number of "*novus ordo*" Communist states.

I may be mistaken, but, in my opinion, these constitute the innermost thoughts of Stalin and his comrades.[19]

This rather remarkable letter from the Italian Ambassador in Moscow is worth serious consideration from three points of view: the origins of Moscow's suspicions of London, the limitations of an eventual Italo-Soviet collaboration, and overall Soviet foreign policy. The fact that Potemkin did not hesitate to apprise Rosso of the information he possessed on Chamberlain's Rome talks in support of the accusation that Great Britain had worked to provoke a German attack against Russia merits further examination. In the first place, the return to it confirms the intensity of the conviction in the Soviet mind. In fact, if the Narkomindiel had had the slightest doubt of the truth of its information, it would have been very careful not to mention the matter to one who was in a position to confirm its inaccuracy, if such were the case, and thus destroy the entire Soviet case. Second, it is clear that the source of the information possessed by the Soviet was not an Italian one because such a revelation would have seriously imperiled its informant's future effectiveness. As was learned some time after the end of World War II, the documents contained in the safe at the British Embassy in Rome were regularly photographed and copies consigned to the Italian Intelligence Service and to the Counsellor in the Soviet Embassy in Rome, Helfand.[20]

Nevertheless, a reading of both the English and Italian versions of the minutes of the Chamberlain-Mussolini talks of January 12, now available to us,[21] still leaves the accuracy of the Soviet thesis open to question.

[19] Rosso to Ciano, personal letter, April 6, 1939, no number.

[20] See pp. 409–10 below.

[21] Ciano, *L'Europa verso la catastrofe*, pp. 400–1; B.D., 3rd series, III, pp. 524–29.

There is no question that the British Prime Minister referred to a possible
Nazi venture toward the Ukraine, implying a localized conflict between
Germany and the U.S.S.R.[22] Chamberlain's approach to this question
grew out of his anxiety concerning the Führer's real intention, and it is
not easy to read into this approach anything designed to suggest that
German expansionism should be directed toward the east. Chamberlain's
affirmation that a Soviet-German, a German-Polish, or a Russo-German-
Polish war would not necessarily involve the western powers and his

[22] The opening phase of the discussion on the subject is recorded in the English
version as follows:

The Duce then enquired whether there was any point which British Ministers
wished to raise. The Prime Minister replied that he would like to elicit the
Duce's opinion upon a matter of some delicacy, although if Signor Mussolini felt
that he preferred not to answer the question, no doubt he would say so. As he
had said yesterday, he had hoped that after Munich, and particularly after the
Declaration signed by Herr Hitler, it would be possible to proceed with discussion
designed to put relations between Germany and Great Britain on a better footing.
Unfortunately, this had not been found practicable and the attitude of Germany
was giving rise to a great deal of anxiety and doubt, not only in his mind but all
over Europe. Armament was proceeding not only unchecked, but at an increased
pace. There was talk of massing troops, and a general suspicion that Herr Hitler
had it in mind to make some further move in the near future which would be
likely to upset a great part of Europe.

There were different suggestions as to the nature of such a move. Some people
thought it would be in the direction of the Ukraine; others that although that
might be the ultimate aim, it would be preceded by a sudden attack in the west.
Here Signor Mussolini shook his head emphatically. Probably most people thought
that the move, if made, would be towards the East, and they feared that it might
mean a war between Germany and Poland, or Germany and Russia, or Germany
with Poland and Russia combined. The Prime Minister would not say that such
a war would necessarily involve Western Powers also, but once war began one
never could tell when or where it would stop. Here Signor Mussolini indicated
his assent. Therefore, the Prime Minister concluded, these rumours and suspicions
were undermining all confidence in Europe; they were driving every country into
increased programmes of rearmament and as long as they continued there seemed
little hope of improvement in the situation. What he would like to know was
whether the Duce could give him any assurances which would do something to
mitigate his anxiety on this very important matter.

B.D., 3rd series, III, pp. 524–25.
For the background leading to Chamberlain's question to Mussolini, see the information which had been transmitted to London earlier, in *ibid.*, Docs. 503, 526,
529. The Italian minutes for the same colloquy read as follows:

Thereupon Chamberlain asked to speak on a question which he defined as
being delicate. As he had the occasion to say yesterday, he had hoped, after
Munich, to be able to establish the basis for greater international collaboration
and particularly for a more deep-rooted understanding with Germany. This has
not been possible. At the same time, he was forced to admit that in world public
opinion there is increasing anxiety regarding Hitler's true intentions. The feverish
tempo of rearmament in Germany and the rumors concerning mobilization ac-

insistence on certain presumed Soviet weaknesses[23] could be interpreted in various ways, particularly if it is recalled that the policy emerging from the Munich meetings appeared, in the eyes of the totalitarian states as well as in many Anglo-French circles, to make sense only if there was at the same time a tacit understanding that Hitler would be allowed a free hand in the east.[24] However, while Mussolini's reply firmly denied the existence of a Nazi threat to the Ukraine, he accompanied this statement, according to the English minutes of the meeting, with a declaration that he was not particularly opposed to the creation of an independent Ukraine.[25] In any event, it was clear that the Kremlin also considered that

---

tivities are leading the world to conclude that Hitler intends new coups which could be dangerous to the peace of the world. A number of people believe that Hitler is contemplating an action toward the Ukraine to create an independent state which could then be used to drive back the Russians. Others believe that an attack will come in the west against the French, and still others believe the attack will occur in the east against Poland. Such actions would provoke a war with Poland or Russia or both. There is no proof that such a conflict can be localized, but, in any event, the situation is dangerous, just as the anxiety created by the uncertainty regarding the true intentions of the Germans produces a sense of disquietude. Can the Duce provide some clarification on the situation?

Ciano, *L'Europa verso la catastrofe*, pp. 400–1.

[23] As the discussion developed Chamberlain added, "Russia could not be an enemy to be feared by Germany for she was too weak internally to take the offensive, although she might put up a very good defense if she were attacked." *B.D.*, 3rd series, III, p. 526.

[24] The German Ambassador to London at the time wrote as follows:

It can be assumed that, in accordance with the basic trend of Chamberlain's policy, they will accept a German expansionist policy in eastern Europe. In this connection the Polish question recedes into the background as compared with the Ukrainian question. It is expected that the first move for a new order in eastern Europe will arise out of the Ukrainian question, which would be tackled by Germany and brought to a head. Those who know Russia express the opinion that a rising in the Russian Ukraine has never, since the revolution, had so much chance of success as today, provided that it receives support from outside. Such support could only come from Germany.

Dirksen to Von Ribbentrop, report, January 4, 1939, *G.D.*, Series D, IV, Doc. 287.

[25] *B.D.*, 3rd series, III, p. 525:

Signor Mussolini appeared to consider his answer carefully and then he replied slowly and with pauses between the sentences. He said it was true that Germany had rearmed and was still rearming, but that he was convinced that this was only for defensive purposes and that Herr Hitler desired a long period of peace in order that he might fuse together the component parts of the expanded Reich and develop its productive forces. He thought it was very possible that these rumours were being spread about by propagandists anxious to make mischief and to put Germany in the wrong. He did not believe that Hitler had any intention of setting up an independent Ukraine or of attempting to bring about the disruption of Russia, although he, Mussolini, would not feel that it would be a bad thing if an independent Ukraine were created and it certainly would not be to

its security was being threatened by London and was moved by this consideration to do what was necessary to neutralize this threat.[26]

That portion of Rosso's letter referring to the eventual Italo-Soviet rapprochement is also of interest. The Peoples' Vice Commissar repeats the
arguments advanced on March 18 in support of the common interests of
the two countries, but he eliminates every anti-German reference made in
the earlier approach. This was extremely significant. The Italian Ambassador did not ignore the change in the Soviet position, but he perhaps
did not draw all of the possible conclusions from his correct diagnosis of
the tactical value of certain requirements of Soviet policy. In conclusion,
he did note what he believed to be the ultimate Soviet goals, but he fails
to ask himself the question of whether an understanding with Berlin or

---

the disadvantage of the Russians. He would like to mention that Italy did not
favour a common frontier between Hungary and Poland because the frontiers
had been laid down on ethnical principles and the Ruthenians were neither Poles
nor Hungarians. The interview which Hitler and Beck had had recently at
Berchtesgaden had improved the situation between these two parties and again
he repeated that in his view these stories about a move eastward by Germany
were without foundation and probably started deliberately by propagandists. As
to any idea of a German attack in the West, such a thing was absolutely out of
the question.

The Italian version is as follows (Ciano, *L'Europa verso la catastrofe*, pp. 401–2):

The Duce recognizes that Germany has rearmed and is rearming on an imposing scale, but this rearmament must be considered in relation to Russian rearmament, about which we have no precise information but which must be
considered to be of major proportions. He believes that Hitler desires a long
period of peace in order to better merge the new territories acquired by the Reich
and to develop Germany's great productive force. It is also likely that elements
not in responsible positions desire the breakup of Soviet Russia, and he personally
added that if Bolshevism was to disappear it would not be a disaster for humanity
and it would certainly be a blessing for the Russian people. But, from the information in his possession, he is in a position to exclude the possibility that
Hitler is contemplating an attack on the Ukraine. This rumor may well have
grown out of the Ruthenian question. It should also be made clear that Italy
also opposes a common frontier between Poland and Hungary, since the Vienna
Arbitrage is based on ethnic concepts, and Ruthenians are neither Poles nor Hungarians. He excludes categorically an attack against the west.

[26] In effect—and this could also explain the timing of Potemkin's confidential
comment to Rosso—until the occupation of Ruthenia by Hungarian forces and the
period following the coup against Prague, Moscow's anxiety about Hitler's plans for
the Ukraine was increased by a series of rumors which were constantly repeated
throughout the West. Stalin had denounced the validity of the rumors in his speech
of March 10, and it cannot be denied that the number and variety of rumors all
hinting at very much the same thing would have left anyone perplexed. On this
point, see Beloff, *The Foreign Policy of Soviet Russia* (London: Oxford University
Press, 1949), II, pp. 213–18, 222, and the references cited therein; Leon Noël,
L'Agression allemonde contre la Pologne (Paris: Flammarion, 1946), pp. 260–65,

with Rome, albeit temporary, would not facilitate the achievement of these goals. In any case, both the information and the commentary contained in Rosso's communiqué were bound to give Ciano much to think about regarding the various political combinations which the Kremlin could realistically consider in facing the critical international situation.

3

The possibility of a marked change in German policy toward the Soviet Union was first touched upon by Goering in a conversation with Mussolini during the former's visit to Rome in mid-April, 1939. The German minutes on this point read as follows:

In connection with the change in Polish foreign policy as regards the attitude of that country towards Germany, which Field Marshal Goering emphasized, the conversation then turned to Russia. In this connection the Field Marshal referred to Stalin's speech at the last Conference of the Communist Party, in which Stalin had stated that the Russians would not allow themselves to be used as cannon fodder for the capitalist powers. He (the Field Marshal) would ask the Führer whether it would not be possible to put out feelers cautiously to Russia through certain intermediaries with a view to a rapprochement so as to cause Poland anxiety over Russia as well.

The Duce welcomed this idea most warmly and said that in Italy too they had similar ideas for some time and, without saying anything definite, also had already adopted a more friendly tone towards the Russians through the Italian Ambassador in Moscow in connection with economic negotiations, a gesture which met with a very keen response from Potemkin, the Secretary of State in the Russian Foreign Ministry.

292; *B.D.*, 3rd series, III, Doc. 534, IV, Docs. 24, 38, 40, 76; Keith Feiling, *The Life of Neville Chamberlain* (London: MacMillan, 1947), pp. 391, 395.

Alexander Henderson's notation on the matter was typical: "The day the Nazis decide that the dream of colonizing the Ukraine, to make a German dominion of it, is a dream which can never be realized, will indeed be a dangerous one for Great Britain and France." *Eyewitness in Czechoslovakia* (London: Harrap, 1939), p. 287. In the summer of 1939 Salazar, in a conversation with the Italian Minister to Lisbon, repeatedly referred to his conviction that Germany aimed at acquiring the Ukraine. Mameli to Ciano, report, July 16, 1939, *I.D.*, 8th series, XII, Doc. 592.

The German diplomatic documents concerning the period between Munich and the occupation of Prague indicate that Berlin was directed to adopt a position of wait and see, leaving the Ruthenian question open to all possible solutions, while resisting vigorously the pressing claims of the Hungarians to the region. At the same time, the documents contain a long report from the German Ambassador in London, Dirksen, in which he analyzed, on the eve of Chamberlain's departure for Rome, the attitude of British governing circles and the press toward an eventual German action in the Ukraine and in which he came to the conclusion that, if the act were preceded by adequate psychological preparation, it would be accepted by Great Britain. Dirksen to Von Ribbentrop, report, June 4, 1939, *G.D.*, Series D, IV, Doc. 287.

On this point Count Ciano said that the Russian Chargé d'Affaires who had often failed to call on him for months on end, had called on him twice in one week in a very friendly manner, apparently in this very connection.

The Duce stated that a rapprochement between the Axis powers and Russia was naturally dependent on the attitude Japan would adopt. If Japan had no objections to such matters, this rapprochement could, as Count Ciano had already stated, be effected with comparative ease. The object of such a rapprochement would be to induce Russia to react coolly and unfavourably to Britain's efforts at encirclement, on the lines of Stalin's aforementioned speech, and to take up a neutral position. That would make a very great impression in the democratic world. The Axis Powers could tell the Russians that they had no intention of attacking Russia. Since Bolshevism was not tolerated in Italy and Germany, Russia would naturally not be expected to tolerate National Socialism and Fascism within her own territory. Moreover in their ideological struggle against plutocracy and capitalism the Axis Powers had to a certain extent the same objectives as the Russian régime. It was, however, important to know what Germany's attitude towards the Ukraine was.

In reply to the Duce's last question, the Field Marshal said that, according to the statements by the Führer, Germany had no designs whatsoever on the Ukraine, and that ever since he had been a member of the Cabinet he (the Field Marshal) had not set eyes on a single document dealing with the Ukraine and the whole question had only been raised in British newspapers for propaganda purposes against Germany. Only recently the Führer had told the Field Marshal again that he had no designs whatsoever on the Ukraine. It was moreover interesting to note that there had been absolutely no further mention of Russia in the Führer's latest speeches. Any declaration of neutrality on the part of Russia would in any case not fail to make a deep impression on Poland and the Western Powers. If Russia declared her neutrality Poland would then not lift a finger in a general conflict.

In reply to a question by the Duce, the Field Marshal went on to say that, of the 35 million inhabitants of Poland, only 14 million were real Poles. Poland's air armaments were not particularly good and consisted mostly of obsolete French and British aircraft. The Polish artillery dated for the most part from the war.

In the event of the Axis Powers reaching a decision to seek a rapprochement with Russia, the Duce thought that Italy's method might be through a trade treaty with Russia. The Field Marshal also referred to the Russian desire to expand the scope of the Russo-German economic treaty. If Germany gave her consent to this, talks with Russia would be possible immediately. The Duce considered the matter to be important because Britain was also making advances to the Russians at the moment.[27]

The exchange of views on that occasion is obviously of great interest. First, it is noteworthy that the initiative to discuss a possible amelioration of relations with the U.S.S.R. came from Goering, who introduced the subject "in connection with the change in Polish foreign policy as regards

[27] Schmidt, promemorial, April 18, 1939, *G.D.*, Series D, IV, Doc. 226.

the attitude of that country towards Germany." This point was significant because it suggested grounds for a possible political entente between Berlin and Moscow. Second, Mussolini's positive reaction to the Field Marshal's idea (Goering had affirmed that he had not yet spoken of the project to Hitler) should be kept in mind because later on it becomes understandable for the Germans to say that the rapprochement to the Soviet Union had been approved by the Duce,[28] even though it was incorrect to state that it was Mussolini who had made the suggestion or that he foresaw the totality of the diplomatic revolution brought about by the Nazi-Soviet Pact of August 23, 1939. In fact, Mussolini had not suggested any guidelines to the nature of the rapprochement with the Soviets, probably because at that moment he considered it impossible for Berlin and Moscow to go much beyond a general amelioration. In any case, while not insisting on this point, he did consider the maneuver to be an entirely negative one designed to prevent the Soviet Union from joining in the encirclement of Germany, and this belief was sufficient to determine the limits of his conception, limits which were further defined in his observation concerning Japan's position. On this point it should also be noted that neither Mussolini nor Goering seemed to realize that the proposed rapprochement with Russia would render the Anti-Comintern Pact devoid of meaning. It was also true that neither leader was aware of the secret protocol annexed to the German-Japanese Pact of November, 1937 (this protocol was never revealed to the Italians, and Goering himself only learned of it during the Nuremberg Trials). In any event, it was significant that neither Mussolini nor Goering paused to consider the effect of their proposed project on the negotiations then under way in Tokyo, which indicates that, as late as April, 1939, neither Rome nor Berlin understood the position of the Japanese government. And finally, attention should be called to Mussolini's and Ciano's repeated references to the increasingly friendly attitude of the Soviet Union toward Italy. Such references, while they immediately attracted the attention of Berlin at a time when the Germans were anxiously looking for any symptoms

[28] Shortly before the conclusion of the Nazi-Soviet Pact of August 23, 1939, the Italian Minister-Counsellor in Berlin, Magistrati, wrote to Ciano: "Do you know that, in a certain sense, this Nazi-Soviet rapprochement originated, as Schmidt has told me, in a phrase uttered by the Duce to Goering in Rome in mid-April when he said, 'Why don't you find a way to come to terms with Moscow?'" Magistrati to Ciano, personal letter, August 21, 1939, I.D., 8th series, XIII, Doc. 140. Von Ribbentrop too, in speaking with Rosso on August 25, attributed the idea of a rapprochement between Germany and the Soviet Union to Mussolini. Rosso to Ciano, telegram, August 25, 1939, ibid., Doc. 264. Goering made a similar comment in a conversation some time later with Magistrati. Magistrati to Ciano, letter, September 12, 1939, ibid., 9th series, I, Doc. 170.

that Russia was well disposed toward an agreement with Germany, may
be the basis of an idea subsequently developed by Von Ribbentrop: to
use the good offices of Italian diplomats as a means of reopening negotiations with Moscow.

There is no evidence that, in the period immediately following Goering's visit to Rome, the Wilhelmstrasse informed the Italian government
of the approaches to Moscow then being made by the Nazis.[29] However,
in drafting a memorandum for Ciano's use in a meeting with Von Ribbentrop in Milan, Mussolini, on May 4, 1939, thought it pertinent to spell
out his views on what the nature and limits of an eventual rapprochement
with the U.S.S.R. should be: *"Policy toward Russia?* Yes to a policy that
would prevent Russia from joining the anti-Axis bloc but nothing more,
since such a policy would be totally antithetic to present positions, completely incomprehensible internally, and would weaken the fabric of the
Axis."[30]

Despite its brevity, this passage made several significant points. First, it
clarified the meaning of the statements made by the Fascist Chief of State
to Goering on April 16 and defined the guidelines which, in Mussolini's
view, should be used in the approach to Moscow. Second, even if the
news that Litvinov was to be dismissed had a certain effect on the situation, the fact that Mussolini returned to the subject of a rapprochement
with the U.S.S.R. for a second time in so brief a period demonstrated that
he had been struck by Goering's proposal and that his receptiveness to
the idea was not simply a momentary fancy. Finally, the desire to examine the problem with Von Ribbentrop, while it revealed his conviction
that the maneuver would be undertaken by the two Axis powers at the
same time and each in full accord with the other, nevertheless seemed to
reveal a certain concern regarding the character the Germans might seek
to give to the undertaking, even though there is no evidence to indicate
just how such a concern arose.

Meanwhile, the elevation of Molotov to the post held by Litvinov
prompted a number of interesting comments from the Italian Ambassador
in Moscow, who reported his first impressions as follows:

It is possible only to guess as to the causes prompting Litvinov's retirement
since, to date, Russian sources have revealed nothing specific on this sensational
stroke.

[29] For example, Attolico was not even informed of the important colloquy between Von Weizsäcker and Merekalov of April 17. See *G.D.*, Series D, VI, Doc.
215.

[30] For the text of the Mussolini note, see Toscano, *Origins of the Pact of Steel*,
pp. 289–91.

I am convinced that it is a matter of profound differences between Stalin and the Politbureau on the one hand and Litvinov on the other regarding the question of the fundamental lines of Soviet foreign policy.

I have reason to believe that during recent months Litvinov had worked strenuously to achieve a close military-political collaboration with England and France, while the Kremlin leaders continue to be very suspicious of the western democracies. Therefore, I am inclined to believe that the fall of Litvinov indicates the failure of the Anglo-Soviet negotiations. It is also possible that there are differences connected with Potemkin's mission to Ankara.

However, I have the impression that the departure of Litvinov marks the failure of the collaborationist forces who wished to strengthen the democratic bloc and the success of the isolationist bloc which desires war between the totalitarian powers and the democratic powers (both regarded as enemies because both are capitalist and therefore anti-Communist) in the hope of seeing a violent social crisis emerge therefrom as the necessary condition for a successful proletarian revolution in Europe.

The preceding is simply the reflection of my intuition, since I have not the slightest bit of positive information at hand. Therefore, I do not exclude the possibility of having to modify some of my views expressed herein.[31]

It must be recognized that, despite Rosso's final reservation, he did have an excellent grasp of what was actually happening, and the accuracy of his conclusions differs markedly from the comment sent to Berlin by the German Chargé d'Affaires in Moscow, who simply noted the possibility of a difference of opinion in the Kremlin on the negotiations conducted by Litvinov.[32] Rosso's telegram reached Palazzo Chigi prior to Ciano's departure for Milan, that is, in time to be considered by him in conducting his discussions with Von Ribbentrop.

From the minutes of the meeting between the two Axis Foreign Ministers, a meeting at which the decision was made to proceed with the Italo-German alliance, it appears that Mussolini's thesis was accepted in substance by the Germans. The pertinent passage in the Italian minutes of the meeting is as follows: "Von Ribbentrop is convinced that we should take advantage of the favorable opportunity presented to us at this time to prevent Russia's joining the anti-totalitarian bloc, but he is also in complete agreement that it is absolutely necessary that we carry out such a plan with the greatest discretion and within carefully defined limits. Any exaggerated manifestation, in a Russophile sense, would have negative results. However, he insists that it is necessary to continue to em-

---

[31] Rosso to Ciano, telegram, May 5, 1939, No. 51.

[32] Tippelskirch to Von Ribbentrop, telegram, May 4, 1939, *G.D.*, Series D, VI, Doc. 325. The Italian Minister to Finland also reported immediately to Ciano that "replacing with Molotov should indicate Moscow's desire to avoid concluding agreements which would draw the U.S.S.R. into the tinder box of European politics." Koch to Ciano, telegram, May 5, 1939, No. 35.

phasize the amelioration evident in the relations between the Axis and the U.S.S.R."[33]

The minutes prepared by Von Ribbentrop indicate only a difference in details: "It was agreed by the Reich Foreign Minister and Count Ciano that a *detente* should be brought about in political relations between the Axis Powers and the Soviet Union. Such a *detente*, however, should not be pushed too far, since it was the Duce's view that friendly relations with the Soviet Union were not possible for reasons of Italian domestic policy."[34]

In effect, the only significant difference between the two minutes was that Von Ribbentrop stressed the point that the limits to the rapprochement with the Soviet Union were set by Mussolini, apparently not for reasons common to both powers, but solely for reasons of Italian internal policy.

None of the German documents which were eventually brought to light suggests that, on that occasion, Von Ribbentrop was anything less than sincere. During that period in Berlin, despite the uncertainty regarding the real intentions of the Soviets, it is certain that there was as yet no clear idea of the scope of Moscow's possible action, nor had all hope that the Japanese would accept the offer to join the Italo-German alliance been abandoned at that time.[35] The final moment for the settling of accounts with Poland, upon which Hitler was to base his irrevocable decisions, was still far from established. Therefore, in the early stages, the policy of rapprochement with Russia by the Axis, within the limits set by Mussolini and accepted by Von Ribbentrop, seems to have been fully agreed upon by Rome and Berlin.

When Ciano returned to Rome from Milan, a detailed report from Rosso on Litvinov's resignation awaited him. Despite its length, it is worth reproducing in full here:

In my telegram to Your Excellency yesterday I gave my interpretation of the dramatic resignation of Litvinov as Peoples' Commissar for Foreign Affairs and the nomination of Molotov, President of the Council of Peoples' Commissars, to the post.

I speak of "interpretation" because it has not been possible for me or for any of my colleagues to obtain from Soviet sources the slightest information on the reasons for the sudden—or at least unexpected—change.

I have considered it necessary to view this change in relation to the Anglo-Soviet negotiations, and I expressed the opinion that the fall of Litvinov signi-

[33] Ciano, *L'Europa verso la catastrofe*, p. 432.
[34] Von Ribbentrop, promemorial, May 18, 1939, *G.D.*, Series D, VI, Doc. 341.
[35] In this sense see Hitler to Mussolini, letter, August 25, 1939, *G.D.*, Series D, VII, Doc. 266.

fied the probable failure of the negotiations between London and Moscow. I would not know how to explain the retirement of the principal Soviet negotiator (a retirement which has been portrayed as being entirely voluntary) otherwise than as a rejection of his policy; and since there is reason to believe that Litvinov was *personally* favorable to collaboration with London and anxious to reach an accord with the western democracies, I must conclude that the Soviet leaders, that is, Stalin and the Politbureau, decided, instead, to abort the negotiations.

Not knowing what the precise proposals and counterproposals of both London and Moscow involved, although the British press has alluded repeatedly to the subject in recent days, I can do no more than offer conjectures. However, I do not believe that I am far from the truth in explaining the events as follows: when the Czechoslovakian crisis reached its height, and constant reference was made to Germain aims in the Ukraine, Litvinov launched his proposal for a conference, which Chamberlain hurriedly declined, suggesting that negotiations be conducted via the usual diplomatic channels. At first, these negotiations excluded or at least permitted only marginal Soviet participation. Meanwhile, Moscow had begun to feel that it was not really threatened by Germany and that, therefore, it was no longer in the position of having to solicit but, rather, in the position of being solicited. This was reason enough to prompt the Soviet government, when pressed by the British government to join in an antitotalitarian bloc, to state its conditions, excluding any limited or partial obligations and insisting instead on the creation of an encompassing system of collective security.

However, it is reasonable to believe that the insistence on collective security was purely a tactical move by Moscow, that is, one made without any real intent of posing this principle as a sine qua non. In other words, I believe that the Soviet proposals were made in the conviction that, given their all-encompassing nature, the British government would never agree to accept them.

I am prompted to advance the following hypothesis to explain Litvinov's fall, although I am fully aware that I have no concrete evidence to support it. During the final phase of the diplomatic negotiations, Litvinov allowed himself to be dragged along by his personal sympathies and committed himself too deeply for compromise, in this manner provoking the rejection of his policy by both Stalin and the Politbureau.

However, the logic of my interpretation is based on the following facts, which I regard as irrefutable:

1. The U.S.S.R. has no desire to participate in a war because it fears both the internal and external consequences. The Kremlin leaders probably hope for a war between the capitalist powers but are determined that Russia remain out of such a conflict, at least until such time as they judge it to be to their advantage to enter it. On this point I refer to Stalin's words of last March 10 when, outlining the obligations of the Communist Party in the field of foreign affairs, he stated: "It is necessary that we act prudently and that we *do not allow* the warmongers, accustomed to having others pick their chestnuts out of the fire for them, to involve the U.S.S.R. in international conflicts."

2. In assuming the obligation to assist Poland, Great Britain has virtually eliminated the prospect of Polish-German military collaboration. By this act Great Britain has indirectly furnished the U.S.S.R.—free of charge—with an

important guarantee to her security, in that for the moment the Soviet Union does not have to concern herself with the threat of a German attack across Poland or, perhaps, with the threat of such an attack with the cooperation of the latter.

Now, at a time when the U.S.S.R. does not feel directly menaced, it is difficult to see just what the Soviet interest would be in concluding political and military accords which, without substantially increasing her security, would probably have the effect of provoking the hostility of Germany and thus pave the way for future threats to Soviet security.

Considering the situation from the Soviet point of view, both as it may concern the ultimate revolutionary aims of communism and the effect it might have on the immediate national interests of the U.S.S.R., the most logical presumption is, therefore, that Moscow has no desire to be dragged into the complications of an anti-totalitarian maneuver.

Now that I have presented my opinions and considerations, I must also point out that a number of my diplomatic colleagues are offering different interpretations for Litvinov's dismissal.

There are those who seek to explain the change in the leadership of the Narkomindiel solely on the basis of Stalin's desire to have someone at the helm of Soviet foreign policy in whom both he and the Politbureau have complete trust and faith during the course of the negotiations with Great Britain.

Then there are those who regard the change as a simple "changing of the guard," a matter that is entirely foreign to policy motives and brought about by personal reasons, and that, therefore, Litvinov's policies will not be changed. This is the opinion advanced by certain members of the British Embassy, which apparently continues to believe in a favorable conclusion to the Anglo-Soviet negotiations and may believe that such a resolution might be hastened by the appointment of Molotov as Commissar for Foreign Affairs.

In conclusion, I may say that these varying interpretations appear to have one point in common: that of being based exclusively on conjecture and individual intuition.[36]

In developing, with his usual final reservations, the preceding arguments,[37] which served him as the basis for his conclusion that the U.S.S.R. had no intention of allowing herself to be dragged into an antitotalitarian

[36] Rosso to Ciano, report, May 5, 1939, No. 1816/751.

[37] The considerations regarding the link existing between the feared German action in the Ukraine and Litvinov's proposal for the convocation of an international conference are apparently noteworthy. Rosso's interpretation of the first phase of the Anglo-Soviet negotiations is also suggestive, while special attention should be paid to his statement regarding the feeling in the U.S.S.R. that it was no longer really threatened by Germany. However, it should be noted that the Italian Ambassador to Moscow, accepting the viewpoint earlier expressed by Togo to Von Schulenburg, ever since March 3, 1939, had reported that he had gained the impression that the Kremlin no longer considered itself to be menaced by Germany. Rosso to Ciano, report, March 3, 1939, No. 913/343. Obviously this contradicted the interpretation regarding the origins of Litvinov's first proposals, unless—and in this case the circumstance was not clearly revealed—the Prague coup had, for a brief time, reawakened in Moscow those suspicions toward Berlin which only a few days previously seemed to be entirely dissipated.

maneuver, the Italian Ambassador undoubtedly correctly deduced the indirect consequences, for both Moscow and Berlin, of Great Britain's decision to conclude a mutual assistance pact with Poland. With the collapse of the possibility of anti-Soviet military collaboration by Poland and Germany, it was logical that the Soviet Union would no longer be interested in openly joining an anti-German camp. This reason would have been sufficient to account for the principal elements in the situation, had it been purely static. If Rosso then chose to draw conclusions about all of the possible consequences of the inference that the Kremlin favored a clash between capitalist powers, he would then have had to consider the possibility of a Russo-German understanding as anything but remote.

At about this time further information arrived in Rome from the Italian legation in Teheran. Minister Petrucci telegraphed on May 8 as follows:

> Count Von Schulenburg, German Ambassador to Moscow, who was waiting here to be received by the Shah, has been urgently recalled to Munich to confer with Von Ribbentrop regarding the new situation created in Moscow by the Litvinov resignation. He will leave tomorrow morning via Lufthansa and will stay at the Hotel Continental in Munich in order to maintain his incognito. He told me that the Litvinov resignation had not been expected, although Stalin's last speech indicated that there would be a change in Soviet foreign policy. He said that he did not dare make any predictions but the fact is that the Soviet Union has been seeking a rapprochement with Germany for some time, and that if this has not yet come to pass, it is the fault of Germany's intemperate official language and press. He suggested three possible hypotheses:
> 1. Stalin desired to get rid of Litvinov because he was too closely identified with a system of collective security which has failed completely.
> 2. The weakness demonstrated by Litvinov and his fear of committing himself too deeply in support of China against Japan, his support of Czechoslovakia against Germany, and his last-minute support of Poland irritated Stalin, who now intends to commit himself fully.
> 3. The imprudent action of the British and the Polish attitude, which is decidedly anti-German, made the threat of war in the east increasingly real, and these factors convinced Stalin to abandon the policy pursued by Litvinov in order to seek an understanding with the Rome-Berlin Axis.
> He regards the third hypothesis as the most probable.[38]

When Count Ciano returned from Milan he found before him Rosso's report on the significance of Litvinov's resignation, along with the opinion on the action advanced by the German Ambassador to Moscow. The latter blamed Germany for the failure of Russia and Germany to reach an understanding, an understanding which the Kremlin apparently had been wanting for some time. He believed that Stalin intended to seek an entente with the Axis. Von Schulenburg's urgent recall to Munich indicated that Von Ribbentrop planned to implement as soon as possible the

---

[38] Petrucci to Ciano, telegram, May 8, 1939, No. 55.

policy agreed upon at Milan a few days earlier. Therefore, there was sufficient evidence to suggest that future Berlin-Moscow relations merited careful scrutiny even though Berlin had not transmitted any information on this particular issue.[39]

[39] As a matter of fact, the Italian Consul General in Berlin had prepared for Attolico the note which is reproduced below. There is no evidence, however, that it was transmitted to Rome, as was the Ambassador's customary habit. It is likely that, first, Attolico's absence from the German capital and, later, the intense activity at the Embassy in preparation for the signing of the Pact of Steel were responsible for this oversight.

Renzetti's note read as follows:

From the comments and evaluations expressed in conversation and in colloquies with German leaders, I have gathered the impression that the attention of political, military, and economic circles is more clearly focused on the study and examination of the possibility and the advantage of an understanding with Russia. I have also been able to confirm that some of those to whom I talked several months ago who, when I suggested the possible advantages to be gained by normalizing relations with Moscow (and I did this in order to learn the German thinking on the matter), unequivocally stated that any such idea was out of the question now either do not comment on the subject or seem to be much less adamant in their positions.

The problem of German-Russian relations has always been closely followed and studied in absolute secrecy by a very few elements in the military, in an occasional political bureau, and by a number of businessmen who, in the past, had exported their products to Russia; in addition, of course, to the appropriate office of the Economics Ministry. This was done in the strictest secrecy when the order of the day in Germany was, and officially at least it remains today, war to the death against Bolshevik Russia. With the deepening of the economic and political crisis, the problem is slowly but inexorably coming to the surface, not publicly of course, but in conversations, in discussions between the knowledgeable and the leaders, occurring in places not frequented by the curious or the indiscreet.

Personally, I believe that Hitler has given the problem serious study during recent months. As the prospects for realizing profitable accords with the British and the Poles appeared to fade away, he, overcoming his strong aversion for modern Russia, has obviously turned his attention to the problem of intensifying commercial exchanges with the Soviets and to an eventual Nazi-Soviet Pact. It should be noted that Hitler no longer refers to Russia in his speeches nor do those closest to him, beginning with Rosenberg, who was the author of the plan to divide the Ukraine between Germany and Poland. I found a confirmation of my suppositions in a comment or, rather, a brusque observation made to me by one who is often in close contact with Hitler. Some weeks ago in conversing with this person, in order to hear what he had to say on the matter, I suggested that one day in the not too distant future Germany would reach an accord with Russia. This person was visibly surprised and exclaimed, "But how did you learn that Germany intends to reach an agreement with Russia?" Of course I replied that this represented nothing more than my personal opinion, but I was not at all certain that I convinced him of this, since he evidently continued to believe that I had been informed of this development.

I don't know for certain whether Hitler has seriously considered the possibility of a long-lasting agreement with Poland. I doubt that he has. I recall that on

4

It is clear that the Nazi government did not directly inform Italy of the soundings made in Berlin by the Soviet Chargé d'Affaires in his interesting colloquies with Schnurre and with Baron Von Stumm on May 5, 9, and 17,[40] but the correspondence from the Italian Embassy in Moscow—which had, in the meantime, reported in detail on the course of the

---

past occasions he has mentioned to me more than once that any treaty concluded could not resolve the territorial questions—that these could not be resolved through diplomatic negotiations. On the other hand, Hitler has never lost sight of the question of German expansion toward the northeast. He is too thoroughly convinced—and he repeated this to me on a number of occasions—that Germany must follow the routes traced in past centuries by the Teutonic knights, routes which suited the attitudes and habits of the German people. Perhaps it should be concluded that Hitler desires to attempt to realize the plans advocated by Rosenberg and by Goering himself because the existence of a friendly state between Germany and Russia appears to be useful to Germany and also because the dream of the fall of Russia appeals to him (what role did Himmler play in this?) and the idea of pursuing a policy different from that of his predecessors fascinates him.

There are many obstacles facing an entente with Russia, such as the explicit statements by Hitler about the impossibility of a Nazi-Soviet accord, Goering's action in Poland, Himmler's maneuvers, Von Ribbentrop's plans, etc., but these difficulties are not considered to be insurmountable.

It is said here that Russia, like Germany, needs to avoid any entente with England. There is a wider chasm between democracy and bolshevism than between National Socialism and bolshevism; both of the latter are engaged in combating capitalism in the interest of the wellbeing of the people. Once Russia has reached an understanding with Germany, it will direct all its energies toward the Orient rather than toward the west. Japan is presently in difficulty. On the other hand, if Japan should win, it would direct all of its energy against all whites, Germans and Italians included. China could become an excellent market for Germany, particularly if the English and American position in China were made more difficult by Soviet pressure. Russia could become an excellent outlet for Germany and could furnish her needed raw materials. The Balkan markets are insufficient; more important ones are required both because their purchasing power is limited and because German products appearing on these markets must compete with those of other countries including Italy. East Prussia can prosper again only if Russo-German trade is re-established. Once Germany's eastern front is secured, German armament expenditures can be reduced, and Germany will be able to exert greater pressure on France and England. The Anti-Comintern Pact is no obstacle to a Nazi-Soviet trade agreement: in this regard, the example furnished by Mussolini set the pace when he furnished the Russians with the fastest cruiser in the world in exchange for Russian products.

Renzetti to Attolico, note, May 7, 1939, no number. The individual referred to by Renzetti as being in frequent contact with Hitler was the Gauleiter of East Prussia.

[40] Schnurre, promemorial, May 5, 1939, *G.D.*, Series D, VI, Doc. 332; Braun Von Stumm, promemorial, May 9, 1939, *ibid.*, Doc. 351; Schnurre, promemorial, May 17, 1939, *ibid.*, Doc. 406. It is noteworthy that in these Astakhov repeated to Schnurre what Potemkin had already told Rosso, i.e., that ideological differences had not prevented Italo-Soviet collaboration.

Anglo-Soviet negotiations[41]—reveals that Rosso had received detailed information from his German colleague on his conversation with Molotov on May 20, 1939. Rosso was informed early on May 24 and telegraphed to Rome as follows:

The German Ambassador has seen Molotov and declared that the German government would be pleased to reopen talks leading to a trade treaty.

Molotov replied that the Soviet government had no objections to such a proposal but believed that a commercial agreement could not be of real interest unless it was founded on a "political base." My German colleague went to great pains to get Molotov to clarify his ideas, but the Russian continued to repeat the phrase "political base" without specifying what this might mean, limiting himself to the statement that both governments could reflect on the matter.

The German Ambassador immediately referred the above to Berlin and in bringing me up to date on the developments did so in the strictest confidence.[42]

The following day Rosso completed his comment on the confidential information given to him by Von Schulenburg:

In my telegram dispatched yesterday I provided Your Excellency with a brief summary of the information imparted to me by the German Ambassador here regarding his colloquy with the President of the Council of Peoples' Commissars and new Commissar for Foreign Affairs, Molotov. With the following report I complete and confirm what I transmitted via telegram.

While he was still in Berlin, Von Schulenburg had asked his staff here in Moscow to arrange a meeting for him with Molotov. This was on the eve of his return to Moscow and after the completion of his mission to Teheran on the occasion of the marriage of the Crown Prince of Iran.

My colleague informed me that he had planned to return to Moscow directly from Teheran via Baku but that at the last moment he had been urgently recalled to Berlin to receive new instructions.

At the Wilhelmstrasse, Von Ribbentrop directed him to leave for Moscow as soon as possible in order to see Molotov for the purpose of proposing a reopening of talks for a trade agreement.

The day after his return to Moscow, Von Schulenburg went to see the Commissar for Foreign Affairs and transmitted Berlin's proposal to him.

My German colleague has brought me up to date on what transpired in the most detailed way—in the strictest confidence of course—and it is as follows:

Von Schulenburg opened the conversation with Molotov by recalling the negotiations undertaken some months ago, at first unofficially and later officially, and pointed out that in the last conversations with the Commissar for Foreign Trade, Mikoyan, an agreement had been reached in principle that both governments favored the conclusion of an accord on a very large scale which would greatly increase the total volume of exchanges between the two countries. Then some difficulty had developed regarding Germany's ability to pay for her pur-

---

[41] Rosso to Ciano, telegrams May 10, 11, and 16, 1939, Nos. 52, 53, 1858, 57.
[42] Rosso to Ciano, telegram, May 23, 1939, No. 60.

chases of raw materials in the Soviet Union because, at that time, German manufacturers could not guarantee delivery of the products requested by the Soviets in exchange on the terms desired (Schulenburg spoke of machinery but I believe that war materials were also included). However, today, the German government believes that the difficulties could be overcome and therefore proposed that the trade talks be reopened.

Molotov replied that, while he wanted it clearly understood that the Soviet government agreed to discuss the trade question, he could, at this moment, see an interest in the commercial accord *only if it were founded on a political base.*

Von Schulenburg was fully cognizant of the importance of such a statement and promptly asked what Molotov meant by the "political base" to which he alluded. However, Molotov did not want to be any more explicit than that and simply repeated the phrase literally.

My colleague insisted that the Commissar spell out more clearly the desires and intentions of the Soviet government. To this end he pointed out that while he (Schulenburg) as an ambassador, and therefore merely an executor of orders, was in no position to suggest plans or proposals not previously approved by his government, Molotov, in his dual role as President of the Council of Peoples' Commissars (and therefore Chief of State) and Commissar for Foreign Affairs, could express the thinking of the Soviet government directly. In any event, he could, if only on an unofficial basis, provide him with some elements on which to base a correct judgment of the Soviet wishes in the matter. This insistence did not penetrate Molotov's reserve, and the latter concluded the conversation by simply stating that the opportunity existed and that both governments should carefully meditate on the question.

My German colleague gained the clear impression from this colloquy that Molotov had received instructions from above to pursue the idea of a "political base" as a preliminary condition to the conclusion of a trade agreement but to offer no specifics on the suggestion and to make no comment on it. This was done for the obvious purpose of forcing the German government to make concrete proposals.

In reflecting with Schulenburg on the meaning and implications of the statement by the Soviet Commissar, I posed the hypothesis that the Soviet government, in making this move, was considering the immediate objective of "maneuver," i.e., to probe for what political guarantees it might eventually obtain from Germany and, at the same time, to determine to what lengths the British are willing to go to obtain a military alliance with the U.S.S.R.

My colleague agreed that such a hypothesis could be well founded. However, he asked himself what Berlin can offer to Moscow in the political area at the very time when—according to his information—talks are going on between the Rome-Berlin alliance on the one hand and the Tokyo government on the other to strengthen the politico-military solidarity of the three friendly powers.

I, too, share this view because I believe that the minimum demand the Soviets will make will be a formal nonaggression pact, and I fail to see how this could be reconciled with a policy of closer collaboration with Japan. Of course, it is understood that this reasoning is made independent of any consideration of events which, at this very moment, might block, either for the Italo-German combine or the Soviets, any measurable radical and sudden shift in the foreign policies of the three countries.

Von Schulenburg reported in detail to Berlin on the colloquy and is now awaiting instructions.

In order for me to keep close tabs on the further developments of this interesting phase of diplomatic activity, I would be grateful if Your Excellency would, within reasonable limits, provide me via telegraph every useful bit of information, and particularly that information which the Royal Ambassador to Berlin might be able to furnish on the attitude and the decisions taken by the German government.

I need not add that I am continuing to maintain close rapport with the German Ambassador here, with whom I have always had a very cordial relationship. Nevertheless, my task of providing information will be greatly facilitated if my German colleague gets the idea that Your Excellency is keeping me informed of the problems which are of interest to Italo-German policy.[43]

Both of Rosso's communiqués are noteworthy. First, despite the fact that Von Schulenburg's confidential observations failed to include the colloquy with Potemkin requested by the German Ambassador in order to clarify the statements made by Molotov, which also occurred on May 20,[44] and although he also failed to mention his first instructions from Berlin to assume a prudent attitude of watchful waiting,[45] they do agree exactly with the summary account of his colloquy with Molotov transmitted by him to the Wilhelmstrasse. Second, Rosso's evaluation of the situation reveals certain reservations and a degree of skepticism that correspond with Mussolini's instructions to Ciano on May 4, but of which the Italian Ambassador to Moscow knew nothing. This attitude, while based on very persuasive considerations, nevertheless should be kept in mind for the weight it may have had on Ciano's overall evaluation, particularly as it concerns the closeness of the collaboration between the two Axis ambassadors in Moscow; at this very time the directives of the Wilhelmstrasse underwent a considerable evolution in evaluating the limits of the possibilities and the advantages of any action toward the U.S.S.R. Third, the first instructions sent by Von Ribbentrop to Von Schulenburg, limited to a simple reopening of commercial talks, did not go beyond what had been agreed upon at Milan, and both these and the comments of the German Ambassador on Molotov's observations confirmed that Berlin did not, at that time, have a well-defined Russian policy. Last, Von Schulenburg's words as well as his reports to Berlin seem to suggest that, initially, his confidential comments to Rosso were based on a purely personal relationship. From this stems Rosso's anxiety about being kept informed of the information transmitted by Attolico from Berlin. In any

---

[43] Rosso to Ciano, report, May 24, 1939, I.D., 8th series, XII, Doc. 13.

[44] Von Schulenburg, promemorial, May 20, 1939, attached to Von Schulenburg to Von Weizsäcker, letter, May 22, 1939, G.D., Series D, VI, Doc. 424.

[45] Von Weizsäcker to Von Schulenburg, telegram, May 21, 1939, ibid., Doc. 414.

event, the first overture by Berlin to Moscow did not alter the common policy established by the Axis and, as will be noted below, led to parallel policies toward the U.S.S.R.

Confirmation of the initial Italo-German collaboration was not long in coming. From the evidence it is apparent that Von Ribbentrop, by May 25, had prepared instructions authorizing Von Schulenburg to enter into a frank political discussion with Molotov.[46] However, these instructions were not sent to Moscow, and, on May 27, they were replaced by others which strengthened those sent on May 21.[47] The reasons for this change are to be sought in the two conversations the Reich Foreign Minister had on May 26 with the Italian and Japanese ambassadors. Attolico reported their substance as follows:

Yesterday, Ribbentrop repeatedly called me on the telephone from Sonnenburg to keep me informed of a conversation he was having with Oshima, the essentials of which are reported here.

Ribbentrop was concerned by the progress made toward an Anglo-French-Russian accord and considered it unwise to assist the enemies of the Axis by standing aside with folded arms. Rather, action should be countered by action and pressure by pressure. Why, Ribbentrop argued, does Russia lend a willing ear to England and France? Because it fears Germany and Japan. *If this is the case, it would suffice to inform Russia that she has no reason to fear one or the other, and she would avoid becoming enmeshed with England and France.*

Meanwhile, it would be necessary, Ribbentrop continued, for both Germany and Japan to take action immediately in Moscow. Assurance from Germany alone would be insufficient. It was absolutely necessary, and perhaps even more important, to have the Japanese assurance. It was this thinking that led the conversation with Oshima along these lines and—taking advantage of the more or less enigmatic 'statement by Molotov to Schulenburg—to Ribbentrop's request that Oshima telegraph to Tokyo to this effect.

Oshima replied in clear terms that he could *not* agree with him, for two reasons:

1. *the Kremlin was extremely suspicious, and any overture by us would, at this time, produce an effect opposite to that desired;*

2. *in any event, proposals of this sort would lose the support for the Axis in Tokyo even of the military and thus permanently eliminate any prospect for the realization of a three-power pact.*

Ribbentrop informed me of all of this not because of my position as ambassador (as a matter of fact he expressly urged that I *not* refer this matter to Your Excellency, which is why I chose not to telegraph), but because of my expertise in Russian affairs, and he was asking my views on the subject.

While expressing all of the reservations normal to protocol—and recalling the general lines laid down by Your Excellency on the matter—I did not hesitate to say that I agreed with Oshima, noting that in the present situation, aside from

[46] *Ibid.*, Doc. 441.
[47] Von Weizsäcker to Von Schulenburg, letter, May 27, 1939, *ibid.*, Doc. 446.

any domestic political considerations, any overture made by us would be used by the Kremlin to wrest a better bargain from London and Paris. Instead (I had received your telephone call a few moments earlier), I added that it seemed to me that the moment had come for us to "link up" with Japan and that we should make it clear to Tokyo that if it ever wished to join in an accord with the Axis, it should do so now and not later.

Ribbentrop replied that (a) as to the first question—overtures to Russia—he was inclined, barring second thoughts, not to insist on them for the moment; (b) as to the second question, he would discuss it immediately with Oshima.[48]

This three-way conversation is important because it explains how, in the beginning, Von Ribbentrop conceived the negotiations with the U.S.S.R. only with the agreement of Tokyo and Rome, to the extent of regarding Japan's role to be pre-eminent,[49] both because of the latter's influence on later developments in the negotiations and, conversely, on their evaluation by Mussolini and Ciano. In fact, with his clearly negative statements of May 26, Oshima eliminated virtually all possibility of participating in the later phases of the discussion and, unknowingly, rashly laid the groundwork for the isolation of his country on the day that the difficult negotiations for a tripartite alliance of Italy-Germany-Japan were to fail.[50] As for Attolico, if his negative judgment did not have immediate consequences in Berlin, it did have the subsequent effect of reducing the Italian Embassy's rapport with the Germans on this specific problem. Since Von Ribbentrop chose to follow the path not recommended by Attolico, he was to find himself psychologically in a difficult position, aggravated not only by the fact that he was venturing on a course that did not fully reflect the understanding reached in Milan but, moreover, that he possessed no guarantee that he could successfully realize his goal.[51] When he did achieve this guarantee, it was not only too late (it was already the eve of August 23), but other elements of discord had already appeared in the relations between the two Axis governments. These factors explain, but obviously do not justify, the attitude of reserve maintained by Von Ribbentrop toward the Italian Embassy and, therefore, toward the Italian government. Conversely, in view of Attolico's apparent lack of faith in the

[48] Attolico to Ciano, report, May 27, 1939, *I.D.*, 8th series, XII, Doc. 48.

[49] In his letter to Von Schulenburg of May 27, Weizsäcker referred to the reservations advanced by Tokyo and Rome without, however, specifying the circumstance under which they were made or the personal nature of the reservations themselves.

[50] In justifying the comportment of the Japanese Ambassador, it must be pointed out that he did not foresee so flagrant a violation by Germany of the obligation for reciprocal consultations before concluding accords with the Soviet Union, an obligation contained in a secret annex to the Anti-Comintern Pact.

[51] In this sense, see also Hitler's letter to Mussolini of August 25, 1939.

possibility of the Reich's reaching an understanding with the U.S.S.R., the Italian Embassy in Berlin lacked the stimulus to intensify its investigative activities and then to estimate quickly and accurately the importance of subsequent developments. The fact that Attolico, Italy's representative in the German capital, declared his pessimism[52] and that the information on the Nazi-Soviet negotiations came largely from the Italian Embassy in Moscow and not from Berlin induced both Mussolini and Ciano to underestimate them. This reasoning sets the scene for Rome's surprise at the news which reached the government on August 21 of the imminent conclusion of the Nazi-Soviet Pact. This explanation is also borne out by a technical factor which has major significance for the professional diplomat. The entire correspondence from Moscow on the Russo-German negotiations was not routed to the Cabinet of the Ministry for Foreign Affairs but rather to the area desks along with all other dispatches of ordinary interest because the entire matter was not considered to be secret or particularly important.

Von Ribbentrop was not discouraged by Attolico's negative attitude toward an overture to Moscow. Moreover, faced with the problem of finding a quick way to re-establish contact with Moscow on this particular matter, the Nazi Foreign Minister accepted Von Weizsäcker's suggestion that Ambassador Rosso's good offices be used to inform the Soviets that the Germans were disposed to discuss the possibility of an accord with the Soviets.[53] For this reason Von Ribbentrop had a second meeting with Attolico on May 29, which the latter reported to Rome as follows:

> As I wrote to Your Excellency in my report of May 27, it seemed to me that Ribbentrop had, at least for the moment, abandoned the idea of pressing further on the matter of making direct overtures to the Soviet Union. In reporting this, I had, however, added the phrase—and how right I was in doing so, given the nature of the man—that he had arrived at that conclusion "barring second thoughts."
> Evidently, Ribbentrop has had these second thoughts, and this morning he again conversed with me by telephone at great length on the issue. He was of the opinion that if a direct approach either by Germany or Japan was out of

[52] It is impossible to exclude a priori the hypothesis that Attolico's attitude (which he officially justified by referring to directives in principle which he had supposedly received from Ciano, perhaps orally) was conditioned by the desire to restrain the Nazi government from plunging down a road which, if followed to its logical end, would have further compromised the already limited prospects for peace in both Rome and Berlin. However, in opposition to this hypothesis, there is no evidence that Attolico confided this purpose to any of his colleagues either before or after World War II, and when, despite everything, Von Ribbentrop decided to act resolutely against Moscow, Attolico failed to point out the uselessness of the Soviet card as a factor in localizing an eventual German-Polish conflict.

[53] Von Weizsäcker, promemorial, May 25, 1939, G.D., Series D, VI, Doc. 437.

the question, an "indirect approach" through Italy might be entirely feasible. In other words, he would desire, for example, that eventually our Ambassador to Moscow be directed by Your Excellency to see Potemkin and, perhaps taking advantage of a general request for information on the course of Anglo-Soviet negotiations, drop the hint that it would be a great shame if Russia were to tie herself to England definitely at the very moment when there were unmistakable signs of a natural evolution in the situation at Berlin.

Ribbentrop then insisted that I join him in the country in order to discuss the matter further in person *without referring it to Rome.*

I went to Sonnenburg and, after giving Ribbentrop the opportunity to explain his point of view once again, I told him that before I could express even as much as a personal opinion on the matter, I would have to know exactly what the nature of Molotov's reply to Von Schulenburg was with reference to the German proposal to reopen the negotiations for a trade agreement.

Ribbentrop, in the presence of Weizsäcker and Gaus, who had also arrived, replied that after all of them had carefully examined the report made by Schulenburg on his colloquy with Molotov, they had all come to the conclusion that Molotov's attitude had been rather sibylline. In the final analysis, if Molotov wanted to enter into conversations, he could have accepted the proposal to reopen trade negotiations. Instead, he chose not to do so, barricading himself behind the objection that at this moment, "the necessary precise political premises" were lacking. To Schulenburg's pointed requests that he clarify the meaning of this sentence, Molotov chose not to reply.

I noted that Molotov's reply could have undoubtedly been interpreted in two different ways: that is, simply as a means of rejecting the German proposal to reopen trade negotiations without further ado, or as an invitation to the Germans to make proposals of a political nature.

Naturally, I did not possess sufficient evidence to ascribe one interpretation rather than the other to Molotov's reply. It was up to Ribbentrop to tell me whether he had any such information and whether, with it, he could determine that the reply itself constituted an overture.

After Ribbentrop and Weizsäcker had replied in unison that they possessed no such information, I ventured to observe that I could not see how a German direct or indirect attempt, necessarily timid because of the circumstances, could bring about any practical results in the few short days that apparently remained before the conclusion of the Anglo-Soviet treaty. I added that it was a situation which, in the best of circumstances and in the interest of our own self-respect, can be improved only slowly and then only up to a point.

Both Ribbentrop and Weizsäcker admitted that my point of view was correct. Thereupon, it was decided that tomorrow Weizsäcker would meet with the Soviet Chargé d'Affaires in Berlin who had requested the Auswärtiges Amt to reach a friendly agreement in the matter of trade relations for the Protectorate of Bohemia and Moravia where it appears that the Soviets have important interests at stake. In replying to the Chargé d'Affaires, Weizsäcker will state that insofar as Germany is concerned there would be no difficulty in reaching a friendly solution to the problem but that Germany could not understand how this request could be squared with what amounts to a rejection by Molotov of the suggestion that negotiations on overall trade relations between the two countries be activated. And since it appears that this same Soviet Chargé d'Affaires has, on other occasions, talked of the possibility of a relative "normalization" of the political relations between the two countries, Weizsäcker will take the opportunity to repeat that insofar as Germany is concerned—particularly after the resignation of Litvinov—there exists no insurmountable obstacle to normalizing these relations but that, before Germany can decide on the matter, it must know what Russia's precise intentions are. These were Ribbentrop's instructions to Weizsäcker. Therefore, he has decided to await the results of this conversation and to learn of the Kremlin's reaction to these statements.

However, Ribbentrop urged me to consider this entire conversation as being entirely personal and begged me not to inform Your Excellency about it quite yet because he had neither clarified his own thinking on the subject nor submitted the matter to the Führer for consideration. (He also made it very clear that any allusion I might make to the subject on the telephone would seriously embarrass him.) If and when he becomes convinced, after further reflection on the matter and when the moment seems opportune, that in fact such a step by our ambassador in Moscow would be useful, he would then submit the necessary request to Your Excellency. However, I do not think this will come to pass, at least for the moment.[54]

On this occasion the Germans had been rather precise in explaining to Attolico the nature of the problem, as well as their uncertainties. Undoubtedly, their action was also dictated by necessity, because in seeking to use Rosso's good offices to reopen contacts with Moscow, they could not hide the facts in the case. The fact remains that, despite Attolico's negative attitude expressed in the meeting of May 26, Von Ribbentrop, up to that time, had considered the question within the context of an agreement and accord with the Fascist government. The suggestion that Rosso step in was abandoned, but the instructions given to Von Weizsäcker on how he should handle the matter with the Soviet Chargé d'Affaires in Berlin, Astakhov, were the product of a joint decision and were approved by Attolico.[55]

The two reports from the Italian Ambassador in Berlin were not extraneous to the negative development of Mussolini's thoughts on the matter. He had seen these reports on May 30, when he was preparing his notes on the nature and limits of the Pact of Steel for Hitler's consideration.[56] In these notes it is evident that the Duce considered probable the conclusion of an Anglo-French-Soviet pact as reference is made to a "London-Paris-Moscow triangle" and to "concrete aid" by Russia to Poland. Between May 4 and May 30 Mussolini's hopes regarding the efficacy of an Axis action in Moscow had, therefore, gradually been dis-

[54] Attolico to Ciano, report, May 29, 1939, I.D., 8th series, XII, Doc. 53.
[55] On this point see Von Weizsäcker, memorandum, May 29, 1939, G.D., Series D, VI, Doc. 450.
[56] Text in I.D., 8th series, XII, Doc. 49.

sipated. The change in Ciano's thinking, keeping in mind his oral instructions to Attolico, was probably somewhat slower, but in his activity it was also possible to perceive an absence of real conviction. Nevertheless, it may be affirmed that by the end of May, without breaking the specific understanding with Berlin, a change did take place in Rome on the problem of a Russo-German rapprochement. Even Germany, while continuing its contacts with Moscow, did not at that time regard their conclusion with any optimism.

On May 30 the German Secretary of State met with the Soviet Chargé d'Affaires and spoke to him along the lines agreed upon.[57] Following this colloquy, the Wilhelmstrasse immediately imparted new instructions to Von Schulenburg,[58] and Rosso was promptly informed of them.[59] Accordingly, the Italian Ambassador reported in detail on these events the same day:

> Yesterday the German Ambassador here informed me that he had received instructions to drop for the moment any discussion of the "political bases" alluded to by Molotov as conditions for a renewal of the trade negotiations.
>
> Mr. Von Ribbentrop, according to what Von Schulenburg told me, had reached this negative decision after consultation with His Excellency Attolico and with the Japanese Ambassador to Berlin.
>
> My German colleague regards the decision as wise and opportune because he cannot see what useful purpose would be served at the present time by an overture to the U.S.S.R. for a political rapprochement. In any event, it seems to him necessary to await Molotov's speech, which has been announced, from which it may be possible to discern the point reached by the Anglo-French-Soviet negotiations.
>
> This afternoon, prior to Molotov's speech, Von Schulenburg informed me that he had received new instructions from Berlin.
>
> First of all, Von Ribbentrop informed him of a colloquy he had had[60] with the Soviet Chargé d'Affaires in Berlin, to whom he had expressed, in a general way, the desire of the German government to "normalize" its relations with the U.S.S.R. He then proceeded to give him instructions to direct the German Commercial Attaché to make contact with the Peoples' Commissar for Foreign Trade for the purpose of arriving at a de facto renewal of trade negotiations.
>
> In bringing me up to date on the above, Von Schulenburg expressed his doubts as to the success of this attempt because he foresaw that the "political bases" condition would be brought up in much the same way it had been by Molotov to the Ambassador. However, he would carry through on the instructions he had received from Berlin and, in due time, would let me know the results.

[57] Von Weizsäcker, memorandum, May 30, 1939, G.D., Series D, VI, Doc. 451.
[58] Von Weizsäcker to Von Schulenburg, telegram, May 30, 1939, ibid., Doc. 452.
[59] Rosso to Ciano, telegram, June 1, 1939, No. 64.
[60] The mistaken reference to Von Ribbentrop instead of Von Weizsäcker was corrected by Rosso in a later report to Ciano on June 4, 1939, I.D., 8th series, XII, Doc. 107.

I believe that, after Molotov's speech—he made it very clear that political negotiations with England and France are far from a positive conclusion—the situation today is less favorable than heretofore and that, therefore, a contact between the German Embassy and the Commissar for Foreign Trade might produce something positive; if nothing else, it might serve to clarify the real intentions of the Soviet government.[61]

Once again the two Axis governments were working together. Especially interesting is the less pessimistic note in Rosso's comment, in contrast to the persistently negative attitude maintained by his German colleague, who, among other things, would have approved of the position taken by Attolico and Oshima.

The Italian Ambassador's views had been altered by his impressions of Molotov's speech on May 31, a speech which appeared to him to be characterized by coolness toward London and Paris, revealing the persistent Soviet suspicions of these governments. Moreover, the President of the Council of Peoples' Commissars had repeated the familiar phrases of Stalin regarding the necessity for the Soviet Union to guard against being dragged into conflicts by the maneuvers of others, and this seemed particularly significant to Rosso, leading him to the conclusion that the speech was entirely dominated by the concept of the defense of Soviet territory.[62] Moreover, this evaluation was fully supported by the Italian Embassy in Warsaw.[63]

However, insofar as Von Schulenburg is concerned, some divergences appear between the impression he conveyed to Rosso and the point of view he defended in Berlin.[64] It could be that the German Ambassador, like his Italian colleague, wanted, at least initially, to assume a cautious and uncritical attitude, or that he had been induced to take a stronger position toward his own superiors than he had originally planned in order to counteract more effectively the negative influence exerted by Attolico and Oshima on the Wilhelmstrasse.

On June 4 Rosso had been briefed by his German colleague on the outcome of the Hilgar-Mikoyan colloquy.[65] Rosso reported in detail the same day on this colloquy as follows:

Mr. Hilgar, the German Commercial Attaché here, went to see Mikoyan at the Commissariat for Foreign Trade and submitted to him Berlin's proposal to reopen negotiations for the conclusion of a trade agreement.

[61] Rosso to Ciano, report May 31, 1939, *ibid.*, Doc. 73.

[62] Rosso to Ciano, telegram, June 1, 1939, and report, June 1, 1939, *ibid.*, Docs. 80 and 86.

[63] Arone to Ciano, courier telegram, June 2, 1939, *ibid.*, Doc. 92.

[64] Von Schulenburg to Von Weizsäcker, letter, June 5, 1939, *G.D.*, Series D, VI, Doc. 478.

[65] Rosso to Ciano, telegram, June 4, 1939, No. 66.

When Hilgar referred to the previous negotiations as having been simply "interrupted," Mikoyan was quick to point out that it was, instead, a matter of a "breaking off" of negotiations and defended his definition by pointing out that Schnurre's failure to come to Moscow last January was a unilateral decision made by Germany which, in effect, had terminated the negotiations.

Hilgar then explained that four months ago there existed technical and practical reasons why the German government could not accept the Soviet conditions and that for these reasons alone Berlin at that time had decided to postpone the negotiations. Today, on the other hand, Germany saw the possibility of satisfying certain requests which earlier she could not do and, therefore, she believed that the time had come to reopen these talks.

At this point Mikoyan asked the Commercial Attaché if he was in a position to "guarantee" that the new negotiations would be carried through to a positive conclusion.

Hilgar replied that, naturally, he was in no position to offer such a guarantee. However, he could confirm that, insofar as Germany was concerned, the obstacles in existence last January had since disappeared (difficulty of delivery of certain items within stated periods) and that, therefore, a favorable result could reasonably be expected.

It was at that point that Mikoyan also referred (as Molotov had done to Von Schulenburg) to the "necessary political premises."

Hilgar then pointed out that in his position as Commercial Attaché he could make no comment on matters of this nature because they were beyond his competence. However, it seemed to him that the relations between the two countries were sufficiently normal to permit, without further delay, useful negotiations to improve commercial exchanges, while he personally could not understand what the Soviet government had in mind when referring to political premises.

Evidently Mikoyan listened attentively to these considerations and closed the colloquy with the promise to give careful thought to what had been outlined to him by Mr. Hilgar.

The German Embassy has judged these contacts with Mikoyan to have produced rather favorable results, in that Mikoyan did not refuse to reopen negotiations for a trade agreement and, therefore, the door apparently remains open for further discussions.

Insofar as I am concerned, I find Mikoyan's request that the positive results of eventual new negotiations be guaranteed very significant. It seems to me to be obvious that with this statement he could not have pretended that the Germans would assume an a priori obligation to accept whatever conditions the Soviets cared to impose. Thus, it seems likely that he simply sought assurance that the German overture to reopen negotiations was not a mere political maneuver, but that Berlin, in fact, seriously sought a commercial accord.[66]

Aside from the interest this document presents for a reconstruction of the steps leading to the Nazi-Soviet rapprochement,[67] it could also serve

[66] Rosso to Ciano, report, June 4, 1939, I.D., 8th series, XII, Doc. 107.
[67] The telegram in which Von Schulenburg informed the Wilhelmstrasse of this conversation contains a much less detailed summary. Von Schulenburg to Von Ribbentrop, telegram, June 2, 1939, G.D., Series D, VI, Doc. 465.

to explain Von Schulenburg's evolution toward a positive position on the question. Moreover, Rosso's acute concluding observations regarding the real significance of Mikoyan's question helps to place the event in its proper perspective.

The information transmitted by Rosso to Rome was promptly passed on to Attolico, who commented on it on June 8 as follows:

> It is believed here that a renewal of negotiations for a trade agreement with the Soviets is now possible.
> The German Military Attaché in Moscow has been recalled to Berlin *ad audiedum* for the purpose of determining what discreet approaches might be made through him to Voroshilov.
> I do not say that all of this, in the long run, might not produce something positive. However, I do exclude the possibility that this might, in some way, influence the accords being negotiated between London, Paris, and Moscow. Nor do I, for that matter, believe, as the Germans seem to, that the Baltic non-aggression pacts stipulated yesterday are an effective obstacle to a conclusion of the accords themselves.[68]

As is evident, the Italian Ambassador in Berlin, while confirming and amplifying the information provided by his colleague in Moscow and not excluding the possibility of an eventual commercial accord between Russia and Germany, was restating in an unusually categorical form his clearly negative opinion of the possibility of blocking the Anglo-Russian rapprochement. In choosing between the two views, Ciano was undoubtedly drawn to side with Attolico, particularly since the several discreet overtures Rosso had made toward an improvement in Italo-Soviet relations on the occasion of his first visit to Molotov, after the latter had replaced Litvinov, had received a rather cool reception.[69]

Shortly afterward, the Italian Ambassador to Moscow reported to Rome the substance of a colloquy he had had with Potemkin in which the latter made it clear that Moscow's negotiations with London, far from having reached their conclusive phase—as some were led to believe by the departure of Strang from Moscow for London—"had not yet overcome serious basic difficulties."[70]

---

[68] Attolico to Ciano, telegram, June 8, 1939, *I.D.*, 8th series, XII, Doc. 155. Regarding the anticipated approaches to Voroshilov, see the comments in Rosso's report to Ciano of June 22, 1939, as given in n. 79 below.

[69] Rosso to Ciano, report, June 10, 1939, *ibid.*, Doc. 183. The following day the Italian Minister to Kabul reported that the prevailing opinion in Afghanistan was that the Anglo-Russian accord would be signed, but he added, "According to the Afghans, if the Anglo-Russian accord is not signed, given the usual reactions of Soviet policy, in a short time an overturn of the alliances would occur: the U.S.S.R. would draw closer to the Rome-Berlin Axis and then, they think, war would soon come." Quaroni to Ciano, telexpress, June 11, 1939, *ibid.*, Doc. 189.

[70] Rosso to Ciano, telegram, June 11, 1939, *ibid.*, Doc. 187.

The following day Rosso informed Palazzo Chigi of Mikoyan's decision
to renew trade negotiations with Germany and of his insistence on the
necessity of realizing the political premises, Von Schulenburg's departure,
and Hilgar's recall to Berlin for consultations.[71] In a telegram of June 12,
Rosso informed Rome that he had learned from an extremely confidential
source that his German colleague planned to submit to his government for
study the following proposals as possible offerings to be made to Moscow
in the political field in exchange for the U.S.S.R.'s abandonment of the
proposed accords with Paris and London: "(1) Germany's formal assurance that the Reich has no aggressive designs against the Soviet Union;
(2) a declaration that confirms the validity and the content of the Treaty
of Berlin, which remains in effect between the two countries; (3) an
eventual naval accord for the Baltic; (4) eventual guarantees to Poland
(excluding Danzig) and Rumania."[72]

Rosso reported on the situation on June 13 as follows:

Count Von Schulenburg left for Berlin the day before yesterday, where he
will be joined by the Commercial Attaché, Hilgar, who departs tonight.

The trip of the Ambassador and his collaborator was decided upon as a result
of the new colloquy between Hilgar and Mikoyan.

According to the confidential information transmitted to me by the German
Embassy, Mikoyan called Hilgar to his office and told him that, having accepted
the recent German proposal, the Soviet government was prepared to reopen the
trade negotiations without further delay. Mikoyan suggested that Schnurre be
sent to Moscow as soon as possible. However, he was forced to make it clear
that insofar as the Soviet government was concerned, the conditions advanced
during the preliminary negotiations of the past winter would still be in effect.

Hilgar objected that, since the German government had decided to make
concessions, similar concessions were also to be expected from the Soviet side.

Mikoyan made no formal concession, but he finally did lead Hilgar to believe
that the possibility for some compromise was not excluded. This prompted
Hilgar's decision to return to Berlin to study the situation with the offices concerned. (It is understood to be primarily a question of determining whether
Germany, instead of requiring payment for her manufactures in raw materials
such as manganese and oil, which Russia does not seem to be able to provide,
would accept payment in cash or in other products.)

In his colloquy with Hilgar the Commissar again returned to the theme of
"political premises," and this convinced Von Schulenburg to make the journey
to confer with the Wilhelmstrasse.

From what I have been able to understand, my German colleague seems to
be inclined to give Moscow some satisfaction in the political area. He has several ideas on this question which he wishes to propose to Von Ribbentrop.
Among others, he proposes to suggest that Berlin make a formal declaration
that Germany has no aggressive designs against the Soviet Union.

Von Schulenburg also views as a possibility a public statement which would

[71] Rosso to Ciano, telegram, June 12, 1939, No. 70.
[72] Rosso to Ciano, telegram, June 12, 1939, No. 71.

confirm the full validity and the friendly spirit of the Treaty of Berlin which remains in effect between Berlin and Moscow. (I presume that my colleague has in mind something similar to the declaration made last November jointly by Moscow and Warsaw.)

Von Schulenburg wonders whether it is not the time to propose to the U.S.S.R. a naval pact for the Baltic and, perhaps, an accord offering guarantees to Poland (excluding Danzig) and Rumania alike.

Of course, the proposals my German colleague has in mind to make eventually to Moscow would be subordinated to the condition that the Soviets abandon the negotiations now under way for an accord with Paris and London.

I must make it clear that what I have noted above was given to me in the strictest confidence, not by Von Schulenburg, who had already departed for Berlin, but by one of his collaborators. Therefore, I cannot guarantee the absolute accuracy of the intentions attributed to my colleague.

However, it is certain that he did go to Berlin to force a decision on a delicate and important problem: that of learning whether, at this particular time, Germany would find it advantageous to consider the Soviet hints seriously and to act accordingly.

Insofar as I am concerned, the tactics of the U.S.S.R. are clear: Moscow notes that London and Paris are anxious to win Russian collaboration and that the German government is preoccupied by the prospect of an Anglo-French-Soviet pact which—call it a mutual guarantee against aggression if you will—in effect would be a military alliance. Thus, the situation is favorable for the Soviet Union to bet on two hands and to seek to obtain at one and the same time an Anglo-French guarantee and a German guarantee.

I remain convinced—my views are unchanged since the beginning of the negotiations with England—that the Kremlin leaders have never really desired to assume hard and fast obligations with the western powers, fearing that this would provoke a worsening of their own position vis-à-vis Germany and Japan. For this reason I expressed the opinion that the U.S.S.R. had presented London with excessively strong demands which it was certain would be rejected.

The incredible British tendency toward compliance has, however, created a new situation, and as a result, the U.S.S.R. today finds herself trapped by her own game, and if Mr. Strang, whose arrival here in Moscow is expected at any moment, were to return with further concessions to the Russian demands, I fail to see how Moscow could gracefully refuse them.

Therefore, I wonder whether eventual German offers will actually arrive in time and, if they did, whether they would be adequate to convince the Soviet government that it should renounce its pact of guarantee with London and Paris.

In conclusion, it seems to me to be clear that the U.S.S.R. will maneuver to attain both of its objectives, that is, I repeat, the Anglo-French guarantee and the German assurance.[73]

Once again it is the confidential information furnished by Schulenburg to the Italian Embassy in Moscow that kept Rome informed while the

---

[73] Rosso to Ciano, report, June 12, 1939, I.D., Doc. 201. In his own handwriting Rosso added a postscript to the report noting that he had just learned that the German Military Attaché had been recalled to Berlin for consultations.

Auswärtiges Amt reported nothing to Attolico. Once again it is the Italian documentation which fills the lacunae of the German documentary collection, which contains only a very brief reference to the Hilgar-Mikoyan colloquy of June 8, 1939.[74] Several other observations may be made concerning the substance of Rosso's dispatches to Rome.

First, from the content of the proposals which the German Ambassador to Moscow planned to recommend to Von Ribbentrop, it is evident that, even before the references which Astakhov furnished on June 14 to the Bulgarian Minister in Berlin[75] and which he regarded as being decisive factors in later Nazi-Soviet political negotiations, Von Schulenburg sought to devise a solution of his own to the condition advanced by Molotov and Mikoyan regarding the famous "political premises." In this attempt, the German Ambassador revealed that if, in certain cases (assurances of non-aggression, an accord on the Baltic) he had anticipated Moscow's later demands, in others (Polish guarantees) he had no concept of Hitler's intentions nor any idea where the Soviet Union's real interest lay—an interest which the Germans were in a much better position to satisfy than were the British. In any event, it seems likely that toward the end of June, when Count Ciano outlined to the Soviet Chargé d'Affaires in Rome his own ideas concerning the content of the proposals which the Germans might possibly offer the Russians,[76] he had these and other comments from Rosso in mind.

A note of skepticism becomes clearly discernible when one considers a diagnosis of the Soviet tactics contained in the Italian Ambassador's report. In all probability, Von Schulenburg's statements, as well as the latest information on the course of Soviet negotiations with Paris and London, influenced Rosso's judgment to the point of permitting him to under-

---

[74] Cf. Von Schulenburg to Von Ribbentrop, telegram, June 9, 1939, *G.D.*, Series D, VI, Doc. 499.

[75] Woermann, memorandum, June 15, 1939, *ibid.*, Doc. 529.

[76] Von Schulenburg, memorandum, August 16, 1939, *G.D.*, Series D, VII, Doc. 79. There is no trace whatsoever in the archives of Palazzo Chigi of the above-mentioned Ciano-Helfand colloquy explicitly referred to by Molotov to Von Schulenburg on August 15. It is not clear whether this is a lacuna or an omission, but the second hypothesis is the more plausible because not all of the Italian Foreign Minister's conversations were recorded in minutes. Much more serious is the fact that neither Rosso nor Attolico were informed of this colloquy. However, there is reason to believe that Ciano did refer directly to the German Ambassador in Rome, as Von Schulenburg was sufficiently well aware of the colloquy to explain to Molotov that it originated in a report made by Rosso. The detailed reference both to its time and content by Molotov and the fact that his observations correspond precisely to what Rosso reported excludes any doubt about either the existence or the content of the Ciano-Helfand colloquy.

estimate his earlier acute diagnosis in the report of May 5 regarding the practical effects on the U.S.S.R. of a British guarantee to Poland. It is possible that from the moment when the Franco-British guarantee was, albeit indirectly, achieved by Moscow, further pursuit of negotiations with London and Paris was primarily aimed at inducing Berlin to shift its offers for a rapprochement with the Soviet Union to a different and much more fruitful plane insofar as the U.S.S.R. was concerned.

With the arrival in the German capital of the principal personnel of the German Embassy in Moscow, discussions began at the Wilhelmstrasse to determine what policy should be adopted. To date, little is known about these talks. However, an interesting clue is provided in a report dispatched to Rome by Attolico on June 14:

I am reporting below several statements made by Goering to Renzetti on the subject of relations with Russia and Japan.

Goering spoke at length regarding the great possibilities of an expansion in Germany's trade if she were to succeed in concluding a trade pact with the U.S.S.R. He said that he had spoken at length on the same problem with the Duce.

In Goering's judgment, Stalin fears war because, in the event of victory, power would pass to the military, while a defeat would mean the collapse of the Bolshevik regime. Thus, Goering concluded that an intelligent management of these negotiations would make it possible to arrive at a German-Russian understanding. It is understood, of course, that both sides will have to renounce every form of propaganda.

Goering added that thus far we have gained nothing tangible from the accord with Japan. The Japanese are always demanding something but give nothing in return; they do not pay for the materials furnished by Germany and probably are not paying for what the Italians furnish either. Germany has lost two or three hundred million uniforms because of the Japanese, who, in turn, then purchase whatever they need from the English, paying, of course, in hard currencies. To this must be added the fact that, because of Japan, Italy and Germany have lost the important Chinese market, and the final blow is that the Japanese then declare that they are not interested in European problems! Some weeks ago, Goering continued, the Japanese Ambassador informed Ribbentrop that Japan could not tolerate the creation of a Nazi-Soviet entente. Ribbentrop, Goering noted, remained calm and did not take him to task. It is true that he finds himself in a rather difficult position because of the anti-Bolshevik pact, but it is also true that, at certain times, one must not avoid showing concern toward nations who act as Japan does.

"Insofar as I am concerned," Goering concluded, "I could not care less what the Japanese Ambassador says or does. I will continue on my road to arrive at a good accord with the Russian market, which is vital for Germany."

I need not point out to Your Excellency that everything reported above must be regarded with serious reservations because, we know, German foreign policy is no longer directly influenced by the Field Marshal. However, it is always interesting to have confirmation of the direction in which Goering is going.

And since I have learned that Von Schulenburg is here in Berlin, I will seek to learn from him just how things are going.

Insofar as the negotiations with Japan are concerned I can say that, for the moment, they are not being pressed. A week ago a new reply arrived from Tokyo, which, as usual, Oshima regarded as unsatisfactory and refused to transmit. On the other hand, Ribbentrop does not believe it to be opportune to press for action from this quarter at this particular time because he desires to wait to see how the Anglo-Soviet negotiations proceed. If and when these are concluded, it will then be the time, according to him, to apply pressure to Tokyo, eventually even starting *ex novo* on more precise and specific bases, as the Japanese will be in a better position to know exactly where their interests lie.[77]

The statements by Goering to the Italian Consul General in Berlin merit attention in that, in addition to confirming the content of the Rome talks, they clearly show the course Goering was pursuing and his determination not to be thwarted even by the stipulations of the Anti-Comintern Pact. Giving due consideration to the observations of the Italian Ambassador regarding the limits of Goering's political influence, it is still possible to discern the source of the major pressures exerted upon Hitler and Von Ribbentrop in favor of an arrangement with the Soviet Union.[78] At the same time, we note that Attolico again affirmed his negative attitude toward the Soviet overture, while the recent conclusive information regarding the German Foreign Minister's state of mind toward Japan provides another element for an evaluation of Von Ribbentrop's thinking.

5

Meanwhile, from Moscow,[79] Helsinki,[80] and Warsaw[81] reports continued to pour into Rome reflecting great skepticism regarding the outcome of the Anglo-French-Soviet negotiations. This situation induced Ciano to

[77] Attolico to Ciano, report, June 14, 1939, *I.D.*, 8th series, XII, Doc. 231.

[78] The German diplomatic documents collection (*G.D.*, Series D, IV, Docs. 479, 488, 493) not only confirm the part played by Goering in the decision to begin commercial relations with the U.S.S.R. during the winter of 1938–39 but also indicate that the Japanese attempted to get Berlin to delay the conclusion of these negotiations until Tokyo had reached agreement with Moscow on the question of fishing rights in Siberian waters.

[79] Rosso to Ciano, telegrams, June 16 and 19, 1939, *I.D.*, 8th series, XII, Docs. 247 and 275; telegram, June 20, 1939, No. 75; telegrams, June 22, 1939, *I.D.*, 8th series, XII, Docs. 307 and 309; report, June 22, 1939, *ibid.*, Doc. 314. At the close of this report Rosso added,

I have recently read in an Italian newspaper a report from Warsaw in which it is noted that two diametrically opposed currents exist within the Politbureau insofar as negotiations with England and France are concerned: one (represented by Molotov, Mikoyan, and Zdanov) which would be in favor of the accord, sub-

break his silence and to instruct Rosso to collaborate in the German overtures. The Fascist Foreign Minister telegraphed to Rosso as follows:

We are following with great interest all of the information regarding the
attitude being adopted by that government in the face of Anglo-French
pressures.
It is a propitious time for you to develop by all means available to you,
observing proper caution of course, every useful approach designed to strengthen
that resistance in view of the possible collapse of the proposed Anglo-Russian
alliance and for the purpose of assisting the eventual rapprochement between
the Soviets and the Nazis.
Reply by telegraph.[82]

If the timing for an Italian diplomatic effort in Moscow was propitious,
the instructions imparted by Ciano were very general indeed. These directives do not contain even a reference to the Von Ribbentrop-Attolico
talks of May 29 but simply indicate the Fascist government's keen interest.
Yet, despite the usual silence that Palazzo Chigi maintained toward its
representatives abroad and the peak of skepticism noted in Rome several
weeks earlier, as Mussolini was preparing his notes on the Pact of Steel,
even these instructions were not insignificant. On the other hand, given
the absence of any correspondence with Attolico on the matter and the
tone of Von Schulenburg's first colloquy with Rosso after his return from
Berlin, it must be assumed that Ciano had not discussed his initiative
with Von Ribbentrop prior to telegraphing the instructions to Rosso. This
would explain the necessarily vague character of the directives.

Thus the Italian Ambassador in Moscow found himself in the not
unusual situation of having to use his own judgment in developing the
details necessary to implement the directives received from Ciano. This
Rosso did in a telegram to Palazzo Chigi on June 25. After mentioning his
earlier fruitless visits to Molotov,[83] he commented as follows:

It seems obvious to me that if some possibility exists for action in the desired
manner it can only be realized by a German approach based on two points:

---

ject of course to the western powers' satisfying Soviet needs in their entirety,
the other, led by Marshal Voroshilov, is definitely hostile to assuming any obligation. To date, Stalin has not taken a stand. I am in no position to check on the
accuracy of the information, but I do find in the account certain elements of
truth which, in my opinion, make it a perfectly plausible approach. I must add
that I am convinced that the reluctance to involve the U.S.S.R. in an eventual
world war is especially strong within the ranks of the high command of the
Red Army.

[80] Bonarelli to Ciano, telegram, June 17, 1939, *ibid.*, Doc. 261.
[81] Arone to Ciano, telegram, June 16, 1939, *ibid.*, Doc. 243.
[82] Ciano to Rosso, telegram, June 23, 1939, *ibid.*, Doc. 317.
[83] See Rosso to Ciano, report, June 10, 1939, *ibid.*, Doc. 183.

(1) assurances and guarantees that German policy does not menace Soviet policy; (2) a warning that an eventual Moscow accord with London and Paris will be considered as Soviet participation in the policy of encirclement and will therefore be regarded as a hostile act. Thus, I interpret Your Excellency's instructions to mean that my actions should be that of supporting my German colleague in his approaches, and, in order to determine what my action should be, I will await the return of the German Ambassador, who I presume will be armed with precise instructions from his government.

I would appreciate knowing whether the above meets with Your Excellency's approval.

I must add that in my past conversations I have always stressed the view that an accord with France and England would create serious dangers for the U.S.S.R., both in the east and in the west.[84]

Rosso's suggestions (apparently he was not aware of what had transpired in the Hilgar-Mikoyan conversation of June 17[85]) indicated an awareness of the considerations previously put forth by Von Ribbentrop to Attolico and strike a note of realism and objectivity. On the following day, after having transmitted to Rome other interesting information regarding the difficulties being encountered by the Anglo-French-Soviet negotiations,[86] Von Schulenburg supplied Rosso with many details of his meetings in Berlin.

In a telegram on June 27 Rosso advised Rome as follows:

My German colleague returned to Moscow yesterday and came to see me to bring me up to date on the instructions received by his government. In his conversations in Berlin he learned that Ribbentrop was very skeptical regarding the possibilities of blocking the Anglo-French-Soviet accord, which is considered to be almost inevitable, and, moreover, that Ribbentrop is very much concerned about the repercussions which an eventual Nazi-Soviet rapprochement would have on the Japanese. The German Ambassador, in turn, was successful in his efforts to convince the Wilhelmstrasse that it would be worthwhile to try to effect a rapprochement with Moscow. He received authorization to inform Molotov formally that Germany has no intention of attacking the Soviet Union. At the same time, he will let the President of the Council of Peoples' Commissars know that the stipulation of a pact with France and England would make the desired improvement in relations between Berlin and Moscow much more difficult.

My colleague foresees that Molotov will ask for something more concrete and a confirmation of Germany's friendly intentions, and, in that event, he will seek to have Molotov spell out the Soviet wishes, while reserving the right to refer them to Berlin.

As is apparent, my colleague returned from Berlin with rather vague direc-

[84] Rosso to Ciano, telegram, June 25, 1939, *ibid.*, Doc. 341.

[85] Hilgar, memorandum, June 17, 1939, attached to Tippelskirch, report, June 18, 1939, *G.D.*, Series D, VI, Doc. 543.

[86] Rosso to Ciano, telegram, June 26, 1939, *I.D.*, 8th series, XII, Doc. 352.

tives which do not yet permit him to act decisively, but he agrees that any approaches should be made cautiously, being constantly mindful of the psychological factor, i.e., the extremely suspicious attitude of the Soviets. Tomorrow he will request an audience with Molotov, and he promised to keep me informed of developments, which I will telegraph.[87]

At the same time Attolico telegraphed from Berlin as follows:

Count Schulenburg has returned to Moscow. In the final analysis, he does not carry any completely new instructions.

In the economic field he must seek to obtain from the Russians a guarantee of a common base for negotiations. If and when this base can be demonstrated to exist, Germany will send its delegates to Moscow.

In the political area, the German Ambassador must show a friendly face to the Russians, letting them know that Germany is well disposed toward the U.S.S.R., albeit with the understanding that the Soviet Union also prefers to have Germany as a friend rather than an enemy. Naturally, that choice is left to the U.S.S.R.[88]

In substance, the dispatches of the two Italian ambassadors are very similar, although in the one from Rosso the origins of Von Ribbentrop's attitude are defined.

The overall view of the situation was completed by the following data sent by Rosso the next day to Palazzo Chigi:

Before leaving Berlin my German colleague had a long conversation with the Soviet Chargé d'Affaires there, and he spoke to him very openly on the subject of German-Russian relations. He assured him that the U.S.S.R. had no reason to fear an attack from Germany, that the supposed plan against the Scandinavian states was a figment of the imagination, that regarding Poland the German program was moderate and clearly limited, etc. He told him that, within the limits possible, Berlin desired to collaborate with the U.S.S.R., but that an accord with England and France would be interpreted as a hostile act and would make collaboration difficult, if not impossible.

The Ambassador then told the Chargé d'Affaires that he was personally in favor of Molotov's request for "political bases" but that the Soviet government should abandon its suspicious attitude and extreme reserve and divulge exactly what it was that was wanted. On this point, my German colleague told me that he had discussed with Berlin the possibility of transforming the existing "neutrality pact" into a "non-aggression pact," and I seem to have understood that he also mentioned this to the Soviet Chargé d'Affaires. In conclusion, in his unofficial and personal conversation, the German Ambassador has let the Soviet government know indirectly far more than what he was authorized to state officially to Molotov.

Regarding the serious difficulties represented by the attitude of Japan, which wants to hear nothing of Russo-German economic negotiations, my colleague told me very confidentially (begging me not to repeat it) that during the Berlin

[87] Rosso to Ciano, telegram, June 27, 1939, *ibid.*, Doc. 376.
[88] Attolico to Ciano, courier-telegram, June 27, 1939, *ibid.*, Doc. 376.

consultations the idea of a "triangular guarantee"—that is, reciprocal guarantees between Germany, the Soviet Union and Japan—was also discussed very generally. However, the practical implementation of such a plan was considered to be highly problematical.

My German colleague and I examined the possibility of my taking a step in line with Your Excellency's instruction in your telegram No. 48. The German Ambassador observed that, since I could offer nothing concrete, my effort could only be an indirectly supporting one, but that I could exert a useful influence by letting the leaders of the Soviet Foreign Office know that Germany is sincere in its desire to ameliorate relations with the U.S.S.R. We agreed that after his colloquy with Molotov takes place (not yet set), I will go to see Potemkin and speak in the sense indicated.[89]

Once again the dispatches from the Italian Embassy in Moscow complete the data furnished by the German diplomatic document collection,[90] and, in a certain sense, they are more complete than what was furnished by the German Embassy in Moscow. As usual, Rome was kept informed via Von Schulenburg rather than Von Ribbentrop. Von Schulenburg's version of the Berlin consultations reveals a Von Ribbentrop caught in the grip of uncertainty and fundamentally in much the same state of mind toward the possibility of an accord with Russia as he was during his conversations with Attolico and Oshima. Not having lost hope for Japan's prompt adhesion to the Italo-German alliance and still very skeptical about the chances of blocking the stipulation of the Anglo-French-Russian accord, the Nazi Foreign Minister seemed to want to proceed with extreme caution. This time, in contrast to what occurred during the initial phases, it was the German Ambassador to Moscow who assumed a positive stance and wrested from Von Ribbentrop the authorization to make those modest statements to Molotov which were indispensable in preventing the abandonment of the talks with the Soviets. In pursuing his program of action, Von Schulenburg, in his meeting with Astakhov, went beyond the instructions received from his Foreign Minister. The Rosso-Schulenburg talks, in addition to reasserting the collaboration of the two Axis diplomats in Moscow and confirming the hypothesis that the instructions sent from Rome to Rosso on June 23 had not been previously cleared with Berlin, were to serve as a vital orientation for Ciano in his contacts with Helfand, from which Molotov derived the impression that the Fascist government was acting as the spokesman for Von Ribbentrop[91] while, in reality, for that moment at least, Von Schulenburg was the only spokesman.

[89] Rosso to Ciano, telegram, June 28, 1939, *ibid.*, Doc. 386.

[90] On the Von Schulenburg-Astakhov colloquy of June 17, 1939, see Von Schulenburg, memorandum, June 17, 1939, *G.D.*, Series D, VI, Doc. 540.

[91] Cf. Von Schulenburg, memorandum, August 16, 1939, *ibid.*, VII, Doc. 79. The portion of the Von Schulenburg memorandum relative to the Molotov declarations regarding the action taken by Ciano with Helfand reads as follows:

The Soviet government at the end of June received a telegraphic report from

The Schulenburg-Molotov colloquy (of which Rosso was promptly informed) occurred on June 28,[92] that is, one day before the appearance in *Pravda* of Zdanov's article strongly critical of the British and French, an article which Rosso regarded as inspired by Stalin, as a sign of differences within the Politbureau, and as either a last attempt to bring Paris and London into line with the Soviet views or a clear hint that a break in the negotiations was imminent.[93]

The Italian Ambassador's account of that meeting is as follows:

The German Ambassador met with Molotov and talked to him as planned. Molotov stated that he took note with satisfaction of the German assurances and added that the policy of the U.S.S.R. was to remain on good terms with all countries and that this included Germany. He did not repeat the well-known phrase "political bases," and demonstrated that he wanted to keep the discussion limited to generalities. When Schulenburg referred to the Soviet-

---

their Chargé d'Affaires in Rome about his conversation with the Italian Foreign Minister, Ciano. In this conversation Ciano had said that there was a German plan which had as its goal a decisive improvement in German-Soviet relations. In that connection Ciano had referred to the following items in the plan: (1) Germany would not be disinclined to exercize influence on Japan for the purpose of improving her relations with the Soviet Union and eliminating frontier conflicts. (2) Further, the possibility was envisaged of concluding a non-aggression pact with the Soviet Union and jointly guaranteeing the Baltic States. (3) Germany was prepared for an economic treaty with the Soviet Union on a broad basis. The contents of the foregoing points has aroused great interest on the part of the Soviet Government and he, Molotov, would very much like to know how much of the plan which Ciano had outlined in the form just mentioned to the Soviet Chargé d'Affaires was true. I replied that the statements of Ciano apparently rested on a report by the Italian Ambassador here, Rosso, of which we have already heard. The contents of this report rested principally on Rosso's deductions.

[92] Von Schulenburg to Von Ribbentrop, telegram, June 22, 1939, *ibid.*, VI, Doc. 579.

[93] Rosso to Ciano, telegram, June 29, 1939, *I.D.*, 8th series, XII, Doc. 395; report, June 29, 1939, *ibid.*, Doc. 403. On the same day the Italian Chargé d'Affaires reported from London, referring to a conversation with the Japanese Ambassador and concluding as follows:

As to the question of knowing whether, in the final analysis, the Pact of Moscow will or will not be signed, which is the same as saying whether the Soviet government wants it, even at a high price, or does not want it at all, Shigemitsu told me that he didn't care to comment; however, he did want to inform me that all of the information he had been receiving from the Japanese Ambassador to Moscow seemed to indicate that Stalin was far from being convinced that the proposed pact was a good thing; while Soviet propaganda abroad very ably seeks to convince the public that the Russians desire the accord but that it is the English who are not willing to pay a fair price for it.

Crolla to Ciano, report, June 29, 1939, *ibid.*, Doc. 402.

German treaty of 1936 as still being in effect, Molotov seemed to be astonished "because he believed that events of recent months destroyed whatever value it had" (my colleague was not sure whether Molotov was alluding to the Anti-Comintern Pact or to the alliance with Italy). Schulenburg challenged this view, but Molotov refused to comment on the matter further.

Despite the fact that the discussion was little more than academic, accomplishing nothing positive, the German Ambassador is reasonably well satisfied with the results, especially because of the cordial, almost friendly, attitude displayed by Molotov.

He too shares the opinion that it would be wise to proceed cautiously without pressing the issue. He is also asking himself whether the Zdanov article is simply a maneuver or really signifies that a rupture in the negotiations with England and France is imminent. However, in the case of the first hypothesis, the Soviet government is very familiar with the German view and is undoubtedly keeping it in mind.[94]

Despite the fact that the account given to Rosso by Schulenburg was much less detailed than that which he transmitted to Berlin, nothing of importance was omitted. However, the German Ambassador failed to mention to Rosso the instructions he had received from Von Weizsäcker on June 30 containing Von Ribbentrop's invitation to abstain temporarily from any further contact with the Soviets.[95] Meanwhile, Rosso, with what was apparently the concurrence of Von Schulenburg, approached Potemkin on July 4. Immediately afterward he telegraphed to Rome as follows:

During the course of the conversation I had this morning with the Vice Commissar about timely matters, I alluded to the conversation between Molotov and my German colleague, and I pointed out that I had the impression that the German government was genuinely interested in improving its relations with the U.S.S.R.

Potemkin noted that "good relations between the two countries would undoubtedly constitute one of the guarantees for effective tranquillity to defend the peace," but he made no further comment. I did not press the matter further since, in agreement with my German colleague, it was decided that I should limit myself to confirming the fact that Germany was well disposed toward the U.S.S.R. I then asked the Vice Commissar whether or not today's communiqué regarding Molotov's reply to the most recent Anglo-French proposals indicated an imminent conclusion of the pact. The Vice Commissar was very reticent and said only that "a point yet remains to be resolved." He then referred to the speech made by the head of state before the Council, noting that the Soviet

[94] Rosso to Ciano, telegram, June 30, 1939, ibid., Doc. 406.

[95] Von Weizsäcker to Von Schulenburg, telegram, June 30, 1939, G.D., Series D, VI, Doc. 588. The fact that Berlin continued to maintain silence on the matter insofar as Attolico was concerned is understandable only if the hypothesis discussed earlier is accepted, i.e., that Ciano's instructions to Rosso in Moscow to support the German action had not been cleared with Von Ribbentrop.

government would sign only when all (and he emphasized the word "all") of the conditions stipulated by the President of the Council of Peoples' Commissars were accepted.[96]

The step taken by the Italian Ambassador at the Narkomindiel, agreed upon locally by the two Axis ambassadors and not at higher levels between the two ministers of foreign affairs, was more discreet and limited in nature than what had been initially considered in Berlin and certainly was on a much lower level than that taken by Ciano in his talks with Helfand a few days earlier. It should be particularly noted that in this case the repetition of the warning regarding the consequences of an eventual Anglo-French-Soviet accord on relations with the Axis was omitted, a warning which Rosso had studiously avoided making but which he had promised to advance at some future time. In addition, the spontaneity of the Italian initiative seems to indicate a strong support of the venture as well as a certain degree of impatience with the Fascist government's efforts to hurry the Russo-German approaches to a successful conclusion. While the reactions of the Vice Commissar for Foreign Affairs were reserved, they were significant, and undoubtedly Moscow was convinced that Italo-German diplomacy was in perfect unison.

[96] Rosso to Ciano, telegram, July 4, 1939, I.D., 8th series, XII, Doc. 451. In his report of July 5 Rosso enlarged on this summary:

I referred to "communications received from Rome" at Von Schulenburg's suggestion because he believed that a statement made in this fashion would have greater impact in that it would demonstrate that the Italian government knew and approved of Berlin's intentions.... Von Schulenburg indicated his satisfaction with this "supportive" gesture and believes, that, for the moment, it is sufficient. He has had no further contact with Molotov and continues to hold the view that it is not wise to suddenly press forward for an immediate solution. Rather, he notes, it would be wiser to let the seeds which he has sown mature—if a possibility for maturing exists—in his conversation in Berlin with the Soviet Chargé d'Affaires and in his talks with Molotov upon his return to Moscow.

It is probable that the cautious attitude adopted by the German Ambassador was prompted by the suggestions confidentially transmitted to him by Von Weizsäcker urging him to move slowly to give Hitler sufficient time to play the Soviet card during the month of August in the Danzig issue. (On this point, see Ernst Von Weizsäcker, Erinnerungen [Munich: Paul List Verlag, 1950], p. 247.) On the other hand, according to the hypothesis I suggested above, confirmation that Hitler had no aggressive intentions against the U.S.S.R. reached Moscow secretly via the spy Sorge in his commentary on the progress of the Italo-German-Japanese negotiations for a tripartite alliance. It is known that these negotiations failed precisely because of the differences of opinion between Tokyo and Berlin regarding the aims of the alliance. Japan sought to limit it exclusively to the casus foederis against the U.S.S.R., while Germany was particularly interested in an obligation directed against the democratic powers.

6

During this same period, Ciano and Attolico were beginning to note the first discrepancy between the correct interpretation given by Rome of the Milan agreement on Poland and the immediate aims of the alliance and Von Ribbentrop's interpretation. This discrepancy prompted Ciano to instruct Attolico to seek reassurance from Von Ribbentrop as to the latter's views on the Polish problem.[97] The Attolico-Ribbentrop conversation occurred on July 6. During the course of that long conversation, the Nazi Foreign Minister described the situation as he saw it in optimistic terms. In this exposition, as reported by Attolico, he also discussed the role of the U.S.S.R. as follows: "Russia? What could Russia do? Nothing. She has no desire to do anything. Even if she signs a treaty, she will not march. As for the rest—today I sent new instructions to Schulenburg (which I [Attolico] later ascertained were concerned only with eventual commercial negotiations) which will be sufficient to put a new bug in Stalin's ear."[98]

Though he had obviously not yet completely freed himself of the idea that the U.S.S.R. would sign the Anglo-French-Soviet accord, in these words there emerges for the first time a note of optimism regarding the U.S.S.R.'s ultimate position. It is possible that Von Ribbentrop was thinking of the favorable impression of his meeting with Molotov on June 28 reported by Von Schulenburg.[99] It is interesting that this time the Fascist government was promptly informed of this evolution directly by the Nazi Foreign Minister. Ciano should have had good reason to give the matter careful thought since, contrary to Von Ribbentrop's assumption, the information reaching Rome at the same time from Rosso always reflected the latter's lack of faith in a successful conclusion of the Anglo-French-Soviet Pact.[100]

On July 9, 1939, reporting by telegraph on the hypothesis prevalent in all quarters that the tripartite negotiations would be given a new and simplified direction as a result of the meeting between Molotov and the French and British diplomats on the previous day, Rosso added:

However, I doubt that the Soviet government is inclined to obligate itself in this sense because what seems to interest the U.S.S.R. most at this moment is

[97] Ciano to Attolico, personal letter, July 2, 1939, I.D., 8th series, XII, Doc. 432.
[98] Attolico to Ciano, report, July 7, 1939, ibid., Doc. 503. (On this colloquy see also Von Ribbentrop, minutes, July 8, 1939, G.D., Series D, VI, Doc. 636, where, however, there is no reference to the Soviet Union.)
[99] Von Schulenburg to Von Ribbentrop, telegram, July 3, 1939, ibid., Doc. 607. It is worth noting that Von Ribbentrop requested Von Schulenburg to enlarge upon his first summary account telegraphed to Berlin on June 28.
[100] Rosso to Ciano, telegram, July 6, 1939; report, July 6, 1939, I.D., 8th series, XII, Docs. 483, 491.

a guarantee against indirect aggression. On the other hand, it is important to keep in mind Molotov's speech to the Supreme Council in which he announced the *sine qua non* condition for the stipulation of the accord: "Anglo-French-Soviet guarantee of the central and eastern European states including, without exception, all of the European countries bordering on the U.S.S.R." I must conclude that Moscow will remain adamant on this point and will insist on receiving from France and England general commitments in precise and absolute terms. I remain of the opinion that the Kremlin leaders are fundamentally opposed to tying themselves to the two countries that are the typical representatives of the capitalist system and of the bourgeoisie and that their tactics aim, in fact, at realizing the following objectives: (1) humiliation of England and revenge for Munich; (2) provocation of the fall of Chamberlain; (3) encouragement of a European conflict in the hope of exploiting it in favor of the ideological and political interests of the Bolshevik regime.[101]

A brief official communiqué published the following day in the Soviet press, affirming that the Molotov conversations with the French and British diplomats had not produced positive results, immediately confirmed the Italian Ambassador's accuracy of observation. The Ambassador noted, moreover, that in Moscow the word was spreading that the Soviet attitude was being strongly influenced by a German intervention.[102]

The exact status of the Russo-German conversations at that time is given in another report drafted by Rosso and based on confidential information received from Von Schulenburg:

Count Von Schulenburg has informed me that his Commercial Attaché, Hilgar, went to see Mikoyan yesterday bearing new proposals for the conclusions of a trade agreement.

From what I was able to understand, these proposals contain further concessions to meet Soviet requests and would demonstrate the German willingness for an agreement.

Mikoyan promised to discuss the new proposals in a future meeting, evidently because he needs to have the concurrence of the Kremlin leaders on the policy line to be pursued with the Germans.

On the political plane, since the Molotov-Schulenburg conversation of June 28 there has been no new development, and my colleague does not believe it necessary to take any action toward further discussions at this time.[103]

This report demonstrates that the information transmitted by Von Schulenburg reflected Von Ribbentrop's current opinions; the latter was to outline them in a personal letter to his Chief of Mission, the Embassy Counsellor in Moscow, Tippelskirch.[104]

[101] Rosso to Ciano, telegram, July 9, 1939, *ibid.*, Doc. 516.

[102] Rosso to Ciano, telegram, July 10, 1939, *ibid.*, Doc. 522.

[103] Rosso to Ciano, report, July 11, 1939, *ibid.*, Doc. 537; cf. Von Schulenburg to Von Weizsäcker, telegram, July 10, 1939, G.D., Series D, VI, Doc. 642. For the content of the colloquy, see the instructions sent by Von Weizsäcker to Von Schulenburg, telegram, July 7, 1939, *ibid.*, Doc. 628.

[104] Tippelskirch to Von Schulenburg, letter, July 12, 1939, *ibid.*, Doc. 661.

At first glance it appears very strange that, despite this and other such data transmitted to Rome,[105] Mussolini, in his instructions to Attolico to induce Hitler to accept the idea of an international conference on the Polish question and thus to eliminate the threat of war, considered it opportune to exclude the U.S.S.R. from such a conference.[106] The obvious conclusion is that the Duce and Ciano, after a brief period of urging Rosso to take certain steps and of colloquies with Helfand, returned to the position stated in the notes of May 30 implying faith in the counter-measures of the Axis in Moscow, and gave no thought to the succeeding developments that Rosso reported diligently and frequently, considering them of insufficient importance to warrant a re-examination of the skepticism adopted after the first phase of action.

Attolico and Magistrati met once with Von Ribbentrop on July 25 and found their reception to be substantially negative, even making due allowances for the fact that the latter wanted to wait until Hitler had personally stated his views.[107] Attolico took advantage of this period of waiting to report to Rome the substance of his colloquy with the Minister of Estonia on the question of the Anglo-Soviet negotiations:

Today, upon returning from his vacation, the Minister of Estonia, Mr. Tofer, came to see me.

I asked him what he thought of the developments in the Anglo-Soviet nego-

---

[105] Coppini to Ciano, courier telegram, July 8, 1939, *I.D.*, 8th series, XII, Doc. 511; Rogeri to Ciano, telegram, July 15, 1939, *ibid.*, Doc. 580; Bonarelli to Ciano, telegrams, July 17, 21, 1939, *ibid.*, Docs. 594, 625; Rosso to Ciano, telegram, July 22, 1939, *ibid.*, Doc. 638. In this last telegram Rosso reported a colloquy he had with Potemkin in which the latter stated that it was his impression that the negotiations with London and Paris would go on for some time to come because there was still a great deal of discussion on a number of points. Moreover, on July 22, 1939, the entire Soviet press published an official communiqué announcing the reopening of the Nazi-Soviet trade negotiations. Von Schulenburg to Von Ribbentrop, telegram, July 22, 1939, *G.D.*, Series D, VI, Doc. 699. On the other hand, after noting the unusual presence of the Soviet Chargé d'Affaires at the Munich Arts Festival (the latter, in his search for new contacts, had also met with Hitler), Attolico also reported that "there is no evidence as yet that the Führer himself has accepted this view. He ascribes a very nearly decisive importance to the position about to be taken by the Soviet Union. Moreover, he would have no plan to attempt a coup against Danzig and the Corridor until he was certain of being able to 'isolate' Poland." Attolico to Ciano, report, July 17, 1939, *I.D.*, 8th series, XII, Doc. 598. The Italian Ambassador to Berlin five days later added the following: "It is confirmed that in high places an eventual failure of the Anglo-French-Soviet negotiations would be regarded as a chance to 'isolate' Poland from her allies and thus could be construed as a sign to launch a new German coup." Attolico to Ciano, report, July 22, 1939, *ibid.*, Doc. 649.

[106] Magistrati, note, July 22, 1939, *ibid.*, Doc. 647.

[107] For this colloquy, see Attolico to Ciano, telegrams, July 26, 1939, and report, July 26, 1939, *ibid.*, Docs. 677, 678, 687.

tiations. He declared that the U.S.S.R. could not possibly have any interest in joining an Anglo-French military alliance since—with the Maginot and Siegfried lines—in an eventual war it would be Russia who would have to bear the brunt of an attack. Moreover, while Russia's prospective allies can withstand a long war and are basing their preparations and their strategy on this premise, Russia has everything to fear from a long war. For these reasons—which are crystal clear—Russia should have no desire to participate in a European conflict —at least from the beginning.

However, Mr. Tofer continued, it now seems evident—in view of the unexpected British acceptance of all of the Russian conditions—that the Soviet government is about to tie herself to the British. Perhaps the Russians were influenced in this decision by news of an Anglo-Japanese understanding, which has once again raised the specter of isolation of the Soviets in the event that the present negotiations with England should fail.

In reply to my question as to whether he thought Finland, in the event of the conclusion of an Anglo-French-Soviet alliance, would be disposed to move closer to Germany, Mr. Tofer stated that he could not answer with certainty, but that he could say that, as of this time, Finland already regretted not having accepted the non-aggression pact offered to her by the Germans months ago.[108]

The startling note in this report is the absence of comment by Attolico. The reasoning used by the Estonian Minister to support his view that the Soviet Union had no real interest in joining an Anglo-French alliance, while somewhat different from that advanced by Rosso, seems to be rather consistent. However, his arguments justifying his optimism about the outcome of the Moscow negotiations were either so questionable (such as that a favorable outcome would be the consequence of an Anglo-Japanese accord) as to be used by Rosso to arrive at diametrically opposite conclusions or entirely without foundation (such as the Soviet fear of isolation). With the information he possessed on the true position of the Japanese and on the German-Soviet negotiations, Attolico could easily have corrected his Estonian colleague. However, he abstained from doing so and did no more than transmit to Rome what amounts to an optimistic judgment on the outcome of the Anglo-French-Soviet negotiations, which apparently corresponded with his own convictions.

Three days later, through his Foreign Minister, the Führer opposed Mussolini's recommendations on the basis of the following considerations, transmitted to Rome by the Italian Ambassador to Berlin:

As to the conference, Hitler is of the opinion that it would present difficulties and disadvantages.
Despite propaganda to the contrary, the position of the Axis in the world is very strong. Any such undertaking on the part of the Axis powers would serve

---

[108] Attolico to Ciano, telexpress, July 27, 1939, *ibid.*, Doc. 703.

the opposition's propaganda and would be fatally interpreted as a sign of weakness.

Moreover (Ribbentrop regards this point as being very important), a proposal for an international conference launched at a time when the Anglo-Soviet negotiations are reaching a climax would alarm the Russians, who, fearing the threat of isolation, would tend to abandon all resistance and fall into the arms of the English and French.

Limiting the conference to the same powers (as were at Munich) would not be easy, even if it were possible to have Spain admitted, and it would certainly require the inclusion of Russia without any assurance that Japan would be able to participate.[109]

Commenting on that part of the report which is of primary interest to us, Attolico observed:

It is true that Von Ribbentrop seeks to calm the Führer's anxieties and to allay his doubts by insinuating that, after all, a conflict with Poland could be localized. Until a short time ago, he even deluded himself that Poland could choose not to react to a coup against Danzig. Moltke had been charged with looking into this possibility. When these soundings proved to be negative, hopes and illusions were directed elsewhere. Von Ribbentrop was correct when he told me yesterday—I commented on it much earlier in my reports—that the Führer is attaching ever greater significance to the Anglo-Russian situation. In the event that the Moscow negotiations fail, the thinking here is that Poland could be attacked with impunity without others coming to her aid. This too is an error. With or without a treaty, in a war that broke out now, it is unlikely that the U.S.S.R. would move; at least, it would not participate in military operations immediately.

On the other hand, with or without a treaty—given the present state of affairs—Russia's material aid to Poland is certain. Moreover, the fact that Poland is not actively supported by Russia does not mean that Poland could not draw France and England into the war on her side, particularly the English, who are showing signs of being far more aggressive than France.[110]

The Attolico-Von Ribbentrop meeting of July 25 seems to mark an important turning point in the relations between the two countries. For the first time, Mussolini's suggestions gave Von Ribbentrop a clear idea of the extent of Italy's opposition to the Polish adventure, and Attolico's observations confirmed the Italian reluctance to share his views on the position of the U.S.S.R. On the one hand, then, he sought to ascertain exactly what the Soviet intentions were and to hasten the relaxation of the Kremlin position toward Berlin; on the other, he avoided a detailed discussion with the Italian Ambassador on Soviet-German relations until such time as he could be sure to have the upper hand. This explains the

[109] Attolico to Ciano, telegram, July 31, 1939, *ibid.*, Doc. 732.
[110] Attolico to Ciano, report, August 1, 1939, *ibid.*, Doc. 743.

particularly important Schnurre-Astakhov conversations of July 26, *the day after the first Ribbentrop-Attolico talks,* the Ribbentrop-Astakhov meeting of August 2, and the new instructions from Von Weizsäcker to Von Schulenburg of August 3,[111] of which the Italian Embassy was not informed.[112]

7

In contrast to what was happening in Berlin, Von Schulenburg continued to keep Rosso informed (and there is no evidence that this was done at Von Ribbentrop's instruction), and the Italian Ambassador became Palazzo Chigi's principal source of information on the course of the Nazi-Soviet talks.

On July 25, 1939, Rosso concluded his morning telegram[113] with the following observations:

I had noted that for some days several foreign newspapers (particularly the French and English press) had referred to a trip to Berlin my German colleague was about to take for consultations. The *Temps* of July 22, which arrived here last night, also published a telegraphic report from *Havas* in London indicating that the journey had already taken place and noted that Von Schulenburg had probably been recalled to Berlin not to report on the course of the trade negotiations but, rather, to give the Führer his views on what the Soviet position might be in the event that a world war broke out.

[111] Schnurre, memorandum, July 27, 1939, *G.D.*, Series D, VI, Doc. 729; Von Ribbentrop to Von Schulenburg, telegram, August 3, 1939, *ibid.*, Doc. 760; Von Weizsäcker to Von Schulenburg, telegram, August 3, 1939, *ibid.*, Doc. 759.

[112] Instead, on July 28 Attolico referred to Rome certain confidential information, also regarding Russia, in which it appeared that Litvinov's departure from the Narkomindiel had not marked the end of Jewish influence in the Russian Foreign Office. Attolico to Ciano, report, July 28, 1939, *I.D.*, 8th series, XII, Doc. 716.

[113] Rosso to Ciano, telegram, July 25, 1939, No. 97. The day before, at the conclusion of a long report on the status of the Anglo-French-Soviet negotiations, the Italian Ambassador to Moscow commented as follows:

It would be even more dangerous today than it was at the beginning of these negotiations to hazard a guess as to how they might come out. It is evident that the U.S.S.R. is not anxious to assume binding obligations, and I must assume that, at long last, the British negotiators are becoming aware of this. On the other hand, the Kremlin leaders must also be concerned about the damaging effect it would have on the U.S.S.R.'s international position in the event that the failure of these negotiations could be clearly laid at the Russian doorstep. Given these circumstances, it is easy to explain the drawn-out negotiations and the series of obstacles raised by Moscow, particularly since these negotiations have been characterized from the beginning by one factor: mutual suspicion.

In addition, I continue to believe that the situation in the Far East, even if not discussed formally in Moscow, is a decisive factor in the Soviet Union's decisions.

Rosso to Ciano, report, July 24, 1939, *ibid.*, Doc. 665.

Since my German colleague had never mentioned the possibility of an imminent journey to Berlin, I went to see him this morning to find out whether the rumor had any basis in fact.

Von Schulenburg told me that he was the first to be surprised by the news story because he had received no invitation from the Wilhelmstrasse to return to Germany for conferences and, moreover, he saw no reason which would justify his going to Berlin at this particular time. . . . His astonishment increased even more after he heard the German radio mention this supposed trip, not to deny it, but simply to indicate that it was merely a routine visit which German diplomats make from time to time to maintain close liaison with the central offices.

My colleague is at a loss to explain these rumors and is awaiting clarification on the matter from Berlin.

He then confirmed the news in a communiqué issued by the Narkomindiel that read as follows: "During recent days negotiations have been reopened between Germany and the U.S.S.R. on matters of trade and credits. The Delegate Adjunct in Berlin, Barbarin, is conducting the negotiations in the name of the Commissariat for Foreign Trade, and Mr. Schnurre is representing Germany."

Von Schulenburg told me that the shift in the scene of the negotiations from Moscow to Berlin had come at the request of the Soviet government and that this request was rather strange because the Soviets had always insisted that these negotiations take place in Moscow. My colleague cannot explain this change in attitude except by offering conjectures, which he preferred not to do —one being that the change was requested in order to avoid having the trade negotiations interpreted as political negotiations.

This explanation may not appear to be entirely convincing in that it would seem to be rather convenient for the U.S.S.R., in the present stage of the negotiations with France and England, to let it be believed that a possibility existed for a political agreement between Russia and Germany. Nevertheless, I regard it as probably the most plausible one.

Meanwhile, it is interesting to note that neither Molotov nor Mikoyan have made the slightest reference to those "political bases" upon which they so strongly insisted some months ago and set as the *sine qua non* condition for trade talks with Germany.

Von Schulenburg personally informed me that the Berlin conversations are proceeding satisfactorily and that the trade agreement seems to be approaching a satisfactory conclusion.

The crux of the negotiations seems to be—according to what Von Schulenburg told me—a credit of two hundred million marks in favor of the U.S.S.R. The past difficulties regarding German exports seem to have been overcome; it remains to be determined whether the Soviet Union will be in a position to furnish Germany with a quantity of material equal to that imported from Germany.[114]

[114] Rosso to Ciano, report, July 25, 1939, *ibid.*, Doc. 674. It is interesting to note that in January, against the wishes of the German government, the U.S.S.R. insisted on shifting the seat of the trade negotiations to Moscow after they had unofficially begun in Berlin. At the time, the action taken by the Soviet Ambassador,

This report should have interested Ciano and helped him to interpret the apparently singular decision taken by the Wilhelmstrasse to censor both the news of the meeting at the Villa d'Este between the Japanese ambassadors to Rome and to Berlin and their statements favoring a tripartite alliance but "postponing their taking a position on the matter because the Anglo-Russian negotiations were entering a delicate phase."[115] There must have been sound new reasons why Ribbentrop adopted this delaying tactic, since it was he who had constantly applied pressure on Tokyo to hasten the conclusion of the tripartite agreement and, up to that time, had always regarded as highly probable the conclusion of an Anglo-French-Soviet pact.

In effect, then, an interesting phenomenon had developed. After a first phase in which the Italians took some action and were optimistic regarding the possibility that the Anglo-Soviet negotiations could be forced to fail, Rome subsequently fell into a kind of torpor that reflected Attolico's attitude—a skepticism so overwhelming that it was apparently unaffected by later reports coming from Moscow and, ultimately, from Berlin itself.[116]

Merekalov, was interpreted by the Director of the Economics Section of the Wilhelmstrasse, Wiehl, as follows: "The strong desire to have a German delegation come to Moscow can therefore only be interpreted in the sense that the Soviet government would like to demonstrate to the outside world the value placed also by the Third Reich on the continuation of economic relations." Wiehl, memorandum, January 12, 1939, G.D., Series D, IV, Doc. 484. The Soviet request was no small factor in the interruption of the Russo-German negotiations. Although it suggests that the reversal in the position taken on the matter by the Narkomindiel only a few months later, after an initial basic position had been adopted, must be assumed to indicate a more intense desire to bring the negotiations to a successful conclusion, it is nevertheless necessary to note that this fact was not sufficiently stressed by either Von Schulenburg or the Wilhelmstrasse.

[115] Attolico to Ciano, phonogram, August 4, 1939, I.D., 8th series, XII, Doc. 769. On the Anglo-Soviet-French crisis, see also Migone to Ciano, telegram, August 2, 1939, ibid., Doc. 748; Bonarelli to Ciano, telegram, August 4, 1939, ibid., Doc. 770; Crolla to Ciano, report, August 11, 1939, ibid., Doc. 844.

[116] The Italian Ambassador to Paris, referring to a conversation he had had with his German counterpart, reported as follows:

During the same visit to Germany, Welczeck also conferred with Coulondre, the French Ambassador to Berlin, who purportedly expressed the conviction that Russia would never accept the Anglo-French proposals. The reason for this was that either in victory or in defeat the present Russian regime would be transformed. Another reason was that Russia has no interest in assuming military obligations to guarantee the status quo for those very Baltic States and Poland toward which she has not abandoned the hope of eventually reactivating a policy of absorption.

Guariglia to Ciano, report, July 4, 1939, ibid., Doc. 464. The information should have been given the most serious consideration because it reflects the opinion of one of the most qualified of the opposition's diplomats.

It is possible that this static attitude was also prompted by a desire to give the Germans no new arguments in favor of their proposed Polish adventure. On the other hand, Von Ribbentrop, who, under the influence of the Italians, had moved from initial optimism to an attitude of extreme caution, ultimately decided, either because of developments in the twofold negotiations in Moscow or because of his interest in overcoming Italian resistance to his plan of action for Poland, to re-examine his position and to intensify the action of the Wilhelmstrasse in Moscow. However, he did not directly inform Rome of his decision, nor for that matter, did he trouble to consult with the Italians.

Moreover, on August 5 dispatches from Attolico and from Rosso arrived simultaneously at Palazzo Chigi, and if they cannot be considered clearly contradictory in every detail, they certainly provided matter for serious reflection. Attolico commented as follows:

Today I asked Weizsäcker what he thought of the Shiratori-Oshima meeting. He told me that he had learned of it only through the Italian newspapers. In addition, he had cabled Tokyo asking for an explanation and inquiring whether this might be considered a move to sabotage a possible Soviet-German rapprochement.

While awaiting clarification, Weizsäcker is inclined to believe that the meeting was simply attributable to the initiative of the two ambassadors, who, having staked their positions on the successful conclusion of a tripartite agreement, sought to take advantage of what they regarded as a good opportunity to force Tokyo's hand.

I asked what there was between Russia and Germany of a serious nature, and Weizsäcker replied that the trade negotiations were proceeding reasonably well, and that the question of political contact was continually raised by the Russians, who ask why not? Let us know what your intentions are, etc., etc.

It is obvious that the Russians want to play the game with two balls, and they will continue to do so—according to Weizsäcker—until the present crisis is resolved in one way or another. Therefore, it is believed here that the Anglo-Soviet negotiations will continue for months.[117]

On the other hand, the Italian Ambassador to Moscow reported as follows:

The German Ambassador confidentially informed me of a long conversation he had yesterday with Molotov. It must be assumed that Von Schulenburg spoke under instructions from Berlin when he told Molotov that his government was always anxious to improve relations with the U.S.S.R. and that it viewed this goal as being attainable in three stages: (1) the satisfactory conclusion of the trade agreement; (2) cessation by both sides of their press campaigns against each other and initiation of exchanges on cultural levels; and

[117] Attolico to Ciano, report, August 5, 1939, *ibid.*, Doc. 787.

(3) political rapprochement, undertaken either by reconfirming existing agreements or drawing up new ones.

Molotov replied that he shared the German desire for an amelioration of relations between Germany and the U.S.S.R. and that, in the main, he concurred on the question as it had been submitted to him. However, while he regarded it to be a relatively simple matter to reach a satisfactory agreement at the economic level, on matters of the press, and on cultural exchanges, there were certain political obstacles represented by the following factors: (1) the signing of the Anti-Comintern Pact; (2) German support of Japan; and (3) German opposition to the participation of the U.S.S.R. in international conferences.

My colleague stated that he was not aware of what was meant by the third point, and Molotov mentioned the Munich meetings, which the U.S.S.R. could not attend because of the German veto. Schulenburg replied that Chamberlain had refrained from inviting the Soviet Union because he realized that its presence would have blocked the desired accord.

The above is the essential part of the colloquy, which lasted one and a half hours. Schulenburg has reported it to Berlin in great detail and is now awaiting instructions which will permit him to continue and possibly to develop these conversations further. Meanwhile, he is satisfied with the way yesterday's colloquy went because Molotov, instead of demonstrating his usual reticence and reserve, spoke to him frankly and in clear terms and always very cordially.

During the course of the conversation Von Schulenburg sought to learn something about how the negotiations with France and England were going, but on this matter Molotov maintained his normal reserve, restricting his comment to stating that "the objective of the negotiations was purely a defensive one."[118]

It was evident that, notwithstanding the alliance agreement, the Wilhelmstrasse continued to maintain a very reserved attitude toward Attolico insofar as the subject of Russo-German negotiations was concerned. This was also true of Von Weizsäcker, who, while he did not hesitate to put Attolico on guard against Von Ribbentrop's real aggressive aims toward Poland, chose not to mention the Schulenburg-Molotov conversation of August 4 or even the instructions which he had sent to Moscow and which had set the stage for these talks.[119]

[118] Rosso to Ciano, telegram, August 5, 1939, ibid., Doc. 780. On this colloquy, see also Von Schulenburg to Von Ribbentrop, telegram, August 4, 1939, G.D., Series D, VI, Doc. 766.

[119] At this point the question arises as to whether or not the explanation of Von Weizsäcker's actions might lie in his fear that, given the prospect of a German-Soviet accord, the resistance of the Fascist government to an adventure in Poland might be weakened. As a matter of fact, the same Von Weizsäcker was to pay less and less attention to Von Ribbentrop's instructions, personally informing the British Ambassador to Berlin, Henderson, of the possibility of the Nazi Foreign Minister's going to Moscow and of possible Russian participation in a partition of Poland and authorizing the Chief of Cabinet, Kordt, to go to London to pass on similar informa-

However, in this case too, the confidential statements by the German Ambassador to Rosso put Palazzo Chigi in a position to know the essentials of German activity in Moscow and to measure the degree of German reticence in divulging information to its ally. Since the differences existing between Rome and Berlin in evaluating the possibility of localizing a German action in Danzig were becoming more profound and increasingly clear, one could ask whether one of the precise causes for this development might not be the evolution of Nazi-Soviet relations.

On the other hand, on August 7, Magistrati, in a personal letter to Ciano, commented as follows:

Two circumstances could precipitate the situation and drive the Germans to attempt the coup: (1) some intemperate gesture by the Poles, brought to a high emotional pitch by the press in the democratic countries, as they were today over the matter of the customs officers, which would appear to be extremely threatening to German "prestige"; (2) the failure *apertis verbis* of the Anglo-French-Soviet conversations, which, in creating serious perplexity in London and Paris and forcing Russia to remain immobile, might give strong support to the arguments of the "interventionists." But this situation, particularly after the dispatch of the Franco-British military missions to Moscow, seems today to be far from coming to pass. Even if the accord is not signed, it is unlikely that it will be declared to be an impossibility.

In this context, the present Russo-German situation is strange and interesting. The intensification of the difficulties between Berlin and Warsaw is linked to the renewal of German hopes for greater understanding in Moscow. In a special way there is an identity of views among the traditional forces—I would like to call them "Bismarkian"—of the Wilhelmstrasse, the traditionally Russophile army, representatives of the industrial community, and even new elements who see in the authoritarian nature and the organization of the Stalinist regime certain similarities with National Socialism. And even Ribbentrop, that prophet of the anti-Comintern, today makes no mention of his pro-Japanese feelings. The characteristic episode which took place yesterday, in which the Wilhelmstrasse, intent on avoiding raising the slightest suspicion in the minds of the Kremlin leaders, banned any mention of the Shiratori-Oshima meeting at Villa d'Este, is truly significant, and this without adding that the German press for the past six months has not criticized Russia or Bolshevism. How long ago seem

tion. Von Weizsäcker, *Erinnerungen*, pp. 247–48; Erich Kordt, *Nicht aus den Akten* (Stuttgart: Union Deutsche Verlagsgesellschaft, 1950), pp. 312, 316. Contrariwise, when Attolico returned from Salzburg and saw Rosso's telegram of August 5, he went to see Von Weizsäcker to confirm its accuracy and was told that the information transmitted by Rosso was correct but with the added note that the "information given to Your Excellency verbally [to Ciano at Salzburg] had been greatly, very greatly exaggerated." Attolico to Ciano, telegram, August 14, 1939, *I.D.*, 8th series, XIII, Doc. 32. Evidently Von Weizsäcker hoped to neutralize the possible psychological effects of the optimistic statements by Hitler and Von Ribbentrop regarding the Italian opposition to an attack against Poland. Von Weizsäcker was shortly to comment on these statements.

the days of Hitler's thunderous speeches larded with stentorian accusations against the "destroyers of humanity"!

Conclusions? Deductions? The German ship of state, despite the fact that the hand of the pilot is anything but steady, seems to be sailing toward Nuremburg without the threat of tragedy. From that tribunal the world will receive the official definition of the problem: war or peace in 1939?[120]

Not even this somewhat optimistic analysis of the situation contains any new elements. The prospects of an open collapse of the Anglo-French-Soviet negotiations were considered to be remote. And if the effect of such a failure on Hitler's decisions was clearly understood, it was regarded as being independent of the possibility of a Russo-German understanding. The Italian Minister Counsellor in Berlin detailed the nature of the existing pressure for "a policy of greater understanding with Moscow," but he failed to discuss ways in which this tendency might be realized, the extent of the desired rapprochement, or its prospects of success. In any event, this was the information available to Ciano when he arrived in Salzburg to meet with Hitler and Von Ribbentrop.

8

During the course of the Italo-German conference of August 11–13, the German Foreign Minister and the Führer spoke openly about the German-Soviet negotiations. These statements, taken from Ciano's minutes of the meeting, were as follows:

Russia will not intervene in the conflict because the Moscow negotiations have failed completely and because (and this was told to me in strictest confidence) rather specific talks are now under way between Moscow and Berlin. (I point out that this secrecy so closely guarded during the development of these negotiations is hardly in keeping with the terms of the alliance and with the complete loyalty we have shown toward Germany.)[121]

... Russia will not move. The Moscow negotiations have been a total failure. The Franco-British military missions were sent to Russia simply to mask the total collapse of the political talks. On the other hand, the Russo-German contacts are proceeding very favorably, and recently a request has been received for the name of a plenipotentiary to go to Moscow to discuss the friendship pact.[122]

[120] Magistrati to Ciano, personal letter, August 7, 1939, *ibid.*, XII, Doc. 798.

[121] Minutes of the Ciano-Ribbentrop meeting in Salzburg, August 11, 1939, *ibid.*, XIII, Doc. 1. The German minutes of this meeting have not been located.

[122] Minutes of the Ciano-Hitler colloquy at Berchtesgaden, August 12, 1939, *ibid.*, Doc. 4. Moreover, regarding the motives which induced Ciano to eliminate from his minutes every reference to the episode of the arrival of the communication concerning the request for a German plenipotentiary to be sent to Moscow just at the time of the Berchtesgaden talks, see Mario Toscano, "Fonti documentarie e memorialistiche per la storia diplomatica della seconda guerra mondiale," *Rivista storica italiana* (1948), II, pp. 105–6.

The minutes kept by Schmidt at the Berchtesgaden meeting read as follows:

Concerning the plan for a conference, the Führer stated that Russia could no longer be excluded from future meetings of the Powers. During the Russo-German talks the Russians, referring to Munich and other occasions on which they had been excluded, had let it be understood that in the future they would not tolerate this. . . .

During this exchange of views the Führer was handed a telegram from Moscow and one from Tokyo. The conversation was interrupted for a short time and Count Ciano was then informed of the contents of the Moscow telegram. The Russians agreed to a German political negotiator being sent to Moscow. The Reich Foreign Minister added that the Russians were fully informed about Germany's designs on Poland. He himself, on orders from the Führer, had informed the Russian Chargé d'Affaires.

Regarding this, the Führer remarked that in his opinion Russia would not be prepared to pull the Western Powers' chestnuts out of the fire. Stalin's position was just as much in danger from a victorious as from a defeated Russian army. Russia was at the most interested in extending her borders to the Baltic Sea. Germany had no objection to this. Besides, Russia would probably never intervene on behalf of Poland whom she thoroughly detested. The sole purpose of sending the Anglo-French Military Mission to Moscow was to conceal the catastrophic state of the political negotiations.[123]

Von Ribbentrop abandoned the reserve that he had maintained toward Attolico during recent weeks, and both he and Hitler, on August 11 and 12, 1939, clearly and officially expressed to Ciano what they believed the situation in Moscow to be and what Germany proposed to do with regard to the U.S.S.R. Obviously, in their presentation both of them made it clear that they considered the prospects of immediate Russo-German relations in far more optimistic terms than they had in the past, but they did not yet choose to indicate—perhaps because they were not in a position to measure just how far the Kremlin was willing to go—their intention of abandoning the understanding reached at Milan on the policy to be followed in Moscow to block the conclusion of a pact with London.[124] A comparison of the German documents published to date with the Italian ones reproduced here demonstrates that, at the moment of the Salzburg meeting, Ciano was informed about much of the negotiations going on between Moscow and Berlin, if not through Von Ribbentrop's communica-

[123] Schmidt, memorandum concerning the Ciano-Hitler colloquy of August 12, 1939, at Berchtesgaden, *G.D.*, Series D, VII, Doc. 43.

[124] In his above-cited letter to Mussolini of August 25, 1939, Hitler implicitly confirms this interpretation when he affirms that before Von Ribbentrop's journey to Moscow he "had no idea of the possible extent of these conversations, or any assurance of the possibility of their success." Hitler to Mussolini, letter, August 25, 1939, *ibid.*, Doc. 266.

tions to Attolico, certainly through Von Schulenburg's confidential statements to Rosso. The minutes reveal a keen understanding of the Anglo-French-Soviet negotiations, and they emphasize the possibilities inherent in the situation. The complete confidence expressed by Hitler and Von Ribbentrop, even within the exposition made to Ciano, appears to have been excessive, in that the "famous" communication from Moscow which caused the interruption of the conversations at Berchtesgaden[125] appears to have been nothing more than a summary account of the Schnurre-Astakhov meeting which had taken place that same day.[126] There the Soviet Chargé d'Affaires declared that he had received instructions from his government to emphasize its desire to improve relations with Germany and then unofficially discussed several possible subjects which might be included in the negotiations. Evidently, the Führer and his Foreign Minister, in order to impress Ciano, to induce him to re-examine his views on the international situation, and to exclude the possibility of localizing a German-Polish conflict, not only abandoned their usual reserve but went to the opposite extreme, giving the impression that there was much more between Berlin and Moscow than, in fact, there was. However, it appears unrealistic to assume that Ciano could have taken them to task for being silent on what was transpiring between Moscow and Berlin.

One cannot help but be astonished that the Hitler-Ribbentrop statements provoked no reaction in Rome and apparently were all but ignored by the Italian leadership. One's surprise is not so much at what was done but, rather, at what was not done to prevent Germany from setting out to accomplish her indicated goals. The meeting had been desired by both governments, primarily to counteract the Anglo-Russian negotiations. Now it was apparently evolving into an agreement concerning an attack on Poland, and the Italians continued to refrain from protesting the course events were taking.

As a matter of fact, all Ciano's and Attolico's efforts at this point were focused on proving that, in the event of an attack on Poland, Great Britain would not remain aloof and that the conflict would become a general one. The negotiations with Moscow, which even then appeared to be increas-

[125] The episode referred to by Schmidt is confirmed in all of its details by Eugenio Dollmann, *Roma Nazista* (Milan: Longanesi, 1949), pp. 225–26; Erich Kordt, *Wahn und Wirklichkeit* (Stuttgart: Union Deutsche Verlagsgesellschaft, 1948), p. 163; Massimo Magistrati, *L'Italia a Berlino: 1937–1939* (Milan: Mondadori, 1956), pp. 399–400. The episode perplexed the Italians, who were left to conclude that it was a German maneuver intended to intimidate.

[126] Cf. Schnurre to Von Schulenburg, telegram, August 14, 1939, *G.D.*, Series D, VII, Doc. 50. There is the possibility that reference is made to another communication, but there is no trace of any such communication in the German documents.

ingly important, were disregarded. The consequences of such apathy are difficult to evaluate, but the least that can be said is that it did not discourage Hitler, *after the Salzburg meeting*, from seeking support from Russia for his proposed attack on Poland, as the Fascist government's negative attitude had rendered such support necessary.[127] However, it is doubtful that even heavy pressure from the Italians would have had a significant effect. It would certainly have been no more effective than the warnings and apprehensions Rome expressed regarding an attack against Poland, the issue conditioning every other action.

Moreover—and this new element finally took shape at Salzburg—the second telegram, the one from Tokyo which arrived at Berchtesgaden on August 12, brought an end to the hopes of an early Japanese adherence to the Italo-German alliance,[128] removing yet another obstacle to Von Ribbentrop's action in Moscow.

In conclusion, the Germans at Salzburg informed the Italians in detail of what they had done up to that time and what they proposed to do. However, the situation that evolved out of the unresolved differences between Rome and Berlin regarding the action against Poland drove the Germans to go beyond what they had outlined as their new position, even concerning the rapprochement with the U.S.S.R. Moreover, Hitler's fixation on the date of the attack constituted, even taking Ciano's attitude into consideration, another determining factor in setting the pattern for the Reich's policy toward Russia. On a technical diplomatic plane, rather than a political one, the Germans were aided by the absence of any Italian comment on the new direction. However, the letter of the Milan agreement was crystal clear, and its spirit left no doubt of Italian opposition to the Polish undertaking.

9

After Ciano returned to Rome, he and Mussolini searched for the best policy line to observe toward Italy's ally, and just as they were drafting new instructions for Attolico, this telegram arrived from the latter in

---

[127] The Bonnet thesis, according to which until August 11 Hitler thought that he might also have to fight against the Soviet Union at the same time, is not acceptable. Nevertheless, Bonnet did recognize the effect the Salzburg meeting had on the Nazi-Soviet negotiations. Georges Bonnet, *Fin d'une Europe* (Geneva: Cheval Ailé, 1948), p. 274.

[128] Kordt, *Wahn und Wirklichkeit*, p. 163. While much attention has been given to the communication from Moscow, little has been devoted to the no less important one from Tokyo. Perhaps it was the telegram from Ambassador Ott to Von Ribbentrop of August 11 (*G.D.*, Series D, VII, Doc. 25). It should be noted that Ciano was not informed of this dispatch, for reasons about which one can only conjecture but which, in any event, reveal at once the German reticence toward Italy and the German desire to concentrate the attention of the Fascist Minister for Foreign Affairs on the important Soviet negotiations.

Berlin: "I am in a position to confirm without equivocation the information furnished by our Ambassador in his report re-transmitted to me. Information given to Your Excellency orally on the matter has been very highly exaggerated."[129]

The importance of this brief telegram, which was not followed by a detailed report, should not be underestimated. It served, in fact, to confirm the impression of Ciano and his associates that both Hitler and Von Ribbentrop had described the state of Russo-German negotiations with excessive optimism. In reality, it was only on August 14, the date of the telegram, that Von Ribbentrop telegraphed instructions to Von Schulenburg to step up the tempo of the negotiations with the Russians, and at that late date the reaction of the Kremlin was still unpredictable.[130] If the

---

[129] Attolico to Ciano, telegram, August 14, 1939, *I.D.*, 8th series, XIII, Doc. 32. This telegram was sent at 2:30 P.M. and reached Rome at 5 P.M. The "report referred to" was a telexpress from the Ministry which transmitted to Berlin Rosso's telegram of August 5, 1939 (see *ibid.*, XII, Doc. 780). Upon his arrival in Rome, Ciano was also able to see the above-cited Crolla report of August 11 from London, in which the Italian Chargé d'Affaires referred to one of his conversations with the German Ambassador in which the latter had mentioned the reasons for his skepticism regarding the outcome of the Anglo-Soviet negotiations. The report read as follows:

> Dirksen began by citing examples, speaking to me primarily of the Anglo-Russian negotiations. He told me that his first impression, when he learned that an Anglo-French military mission was being sent to Moscow, was that they were now talking seriously. However, immediately afterward he changed his mind completely. Furthermore, the names of the three British delegates representing the army, navy, and air force leads one to conclude that the mission has scant hope of success. They are the names of brilliant officers, valorous naval commanders, excellent instructors for recruits at air bases, but they are totally lacking in experience in matters of strategy. In fact, they are not general staff officers and are therefore the worst possible choices for the difficult, delicate, and complex negotiations which should be anticipated in Moscow. What will these officers do there? They will go to satisfy English and world public opinion and to fill the void left by the suspension or, at the very least, by the slowdown of the political negotiations after Strang's return to London. They will possibly go there to provide some exact judgments on the war potential of the Soviet armed forces. If there was hope of doing more, the British mission, as presently composed, would be obviously inadequate.
>
> On the other hand, the enlarging of the scope of the Moscow conversations to include the military will offer the Soviets greater opportunities to carry on their obstructionist tactics, if that continues to be the tactical objective of the Soviet government. For the moment, putting aside the difficulties relative to the definition of the so-called indirect aggression, the Russians will be able to raise a thousand other difficulties concerning military collaboration in case of war. Thus the negotiations will be dragged on into an indeterminate future.

Crolla to Ciano, report, August 11, 1939, *ibid.*, XII, Doc. 844.

[130] Von Weizsäcker to Von Schulenburg, telegram, August 14, 1939, *G.D.*, Series D, VII, Doc. 51; Von Ribbentrop to Von Schulenburg, telegram, August 14, 1939, *ibid.*, Doc. 56. Von Schulenburg's reply reached Berlin at 5:25 A.M. on August 16.

information learned at the Wilhelmstrasse by the Italian Embassy confirming that transmitted by Rosso on August 5 was accurate insofar as the *past* was concerned, it was inevitable that it was psychologically misleading concerning the *future*.

Not withstanding this consideration, two days later Magistrati, the Chargé d'Affaires in Berlin, reported to Rome as follows:

> This morning the Soviet Chargé d'Affaires came to see me. He has been running the Soviet Embassy for several months in the absence of the Ambassador.
>
> He confirmed that the trade negotiations between Germany and Russia which are taking place in Berlin are about to be concluded and that, in all likelihood, the accord will be signed within a few days.
>
> According to the Chargé d'Affaires, "It could serve as a good base for further developments."
>
> On the whole, the Russian seemed to be optimistic concerning relations between Germany and Russia, and he stated that he is convinced that the Polish crisis will break out within approximately ten days.[131]

Given the habitual reserve of the Soviet diplomats, this conversation with Magistrati should have been recognized as sufficiently important to warrant querying the Wilhelmstrasse to learn whether the information received on August 14 continued to reflect the situation as it actually existed, particularly in view of the fact that Rome had just received a telegram from Rosso describing the latest developments in the German action at Moscow, as follows:

> Following new instructions received from Berlin, the German Ambassador requested to confer again with Molotov, and he was received by the latter late last night.
>
> I will say that in reporting on his colloquy, my German colleague was rather reticent and vague and that I received more precise information on the conversation from another official in his embassy in the strictest confidence and with the request that no mention (repeat) no mention be made of this in Rome to Ambassador Von Mackensen. The reason is understood to be that Von Ribbentrop wants to keep Your Excellency informed directly rather than through Moscow.
>
> The substance of the colloquy was as follows: Von Schulenburg referred to the mutual interest in arriving at a prompt conclusion on the matter of improving political relations and referred to the nonaggression pact which Germany was prepared to sign.
>
> Molotov took note of the German overture with satisfaction and made two other requests: (1) German guarantee to the Baltic States; (2) a German agreement to act as a "moderating influence" on Japan. Von Schulenburg promised to refer the matter to Berlin.

[131] Magistrati to Ciano, telegram, August 16, 1939, *I.D.*, 8th series, XIII, Doc. 55; see also Magistrati, *L'Italia a Berlino*, p. 412.

At the same time, Schulenburg declared that it was his personal opinion that a "major figure" in the Nazi government (evidently Von Ribbentrop) would have no difficulty in coming to Moscow to sign the accord. Molotov was pleased by this declaration because he viewed this gesture as further proof that "Germany was serious."

During the course of the conversation Molotov mentioned that the Italian Foreign Minister had mentioned to the Soviet Chargé d'Affaires in Rome that the Fascist government viewed the present Russo-German negotiations with favor and expressed the hope that they would be crowned with success. It is clear to me that the Soviet government is exploiting the favorable moment to extract the maximum in the way of advantages from both Germany and England and France in the way of prestige as well as in the area of security. Despite the fact that I see the possibility today of a Nazi-Soviet nonaggression pact being realized, I continue to believe that the Soviet government still objects to assuming any hard and fast obligations insofar as its intervention or nonintervention in a European conflict is concerned, and that its primary objective is to preserve its freedom of action.[132]

In comparing the summary account of the Schulenburg-Molotov colloquy sent to the Wilhelmstrasse by the German Ambassador[133] with the version transmitted by Rosso, it becomes very clear that the staff of the German Embassy in Moscow made some omissions, particularly concerning the secret adjunct to the nonaggression pact, while (and this was a very significant coincidence) very little or nothing was omitted in the report concerning that part of the negotiation that coincided with understandings reached previously at Milan. However, the information sent to Rome was sufficiently clear to indicate to the Italians that the negotiations as outlined by Hitler and Von Ribbentrop at Salzburg and Berchtesgaden were progressing favorably along the lines suggested by Ciano.[134] Here too, from a diplomatic point of view, a serious request should have been made for a high-level clarification of what was going on in Moscow. In examining the Rosso forecasts, which were favorable concerning the possibility of a positive conclusion of the Nazi-Soviet negotiations for a nonaggression pact but negative concerning Russia's assumption of precise obligations in a European conflict, it would have been logical to ask

[132] Rosso to Ciano, telegram, August 17, 1939, I.D., 8th series, XIII, Doc. 69. The telegram was sent shortly after midnight. Therefore it must have been drafted on the 16th.

[133] Von Schulenburg to Von Ribbentrop, telegram, August 16, 1939, G.D., Series D, VII, Doc. 70.

[134] It is interesting to note that Von Schulenburg's account to Rosso (confirming that appearing in the German documents) contrasted with Ciano's version of what Hitler told him at Berchtesgaden, that the dispatch of a German plenipotentiary to Moscow did not originate in a Soviet invitation but reflected Kremlin acceptance of a Wilhelmstrasse suggestion to do so.

whether Berlin's apparent absolute certainty of being able to localize the conflict with Poland was due to a total incapacity to evaluate the situation or to an overly optimistic interpretation of factors which had not been made entirely clear to the Fascist government.[135]

The Rosso evaluation was not given sufficient consideration in Rome, where no effort was made to call the attention of the Wilhelmstrasse to the necessity of observing the Milan agreement regarding the rapprochement policy with the U.S.S.R. Instead, every effort was concentrated on emphasizing the existing disagreement between the two governments as to the degree to which the western powers would react to a German attack on Poland. Even though Italy's greater "maritime" sensibility contrasted with Germany's "continental" one—and this may have been at the root of their differences—the conduct of the Fascist government was indeed perplexing and cannot be explained in such general terms. More important, perhaps, was Ciano's continued deep skepticism regarding the prospects of Von Ribbentrop's success in Moscow and the Fascists' superficial treatment of the entire question, which perhaps stemmed from a desire to avoid the complications of a risky and uncertain maneuver.

These considerations may explain, even if they do not justify, the fact that, after having discussed the results of the Salzburg and Berchtesgaden meetings at length in Rome, Mussolini issued oral instructions to Attolico to say to Von Ribbentrop that he felt it would be extremely difficult to localize a German-Polish conflict and that, therefore, the present situation was not favorable for an Italian intervention, but that Italy was not taking a position relative to those German-Soviet negotiations which were foremost in the German Foreign Minister's considerations.

Attolico and Magistrati were received by Von Ribbentrop at Fuschl on August 18, but the stormy session that followed left matters politically unchanged.[136] During the course of these talks Von Ribbentrop again observed, "But the most important element consists of the fact that Russia herself, and it can now be said with certainty, will never oppose Axis

---

[135] Magistrati, L'Italia a Berlino, p. 410. Magistrati notes that he raised the issue in his discussions with Attolico, but the correspondence of the Italian Embassy in Berlin does not reveal that these questions were raised or developed in an official way.

[136] Pittalis to Ciano, telegrams, August 19, 1939, I.D., 8th series, XIII, Docs. 100, 101, 108; telegram, August 20, 1939, ibid., Doc. 116; Magistrati, promemorial of August 19, 1939, relative to the Ribbentrop-Attolico colloquy of August 18, 1939, ibid., Doc. 102; Magistrati, L'Italia a Berlino, pp. 416–19. Before leaving Berlin, Magistrati saw Von Weizsäcker, and the latter told the Italian Chargé d'Affaires (Attolico was in Rome to receive oral instructions from Mussolini) that the contacts between Berlin and Moscow were "constantly improving" and that the stipulation of the trade agreement seemed to be imminent. Ibid., p. 415.

actions. The matter must still remain secret, but the effective improvement in Russo-German relations is a certainty. Tomorrow or the day after, the commercial accord between the two countries will be signed,[137] and the first contacts for an accord in the political field have been launched successfully."[138]

In the absence of instructions, the two Italian diplomats took no stand on this particular point. In any event, the arguments of the Fascist government lacked one essential point to which the Germans might have reacted, that is, the affirmation that, whatever the content of future Russo-German understandings might be, they would not be powerful enough to localize a German-Polish conflict. There is no trace of any such consideration in the instructions issued by Rome or in the correspondence of the embassies in Berlin and Moscow. Probably this consideration and a clear-cut position on the matter were lacking because the Italians believed an entente to be highly unlikely and so never considered the matter in all of its ramifications thoroughly and officially.

Yet such a position would have been extremely natural because Mussolini's notes to Hitler of May 30, designed to interpret the Pact of Steel and which the Fascist government quite correctly cited to justify its opposition to the outbreak of a general war before the specified period of time had lapsed, explicitly mentioned the possibility of successful Anglo-French-Soviet negotiations for an alliance.

Attolico left Berlin for Rome and arrived at 11:20 A.M. on August 20, at which time Rosso was sending the following telegram to Rome: "The German Ambassador has seen Molotov two more times. My colleague is pleased by the outcome of these conversations, which apparently have made a slow but satisfactory progress. He has promised to give me greater details later."[139] This was the last information on the subject transmitted to Palazzo Chigi prior to the *coup de scene* of August 21.

10

The news of Von Ribbentrop's imminent departure for Moscow to sign a political accord with the U.S.S.R. was telephoned to Ciano by the Nazi Foreign Minister himself at 10:30 P.M. on August 21. The surprise in

---

[137] It was signed on August 19, 1939.

[138] Magistrati, promemorial, August 19, 1939, n. 136. This point was summarized as follows in Attolico's telegraphic account: "I wouldn't know what else to add except that ... further assurances have been provided by the U.S.S.R. regarding its disposition to conclude with Germany a political accord ... (in addition to the commercial accord which will be signed tomorrow)." Pittalis to Ciano, telegram, August 19, 1939, *I.D.*, 8th series, XIII, Doc. 100.

[139] Rosso to Ciano, telegram, August 20, 1939, *ibid.*, Doc. 122.

Rome at this announcement was enormous, even though no details were offered as to the probable content of the agreement.[140] Mussolini immediately arranged to cancel Ciano's projected trip to Berlin to explain Italy's plan to remain out of any conflict provoked by a German attack against Poland. The astonishment of both the Duce and Ciano was such that for twenty-four hours the two not only regarded Berlin's belief that a German-Polish conflict could be localized as a possibility but thought that it might be possible to profit from such a contingency to make some territorial gains. At the moment, it did not occur to either of the Fascist leaders to criticize Berlin for its action and to request clarification. Instead, Ciano congratulated Von Ribbentrop and wished him a successful journey.

After what has been noted in the preceding pages, little can be added by way of explaining this singular phenomenon. Despite all of the advance warnings by Germany and the precise information transmitted by Rosso, Mussolini's and Ciano's total skepticism, aided and abetted by the reports from the Italian Embassy in Berlin, prevented them from seriously examining the problem of Russo-German relations. Hence the news from Von Ribbentrop produced shock and confusion, followed immediately by a confirmation of Italy's opposition to the Polish adventure.

However, the mere announcement of Von Ribbentrop's trip to Moscow did not mean that the pact was a foregone conclusion, and therefore it is relevant to pursue the investigation to learn what further developments in the negotiations came to the attention of Palazzo Chigi. The first report from Berlin furnished no indication as to the nature of the proposed accord. The Italian Chargé d'Affaires (Attolico had immediately departed for Berlin from Rome) limited his account to a report of Germany's internal reaction to the news of the imminent conclusion of the pact with the Soviets, as follows:

> As I reported via telegraph from Munich and Berlin, the announcement,

[140] For details on this point, see Ciano, *Diaries*, p. 126; Mario Donosti [Luciolli], *Mussolini e l'Europa* (Rome: Leonardo, 1945), pp. 209–10. As for the impression this created at the Italian Embassy in Berlin, it may be of interest to report what Magistrati wrote to Ciano:

> The news of the imminent conclusion of the Nazi-Soviet nonaggression pact and of Von Ribbentrop's imminent departure for Moscow has produced general satisfaction here. All see *"finis Poloniae"* and look to the Poland of the Congress of Vienna. It cannot be denied that it is a master stroke and that the Franco-British failure in Moscow is a major blow. With Japan as her friend (even though in one fell swoop the Anti-Comintern Pact is void of meaning) and Russia neutralized, Germany holds trump cards. How can she be stopped? Is there any advantage in doing so?

Magistrati to Ciano, personal letter, August 22, 1939, *I.D.*, 8th series, XIII, Doc. 140. Cf. Magistrati, *L'Italia a Berlino*, pp. 422–23.

given to the press in an effective and dramatic way, of the upcoming stipulation of the nonaggression pact between Berlin and Moscow and the departure of Von Ribbentrop for the Soviet capital has brought a general sense of relief to an atmosphere which has been externally calm but internally tense.

In the final analysis, the rapprochement with the Soviet Union has always been welcome here, and the most diverse elements are in accord on this point, elements which range from the traditional Bismarckian Russophiles (the army and the Foreign Office) to the extremists in the Nazi Party itself. Then the fact that it will be Von Ribbentrop himself, the creator of the Anti-Comintern Pact, who will sign for Germany, and for Von Ribbentrop that the *"Horst Wessel Lied"* will be played in the streets of Moscow tomorrow (the song that contains the phrase "comrades murdered by the Red Front and the reaction"), forced even those who opposed the pact on ideological grounds, chiefly among them Alfred Rosenberg, to abandon their opposition.

In addition to being a master political stroke, the event constitutes a decisive blow to the British policy of encirclement, and this just on the eve of the Danzig crisis. The signing of the pact will undoubtedly provide the Nazi government with a success in the field of practical politics, if not an ideological one, sufficiently strong to put to rest all movements to stimulate discontent among the masses of the people, particularly in large cities such as Hamburg, where these movements seem to have their roots in the secret Communist cells.

The press, as noted above, has effectively handled the announcement as one of a sensational nature. The first information was made public very late in the evening and this morning all of the papers carried the brief and concise statement in banner headlines without comment, which strengthens the sense of "surprise," that is, of a very pleasant surprise.

Only in the afternoon did the first comments begin to appear in the news accounts, and all of these contained an anti-British overtone. In effect, the releases state that the general political situation has been overturned and the system of encirclement smashed. Germany has not let herself be taken by surprise, as she did in 1914.

It is important to note that the emergence of the pact has already begun to alter the situation concerning Danzig. A great deal of space is being given to an article which appeared in the *Danziger Vorposten* which asserts that the city of Danzig cannot live without being linked to its natural hinterland, since, in the present situation, it is always at the mercy of a Polish blockade, which could reduce it to starvation.[141]

This report reached Rome at a time when, in the light of the reactions from London and Paris, Mussolini and Ciano were concluding that the Moscow accord had not substantially changed the situation in the West.[142] Because of the increase in the German demands against Poland, the

---

[141] Magistrati to Ciano, report, August 22, 1939, *I.D.*, 8th series, XIII, Doc. 163.

[142] Ciano, *Diaries*, pp. 126–27. The first reservations expressed by Ciano on the efficacy of the Nazi-Soviet pact in localizing an eventual conflict with Poland were made on the morning of August 23 to the German Minister of Finance, Schwerin-Krosigk, at Palazzo Chigi. Schwerin-Krosigk to Von Ribbentrop, letter, August 23, 1939, *G.D.*, Series D, VII, Doc. 227.

Fascist government was more and more concerned about Italy's position in the matter, and its entire attention was absorbed in an effort to avoid Italian involvement in any German-Polish conflict. Consequently, Italian disinterest in what was occurring in Moscow tended to increase. However, Magistrati[143] and Attolico,[144] without dwelling too heavily on the substance of the Nazi-Soviet pact, immediately concerned themselves with the best way to use the event to make the noninterventionist position of Italy absolutely clear without precipitating a dissolution of the Pact of Steel. Such a dissolution had been seriously considered immediately after the Salzburg meeting.

At the same time, Rosso telegraphed the first information from Moscow concerning Von Ribbentrop's visit to that capital. "This afternoon Von Ribbentrop had his first colloquy with Stalin and Molotov. He will meet with them again this evening, and for this reason begged to be excused for not keeping his appointment to dine with me. He informed me that he was very satisfied with the way things went today in the talks and predicts an imminent satisfactory conclusion, possibly even this evening. He told me that as soon as it is materially possible, he will bring me up to date on the results in order that I may inform Your Excellency."[145]

Encouraged by this apparent success, Von Ribbentrop, despite the disagreements evident at Salzburg, proposed to inform Ciano of his activities immediately. He apparently maintained this attitude throughout his entire stay in Moscow; in fact, on August 25, Rosso telegraphed as follows:

I conferred at length with Von Ribbentrop this morning. He told me that the discussions at the Kremlin lasted almost without interruption until two o'clock in the morning before the pact was signed.

He had a friendly conversation with Stalin and Molotov in an extremely cordial atmosphere. He commented on the text of the pact, noting the particularly important clause relative to reciprocal consultation. I indicated my interest in the wording of Article 2, which affirms the obligation of neutrality independent of the fact that the other contracting party may or may not be accused of an act of aggression against third parties.

On this point Von Ribbentrop told me that he is firmly convinced that the U.S.S.R. will in no case oppose Germany during an eventual German conflict with Poland. He added that he had had a very frank exchange of ideas with Stalin regarding Poland and Turkey and that, insofar as Danzig was concerned, the Soviet government was fully satisfied with the inevitability of the solution demanded by Berlin.

As for Japan, Von Ribbentrop assured the Soviets that the German govern-

---

[143] Magistrati to Ciano, personal letter, August 23, 1939, *I.D.*, 8th series, XIII, Doc. 187.

[144] Attolico to Ciano, report, August 24, 1939, *ibid.*, Doc. 218.

[145] Rosso to Ciano, telegram, August 23, 1939, *ibid.*, Doc. 181.

ment would use its influence toward an improvement in Russo-Japanese relations; he foresees strong discontent in Tokyo, but he is hopeful of being able
to persuade the Japanese government that it would be in its own interest to
modify its anti-Russian policy in north China in order to devote its entire effort
to south China.

As for Turkey, it will be up to that government to examine the new situation and to decide whether or not it wants to be a friend of the Axis.[146] I am
abstaining from referring to other matters discussed with me because he mentioned that he had conferred with Your Excellency in detail on them at
Salzburg.

In conclusion, he regards the new pact as a decisive turn in the course of
events for Europe and the world, a turn decidedly in favor of the Italo-German
alliance.

He is pleased by the thought that his mission will be approved by the Duce,
to whom he attributes the first step toward the rapprochement with the
U.S.S.R. He added that the alliance pact was referred to by Molotov as a factor
already making its effect felt [two groups of undecipherable words occur here]
the possibility of an amelioration of relations with the Axis powers.

The formal pact will have a protocol or exchange of notes appended on
which Von Ribbentrop promises to inform Your Excellency fully as soon as
possible. Von Ribbentrop's impressions of Stalin were summarized as follows:
"A personality of major caliber, gifted with a revolutionary sense of the
highest order."

Von Ribbentrop hopes to be able to reach Munich in time to see Hitler
before the day is out.

I note that, at the moment of the German Minister's departure, I took the
occasion to congratulate Potemkin on the conclusion of the accord with Germany. The Vice Commissar replied that he reciprocated the Italian Ambassa-

---

[146] The Chargé d'Affaires in Ankara had already telegraphed to Rome on the
subject as follows:

The news of the conclusion of the Nazi-Soviet nonaggression pact as being
imminent has produced a sensation here. The Turkish press has published, in
extraordinary headlines, the information coming in from the news agencies; comments, however, are scarce, an obvious sign that local circles were caught un-
awares. Only the *Republique* and the *Vakit* this morning published detailed
articles on the subject. In their attempt to diminish the importance of the event
in the eyes of the public, these articles reveal a grave concern and a sense of
embarrassment.

In diplomatic circles here focus is on the fact that Turkey is one of the countries most directly affected by the dramatic upheaval in the political orientation
of eastern Europe brought about by the lightning diplomatic victory of the Axis.
It is also believed that among the factors influencing the Soviet decision is included the Soviet government's concern that England, by virtue of its accords
with Turkey, can remain in control of the Straits.

For the moment, there has been no indication of the attitude of the government here with respect to the new situation, but it is understandable that it must
be concerned, since this government is about to sign definitive accords with
England and France which have been in preparation.

Berio to Ciano, telegram, August 23, 1939, *ibid.*, Doc. 172.

dor's felicitations and was convinced that rapprochement with Berlin will facilitate further improvement in the already good relations existing between Italy and the U.S.S.R.

The French and English military missions will leave Moscow as soon as possible.[147]

It must be recognized that the information given by Von Ribbentrop to Rosso, while failing to provide the details of the understandings reached with Stalin and Molotov, in contrast to that gathered by the Italian Embassy in Berlin,[148] was at least sufficient to call the attention of Palazzo Chigi to the existence of a secret Russo-German protocol, the nature and terms of which Von Ribbentrop promised to discuss orally with Ciano, a matter of no mean importance.

The subsequent Italian non-belligerence, which was certainly unforeseen by Von Ribbentrop, immediately introduced a decided chill into the relations between the two allies, and no further mention is made of the pact or of the protocol. On the other hand, it does not appear that the Fascist government utilized the information to request further clarification.[149] The Ribbentrop-Rosso meeting was the last manifestation of Berlin's trust in Rome for a very long time. On the Italian side, the expository statement by Hitler in his letter to Mussolini of August 25 was used as the point of departure for communicating to Berlin Italy's decision not to intervene in the imminent conflict.

[147] Rosso to Ciano, telegram, August 25, 1939, *ibid.*, Doc. 264.

[148] The day before Attolico telegraphed as follows: "In reply to my question as to whether the U.S.S.R. had imposed collateral conditions to the nonaggression pact implying eventual German-Polish settlements, Woermann replied that he had no information on the matter. He is certain that other matters—beyond those of the pact—were discussed, but perhaps not that particular point." Attolico to Ciano, telegram, August 24, 1939, *ibid.*, Doc. 201. Immediately afterward, in response to a request from Rome, Attolico noted that "Ribbentrop has had the D.N.B. release a communiqué from Moscow in which he expressed the hope that the new Russo-German pact may serve to improve Russo-Japanese relations, thus strengthening German-Japanese rapport. This was obviously released with the consent of the Soviets." Attolico to Ciano, telegram, August 24, 1939, *ibid.*, Doc. 201. From these dispatches it appears evident that the Wilhelmstrasse was aware of the issues discussed by Von Ribbentrop in drafting the secret protocol to the Nazi-Soviet pact, but it carefully observed the dictum of silence imposed on it by the Nazi Foreign Minister.

[149] While the Undersecretary of State of the Italian Foreign Ministry, on the day before the arrival of the telegram from Moscow, telegraphed to Moscow and Berlin: "Please telegraph immediately text of the Russo-German accord" (Bastianini to Rosso and to Attolico, telegrams, August 24, 1939, *ibid.*, Doc. 211), it seems noteworthy that even Rosso, in his long analysis of the public text of the Nazi-Soviet pact, refrained from raising the question of the probable content of the secret protocol. From Berlin nothing more reached Rome regarding the significance of the Moscow accords of August 23.

11

In summary, the Italian diplomatic documents not only make it possible to examine the role of the Fascist government in the Nazi-Soviet negotiations, but also permit us for the first time to settle the historical questions raised by the several apparently contradictory actions of Mussolini and Ciano. They also cast new light on the negotiations between Moscow and Berlin and upon the factors motivating Soviet policy.

As far as the latter is concerned, the data concerning the reactions of the Kremlin to Chamberlain's visit to Rome are singularly interesting. Undoubtedly, Moscow's suspicions concerning the existence of a British plan tending to channel German expansionist desires toward the east have their origin prior to January, 1939, at least as early as the Chamberlain-Hilgar meetings during the Czechoslovak crisis[150] and the Bonnet-Ribbentrop meeting on the occasion of the signing of the Franco-German accords of December, 1938. However, the leaking of information to the Kremlin on the British Prime Minister's Rome meetings was to eliminate any remaining Soviet doubts and produced the decision to smash the purported British plan. Yet in analyzing the Soviet motives in signing the agreements of August 23, 1939, the importance of the defensive interests of the Soviet Union cannot be ignored.

In turning to an examination of the German attitude, Berlin's initial uncertainty seems to be established beyond doubt. This uncertainty, it appears upon closer examination, was greatly enhanced by the persistent ignoring of Tokyo's real position. Without realizing it, the Nazi leaders were moving toward a choice which was later to have a decisive bearing on the military and diplomatic developments of World War II. Even when the Japanese position was finally defined, they misunderstood the choice in favor of Moscow. In reality, the search for the means to isolate a conflict in Poland became the dominant motivating factor, thereby assuring that local and immediate requirements would take precedence over global and long-range ones, a conclusion which finds its logical explanation in the fact that Berlin did not believe, up to the very last minute, that the western powers would come to the defense of Poland. Thus, while the Polish conflict was quickly resolved on the military plane, its consequences, which were of a much greater magnitude and derived from a

---

[150] On the day after the Munich agreements were signed, in commenting on Hitler's solemn declarations that he had no further territorial claims in Europe, the German Embassy Counsellor in Moscow observed: "It is significant that the Soviets are obviously of the opinion that the Führer's assurances do not apply to the Ukraine since, according to the National Socialist point of view, the Soviet Union is not a part of Europe." Tippelskirch to Schliep, letter, October 10, 1938, *G.D.*, Series D, IV, Doc. 477.

choice made in August, 1939, continued to be felt. Before undertaking the negotiations with Moscow, Von Ribbentrop repeatedly consulted with Attolico and Oshima, both of whom contributed to his doubts and to a delay in the political discussions. Finally, however, when the Nazi Foreign Minister determined his policy toward Poland and took the decision to see it through to the end, he adopted a policy of reserve toward the two ambassadors. He never entirely abandoned it, not even with Attolico, and the contact between Rome and Berlin on the matter was neither continuous nor frequent. On the other hand, his noteworthy reticence with Rome, (at this time Von Weizsäcker did not believe it to be necessary to question it) was not nearly as encompassing as heretofore suspected. Ciano offered no objection, and the last hope that Japan would promptly join the Italo-German alliance dimmed. The decisive turn came at Salzburg when Italy resisted Hitler's pleas that Rome abandon its reservations about the plans for an attack on Poland. But on August 25 in Moscow Von Ribbentrop, who always believed he could count on the military solidarity of the Fascists, probably planned to bring his ally up to date on what had transpired in the Moscow negotiations. Mussolini's letter to Hitler of the same day brought that plan to an abrupt end.

The idea of a Russo-German rapprochement, which had been considered in Berlin,[151] found in Mussolini its first supporter outside of Germany. During his talks with Goering in April, he did not hesitate to include the question in an official conversation. This circumstance had much greater repercussions in Germany than might have been expected.

While the Italian Embassy in Moscow distinguished itself for the soundness and lucidity of its interpretation of the evolution of Soviet foreign policy, the birth of the Pact of Steel was accompanied by an Italo-German understanding regarding the propriety and the limits of an accord with the U.S.S.R. for the purpose of trying to block the successful conclusion of the Anglo-Russian negotiations.

Up to the time of the Salzburg meeting, the Fascist government was aware of virtually all of the essential elements of the Moscow-Berlin negotiations. It sought to facilitate their progress by supporting them at the Narkomindiel; it transmitted to the Russians the first concrete proposals made by the Axis regarding the possible content of the proposed political accord; and it cultivated the possibility of a parallel Italo-Soviet understanding. Nevertheless, the apparent skepticism of the Italian Ambassador to Berlin about the real significance of the Axis negotiations in Moscow, which was, in the final analysis, fully shared by Mussolini and Ciano,

---

[151] For the first reference to this problem after Munich, see *ibid.*, Docs. 476, 477.

paralyzed Fascist diplomacy and induced the Duce to consider the Anglo-Russian accord possible. Similar skepticism on the part of the German leadership led the latter to hold similar views for some time.

At Salzburg, when Hitler and Ribbentrop brought Ciano up to date not only on the status of the negotiations but also on the goals to be attained, the impossibility of localizing the conflict absorbed the Italian Foreign Minister's entire attention. Thus he did not take the time to point out the probable violation of the Milan agreement or to suggest that the Soviet strength might not be sufficient to keep the conflict localized, even though, at the time, he did consider this aspect of the question.

The treaty of August 23 (excluding the protocol) was, in fact, a great surprise to Mussolini and Ciano and to the Italian Embassy in Berlin. For a variety of reasons which have been discussed here, the detailed information transmitted by the Italian Embassy in Moscow went unnoticed, while the discussions between Attolico and Von Ribbentrop on Russo-German relations psychologically supported rather than discouraged or eliminated German reticence. It must be admitted that after the initial postulation and launching of the proposal, Mussolini and Ciano treated the question rather superficially and only occasionally, and the isolation of the offices of the ministry and of the legations abroad did the rest. There are few cases in diplomatic history in which appearance and reality had so little in common. In Moscow, until almost the last minute, Axis diplomacy seemed to be functioning in perfect unison while, in fact, the evaluation of events and the aims pursued by the two allies were drifting further apart. Elsewhere, beginning with Italy, the agreement was credited with being an unforeseen German action, while, in fact, the Soviet-German accord had been predicted. However, it had been considered to have aims and objectives far different from those which were suddenly, or almost suddenly, made public. In fact, however, a majority of Berlin's moves were indirectly brought to the attention of Rome through the efforts of the Germans.

III.

ITALO-SOVIET RELATIONS, 1940–1941:
FAILURE OF AN ACCORD

Summary: 1. Premise. Purpose and limits of this investigation. 2. Relations between Rome and Moscow during the period of Italy's nonbelligerence. Did Palazzo Chigi consider aligning with the Wilhelmstrasse on August 22, 1939? Italy chooses to wait. On October 1, Von Ribbentrop for the first time describes to Ciano his Moscow experiences in enthusiastic terms. Anfuso's queries to Ambassador Rosso regarding the essence of Soviet foreign policy. The Finnish crisis and the anti-Soviet attitude of the Fascist government. The recall of the Soviet Ambassador to Rome and his probable clarifying summary report. Helfand's unsuccessful soundings of Anfuso on December 18. Rosso's recall from Moscow and his eventual anti-German aims. Further conciliatory overtures by the Narkomindiel and Ciano's negative reaction. The bitter polemics exchanged by the Fascist and Soviet presses. Germany's conciliatory action. Hitler's letter to Mussolini of March 6, 1940, and Von Ribbentrop's statements at Palazzo Venezia on March 11. The favorable reply by the Fascist head of state. Steps taken by the Wilhelmstrasse to ameliorate Italo-Soviet relations. Italy's intervention in the war and the return of Rosso and Gorelkin to their respective ambassadorial posts. 3. The cordial Soviet reception of the Italian Ambassador. His colloquy with Molotov of June 13. Mussolini's instructions of June 16 for a rapprochement with the U.S.S.R. Hypotheses regarding their ultimate aims. The second Rosso-Molotov meeting of June 20. New statements and new questions posed by the President of the Council of Peoples' Commissars to the Italian Ambassador on June 25. Probable aims of the Soviet initiative. Limited echo at Palazzo Chigi. Rosso presses Rome for a reply, but on July 5 Ciano directs that further political conversations with Moscow be avoided. His instructions of July 23 to initiate economic negotiations with the U.S.S.R. and the reservations expressed by the Italian Ambassador to Moscow. The Rosso-Mikoyan meeting of July 27 and the Soviet request for a complete clarification of Italo-Soviet political relations prior to entering into any economic negotiations. Molotov's speech to the Supreme Soviet of August 1. On August 4 Ciano discusses the problem of relations with the U.S.S.R. with Mussolini and proposes a favorable reply to Molotov's questions and consultation with Berlin. Von Ribbentrop's veto of August 16. Immediate acquiescence by Mussolini. 4. Soviet dissatisfaction with the Vienna Arbitrage and the absence of Italy's reply to the questions raised by Molotov. The precipitous recall of Rosso and Mussolini's initiative of September 10. Birth of the Tripartite Agreement and the Italo-German exchange of views regarding the adoption of a common circumspect policy vis-à-vis the U.S.S.R. The German occupation of Rumania and its influence on new German and Italian plans for a

* An earlier version of this chapter was published by Sansoni of Florence in 1955 as Una mancata intesa Italo-Sovietica nel 1940 e 1941.

four-power pact with Moscow. The Italo-German conversations in Florence and in Schönhof on October 28 and November 4 to draft the proposals to be presented to the Soviet Union by the Tripartite Powers. 5. The fiasco of Molotov's visit to Berlin and its influence on the German attitude. Effects of the Greek campaign on Italy's relations with Germany and the U.S.S.R. The Kremlin's extreme cordiality toward Italy. Probable reasons for such an attitude. Ciano's decision to reopen the negotiations with Moscow. Motivations and aims. Equivocal consultation with Berlin. 6. The declarations of the Fascist Foreign Minister to the Soviet Ambassador to Rome on December 26. Their immediate and favorable echo in Moscow. The Rosso-Molotov colloquy of December 30. Importance of the questions posed by the President of the Council of Peoples' Commissars to the Fascist government. 7. Ciano's letter to Alfieri of January 1, 1941. The Ribbentrop-Alfieri conversations of January 6. Contemporaneous proposals by Rosso to Palazzo Chigi for the conduct of negotiations with the Soviet Union. Dilatory attitude of the Wilhelmstrasse and the Italian Ambassador toward Moscow's requests for action in Rome. On January 19, Von Ribbentrop personally informs Ciano of the basically negative attitude of the German government and proposes to have his office prepare the replies to Molotov's questions. The passive attitude of the Fascist Foreign Minister. 8. The German note to Italy of January 22 and the Wilhelmstrasse formula for the Moscow talks. Its immediate acceptance by Palazzo Chigi. Ciano's instructions to Rosso of January 24. 9. The Rosso-Molotov colloquy of January 27. The new questions raised by the President of the Council of Peoples' Commissars and the views of the Italian Ambassador to Moscow. Mussolini's favorable reaction and his conciliatory proposals transmitted to Berlin for German approval on January 29. Von Weizsäcker's attitude of reserve. Von Ribbentrop's critical comments expressed to the Italian Chargé d'Affaires in Berlin on February 6. Their acceptance at Palazzo Venezia and the new formula proposed by Mussolini on February 14. The last instructions by the Fascist head of state to Rosso, February 20. 10. The Rosso-Molotov colloquy of February 24. Hypotheses regarding the origin of the negative position assumed by the President of the Council of Peoples' Commissars. End of the Italo-Soviet conversations. 11. Conclusions.

1

A conspicuous number of memoirs and documents have gradually appeared which cast considerable light on the secret negotiations undertaken by the governments of Rome and Moscow in 1940 and 1941 leading toward an accord which should have included a reciprocal recognition of the particular political interests of Italy and of the U.S.S.R. in the Mediterranean, the Balkans, the Straits, and the Black Sea, respectively.[1]

[1] Gregorio Gafencu, *Preliminari della guerra all'Est* (Milan: Mondadori, 1946); Augusto Rosso, "Obbietivi e metodi della politica estera sovietica," *Rivista di studi politici internazionali*, I (1946); Mario Donosti, *Mussolini e l'Europa* (Rome: Leonardo, 1945); Galeazzo Ciano, *Diario*, 2 vols. (Milan: Rizzoli, 1946); Galeazzo Ciano, *L'Europa verso la catastrofe* (Milan: Mondadori, 1948); *Hitler e Mussolini: Lettere e documenti* (Milan: Rizzoli, 1946); Leonardo Simoni, *Berlino: ambasciata d'Italia 1939–1943* (Rome: Migliaresi, 1946); Dino Alfieri, *Due dittatori di fronte* (Milan: Rizzoli, 1948). Some documents concerning this episode have been pub-

These publications have made it possible for some scholars[2] to comment, at least briefly, on the episode. The subject merits further and more detailed study based on the documentary files, only partially published, and preserved in the Historical Archives of the Italian Ministry for Foreign Affairs,[3] documents which cast new light on this strange and incomplete page of Fascist foreign policy during World War II. The present inquiry, subject to correction by the Soviet documentary material yet unpublished and clearly indispensable for an exhaustive general evaluation of the entire negotiation, aims to reconstruct its origins and development within the limited profile of Italian diplomatic action.

2

During the period between the conclusion of the Nazi-Soviet Pact of August 23, 1939,[4] and Italy's intervention in the war, relations between Rome and Moscow were anything but smooth. Periods of cordiality were offset by others of cold suspicion caused not so much by any specific agreement or divergence of view between Rome and Moscow as by developments in German-Russian relations.[5]

The fact that among the papers in the archives of the Cabinet of the Italian Minister of Foreign Affairs there is a note—compiled by the office of the Director General for Political Affairs on August 22, 1939—regarding the origins of the pact of friendship, nonaggression, and neutrality signed between Italy and the U.S.S.R. on September 2, 1933,[6] and that

---

lished in *I documenti diplomatici italiani*, Series IX, 5 vols. (Rome: La Libreria dello Stato, 1954–1965), hereafter cited as *I.D.*, and in *Documents on German Foreign Policy 1918–1945*, Series D, Volumes VIII–XII (London: Her Majesty's Stationery Office, 1954–1962), hereafter cited as *G.D.*

[2] Max Beloff, *The Foreign Policy of Soviet Russia 1929–1941*, 2 vols. (London: Oxford University Press, 1952); Angelo Tasca, *Due anni di alleanza germano-sovietica 1939–1941* (Florence: La Nuova Italia, 1951); Philip W. Fabry, *Der Hitler-Stalin Pakt, 1939–1941* (Darmstadt: Fundus Verlag, 1962).

[3] The unpublished Italian documents will be cited by the original general registration number given to each dispatch, since the entire historical archive of the Italian Foreign Ministry is undergoing a complete reorganization, and it is impossible to include references to the numeration of the various packages.

[4] For the part played by Fascist diplomacy see Chapter II above.

[5] Ciano, *Diario*, I, pp. 193, 196, 203; Donosti, *Mussolini e l'Europa*, p. 228.

[6] According to this note it appears that the pact in question was first touched upon in a conversation between Mussolini and the Soviet Ambassador, Potemkin, at Palazzo Venezia on May 28, 1933. During these talks, both parties reaffirmed their desire to maintain and to consolidate the cordial relations existing between the two countries. Mussolini was particularly interested in calming the Soviet government's fears regarding an eventual anti-Bolshevik orientation of the Hitler government, assuring the Soviet representative that he had urged moderation on Berlin and that

Litvinov journeyed to Rome in December of the same year could suggest that the announcement of Von Ribbentrop's journey to Moscow led the Fascist government to consider momentarily the possibility of aligning itself with the new Nazi policy vis-à-vis the Soviets. In any event, the outbreak of World War II and the Italian declaration of nonbelligerence promptly altered the situation. The Fascist government assumed a position of watchful waiting, and, for a time, Rome avoided any serious and thorough evaluation of the problem of its relations with Moscow. It was probably during the Ciano visit to Berlin on October 1, 1939, that Von Ribbentrop, who shortly before informed Moscow of his desire to consult with the Italians on the matter of the proposed Soviet-Turkish mutual assistance pact,[7] first described the new Kremlin policy in enthusiastic, glowing terms.[8]

Despite the fact that the Nazi Foreign Minister's words were not particularly appreciated by his Axis colleague,[9] evidence seems to indicate that it was precisely this enthusiasm which prompted Ciano's Chief of

---

he would continue to do so. Returning to Moscow the following June, Ambassador Potemkin discussed with his government as well as with Ambassador Attolico the question of consolidating good relations with Italy and received a favorable response. Returning to Rome in July, the Soviet Ambassador presented to the Fascist government the draft of a pact. With few modifications this draft was adopted as the definitive text. On the occasion of its signature, its significance was illustrated in a communiqué to the press on September 30 and by Mussolini in an article entitled "Italia e Russia" appearing in Il Popolo d'Italia. It should be noted that the essential information contained in this ministerial note of August 22 was reproduced in an article entitled "Italy and the Soviet Union" published in the Messaggiero for September 5.

[7] Von Weizsäcker memorandum of September 18, 1939, G.D., Series D, VIII, Doc. 91.

[8] On these talks, see Ciano's minutes, October 1, 1939, I.D., 9th series, I, Doc. 552. For the German version, see Paul Schmidt, promemorial, October 2, 1939, G.D., Series D, VIII, Doc. 176.

[9] With reference to his Berlin talks, Ciano wrote: "Von Ribbentrop is becoming increasingly infatuated with Russia, to which he refers in apologetic terms, although maintaining numerous reservations regarding Soviet military efficiency. He reached the point of saying that in the midst of the members of the Politburo he found himself as comfortable as amongst Nazism's Old Guard or old Squadristi." Ciano, minutes, October 1, 1939, I.D., 9th series, I, Doc. 552. On the same date, Ciano noted in his diary: "He [Ribbentrop] is overcome by Russophilia, and he expresses himself in favor of the Communists imprudently and with such vulgarity as to puzzle anyone who listens to him." Ciano, Diario, I, p. 175.

Von Ribbentrop's attitude evidently provoked a negative reaction from Mussolini as well. A few days later, in speaking to Ambassador Von Mackensen, Mussolini reemphasized in very strong terms his aversion for communism and for the Soviet Union. Cf. Von Mackensen to Von Ribbentrop, telegram, October 6, 1939, G.D., Series D, VIII, Doc. 205.

Cabinet to send the following personal letter to the Italian Ambassador in Moscow:

> In view of the present international situation I believe it would be extremely useful to the Minister to have your personal views on the principal aspects of Russia's new and intense diplomatic-military activity.
>
> I am fully cognizant of the obstacles you encounter in those circles in seeking to obtain accurate information which will permit an objective judgment regarding the real intentions and the activities of the Soviets.
>
> While I can assure you that what you have reported in your telegrams and dispatches has been read here with great interest, may I suggest that, even in the absence of precise and corroborative data, you give us your personal judgment on matters of primary concern to us. For example:
>
> 1. Can the present Russian activity be attributed to motives of Bolshevik internationalism, or does it mark a reawakening of old Muscovite imperialism?
>
> 2. Is this dynamism Slavic or Bolshevik or a fusion of the two?
>
> 3. What are the probable objectives of Soviet expansion?
>
> 4. Can the Soviet-German alliance be interpreted as susceptible to possible further development in the future or simply as an accord *ex delictu*, having an immediate goal as its objective, i.e., the division of the recent territorial acquisitions?
>
> 5. If the alliance is susceptible to further development, what do you think its immediate objectives might be?
>
> 6. Is it possible that, in the event of a spreading of the European conflict, Russia may direct her expansionist energies toward her historic objectives in the Near and Middle East?
>
> 7. Does the present intensification of Soviet activity in the west imply a real and long-lasting shift away from an active Far Eastern policy?
>
> 8. What were the repercussions of public opinion to the Soviet alliance with the Reich, to the recent successes in Poland and in the Baltic States, and, lastly, to the anti-Communist activity undertaken by the western powers and particularly by France?
>
> Your impressions on these matters would be considered most useful here, and I wish to place my emphasis on the word "impressions" because it is obvious that in a political world such as that of the Soviets one can hardly expect a reply to a questionnaire. What you are able to send will serve to give us a general idea of the situation as seen by a perspicacious observer such as yourself.[10]

Evidently, the long series of questions posed for Rosso's consideration, while revealing the uncertainties and the absence of definite opinions in the mind of the author, were nevertheless, aimed at obtaining an objective point of view for the purpose of comparing it with the extremely partisan impressions voiced by the Nazi Foreign Minister. On the other hand, the descriptive *"ex delictu"* used in reference to the Nazi-Soviet Pact could have been an indication of Ciano's attitude toward it.

[10] Anfuso to Rosso, personal letter, October 18, 1939, *I.D.*, 9th series, I, Doc. 796.

Anfuso's letter to Rosso, sent by courier, arrived in Moscow on November 12. Rosso replied immediately as follows:

I am replying immediately to your letter of October 1, which arrived via courier only yesterday.

In giving you my opinions on the present Soviet diplomatic-military activity, I will observe the order of the questions which you raise and which adequately cover the main aspects of the situation.

1. Can the present Russian activity be attributed to motives of Bolshevik internationalism, or does it mark a reawakening of old Muscovite imperialism?

Despite the apparent contradiction, perhaps in the final analysis both factors play a role. We are witnessing a movement that is substantially imperialist in character, but carried out under the banner of international bolshevism.

There is no doubt that the present Soviet actions are clearly internationalist in nature. In this respect, Molotov's speech of November 6 in which he accepted in toto the Comintern thesis is significant.

I view Russian expansionism as a natural phenomenon and very nearly spontaneous: that is, it is the effect of the dynamism of a relatively young people rich in resources. However, the present structure of the U.S.S.R. presses its leaders—or, rather, obligates them—to follow for the moment the course set by a revolution that is of the recent past, that of Communist ideology and internationalism.

I state that it "obligates them" because not even Stalin, with all his dictatorial power, could cast aside the banner he has waved up to the present day.

It is often said that in recent years Stalin has become increasingly "nationalistic." The assertion is partially true in the sense that—certainly more than the old-guard Bolsheviks and the Trotskyites—Stalin has fashioned a policy that has taken into far greater account the needs and interests of the Soviet Union than those of the proletariat of the world. He has done this, nevertheless, to consolidate a "socialist state" which, despite possible temporary alliances, continues to remain an isolated organism in a bourgeois-capitalist world. Thus, because of circumstances, he is forced to combat this capitalist world, and he must of necessity do so under the banner of the proletarian revolution.

2. Is this dynamism Slavic or Bolshevik or a fusion of the two?

The U.S.S.R. is a conglomerate of peoples in which the Slavic element is by far the largest (130 million out of 183 million), and since the racial factor exerts its influence in any regime, there is no doubt that the Soviet political and social currents have many characteristics which are typically Slavic. Yet I do not believe that we can speak of a "Pan-Slav movement" such as existed in Tsarist Russia and which was nurtured by the aristocracy and by the patriotic bourgeoisie, both of which were destroyed by the revolution.

Today, above all else, there exists a "Soviet patriotism," and it is ingrained particularly in the new generation, which has grown up in a Bolshevik climate and which is the most acutely alive and energetic element in the country. Therefore, the principal factor, the true motivating force of the present Soviet dynamism, is essentially Bolshevik in nature.

3. What are the probable objectives of Soviet imperialism?

I must state beforehand that I see Soviet expansionism not primarily in the form of "territorial conquests" but rather in the guise of "political penetration" and the acquisition of "areas of influence."

The U.S.S.R. has no need of "vital living space" because it possesses, particularly in Asia, rich and immense territories yet to be colonized and exploited. It is my opinion that Stalin's principal objective is precisely one of exploiting the enormous resources of the Asiatic holdings and that his attention is focused on the Far East.

I would add one further observation: thus far, Stalin has demonstrated that he acts very prudently, pragmatically, and with a sense of realism.

Therefore, I do not believe that, as long as he is at the head of the government, the U.S.S.R. will undertake any dangerous adventures.

The occupation of the Ukraine and of western White Russia and the territorial concessions obtained in the three Baltic States cannot, in the strictest sense, be considered as manifestations of a true expansionist policy because this is essentially a reconstruction of a pre-existing Russian unity. It must also be recognized that the requests for naval bases in Latvia, Estonia, and Finland are justified in part by realistic considerations of military security and geographic necessity.

Therefore, I tend to believe that the U.S.S.R.'s only territorial aspiration (aside from the frontier rectification requested of Finland) lies in acquiring Bessarabia. Moreover, I am convinced that Stalin will not miss any favorable opportunity to demand the restitution of that old Russian province.

Once Russia acquires its old frontiers I would suppose that it will consider itself *territorially* satisfied.

At the same time, however, I am also convinced that we are witnessing a reawakening of Soviet "political expansionism" which will seek to extend itself in all directions but particularly in the following areas: (1) the Balkans; (2) Persia and Afghanistan; (3) China.

In the Balkan sector the most likely objective at this moment seems to me to be Bulgaria, which the U.S.S.R. is ardently trying to influence with promises regarding the Dobrudja.

4. Can the Soviet-German alliance be considered capable of further development in the future or simply as an accord *ex delictu*, having an immediate goal as its objective, i.e., the division of the recent territorial acquisitions?

Before replying to this question I would like to call attention to what were, in my opinion, the real motives that attracted the U.S.S.R. to the alliance with Germany.

(1) The U.S.S.R. regarded herself as militarily unprepared and feared German attack. Therefore, she gladly accepted a friendship pact with her potential adversary;

(2) The U.S.S.R. *desired* a European war and knew that a Soviet accord with Germany would unleash it.

The U.S.S.R. encouraged the outbreak of war, and today she desires to see it spread as far as possible because it is in the interest of the Soviet regime that all of the bourgeois-capitalist countries enmesh themselves completely in a life-and-death struggle. When they are completely exhausted and bankrupted, the work of the Third International will be greatly simplified!

This is the opinion I have expressed ever since the Czechoslovak crisis and which I later repeated during the course of the Anglo-French-Soviet negotiations in Moscow and again on the eve of the beginning of military operations in Poland. I continue to hold this opinion because if I were a member of the Politburo I would not reason otherwise.

The problem of the possible developments of the Nazi-Soviet Pact must therefore be studied in the light of Moscow's objectives: the desire to spread and lengthen the war:

I could be mistaken, but I do not believe that the U.S.S.R. has any intention of helping Germany win the war. I do not believe it because a victorious Nazi Germany could, perhaps, tomorrow become a new threat to the U.S.S.R.

I do not possess positive information, but I believe that, to date, the U.S.S.R. has assumed obligations to provide the Nazis with no more than diplomatic and economic aid. Perhaps in certain circumstances she might furnish the Germans a contingent of fighter aircraft.

I have strong doubts, however, that the U.S.S.R. will ever reach the point of agreeing to provide military aid to the Reich on a grand scale (at least as long as the outcome of the conflict remains in doubt). Instead, I believe that she will continue to exploit the favorable situation created for her by the alliance with Germany, preserving intact her own freedom of action and maneuver.

Furthermore, I would not exclude the possibility that the Soviet leaders nurture the secret hope for a semi-bolshevization of Nazi Germany itself.

5. If the alliance is susceptible to further development, what do you think its immediate objectives might be?

Assuming that I see the possibility of the U.S.S.R. entering the war only in the event of decisive Nazi successes on the western front, I do not believe that one should exclude, in such circumstances, Soviet military action against Turkey as a potential ally of France and England, and eventually in the Balkans.

Faced with the beginnings of a collapse of the British Empire, I would not even exclude the possibility of a Soviet military action against India via Iran and Iraq.

6. Is it possible that, in the event of a widening of the European conflict, Russia may direct her expansionist energies toward her historic objectives in the Near and Middle East?

Subordinate to the observation I made in question number three (policy of prudence), I believe that if, at a given moment, the U.S.S.R. concluded that she could obtain important results *without incurring undue risks*, she would certainly take advantage of favorable opportunities to extend her influence particularly in the Balkans, in Constantinople, and in Teheran.

7. Does the present intensification of Soviet activity in the West imply a real and long-lasting shift away from an active Far Eastern policy? Viewed from Moscow, the Far Eastern policy of the U.S.S.R. has always appeared to be essentially conservative and defensive in character. It was Japan who menaced the Soviet Union and not vice versa. I believe that the intitiative will continue to be allowed to remain in Japanese hands. If Tokyo renounced her policy of expansion in those Chinese areas of particular interest to the U.S.S.R. (especially Outer Mongolia), I must conclude that the U.S.S.R. would gladly maintain her present policy.

8. What was the reaction of public opinion to the Soviet alliance with the

Reich, to the recent successes in Poland and in the Baltic States, and, lastly, to the anti-Communist activity undertaken by the western powers and particularly by France?

Public opinion in the U.S.S.R. (if we take this to mean the real sentiments of the masses) cannot be ascertained because it cannot express itself freely. The foreign diplomat has no contact with the people and can arrive at a conclusion about what the people are thinking only with great difficulty. In general, the Soviet masses are indifferent to developments in foreign affairs.

Within the party, the accord with Germany originally created a profound sense of bewilderment. However, I believe that it has since been accepted favorably, particularly when the undisputed advantages accruing to the U.S.S.R. were noted (especially that of permitting the U.S.S.R. to remain out of the war).

In government circles there is a deep admiration for German organizational ability and for German military strength.

The occupation of the Ukraine and western White Russia was naturally greeted with satisfaction, in that it was regarded as "restitution that was due." The same may be said for the concessions obtained in the Baltic States.

As for the anti-Communist repressions in France and in other western countries, party members were very indignant, and almost every day the local press violently attacks the "reactionary governments." On this matter the masses remain supremely apathetic.[11]

The detailed analysis presented by the Italian Ambassador to Moscow (to be kept constantly in mind in evaluating Rosso's subsequent activity, which obviously occurred within the framework of what he had described, and in discussing the importance of the negotiations with Moscow) differed greatly from that presented by Von Ribbentrop. Moreover, Rosso's report arrived in Rome at the very time when relations between Rome and Moscow were entering a period of extreme tension. A first indication

[11] Rosso to Anfuso, personal letter, November 13, 1939, ibid., II, Doc. 207. In addition to this semiofficial letter, Rosso at the same time wrote a second private letter to Anfuso in which, after explaining that the letter from the Chief of Cabinet was the first indication of interest that he had received from the Ministry in three years, he added that he was fully aware that he, who worked abroad, could not expect complete agreement with each opinion he expressed, but that there were periods in which the Chief of Mission needed to receive directives, to obtain information, and to be oriented. This had never been done for the Moscow mission despite the exceptional importance of the events of the past two years. Given the rapidity with which he had prepared his replies to Anfuso's questions, Rosso had found it impossible to present all of his views on Soviet policy. Therefore, he believed that it would be very useful if he were authorized to return to Rome for a brief visit in order to complete his presentation and to gain some insight into the intentions of the Rome government. Rosso to Anfuso, personal letter, November 13, 1939, ibid., Doc. 208. Ciano directed that Ambassador Rosso's request to return to Italy for a brief visit be rejected. Given the existing situation, Ciano felt that an official journey to Rome might lend itself to rumors and erroneous interpretations. Anfuso to Rosso, telegram, November 21, 1939, ibid., Doc. 276.

of this tension was a statement from the Comintern of November 7, in which all of the bourgeois classes were attacked. Ciano convinced Mussolini to direct Gayda to reply with a strongly worded article in *Il Giornale d'Italia*.[12]

A short time later, the outbreak of the Finno-Soviet War provoked a series of student demonstrations in Italy against the Soviet Union and in support of Helsinki.[13] While the anti-Soviet attacks in the Fascist press were intensified,[14] the Italian government began shipping military supplies to Finland.[15] Almost simultaneously, the Narkomindiel decided to suspend all shipments of fuel oil to Italy, and on December 8, the Fascist Grand Council reaffirmed Italy's continuing interest in all problems affecting the Danube Basin.

All of these actions were in obvious contrast with the friendly relations existing between Moscow and Berlin, but, at least within certain limits, they were to be considered as a direct reaction of the Fascist leadership to the excessively pro-Soviet policy of the Nazis. This dissatisfaction was expressed very clearly by Mussolini during the course of his conversation with Ambassador Von Mackensen on December 2, which the latter reported as follows:

He condemned in the sharpest terms the conduct of Russia, which, if it continued, would give rise to the worst dangers. As far as Italy was concerned, bolshevism remained enemy Number One, and bolshevism and the Moscow government were very hard to distinguish. He himself had at one time advised us to relax to some degree the tension of our relations with Russia, but only to a certain point—a policy, moreover, for which he had found complete understanding on the part of Marshal Goering. There could be no question that the

---

[12] Ciano, *Diario*, I, p. 186. The Gayda article was entitled "Il falso e il vero" and was published in the edition of November 8, 1939. Simultaneous with the publication of the Comintern's statement, a no less significant article by Dimitrov, "La guerra e la classe operaia dei paesi capitalistici," appeared in the volume for August–September, 1939, of *Kommunisticeski International*.

[13] Ciano, *Diario*, I, p. 193. Ciano noted that the people cry "Death to Russia" and really mean "Death to Germany." In the same sense, see Donosti, *Mussolini e l'Europa*, p. 228.

[14] For important details, see Beloff, *Soviet Russia*, II, pp. 302–03; D. J. Dallin, *Soviet Russia's Foreign Policy 1939–1942* (New Haven: Yale University Press, 1942), pp. 175–76. A typical illustration is the editorial "La politica della Russia" in the semiofficial *Relazioni internazionali* for December 16, 1939, and the article "Cosa vuole la Russia" which appeared in *La Stampa* of Turin on December 3, 1939.

[15] Ciano, *Diario*, I, pp. 195–96; Simoni, *Berlino: ambasciata d'Italia*, p. 36. Part of the material shipped by Italy to Finland was blocked in German territory and returned to Italy. On this episode, see *I.D.*, 9th series, I, Docs. 817, 838; II, Docs. 443, 477, 490, 555, 570, 579, 582, 588, 602, 633, 651, 661, 662, 671, 673, 682, 765; *G.D.*, Series D, VIII, Docs. 439, 444, 519.

main responsibility for the present development lay with England and France, who had for weeks been on their knees at Stalin's door, and he did not for a moment fail to recognize the necessity which had determined our later decisions, but he hoped that the present temperature of our relations with Moscow would not be raised further. The greed of these crooks [*"Schieber"*—he used the German expression] was insatiable. They had taken advantage of tremendous feats of German arms to pocket their gains without fighting and effort.[16]

Notwithstanding this, a few days later Mussolini appeared to be inclined to lessen the tension with Moscow and suggested to Ciano that he should insert a friendly statement toward the U.S.S.R. in a speech he was preparing on Fascist foreign policy.[17] However, later that day the Soviet Ambassador, who, on December 12, was to have presented his credentials to the Italian head of state, consigned a note to Palazzo Chigi in which he announced that he had been recalled to Moscow.[18] The Fascist Foreign Minister was to take advantage of this gesture of the Kremlin's displeasure by speaking in strongly anti-Communist terms before the Chamber of Fasces and Corporations on December 16.[19]

Later Molotov explained to Von Schulenburg some of the reasons prompting the Peoples' Commissar to recall Gorelkin by referring to the student demonstrations, "which in a totalitarian regime could not be anything but prearranged," and to the "sudden and incomprehensible anti-Soviet campaign initiated by the Italian press."[20]

However, it did not appear, at least in the beginning, that Moscow had any intention of moving toward a break in relations, but rather toward a

[16] Von Mackensen to Von Ribbentrop, telegram, December 2, 1939, *G.D.*, Series D, VIII, Doc. 410.

[17] Ciano, *Diario*, I, p. 196.

[18] The text of the Soviet note was as follows: "I have received orders from my government to return immediately to Moscow, and therefore, given this circumstance, I must inform you that I will not be able to present my credentials on December 12 to His Majesty the King of Italy and Albania, Emperor of Ethiopia. For the above-mentioned reasons, I beg you, Mr. Minister, to present my apologies to his Majesty. I take this occasion, Excellency, to express again my feelings of the highest esteem." *I.D.*, Series IX, II, Doc. 538. This note was transmitted to Rosso in Moscow only on December 14 in response to his request for information; Rosso had learned of Gorelkin's departure from Rome from a casual comment made by the Lithuanian Minister. Rosso to Ciano, telegram, December 14, 1939, No. 317; Ciano to Rosso, telexpress, December 14, 1939, No. 243555/41, and telegram, December 18, 1939, No. 125.

[19] Several days later in a conversation with Ambassador Attolico and in reference to Ciano's speech, Von Ribbentrop expressed his surprise "at the extreme anti-Russian attitude of Italy, since the Russian expansion did not, after all, threaten either Germany or Italy." Von Ribbentrop, memorandum, December 28, 1939, *G.D.*, Series D, VIII, Doc. 493. On this conversation see also Attolico to Ciano, telexpress, December 29, 1939, *I.D.*, 9th series, II, Doc. 759.

[20] Mascia to Ciano, telegram, January 10, 1940, *I.D.*, 9th series, III, Doc. 68; cf. *G.D.*, Series D, VIII, Doc. 494, note 1.

clarification of them. On this point a conversation which took place on December 18 between the Soviet Chargé d'Affaires in Rome and Ciano's Chief of Cabinet may be of considerable significance. The substance of this conversation was summarized on the same day by Anfuso in the following note for Ciano:

The Soviet Chargé d'Affaires, after a hurried trip from Geneva upon learning of the Soviet Ambassador's departure from Rome, came to see me.

Helfand made it clear that he had not received instructions to see Your Excellency and that, therefore, "on his own initiative" he chose to speak with me on a *purely personal basis* on the actual state of Italo-Soviet relations. He immediately made it clear that Moscow was annoyed and irritated by what has happened in Italy: "One would only have to read the telegrams sent to me by the Narkomindiel to confirm this point." Helfand stated that "Ciano's speech distressed me. The anti-Soviet student demonstrations, the attitude of the Italian press, the continued and ostentatious presence of a rather large military unit in front of the offices on Via Gaeta, and the abolition of all Italo-Soviet trade have, as I have noted, disturbed Moscow and threaten to worsen Italo-Soviet relations perhaps even beyond the nadir reached during the Spanish war. I repeat that I am not here to protest, because my government has not charged me with such a task, but I would like to know what it is that has so seriously inflamed Italian public opinion? And how was it possible to eliminate so casually the economic exchanges which had been arranged only after long and laborious effort? And why did the Italian government tolerate such violent anti-Soviet demonstrations and permit Italian public opinion to become so emotionally involved on behalf of the Finnish cause, which to Italy, for any number of reasons, could hardly be interpreted as vital?"

I replied to Helfand that, since he was permitting me to speak to him strictly unofficially, I desired to make it clear that the U.S.S.R. had not made any particular effort to ingratiate itself with Italian or world public opinion. Therefore, it seemed strange to me that he was surprised by his country's lack of popularity. Insofar as Italy was concerned, it had always been anti-Bolshevik in both theory and practice. When the Soviets shift from words to action, Italy reacts. It has always been thus.

Replying to what he told me we had done in Albania, I made it clear to him that the difference between our policy in Albania and the Soviet policy being applied at this moment in Finland lay in the fact that the Albanians asked for nothing more than to be placed under the protection of the Italian crown, while the Finns preferred to be shot one by one rather than accept Bolshevik domination. I then took the occasion to tell him, in view of the recall of the Soviet Ambassador from Rome and the manner in which it came about, that this act was hardly one to be termed good diplomatic form and that, moreover, it had been downright inconvenient.

Regarding the student demonstrations, I made it clear to Helfand that these were entirely spontaneous manifestations of popular indignation provoked by the attack of a gigantic power such as Russia against a small patriarchal nation such as Finland. Nothing had been done to provoke these manifestations. Nothing had been done to ignite these demonstrations. These are common to the youth of all countries who rise like cavaliers in defense of the weaker elements. As for the troops in Via Gaeta, they were ordered there in the interest of the Soviet Embassy and, for this reason, I expected thanks rather than protests.

Helfand continued by saying that it was not within his province to judge the action taken by the Ambassador. Of course, he had acted upon instructions from Moscow, where it has been noted with chagrin that Italy had provided for the shipment of arms and aircraft to Finland and enrolled volunteers for battle against the Soviets.

I was forced to say to Helfand that he should not make such accusations without proof to support them, and I asked him to check on the sources of his information.

Helfand insisted that what he was saying should not be in any way construed as a protest but only as an expression of his personal views to a friend. It pained him to see the possibility of Italo-Soviet friendship destroyed, a goal to which he had dedicated years of work during his assignment in Rome, and he asked me what could be done to correct the situation. Your Excellency's speech, he added, had reached the point of irreparably widening the abyss that divided the two countries, but he preferred to believe that there was something that could be done to prevent relations from becoming hostile.

At the conclusion of this detailed expression of his feelings, during the course of which he never mentioned Germany nor made reference to Italo-German relations, Helfand told me that he was permitting himself the privilege of asking my advice on the following: "I am considering telegraphing to Moscow that, since the anti-Soviet manifestations in Italy have diminished, I could assume the obligation of seeking to normalize relations between the two countries if Molotov would promise to make it known, via the usual diplomatic channels, that the U.S.S.R. intended to respect in every way Italy's interests in the Balkans."

Helfand added that he did not have the slightest suggestion of an instruction from his government to make such an overture, but that he was aware that the anti-Soviet agitation in Italy was determined by the very fact that Italy could see that her Balkan interests might be threatened by the U.S.S.R. He knew that the Soviet government not only considered it in its own interest but intended to respect the Italian position in the Balkans and that he would do his best to furnish us with formal reassurance on this matter, which would lead to a lessening of tension in and a clarification of Italo-Soviet relations.

I replied to Helfand that the attitude of the Soviet Union not only in the Balkans but throughout the world was the object of concern to Italy as well as to the entire civilized world. The last article in the journal *Kommunisticeski International* on the Rumanian question, for example, was not designed to quiet the apprehensions of those who, unaware of the Soviet expansionist program and incapable of understanding its claims because they do not know whether these are based on Marxist rights or on the needs of the Russian people, are concerned to see brush fires cropping up all over which ultimately will be difficult to stamp out. As for the advice he sought, I replied that it was difficult for me to provide it since I could not see the possible basis for such a declaration from the U.S.S.R. Italy is a Balkan nation by virtue of its presence in Albania. Her interests in the Balkan peninsula, other than her position in Albania, are predominant. Given this premise, Italy will know how to have her rights and interests respected without requiring assurances from third parties. A guarantee of this nature on the part of the U.S.S.R. in exchange for a tolerant attitude on the part of Italy in the face of an increased momentum in Slavic imperialism does not seem to me to be, at this moment, of any particular urgency. In any event, these were my personal views.

Helfand asked whether he might see me again and whether I was in a position to promise to give his proposals some thought because only on the basis of a suggestion from me would he be able to telegraph to Moscow proposing that the Soviet Union move toward a possible amelioration of relations founded on a precise guarantee from the U.S.S.R.

I told him that I would be pleased to see him again whenever he desired, but that insofar as a reply to what he had suggested was concerned, I could not see what I could possibly add to what I had already said.

He insisted in knowing whether we could dine together to discuss the question.

The conversation left me with the impression that he was reflecting the Soviet fear of seeing the gap that separates the Soviet Union from Europe spread even further and that Moscow finds it necessary to circumscribe its actions within the realm of her immediate interests and to avoid complications with countries which can most easily promote an anti-Bolshevik campaign.[21]

Apart from permitting an overall examination of the arguments adopted by both sides to justify the policies of their respective governments, three points brought out in the summary of the Anfuso-Helfand conversation merit particular attention: first, the ductile position of the Soviet Chargé d'Affaires; second, the formula proposed by him to resolve the crisis in Italo-Soviet relations; and third, the polemical and negative attitude of the Chief of Cabinet of the Fascist Foreign Ministry. Many elements suggest that the move made by Helfand was prompted by the Narkomindiel. In fact, it is in complete harmony with the subsequent declarations made by Molotov to Von Schulenburg and by Potemkin to the Italian Chargé d'Affaires in Moscow, Mascia, which will be noted below. The proposed assurance on the part of the Soviets that Italian interests would be respected in the Balkans appeared to be too binding in nature and too close to the position assumed in the summer of 1940 by the Soviet Foreign Minister in his conversation with Rosso to have been improvised by Helfand in conversation with Anfuso. Therefore, it might be assumed that toward the end of 1939 and early in 1940, the Kremlin, having placed great weight on its tie with Germany, did not desire to see the German position weakened to any degree by Italo-German dissension and viewed an understanding with Rome as also having a positive effect vis-à-vis Berlin. Insofar as Anfuso was concerned, the strengthening of his anti-Bolshevik position after his exchange of letters with the Italian Ambassador to Moscow apparently should be seen in the context of the increasingly anti-Soviet position—coherent from a doctrinal point of

[21] Anfuso to Ciano, note, December 18, 1939, *I.D.*, 9th series, II, Doc. 646.

view—taken by his superior, Count Ciano.[22] The latter, on December 23, in speaking to Antonescu, went so far as to assure the Rumanian diplomat that "in the event that Russia should attack Rumania and the latter offered armed resistance, Italy would not fail to come to her aid with all the means at her disposal."[23]

The waning days of 1939 registered the nadir of Nazi-Fascist relations.[24] Despite the fact that the official documents contain no indication of this nature, it seems likely that Ciano's sudden decision on December 28 to recall Rosso from Moscow may be explained not as a desire to reply in kind to the action by the Kremlin[25] but as a desire to accentuate the divergences between Rome and Berlin.[26] Mussolini himself evidently shared his son-in-law's views and in his letter to Hitler of January 5, 1940, expressed substantial disagreement with the policy pursued by the German government. In all likelihood, the message of the Italian Chief of State was aimed principally at preventing Hitler from moving to the offensive on the western front, thus leaving the door open to a possible compromise peace with the western powers. Nevertheless, it should be noted that

[22] Ciano, *Diario*, II, pp. 186–98.

[23] Ciano, *L'Europa verso la catastrofe*, p. 500. These minutes contradict the affirmation made by Ciano in his *Diario*, I, p. 200, according to which he avoided assuming obligations and confirms, instead, the version offered by Gafencu (*Preliminari*, pp. 341, 342). The probable explanation for this divergence of view lies in the fact that there were two Ciano-Antonescu colloquies and that the observation made by Ciano on this point refers only to what transpired in the first of these two meetings. In his colloquy with Csáky of January 4, 1940, Ciano also spoke of Italian aid in the form of "armed masses" in the event of a Russian attack on Hungary, aid which, however, was subject to the resolution of the problem of unrestricted communications between the two powers. Ciano, minutes, January 7, 1940, *I.D.*, 9th series, III, Doc. 44.

[24] Ciano, *Diario*, I, pp. 198, 201, 202.

[25] In his telegram to Rosso on December 28, 1939 (*I.D.*, 9th series, II, Doc. 741), Ciano stated: "Given the fact that the Soviet Ambassador has been recalled to Moscow by his government and that he left Rome on December 9 without taking leave of the Minister of Foreign Affairs, Your Excellency is being recalled to Rome. Your departure from Moscow should take place under the same conditions, that is, without leave-taking of the Peoples' Commissar for Foreign Affairs and without furnishing any explanation whatsoever. You will limit yourself to informing that government in writing of your departure precisely as Gorelkin did. Confirm." Rosso's recall was not immediately communicated to the Italian Embassy in Berlin. Attolico telegraphed to Anfuso for confirmation of the information transmitted by foreign radio stations. The Chief of Cabinet confirmed the fact in a personal letter to Attolico. Attolico to Anfuso, telegram, January 2, 1940, No. 3; Anfuso to Attolico, letter, January 2, 1940, No. 1/000008.

[26] On December 29, 1939, Ciano informed the German Chargé d'Affaires in Rome of Rosso's departure from Moscow, indicating that the action taken, "which was the minimum that Italy had to do in view of the conduct of the Russian Ambassador, does not indicate any change in Italian policy vis-à-vis Russia." Von Plessen to Von Ribbentrop, telegram, December 29, 1939, *G.D.*, Series D, VIII, Doc. 494.

Mussolini, developing the concepts already expressed to Von Mackensen on December 2, 1939, repeated in peremptory terms his anti-communism and reaffirmed his conviction that an understanding with the U.S.S.R. could have only a tactical value because, if it were pressed beyond a certain limit, it would provoke a catastrophic reaction among the Italian public. But Mussolini did not stop there. He indicated those portions of Russian territory which were logical areas of expansion for the German people and pointed to the Soviet Union as the principal enemy of the two revolutions—the adversary that must be defeated *before* destroying the two democracies, which contained in their very structures the seeds of decadence.[27]

On the other hand, there is no evidence to demonstrate that, in those days, Moscow had reached the point of regarding Italo-Soviet relations in such pessimistic terms. On January 11, 1940, returning to the subject of the Schulenburg-Molotov conversation referred to above, the Italian Chargé d'Affaires in Moscow had, among other things, this to say in his telegraphic report to Rome:

> In a colloquy last night with the German Ambassador, the latter confirmed the news of my telegram cited above, adding that from the nature of the conversation it seemed to him that the Soviets were anxious for Germany to use its good offices to help re-establish good relations between Italy and the U.S.S.R. The German Ambassador apparently replied that it was necessary to allow some time to elapse before initiating any action along these lines. Naturally, the German Ambassador was fully aware of the fact that it was up to the U.S.S.R. to nominate a new ambassador to Rome and that evidently it could no longer be Gorelkin. I made no comment.[28]

The version offered by the German Ambassador suggested that Molotov's appeal to the good offices of the German government was more explicit than he, observing the usual diplomatic caution, was willing to admit.[29] However, the interest of the Narkomindiel in ameliorating Italo-Soviet relations appears to be confirmed both by the attitude assumed by

[27] Mussolini to Hitler, letter, January 5, 1940, *I.D.*, 9th series, III, Doc. 33; *G.D.*, Series D, VIII, Doc. 504. On the same day Mussolini told Ciano that "Italy has no sympathy for Germany, indifference towards France, hatred for Great Britain and Russia." Ciano, *Diario*, I, p. 210.

[28] Mascia to Ciano, telegram, January 11, 1940, *I.D.*, 9th series, III, Doc. 85.

[29] In his colloquy with the German Ambassador, Molotov limited himself to emphasizing that Rosso's departure had been exploited for propaganda purposes by the enemies of Germany and that the Soviet government could not fathom the reasons for Italy's hostility. The following day, the Peoples' Vice Commissar for Foreign Affairs, Potemkin, was more explicit in speaking to Von Schulenburg, asking that the German government use its influence to induce Ciano to modify his attitude toward the Soviet Union. Von Schulenburg to Von Weizsäcker, letter, January 10, 1940, *G.D.*, Series D, VIII, Doc. 521.

the Soviet press and by Potemkin's subsequent colloquy with Mascia. The Italian Chargé d'Affaires sent a summary account of these talks to Rome on January 15, 1940. (In the meantime the Ciano-Csáky meeting at Venice had taken place, in which the Danubian situation and Hungarian-Soviet relations had been discussed.) Mascia's summary was as follows:

> As mentioned in my telegram No. 30, this morning I called on the Vice Commissar for Foreign Affairs in regard to the fuel oil problem. Before my departure, the Vice Commissar asked me whether the statements made yesterday by the Hungarian Minister had been agreed to by the Italian government. I replied that I had ·no knowledge of the matter. Potemkin, evidently very pleased by the Hungarian statements, continued his remarks by asking himself who would gain by spreading such rumors as that abroad after the Venice meeting regarding "Soviet expansionist aims in Central Europe and in the Balkans and eventual Italian resistance." I replied, "Evidently our ex-friends the English and the French." Thereupon, he recalled in detail the conversation he had with the Duce during which it was agreed that between the U.S.S.R. and Italy there was no motive for dissension, while there were many reasons for their reaching an accord, even if only in the economic sphere.
>
> I pass on these statements, made in a very cordial tone but always in the presence of the Chief of the Political Bureau of the Foreign Office, who took notes, because they seem to confirm what the German Ambassador told me concerning the desire of this government to ameliorate its relations with Italy.
>
> It is significant to note that Potemkin made no reference to the anti-Soviet campaign in the Italian press and that the major newspapers here continue to maintain a very reserved attitude in this regard.[30]

This clear overture by Moscow also fell on deaf ears at Palazzo Chigi. Ciano telegraphed to Mascia ordering him to reduce to the necessary minimum his contacts with the Soviet government and noting that the Soviet Chargé d'Affaires in Rome had had no contact with the Ministry for Foreign Affairs for several weeks.[31] Meanwhile, the Fascist press continued its anti-Soviet campaign with regard to the Russo-Finnish war, and, in time, the Narkomindiel allowed the Soviet press free rein to conduct an energetic anti-Italian attack.[32]

The German government could not remain indifferent to the further worsening of relations between Rome and Moscow, particularly since it was obliged to accompany its attempt at a rapprochement with its Fascist ally by an attempt to reduce the Italo-Soviet tension.

This conciliatory action was initiated by Hitler himself in a letter to Mussolini of March 8, carried to Rome personally by Von Ribbentrop. In

---

[30] Mascia to Ciano, telegram, January 15, 1940, *I.D.*, 9th series, III, Doc. 125.

[31] Ciano to Mascia, telegram, January 16, 1940, *ibid.*, Doc. 132.

[32] Mascia to Ciano, telegrams, January 26, 28, 29, and 31, and February 3, 5, 7, and 9, 1940, *ibid.*, Docs. 210, 220, 222, 224, 225, 235, 248, 257, 258, 269, 279.

this note, after having depicted Nazi-Soviet relations and the new Soviet policy in exceptionally optimistic terms, he charged his Foreign Minister with pointing out to the head of the Fascist government, drawing on the fund of his impressions and personal experiences, "the extent to which Russia had undergone—in his view—a profound and historic change."[33]

Von Ribbentrop faithfully carried out his instructions in his conversations at Palazzo Venezia on March 10 and 11.[34] He reiterated his well-known interpretation of Soviet policy, which, in his view, had finally abandoned all idea of world revolution and had become nationalistically Russian. Mussolini, who during the early phases of the colloquy seemed to regard Von Ribbentrop's statements with considerable skepticism, apparently was convinced to a degree by the German's arguments before the end of the second day of talks and assured the Nazi Foreign Minister that "if the Russians wished to resume normal relations he, for his part, was entirely willing." Von Ribbentrop was so obsessed by the virtue of his views that he returned to this particular argument many times during the course of the talks and, finally, in the interest of eliminating every possibility of equivocation regarding Mussolini's disposition to ameliorate relations with Moscow, noted in the minutes: "Another question by the Foreign Minister referred to the Italo-Russian relations. If he had correctly understood the Duce, there was a possibility that these relations would improve. The Duce stated that such an improvement was entirely possible and pointed to the anxiety voiced in the press of the Western Powers in connection with the Foreign Minister's visit to Rome, to the effect that it might lead to the formation of a Spanish-Italian-Russian-German-Japanese bloc. And perhaps this was a possibility."[35]

Again during the Brenner meeting of March 18, 1940, between Mussolini and Hitler which rekindled the Italo-German alliance, the two dic-

[33] Hitler to Mussolini, letter, March 8, 1940, *G.D.*, Series D, VIII, Doc. 633; *I.D.*, 9th series, III, Doc. 492.

[34] As the moment for Von Ribbentrop's journey to Italy approached, Ambassador Attolico listed the principal motives which, according to the information gathered by him, could have induced Hitler to send his Foreign Minister to the Italian capital. Among these, he noted the need to better explain Germany's position vis-à-vis the Soviet Union "and to place it within the framework of the general interests of the Axis while searching to modify Italy's position with respect to the Soviet Union, a position which at present indirectly creates some embarrassment for Germany." Attolico to Ciano, telexpress, March 9, 1940, *I.D.*, 9th series, III, Doc. 502.

[35] For Von Ribbentrop's colloquies in Rome, see the minutes kept by Schmidt for the talks of March 10–11, 1940. *G.D.*, Series D, VIII, Docs. 665 and 699. The minutes published in *I.D.*, 9th series, III, Docs. 512 and 524, are a translation of minutes drafted by the Germans. In addition, see Von Ribbentrop's telegrams of March 11 and 12, 1940, to the German Foreign Ministry for transmittal to Hitler. *G.D.*, Series D, VIII, Docs. 667 and 670.

tators devoted considerable time to the theme of their relations with the U.S.S.R. However, the Germans did not invite the Italians to seek a rapprochement with the Soviets in the explicit terms used in Rome by Von Ribbentrop, and, at the same time, Mussolini did not reassert his disposition to improve relations with Moscow.[36]

In any event, Mussolini apparently conceded enough in his conversation with Von Ribbentrop on March 11 to prompt the latter to take concrete steps leading toward a normalization of Italo-Soviet relations. Since Molotov had expressly requested to be informed regarding the results of the Rome conversations,[37] Von Ribbentrop immediately directed Ambassador Von Schulenburg to provide the Russian with a summary of what had transpired in Rome and to emphasize that Mussolini's statements reflected a real desire on the part of the Italian government to build a cordial rapport with the Soviet Union.[38]

This communication was received by Molotov with interest, but the Peoples' Commissar was quick to add that if Mussolini's words were encouraging, "concrete proof was as yet lacking that Italy was seriously determined to alter her relations with the Soviet Union; consequently the Soviet government was for the present adopting a waiting attitude."[39] This cautious reserve is entirely comprehensible in view of the position taken by the Fascist government toward the earlier Moscow overtures.

Nevertheless, a few days later, Von Ribbentrop transmitted a summary of what had transpired at the Brenner meeting to Von Schulenburg, to be communicated to Molotov,[40] and added that the German Ambassador should take the occasion to press again for an amelioration of Italo-Soviet

[36] Schmidt, memorandum, March 17, 1940, G.D., Series D, IX, Doc. 1. (The minutes published in I.D., 9th series, III, Doc. 578, are the translation of a memorandum prepared in the offices of the Wilhelmstrasse and consigned to the Italians.) In transmitting the impressions provoked in Germany by the meeting at the Brenner Pass, Attolico also noted: "I believe it superfluous to indicate the enormous interest aroused in diplomatic circles here by the Führer's visit to the Duce. Their attention is primarily focused on Italo-Soviet relations, believing that the Soviets want to demonstrate their desire, as indicated by a recent article in Izvestia, to recognize Italy's interests in the Balkans, while the resolution of the Russo-Finish conflict has eliminated a powerful moral block to Italy's normalizing her relations with the U.S.S.R." Attolico to Ciano, telexpress, March 19, 1940, ibid., Doc. 585.

[37] Von Schulenburg to Von Ribbentrop, telegram, March 11, 1940, G.D., Series D, VIII, Doc. 675, note 1.

[38] Von Ribbentrop to Von Schulenburg, telegram, March 14, 1940, ibid., Doc. 675. On March 13 Von Ribbentrop had discussed Italo-Soviet relations at length with the Soviet Ambassador to Berlin, Shkvartsev. Ibid., note 2.

[39] Von Schulenburg to Von Ribbentrop, telegram, March 18, 1940, ibid., Doc. 684.

[40] Von Ribbentrop to Von Schulenburg, telegram, March 21, 1940, ibid., IX, Doc. 7.

relations. He insisted that, based on what Mussolini had said in Rome, there could be no doubt of the disposition of the Fascist head of state to move toward this goal and that, as a first step, it would be advisable to have the ambassadors of the two countries return to their respective posts. He, Von Ribbentrop, would be pleased to facilitate this step by serving as liaison between the two governments.[41] This gesture was also received with guarded reserve by Molotov, who, while stating that he would refer the German offer to his government, noted that "concrete public proofs of a change of mind on the part of the Italian government would be very desirable."[42]

The Italian government was promptly informed of these German initiatives by the German Ambassador to Moscow.[43] On April 1 Von Mackensen also discussed the matter with Ciano. Ciano also treated the matter with cold detachment, noting that it "needed time." With, as a pretext, several phrases used by Molotov in a recent speech which were considered offensive, Ciano declared that it was not an easy matter to alter suddenly the Italian position vis-à-vis the U.S.S.R. The best he could do would be to present the problem to Mussolini.[44] Thus the attempt to normalize Italo-Soviet relations ended, at least for the moment, in failure. Armed with Mussolini's words of approval in principle, Von Ribbentrop approached Molotov, who proved not entirely negative in his reception but made it clear that he had no desire to take the first step to reduce the tension and explicitly stated that he regarded Mussolini's statements as insufficient proof of Italy's good intentions. In order to move toward normalization the Italian government would have to make a concrete and public gesture that would demonstrate its goodwill. At the time, such a gesture was hardly likely. When queried directly by Von Mackensen, Ciano, who was aware of the difficulties raised by the Soviets, thanks to the information which had reached him from the Embassy in Moscow, had clearly decided to procrastinate and was much less receptive than Molotov had been on the fundamental question. It was obvious that in Rome, despite the now famous statements by Mussolini on March 11, it

[41] Von Ribbentrop to Von Schulenburg, telegram, March 21, 1940, *ibid.*, Doc. 6.
[42] Von Schulenburg to Von Ribbentrop, telegram, March 26, 1940, *ibid.*, Doc. 11.
[43] Mascia to Ciano, telegrams, March 23 and 27, 1940, *I.D.*, Series IX, III, Docs. 613 and 626. Attolico also reported from Berlin that a rumor was circulating in that capital of German action to help ameliorate Italo-Soviet relations, and some were even speaking of a Ribbentrop-Molotov-Ciano meeting. Attolico to Ciano, telexpress, March 26, 1940, *ibid.*, Doc. 624.
[44] Von Mackensen to Von Ribbentrop, telegram, April 1, 1940, *G.D.*, Series D, IX, Doc. 34. For Molotov's speech, see Jane Degras, *Soviet Documents on Foreign Policy* (London: Oxford University Press, 1953), III, pp. 436–49.

was not considered opportune to rush toward an amelioration of relations with Moscow. This situation was explainable in part by the desire to avoid giving the appearance of being towed along in the German wake and in part by reasons of internal policy. Ciano had been the most intransigent, probably because he saw in the dissension with the Soviet Union a means whereby, in a larger perspective, Rome's position could be differentiated from that of Berlin. Given these conditions, it was logical that Von Ribbentrop chose to suspend his activity for a time, all the more so because, formally, both Molotov and Ciano were obliged to reply to him, as they had agreed to present the matter to their respective governments.

The German efforts were renewed toward the end of April. Although nothing new had occurred which might have aided an Italo-Soviet rapprochement, the Wilhelmstrasse could now exploit the impressions created in both Rome and Moscow by the success of the Norwegian campaign, which undoubtedly lent greater strength to the German pressures. On April 28, therefore, Von Schulenburg was directed to ask the Soviet government whether a decision had been reached on the question of Soviet relations with Italy.[45] In the colloquy which he had with Molotov on May 6 it was clear that the Peoples' Commissar had not budged at all from his previous position of detachment and reserve. However, in the face of the German Ambassador's insistence, Molotov finally asked whether "he could inform his government to the effect that the Italian government through the good offices of the Foreign Minister had expressed its willingness to normalize relations by the dispatch again of ambassadors on both sides," and Von Schulenburg, deviating considerably from the truth, answered in the affirmative.[46]

It remained to be seen whether Rome had altered its position to any appreciable degree.[47] A first sounding, made by Von Mackensen in a conversation with Ciano on May 20, revealed the Italian Foreign Minister to be less intransigent but still firm in insisting that it be the Soviets who take the first step by requesting l'agrément for a new ambassador.[48] Several days later Ciano returned to the question in a colloquy with Von Mackensen, stating that, at Mussolini's behest, he was now disposed to agree

[45] Friedrich Gaus to Von Schulenburg, telegram, April 28, 1940, G.D., Series D, IX, Doc. 177.

[46] Von Schulenburg to Von Ribbentrop, telegram, May 6, 1940, as reported in Woermann to Von Mackensen, telegram, May 17, 1940, ibid., Doc. 263.

[47] Instructions to this effect were imparted to Von Mackensen in the Woermann telegram cited above.

[48] Von Mackensen to Von Ribbentrop, telegram, May 20, 1940, ibid., Doc. 279. See also Anfuso note, May 19, 1940, I.D., 9th series, IV, Doc. 499.

that the two ambassadors return to their respective posts simultaneously, thereby eliminating the problem of who was to take the first step.[49] The proposal was immediately transmitted to Moscow via the German Embassy, and Molotov, after some hesitation, agreed to it.[50]

If the change of heart in the Italian Foreign Ministry is easily explained by the need to re-examine previous directives in the light of Italy's imminent entry into the war and by the need to pave the way for an economic agreement with the U.S.S.R.,[51] the origins of the Soviet decision to accept Ciano's proposal are less clear. It is probable that considerable influence on the decision was exercised by the information transmitted to Moscow by Helfand, according to whom Ambassador Von Mackensen had declared that the Balkan problems were to be resolved "through mutual cooperation by Germany, the Soviet Union and Italy." This statement was received with great interest by Molotov, who, on two occasions, asked Von Schulenburg whether this statement truly reflected the opinion of both the German and Italian governments.[52] In reality, Von Mackensen had carefully avoided making any such statement,[53] but Von Ribbentrop, once he had ascertained Molotov's great interest in the matter,[54] preferred to deny the information in vague terms, limiting himself to repeating that Germany remained faithful to the accords of August, 1939, that she was interested in the Balkan countries only from an economic point of view, and that Italy most certainly had no intention of extending the war to the Balkans.[55] This episode—of which the Italian government was promptly informed through its embassy in Moscow[56]—almost certainly had its effect in inducing the Soviet government to normalize its relations with Italy, but it is particularly significant because it forecast the direction in which

---

[49] Von Mackensen to Von Ribbentrop, telegram, May 29, 1940, *G.D.*, Series D, IX, Doc. 344.

[50] Von Ribbentrop to Von Schulenburg, telegram, May 30, 1940, *ibid.*, Doc. 349; Von Schulenburg to Von Ribbentrop, telegrams, June 1, 4, 1940, *ibid.*, Docs. 359 and 381. See also Mascia to Ciano, telegrams, May 30, June 4, 1940, *I.D.*, 9th series, IV, Docs. 649 and 732.

[51] On this point see Giannini, circular telegram, May 27, 1940, *ibid.*, Doc. 601; Mascia to Ciano, telegrams, May 29, 31, and June 2, 3, 4, 1940, *ibid.*, Docs. 624, 671, 709, 716, and 732.

[52] Von Schulenburg to Von Ribbentrop, telegrams, June 4, 7, 1940, *G.D.*, Series D, IX, Docs. 382, 392, note 2.

[53] Von Mackensen to Von Ribbentrop, telegram, June 6, 1940, *ibid.*, Doc. 382, note 2.

[54] Von Ribbentrop to Von Schulenburg, telegram, June 5, 1940, *ibid.*, Doc. 388; Von Schulenburg to Von Ribbentrop, telegram, June 6, 1940, *ibid.*, Doc. 392.

[55] Von Ribbentrop to Von Schulenburg, telegram, June 16, 1940, *ibid.*, Doc. 454.

[56] Mascia to Ciano, telegrams, June 4, 8, 1940, *I.D.*, 9th series, IV, Docs. 738, 803.

the talks with Moscow would shift—talks of an economic nature which Palazzo Chigi hoped to initiate with the Soviets.[57]

The initial phase of Italo-Soviet relations during Italy's nonbelligerence came to a close on this plane. During this period relations between the two governments were tense but never reached the point of final rupture, and both Rome and Moscow had, in effect, assumed positions of cautious, watchful waiting.

3

Prior to his rather unexpected departure for Moscow, the Italian Ambassador received merely general instructions to "normalize" relations with the U.S.S.R., and only during his stopover in Berlin did he learn of Italy's declaration of war against France and Great Britain.[58] He arrived in Moscow on the afternoon of June 12 and was greeted cordially. He was received by Molotov at the Kremlin during the evening of June 13[59] and telegraphed the salient points of this conversation to Rome that same night.[60] On June 14 he reported to Rome in greater detail, as follows:

I am forwarding this more detailed account of the colloquy of June 13 with the Soviet President of the Council of Ministers and Commissar for Foreign Affairs.

Returning to my post the afternoon of the 12th inst., the following day I requested an audience with Molotov. An appointment was set for 9:30 that evening at the Kremlin.

I was greeted with unusual cordiality, and I stated that I was pleased to have returned to my post in Moscow and expressed satisfaction that with the simultaneous arrival of Ambassador Gorelkin in Rome an abnormal parenthesis in the diplomatic relations between our two countries had been brought to a close. I added that I was stirred by a sincere desire to work toward an improvement in these relations and that I hoped he would facilitate the fulfillment of my task.

---

[57] The Italian government had received numerous indications of the growing Soviet interest in the Balkans. See, for example, Mascia to Ciano, telegrams, May 18, 21, 1940, *ibid.*, Docs. 461 and 522; Magistrati to Ciano, telegram via courier, May 27, and telegram, June 8, 1940, *ibid.*, Docs. 605 and 810; De Peppo to Ciano, telegram, June 4, 1940, *ibid.*, Doc. 737; Mameli to Ciano, telegram via courier, June 8, 1940, *ibid.*, Doc. 815. It is also noteworthy that Ambassador Gorelkin on his way back to Rome took the occasion to stop in Sofia. Mascia to Ciano, telegram, June 10, 1940, *ibid.*, Doc. 835. On the other hand, the Italian Chargé d'Affaires in Moscow promptly made it clear that the commercial policy of the U.S.S.R. was closely linked to its general policy and that the Soviet government used its ability to provide raw materials to obtain political concessions in exchange. Mascia to Ciano, telegram, May 31, 1940, *ibid.*, Doc. 671.

[58] Rosso, "Obbietivi e metodi," p. 18.

[59] Rosso to Ciano, telegram, June 14, 1940, *I.D.*, 9th series, V, Doc. 19.

[60] Rosso to Ciano, telegram, June 14, 1940, *ibid.*, Doc. 23.

Molotov replied that he, too, was equally pleased and that I could count on his cooperation.

After the exchange of these diplomatic courtesies Molotov remained silent. I took the occasion to direct the conversation toward a discussion of the European situation by commenting on our declaration of war.

Citing the Duce's words, I described the historic, political, and moral reasons for our intervention, and I quoted literally the phrases used by the Duce in addressing himself to "other nations who share Italy's land and sea frontiers."

At this point I noted an expression of intense interest and obvious anticipation on Molotov's face. Because I did not feel myself at liberty to go beyond a paraphrase of the concepts defined by the Duce, Molotov took the initiative in the conversation, with the obvious intention of extracting further information from me regarding the objectives of Italian policy.

Molotov stated that he was very familiar with the speech delivered from the balcony of Palazzo Venezia. He considered Italy's entrance into the war as an event of major importance in the economy of the war in progress. After the serious defeats inflicted on the British and French forces by German arms in Belgium and France, the Italian intervention assumed decisive importance. He was convinced that France and England were destined to be totally defeated and that their political prestige would be destroyed.

At this point, Molotov asked me what Italy's "program of action" happened to be. The question was probably designed to sound me out regarding our political as well as our military objectives.

Once again I referred to the Duce's words and drew attention to the fact that Mussolini made it clear that he proposed to resolve the problem of Italy's sea frontiers and that our action was directed solely against France and England.

He then asked for my prognostications, and I replied that the Italian people, though fully aware of the difficulties arising from the strong strategic positions the enemy powers controlled in the Mediterranean, were certain of final victory for the two totalitarian nations—that is, young and vigorous nations, animated by the spirit of the Fascist revolution—against the two old plutocratic western democracies. This was a conflict between the old and the new worlds, between static and conservative social and political concepts on the one hand and dynamic ideals of progress and greater distributive justice on the other. There could be no doubt that historical evolution clearly indicated the success of the latter.

Molotov repeatedly nodded his assent and was visibly pleased when I characterized the Soviet Union as a young and dynamic nation.

When the conversation, up to that moment sustained on a somewhat academic plane, tended to lapse, Molotov asked me—pressing the point—whether I had any specific questions to discuss with him, and he appeared to me to be disappointed when I replied that "for the moment" I had none. I had the sensation that he expected me to say something more on Italian policy. Not wanting to assume the initiative himself, Molotov probably desired that I provide him with an opportunity to discuss Italo-Soviet relations and their possible future developments in great detail.

Instead, I did not believe that I could venture into this particular area because, in Rome, I had received only the general directive to "re-normalize" our diplomatic relations with Moscow, something that has automatically come to pass with the return of the two ambassadors to their respective posts.

Nevertheless, I believe it to be my duty to call Your Excellency's attention to the fact that at this moment the Soviet government seems to be anxious to strengthen its ties to us, perhaps having in mind the possibility—under given circumstances—of collaborating with us or of reaching a political understanding regarding a sector of Europe in which we have common interests, either the Balkans or the Black Sea area.

Naturally, I cannot offer an opinion on the timeliness of encouraging this tendency and eventually profiting by it, since I am fully aware that Italo-Soviet relations cannot be considered per se but rather that they must be considered within the overall framework of Italian foreign policy. For guidelines in my future conduct and in the phraseology to be employed, it would be particularly useful to me to receive some directives from Rome, regardless of how general. This is especially important because my German colleague, Count Von Schulenburg, having actively involved himself in the efforts leading to a return of the two ambassadors to their posts, is extremely anxious to know which direction our relations with Moscow are apt to take.

Before closing, I believe it to be useful to note that the same Von Schulenburg, acting on precise instructions from his government, some days ago presented Molotov with a request that the Soviets recommence furnishing the Royal Italian Navy with fuel oil.

The reply at that time from Molotov was negative, but he did observe that this was a matter with which the Italian Ambassador would and should concern himself upon his return to Moscow.

I did not believe that I should mention the matter during my conversation with Molotov because I had received no instructions on the question, nor did I have the necessary data to formulate the request in the precise terms desired by the Royal government. However, I wish to repeat at this time what I have already mentioned in my telegram; that is, it is useless to expect any satisfactory results from economic negotiations with this country if we are not, at the same time, in a position to satisfy those "political premises" to which the government of the U.S.S.R. constantly and rigidly subordinates its commercial policy (see the Nazi-Soviet negotiations of last summer).[61]

Two distinct motives lie at the base of the position assumed by the President of the Council of Peoples' Commissars. These are evident in his reply to Rosso. The first of these is general, the second specific. The first evolved from the military situation which, with the collapse of France and the abandonment of the Continent by the British armed forces, temporarily gave Germany hegemony in Europe. On the eve of re-establishing a certain equilibrium, with the annexation of the Baltic States and Bessarabia to the U.S.S.R., the Soviets did not ignore the possibility of some

---

[61] Rosso to Ciano, report, June 14, 1940, ibid., Doc. 22. Rosso informed Von Schulenburg of the contents of this communication. Cf. Von Schulenburg to Von Ribbentrop, telegram, June 22, 1940, G.D., Series D, IX, Doc. 520.

new tripartite combination—Russo-German-Italian or perhaps a bipartite one, an Italo-Soviet combination (the latter a more remote possibility, given the existence of the Italo-German alliance)—which would allow the U.S.S.R. greater maneuverability, if not actual resistance to Berlin.

The specific motive is suggested by the above-cited information transmitted by Helfand regarding the statements presumably made by Von Mackensen, a point on which, as has been noted, Von Ribbentrop was rather evasive. If, in fact, there had been an Italo-German plan for the peaceful solution of Balkan problems, Rosso should have known something about it and should eventually have been the bearer of one or more proposals. His failure to transmit any specific proposals probably tempered Molotov's satisfaction with the re-confirmation of Mussolini's statements on the maintenance of peace in the Balkans. Rosso's replies to Molotov had been most adequate and, insofar as Rome was concerned, it was clear that he intended to focus his own government's attention on reality by immediately taking a position against any illusion that might develop in Rome that it would be possible to intensify commercial exchange between the two powers without assuming political obligations. Finally, Von Schulenburg's positive attitude is worth noting. This factor is interesting not only because a short time later the German executed a complete about-face, but also because of the influence he may have had on the thinking of the Italian Ambassador.

Rosso's telegrams arrived in Rome during Ciano's absence because of military service. The Fascist head of state, who had temporarily assumed the Foreign Ministry portfolio,[62] replied immediately as follows:

> Insofar as Italo-Russian relations are concerned, on the political terrain we can move very far along, given the present direction of Soviet policy and the liquidation of the Communist movement in the West.
>
> The records contain a political treaty signed by me and Potemkin some years ago, and to all intents and purposes it is still in force.
>
> This might be used as a point of departure in order to define the respective lines of foreign policy of the two countries, particularly as they concern the Danube-Balkan Basin.
>
> Now that I have given the general outlines, reopen the talks with Molotov on this basis, urge him to speak, assure him that the Fascist government is stimulated only by goodwill, and then report.[63]

Mussolini's instructions are worth examining from two points of view: their specific technical aspects and their general political implications. Inso-

---

[62] This is only technically correct. In the substantive sense, Mussolini always directed Italian foreign policy even when he was not Minister for Foreign Affairs.

[63] Anfuso to Rosso, telegram, June 16, 1940, I.D., 9th series, V, Doc. 29.

far as the first of these is concerned, it is difficult not to concur with the criticism advanced by Rosso,[64] who quite correctly pointed out how excessively general and vague they were, which placed the Ambassador to Moscow in serious difficulty in seeking concrete and productive conversations with Molotov. This technical deficiency should not have been too surprising. It was the product of the extemporaneous nature of the decision made by the Duce.

The search for Mussolini's motives is much more interesting. France had not yet formulated its request for an armistice; therefore the armistice as such could not have been a motivating factor. It is likely, therefore, that the explanation is to be found in the Duce's earlier statements to Von Ribbentrop and Hitler during the Rome and Brenner Pass meeetings and in the correspondence exchanged with the Führer, that is, the desire to harmonize Italian policy toward the U.S.S.R. with that of Germany. It is possible, however, that Mussolini may have had other, or at least more complex, reasons. It is not impossible that, attracted by the cordiality of the Russians and their indications of willingness to treat realistically with the Italians (following a near-rupture in relations) and by the presentation made by Rosso, Mussolini wanted to take advantage of the situation in order to achieve a personal diplomatic victory in emulation of Hitler and to retain for himself—an aspiration similar to Molotov's—a certain freedom of maneuver vis-à-vis Berlin. Concrete evidence to confirm this view is lacking, but such an interpretation would explain the warmth of his telegram and the absence of any reference whatsoever to his German ally. That he wanted to acquire a certain autonomy of action with respect to Berlin seems also to be demonstrated by the Duce's sudden personal decision (taken six days later) not to include among the conditions for the Italo-French armistice the Italian occupation of the Rhone valley, Corsica, Djibuti, and Tunisia, conditions previously agreed upon with Hitler at Munich.[65]

Rosso—also revealing a certain degree of naïveté—considered "the pos-

[64] Rosso, "Obbietivi e metodi," p. 19. It is true that Rosso himself in the report of June 14 had requested a "directive, even the most general," but evidently what he received, although it was the minimum sufficient for proper orientation, would not carry a conversation "very far along" on a political plane.

[65] Simoni, *Berlino: ambasciata d'Italia*, p. 133. Mussolini to Hitler, letter, June 22, 1940, *I.D.*, 9th series, V, Doc. 83. The interpretation given for Mussolini's decision to renounce certain of the armistice conditions agreed upon at Munich is based on my own personal deductions. See also Donosti, *Mussolini e l'Europa*, p. 233. The text of the Italo-German agreement for the inclusion of the above-mentioned areas to be occupied by the Italians under the terms of the armistice with France is drawn from the minutes of the Munich meeting of June 18 which were drafted personally by Mussolini and published in *Hitler e Mussolini*, pp. 51–54.

sibility of gaining greater independence of action with respect to Berlin" and the "advantage of not remaining tied exclusively to the Axis partner who was already threatening to transform the alliance relationship into one of semi-vassalage."[66] While awaiting his audience with Molotov, he sought to obtain more precise directives from Rome and to this end telegraphed to Palazzo Chigi on June 17 as follows:

I have received the telegram dispatched yesterday containing the Duce's instructions regarding Italo-Russian relations.

I will see Molotov, and I will speak according to the directives sent.

However, with reference to *specifying* the lines of political action of the two countries, and in anticipation of the questions which *Molotov* will most certainly ask me regarding *our* objectives and *our* program, it would be extremely useful to me to have some precise instructions on the subject, particularly concerning the Danubian-Balkan Basin.

My soundings will have a greater chance for success if, in asking Molotov what the Soviet intentions are, I am in a position to tell him—albeit in general terms—what the Italian intentions are.

Since I will not be able to meet with the President of the Council of Peoples' Commissars before the day after tomorrow (tomorrow being a holiday in the U.S.S.R.), I beg you to telegraph your reply by next Wednesday at the latest if at all possible.[67]

As was predictable, since both Mussolini and Ciano were en route to Munich,[68] Rosso received no reply to his request from Rome, and in the evening of June 20 he was received by Molotov at the Kremlin and held in conversation for over an hour. The Ambassador immediately dispatched three telegrams on what had transpired in this important colloquy.[69] The next day he provided greater detail, as follows:

To the necessarily succinct information furnished in my above-mentioned telegrams I am adding this more detailed account of my colloquy with Molotov at the Kremlin last night.

By way of preamble, I must say that to reopen conversation with the President of the Council and to "make him speak" according to the instructions sent to me by the Duce, I judged it necessary to make it clear that I had come to transmit a communication from the Duce himself.

I must add that I interpreted my instructions to mean that I was authorized

---

[66] Rosso, "Obbietivi e metodi," p. 19.

[67] Rosso to Anfuso, telegram, June 17, 1940, *I.D.*, 9th series, V, Doc. 35.

[68] In the above-mentioned minutes of the Munich meeting (see note 65), the Fascist Chief of State noted Hitler's "irony and scorn" in the latter's comments on Russia. In contrast, Ciano observed, "He [Von Ribbentrop] referred in formally correct terms, albeit no longer cordial, to Russia, toward whom he believes that Germany can maintain the present policy line for a long time to come." Ciano, note, June 19, 1940, *ibid.*, Doc. 65.

[69] Rosso to Ciano, telegrams, June 20, 1940, *ibid.*, Doc. 73.

to develop the concepts contained therein in such a way as not to give my interlocutor the impression that this was to be a superficial and academic conversation. Only in this way could I hope that Molotov might abandon his habitual
reserve, something I believe I accomplished. For this reason I amplified the
declaration concerning the Italo-Soviet Treaty of 1933.

And finally, I note that, in the absence of specific directives, yet finding
myself in the position of having to take the initiative in the matter of a
"reciprocal clarification of our respective positions," I explained to Molotov the
directives of Italian policy, basing my arguments—for Italy's participation in the
war—on the Duce's speech of June 10.

As for our position regarding the problems of the Danubian-Balkan Basin,
I was forced to base my comments on my general knowledge of the fundamental lines of Fascist policy and on my personal impressions and deductions.

With this as premise, I transmit herewith—based on the notes I had prepared prior to the conversation—the gist of my oral communication to Molotov,
who heard me through without interruption.

After having explained that because of the suddenness of my departure from
Italy I had not had the time for the necessary contacts with my superiors (and
that this explained why I had not been able to say very much to him during
our first conversation), I informed him that I had received instructions from
Rome and that for this reason I had requested a second meeting.

The substance of what I said to him is as follows:

The communication I received from Rome is signed by Mussolini and contains his instructions to me on the subject of Italo-Soviet relations.

The Duce begins by recalling the existence of a pact which was signed on
September 2, 1933, in Rome by him and by the then Ambassador of the
U.S.S.R., that is, the Italo-Soviet pact of friendship, nonaggression, and
neutrality.

This pact has never been repudiated and therefore continues to remain in
effect.

At this point I would like to note—and this is purely a personal observation—
that recent European events have, on occasion, cast a shadow over this pact and
prevented it from functioning in the spirit in which it was created.

It seems to me that it would be useless to dig up the past and equally useless for one or the other of the parties to engage in recriminations. What is of
vital concern is the present and the future.

So much for my personal observation, and I now return to the Duce's
communication.

In the instructions he gave me, Mussolini expressed an opinion which I
consider to be important, and it is as follows:

He is convinced that the Italo-Soviet pact of friendship, nonaggression, and
neutrality of 1933 can—if there is goodwill on both sides—be, in a manner of
speaking, "revitalized," not only in words but also in spirit, and can be transformed into something vibrant and alive instead of being allowed to remain
inert or to die.

Mussolini has instructed me to tell you that, insofar as he is concerned, the
goodwill exists.

Therefore, I am interested in learning if you are, in the main, in agreement on the advisability of revitalizing our pact and if you are inspired by the same goodwill demonstrated to me by my head of state.

If I may, I would like to proceed with an exposition of the ideas transmitted to me by Mussolini.

The Duce believes—and I believe that you would concur on this point—that the necessary premise for a satisfactory development of the relations between our two countries consists, fundamentally, in a reciprocal clarification of our respective positions regarding the political problems of common interest. Mussolini proposes a frank clarification of our position. The aim of this clarification would be that of ensuring that the interests of our two countries will not conflict in the future but that, instead, they may be reconciled and that they may be also reconciled with the interests of third parties.

I do not know whether you are in a position at this time to tell me something of the aims of Soviet policy. However, let me assure you immediately that whatever you may say to me will be communicated to Rome with absolute fidelity and precision and, of course, in the strictest confidence.

On the other hand, I can tell you that the instructions I received allow me to explain the main lines of Italian policy, whose general nature was outlined in the Duce's speech announcing Italy's entrance into the war.

Italy—and I mentioned this in our last conversation—has declared war against France and England in order to reach one main objective: that of breaking the chains which have heretofore enslaved her in the Mediterranean.

The Anglo-French blockade of recent months, applied in the most oppressive way imaginable, has made us acutely aware of this slavery, which we are determined to end.

This means that our objective in the war is to force France and England to abandon the idea of dominating the Mediterranean. We want to destroy the Anglo-French hegemony so that the Mediterranean will become a free sea. We are at war, therefore, with England and France primarily to liberate the Mediterranean—in our interest, of course, but also in the interest of all nations who need this freedom.

Aside from the demands which she intends to impose on the enemy countries, Italy has no claims against other states.

Therefore, this signifies that we have no aggressive intentions toward anyone. Mussolini has stated this clearly when he made his now well-known declaration, not only to Switzerland, but also to Yugoslavia, Greece, and Turkey.

Some time ago rumors were rife that Italy harbored hostile intentions toward Yugoslavia and toward Greece. I can assure you that they were absolutely false.

Naturally, we are politically as well as economically interested in the countries that lie in the Balkan-Danube Basin: Hungary, Yugoslavia, Rumania, Bulgaria, and Greece.

However, our interest is essentially friendly in character: we are solely interested in placing our political relations on a sound footing and developing our economic rapport.

We have not the slightest intention of seeking to exert an exclusive influence on these countries and even less of threatening their independence or their territorial integrity.

Our objectives in the Danubian countries and in the Balkans may be summarized in the phrase "friendly collaboration." We are aware that divergencies between some of these countries exist and that numerous territorial claims which are the inheritance from the last war remain unresolved.

I wish to allude specifically to Hungary's claims against Rumania in Transylvania and Bulgaria's claims to the Dobrudja.

We also know that an unresolved problem exists between the U.S.S.R. and Rumania, one that you have mentioned publicly in one of your speeches to the Supreme Council of the U.S.S.R., namely, that of Bessarabia.

In the face of all of these problems which do not affect Italy directly but only in an indirect sense, the policy of the Italian government has always been inspired by the desire to see these resolved peacefully. Mussolini intends to continue this policy of "friendly cooperation."

In summary, I have outlined the general aspects of Italian policy. And now I would like to ask whether you would care to comment on the general lines of Soviet policy regarding the above-mentioned countries.

Having listened to me carefully, Molotov asked me to repeat what I had said regarding the Danubian and Balkan countries. He listened attentively, reflected for a moment with an expression of great concentration, and finally replied slowly, weighing every word carefully.

He began by telling me that he greatly appreciated my comments made upon instructions from the Duce. They were unquestionably "important and worthy of careful attention." For this reason he desired to reflect further on the entire problem of Italo-Soviet relations and to discuss them again at a future colloquy. (I note that, in all matters of major importance, Molotov always reserves his final judgment until he has had a chance to speak of them with Stalin and to receive his instructions.)

However, Molotov did not say that he was in complete accord with us regarding the Italo-Soviet pact of 1933 as being fully in effect.

He added that the U.S.S.R. had not been able to explain the Italian attitude of recent months, particularly that of the past winter (an evident allusion to the pro-Finnish demonstrations in Italy), "especially since the change in relations between the U.S.S.R. and Germany." However, he was in agreement with me that it was useless to dwell on the past and to become involved in recriminations: it was much more useful and important to concern ourselves with the present and the future.

Molotov continued by saying that he was delighted to accept the Duce's proposal and that he was, therefore, ready to exchange points of view, particularly on questions that involved the Danubian-Balkan sector—"questions," he noted, "that are of concern to both of our countries." Moreover, he expressed his desire that this exchange "be continued and developed in concrete form."

In reference to what I had had to say about Italy's war aims, Molotov indirectly led me to conclude that the U.S.S.R. found nothing in these with which to find fault. In fact, he stated that the U.S.S.R. was not responsible for the existing situation (literally, that the U.S.S.R. was not the defender of the status quo as it has existed up to the present).

Turning to the Balkans, the President of the Council stated that he was pleased to note my comments relative to Italian policy in the Balkans and our desire to facilitate a friendly solution to the territorial problems existing between the countries of the Danubian-Balkan Basin. He added that he "appreciated the understanding Italy had of the problems regarding Rumania."

Insofar as Bessarabia was concerned, he declared that the U.S.S.R. intended to resolve the question peacefully. It was imperative, however, that the solution not be delayed for long because he judged the situation to be "ripe."

As for the Hungarian and Bulgarian claims, to which I had alluded only in passing, Molotov made no comment, and I believe that to induce him to commit himself on the matter it will be necessary that I tell him something of the Italian point of view.

At this point Molotov asked if he might raise some questions, to which I replied to the affirmative. He then asked:

1. "Can you tell me whether Italy is bound by some specific obligations to any of the Danubian-Balkan powers?"

I replied that I was aware only of the obligations assumed by Italy in the friendship and non-aggression pacts concluded with practically all of those countries. I did not believe that other obligations existed.

It may be presumed that with this question Molotov sought to learn whether there existed any secret pacts which obligated Italy to support the claims of one of the Balkan states against others. Perhaps he was interested also in learning whether we are bound by some promise to Rumania in the matter of Bessarabia.

2. "What form do you think your relations with Turkey will take? Do you consider a war with Turkey as possible or inevitable?"

I replied that I certainly did not regard it as inevitable since—at least insofar as we were concerned—we had no intention of provoking it. All would depend on the way Turkey conducted herself and on how she would implement her agreements with France and England. If Turkey did not undertake any hostile act against us, the prospect of war could be excluded. Italy's position had been made crystal clear by the Duce.

In turn, I asked Molotov what he believed the Turkish position would be. He replied that, according to his information, and particularly after the improvement of relations between Berlin and Ankara, he had reason to believe that Turkey had no desire to be drawn into the conflict.

3. The third question concerned Egypt. Molotov stated that he had noted that I, citing the Duce's declarations to the neighboring countries, had not mentioned Egypt. He stated that he thought he could understand my omission. Nevertheless, he was interested in what I thought about how our situation might develop with respect to that country. Insofar as he was concerned, he failed to see how things could remain as they were on the day the Duce made his speech.

I replied that I agreed with him about the complexity of the situation because Egypt, in fact, was not an independent country. It was obvious that prompt acquiescence by the Egyptian government to England's will and demands in the area of military operations could have repercussions on the attitude of the Fascist government.

Molotov frequently indicated his comprehension.

Before taking my leave I asked, in a semi-serious tone, whether the new ambassadors from France and England, only recently arrived in Moscow, had begun to "flirt" with the Soviet government.

Molotov replied that both Labonne and Cripps impressed him as being "beaten" men, particularly the former. He added sarcastically that the French Ambassador had gone to great pains to demonstrate that the U.S.S.R. must concern itself with the problem of European equilibrium, which was being threatened by excessive German power. Molotov replied that European equilibrium had never been a fetish to the U.S.S.R. and that, moreover, the U.S.S.R. had no intention of defending the European equilibrium as it had existed up to recent days.

As for the English Ambassador, Molotov stated that Cripps had dwelled at length on "those commercial questions which had been discussed in vain for months between London and Moscow." Then Cripps had touched on the Balkan question, suggesting that the U.S.S.R. assume the role of "leading power" in that area.

Molotov told me all of this with an ironical smile, by which he obviously wanted me to understand that the promises and blandishments of the two ambassadors had not had any effect.

As I prepared to leave, Molotov renewed his thanks for my visit and expressed the hope that I would return soon.

In my telegram No. 295 I have already summarized my impressions, which I repeat here:

1. Molotov had a strong interest in my communication to him and was obviously satisfied to learn that the Fascist government was disposed to maintain cordial relations and to exchange viewpoints with the U.S.S.R.

2. Molotov wanted to make it clear that the U.S.S.R. intends to concern itself with Balkan problems but, at the same time, has recognized Italy's interest therein.

3. When Molotov stated that the Bessarabian problem was "ripe," I realized that the statement was significant.

4. There was nothing subtle about Molotov's curiosity regarding our intentions vis-à-vis Turkey and Egypt.

5. And finally, I wish to add that the tone used by Molotov in speaking of England and France evidently was used for the purpose of demonstrating that the U.S.S.R. does not intend to change its policy toward Germany.[70]

When Mussolini's telegram is compared with the text of the statement made by Rosso to Molotov, it is clear that the Italian Ambassador had made great use of the latitude granted to him by the general nature of his instructions and that, as he had earlier warned, he had "interpreted" Mussolini's speech made on the occasion of Italy's entrance into the war in reference to specific problems regarding which he had received no instructions.[71] Evidently, he had plunged ahead with great enthusiasm, convinced that from the conversations some accord might be reached or something advantageous might be derived for his homeland. He had succeeded in getting Molotov to "talk," but when he himself spoke, notwithstanding his good intentions, he had permitted Molotov to conclude that portions of his statements were Mussolini's when they were merely the Ambassador's

[70] Rosso to Ciano, report, June 21, 1940, ibid., Doc. 81.
[71] Concerning Rumania, his interpretation of the policy lines of the Fascist government was politically correct but historically erroneous.

interpretations and embellishments. Thus, aside from the actual merit of the statements, these were bound to convey a certain significance to Molotov. On the other hand, Rosso was absolutely right to note that the hurried instructions given to him (the text of these is sufficient indication of the haste in which they were dashed off) put him in an extremely difficult position. As for the interpretation to be given to Molotov's position, Rosso commented in his courier telegram of June 22 as follows:

I call your attention again to my conversation with Molotov in order to present the following observations for your consideration:

1. There is no doubt that the government of the U.S.S.R. has been impressed by the German military success in the west, which here was not expected to be so rapid or so complete. The Kremlin predicted a longer war and, perhaps, desired less decisive results.

I believe that today the U.S.S.R. is beginning to concern herself with Germany's extraordinary power and for this reason is beginning to take the necessary precautions. This is the explanation for her rush to strengthen her positions in the Baltic with the effective occupation of Lithuania, Latvia, and Estonia and for maintaining her armed forces mobilized.

It is my judgment that this Soviet preoccupation does not yet carry with it any intention to modify policy toward Germany. Moreover, I consider the Anglo-French hopes of effecting such a change as being naïve. The irony with which Molotov commented on the vague suggestions of the English and French ambassadors (the former suggesting that the U.S.S.R. assume the leading role in the Balkans and the latter seeking to attract the U.S.S.R. by the argument of European equilibrium) left me with the clear impression that the Kremlin is far from any desire to execute an about-face, and, further, is fully aware of the grave risks involved in terminating the accord with Germany.

Nevertheless, I believe that the U.S.S.R. is looking for outside support, and I consider that a rapprochement with Italy should be thought of in these terms.

This is apparently the reason for Molotov's evident satisfaction with the demonstration of good will on the part of the Fascist government and his own desire to strengthen contacts with Rome.

2. Molotov made it very clear that the U.S.S.R. is very much interested in and wants to become involved in the Balkans. However, he also let me know that she had no pretensions of exercising a predominant influence, least of all an exclusive one. Moreover, it is my feeling that he wants to reach agreement with Italy and Germany on the problems of the Danubian-Balkan Basin or, at the very least, to participate in eventual Italo-German consultations on the questions involving that part of Europe.

3. I must stress that these are simply my "impressions," based, thus far, on rather tenuous data, yet worthy of consideration. In any event, I hope to be able to confirm them in my future conversations with Molotov.

4. Until such time as the rapport with Molotov can be developed in the sense indicated by the instructions contained in the Duce's telegram, it is necessary that I be in the position to "nurture" the conversation. Molotov will "sing" only in response to the degree that I entrust him with what information and confidences I may.

In my conversation with Molotov on June 20, in the absence of specific instructions, I explained the Italian point of view on the Mediterranean question and on the Danubian-Balkan problems on my general knowledge of the Fascist directives on policy and, on occasion, drawing from inductive reasoning.

My task would be greatly simplified and the results I obtain from my soundings could be much more profitable if I were in a position to speak with greater knowledge, based on any instructions you care to send to me.

5. In reference to what I have outlined above, therefore, I would appreciate knowing: (a) whether my explanation to Molotov of Italy's war aims and of Italian policy in the Danubian-Balkan Basin reflects, in the main, what is desired; (b) what further information I may eventually furnish Molotov on the following points: 1) our attitude on the Bessarabian problem and on the Rumanian problem generally; 2) our attitude toward Hungary's territorial claims and any eventual obligations we may have in the matter; 3) our attitude toward Bulgarian claims to the Dobrudja and to access to the Aegean Sea; 4) our policy toward Greece, Turkey, and on the Straits Question; 5) our agreements and our attitude toward Yugoslavia; 6) the predictable development of events concerning Egypt.

At the same time it would be useful for me to know on what other points, in addition to those touched on during my conversation with Molotov on June 20, I should continue to sound out possible Soviet intentions.

Molotov provided some information on the Bessarabian problem. I would propose to sound him out on the theme of Bulgarian and Hungarian claims in addition to the Straits Question and, eventually, on U.S.S.R. relations with Iran and Afghanistan.

Naturally, if the occasion offers, I shall seek to learn what I can on Soviet relations with Japan as well as with the northern countries. I would like to know whether you are in agreement. Permit me to repeat that in order to keep the conversation alive I too will have to speak, and, of course, I want to be able to do so in accordance with your instructions. I would be grateful if you would send me your instructions as soon as possible.[72]

Rosso's two reports, as always, had the merit of frankness and clarity. His observations made sense, and his insistence on receiving instructions was perfectly reasonable. In the second point of the second report Rosso correctly touched upon the key point of Molotov's comments, i.e., the Soviet Union's preoccupation with being cut off from the Danubian-Balkan Basin and (he might have added) her aspirations for the Straits. Equally sound was Rosso's judgment that Molotov was seeking "outside support." It remained to be seen just how far it would be possible for Italy to follow Molotov along this road without taking into consideration and resolving beforehand what might be termed the "German aspect" of Italo-Soviet relations—that is, at a certain point, what would be the repercussions on the Axis alliance of Rome's negotiations with Moscow—this aspect of the question did not appear among those stressed by Rosso. True,

[72] Rosso to Ciano, telegram via courier, June 22, 1940, *ibid.*, Doc. 90.

he was not the Ambassador to Berlin, much less the Minister for Foreign Affairs, and, in the final analysis, it was the latter who should have asked himself this question. Nevertheless, in pressing for instructions in order to continue the conversations with Molotov, or at least for a decision, he felt (as is clear from his admissions and his contacts with Von Schulenburg) that it was unlikely that he could go beyond general statements in responding to the complex questions raised by the precise and demanding Molotov unless this point were first clarified. In addition, Rosso did not seem to grasp the real significance of the question Molotov raised regarding the Fascist government's intentions toward Egypt and Turkey. It was perhaps insufficient to explain Molotov's questions on this point as being inspired by simple curiosity, even though the response given by him to Rosso's counter-question regarding the Soviet Union's attitude toward Turkey was such as to lead anyone to an erroneous conclusion. Yet the notable lack of success that marked the Turkish Foreign Minister's long stay in Moscow during the fall of 1939 should have indicated that Molotov's question was much more complex than it appeared to be at first glance. Moreover, there is no evidence that Rosso recognized the full significance of the fact that Molotov had selected the Italian Ambassador, long before Von Schulenburg,[73] in whom to confide that the Soviet Union considered the Bessarabian question to be "ripe." Was this a simple desire to test Rome's reaction, or was it the first manifestation of a real disposition for a preference and for concrete collaboration? Of course the evidence which might make it possible to reply accurately to this interesting question is not available, but, since it is highly unlikely that the assurances of assistance made by Ciano to Antonescu in December, 1939 (assurances which Rosso himself seems to have ignored) were known to Moscow, the last hypothesis may be most nearly correct.

To his report of June 21 and telegram of June 22 sent to Rome via air courier, Rosso also added the following personal letter to Anfuso:

Via special courier who will leave for Rome by air tomorrow, I am sending a detailed report of my recent colloquy with Molotov along with a long telegram on the subject, which I believe will be clearer if it reaches you without danger of alteration resulting from coding and decoding.

I believed the argument to have been sufficiently important and of a sufficient urgent nature to justify the dispatch of an ad hoc courier to Venice. I have noted faithfully—very nearly verbatim—what I said to Molotov and what he said to me.

[73] Molotov informed the German Ambassador of the Soviet decision regarding Rumania only on June 23, 1940. Von Schulenburg to Von Ribbentrop, telegram, June 23, 1940, G.D., Series D, X, Doc. 4.

On the question of getting him to talk, I myself had to take the initiative by confiding in him—or at least giving the impression of doing so. And since I had received nothing more than the telegram by way of instructions—very clear and significant but, at the same time, very sketchy—from the Duce, I found myself obliged to guess about Rome's wishes on many points.

I ask myself whether I did so satisfactorily, and I would like to know whether or not this is so in order that I may be better able to judge in the future.

If you feel that I ventured too far with Molotov, I urge you to so inform me so that I may bite my tongue. If, instead, I should push forward, I urge you to let me know this.

I have no fear of assuming responsibilities, and if you leave me with freedom of maneuver, I will do the very best that I can. But because I am aware that this is a gambit that could become rather important, I would like to know what our policy goals are. Moreover, may I urge you to see to it that the Minister provides me with the material to "nurture" my future conversations with Molotov?

You will note that in my telegram I ask a certain number of questions of the Ministry. I presume that it will not be possible to provide me with precise answers on some of these. It would suffice if I knew this, so that I might avoid such subjects if at all possible. On the other hand, in those instances where you can give me precise answers, I beg you to do so via telegraph so that I can approach Molotov with something to exchange.[74]

While this letter focuses attention on the difficulties encountered by Rosso in carrying out his duties, it does not indicate to Palazzo Chigi how he viewed the future development of the conversations nor that he proposed to lead them toward certain objectives. If it indicates the author's frankness and honesty, at the same time it reveals his perplexity regarding the specific aims of Italian policy vis-à-vis the U.S.S.R. and the precise steps to be taken after carrying out the imprecise and general directives in Mussolini's telegram.

On June 22 Ciano also met with Gorelkin.[75] The cordial statements made on that occasion by the Minister for Foreign Affairs, while limited to generalities, had a favorable echo in Moscow, as will be noted below, particularly for the conservative policy Italy proposed for the Balkans. Thus, Molotov had—or had reason to believe he had—an immediate confirmation of the assurances given to him by Rosso two days previously.

On the basis of this data, during the afternoon of June 25, the Presi-

[74] Rosso to Anfuso, personal letter, June 21, 1940, I.D., 9th series, Doc. 82. This document is included in the ministerial proceedings and is initialed by Ciano.

[75] Ciano, Diario, I, pp. 281–82. It is also possible that Ciano's friendly attitude stemmed from the first indications of a negative German position regarding the Soviets, as observed at Munich.

dent of the Council of Peoples' Commissars called the Italian Ambassador
to the Kremlin and read the following note to him in Russian:

It is the opinion of the U.S.S.R. that the war is not likely to be terminated
prior to the arrival of winter, if indeed it does end this year. With respect to
this situation, we will raise all of the questions which remain unresolved and
seek to resolve them by one means or another.

With respect to the questions posed by the Italian government both in
Signor Rosso's colloquy of June 20 with me and in that of Signor Ciano with
Gorelkin on June 22, the position of the U.S.S.R. can be summarized as
follows:

The U.S.S.R. has no claims to make with respect to Hungary. We have
normal relations with Hungary. The U.S.S.R. holds that the claims (literally,
"pretensions") of Hungary against Rumania have a valid base.

With Bulgaria the U.S.S.R. has the good relations of a good neighbor. There
is a basis for becoming closer. Bulgaria's claims against Rumania and against
Greece have a valid basis.

The basic claims of the U.S.S.R. against Rumania are well known. The
U.S.S.R. would like to obtain from Rumania what belongs by right to the
U.S.S.R. without having to resort to force, but this will become inevitable if
Rumania proves to be intransigent.

As to the other areas of Rumania, the U.S.S.R. recognizes Italian and German interests in them and is ready to reach an accord with the two powers on
this question.

Turkey arouses concern, given the unfriendly attitude it displays toward the
U.S.S.R. (and not only toward the U.S.S.R.) as exemplified by its conclusion
of a pact with England and France.

This concern is magnified because of Turkish tendencies to dictate terms to
the Soviet Union regarding the Black Sea, claiming to be the sole sovereign of
the Straits, and also by her practice of menacing the Soviet Union in the area
southeast of Batum.

As for the other areas of Turkey, the U.S.S.R. recognizes the rights of Italy
and, therefore, also those of Germany, and is ready to reach an accord with
these two powers on this question.

Insofar as the Mediterranean is concerned, the U.S.S.R. regards it as being
entirely equitable that Italy have the pre-eminent position in this sea. Here the
U.S.S.R. hopes that Italy will recognize the U.S.S.R.'s rights as the major
power on the Black Sea.[76]

---

[76] Rosso to Ciano, telegram, June 25, 1940, I.D., 9th series, V, Doc. 104, and
report, ibid., note 1. The text reproduced above is that of the report because, for
code security reasons, the text in the telegram was only a summary. Rosso immediately informed his colleague, Von Schulenburg, of the nature of his colloquy with
Molotov, and the latter promptly notified Berlin. Von Schulenburg to Von Ribbentrop, telegram, June 26, 1940, G.D., Series D, X, Doc. 21. The Rumanian Minister
in Moscow, Gafencu, also learned of the event, but it is not known from whom or
when. Gafencu, Preliminari, p. 62.

As Rosso telegraphed the same day:

After having read the statements outlined in the preceding paragraph, Molotov urged me to communicate them to Rome and expressed the hope that the Royal Government would inform him as soon as possible of its point of view on the questions mentioned by him.

Molotov continued by recalling that the Nazi-Soviet negotiations of last September proceeded with rapidity and led to a satisfactory conclusion because both governments spoke with absolute sincerity and clarity. He added that the excellent political relations with Germany established at that time "continued to flourish." He hoped to be able to proceed in the same spirit and with the same results with Italy.

I thanked Molotov for his statement, whose clarity and importance I appreciated. I expressed pleasure at the results obtained by the Duce's initiative, in which he had proposed the exchange of views on questions of common interest. I assured Molotov that I would urge Your Excellency to examine his declaration promptly and to give the Fascist government's point of view with equal dispatch.

In summary, I believe I should emphasize the following points:

1. The U.S.S.R. recognizes the Hungarian and Bulgarian claims against Rumania as well as the Bulgarian claims against Greece, and—aside from the Bessarabian question, which it considers to be a matter of exclusive interest to the Soviet Union—declares itself to be ready to reach agreement with both Italy and Germany on questions regarding the Danubian-Balkan Basin.

2. The U.S.S.R. proposes to reopen the question of the Straits with the Turks and probably contemplates territorial claims against Turkish Armenia and Georgia, in order to re-establish the frontiers of 1914.

3. Molotov suggests a three-power accord on policy vis-à-vis Turkey.

4. The U.S.S.R. recognizes Italy's pre-eminent position in the Mediterranean but desires that her position of pre-eminence in the Black Sea also be recognized.

I call attention to the nuances in Molotov's statements when he mentions German interests in Rumania and Turkey. German interests are placed on the same plane with Italy's in Rumania; for Turkey, he spoke instead of German interests as a consequence of Italian interests.[77]

Molotov's statements can be examined from two points of view: their content and their motivation. Regarding content, it should be noted that once again Italy was the first to be informed of the objectives of the Soviet Union's future policy toward Bulgaria as well as Turkey. On this point, one should not overlook the fact that Molotov had not yet raised the Straits Question or the Georgian and Armenian problems with Von Schulenburg in such peremptory terms, nor had he declared his hope for closer rapport with Bulgaria (a formula which indicated Soviet desire to look upon Bulgaria as the area of the U.S.S.R.'s strongest influence). In addition, the

[77] Rosso to Ciano, telegram, June 25, 1940, *I.D.*, 9th series, V, Doc. 104.

passage concerning the claims against Rumania, when related to the declarations of the President of the Council of Peoples' Commissars in his colloquy with the Italian Ambassador on June 20, anticipated Soviet renunciation of the whole of Bukowina, which was communicated to Von Schulenburg by Molotov only on the following day[78] (the claim to northern Bukowina was not mentioned). The approval given to the Magyar and Bulgarian claims against Bucharest was certainly related to the imminent precipitation of the Rumanian crisis. But the sanctioning of the Sofia government's claims against Athens, in addition to supporting the Russian desire to attract Bulgaria into the Soviet orbit, could be related equally well both to the question of the Straits and to the tacit scheme to raise the entire Greek problem indirectly in the hope of doing Italy a favor.[79] The silence observed with regard to Yugoslavia (the only Balkan state not mentioned in the Molotov statement) was worthy of note, as was the problem of Egypt—also unmentioned—about which Molotov, after the questions raised by him during the June 20 colloquy, was most anxious to have the Fascist government's point of view.

On the other hand, the recognition of the legitimacy of Italian aspirations to pre-eminence in the Mediterranean represented a significant retreat from the position taken earlier by that same Molotov, who on January 15, 1938, had declared in a speech before the Supreme Soviet that such an aspiration was one of the principal reasons why the U.S.S.R. should increase the size of its navy.[80] The explicit confirmation of the good relations existing with Berlin was apparently aimed at reassuring the Fascist government regarding the objectives of the desired accords, while the reference to the rapidity with which the pact with Germany was concluded a year earlier could be interpreted as a discreet invitation to accelerate the tempo of the negotiations. Finally, it should also be noted that the Soviet statesman, while explicitly indicating his wish for a three-power accord (Italy-U.S.S.R.-Germany) on Turkish and Rumanian problems, also referred at the same time to matters which should find their place in a bilateral agreement between Rome and Moscow.

Turning now to an investigation of what might have motivated Molotov, the first factor concerns the reasons why he took the initiative in revealing to Italy his own government's future plans when the course of his last conversation with Rosso should have prompted him to await some kind of a reply to his questions. Undoubtedly, the imminent squaring of

78 Von Schulenburg to Von Ribbentrop, telegram, June 26, 1940, G.D., Series D, X, Doc. 25.
79 The first crisis in Italo-Greek relations developed shortly thereafter.
80 Beloff, Soviet Russia, II, p. 110.

accounts with Germany must have had considerable weight in the decision of the Narkomindiel, but perhaps it was not the only influence. On the eve of the occupation of Bessarabia and northern Bukowina, which was effected twenty-four hours later (and even though the occupation of Bessarabia had been taken into account in the Nazi-Soviet accord of 1939), the U.S.S.R. was evidently preoccupied by the existence of an Italo-German understanding or at least of plans of the two countries for the Danubian-Balkan Basin, which the occupation itself might have activated.[81] Therefore, it is likely that Molotov considered it good policy to confide in Italy and to demonstrate that he was disposed to recognize Italian interests in the Basin and in Turkey. In the event that Italian reaction was favorable, this would facilitate the conclusion of a tripartite agreement, aid Moscow in its discussions with Berlin, and, perhaps, even create some areas of dissension between Rome and Berlin which could work to Moscow's advantage. In any event, in dealing with Rome (and Molotov had every reason to believe that Rome was anxious for this) he could hope to acquire useful information and data on which to base a judgment.

Rosso's telegram did not produce any unusual echo in Italy. Ciano, who on the preceding day had commented unfavorably on news from German sources of an imminent Russian attack against Rumania and who continued to regard Soviet policy as "increasingly anti-German,"[82] did not consider the Molotov overtures important enough to merit notation in his diary. However, in a colloquy with Gorelkin on June 26 on the Bessarabian question and in informing the latter that Italy, while it had no objection to the liquidation of that particular problem, hoped for a peaceful solution,[83] the Fascist Foreign Minister touched on the majority of the problems discussed by Molotov with Rosso but avoided going beyond generalities on any of them.[84] No communication was sent to the Italian Embassy in Moscow.

The continued silence from Rome prompted Rosso to again ask for the

[81] For Molotov's constant preoccupation with this matter, see his statements to Von Schulenburg of July 29, 1940. Von Schulenburg to Von Ribbentrop, telegram, July 29, 1940, *G.D.*, Series D, X, Doc. 249.

[82] Von Mackensen to Von Ribbentrop, telegram, June 26, 1940, *ibid.*, Doc. 18; Ciano, *Diario*, I, p. 283. It should also be noted that the Germans again failed to inform the Fascist government of their secret agreement of August, 1939, with the Soviets which recognized the Soviet claims to Bessarabia.

[83] Ciano, *Diario*, I, pp. 283–84.

[84] Ciano to Rosso, telegram, July 5, 1940, *I.D.*, 9th series, V, Doc. 187. A Ciano note of August 4, 1940, attached to the cabinet proceedings indicates that this colloquy occurred on June 28. Ciano, note, August 4, 1940, *ibid.*, Doc. 356.

long-awaited instructions, in the following telegram to Palazzo Chigi on July 3:

With your telegram of June 16, the Royal Government has taken the initiative in proposing an exchange of views with the Soviet government in order to formulate the respective outlines of political policy, particularly for the Danubian-Balkan Basin. Molotov promptly accepted our proposal and, moreover, expressed the desire that the exchange of views begin early and in concrete form (conversation of June 20).

In a colloquy on June 25 Molotov made several important declarations regarding the attitude of the Soviet Union toward the problem of Bessarabia, the Hungarian and Bulgarian claims against Rumania, and Soviet-Turkish relations. He also suggested the timeliness of an accord between the U.S.S.R., Germany, and Italy on the Danubian-Balkan Basin and Black Sea questions. Molotov then expressed his desire to learn the Italian position on these problems.

After my last conversation with Molotov, the occupation of Bessarabia and northern Bukowina took place, which, in encouraging the Hungarians and Bulgarians to press their claims, appears to be destined to trigger a serious crisis in the Danubian-Balkan Basin.

In my telegram dispatched yesterday, I reported the instructions received here by the Hungarian Minister, who has been instructed to request Soviet intervention in Belgrade to advise the Yugoslav government to maintain its neutrality in the event of a Hungarian-Rumanian conflict.

In view of the present delicate situation and in anticipation of a possible question from Molotov regarding the Italian point of view and intentions, I renew my plea that I be furnished instructions and orientation guidelines on the various points referred to in my earlier telegrams.[85]

The insistence of the Italian Ambassador to Moscow appeared to be fully justified not only by the widening of the Balkan crisis but also by the realization of the probably negative future consequences of failure to come to an immediate tripartite accord. In effect, the Vienna Arbitrage was to constitute the point of departure for the final Nazi-Soviet crisis.

Rosso's request was not favorably received by Ciano, who on July 5, the eve of his departure for Berlin, replied as follows: "There is no point in pursuing the conversations further, and any attempt to probe deeper into the proposals presented by the Soviets should be avoided. I have had a reasonably detailed conversation with Gorelkin during the course of which we touched upon the majority of those subjects discussed by you and Molotov, without, however, going beyond generalities. In conclusion,

---

[85] Rosso to Ciano, telegram, July 3, 1940, *ibid.*, Doc. 170. Note the failure to refer to the Soviet support of the Bulgarian claims against Greece and to the closer relations with Sofia. As for the step taken by the Hungarian Minister, I have learned that, at the same time, Regent Horthy sent a personal letter to Prince Paul of Yugoslavia expressing much the same ideas.

maintain an atmosphere of comprehension, but what has been done is enough, at least for the moment."[86]

No document has been uncovered to explain this sudden slowdown. However, several facts should be kept in mind. As has been noted, behind Mussolini's instructions lay his personal desire to undertake an action of his own. Prior to the French request for an armistice, he immediately and with pleasure accepted the Soviet invitation. However, on impulse and without having a precise plan, he urged Rosso to "get him to talk." It is clear that his telegram reveals a desire and hope to receive rather than to advance information and proposals. Instead, Molotov had replied not only with proposals but also with questions which were, moreover, precise and not at all restrictive: Bulgaria, Greece, Turkey, the Mediterranean. To reply, it was necessary to abandon vague generalizations and formulate a precise thought, which Mussolini evidently was not prepared to do. The maneuver may now have appeared in an entirely different light. In fact, two days earlier "a great deal of information from various sources suggesting that Russia was steadily increasing her preparations to take a hostile position toward the Axis" arrived in Rome.[87] On the other hand, it was precisely on July 5 that Mussolini, in giving Ciano his instructions on the eve of the latter's departure for Germany, had advanced the proposal for a landing on the Ionian Islands and for splitting up Yugoslavia,[88] and requested Hitler's opinion on the matter in advance (which might explain the expression "for the moment" at the close of Ciano's telegram to Rosso). Finally, the present uncertainty regarding the immediate course of Axis policy in the Balkans was similar to the uncertainty existing over the Battle of Britain, which could also have brought about a rapid military or diplomatic end to the conflict. Ciano, on the other hand, was not sympathetic to Berlin and had no faith in Moscow, which (added to the rest) had tied itself tô Berlin; thus he did not encourage the negotiations. Since a reply had to be sent to Rosso, it was drafted in the same generalities that had characterized the first instructions.

The sudden slowdown does not appear to have been related to the desire to consult with the Germans on this specific point during the Fascist Foreign Minister's visit to Germany, since neither Ciano's diary nor the minutes of his colloquy with Hitler indicate that the subject was mentioned.[89]

[86] Ciano to Rosso, telegram, July 5, 1940, *ibid.*, Doc. 187.
[87] Ciano, *Diario*, I, p. 290.
[88] *Ibid.*, p. 291.
[89] The minutes drafted by Ciano contain only one passage referring to the Soviet Union: "It should be noted that, while he avoided speaking of Russia in any detail, Hitler nevertheless lost no opportunity to reveal his distrust of that country. And

What can be said at this point about the way Ciano replied to the accurate information and observations provided by his Ambassador and to the latter's fervent pleas? No word of explanation, not a shred of information either general or specific—this was Ciano's usual method of dealing with the departments of the Ministry and with all of the legations abroad, and the results are familiar to everyone.

It is likely that there would have been no change in the Fascist position for a considerable time if the urgency of re-establishing normal trade relations with the Soviet Union had not introduced a new element into the issue, forcing Ciano to turn to Moscow with his telegram of July 23, which read as follows:

The Soviet Ambassador here told Senator Giannini that his government is in accord with the idea of re-establishing trade relations with Italy but desires that the negotiations take place in Moscow and that the new agreements be established on a different basis from those which expired December 30 last.

Not having received instructions on the point, the Soviet Ambassador was unable to specify what this new basis might be.

For the purpose of evaluating the advisability of undertaking new negotiations in terms of the practical utility they might offer, it is important that we have a reasonably accurate idea of the bases which the Soviet Union intends to establish for the new accord.

Therefore, I would appreciate Your Excellency's raising this matter with the Soviet authorities and reporting.[90]

Given the German experiences in this area the year before—experiences which were well known to Rome—given the fact that Molotov was ignoring certain overtures and that the Rumanian crisis was fully developed, it required a certain amount of impudence to take such an approach, which, among other things, implied the reopening of political conversations which

---

Von Ribbentrop seconded this." Ciano, note, July 7, 1940, I.D., 9th series, V, Doc. 200. From the German minutes it appears that, in order to prevent the Italians from attacking Yugoslavia, Hitler used the argument of the danger of a Soviet intervention in the Balkans aimed at reaching Bulgaria and the Turkish Straits, and added that "England and Russia, under the influence of these events, would discover a community of interests." Schmidt memorandum, July 8, 1940, G.D., Series D, X, Doc. 129. It should be recalled that some days earlier Hitler had told Ambassador Alfieri that Great Britain had not abandoned the idea of drawing the Soviet Union into its camp. Alfieri to Ciano, report, July 1, 1940, I.D., 9th series, V, Doc. 161; however, cf. Schmidt memorandum, July 1, 1940, G.D., Series D, X, Doc. 73, where the reference to the U.S.S.R. is less emphatic.

[90] Ciano to Rosso, telegram, July 23, 1940, I.D., 9th series, V, Doc. 285. The Giannini-Gorelkin conversation, according to the above note of August 4, 1940, occurred on July 18, but a preliminary encounter took place earlier. Cf. Ciano to Rosso, telegram, July 12, 1940, ibid., Doc. 230.

Palazzo Chigi just a short time before had decided to forego. Rosso did not fail to point this out the next day in his telegram to Rome:

Before trying to implement the instructions in your telegram No. 99, I believe it to be my duty to point out the following:

Even without questioning the Soviet authorities, one can predict with almost absolute certainty that the "different basis" required for the trade negotiations as mentioned, but not defined, by the Soviet Ambassador will be of a political rather than of a technical nature.

This embassy has repeatedly noted that every commercial accord entered into by the government of the U.S.S.R. is always subordinated to certain political conditions. In this context, I recall the well-known "political premises" which Molotov repeatedly insisted on with Von Schulenburg during the preliminary phases of the Nazi-Soviet negotiations in the summer of 1939 and which later appeared in the accord for political collaboration, an almost simultaneous concomitant of the trade pact.

It is clear to me that this government is seeking to employ a similar approach in dealing with us. Therefore, I am convinced that any request for clarification regarding the new bases for a trade agreement which I may make to the Soviets will be answered by reference to the need to clarify the political situation first. Moreover, since Molotov in his colloquy with me on June 25 made some important declarations which implied the Soviet desire to confer with us with a view to arriving at an accord on the Danubian-Balkan and the Black Sea issues, it is not illogical to assume that he will insist upon knowing the Italian point of view and intentions on these matters.

I thought it necessary to raise the prospect of this eventuality because the instructions given me in your telegram No. 99 will in all likelihood have the effect of prompting the reopening of the conversation along political lines which, according to the directives contained in your telegram No. 75, Your Excellency has considered opportune to abandon for the moment.

I would appreciate knowing whether, notwithstanding the above, I am to request clarification regarding the trade negotiations. If your reply is in the affirmative, I beg you to telegraph your instructions as to how you wish me to reply to the likely insistence of the Soviets that the "political premises" be clarified first.[91]

Ciano promptly replied curtly, "Carry out instructions contained in my telegram No. 99."[92] The directive from the Fascist Foreign Minister arrived in Moscow after Rosso had been called to confer with the Commissar for Foreign Trade, Mikoyan. On July 27 Rosso sent the following summary report of these conversations to Rome:

This morning I was invited to meet with Mikoyan at the Commissariat for Foreign Trade. By way of introduction, he recapitulated the essentials of the preliminary conversations in Rome between Gorelkin and Giannini regarding a

---

[91] Rosso to Ciano, telegram, July 24, 1940, *ibid.*, Doc. 298.

[92] Ciano to Rosso, telegram, July 27, 1940, *ibid.*, Doc. 272, note 4. In a marginal note Rosso observed, "This is a reply that does not meet my needs!"

trade agreement and noted that the Soviet government had already stated that it was ready to negotiate with the Italian government and that the latter, in turn, had agreed to negotiate in Moscow. He then mentioned the declarations made by the Soviet Foreign Minister regarding the "new bases" and Giannini's questions concerning the nature of the latter. He made it clear that he called me to his office specifically to answer this question.

Mikoyan informed me that the Soviet government saw the possibility of great growth in Italo-Soviet trade. However, this possibility depended on "a complete clarification of the political relations between the two countries." At this point, he asked me for my thoughts on the subject. I replied that my recent conversations with President Molotov and those between Gorelkin and Ciano had touched upon the political situation and had already produced further clarification.

Mikoyan repeated that in order to give the Italo-Soviet exchanges the desired scope, a "complete" clarification was necessary together with a "political accord" such as had taken place last year between the U.S.S.R. and Germany. In turn, I replied that I would refer his statement to my government.

Before terminating the conversation, the Commissar asked me whether I could tell him what products the Italian government was seeking to obtain. I replied that I was not in a position to specify but that I supposed, in the main, Italy would be interested in the products imported from the Soviet Union during the life of the commercial accords of February, 1939, principally fuel oil. I then asked whether, in the light of the various agreements concluded recently by the U.S.S.R. with other countries, this product was still available. The commissar replied that the Soviet resources were very great and that "in the event of need, fuel oil could be found also for Italy."

My predictions were, therefore, well founded because the Soviet government has now formally made it clear that it intends to insist upon a political agreement as a condition for a trade pact.

I call attention to the fact that Mikoyan is an influential member of the Politburo. His statements made today were obviously designed to inform us not only of the views of the competent technical staffs but also of the position taken by the entire government.[93]

Aside from the obvious fact that Rosso was forced to begin his discussion with the Commissar for Foreign Trade without proper briefing, the Italian Ambassador's predictions had come true: the Fascist government was again faced with the problem of its relations with the U.S.S.R., while the pressure from Moscow was increasing. Further pressure on the Fascist government to take a positive decision was evident in Rosso's telegram of July 30 and in Molotov's speech to the Supreme Soviet on August 1.

In his telegram Rosso included his observation that it was clear that the Soviet Union desired to participate in consultations and decisions concerning the Danubian-Balkan area. The German Ambassador to Moscow was personally of the opinion that it would be good policy for Germany

[93] Rosso to Ciano, telegram, July 27, 1940, *ibid.*, Doc. 317.

and Italy to accept the Soviet overtures for collaboration of the three powers in examining the problems of southeastern Europe. Von Schulenburg believed that it would be easier to control and moderate Soviet aspirations through a policy of cooperation than to ignore or reject its proposals for an accord. The Italian Ambassador was in agreement with this view, particularly as it concerned the Straits Question, because he was convinced that the Soviets would seek to resolve that question at the first favorable opportunity.[94]

In his speech, Molotov stated: "It should also be noted that our relations with Italy have lately improved. An exchange of views with Italy has revealed that there is every possibility for our countries to ensure mutual understanding in the sphere of foreign policy. There is also every reason to expect an extension of our trade relations."[95]

Count Ciano finally decided to discuss the question with Mussolini and prepared a memorandum on the matter after having outlined the chronological development of the principal exchanges of views between Moscow and Rome. He concluded as follows:

For each of the points indicated above I note the following:
Danube-Balkan countries: Since the time of the Molotov-Rosso conversations the U.S.S.R. has annexed Bessarabia and northern Bukowina. Germany and Italy have demonstrated by their behavior the greatest comprehension of the Soviet action. They have not raised objections. Indeed, they have applied a certain pressure on Rumania. The renewal of relations with the Soviets has, therefore, already produced the desired results at least insofar as the Russians are concerned.
On the other hand, the basic policy lines of the Soviet Union as furnished to us by Molotov with regard to Hungary, Bulgaria, and Rumania generally agree with those of the Axis.
Turkey: We can also say to the Soviets that insofar as Turkey is concerned Italy has no aggressive designs toward her, that Ankara's policy also appears to us to be anything but clear, and that we are aware of the Soviet dissatisfaction and suspicions vis-à-vis the Turks.
The Mediterranean and the Black Sea: On this question, too, I can see no reason for objecting to a general declaration to the U.S.S.R. that Italy will keep in mind the interests of the Soviet Union as the principal power in the Black Sea. Nevertheless, we could ask for further clarification of the precise meaning of this statement. Where, in response to this request, the U.S.S.R. notes that it intends to reserve, as it seems logical to assume, *the right to demand and obtain a return to the demilitarization of the Straits, we can encourage her in these aims.*

[94] Rosso to Ciano, telegram, July 30, 1940, *ibid.*, Doc. 324.
[95] For the text of the speech see Degras, *Soviet Documents on Foreign Policy*, III, pp. 461–69. See also Rosso to Ciano, telegram, August 2, 1940, I.D., 9th series, V, Doc. 343.

Yugoslavia: Molotov did not mention Yugoslav-Soviet relations. Rosso also remains silent on the matter. It could be of interest to ascertain the Soviet position on the question.

Given the status of German-Soviet relations, it can be assumed that similar communications have also been made to that government, or, in any event, it may be assumed that Berlin is informed of them. For this reason, before replying to Molotov, *it might be opportune to speak of the matter to the German government for the purpose of establishing a common policy for the Axis.*[96]

Ciano's memorandum, like similar earlier documents, may be examined both from a general and a specific point of view. As to the former, one notes his persistence in considering problems within a restricted framework, without a detailed and complete study of their interconnection. Insofar as the specifics were concerned, the Fascist Foreign Minister's observations were based on a certain prudence and a sense of being well-disposed toward the Soviets.[97] In contrast to the instructions sent by Mussolini to Rosso on June 16, they were not prompted by an impulse for complete autonomy of action in the political sense. Instead, in this case the motivating factor was economic, and the conclusions reached in this memorandum were based on respect for the obligation to consult with the Axis partner. The Ciano memorandum was discussed at Palazzo Venezia on August 4, and the Fascist Chief of State, without making any further clarification of the fundamental objectives to be pursued or the reasons for his decision, expressed the general opinion that the "time had come to take further steps toward an amelioration of Italo-Soviet relations." Ciano expressed his agreement.[98] Two days later Mussolini returned again to the subject, indicating his desire for a rapid realization of a major accord with the U.S.S.R. He also referred to a possible journey to Moscow by Ciano. Ciano did not appear to be entirely convinced by Mussolini's approach, but, in any case, he decided to discuss the matter with Von Mackensen, with whom he conferred on August 6. On that occasion, the Italian Foreign Minister allowed the German Ambassador to read the memorandum prepared by him on August 4 for discussion with Mussolini, and Von Mackensen transmitted the text to Berlin almost verbatim, putting the German government in the position of knowing the precise extent of the

[96] Ciano to Mussolini, memorandum, August 4, 1940, *ibid.*, Doc. 356. The italics appear in the original.

[97] It should be noted how the reference to Bessarabia's demonstration of comprehension for the Soviet action confirms the persistent Italian ignorance of the obligations the Germans had assumed in the secret protocol of August 23, 1939.

[98] Ciano, *Diario*, I, p. 297. A week earlier Mussolini had ordered that certain anti-Soviet phrases appearing in the minutes of the meeting with the Rumanian Chief of State, Gigurtu, be eliminated because they might have displeased the Germans.

Italian contacts with the Soviets up to that moment and Rome's ideas
regarding possible development of these negotiations.[99] At the same time,
Ciano instructed Ambassador Alfieri to inform the Wilhelmstrasse that
Von Mackensen would be transmitting the summary text of the Italian
views[100] and telegraphed Rosso that a study was being conducted of the
questions raised by his conversations with the Soviets and that he, Ciano,
would communicate with him further on the matter.[101] Von Ribbentrop's
first reaction, while not committing German policy, appeared to be rather
favorable, to the extent that, on the following day, the Italian Ambassador
telegraphed as follows: "Von Ribbentrop appeared to be very pleased by
the brief summary of the Italian attitude toward the Soviet Union which
I gave him in Your Excellency's name, and he indicated his great interest
in seeing the report which Von Mackensen will transmit."[102]

The difficult course taken by the Rumanian crisis, however, introduced
additional negative elements into this question of relations with the
Soviets. On August 16 the Reich Foreign Minister telegraphed the following definitive reply to Von Mackensen:

Please call on Count Ciano and convey to him the following: It is not quite
clear from Count Ciano's remarks in what direction he would like to reshape
Italy's relationship to Russia. We infer from Ciano's remarks that what he has
in mind is merely a diplomatic exchange of views aiming at a closer friendly
relationship between the two countries, and not any concrete agreements. On
the points brought up by Count Ciano, I would say the following:

1. Any additional improvement in the relations between Italy and Russia
would naturally be welcomed by us from a standpoint of our general policy.

2. Balkans. Now that the Axis has intervened here to the extent of getting
Hungary, Bulgaria and Rumania to start on the path of negotiations, it seems
to me not in our interest at present to bring the Russians into this question in
any form whatsoever. If there were any assurance that Russia's participation
would lead to a further easing of the situation in these areas, there would perhaps be no objection to it. But it seems to us that the course of events (Bessarabia, Dobruja) and the actual state of affairs (Communist agitation in
Bulgaria) do not indicate that this is so. Rather, it seems evident that any further Russian participation not only would not make agreement easier among
these three countries, but on the contrary would make it more difficult because
these countries would try to pit one great power against another. Such an
intervention would tend to inject into the question of purely territorial revision
the factor of ideology, with obvious consequences.

3. As regards the question of Turkey and the Straits, during Ambassador

---

[99] Von Mackensen to Von Ribbentrop, telegram, August 6, 1940, *G.D.*, Series D,
X, Doc. 290. See also Ciano, *Diario*, I, p. 297.

[100] Cf. Alfieri to Ciano, telegram, August 7, 1940, *I.D.*, 9th series, V, Doc. 369.

[101] Ciano to Rosso, telegram, August 6, 1940, *ibid.*, Doc. 367.

[102] Alfieri to Ciano, telegram, August 7, 1940, *ibid.*, Doc. 367.

Von Papen's recent visit, upon mature consideration we reached the conclusion that at this time it would be to the interest of the Axis to keep matters there in as fluid a state as possible. In any event, we have no interest at this time—and this may be even more true for Italy—in getting the Turks and the Russians together. I would in this connection recall M. Saracoglu's diligent efforts in Moscow some time ago and later in Ankara to have Turkey mediate between Russia and England. I should, therefore, recommend that this question not be pursued too far in the forthcoming conversations with the Russians.

4. As regards the question of Russia-Yugoslavia, I believe that in the course of the conversations it would be of interest to ascertain something definite about the real state of their relations.

In conclusion, I would say with respect to Ciano's remarks about the political questions in the last paragraph of your telegram No. 1461, that save for the qualifications outlined above they are in full accord with my own views.[103]

Aside from the rather unfortunate choice of words in formulating the German view,[104] the arguments raised by the Wilhelmstrasse for denying approval of an Italo-Soviet accord appeared to be motivated by serious suspicions of Moscow's intentions and a determination to maintain German control over Axis policy. These arguments were not entirely convincing. In effect, Berlin, contrary to the opinion expressed by Von Schulenburg to Rosso, feared even greater difficulties in the event that the U.S.S.R. were permitted to intervene in bringing the Rumanian crisis under control, but it was illusory to think that the Soviet Union, simply because she was not invited to participate in a three-power understanding which she had proposed, would suddenly abandon her policy of protecting her interests in the Balkans. On the contrary, and what was much more likely, the acts of a Soviet Union not bound by any obligations would be considerably more difficult to control. Undoubtedly, the Wehrmacht's recent smashing victories had created the conviction in Berlin that it would be possible to impose German solutions to problems wherever and whenever desired, but events soon established the limits and the price of such power. In August, 1939, Hitler was disposed to pay for Soviet col-

[103] Von Ribbentrop to Von Mackensen, telegram, August 16, 1940, G.D., Series D, X, Doc. 348.

[104] The section concerning the Straits appears to be somewhat confused, although there is no mistaking the sense of the statement. Regarding the policy to be maintained toward Turkey, Von Papen, some fifteen days earlier, conferred with Hitler and Von Ribbentrop and was determined to "keep the situation between Russia and Turkey fluid, at least to conduct our policy in such a way that Turkey could not in any event become the connecting link between England and Russia." In the event that it became necessary "to be more receptive to Russian desires for a change in the Straits statute so as to prevent the English from constructing the projected triangle in this way, it was decided that in this question, too, we should first await the outcome of the coming weeks in regard to England." Von Papen to Von Weizsäcker, personal letter, August 1, 1940, ibid., Doc. 272.

laboration even to the extent of granting the latter a free hand in the matter of the Straits and southeastern Europe, but this state of mind was profoundly changed under the Arch of Triumph in Paris and in the summer of 1940. Annoyed by Moscow's punctual demand for payment of the promissory notes issued by Berlin a year earlier—with Bessarabia and northern Bukowina as interest—Germany appeared to be ready to maintain good relations with the Soviet Union, but with the understanding that she not demand any further concessions in Europe. This frame of mind was evidently responsible for inducing Von Ribbentrop to ignore his ally's viewpoint. He did confess that he had not completely understood him, but this fact should have prompted him to ask Ciano for further explanation before taking a definitive position.

Finally, it is worth noting that on this occasion the Nazi Foreign Minister expressed for the first time a notion which he was to repeat in the future: he thought it possible for Italy to develop a rapprochement with the Soviet Union without concluding new formal accords and without replying in detail to the questions Molotov had raised with Rosso.

Berlin's veto, undoubtedly made easier by the surfacing, at this same time, of dangerous Italian projects for attacks against Yugoslavia and Greece—also disapproved by Germany and justly so—was communicated personally by Von Ribbentrop to Ambassador Alfieri during the evening of August 16. The Nazi Foreign Minister read the reply sent to Rome via Von Mackensen, dwelling particularly on the attitude to be maintained toward Turkey and emphasizing the danger that once an agreement was reached between Ankara and Moscow the Turkish government could then act as intermediary between London and Moscow. At the same time, Von Ribbentrop reiterated Germany's complete opposition to an attack against Yugoslavia and Greece.[105]

---

[105] Schmidt, memorandum, August 17, 1940, *ibid.*, Doc. 353; Alfieri to Ciano, telegram, August 17, 1940, in *I.D.*, 9th series, V, Doc. 431. The Italian Ambassador, in transmitting the opinion expressed by Von Ribbentrop, concluded that "insofar as Russia is concerned, it is necessary to do everything possible to contain her and to avoid aiding her, through closer political accords with Italy or actions which will rebound to her favor, in her search to realize her expansionist ambitions. Particularly as it concerns the Dardanelles, the problem is extremely delicate and of major importance."

Despite the fact that both the Italian and the German documents carry the August 17 date and that this date is repeated by Simoni (*Berlino: ambasciata d'Italia*, p. 152) and by Von Rintelen (*Mussolini als Bundesgenosse* [Tübingen, 1951], p. 107), the colloquy took place on August 16. This is supported by the fact that Alfieri's telegram was dispatched at 2:20 A.M. on August 17, that during the course of the conversation Von Ribbentrop referred to the telegram to Von Mackensen as

On the following day, therefore, when Von Mackensen transmitted Berlin's reply to Ciano, the Italian Foreign Minister was already aware of the position of the German government and had discussed it with Mussolini. Ciano stated that "he had in mind only an improvement of relations of a very general basis, without envisioning any concrete agreements. He unreservedly concurred in the views as to the consequences of any active Russian participation in Balkan questions," and, of course, he assured Von Mackensen that, for the moment, no action would be taken against Yugoslavia and Greece.[106]

The double German veto—against a military adventure in the Balkans and against a political accord with the U.S.S.R.—was accepted by Rome without protest. Mussolini himself promptly dictated the Italian reply,[107] and the pertinent portion of his message reads as follows: "We take note of Ribbentrop's observations and agree with him that the struggle against Great Britain is at the root of all political arrangements. Inform him that insofar as Russia is concerned, we will make no accords, but we will improve our relations in the general sense, for the purpose also of preventing a decision by the Soviet Union to modify its position toward England."[108]

The Duce promptly cast aside the opportunity afforded him to discuss in detail with Berlin the problem of the Axis relations with the U.S.S.R.; he promised not to conclude any accords with the U.S.S.R. but stated, nevertheless, that he planned to embark on a course intended to improve Italo-Soviet relations. How it would be possible to reconcile the two positions, particularly in view of the precise invitations advanced by Molotov, only Von Ribbentrop, who initiated the idea, could have said. In any case, in order to avoid any mistakes, it was decided in Rome that Rosso need not be informed of Von Ribbentrop's communication or Mussolini's reply,

---

"sent shortly before," and that on August 17 Mussolini and Ciano had already discussed Alfieri's telegram.

It may also be of interest to note that I have been informed by the former Undersecretary for Foreign Affairs of Yugoslavia, Jukic, that the Germans at the same time informed Belgrade that they had saved Yugoslavia from Mussolini's ambitions. This information was given to Yugoslavia through three separate channels: a member of Goering's entourage mentioned it to the Yugoslav Minister to Berlin; a German journalist close to the German Legation in Belgrade informed Jukic; and, finally, the head of the German economic delegation for debt settlement mentioned the information to his Yugoslav counterpart.

[106] Von Mackensen to Von Ribbentrop, telegram, August 17, 1940, *G.D.*, Series D, X, Doc. 357.

[107] Ciano, *Diario*, I, p. 300.

[108] Ciano to Alfieri, telegram, August 17, 1940, *I.D.*, 9th series, V, Doc. 435; see also *G.D.*, Series D, X, Doc. 353, enclosure 1.

and thus, once again, the political negotiations with Moscow were brought
to a halt. Of course, this stalemate implied renouncing, or at least gravely
compromising the renewal of trade relations, which was the basis of
Ciano's original note. Von Ribbentrop's suggestion (which was prompted
by Ciano's comments on August 4) that Italy should sound out the Soviets
on their intentions regarding Yugoslavia, a fact which should have been
of primary interest to Rome, was thereby also ignored. But this failure to
sound out Moscow on its attitude toward Belgrade was, perhaps, inevitable, given the limitations imposed by Berlin upon Mussolini's aggressive designs toward Yugoslavia. Thus, in a peculiar and unique way, and
without ever having clarified the ramifications of the problems raised, the
first phase of the Italo-Soviet conversations of 1940 came to a close.

4

The preparatory negotiations leading to the Arbitrage of Vienna
(which, as has been pointed out, constituted the starting point of the
Nazi-Soviet conflict) offered Ciano the opportunity to learn at first hand
the extent of the change in attitude toward Moscow among the Nazi
leaders. On August 29 he telegraphed to Mussolini: "I must emphasize that Hitler's as well as Von Ribbentrop's speeches reveal a marked
suspicion of Russia, which is supposedly ready to exploit to the maximum
any eventual complications, driving, with the complicity of Bulgaria and
Yugoslavia 'clear to the Straits, to the Aegean, and even to the Adriatic.' "[109] At this point Ciano did not see any real need to join with Hitler
and Von Ribbentrop in a detailed examination of the general problem of
Axis relations with the U.S.S.R. and to resolve it in one way or the other
before evaluating the particulars of the Hungarian-Rumanian controversy,
also of keen interest to the Soviets.

With all of this information available, and in spite of the arrival of a
telegram from the Italian Embassy in Moscow noting the worsening of

[109] Ciano to Mussolini, telegram, August 29, 1940, *I.D.*, 9th series, V, Doc. 516.
According to the German minutes, Hitler stated: "If the conflict started in the
Balkans, it was entirely possible that Russia would likewise attempt to intervene. It
was not known where the Russians would establish the boundary lines of their interests. They would in any case advance as far as circumstances permitted. In this
connection it was immaterial what the Russian political leaders said at the moment
about the boundaries of their interests. As soon as the guns sounded and the armies
were on the march all this would be meaningless and their previous statements (for
instance, that Russia's interest went only up to Moldavia) would be scrapped by
the triumphal march of the armies." Schmidt, memorandum, August 28, 1940, *G.D.*,
Series D, X, Doc. 407.

Italo-Soviet relations,[110] the Fascist Foreign Minister sent the following instructions to Rosso very early on the morning of September 3:

The German Ambassador to Moscow has been instructed by his government to inform Molotov of the Vienna Arbitrage, emphasizing that Russia should also be gratified by the steps taken to promote peace. Without making a special issue of it, find the occasion to express similar ideas to Molotov, emphasizing particularly the common interest of all of the Great Powers, Russia included, in maintaining peace in the Balkans. The equitable normalization of Hungarian-Bulgarian-Rumanian relations, in addition to resolving a dangerous local situation, cannot help but contribute to an overall clarification of the general political atmosphere. Reply via telegraph.[111]

Once again the Italian Foreign Minister had placed his Ambassador to Moscow in an extremely difficult position. Hoping to modify the situation to some extent, Rosso wrote to Anfuso on September 3 as follows:

Last night I telegraphed to indicate to the Ministry the nature of the situation being created by our relations with the U.S.S.R. Perhaps, we cannot yet speak of "tension." However, it is clear that the Soviets are extremely dissatisfied with us, and this dissatisfaction is revealed each day in various ways which I have described in my telegraphic comment of last evening.

This morning I received telegram No. 144, in which the Minister instructs me to describe the Vienna Arbitrage to Molotov but without "using it as a real and concrete step forward."

I am taking advantage of the fact that the courier leaves tonight to write to

[110] Rosso to Ciano, telegram, September 3, 1940, I.D., 9th series, V, Doc. 534. The Italian Ambassador said:

I believe it to be my duty to report that recently the Soviet officials have assumed a rather unfriendly attitude toward us, in contrast to a very courteous one of a few weeks ago. In matters of transit or normal visas, in matters of customs duties, and generally in all administrative and protocol matters they show illwill, with the obvious intent of creating difficulties and being obstructive. The most recent example has been the categorical request for the immediate departure of the Royal Consuls Mammalella, d'Acunzo, and Luciolli, who arrived last night from Tokyo and who had hoped to stop over for a few days of rest. This demand was made despite the fact that their transit visas do not expire for another week.

I must add that in the press I have begun to note a number of articles written in a hostile vein, which may possibly portend the beginning of an anti-Italian press campaign.

The coincidence of these various developments leaves no doubt that they are inspired by directives from the top, based on the dissatisfaction of the Soviet leadership, which may, in turn, be explained by the failure of the Italians to reply to Molotov's entreaties.

I have mentioned the situation as it appears today (which could also worsen) in order that Your Excellency might have this information available during the examination of the question as referred to in your telegram No. 123 of August 7, 1940.

[111] Ciano to Rosso, telegram, September 2, 1940, ibid., Doc. 530.

you now in order to give you my thoughts on the situation. It will be up to you to decide whether these personal views of mine are worthy of being brought to the Minister's attention.

Let me say in advance that, at the time that Molotov assumed the post of Commissar for Foreign Affairs, he made it officially known to all of the foreign legations that the heads of missions could request to see him only if they had some important political problem to discuss with him. Otherwise, they were directed to see one of the vice commissars or the office of the commissariat. This should give you some idea of the difficulty I face in finding an occasion or a pretext for a colloquy with the President of the Council of Peoples' Commissars unless, of course, I go to see him to speak of important matters.

However, aside from this difficulty of a technical nature, I still remain faced with the fact that for over two months we have owed Molotov an answer, expressly requested by him, to questions which we have ignored.

I recapitulate the events:

On June 13, upon my return to Moscow after an absence of five months, I call on Molotov, I have a very academic conversation with him, and I note his expression of marked annoyance with my reticence.

On June 16 the Duce's telegram arrives which states that "in Italo-Soviet relations we can go *much farther* politically." My instructions are to get Molotov to talk, to propose an exchange of views "particularly as they concern the Danubian-Balkan Basin," and to assure him that the Fascist government is motivated by the best of intentions.

On June 20 I see Molotov, who accepts my communication with profound satisfaction and makes some interesting preliminary statements.

On June 25 Molotov invites me to the Kremlin and hands me a document which he discusses in detail and in which the general lines of Soviet policy regarding the Danubian-Balkan Basin are outlined. In effect, Molotov proposes to both the Germans and to us to consult together and to arrive at an accord for a common policy vis-à-vis Rumania, Hungary, Bulgaria, and Turkey. He expresses his hope and his conviction that the Italian government will promptly inform him of its view of the Soviet proposals.

On July 3 I request instructions on the subject, and the Minister, on July 5, directs me to abandon the talks.

On July 25 I receive instructions to question the Soviet government regarding the possibility of negotiating and concluding a trade agreement.

On July 27 the Commissar for Foreign Trade, Mikoyan, pointedly informs me that it will not be possible to arrange trade agreements until the political situation is clarified between the two countries. In other words, he is requesting a reply to Molotov's proposals.

On August 7 a telegram from the Minister informs me that the question is being studied, that the Germans are being consulted, and that in good time I will be given further information on the subject.

After that I received nothing. In going to Molotov to speak of the Vienna Arbitrage, I face the absolute certainty of his asking about a reply to his request of June 25. What can I say to him? And since I will not be able to say anything to him, do you think it wise for me to furnish him with the opportunity to launch into recriminations which—in all honesty—we must recognize as well founded?

I am raising this question with you not because I seek to avoid having a difficult and embarrassing conversation but, rather, because such a step could worsen a situation which is *giving evidence of becoming fairly serious.*

The discourtesies shown us, the difficulties raised, and the minor frustrations caused by the Soviet government departments in the past several weeks are a very clear symptom of their political dissatisfaction. This change in attitude toward us became evident after Molotov's speech of August 1, when the President of the Council spoke optimistically of relations with Italy. Obviously, at the time, he wished once again to encourage us to accept the proposals of collaboration made to us on June 25.

Since we have never replied to their repeated direct and indirect invitations, the Kremlin leaders must have drawn the conclusion that Rome does not want to collaborate with Moscow, and they have begun to show their dissatisfaction with us. This is the situation as it exists today.

Since I remain completely in the dark as to the plans considered at higher levels in Rome, I can only venture some hypotheses regarding the future.

Personally, I have always felt that a political accord with the U.S.S.R. could have some advantages for us, be it in providing a vehicle by which we might control and eventually temper and limit the expansionist Soviet drives, or be it in providing a means by which we might be able to take advantage of the present Soviet anti-Turkish attitude.

However, I am clearly aware that from my Moscow observatory I can only see a portion of our foreign policy problems. I also recognize that there is a certain danger in accepting a Soviet presence in the Balkans.

Obviously, it is a question of weighing the pros and cons of the collaboration offered.

Nevertheless, I wish to call your serious attention to this point. If our decision is to be affirmative, *it will be necessary to lose no time* because situations change rapidly, and it could be that further delay in replying to Molotov's offer might also mean that we will not find the Kremlin to be as well disposed toward us as it was two months ago. (Nor would I exclude, among other things, the possibility that these gentlemen may make some overtures to the Turks and work in Belgrade and perhaps in Sofia in an anti-Italian spirit.)

I believe that my English colleague, Cripps, is watching for every opportunity to create splits between the U.S.S.R. and the Axis.

If, on the other hand, we are determined to refuse the offer of collaboration we must be prepared for a new crisis in Italo-Soviet relations, a worsening which, given the suspicious and vindictive nature of these leaders, could lead to a complete break in relations.

In other words, I have the sensation here that, after the hopes raised by our initiative of June 25, the Soviet government is inclined to go from one extreme to another.

I wished to tell you this more clearly than would have been possible in my telegram dispatched yesterday in order that you could have in your possession all of the factors necessary for an examination of the situation and to arrive at a decision which will be judged to be in our best interests.

Regarding the instructions received this morning concerning the Vienna Arbitrage, I inform you that I was not able to see my German colleague because he has been out of the city since yesterday. I learned, however, that he did see Molotov, that he informed Molotov of the instructions received from Berlin, and *that Molotov's reaction was extremely unfavorable*. Molotov is said to have accused Germany of having violated the pact of friendship of last September for not having consulted the U.S.S.R. on the solution of the Rumanian-Hungarian question.

I hope to be able to see Von Schulenburg tomorrow, and I will telegraph detailed information on the matter. As of this moment I believe I can tell you that any general argument by me to Molotov that the U.S.S.R. should be pleased by the normalization of Hungarian-Bulgarian-Rumanian relations as arranged by the two Axis powers (after the U.S.S.R. had *requested and had not obtained* the right to participate in formulating this solution) is now completely useless and will do nothing more than produce results contrary to those desired.

I could see some usefulness in such a step *only if we desired to reopen the conversations of last June*. But in order to do this I would have to have instructions regarding the reply I should give to the proposals made to me by Molotov, at least those regarding Turkey and the Black Sea if nothing else.

In conclusion, our relations with the U.S.S.R. (and indirectly, perhaps, those between Germany and the U.S.S.R. as well) are at a critical stage and should be given the most serious attention because on the decisions which we take could depend, in one sense or another, the future attitude of the U.S.S.R. toward Axis policy.

I have jotted down my ideas hurriedly here because the courier is leaving in a few hours. I do not know whether I have made these as clear as they should be, but I hope that I have given you a rather precise idea of the situation here as I see it.

If you think it worth while, please have the Minister read my letter.[112]

In this exposition Rosso frankly calls Rome's attention to the seriousness of the situation developing between the U.S.S.R. and Italy as a result of the failure of Rome to reply to Molotov's repeated overtures. He warns of the unknown dangers inherent in the failure to come to an agreement with Moscow and expresses his personal opinion in favor of reaching an accord, or at least of negotiating with the aim of tempering Soviet expansionist tendencies. As he did in June, he concludes by urging, even more insistently now, that a decision be reached, but on this occasion, as in June, while demonstrating its importance, he does not particularly stress "the German aspect" of relations with the U.S.S.R., even though Molotov, in the June 26 conversations, explicitly mentioned a three-power agreement. Rosso was completely unaware of the German veto of the Italian attempt to negotiate, a matter for which Ciano bore the responsibility of not having advised him.

[112] Rosso to Anfuso, personal letter, September 3, 1940, *ibid.*, Doc. 537. The italics appear in the original.

On September 4, Rosso replied to Ciano's telegram as follows:

The German Ambassador here has informed me that he received instructions from his government on August 31 and that on the same day he informed Molotov of the Vienna Arbitrage.

Not only did Molotov fail to thank him for the information, but he expressed his resentment of the methods employed by the German government in the matter and openly accused the Germans of violating the obligations undertaken in the pact of friendship and consultation signed in September, 1939. On the basis of that agreement, Germany was obliged to consult with the U.S.S.R., for she could not ignore the fact that, in having a common frontier with Rumania, the U.S.S.R. was interested in the Rumanian problem, especially when it involved guaranteeing future frontiers. Molotov added that the Soviet government might be in agreement on the substance of the accord reached via the Italo-German Arbitrage, but that it had to protest the failure to be consulted.

Von Schulenburg referred the colloquy to Berlin, and yesterday he received instructions to transmit a further communication to Molotov, the text of which was also telegraphed. This communication tends to justify the German *modus operandi* and to spread oil on troubled waters, but, since it contains many inaccuracies, my colleague thought it his duty to call these to Berlin's attention before seeking a new meeting with Molotov. Moreover, the Ambassador regards the argument advanced by the Wilhelmstrasse, i.e., that the Soviet government had not made its intentions clear to Berlin regarding Bessarabia and northern Bukowina, as ill founded. Today, Von Schulenburg informed me for the first time that in reality, prior to presenting the ultimatum to Rumania, Molotov had informed him of the Soviet government's plans and had allowed him sufficient time to inform Berlin and to receive a reply.

In any event, Von Schulenburg proposed a number of modifications in the text of the communication to be presented to Molotov and is awaiting further instructions.

My German colleague's personal opinion is that in the case under consideration the German government was in fact obligated to consult with the U.S.S.R. and that, therefore, Berlin was at fault in not doing so, all the more because, in all likelihood, the Soviet government would not have raised any objections to the Italo-German Arbitrage and would have settled for the moral satisfaction of having been consulted.

As to the instructions given to me by Your Excellency, I would like to ask whether, given Molotov's known position on the matter, I too should give him the information he received from Von Schulenburg so unfavorably.

While it is true that, insofar as we are concerned, we are not obliged to consult, there does exist the Molotov overture of June 25 proposing that we collaborate on, among other things, the matter of the Hungarian claims against Rumania, to which we, to date, have not replied.

It is easily foreseeable that my communicating with Molotov as instructed would only provoke recriminations because of our failure to reply to his proposals, which, in the final analysis, were the product of our initiative.

In any event, I believe it would be opportune to await the results of Von Schulenburg's second communication to Molotov, which has not yet been made.

Finally, I believe it my duty to call Your Excellency's attention to the following considerations.

There is no doubt that Italo-German action to settle the territorial questions between Hungary, Bulgaria, and Rumania has provoked unfavorable reactions among the Soviet leaders, not because of the substance of the agreements reached (on which Russian acquiescence could have been expected, *a priori*, since Molotov himself told me that he regarded the Hungarian and Bulgarian claims as well founded) so much as because the Soviet Union had been kept entirely in the dark, despite the fact that she had expressed her desire to collaborate.

Therefore, it is more a matter of wounded pride. However, questions of pride can provoke serious reactions among the Kremlin leaders, and it is well to keep in mind that the English Ambassador in Moscow is looking for any opportunity which he can exploit to Great Britain's advantage.

Meanwhile, if in the present international situation Germany and Italy continue to attribute some importance to the Russian factor, it would be wise to act quickly to prevent possible unfavorable shifts in the Soviet attitude.

During the past three months the U.S.S.R. has repeatedly manifested its desire to reach agreement and to collaborate politically with Italy. We have replied with silence and reserve. For these reasons Italo-Soviet relations today are in a state of crisis. This has not yet reached a state of true tension, but the obvious dissatisfaction could easily degenerate into open hostility; in this event one cannot exclude an eventual English maneuver to arrange a Soviet-Turkish rapprochement and to press for anti-Italian diplomatic activity in the Balkans on the part of the Soviets.[113]

Apart from that portion of the dispatch which summarized the several considerations detailed in Rosso's personal letter to Anfuso, it is important to note an error in Rosso's evaluation—an error which, earlier, Von Schulenburg also made. Molotov's negative reactions to the Vienna Arbitrage were not so much due to a question of form or prestige as they were to a two-fold question of substance relative to the guarantee given to Rumania and to the failure to consult the U.S.S.R. The guarantee of Rumania's frontiers could be nothing else than anti-Soviet, and the failure to consult, violating explicit contractual obligations, was interpreted in Moscow as a possible prelude to German opposition to the realization of another important clause of the Russo-German accords which remained to be fulfilled, that concerning Finland. Therefore, the crisis in Soviet-German relations was much graver than Rosso believed it to be, and during the month of September it deepened even more for other reasons, such as the transit of German troops across Finland, the exclusion of the Soviet Union from the Conference of Vienna called by the International Commission for the Danube, and the conclusion of the Tripartite Pact. This time, however, Rosso's appeals created a deep impression in Rome.

[113] Rosso to Ciano, telegram, September 4, 1940, *ibid.*, Doc. 543.

Ciano, on September 10, abandoning his passive attitude, attacked the problem of Italo-Soviet relations with unusual energy in his talks with Von Mackensen. He made it clear that it was impossible to delay further a reply to Molotov's earlier overtures without risking a decisive worsening of relations with the U.S.S.R., which were already gravely compromised by the Vienna Arbitrage. After he had read to Von Mackensen Rosso's letter to Anfuso, Ciano declared that Mussolini fully concurred with Ambassador Rosso's concern and desired to reopen negotiations with the Soviets as soon as possible by sending an economic delegation, as had been proposed to Giannini by Gorelkin. Mussolini, he added, was fully aware of the reservations advanced by the German government, and he did not intend to do anything without prior consultation with Berlin, but he was asking that "due consideration be given to his grave apprehension that Russia's relations with the Axis powers might take a turn which, always assuming that the war with England continues, might make it look possible that Russia one day would drift away." Von Mackensen pointed out that during this time nothing had occurred to modify the negative view expressed by his government, and he emphasized that it would be inopportune to discuss with the Soviets such dangerous subjects as the Straits Question, but Ciano did not waver from his original position and insisted that the German government reply as soon as possible, "in perhaps two or three days."[114]

Undoubtedly, this position was prompted by a streak of independence rarely seen in Italy's dealings with her German ally. Although Ciano made repeated references to Mussolini's views on the subject, which left no doubt that the initiative in the matter stemmed from the Duce, the fact that Mussolini reaffirmed his intention of continuing the negotiations for an accord with the U.S.S.R.—Ciano had referred to the Duce's desire "to renew the Italian-Russian relations on the basis of the Treaty of Friendship of 1933"—was equivalent to stating that the objections raised by Berlin were inconsistent. This implication became even more evident as Ciano continued to insist on his thesis despite the fact that Von Mackensen pointedly repeated the principal reasons for Germany's opposition. Mussolini apparently did not want to discuss the question of whether Italy should or should not reopen the negotiations with Moscow but only to get an agreement on the method of conducting them.

Von Mackensen's assertion that in the meantime nothing had occurred to modify the German position was also inexact. A new development had taken place, and Mussolini himself had noted it as the principal justifica-

[114] Von Mackensen to Von Ribbentrop, telegram, September 10, 1940, *G.D.*, Series D, XI, Doc. 42.

tion for his decision: the now foreseeable extension of the war against Great Britain, which made a worsening of relations with Moscow dangerous in that it might lay the foundation for an Anglo-Russian rapprochement. This was a perfectly logical conclusion, but one which also demonstrated that Rome had not fully understood the gravity of the crisis then developing in Russo-German relations and that it was not aware of Hitler's increasing tendency to look to force as the basis of his policy toward the U.S.S.R.

As has been noted several times above, the Italian Foreign Minister had expressed Mussolini's thoughts: the Duce had taken a position with his usual vigor, but since he had indicated in the recent past that he rarely remained consistent in his actions, doubts were aroused regarding the firmness of this decision.

Berlin's reply was brought to Rome by Von Ribbentrop on the occasion of his visit of September 19–22, on the eve of the conclusion of the Tripartite Pact.[115] The German Foreign Minister was optimistic regarding the effects of the pact on relations with the Soviet Union: in his judgment it was unlikely that the latter would side with Great Britain and the United States because, being almost exclusively a land power, it could not expect to receive effective aid from these allies while at the same time it would expose itself to attack from Germany and Japan. Moreover, Stalin was a prudent statesman. He knew very well that the Red Army was weak and that it could easily be destroyed by the German forces. Turning to the subject of the Italo-Russian conversations, Von Ribbentrop made it clear that Germany had no aggressive intentions against the U.S.S.R. and that it intended to pursue a policy of friendship, but that "on account of the ideological difficulties with Russia" Hitler was determined to maintain a "clear delimitation of interests" and to prevent any "overlapping of respective interests.... For these reasons any Russian advance toward the Balkans and Constantinople appeared to Germany to be a very precarious matter. If Russia should also have a say in matters occurring beyond the Danube, there would, for example, be possible complications in Bulgaria, with its disordered domestic situation.... Also, with respect to the plans regarding Yugoslavia which Italy had for the future, meddling by Russia was undesirable because of the Pan-Slavic tendencies which bound the two countries." As for the Soviet tendency to advance toward the Straits, Von Ribbentrop repeated that a Moscow-Ankara accord was not in Axis interest; however, "the natural aversion of the Turks to having

[115] Von Ribbentrop was the bearer of a letter from Hitler to Mussolini. For the text, see *ibid.*, Doc. 68; I.D., 9th series, V, Doc. 602. However, relations with the Soviet Union were not mentioned in the letter.

Russia too near the Straits was a sufficient brake to prevent the relationship from becoming too close."

In turn, Mussolini—who, during Von Ribbentrop's exposition, had repeatedly indicated his approval—stated that he was convinced that the Soviets would not have reacted in any way to the signing of the Tripartite Pact:

For opportunistic reasons Italy had desired to pursue a policy of rapprochement toward Russia. A rapprochement with Russia had come about contrary to the innermost conviction of Italy, which has no love for Soviet Russia. He [the Duce] did not believe that Russia would undertake anything, if only because Stalin perhaps feared that in a conflict he would lose what he had already gained. Also he (the Duce) shared the Führer's view that a clearcut delimitation of interests between Russia and the Axis would have to be made. By the Japanese alliance they were in a certain sense building on the basis of the old anti-Comintern tendencies, which had in the meantime lain dormant. The pact would come as a bombshell.[116]

In effect, this exchange was based on two points of view. As far as the repercussions which the Tripartite Pact would have had on Kremlin policy were concerned, both speakers were in accord in believing that the Soviet Union would not react because she was faced with the practical impossibility of doing so. As for the second point, the future policy of the two Axis powers toward the U.S.S.R., in emphasizing the deterrent value of the Tripartite Pact, Von Ribbentrop was, in effect, responding to the concern expressed by Ciano on September 10 regarding a possible rapprochement between the Soviet Union and the Anglo-Saxon powers. To Mus-

---

[116] Schmidt, memorandum, September 20, 1940, *G.D.*, Series D, XI, Doc. 73. In the Italian minutes, Mussolini's statements relative to future relations with the Soviet Union are as follows: "There remains Russia. It is not important to seek to establish what the Russians will say: it is important to see what they will do. We may say even now that they will do nothing. In recent weeks Italy has made several references to the policy of rapprochement with the Soviet Union. The only reason for this action was to block the English maneuver of rapprochement with the U.S.S.R. In any event, the practical reaction of the Russians to the alliance will be nil because, today, the Russians are primarily preoccupied with holding on to what they have acquired." Ciano, minutes, September 19, 1940, *I.D.*, 9th series, V, Doc. 617. In the Italian minutes a certain difference of opinion between Mussolini and Von Ribbentrop as to the form of relations with the U.S.S.R. was much more in evidence. The German Foreign Minister declared himself in favor of a policy of friendship with Russia on condition that Moscow not seek to go beyond a clearly defined limit in the Balkans, while Mussolini viewed the rapprochement as a means of circumventing an Anglo-Russian understanding and said nothing about limiting the Russian sphere of interest in the Balkans. It should be noted that Mussolini's position on policy toward the Soviet Union as stated here did not justify the instructions sent to Rosso on June 16 to bring to life the pact of 1933 and to go "much beyond" in seeking rapprochement with the U.S.S.R., since, at that time, there was no danger of Moscow and London coming together.

solini's proposal that an agreement be sought with the Soviet Union, Von Ribbentrop suggested an attitude based on a position of strength. Contrary to every reasonable prediction, Mussolini listened without making any serious objection to this postulation of the problem, and, on this point too, the accord between the Axis members was realized. Thus the position assumed on September 10 by the Italian leaders was abandoned.

This unusually simplistic examination of the problem of Moscow's probable reaction to the Tripartite Pact was repeated again during the Brenner Pass meeting on October 4.[117] However, in a short time Rome and Berlin took another tack, dictated by diverse motives. Germany contemplated new accords with the U.S.S.R. designed to cause the latter to shift her attention from Europe to the Far East, while Italy thought in terms of an accord with Russia to strengthen her own position vis-à-vis the Germans.

The common point of departure for this evolution probably lay in the German military occupation of Rumania, which occurred early in October, 1940 (an occupation which Hitler failed to mention to Mussolini), and which aroused suspicion in Moscow[118] and profound resentment in Rome, to the point of provoking, as a reaction, the attack on Greece.[119] On October 13, that is, the day following the entrance of the Wehrmacht into Bucharest, Von Ribbentrop addressed a letter to Stalin to propose closer relations between the Soviet Union and the members of the Tripartite Pact and to invite Molotov to Berlin to discuss the matter.[120] Apparently Ambassador Alfieri was not informed of this step by the Germans,[121] while

[117] At the Brenner Pass Hitler, after stating that Great Britain continued to resist only because it hoped for aid from the United States and the Soviet Union, affirmed, "Insofar as Russia is concerned, it must be kept in mind that in Moscow calculations had been made on the course of the war which were entirely different from the realities. Undoubtedly Moscow has suspicions concerning the European situation, but the Führer does not believe that Stalin can take an initiative of any sort, particularly because Germany has already massed such forces on her eastern frontiers as to eliminate the possibility of the Bolshevists' attempting any foolhardy adventure." Ciano, minutes, October 4, 1940, *ibid.*, Doc. 677. Cf. Schmidt, memorandum, October 4, 1940, *G.D.*, Series D, XI, Doc. 149. There is no evidence that during Ciano's stay in Berlin for the signing of the Tripartite Pact the problem of relations with the U.S.S.R. was discussed. Schmidt, memorandum, September 29, 1940, *ibid.*, Doc. 124; Ciano, *Diario*, I, pp. 310–11.

[118] Von Tippelskirch to Von Ribbentrop, telegram, October 10, 1940, *G.D.*, Series D, XI, Doc. 170. See also Gafencu, *Preliminari*, p. 89.

[119] Ciano, *Diario*, I, pp. 313–14.

[120] Von Ribbentrop to Stalin, letter, October 13, 1940, *G.D.*, Series D, XI, Doc. 176. Stalin's affirmative reply is dated October 22, 1940. *Ibid.*, Doc. 211.

[121] Simoni (*Berlino: ambasciata d'Italia*, p. 175) asserts the opposite, but the Italian documents reveal no communication on this matter from the Embassy in Berlin. On the other hand, on October 28, when Hitler announced to Mussolini and

the information on the subject gathered by Rosso in Moscow was not very precise. The Italian Ambassador to Moscow telegraphed to Rome on October 16 as follows:

The German Ambassador returned to Moscow last evening from Berlin and told me that his instructions from Von Ribbentrop were to reassure the Soviet government that German policy toward the U.S.S.R. had not changed, nor was there any intention of abandoning the existing collaboration.

The German Ambassador will work primarily to eliminate suspicion caused by the German action in Rumania and to activate the economic accord. In the interest of the latter, Schnurre will soon return to Moscow.

Regarding navigation on the Danube, the Ambassador has received instructions to accept the Soviet proposal for the creation of a single commission comprising all of the riparian states on condition that the U.S.S.R. agrees to Italy's participation.

The Ambassador has promised to keep me informed on the outcome of his future colloquies with Molotov.[122]

Von Schulenburg's reticence was not lost on Rosso, who took the occasion to discuss the matter with Ciano in a personal letter on October 19:

I believe you should know—and it seems best to inform you by personal letter—that since his return from Berlin my German colleague, Von Schulenburg, appears to be more reticent and reserved with me than usual.

During this past week I have had occasion to see him a couple of times, but he has remained tight-lipped regarding any instructions he may have received from Von Ribbentrop, as well as the outcome of his first conversation with Molotov.

From the vague comments he made, I get the impression that the reason is that at the Wilhelmstrasse, in examining Von Mackensen's telegrams from Rome, he learned that certain things which he had reported to me in confidence here in Moscow—and which, of course, were telegraphed by me to Rome —were reported to his colleague in Rome, who then reported them to Berlin.

It may also be that in one or more of my telegrams which Von Mackensen was able to see there were comments or evaluations that were not particularly pleasing to Von Schulenburg and that, therefore, he was not happy about seeing them referred to Berlin.

My relations with my German colleague are excellent; I have never given him the slightest cause for doubt of my absolute loyalty and collaboration, and I hope, therefore, that this reticence is only a matter of temporary pique. Nevertheless, I believed it to be my duty to inform you of this.

Last week I wrote to Anfuso suggesting the usefulness—as I see it—of my

---

Ciano that within a short time Molotov would be going to Berlin, this communication was received "with evident surprise and great interest" by the Italians. Schmidt, memorandum, October 28, 1940, *G.D.*, Series D, XI, Doc. 246.

[122] Rosso to Ciano, telegram, October 16, 1940, *I.D.*, 9th series, V, Doc. 732.

taking a quick trip to Rome for the purposes of orientation. If you concur, I would be very pleased to be able to report orally to you regarding developments in this country.[123]

The lightness with which Ciano revealed to the Wilhelmstrasse the intimate rapport between Rosso and his German colleague deprived the Italian Embassy of a source of information which, particularly during the course of the Moscow talks in the summer of 1939, had proved to be extremely valuable.[124] The reasons, whatever they may have been, for the German Ambassador's dissatisfaction should have restricted only his personal confidential comments. Now it was worthy of note that notwithstanding the importance of Berlin's overture to the U.S.S.R., officially Von Schulenburg had been given no instructions to keep Rosso informed of the negotiations. Rosso's letter (especially as it referred to his Embassy's relations with Rome) is also interesting because of the fact that he again, justifiably, requested to be allowed to return to Rome to discuss the problem of Italo-Soviet relations. This attempt, too, proved to be fruitless. Nevertheless, in those days, unbeknownst to Hitler, the attack on Greece had been decided upon, and Mussolini had approved a Ciano-Gorelkin meeting to take place immediately after the beginning of military operations. The gesture, according to the Fascist Foreign Minister, might have "calmed the waters and laid the groundwork for the future."[125]

It was on the occasion of the Hitler-Mussolini meeting in Florence on October 28 that the Führer more fully informed the Duce of plans to reach agreement with the Soviet Union and to "direct the dynamism of the latter toward the Indies." It was Hitler's judgment that Soviet claims against Finland and Rumania should be resisted and that "undoubtedly there are forces in Russia urging expansion toward the Bosphorus." However, Hitler supposedly discouraged this tendency to go "where there are others" toward inland seas already controlled by others. With a rapprochement between Russia and the Axis, therefore, a solid front would be established from Spain to Japan.

Mussolini added that

a rapprochement of the Axis with the Soviet Union would be a major factor in completing the European coalition against England. He was convinced that Molotov's visit to Berlin would prove to be a serious blow to British hopes. He did not believe that it was necessary for the Soviet Union to join the Axis alliance, but it would be useful if something could be developed which would show that the Soviets had now drawn closer to the Axis. The Führer agreed

[123] Rosso to Ciano, personal letter, October 19, 1940, *ibid.*, Doc. 752.
[124] See pp. 48–123 *passim.*
[125] Ciano, *Diario,* I, p. 317.

with Mussolini and, while he excluded a two-power pact between Germany and the U.S.S.R., he declared that he would favor a three-power agreement between Italy, Germany, and the Soviet Union. Von Ribbentrop then spoke of the possibility of a protocol being signed in Moscow between the foreign ministers of the Axis, Japan, and Russia. This suggestion would be examined and elaborated in a future visit of Ciano to Berlin.[126]

These very sketchy notes are indicative of the illusions Hitler had regarding Moscow's disposition to shift its attention from eastern Europe. Mussolini readily agreed, but he appeared to be concerned with keeping on different planes the relations between the Axis and the U.S.S.R. and those between Italy and Germany (not inclusion in the Axis alliance but creation of "something to show that the Soviets had now drawn closer,"

---

[126] Ciano, minutes, October 28, 1940, *I.D.*, 9th series, V, Doc. 807. The German minutes report Hitler's and Mussolini's statements regarding the Soviet Union as follows:

> The Führer pointed out that Italy and Germany were natural allies, while the partnership with Russia had sprung purely from considerations of expediency. Just as mistrustful as Stalin was toward him (the Führer) so was he also toward Stalin. Molotov would now come to Berlin (this communication was received by the Duce and Count Ciano with evident surprise and great interest) and it would perhaps be possible to divert the activity of the Russians to India. There was a danger that they would again turn to their old goal, the Bosphorous [*sic*], and they had to be kept away from it. It had become necessary to point out to them that they might not step beyond certain definite boundaries. . . . In this connection, stressing again the existing Russian danger to the Bosphorous, the Führer spoke once more of the visit of Molotov to Berlin on November 10 and 11, and stated that it must be made clear to the Russians that there was little sense in their seeking expansion in areas where they would collide with Italy's or Germany's interest and finally gain nothing but an outlet to inland seas. It would doubtless be better for them to expand in other directions. . . . With regard to Russia, the Duce remarked that bringing her into the general front would be very advantageous. The very visit of Molotov would mean a violent blow to England and the foes of the Axis. . . . Shortly before the close of the conversation, the Führer again stressed the fact that he did not construe the entry of Russia into the common front as meaning that an alliance would be concluded with Russia, but, as the Foreign Minister stressed, that a special form of agreement with Russia and the partners to the Tripartite Pact would be found.

Schmidt, memorandum, October 28, 1940, *G.D.*, Series D, XI, Doc. 246.
Thus, there are noteworthy differences between the two sets of minutes. From the German minutes it appears that (a) it was Hitler who emphasized that relations between Germany and Italy would always remain substantially different from those between the Axis and the Soviet Union; (b) Mussolini revealed no reservations regarding an eventual participation of the Soviet Union in an alliance, but rather made a point of noting the advantages to be gained from including the Soviet Union in a "general front" against Great Britain; (c) concerning the eventual accords with Moscow, Hitler expressed himself in much less precise terms than those used in the minutes by Ciano.

etc.). Later, however, it appears that he did not oppose the idea of an accord that would also include Japan.

Ciano's visit to Berlin, agreed upon at Florence, took place at Schönhof on November 4. During this meeting Von Ribbentrop outlined his plan of action toward the Soviet Union as follows:

In the matter of timing and importance the primary problem concerns Russia's relations with the Axis and Japan. Although we are only in the initial phase of action in this sense, Von Ribbentrop believes that it will be possible, after Molotov's visit to Berlin which will take place on November 11, to negotiate an accord between the Tripartite Powers and the U.S.S.R. During the Berlin talks with Molotov, Von Ribbentrop will be in close contact with the governments of Italy and Japan. Since the prospects of concluding a military pact with the U.S.S.R. are to be excluded, Von Ribbentrop believes that a politico-economic pact should be realized, based primarily on a mutual recognition of the existing territorial situation, on the obligation of each party never to aid the enemies of the other parties, and, finally, on a broad clause of friendship and collaboration. Two secret protocols should be appended to this pact. The first of these should define the areas of expansion reserved for each of the contracting powers: Japanese dynamism to be directed toward the south and anti-British in character, while seeking to protect, insofar as possible, the position of Persia and Afghanistan; Italian dynamism to be directed toward North Africa and the Red Sea; German dynamism to be directed toward equatorial Africa. Von Ribbentrop emphasized that he was not mentioning the Balkans because, in the final analysis, he had no intention of discussing Balkan problems with Russia, as he considered them to be an internal problem of the Axis. The second secret protocol should concern itself with Russia's position vis-à-vis the Straits and the Black Sea. Von Ribbentrop believes that, in effect, the Convention of Montreux will have to be abolished and that Russia will have to be given two things: (1) a declaration that the Black Sea is considered a Russian inland sea; (2) freedom of navigation through the Straits. In this way, Von Ribbentrop believes, it will be possible to avoid every Russian attempt to establish herself territorially and militarily on the Dardenelles themselves, a situation which the Axis could not view with indifference. In exchange for the completely free use of the Straits, the four powers of the proposed accord would promise to guarantee Turkey's territorial status quo. Von Ribbentrop emphasizes that the completely free use of the Straits granted to Russia should not in any way disturb Italy because, first of all, Russia has never been a maritime power and never will be one, and, second, because at the end of the war Italy will have acquired so predominant a position in the Mediterranean as to be able to control this sea easily.

Turning to Italo-Russian relations, Von Ribbentrop declared that he was "in agreement on the timeliness of some gesture which would serve to make the relations between the two powers more cordial, but, while awaiting the formalization of the Four-Power Pact, he urged that Italy avoid any attempt to conclude a bilateral agreement."[127]

Aside from the portion of the exposition relating to the offers he proposed to make to Molotov in order to focus Soviet dynamism toward the east—the details of which are known through the minutes of the Nazi-Soviet talks in Berlin[128]—Von Ribbentrop's statements are particularly important for an understanding of the subsequent developments in the Italo-Soviet negotiations.

In effect, the Nazi Foreign Minister stressed three points: the exclusion of the U.S.S.R. from any discussion of Balkan affairs, the revision of the status of the Straits and of the Black Sea, and the suspension by Rome of any initiative designed to conclude bilateral accords between Italy and the U.S.S.R. "while awaiting the formalization of the Four-Power Pact." Now, granted that the German Foreign Minister was certain that the "Moscow Pact" could be realized even under the condition that Russia accept exclusion from Balkan affairs because they were reserved to the Axis powers, it was not clear exactly what the Italo-Soviet bilateral accords could consist of, particularly since what was left—that is, the matter of the Straits—was reserved for solution in the Four-Power Pact. On the other hand, was the suspension of Italo-Soviet negotiations to be considered as indefinite? Finally, it should be noted that Von Ribbentrop's ideas on the matter of the Straits—ideas which differed greatly from those he had advanced on September 19 and which were to undergo other modifications in the proposals presented by him to Molotov[129]—probably influenced the position taken later by the Fascist government in conversations with Moscow.

5

The Hitler-Molotov-Ribbentrop meeting destroyed most of the German illusions, although the negotiations continued, with both sides presenting proposals for accord. Ciano, again in Germany, noted in a letter to Mussolini of November 18: "I will say, first off, that—since Molotov's visit—there is very little talk about Russia, and what there is employs a tone quite different from that used by Von Ribbentrop during my recent stay

---

[127] Ciano, *L'Europa verso la catastrofe*, p. 611. The corresponding German minutes have not been found.

[128] On these conversations see Schmidt, memorandums, November 13, 15, 1940, *G.D.*, Series D, XI, Docs. 325, 326, and 328; Hilger, memorandum, November 18, 1940, *ibid.*, Doc. 329.

[129] *Ibid.*, p. 510.

in the Sudetenland. Russia is again the treacherous country who, given the present situation, is better to have as an enemy than as a friend and whose neutrality must be constantly verified."[130]

Two days later, Hitler himself wrote to the Duce as follows: "With Russia, too, it is more difficult to bring about an agreement on interests and to divert Russian ambitions toward the east. M. Molotov showed, on the contrary, an increased interest in the Balkans.... Every attempt must now be made to draw Russia away from the Balkan sphere and orient her toward the east."[131]

This information, although it could provide an approximate evaluation of the state of mind in a broad and general sense, was inadequate to permit Palazzo Chigi to judge the actual state of Nazi-Soviet relations (which, latently at least, had reached a highly serious level) and the basic aims of the Nazi government.[132] Therefore, the failure to communicate to Italy the exact nature of the Hitler-Molotov conversations and the divergent views evident during their course is responsible for the serious misunderstanding which arose between the two Axis powers regarding the policy to be adopted toward the U.S.S.R.

On the other hand, Italian military failures in Greece had greatly weakened the position of the Fascist government and created dissatisfaction between Rome and Berlin,[133] reflected in the attitude of the German Embassy in Moscow toward its Italian counterpart.[134]

In contrast, the position assumed by the Soviet government toward Italy

[130] Ciano, L'Europa verso la catastrofe, p. 614. During the conversations Ciano had with Hitler on November 18 and 20, 1940, the Soviet Union was not discussed. Hitler limited himself to saying that Molotov "had shown considerable interest in the Balkans at the Berlin talks" and that "efforts must be intensified to divert Russia's aspirations from the Balkans and to orient them to the south." (Schmidt, memorandum, November 19, 1940, G.D., Series D, XI, Doc. 353.)

[131] Hitler to Mussolini, letter, November 20, 1940, ibid., Doc. 369.

[132] The few items of information gathered by the Italian Embassy in Berlin on the Molotov visit did not come from the Wilhelmstrasse but rather from military sources. Alfieri to Ciano, telegram, November 15, 1940, No. 2030. See also Simoni, Berlino: ambasciata d'Italia, pp. 182–83. It is strange, therefore, that after having kept the decision to attack the Soviet Union from the Fascist government to the very end, the former Secretary of State for Foreign Affairs of the Reich should write in his memoirs: "Now that Italy has been at our side in the war for a year, she could have certainly warned us against the campaign in Russia. No warning of this sort was ever given." Weizsäcker, Erinnerungen, p. 308. It should be noted that Von Weizsäcker does not make any reference to the Italo-Soviet negotiations of 1940 and 1941.

[133] Simoni, Berlino: ambasciata d'Italia, pp. 178–88; Ciano, Diario, I, pp. 322, 324, 325, 326, 327, 333; Hitler to Mussolini, letter, November 20, 1940, G.D., Series D. XI, Doc. 369; Donosti, Mussolini e l'Europa, pp. 239–41.

[134] On this matter, see Ciano to Rosso, personal letter, November 11, 1940, No. 1/6479; Rosso to Ciano, personal letter, November 16, 1940, no number.

was correct.[135] It was likely, therefore, that at the Kremlin, in the light of the rigid and hardly reassuring position taken by the Nazis and of the obvious Italo-German differences,[136] it was decided, despite the absence of the anticipated Italian responses, to continue to maintain the position adopted during the preceding June and August. The intention now, more than ever before, was to overcome the obstacles encountered in Berlin to at least a partial recognition of the Soviet program for expansion into the Balkans or, at least, to strengthen the Soviet position vis-à-vis the Reich. Also taken into account was the fact that, as good negotiators, in the event that Russia had to make some concessions, the Kremlin had to rely upon receiving from Rome some useful indications regarding the real intentions of Berlin in order not to concede one inch more than was absolutely necessary.

Furthermore, it should be kept in mind that the Greek crisis, which had as its source, in common with the Russian view, dissastisfaction over the German occupation of Rumania, might have facilitated the realization of Sofia's claims against Greece by a drive towards the Aegean, an area of vital concern to the Soviets. However, in the final analysis, there was one last circumstance that was perhaps pre-eminent in determining the course of Soviet policy. On November 13 in Berlin Molotov heard Hitler state that, in order to reply to the Soviet request for the Straits, Germany would have to consult with Mussolini to make a decision in the matter, since Italy was much more directly concerned with the question than Germany. Therefore, Moscow needed to confirm the accuracy of Hitler's assertion and, in the event that it proved to be true, to take what steps were necessary to win Rome's consent for what was undoubtedly the most important of all of the Russian claims. Obviously, this consent, however problematic, was conceivable only within a framework of very cordial Italo-Soviet relations.

[135] Anfuso to Rosso, telegram, November 2, 1940, No. 200; Rosso to Ciano, telegrams, November 2, 1940; Rosso to Ciano, telegrams, November 3, 1940, Nos. 385, 387, and November 4, 1940, No. 388.

[136] From a telegram from the Minister of Greece in Moscow, intercepted by the Italian intelligence service and retransmitted to Rosso in Moscow in the above-cited personal letter of November 11, it was learned that members of the German Embassy had expressed their satisfaction at the successes of the Greek army. In his reply, Rosso tended to regard the information as correct and cited other equally disturbing cases. Ciano also refers to the matter in his *Diario* (I, p. 322): "From various sources, and particularly from Moscow, information is reaching us regarding an anti-Italian attitude and also a certain anti-Italian traffic which Germany is carrying on in Greece." It would be difficult indeed to believe that the Soviet government was entirely unaware of all of this.

On December 5 Rosso sent to Rome via courier a telegram in which he reported the new situation:

In my telegram No. 523 I reported the correct and objective comportment of the Soviet press in commenting on the Italian military situation, and I noted that this attitude was all the more noteworthy because it is hardly possible that the violent anti-Soviet campaign in the Italian press during the Russo-Finnish war has been forgotten.

Moreover, in this country every manifestation or attitude assumed by the press is always upon instructions from above, so that I can interpret this fact only as a reflection of a political directive from the government, which, very realistically, seeks to avoid provoking, by a hostile attitude of its press, an unfavorable reaction in Italian policy toward the U.S.S.R. Continuing this inductive reasoning, I have concluded by advancing the hypothesis that the Soviet leaders have considered it convenient to leave the door open for an eventual—and perhaps always desired—political rapprochement with Italy.

This interpretation seems to me to be well founded for other reasons as well, symptoms, if you will, whose importance I do not wish to exaggerate but which are, nevertheless, worthy of consideration. These are as follows:

1. Recently the Soviet Commissariat for Defense invited our Military Attaché to make a number of visits to Soviet military units and institutions, more precisely, to a motorized brigade, to an artillery regiment, and to the Frunze Academy (the War College). During all of the visits undertaken by Colonel Weil, he was received with special deference and courtesy, and during the course of the inspection of the Frunze Academy, the Commandant of the War College gave him lunch, during which he offered a toast praising the Italian army and expressing his hope for an increasingly closer rapport between the armed forces of the two countries. In his conversation later he [the Commandant] added that he was fully confident of Italy's ability to achieve complete success in the Greek campaign.

2. The President of the Council, Molotov, who rarely and only in exceptional cases accepts invitations from the foreign diplomatic legations, has recently informed me that he would be pleased to attend a dinner which I am offering in his honor at the Royal Embassy on December 13. He will be joined by the Commissar for Foreign Trade, Mikoyan, the Vice Commissars for Foreign Affairs, Vishinsky and Lozovsky, and a dozen high Soviet officials.

All of these facts are symptomatic, and I believed it to be my duty as well as of interest to report them to Your Excellency for their political significance, which may be summarized at this moment by saying that the attitude of the Soviet leaders toward us is inspired by an obvious desire to better the relations between the two countries.[137]

Uncertain, if not completely in the dark, regarding the origins of the new position assumed by the Soviet government, the Italian Ambassador limited himself to reporting these significant symptoms and refrained from

[137] Rosso to Ciano, courier telegram, December 5, 1940, No. 4514.

going further in his investigation. Limiting himself to a purely expository position, Rosso, on December 14, again reported to Rome as follows:

The dinner in Molotov's honor referred to in my courier telegram No. 4514 of December 5 inst. took place at the Royal Embassy last night. In addition to the President of the Council, it was attended by the Commissar for Foreign Trade, Mikoyan; the First Commissar Adjunct for Foreign Affairs, Vishinsky; the Vice Commissar for Foreign Affairs, Lozovsky, the Chief of Cabinet of the President of the Council, Kosiryev; the Vice Secretary General of the Nar-komindiel, Saxin; the Chief of Protocol, Barkov; the Director General, Kusnet-zov; the Press Chief, Palgunov; and other officials of minor rank, along with the noted composer Prokofiev.

Foreign heads of mission present included the German Ambassador and the Hungarian, Bulgarian, Rumanian, Yugoslav, and Danish ministers.

I have already referred to the rather exceptional nature of Molotov's appearance, he only very rarely accepts invitations from foreign diplomatic missions. I add now that the President of the Council, along with the other Soviet guests, were obviously appreciative of Italian hospitality, showing both Madam Ambassador and myself a degree of cordiality that was noted by all of the diplomats present and which has been the object of much comment in these foreign circles.

I repeat that I do not believe it useful to overestimate the political significance of the success of this evening, a success that was due, in part to the atmosphere which Madam Ambassador has always been able to create for social gatherings at the Royal Embassy. Undoubtedly, however, the desire of the Soviet personalities to demonstrate their friendly attitude toward our country also was an important contributing factor, and, in this regard, the event seemed to me to be worth noting.[138]

This time Rosso's communications were not ignored. However, Ciano's unusually prompt reaction to the information sent by Rosso is not difficult to explain. It was during this precise period that the Italian armies in Greece and in north Africa experienced serious reversals, evoking satisfaction among Italy's enemies and discontent and derision on the part of the Axis ally. Therefore, it was hardly surprising if, from among the many unpleasant reports, one of the very few suggesting a different note was the recipient of special attention. Molotov's courtesy, which Rosso emphasized in his reports, contrasted markedly with the hostile atmosphere which surrounded the Fascist government. But there was more. The military operations then under way had dramatically aggravated the already difficult Italian economic situation. The limited reserves of raw materials had been all but exhausted, and the war industries were producing only on a day-to-day basis. The desperate appeals to Germany for aid were only

[138] Rosso to Ciano, courier telegram, December 14, 1940, No. 4648.

partially satisfied.[139] In this state of affairs, the prospect of finally reactivating commercial and other relations with the U.S.S.R. was to appear most attractive. As was well known, Moscow subordinated all economic agreements to a preliminary solution of the political problem, and the idea of reopening the negotiations interrupted in June must have immediately occurred to Ciano. Thus, on December 16, he addressed the following letter to the Italian Ambassador in Berlin:

> Rosso, in his telegram, a copy of which I attach herewith,[140] comments in detail on the recent Soviet attitude toward us, which seems to be characterized by increasing cordiality.
>
> As you undoubtedly know, on the 13th inst. Molotov dined at the Royal Embassy in the company of the Commissar for Foreign Trade, Mikoyan, the Vice Commissars for Foreign Affairs, Vishinsky, and Lozovsky, and other Soviet functionaries. Rosso concludes by saying that the Soviet leaders, at this moment, demonstrate an obvious desire to improve relations with Italy. I do not think it would be opportune to ignore these good intentions. And since this subject has been considered at various times in our conversations with Von Ribbentrop and with Hitler himself, I would like to know how they regard these Soviet overtures and what they believe should be our next move, recognizing of course, that the Italian interest in improving relations with the U.S.S.R. is *primarily* dictated by the necessity to reopen those commercial exchanges which at the present are practically non-existent and whose reactivation would be of vital importance to our economy at this particular time.
>
> I urge you to discuss the matter with Von Ribbentrop, making clear the practical advantages to be gained and emphasizing, but without going into too much detail, that it would be opportune for us to normalize satisfactorily our relations with Moscow.[141]

This Ciano letter is worthy of close attention because it formed the basis of a serious equivocation between Rome and Berlin. At the outset, one notes the essentially correct position taken toward Italy's ally, requesting her consent prior to proceeding with the undertaking; then, in effect, Ciano pointed out the favorable Soviet disposition and the fact that Italy's primary interest in normalizing relations was primarily economic, adding that such normalizing without going "much beyond" was the object of future negotiations.

Evidently, the formula employed was not a happy one. However, anyone familiar with the type of negotiations possible in Moscow at that time would realize that they could not help but include an exchange of

[139] Schmidt, memorandum, December 20, 1940, *G.D.*, Series D, XI, Doc. 538; Clodius, memorandum, December 23, 1940, *ibid.*, Doc. 554; Donosti, *Mussolini e l'Europa*, p. 141; Simoni, *Berlino: ambasciata d'Italia*, pp. 185–86, 190, 191.

[140] In the original, a note indicates that this refers to a courier telegram from Moscow of December 5, 1940, No. 4514.

[141] Ciano, *L'Europa verso la catastrofe*, p. 617.

ideas on a political plane, regardless of how limited, in addition to the conclusion of a trade pact. On the other hand, on this occasion one cannot say that the Fascist Foreign Minister was much concerned with supporting the Italian position with a wealth of arguments. He settled for a simple summary enunciation, which did not appear to be the best way to convince Berlin of the true importance Rome gave to this question.

The Italian Ambassador to Berlin, who appears to have been apprised of the importance of Rome's instructions to him,[142] carried out the mission given to him and wrote to Ciano on December 23 as follows: "Von Ribbentrop told me that he is in accord with the timeliness of taking advantage of the present Soviet attitude to normalize our relations. He added that an improvement in these relations, moreover, corresponds to the German policy toward Russia."[143]

Alfieri's communication does not give a detailed summary of the colloquy, as Rosso was wont to do, and contained none of the observations and personal considerations which the Ambassador to Moscow was accustomed to add. These details would make it possible today to evaluate the significance of the reply and Von Ribbentrop's intentions more accurately, but it would have been even more important to have had this information at the time so that it might have served to enlighten Ciano not only on the step he was to take immediately afterwards with the Soviet Ambassador but also on the instructions he was to impart to Rosso.

Returning to the exact wording of the Ciano letter, the reply of the Nazi Foreign Minister was as equivocal as the question, with one additional aggravating factor, i.e., the lack of any request whatsoever for a further clarification of the Italian proposals. Von Ribbentrop knew perfectly well what was required in the Soviet demand for "political premises," having himself experienced this at first hand, and he had received from the Italians precise information as to the nature of the earlier conversations with Moscow.

Furthermore—and this circumstance was known only to him—the head of the Wilhelmstrasse knew the nature of the Soviet claims as well as the maximum Hitler would be willing to concede in this area. Notwithstanding all this, Von Ribbentrop not only refrained from asking questions, but also failed to warn Palazzo Chigi of the possible demands Molotov would advance. (Alfieri's telegram leaves no room for doubt on this point even

[142] Simoni, *Berlino: ambasciata d'Italia*, p. 190.

[143] Alfieri to Ciano, telegram, December 23, 1940, No. 2303. In the German documents there is no reference to this colloquy, but in a note dated December 27 Von Weizsäcker wrote that "the Italian Ambassador remarked to me again today that the Duce hoped our political relationship with Russia would not deteriorate." Von Weizsäcker, memorandum, December 27, 1940, *G.D.*, Series D, XI, Doc. 571.

though he did not go into detail on the conversations.) Moreover, Von Ribbentrop went so far as to state that the Italian initiative coincided with German policy toward the Soviet Union.

This strange behavior might well be explained by the Nazi Foreign Minister's limited talents, but this may be too simplistic an explanation. The possibility should not be excluded that Von Ribbentrop purposely avoided becoming involved in details in order to preserve intact his ability to back off from an undertaking which eventually might furnish him with the tools to be used in his attempts to resolve the problem of Nazi-Soviet relations amicably. The communication from Berlin initiated a new and important phase in Italo-Soviet relations.

6

Probably presuming that complete German approval had been received, on the morning of December 26 Count Ciano, with Mussolini's full approval,[144] called Ambassador Gorelkin to Palazzo Chigi. The summary account of this meeting, which was dispatched to Rosso the same day, read as follows:

In connection with what you communicated in your telegram I convened with the Soviet Ambassador this morning and I told him the following:

1. The Fascist government, on the basis of previous colloquies on the matter, considers that the moment has come to further the examination of Italo-Soviet relations both on the political and the economic plane.

2. In our judgment there is no reason for conflict between Italy and the U.S.S.R. The interests of the two countries have no points of friction of any kind and, moreover, in many areas and for many reasons they complement each other.

3. Italy recognizes and is ready to recognize formally the pre-eminence of Soviet interests in the Black Sea in addition to the new frontiers of the Soviet Union. In return, Italy requests that the pre-eminence of her interests in the Mediterranean be recognized.

4. On the basis of these general principles, and with additional questions which the Soviet Union would desire to suggest as objects of discussion, Italy is prepared to bring the Non-Aggression and Neutrality Pact of 1933 up to date, giving it a more precise content.

5. In the event that our proposal meets the approval of the Soviet government, the conversations could take place here in Rome between the Soviet Ambassador and myself or in Moscow between Mr. Molotov and yourself; I also mentioned an eventual conclusive meeting between Molotov and myself.

6. The Soviet Ambassador took note of what I said and made no comment;

[144] Alfieri's telegram also carries Mussolini's initials. In addition to his letter to Alfieri, January 1, 1941, No. 1/0003, Ciano referred to "the detailed instructions of the Duce."

he limited himself to stating that he would immediately inform his government in Moscow. Personally, he stated his agreement and his satisfaction.

7. I am informing Your Excellency of what took place so that you will be aware—in the event that Mr. Molotov refers to this matter—of our proposals, which, for the moment, are general in nature.[145]

Ciano's statements to Gorelkin thus clarified the nature of the negotiations as contemplated by him. Based on them, the Fascist government foresaw the conclusion of a political and an economic accord. But the content of the political accord, despite an attempt to keep in mind both Molotov's declarations of June 25 and Von Ribbentrop's later statements, was, from the beginning, not sufficiently delimited. (Ciano had, of course, in his telegram to Rosso, referred to his proposals as "general.") According to Ciano's version he had carefully avoided touching on the Balkan problem, which Germany intended to reserve to the Axis, but his reference to the earlier colloquies in Moscow and the addition of the phrase "additional questions" which the Soviet government might choose to raise during the course of the negotiations made the omission entirely meaningless.

However, the summary account of the Ciano-Gorelkin conversation sent to Moscow by the Soviet Ambassador (a summary referred to by Molotov in his subsequent conversations with Rosso and not denied by Rome) affirmed that the Fascist Foreign Minister had declared that Italy was ready to recognize "Soviet interests in the Balkans and Soviet interests in Asia."[146] The differences between the two accounts are astonishing. Without questioning the accuracy of the Gorelkin report and recognizing the limitations of the Fascist Foreign Minister, it behooves us to base a critical interpretation strictly on the text of the Ciano telegram because it is indicative of the content which the latter himself believed he had given in the negotiations and because there is absolutely no way of explaining the omission of that portion of his statements to which he had lent little weight. With these reservations and within limits strictly construed, the recognition of the pre-eminence of Soviet interests in the Black Sea was not entirely irreconcilable with the German position on the question. However, the counter-concession requested for the entire Mediterranean seemed to be too great for the U.S.S.R. to accept without something more to redress the imbalance, yet it would have been extremely difficult to win Berlin's approval for any further concessions. But this was not yet sufficiently clear to the Fascist government because Rome was kept in the

[145] Ciano to Rosso, telegram, December 26, 1940, No. 236.
[146] Rosso to Ciano, report, December 31, 1940, No. 4803/1739. It should also be noted that this fact was confirmed by Alfieri to Von Ribbentrop. See Schmidt, memorandum, January 7, 1941, *G.D.*, Series D, XI, Doc. 610.

dark as to the exact nature of the differences between the Soviet Union and Germany.

It remains to be asked whether Ciano's proposals conform exactly to the formula he outlined in his letter to Alfieri on December 16. The answer to the question is not easy to formulate, but cannot be affirmative. It would be difficult to insist that the communication Ciano sent to Alfieri and the latter's reply contained fundamentally the same elements as the communication from Ciano to Rosso, this without even considering the implications of the phrase "eventual conclusive meeting" between the two ministers, which, of course, was mentioned. The formula employed in notifying Berlin of the "renewal of reasonably normal relations" calls to mind that "distension" mentioned at Milan on May 6, 1939, from which the Germans arrived at the Nazi-Soviet Pact of August 23, 1939. But it would be going a bit too far to make such a literal comparison.

It should again be noted how the above-mentioned divergences between the Ciano proposals, the formula presented to Von Ribbentrop, and the limited goals apparently sought by the Fascist government (which gave no indication of deviating from its position of subordination to Germany) were the result of an insufficient study of the entire problem. In effect, if the question of relations with Moscow had been the object of a deep and thorough study, these inconsistencies would not have been possible, and, regardless of the conclusions reached, the ultimate objective could have been sought with an entirely different intensity and continuity of action.

Ciano's statements found a prompt and favorable echo in Moscow. As early as December 28 Gorelkin appeared at Palazzo Chigi to inform the Italian Foreign Ministry of his government's acceptance in principle of the Ciano declaration. Later that day Ciano telegraphed to Rosso as follows:

The Soviet Ambassador came to see me to advise me that the Soviet government is favorable to our proposal for closer political and economic relations and that the Soviet government suggests that the negotiations take place in Moscow. Therefore, please call on Mr. Molotov immediately and express the Duce's satisfaction for the favorable and prompt response, which the Duce considers to be a good omen.

I assume you will, of course, place yourself at Mr. Molotov's disposal to begin the negotiations, which you should conclude along the lines indicated in my telegram to you (No. 236).

While I grant you ample latitude to conclude the negotiations, to which we attribute the greatest importance, I urge you to report as soon as possible on the Soviet government's proposals and your interpretations of these, your suggestions and proposals.[147]

The Kremlin's prompt reply, while certainly indicating a clear interest

[147] Ciano to Rosso, telegram, December 28, 1940, No. 239.

in renewing the conversations with the Fascist government, did not yet clarify the Soviet proposals. However, Rome was optimistic, and, despite the importance apparently attributed to the negotiations, Rosso was given wide powers without being furnished with any details regarding the Italian point of view on the problems, raised previously by the President of the Council of Peoples' Commissars and to which the latter would inevitably refer.

The Italian Ambassador in Moscow asked for an immediate audience with Molotov,[148] which was promptly arranged for the evening of December 30.[149] This important colloquy lasted two hours, and Rosso summarized it as follows in his report to Rome:

I was received by Molotov at the Kremlin at 5:00 P.M. and I left his office at 7:15 P.M.

Ambassador: My government has informed me of the conversations which recently took place in Rome between Foreign Minister Ciano and Ambassador Gorelkin.

Therefore, I am aware of the Italian proposal to begin negotiations for a closer rapport between our two countries, both politically and economically. I have also been informed of your acceptance of the Italian proposal. I am here today primarily to express the Duce's pleasure at your prompt and favorable response. The Duce regards this as a good omen.

You have proposed that the negotiations take place in Moscow, and I have received instructions to place myself at your disposal immediately in order to begin the negotiations without delay.

In his conversations with Ambassador Gorelkin, Minister Ciano described in general terms what, to our minds, could be the basis of the accord. He also transmitted these to me, summarized under four points which—if it is agreeable —I can repeat to you at this time.

[Molotov nodded his agreement and, on the basis of a note previously drafted in Russian, I read these four points to him.]

1. The Italian government, on the basis of the exchange of views which took place in Moscow and Rome last June, holds the view that the time has come to further examine both the political and economic relations between Italy and the U.S.S.R.

2. In the judgment of the Italian government no reasons exist for conflict between the U.S.S.R. and Italy. The interests of the two countries do not conflict. Instead, in many areas and for many reasons these interests complement each other.

3. Italy recognizes, and is ready to do so formally, the pre-eminence of Soviet interests in the Black Sea as well as the new frontiers acquired by the U.S.S.R.

In return, Italy asks that the U.S.S.R. recognize the pre-eminence of Italian interests in the Mediterranean.

4. On the basis of the general principles enunciated in these three points— and with the understanding that the U.S.S.R. is free to bring up other prob-

---

[148] Rosso to Ciano, telegram, December 29, 1940, No. 550.
[149] Rosso to Ciano, telegram, December 30, 1940, No. 552.

lems for discussion if it so desires—Italy is ready to update the Pact of Non-Aggression and Neutrality of 1933 on a more concrete basis.

[After outlining the four points, to which Molotov listened with careful attention, consulting a document he held in his hand—which I later learned was a telegram from Gorelkin—I continued.]

As you note, the Italian government is ready and favorably disposed to examine the suggestions and proposals you may care to make to me in the name of the Soviet government, and I have come to learn your views on the matter.

Personally, I would like to add that I am delighted to reopen with you the conversations of last June, and I will do my utmost to cooperate in reaching a rapid and satisfactory conclusion.

Molotov: I am satisfied with what the Duce has said, and I too am pleased.

Like you, I also hope that our conversations will produce rapid and satisfying results.

We have requested, and Minister Ciano has agreed, that the negotiations take place in Moscow. We have known Ambassador Rosso for years, and we appreciate his efforts in seeking a rapprochement between the two countries.

[After these few introductory sentences, Molotov went directly to the heart of the matter.]

If you will permit, I would like first to ask you a few questions. I will begin with those of a political nature, but this does not mean that we are not also interested in economic problems.

First of all, I would like to have you tell me what Minister Ciano meant, in precise terms, when he spoke to Ambassador Gorelkin of the *"pre-eminence of Soviet interests in the Black Sea."*

Ambassador: It seems clear to me that Minister Ciano meant that we recognize that the U.S.S.R. is the most important power in the Black Sea and that her interests predominate. Therefore, I presume that the statement reflects substantially what you yourself told me in our conversation of June 25 last, when you stated that the U.S.S.R. regarded Italy's claims to pre-eminence in the Mediterranean as just but that, at the same time, you hoped that Italy would regard the interests of the U.S.S.R. as pre-eminent in the Black Sea.

Molotov: You have mentioned the conversations of last June, and it is precisely to these that I wish to speak.

Can you tell me what the views of the Italian government are on the various questions contained in the memorandum I handed to you at that time?

Ambassador: I am not in a position to reply to you. I must, however, presume that my government has made no reference to these since our last conversation in June because, since that time, many events have changed the international situation. Many points included in your memorandum may now be regarded as resolved.

[Molotov proposed that we re-examine the memorandum together.]

For example, the Hungarian claims to Transylvania have been resolved, and the problem no longer exists.

Molotov: I am in perfect accord on this point.

Ambassador: As for Bulgaria, at that time, you stated that you considered its claims against Rumania and Greece as just.

The Bulgarian claims against Rumania have been satisfied with the cession of southern Dobruja to Bulgaria.

As for those claims against Greece, I can tell you that, in the main, Italy is also favorable to a Bulgarian access to the Aegean Sea. It is premature at this time to say whether this aspiration can be satisfied.

[Molotov nodded assent, but without uttering a word.]

Your memorandum also spoke of "problems concerning other areas of Rumania," but you never defined these for me.

Since our conversation of June 25 I have not had the occasion to discuss political problems with you, and, therefore, I did not have the opportunity to ask you to explain this point to me in greater detail. Would you like to do so now?

[At this point Molotov began a long exposition in bitter tones and with evident recriminations. In substance, he said the following.]

Molotov: As the Italian government has been able to confirm, we have acted on the Bessarabian problem as we stated in the memorandum that we would. We made it clear that the problem was real, that it was urgent and that we intended to resolve it without delay.

[At this point I did not regard it opportune to observe that the ultimatum was presented to Rumania only twenty-four hours after Molotov had talked to me about Bessarabia.]

Therefore, our position vis-à-vis Italy was correct. On the other hand, on the other Rumanian problems, on which we had proposed an agreement between the U.S.S.R., Germany, and Italy, the Axis powers acted in a manner *contrary* [Molotov emphasized the word] to what the U.S.S.R. had proposed.

The German and Italian governments have resolved the Transylvania and Dobruja problems without consulting the U.S.S.R. and have guaranteed Rumania's frontiers.

I must inform you, in all sincerity, that the Soviet government regards this guarantee as being directed primarily against the U.S.S.R. We cannot interpret it any other way. Rumania borders on the Soviet Union, and the Italo-German guarantee evidently is directed against the Soviet Union.

We did not hide our views on this matter from the German government, and I personally raised this question during my recent sojourn in Berlin.

What is the purpose of your guarantee to Rumania, keeping in mind that she borders on the Soviet Union?

Naturally, the actions taken by the governments of Rome and Berlin are their affairs. However, I am asking you: why was this guarantee given?

[In the face of these insistent demands I thought it opportune to intervene, and, despite the fact that I had no information on the subject, I made every effort to challenge the anti-Soviet interpretation given to the guarantee. I explained to him that the Vienna meeting, in which the arbitration produced the decision on Transylvania, had occurred at a very critical moment in the general situation affecting the Danube Basin. Hungary was impatient to satisfy her claims—the atmosphere was fraught with peril—and it was necessary to act without delay. Because it was a question of demanding such a major sacrifice from Rumania and getting her government to accept it, it was indispensable to compensate for her wounded pride in some way and to give her some assurance for the future, which was done with the guarantee. To my way of thinking, however, if this guarantee was directed against anyone, it was directed against Hungary and Bulgaria because it offered Rumania a sense of security against these. The guarantee could not have been directed against the U.S.S.R. for the simple reason that the U.S.S.R. had declared, after the annexation of Bessarabia, that her claims against Rumania had been entirely satisfied. Therefore, Italy and Germany knew that they had no need to guarantee Rumania against a nonexistent Soviet threat.]

[Molotov gave no indication that he was convinced by my dialectics and continued with his recriminations.]

Molotov: While we informed the Italian government in due time of the Soviet position regarding Rumania, the Italian government has never informed us of its position, neither before nor after the events which produced the Italo-German guarantee to that country.

Today I am still interested in knowing what the scope and aims of Italian policy are in that area, and I shall be grateful to you if you will ask your government to give me a reply to the following question: *"What is the significance and what are the implications of the guarantee given to Rumania?"*

[I promised to transmit this question to Rome and to communicate the reply to him. Then, in order to learn the full scope of my interlocutor's views, I insisted that he tell me in precise terms what were the other questions to which he alluded in his memorandum of June 25.]

Molotov: Among the other Rumanian problems on which the U.S.S.R. would have wanted to arrive at an agreement with you, I could mention, as an example, that of the *oil fields* which are of particular interest to Italy and Germany. The U.S.S.R. is not directly interested in this question and would, therefore, have easily arrived at an agreement with you. Then there is the *Danubian question.*

[At this point Molotov reflected for an instant and then launched into a long and detailed exposition of the problem from Tsarist times down to the negotiations under way at the Bucharest conference. The most significant excerpts are noted below.]

1. With the restitution of Bessarabia, the U.S.S.R. has become a Danubian power. Today, the U.S.S.R. has a major interest in the question of navigation on the Danube.

2. Thus far, the Bucharest conference has not produced any positive results because Rumania has not yet accepted the change in position of the U.S.S.R. since the annexation of Bessarabia. Rumania continues to believe that because she controls the mouth of the Danube, that the situation has not changed. Her mistake is that of not taking into consideration that today the U.S.S.R. is interested in the question of the control of the mouth of the Danube.

If the attitude of the Rumanian government surprises us, the attitude of the German and Italian delegates who continue to support Rumanian intransigence astonishes us even more.

[Referring to Italy in particular, Molotov continued.]

3. The U.S.S.R. has accepted the presence of Italy on the Control Commission, even though she is not a riparian state, because it is politically opportune. Politically, we are not opposed, although Italy is the *only* [he emphasized the word] country on the Commission without riparian status.

[At this point I interrupted to note that Italy has such imposing interests in the entire Danubian Basin that she could not remain aloof from the control of navigation on a river that is *international*, in that it is an extremely important trade route that involves an area vital to our trade.

I then added that, according to information available to me, the difficulties encountered at Bucharest consisted largely of questions relating to the allocation and definition of the competencies of control organs and of those of a purely administrative nature. Therefore, it seemed to me that the problem could be resolved.]

[Using my comments as a point of departure, Molotov continued.]

Molotov: While insofar as the other problems we have discussed (arbitrage for Transylvania, Rumanian guarantees) are *faits accomplis*, the problem of navigation on the Danube is still under study. Therefore, this is a problem of *actuality*. [He emphasized the word.]

On January 20, 1941, the Conference of Bucharest will meet again. Let us hope that this time it will succeed in concluding its task.

I repeat that the government of the U.S.S.R. cannot comprehend the attitude of the Italian delegate.

I must also formally announce to you that the U.S.S.R. will never accept the solution proposed by Rumania.

I would also appreciate learning your government's precise thinking on this matter.

[With these words, Molotov made it clear that he intended to ask Italy to change its position and to support the Soviet thesis. Turning to other matters, he focused on the Straits Question, which was obviously of major concern to him.]

Molotov: Now, I would like to ask you for clarification on other matters. Can you tell me, in specific terms, what Italy means by the phrase "Italian pre-eminence in the Mediterranean"?

Ambassador: I thought that I had replied to this question at the beginning of our conversation, when you asked for the meaning of the phrase "pre-eminence of Soviet interests in the Black Sea."

I called to your attention then the fact that the terms used by Minister Ciano were substantially the same as those used in your memorandum of June 24.

The general sense, it seems to me, is obvious: it signifies that Italy is the power with major interests in the Mediterranean, as is the U.S.S.R. in the Black Sea.

If you then ask me in what way and with what concrete illustrations this pre-eminence can be explained, I must call your attention to the fact that this aspect of the problem cannot be discussed until the respective countries have specified their vital interests and requirements in the Mediterranean and Black Seas.

Insofar as Italy is concerned I could give you my own point of view in a general way, but I prefer to speak officially on the subject after I have received instructions from my government.

I would appreciate it, however, if you, who are in a position to do so, would tell me what the problems of the U.S.S.R. are in the Black Sea.

[After having observed that the problem of the Straits is the one in which Italian and Soviet interests "come into contact with each other," Molotov continued in approximately these terms.]

Molotov: The Soviet interest in the Straits has roots in the history of the U.S.S.R. and in that of Imperial Russia. As a problem, it is primarily one of national security.

All of the attacks against Russia from the south have come via the Straits. I call to your attention the Crimean War and, more recently, the attacks of England in 1918 and those of France in 1919, during the period of foreign intervention in support of the White Russians.

Turkey owns the Straits and even today is in close rapport with and tied by alliance to England.

England already has powerful military bases in the eastern Mediterranean. We must also recognize that during the past month she has further strengthened her position by exploiting the Greek bases and by occupying the island of Crete.

If this is a matter of grave importance for Italy, Russia cannot ignore it either and must be concerned.

The power that threatens is always England. Not only Italy but Russia as well cannot ignore the problem of naval power in the eastern Mediterranean.

Therefore, I would like to raise this question with your government: "Does Italy understand the interest of the U.S.S.R. in the Straits in relation to the problem of Soviet security in the Black Sea?"

[During the course of his long exposition on the Black Sea problem—briefly summarized above—Molotov repeatedly used the term "Black Sea Straits".]

[Molotov then asked if he could ask me further questions, to which I replied affirmatively.]

Molotov: I have before me Gorelkin's telegram, which he sent to me after his conversation on the 26 inst. with Minister Ciano. In it he states that Italy is ready to recognize "Soviet interests in the Balkans and the U.S.S.R.'s Asiatic interests." Can you tell me what significance should be attributed to this phrase?

Ambassador: It seems to me that the meaning is obvious. Permit me to call your attention to the fact that in our conversations of last June I told you that Italy, while having political as well as economic interests of major importance in the Balkans, has never intended nor does she intend to exercise an exclusive influence in those countries.

I must conclude that Minister Ciano meant that in the Balkans, in addition to Italian interests, there are also Soviet interests.

Insofar as Asia is concerned, you are better able than I am to determine what your vital interests are. Evidently, Minister Ciano chose to say that we recognize and respect these interests.

Molotov: One last question. In the statement that Ciano made to Gorelkin and which you repeated to me, it is noted that Italy is ready to recognize the new frontiers acquired by the U.S.S.R. Would there, perhaps, be any difficulty in doing so? What might the obstacles be?

In Poland the frontier has been established in a convention signed by the U.S.S.R. and Germany, and the latter is your ally. What would be the problem here?

With Rumania and Finland the question of frontiers has been settled between the powers directly concerned.

I am unable to understand why Italy, Germany's ally, would want to delay recognizing the frontiers which have already been accepted by all of the interested parties.

Ambassador: Despite what you have said, the Italian declaration, particularly when formally made, would always be an act of goodwill.

I could cite many cases in which, after a war, and after peace had been concluded by the contending states, third parties have delayed—occasionally for long periods—official recognition of the new territorial changes resulting from military occupation. Therefore, you cannot avoid recognizing our declaration as a friendly manifestation, intended to illustrate the cordial attitude that dominates my government in its relations with the U.S.S.R.

[Molotov did not interrupt, but nodded his head, indicating that he had accepted my explanation.]

With this, yesterday's colloquy came to a close. As I took my leave, Molotov informed me that the conversation could be continued just as soon as I had received communications from Rome regarding the questions discussed or at any time that I requested to be received. I must add that this long conversation took place in an atmosphere that always remained cordial.[150]

To this summary, after asking Rome whether the German government had been apprised of the renewal of the Italo-Soviet negotiations and requesting urgent instructions on the position he should adopt toward Von Schulenburg,[151] Rosso added the following comment:

1. The Soviet government seems to be sincerely anxious to achieve a political agreement with Italy. However, it will not be satisfied with an accord expressed in general terms which contains nothing tangible or positive. Therefore, I do not believe that a simple updating of the Pact of 1933, a declaration of good intent toward collaboration, or confirmation that reasons for conflict do not exist will suffice. It is clear that Molotov intends to establish the negotiations on a basis of *do ut des*, and that he will seek to obtain from us concrete obligations on specific problems.

2. Dissatisfaction remains at our failure to proceed with the conversations of last June, which were started at our suggestion. It is obvious that Molotov intends to see whether, in the present situation, we intend to see the thing through.

3. When he complained about the modus operandi in the Rumanian questions, I had the sensation that more than anything else Molotov wanted us to know of his real resentment against Germany and that, in mentioning the oil

---

[150] Rosso to Ciano, telegrams, December 30, 1940, Nos. 553, 554, 555, and Rosso to Ciano, report, December 31, 1940, No. 4803/1739. The text reproduced here is the more complete because it includes the notes taken at the time by the Embassy interpreter, Relli.

[151] Rosso to Ciano, telegram, December 30, 1940, No. 556. With his telegram No. 9 of January 4, 1941, Rosso again asked for instructions on the position he should maintain toward his German colleague. Ciano replied the following day authorizing the Ambassador to speak with Von Schulenburg regarding the renewal of negotiations and also informed Rosso that Berlin had been brought up to date on the matter. Ciano to Rosso, telegram, January 5, 1941, No. 4.

fields of Rumania, he was really thinking of German military control of that region.

4. It was clear from the detailed exposition of the problem of navigation on the Danube that the U.S.S.R. intends to ask Italy to modify its attitude by abandoning its support of the Rumanian thesis in favor of that of the Soviet Union.

5. There is no question that the nerve center of the Soviet program is the Straits problem. In the insistence with which Molotov spoke of England as the common adversary and of the English naval force as the common danger it is possible to foresee a plan to obtain Italian support in resolving the problem in the interest of Russia.

Until now Molotov has abstained from advancing proposals and suggesting possible solutions, and it is likely that he will continue to do so until a more advanced stage in the negotiations is reached, and only after he has a clear concept of the Italian position. However, in my opinion, the Straits Question will be the fulcrum of the negotiations.

Given this premise, I call attention to the fact that the negotiations which Your Excellency did me the honor of entrusting to me appear destined to develop into very sharp bargaining sessions and that all of the principal questions will have to be studied in depth. The success of the negotiations, in the final analysis, will depend on the decisions which the Royal government adopts regarding the problems which affect the fundamental lines of our general policy.

I add that, given the precedents of last June, the suspicious and sensitive nature of the Soviet leaders, and their coldly realistic policy, the best system to adopt (assuming, of course, that in the light of what has emerged from my first colloquy the Royal government continues to judge it advantageous to reach an accord) will be that of promptly replying in a clear and detailed way to the questions asked by Molotov in order that he be informed of our position and intentions on the various problems raised. At the same time it will be wise to state our demands openly and to establish our conditions right from the start.

Therefore, I urge you to telegraph instructions as soon as possible and provide me with the necessary data regarding the replies I should make to the precise questions posed by Molotov on the following points: (1) guarantees to Rumania; (2) our position on the Danube problem; (3) the Straits Question in relation to Russian security in the Black Sea. It will also be useful to me to have more detailed information and instructions on all of the other points touched on in yesterday's colloquy.

I conclude with a consideration of a general nature. In 1939, in order to obtain concrete political and economic advantages, Germany had to pay the price demanded by the Soviet Union, that is, the abandonment of its own political and demographic positions in the Baltic states (which had been the fruit of a slow and laborious, centuries-old penetration), in addition to portions of Polish territory including the oil resources of Galicia.

In an analogous way, for us today it is a question of weighing the price and the question of whether it is advantageous to pay it to obtain political concessions which Your Excellency has certainly already evaluated, in addition to commercial advantages which I must presume are contemplated by us. As for the latter, it would now be useful for me to know our requirements in order for me to determine whether the Soviet economy is in a position to satisfy our needs.[152]

The Italian Ambassador to Moscow had conducted the discussion with Molotov in the best possible way and had extracted from the latter's comments almost all of the salient points of his position. However, one consideration of some interest should be added regarding the interpretation of the Soviet attitude.

In contrast to the colloquy of June 26, Rosso failed to point out that Molotov did not, at any time during the conversation, or in relation to any of the unresolved questions, refer to the possibility of a tripartite accord, even though a bilateral accord with Italy could not, unlike in the case of the Commission for the Danube and Straits, have assured an immediate solution to the problems. Moscow was apparently content with acquiring only the Fascist government's acquiescense to and collaboration with its thesis. But what could have been the real reasons behind this limitation? (As has been noted, Hitler's statement regarding the preeminence of Italian interests in the Straits, the Nazi-Soviet tension, and the possible impact on Bulgaria of the Greek crisis could all have explained the conduct of the Soviet Foreign Minister.) Evidently, the Italian Ambassador did not consider this point even though the passage in Molotov's declaration relating to his conception that accords with only one ally automatically extend to the other should have given cause for serious reflection.

Rosso was totally unaware of the generalized character which, according to the agreement reached during the Berlin consultation,[153] was to accompany the renewal of negotiations with Moscow, and, again, he concentrated his attention only on the Italo-Soviet aspect of the question. However, it is true that this time he requested or, rather, insisted that Rome tell him whether the Nazi government had been informed of the reopening of negotiations, but he did not go beyond that. As for possible replies to Molotov's questions, Rosso was decidedly in favor of continuing the negotiations.

7

Rosso's telegrams did finally give Ciano some idea of the broad scope that the negotiations had assumed as a result of his own conversation with the Soviet Ambassador and that of Rosso with Molotov. Despite the fact

[152] Rosso to Ciano, telegrams, December 31, 1940, Nos. 658, 659.
[153] Rosso to Alfieri, personal letter, January 16, 1941, partially reproduced in Simoni, *Berlino: ambasciata d'Italia*, pp. 203–7, and in Alfieri, *Due dittatori di fronte*, pp. 230–31.

that his reactions and those of Mussolini were substantially favorable, he immediately became concerned with "not assuming any obligation without first reaching agreement with Germany."[154] In addition, the ideas advanced by Hitler in a letter delivered to Mussolini by Von Mackensen on January 1, 1941, indicated that Berlin continued to entertain the conviction that she could maintain a policy of friendship with the Soviet Union. It is true that the German Chancellor did not fail to emphasize that "the existence of a German Wehrmacht, strong enough to oppose any conceivable eventuality from the East was a prerequisite for any safe conclusion of this war," but the portion of the letter devoted to relations with Russia expressed, on the whole, a certain degree of optimism concerning the possibility of resolving the two principal problems which, according to Hitler, divided Moscow and Berlin, that is, Finland and the Straits.[155] Therefore, in the light of these assertions, a renewal of the Italo-Soviet conversations apparently coincided with the policy pursued by the German government. In fact, Mussolini, commenting to Von Mackensen on Hitler's message, observed that "the conclusion of the Rome-Moscow conversations, now in progress, would create a new element of security in this direction."[156] Accordingly, on January 1 the Fascist Foreign Minister wrote a long letter to the Italian Ambassador in Berlin for the purpose of bringing him up to date on the development of the talks with Moscow "in order to inform Minister Von Ribbentrop with greater precision and clarity."

After listing chronologically the events following Alfieri's "communication" down to the most recent telegrams from Rosso, copies of which were attached to be transmitted to Von Ribbentrop, Ciano continued as follows:

As you will see from reading Rosso's telegram, the Moscow government intends to launch the negotiations, political as well as the economic, with a definition of several political questions which are particularly vital from the Soviet government's point of view.

Apparently, there are three issues which have emerged from the first Molotov-Rosso conversations: (1) guarantees to Rumania, (2) our position on the Danube problems, and (3) the question of the Straits in relation to Russian security in the Black Sea. The Duce's point of view on these three problems is as follows:

1. *Guarantees to Rumania*: These represent the compensation given by the Axis to Rumania following the amputations it suffered, particularly after the Vienna verdict. It is clear that in the eyes of the Axis the guarantees did not have and do not have any anti-Soviet implications: rather, they represent the

154 Ciano, *Diario*, II, p. 11.
155 Hitler to Mussolini, letter, December 31, 1940, *G.D.*, Series D, XI, Doc. 586.
156 Von Mackensen to Von Ribbentrop, telegram, January 1, 1941, *ibid.*, Doc. 589.

limit imposed by Germany and Italy on Magyar ambitions and, perhaps, on Bulgarian ambitions as well.

2. *Our position on the Danube problem*: Within the limits possible, Italy is prepared to consider the Russian requirements, all the more because the Soviets have indicated their comprehension of Italy's interests in the area even though she is not a riparian state of the Danube.

3. *The Straits Question in relation to Russian security in the Black Sea*: This is a fundamental problem. It would be the Duce's intention to have Rosso ask for a precise definition of the problem, at least as the Russians see it, since, as is evident, the Straits Question is subject to several very different solutions (for example, it is possible to go from the extreme of territorial annexation [a solution to be excluded a priori] to simple demilitarization).

Now that you have all of this data available, you can easily see why it is indispensable for us to have Germany's closest cooperation in our negotiations with Moscow. In my opinion, we are treating problems which are much too important and which concern our ally too directly for us to assume obligations without first having obtained Berlin's complete approval.

Therefore, I urge you to immediately contact Von Ribbentrop, inform him completely concerning the above, question him about the problems I have posed, and explain our position on them. Refer his reply, along with any suggestion or direction he may care to give.

The urgency of the matter needs no further emphasis: any excessive delay would arouse Russian suspicions that this time, too, the negotiations are not destined to succeed.[157]

Ciano's letter presents a number of interesting elements. First, it confirmed the plan—at that moment it may have been impossible to do otherwise—to proceed in formulating policy toward the U.S.S.R. only in complete accord with Germany, a fact which automatically put the Italian government in an entirely different position from the Soviets. Second, it was implicit in the recognition of the need for further consultation with Berlin that there had previously been an insufficient exchange on the subject. Ciano gave the impression of crediting Moscow with the main responsibility for the tremendous scope the negotiations had assumed without recognizing that he had largely contributed to this situation by his initial postulation of the problem. Third, the fact that the Duce was well disposed toward Molotov's demands was symptomatic. (The point

[157] Ciano to Alfieri, letter, January 1, 1941, *ibid.*, No. 1/0003. Two days later Ciano conferred with Ambassador Von Mackensen, to whom he read his instructions to Alfieri and also Rosso's telegram concerning the latter's meeting with Molotov. Ciano insisted that Von Ribbentrop inform Rome of the German view as soon as possible, "for we knew just as well as he how suspicious the Russians were and how at every delay they at once suspected intentional procrastination." At the suggestion of the Fascist Foreign Minister, Von Mackensen sent only a brief summary account of this colloquy with Ciano because the question would have been discussed directly by Von Ribbentrop and Alfieri. Von Mackensen to Von Ribbentrop, telegram, January 3, 1941, *G.D.*, Series D, XI, Doc. 599; Ciano, *Diario*, II, p. 12.

concerning the narrow interpretation of the Rumanian guarantees was particularly significant, and, aside from the fact that it had little relation to historical precedents, it went much beyond what Rosso had established in his exposition. Attributing to the U.S.S.R. Italy's permanent membership on the Danube Commission credited Soviet policy with a friendliness toward Italy which, as we shall see below, was to be contested by the Wilhelmstrasse, which claimed exclusive responsibility for this accomplishment.) Fourth, it was clear that Rome had no idea at that time of the nature of the differences existing between Italy and Germany in the matter of policy to be carried out vis-à-vis the Soviet Union. Last, the limited scope within which Italy hoped to deal with the problem of relations with Russia in her consultations with Berlin should be noted once again. The solution of these individual problems should have been preceded by a discussion of the fundamental issue: in the final analysis, what should Axis policy be toward the Soviet Union? It is entirely conceivable that Rosso, from his restricted vantage point in Moscow, had only a hazy grasp of this fundamental question; this assumption is strengthened if one recalls that he was uninformed of his own government's intentions even in the matter of Italo-Soviet relations. But Ciano's comportment cannot be justified, and its consequences soon manifested themselves.

Count Ciano's message to Alfieri arrived in Berlin on January 5 via special courier[158] and appears to have taken Alfieri by surprise[159] and astonished the Embassy staff as well.[160] The fact that one of the secretaries in the Italian legation noted in his diary that the Italo-Soviet negotiation was "undoubtedly prompted by one of the Duce's fits of pique and by his periodic desire to outdo the Germans in any way possible"[161] indicates that the Italian diplomats had not, at the time, given any weight to Ciano's letter of December 16 and to the steps taken at the Wilhelmstrasse a short time later, despite the fact that the contact with Moscow had gone beyond what was touched upon in Alfieri's telegram and letter to Ciano in reply to Ciano's message of December 16.

In any event, Alfieri met with Von Ribbentrop on January 6 and im-

158 Simoni, Berlino: ambasciata d'Italia, p. 197.

159 Alfieri, Due dittatori di fronte, pp. 206, 230. The critical approach taken by Alfieri in his memoirs, in addition to being explicitly contradicted by the telegram which he sent to Ciano on January 6—as will be demonstrated below—appears to be unusually strange if one recalls the sketchy and inadequate information he transmitted to Rome on the results of the Hitler-Molotov meetings.

160 Simoni [Lanza], in fact, noted, "This evening a special courier arrived with documentation that leaves us speechless: Rome is working toward an Italo-Soviet rapprochement!" Simoni, Berlino: ambasciata d'Italia, p. 197. See also Donosti, Mussolini e l'Europa, p. 247.

161 Simoni, Berlino: ambasciata d'Italia, p. 200.

mediately telegraphed to Rome a summary of that colloquy. The sections pertaining to the Moscow negotiations read as follows:

Regarding our relations with Russia, I particularly noted the contents of your letter to him, and I gave him the copy of Rosso's report with the indicated transpositions and pertinent summaries. Von Ribbentrop listened and could not conceal a certain ill-humor as he said, "It is news to me that negotiations are under way."

I immediately and clearly reaffirmed what I had said at the beginning of our conversation, that is, that his statement some time ago in which he recognized the timeliness of our improving our relations with the U.S.S.R. lay at the root of our negotiations with Moscow.

Von Ribbentrop did not reply to this but asked me what our aims were in these negotiations. I replied by referring to Your Excellency's letter, that is, to an updating of the pact of 1933. After rereading the Rosso report, Ribbentrop stated that he desired to reflect on the important problems raised by the Soviets, which would have to be submitted to the Führer. However, he gave me his personal opinion. Referring to the precise statements made to Molotov during the latter's visit to Berlin, i.e., that the Rome-Berlin Axis considered the Balkans as an area of its direct and exclusive influence, justifiable by the vital economic interests of the Axis in the region, he then told me that we should not weaken this policy line. And in the matter of the Danube Question, Von Ribbentrop is of the opinion that making any concession on the presence of Italy and Germany on the Commission would be the source of further complications. In effect, Von Ribbentrop believes that Molotov is playing a double game and is attempting to force in through the window what we have succeeded in pushing out the door. Insofar as the question of the Straits is concerned, Von Ribbentrop recalled that it was he who had suggested the opportuneness of our indicating a certain willingness to compromise with Russia to the point of considering the Black Sea as an inland sea for Russia and the other powers bordering it, and that, in any case, the Convention of Montreux would have to be reexamined. However, he immediately added that the present situation in the eastern Mediterranean demands that we show great prudence and reserve in making concessions to the Russians, particularly because of the reaction they may provoke among Turks.

Clarifying his thoughts further, Von Ribbentrop questioned haste in acting at this particularly delicate moment.

Because of the need to reply to Molotov quickly, I insisted on knowing the opinion of the German government as soon as possible. He told me that it would require three or four days' time.[162]

This time, too, Alfieri limits himself to a summary of the things said to him by Von Ribbentrop and, aside from the firmness of his initial reply, certainly does not add much of his own to the discussion. Yet because of

[162] Alfieri to Ciano, telegram, January 6, 1941, No. 30. For further details on the stormy conversation which took place upon Von Ribbentrop's return from his father's funeral, see Alfieri, *Due dittatori di fronte,* p. 230, Simoni, *Berlino: ambasciata d'Italia,* p. 200, and Donosti, *Mussolini e l'Europa,* p. 247.

its subject matter and tone, the colloquy was unusual, to say the least. It touched on a number of problems and directives of common policy (particularly noteworthy was Von Ribbentrop's question as to what the objectives of the negotiations were), and some comment and observation of a personal nature in the frank and sensible manner employed by Rosso would have been appropriate, all the more so because the diary notation of the Embassy secretary mentioned above, even though it disregarded Ciano's earlier letter, indicated that the Ambassador was severely critical of Rome's initiative. This attitude was confirmed later in Alfieri's memoirs.

There is little to add to what has already been said regarding the position assumed by the Nazi Foreign Minister. His surprise, however, was not entirely justified. His interpretation of Soviet motives and dissatisfaction with Ciano's statements on the Balkans were undoubtedly well founded, while the fundamentally negative attitude he personally expressed regarding other matters is related to facts which had not been communicated to the Fascist government (the projected accord with Turkey, the declarations made to Molotov in Berlin, and the plans to attack the U.S.S.R.). On the other hand, the idea of twisting the Soviet move—of utilizing Fascist diplomacy to ascertain Moscow's real position indirectly—does not correspond with the Nazi Foreign Minister's diagnosis of the Kremlin's aims in its contacts with Rome. Finally, it is worth noting that Von Ribbentrop makes no mention of the problem of recognizing Soviet aspirations in Asia, and that he remained silent on the matter of German preliminary authorization of negotiation when, after Alfieri explained that its aim was to update the pact of 1933, he could have replied that he had been told that it would be "a renewal of reasonably normal relations."

For a more objective reconstruction of what occurred during this colloquy it is also necessary to consider the not indifferent variations in the account of the talks that appear in the German minutes of the meeting.[163] First, they contain not the slightest reference to Alfieri's firm initial reply. Second, according to the German document, in response to Von Ribbentrop's surprise, the Italian Ambassador supposedly added "that it was only a matter of a feeler and that the Duce intended to formulate the conditions for the inauguration of actual negotiations in consultation with Germany." This was a reply that, while reflecting none of that "firmness" mentioned by Alfieri in his telegram, weakened the Italian position because it not only failed to mention Von Ribbentrop's earlier assent on the matter of negotiations, but also left the impression that Rome had not yet arrived at a decision to move ahead with the negotiations with Moscow.

[163] Schmidt, memorandum, January 7, 1941, G.D., Series D, XI, Doc. 610.

It is not easy to determine which version more closely approximates the truth. On the one hand, Alfieri, who had informed Rome of Von Ribbentrop's positive reply on December 23, had a strong motive for mentioning this precedent to the German Minister; on the other, his critical attitude toward the decision taken by Palazzo Chigi and the unimportance with which it was regarded by the Embassy staff in Berlin could have led him to present the matter in the precise way in which it was reported in the German minutes.

Second, the minutes drafted by Schmidt state: "In reply to a question, Alfieri confirmed that Count Ciano had told the Russian Ambassador that Italy would respect Russian interests in the Balkans and in Asia." Obviously, the question was raised after the reading of Rosso's telegram, the text of which had been given to Von Ribbentrop by Alfieri. The reaction of the German Foreign Minister was understandable; Alfieri's reply was less so because in the Ciano version of his colloquy with Gorelkin mention was made of recognizing the new Soviet frontiers, not of recognizing Soviet interests in the Balkans.[164] In any event, this was a point which the Ambassador would have done well to refer to Rome because it goes a long way toward explaining the negative position adopted by Von Ribbentrop toward the Italo-Soviet negotiations.

Last, the Schmidt minutes reveal that, on the whole, the German Minister's reaction was much stronger than reported by Alfieri: rather than having some reservations on the matter of "urgency of the moment," Von Ribbentrop appears to have voiced a clear and unmistakable veto. He reserved the right to transmit a definite reply within a few days, but, after what he said, there should have been no doubt as to the tenor of the forthcoming reply.

Meanwhile, while Palazzo Chigi was waiting for Germany's official reply, a number of communications arrived from Rosso. In the first of these, the Italian Ambassador reported that he had learned from Gafencu that Von Schulenburg had told him of a possible compromise solution to the question of navigation on the Danube.[165] In the second, Rosso transmitted the following summary account of his conversation with his German colleague:

Taking advantage of the authorization contained in Your Excellency's tele-

---

[164] In the memorandum consigned by Alfieri to Von Ribbentrop in which Ciano's statements to Gorelkin were summarized, it was also said that "Italy acknowledges and is ready to recognize formally the predominance of Russian interests in the Black Sea as well as the new frontiers attained by the Soviets." *Ibid.*, enclosure.

[165] Rosso to Ciano, telegram, January 3, 1941, No. 7. While awaiting a reply from Rome to his request for authorization to bring Von Schulenburg up to date on developments, Rosso abstained from asking his German colleague for information.

gram No. 4, I brought my German colleague up to date on the general nature of my meeting with Molotov. In turn, Von Schulenburg gave me the following information:

1. He furnished explanations which he had, in due course, given to Molotov regarding the Rumanian guarantees and which were substantially the same as those I have given to the Soviet Foreign Minister.[166]

2. Recently Von Ribbentrop gave Von Schulenburg instructions of a general nature to confer with Molotov on the Danubian question.[167] The President of the Council of Peoples' Commissars expressed himself to my colleague in the same terms he employed in his talks with me, demonstrating surprise that Germany would seek to block Soviet participation in the maritime administration of the Danube. Von Schulenburg replied that it was rather the attitude of the Soviet delegate to the Bucharest Conference which seemed to demonstrate that the U.S.S.R. was interested in excluding everyone else from this administration. Then, speaking unofficially, he suggested that, in addition to the U.S.S.R. and Rumania, Italy and Germany should also be permitted to participate. Molotov limited himself to observing that, to date, neither Italy nor Germany had advanced any such request but that he would not, at that time, offer any objections. My colleague's thinking is that this idea—which he mentioned only as a personal observation—might serve as a basis for the compromise I mentioned in my telegram No. 7 of January 3.

3. On the matter of the Straits, Von Schulenburg confirmed that this question had been the object of conversation between Molotov and Von Ribbentrop in Berlin. At that time, Von Ribbentrop is reported to have said that, of the two Axis powers, Italy was the one most directly concerned with the matter. Von Schulenburg supposes that Von Ribbentrop has kept Your Excellency precisely informed on this matter.[168]

In examining the problem with my German colleague, we have come to the conclusion that the Soviet objectives are essentially these:

1. To prohibit access to the Black Sea of warships not belonging to powers bordering on that sea either in time of peace or war. With this assurance the

[166] On this point see Von Ribbentrop to Von Schulenburg, telegram, September 3, 1940, *ibid.*, December 7; Von Schulenburg to Von Ribbentrop, telegram, September 4, 1940, *ibid.*, December 13; Von Ribbentrop to Von Schulenburg, telegram, September 6, 1940, *ibid.*, December 24.

[167] Ample detail may be found in Gafencu, *Preliminari*, pp. 79, 102; Beloff, *Soviet Russia*, II, pp. 340–41, 357; Rodolfo Mosca, *Il regime internazionale del Danubio e la guerra* (Budapest: Societas Carpate-Danubiana, 1943), pp. 113–62. The information possessed by Gafencu and by Von Schulenburg concerning the possible solution of the question of the Danubian Commission was also confirmed by Alfieri in one of his talks with the Soviet Ambassador, Dekanov. The latter appeared to be extremely well informed and was obviously very optimistic regarding the successful conclusion of the Italo-Soviet talks. He concluded by offering a toast to the victory of the Axis Powers over their enemies. Alfieri to Ciano, courier telegram, January 8, 1941, No. 3.

[168] Cf. Schmidt, memorandum, November 15, 1940, *G.D.*, Series D, XI, Doc. 328. These minutes record that, on November 13, at the conclusion of the discussion on the Straits problem, Hitler stated to Molotov that "he could not in any circumstances take a position before he had talked with the Duce, since Germany was interested in the matter only secondarily."

Soviet Union would be able to strengthen its security without having to maintain huge naval forces in the Black Sea at the expense of the fleets stationed in the Baltic, at Murmansk, and at Vladivostok.

2. To obtain for herself the right of passage through the Straits at all times of her naval vessels as well as her commercial craft.

Not even Von Schulenburg has been more successful than anyone else in learning whether the U.S.S.R. aims to achieve these objectives by means of an international agreement which will replace the one in effect or by demanding that Turkey allow the U.S.S.R. to participate directly in the military control of the Straits.[169]

This exchange of views was marked by a noticeable reticence on the part of Von Schulenburg.[170] He did not offer Rosso the opportunity to infer that it was Hitler's assertion to Molotov that Italian interests in the Straits Question were the more important of the two powers and that this assertion was the reason—perhaps the principal one—for the Soviet Union's friendly attitude toward the Fascist government. In any event, it is likely that this reticence was the principal reason for Rosso's suggestions regarding the course to take, which he dispatched to Rome the following day. The telegram from Rosso to Ciano on January 6 reads as follows:

In telegram No. 239 Your Excellency invited me to make suggestions concerning the conduct of negotiations for the accord with the U.S.S.R. Taking advantage of this authorization, and in order to amplify what I have said in my telegrams Nos. 557 and 558, I am taking the liberty of making the following suggestions.

For reasons which are to some extent psychological, it is important not to delay replying in some way to Molotov's questions in order to avoid creating suspicion and resentment among the Soviet leaders.

In my opinion we could, in the meantime, make assurances to them along these lines:

1. In the thinking and the intentions of the Italian government the Italo-German guarantees to Rumania were never designed to be anti-Soviet in any way. The guarantees were necessary to induce the Rumanian government to accept the sacrifices demanded for a peaceful settlement of the questions raised

---

[169] Rosso to Ciano, telegram, January 5, 1941, No. 13. The German documentary collection contains no summary report of any kind from Von Schulenburg on these talks.

[170] Aside from the fact that the German Ambassador again fell back on the technique of assuming that Von Ribbentrop had already fully informed Ciano on the matter (on this point see Rosso to Ciano, telegram, December 30, 1940, No. 556), it should also be noted that, in his predictions for the solution to the Straits Question eventually proposed by Moscow, Von Schulenburg not only refrained from stating that he possessed the text of the Soviet project of November 25, 1940 (for the text see G.D., Series D, XI, Doc. 404), but also failed to explain to Rosso that one of the major aspirations of the Kremlin, stated orally and in writing to the German government by Moscow, included the establishment of a military base in the Straits.

by the Hungarian and Bulgarian claims. The Italian government does not foresee that these guarantees can become operative against the Soviet Union because the latter has also declared that, after the restitution of Bessarabia and the incorporation of northern Bukowina into the U.S.S.R., the Soviet Union has no further territorial claims against Rumania.

2. Regarding the Danubian question, the attitude of the Italian government is dictated by the necessity of safeguarding its legitimate interests as a power which recognizes the free navigation of that vitally important river route as the premise necessary to the development of its commercial relations with the nations of the river basin. The Italian government recognizes the increased importance which this river has assumed for the Soviet Union since the latter's acquisition of Bessarabia and is pleased that, in the matter of control of Danubian navigation, the U.S.S.R. is taking its rightful place as a riparian state and as the major power in the Black Sea. As to the differences which have surfaced at the Bucharest conference regarding the administration of traffic on the Danube, the Italian government believes that a satisfactory solution can be attained at that conference if the participating governments will agree on the principle that whatever problem arises in connection with navigation on the Danube must be resolved with the participation of all of the interested powers.

(With this last sentence we would be implying the acceptance of the idea of compromise mentioned in my telegram No. 13, unless, in agreement with the German government, Your Excellency believes that we can proceed with the offer of an explicit proposal in this regard.)

3. The Italian government understands perfectly the interest of the U.S.S.R. in the Straits as related to the problem of Soviet security in the Black Sea and is ready to study with the required attention the ideas and suggestions which the Soviet government may care to propose in connection with the solution to the problem. In this matter, the Soviet government will, of course, want to keep in mind the interests of Italy in its political and commercial relations with the countries bordering on the Black Sea.

(With a declaration of this nature, the Italian government would be assuming no obligation of any kind, while forcing the Soviet Union to reveal its own plans. Your Excellency will then judge whether it is necessary to advance this viewpoint as the most desirable solution to the Straits Question and, at the same time, to furnish the data necessary to demonstrate the concept of the preeminence of Italian interests in the Mediterranean.)

4. In the declaration made to Ambassador Gorelkin on December 26 with respect to Soviet interests in the Balkans and in Asia, Minister Ciano meant that Italy recognizes the existence of these interests and intends to respect them.

5. When he declared that Italy is prepared to recognize the new frontiers acquired by the Soviet Union, Minister Ciano intended to demonstrate to the Soviet Union, through formal recognition, proof of its friendship, which in international practice always takes on the characteristics of a manifestation of goodwill.

These proposals have been based on an understanding of the problems which may be unilateral and incomplete. Nevertheless, I submit them to you in response to Your Excellency's invitation and with the intention of contributing, to the best of my ability, to the drafting of the replies, which will enable me to reopen my conversations with Molotov.[171]

Rosso's proposals did not obligate Rome excessively; they were aimed at extracting further clarifications from the U.S.S.R.; they would have officially confirmed the viewpoints expressed by Rosso unofficially in his colloquy with Molotov; they took into consideration the latest developments in the Danubian question; and, finally, they were designed to gain time without unduly irritating the Soviet government. Their principal defect lay in the fact that, on the one hand, they did not reflect the position assumed at almost the same time by Von Ribbentrop on these problems in his talks with Alfieri (a position which was not described to Rosso in any direct communication),[172] while, on the other, they were not likely to satisfy Molotov. On this point, however, neither Rosso nor the Foreign Ministry in Rome was in a position to judge, given the reticence of the Germans to discuss what transpired in the Hitler-Molotov talks in Berlin. Furthermore, in Rosso's suggestions there was no mention of the need to examine all of the problems in detail. In any event, in Rome, where Von Ribbentrop's rebuff counseled maximum prudence, nothing was done to implement the suggestions of the Italian Ambassador to Moscow. The Italian Foreign Minister did no more than telegraph to Rosso to inform him that "the reply to Molotov's questions, along with the suggestions [by Rosso] regarding the conduct of the Italo-Soviet conversations were the subject of an exchange of views with the German government, and because of the vastness and the complexity of the problems under consideration," the right was being reserved "to send further instructions as soon as possible."[173]

The keenly awaited reply to the questions posed by Palazzo Chigi to

[171] Rosso to Ciano, telegrams, January 6, 1941, Nos. 17, 18. To assist in this activity, aimed at collaborating in searching for a solution of the problems raised by the Soviets, Rosso sent to Rome a very sound historico-political study of the Straits Question. Rosso to Ciano, report, January 11, 1941, N. 112/44. Rosso, on January 10, 1941, prompted by the imminent arrival in Moscow of a Swiss trade delegation, telegraphed to Rome urging that a proposal be forwarded to Moscow to resolve the commercial problems pending between Italy and the Soviet Union, along with a draft of a possible commercial treaty to be proposed to the U.S.S.R. Rosso to Ciano, January 10, 1941, No. 20. The insistence of the Italian Ambassador to Moscow was probably responsible for prompting the Director General for Economic Affairs in the Foreign Ministry, Ambassador Giannini, to draft a detailed brief for Minister Ciano, containing suggestions for possible bases of the desired commercial accord with the U.S.S.R. This brief is dated January 17, 1941.

[172] It appears, instead, that Von Schulenburg not only approved of Rosso's suggestions but also promised to press for Berlin's approval of them. Rosso to Alfieri, personal letter, January 16, 1941. Simoni, Berlino: ambasciata d'Italia, pp. 203–7.

[173] Ciano to Rosso, telegram, January 8, 1941, No. 8.

the Wilhelmstrasse, originally proposed for January 11, was postponed several times, probably because of current developments in Bulgaria, which culminated in the entrance of Wehrmacht troops into Sofia and King Boris' adherence to the Tripartite Pact.

The Weizsäcker-Alfieri meeting was first postponed on the grounds that the German Secretary of State had "received further instructions."[174] On January 13 Weizsäcker informed the Italian Ambassador in Berlin that because of the delay in Von Ribbentrop's return to Berlin the latter had requested that the Moscow talks be handled in a dilatory fashion until the scheduled Hitler-Mussolini meeting.[175] Meanwhile, Rosso, completely unaware of these difficulties and concerned by the prolonged silence from Rome, telegraphed to Ciano the next day as follows:

I believe it my duty to insist on the necessity of avoiding any further delay in giving Molotov an answer, even if only a preliminary one.

Three weeks have passed since the Italian government, for the second time, took the initiative to open political conversations, to which the Soviet government promptly agreed.

It was obvious from the start that these conversations were destined to develop as continuations of those begun last June and then interrupted. Therefore, it was natural to suppose that when I went to the Kremlin on December 30 to see Molotov he would be convinced that the Royal Government was ready to discuss the various points contained in the Soviet memorandum of June 25. Our prolonged delay in replying to questions of a general and preliminary nature posed by Molotov cannot help but create doubts and arouse suspicions damaging to our prestige and position in the eyes of the U.S.S.R.

I am perfectly aware of the need to consult Berlin. I am also aware that the magnitude and complexity of the problems preclude rapid and conclusive decisions, particularly at the present time.

I note, however, that Molotov has not yet probed the heart of these problems and that, therefore, it is possible to reply adequately with formulas that do not imply obligations, such as those I suggested in my telegrams Nos. 17 and 18 of January 6.

A preliminary reply carrying with it no obligations would serve to demonstrate that our initiative was determined by a real desire to arrive at a clarification of our political relations with the U.S.S.R. and would eliminate the doubts and suspicions which may already be making inroads into Molotov's thinking regarding our intentions. At the same time, our reply could lead Molotov to state the Soviet Union's aims and objectives precisely.

When Molotov has made concrete proposals or has raised precise questions,

---

[174] Alfieri to Ciano, telegram, January 11, 1941, No. 52.

[175] Alfieri to Ciano, telegram, January 13, 1941, No. 61. See also Siegfried memorandum, January 13, 1940, G.D., Series D, XI, Doc. 646. A Von Weizsäcker memorandum indicates that the colloquy may have taken place on January 14, 1941. Ibid., note 1. Concerning this communication, which he dated January 16, Simoni incorrectly wrote of a pure and simple German request to suspend the Italo-Soviet negotiations. Simoni, Berlino: ambasciata d'Italia, p. 203.

these can always be carefully scrutinized in conjunction with the German government, in order to determine at that time the feasibility and advantage of pressing forward with the negotiations to reach an accord.[176]

Rosso's arguments were plausible because the difficulty involved in renewing negotiations with Moscow was unknown to him, but Rome's delay in replying appeared quite understandable. The only thing that could be done at that time was to pressure Berlin for a reply, a fact which Rosso deduced for himself and sought to achieve on his own two days later by sending a long personal letter to Alfieri, to which reference has been made above,[177] and by asking Von Schulenburg to press for Berlin's approval of the negotiations.

On January 19, on the occasion of the meeting of the two dictators at Berchtesgaden, Von Ribbentrop finally gave Ciano the reply which he had promised in his conversation with Alfieri on January 6. The pertinent portion, as recorded in the minutes of the meetings between the two Axis foreign ministers, reads as follows:

The most important problem is that concerning Russia. Von Ribbentrop read with great interest what had been communicated to him by Alfieri regarding our negotiations with the Soviets. He stated that while he supported the idea of an improvement in Italo-Soviet relations, he did not believe that a first encounter should have carried the concept as far as it has. He is extremely skeptical of Russia's good faith: he fears that, since Molotov found so many doors closed to him during his visit to Berlin, he is now attempting to enter via the Italian window. This is particularly true in regard to the Balkan problems. Meanwhile, Von Ribbentrop concurs that we should reply to the various questions Molotov raised during his colloquy with Rosso but prefers that our reply be inconclusive, and he himself would like to suggest its general nature in relationship to what was said to Molotov in Berlin. This would serve to maintain a uniform policy between Italy and Germany.

Von Ribbentrop urges that he be kept fully informed of every detail of the development of the Moscow negotiations.[178]

[176] Rosso to Ciano, telegram, January 14, 1941, No. 42.

[177] The cause for this initiative could have been the rumors circulating that very day in Moscow regarding a possible Soviet-Turkish rapprochement as a reaction to the German military movements in the Balkans. Rosso to Ciano, telegram, January 16, 1941, No. 45.

[178] Ciano, L'Europa verso la catastrofe, pp. 628–28 (the corresponding German minutes have not been found). From the minutes of the simultaneous Mussolini-Hitler colloquy (ibid., pp. 628–29) and from the Schmidt memorandum of January 21, 1941 (G.D., Series D, XI, Doc. 672), it does not appear that the problem of relations with the Soviet Union was discussed. Instead, they were discussed two days later, but without explicit reference to the Rome-Moscow conversations. On this second occasion, the words used by Hitler could have been interpreted as an indirect warning to the Italians to proceed very cautiously in their contacts with the Soviets: "It was necessary to be very cautious in dealing with the Russians. They

Von Ribbentrop's reply is clearly that of a superior to an inferior. He failed to refer to his colloquy with Alfieri in which the limits to be set to the Italo-Soviet talks were established (while, at the same time, he had learned from reading the summary of the Rosso-Molotov conversations that Rosso had received instructions allowing him much wider latitude). One might say that he now assumed direction of the negotiations and the determination of their disposition. This control, after all, is what was important to him. The reply was no more than a delaying tactic, as it had become clear that delay and still more delay had thus far characterized the affair, and Von Ribbentrop chose to carry it to the extreme. It is true that he suggested the limits to be imposed on the talks in relation to what was said to Molotov in Berlin, but he would not tell Ciano exactly what was said to Molotov in those talks. Nor was Von Ribbentrop particularly concerned about the fact that, with the postponement of the reply to the Soviets, the conclusion of the Italo-Soviet trade agreement would also necessarily be postponed (it was ultimately not to be realized). This postponement took place at the very time when the Germans concluded with Moscow the most important Nazi-Soviet trade pact since the agreement of August 23, 1939.[179]

Thus, in the final analysis, Italy alone was to pay the price for the differences in points of view between Rome and Berlin,[180] even though the responsibilities were, at the very least, divided, and perhaps even predominantly Berlin's. If the instructions issued by Ciano to Rosso had gone beyond what Ciano had agreed upon with Von Ribbentrop, the reason for postponing a reply to Molotov at this time (a reply that ultimately evaded the questions at issue) lay in the long-standing state of the Nazi-

---

were constantly looking for points in the treaties on which new demands could be based. In their treaty agreements, therefore, like Jewish lawyers, they preferred vague formulations and liked to base their arguments on ambiguous definitions that were capable of various interpretations. In their trade agreements they operated on a big scale but only a part of these had thus far been realized." Schmidt, memorandum, January 21, 1941, *ibid.*, Doc. 679.

[179] The text is in *ibid.*, Doc. 637. The accord is dated January 10, 1941.

[180] On this point it should be noted that in response to Moscow's solicitations for a reply to the note presented on November 25, 1940 (for the text of the note see Von Schulenburg to Von Ribbentrop, telegram, November 26, 1940, *ibid.*, Doc. 404), the Germans continued to repeat that the reply could not be given until Germany had consulted with Italy and Japan. Von Schulenburg to Von Ribbentrop, telegram, January 17, 1941, and Von Ribbentrop to Von Weizsäcker, telegram, January 21, 1941, *ibid.*, Docs. 669, 681. While this fact may have increased Soviet interest in pursuing the conversations with Italy, it could also have induced them to regard Italy as sharing the responsibility for the delaying tactics of the Wilhelmstrasse.

Soviet relationship, a relationship which Von Ribbentrop had never revealed to Ciano and which he did not reveal at this time.

However, Ciano's position in the face of these arguments seems to have been even more ambiguous. Not only did he fail to defend the considerations which had led him to contemplate the rapprochement with the Soviet Union and promptly accepted the German viewpoint as expressed by the Nazi Foreign Minister, but he also refrained from asking for clarification on the Hitler-Molotov-Ribbentrop conversations, which were supposed to form the basis of the reply to the Kremlin. If Ciano's acquiescence in Berlin's wishes was justified by the demands of the alliance and by Italy's extremely difficult military position in Greece and in North Africa, his failure to demand clarification on a problem of fundamental importance to the conduct of a joint foreign policy is far less comprehensible. Realistically, it must be concluded that the last traces of the Fascist government's autonomy were lost in the mountains of Albania and Epirus.

8

The formulas promised by the Wilhelmstrasse were officially consigned to the Italian Chargé d'Affaires in Berlin, Cosmelli, by the German Secretary of State, Von Weizsäcker, on the evening of January 22. The German communiqué consisted of a note to the Fascist government in which the German position on the Italo-Soviet negotiations, the text of the reply which Palazzo Chigi would be expected to give to Molotov's questions, and an oral explanation of the above were outlined. Early the following day, Cosmelli wrote to Rome concerning the German communiqué as follows:

This evening Secretary of State Von Weizsäcker again called me to the Wilhelmstrasse[181] to read to me from the original text of the long memorandum on the conversation with the Soviets, which Minister Von Ribbentrop apparently summarized orally in English for Your Excellency at Berchtesgaden. He has urged me to communicate immediately regarding the correct understanding of the principal points discussed at Berchtesgaden.

Therefore I am briefing the document in question based on the notes I took, and tomorrow I shall report more fully after I have had the opportunity to compare the written texts with what was dictated to me by Von Weizsäcker, since their precise formulation is a vital matter, and in particular regarding those three points touched upon by Your Excellency in your conversation of December 26.[182]

First, the exchanges of views and contacts on these problems between Your Excellency and Von Ribbentrop during last summer have been confirmed. The

181 The previous meeting was for the purpose of communicating the texts of the German-Soviet notes exchanged on the Bulgarian problem.
182 Between Ciano and Gorelkin.

German view is that Berlin, in effect, recognizes the need for an amelioration of Italo-Soviet relations, although it was Germany's view that it would be imperative to avoid arriving at any concrete stipulations on certain questions of a political nature and that, in any case, these talks should be approached with great caution.

These tactics in dealing with the Soviets are all the more necessary now that the Greek campaign has begun.

The three specific questions raised during our recent talks with the Soviets, referred to in Your Excellency's letter 1/003 of January 1,[183] were commented upon as follows:

a. *Rumanian guarantees*: According to the above-mentioned letter, our definition of the guarantees has caused some concern here, in that the guarantees given to the Rumanians are in fact all-inclusive against everyone in defense of the vital interests connected with the maintenance of the status quo and the present Rumanian frontiers.

I have taken some notes on the report given to me orally as it refers to the precedents, meaning, and scope of the Rumanian guarantees.

b. *Navigation on the Danube*: You will recall the Russian demand that only countries bordering on the river participate in discussions relating to and in administration of the river and the subsequent position taken by Germany, who, admitting the vital interests of the riparian states, insisted on an Italian presence based on the close ties of alliance existing between Germany and Italy. Therefore, Italy's permanent position on the Commission is not due to Russian insistence. Since the Soviet objections are judged of more than technical significance, it is considered opportune to postpone the opening of the conference scheduled for January 20 until March. I have transcribed the exact text of the argument presented.

c. *The Straits Question*: Granted their decisive importance in the event of possible German action in the Balkans, they acquire even greater significance in relations with Bulgaria and particularly with Turkey. If it becomes known, as it inevitably will, that Italy is proposing solutions at the expense of Turkey, this could have a grave effect on the Bulgarian territorial questions and, even more seriously, on Turkey.

I am transmitting the text of the German statement. The German memorandum concludes that the German government would look with favor on the realization of concrete results within the limits outlined above, that it would consider opportune an appropriate announcement being made to the press at the moment of reaching an agreement [word undecipherable] in principle, and that, prior to informing the Moscow government of our proposals, Berlin would appreciate being informed of them.[184]

The text of the three formulas presented by the Wilhelmstrasse for inclusion in the Italian reply to Molotov was as follows:

Rumania: The guarantee given to Rumania by the Axis Powers, as is evident from the circumstances under which the guarantee was given, contains

183 From Ciano to Alfieri.
184 Cosmelli to Ciano, telegram, January 23, 1941, No. 93.

nothing aimed against Soviet Russia. Italy, as well as Germany, has a fundamental interest in the preservation of peace and tranquility in Rumania, an interest deriving primarily from the close relationships of both countries with the economy of Rumania. In particular, the extraction of Rumanian oil and its conveyance to Italy and Germany, along with the unimpeded importation of Rumanian grain, are of enduring and vital importance to the Axis powers. Therefore, late last August, in the extremely critical situation at that time, Italy and Germany took on the role of mediators and through their arbitration award ensured the peace that was threatened in the Danube area. However, in order to prevent once and for all the easy recurrence of similar disagreements in that area, the Axis powers undertook to give the guarantee when the Rumanian government at that time expressly requested that it be granted. Inasmuch as the arbitration award necessarily involved cession of a substantial portion of Rumanian national territory, it was entirely natural that Rumania would feel that she ought to be able henceforth to regard both her boundary with Hungary and her national territory generally as finally secured against any outside encroachment. Inasmuch as the territorial demands advanced by the Soviet Government against Rumania had then already found their solution, and the peaceful settlement of Bulgaria's demands also appeared to be assured, the Axis powers no longer had any reservations on these grounds about granting the guarantee.

Danube: . . . Italy first wished to consult with Germany as well as Rumania concerning the future treatment of the Danube question and would gladly cooperate in any practical solution mutually satisfactory to all parties.

Straits: . . . We consider it advisable for the Italian government to confine itself to a statement that it is entirely sympathetic to a modification of the Straits statute in favor of Russia; it would, for example, agree that, as regards passage of naval vessels, such passage should be allowed only to naval vessels of states adjacent to the Black Sea. The details of the arrangement would, of course, have to be left for future negotiations with Turkey.[185]

Finally, the explanatory oral commentary on the German note as well as on the formulas advanced on the three problems was summarized by the Italian Chargé d'Affaires as follows:

Secretary of State Von Weizsäcker, in the presence of Minister Schmidt, who served as interpreter at the Berchtesgaden conversations, made it clear that these formulas are to be considered agreed upon and approved. The text relevant to Rumanian guarantees also is to be regarded as having the value of a formula. These are to be the bases of our communication to Russia.

With reference to the next to the last paragraph of my telegram No. 93 cited above, which is also the concluding portion of the German memorandum, Secretary of State Weizsäcker further specified that "the German government,

---

[185] Cosmelli to Ciano, telegram, January 23, 1941, No. 96. The original German text of the three formulas was transmitted by Cosmelli to Rome on January 25, 1941, along with the report (No. 00830/175). In translating the German version into English some very slight variations from the Italian translation occurred, but these do not in any way alter the meaning of the text.

despite what action has already been taken by us toward the Soviet government, understands that the Italian government must at least achieve a provisional positive result without, however, going into too much detail. In order to achieve such a provisional positive result, it may be necessary to find a formula which, despite its general character, has a certain positive content without infringing upon our common political requirements. Otherwise, undesirable complications might arise for the Axis powers. It would be politically advantageous if the conclusion of the provisional Italo-Russian understanding were publicized in the appropriate news media, without, however, entering into details. The German government would be pleased if the Italian government would inform it of the proposals it intends to make to the Soviet Union for a general political understanding prior to the time it makes them known to the Soviet government."

The above quotation is, in the main, a literal translation of what was told to me by way of clarification and comment or read to me and must be considered an integral part of and a definitive clarification of the next to the last paragraph in my telegram transmitted last night.

As Your Excellency will note, the points repeatedly stressed are an accord that will avoid detail, one that is provisional and general in nature, yet with a certain positive political value; a communication for release to the press without any particular details; prior submission to the German government of our exact proposals before they are transmitted to Moscow.[186]

The memorandum from the Wilhelmstrasse should be examined from three points of view: the overall position toward the Italo-Soviet negotiations, the three formulas relative to the principal questions posed by Molotov to Rosso, and the position to be assumed concerning all other problems to be discussed in arriving at an eventual understanding with Moscow. For the purpose of this analysis the instructions drafted by Von Ribbentrop as a guide for Von Weizsäcker in his colloquy with the Italian Chargé d'Affaires are especially pertinent.[187]

The position taken by Von Ribbentrop toward the entire Italo-Soviet negotiations was actually less rigid than what might have been expected from the statement recorded in the minutes of his colloquy with Ciano on January 19. In effect, the statement reflects a return to his position of August 16, 1940. However, this fact does not in any way justify the sense of optimism suggested by the recommendations being offered regarding statements to be issued to the press, since the matter of the press release was probably a guarantee against the possibility of the Italians taking greater liberties in their negotiations. Moreover, given Von Ribbentrop's experience in negotiating with the Soviets, one might well ask whether he, in all candor, believed that it would be possible that they would be disposed to conclude nothing more than a general and provisional agreement with Italy.

With respect to the three formulas, that concerning the Rumanian

---

[186] Cosmelli to Ciano, telegram, January 23, 1941, No. 95.
[187] Von Ribbentrop, memorandum, no date, *G.D.*, Series D, XI, Doc. 688.

guarantees simply restated the arguments advanced to Molotov by Von Schulenburg and by Rosso, and, in rejecting Mussolini's willingness to make greater concessions on this point, was aimed at preventing any notion from developing in Moscow that the guarantees might not also be applicable against the U.S.S.R.[188] This intransigence might have also been justified by the position taken by Hitler and Von Ribbentrop during the conversations with Molotov on November 12 and 13, 1940, the details of which were unknown to the Italian government, but which indicated that Berlin was persisting in its "hard line" toward Moscow. This attitude became more clearly discernible with regard to the Danube Commission, where some concessions to the Soviets could have been made along the lines suggested by Rosso in agreement with Von Schulenburg.[189] With reference to the Straits, German insistence that Turkey be included in any negotiations to revise the Montreux Convention, even if it simply reiterated the position previously expressed during the Nazi-Soviet conversations in Berlin (which failed) and reflected the change in German policy toward Ankara[190] and Germany's requirements stemming from her imminent military intervention in the Balkans, introduced another very serious obstacle to a solution of the question. Here, too, the Rosso proposal, without further compromising Italy, might have been somewhat easier for Moscow to accept.

Regarding the other problems which were to have been subjects of the Italo-Soviet understanding (Soviet interests in the Balkans and in Asia), the Wilhelmstrasse, obviously taking advantage of the fact that these two

[188] In the memorandum cited in n. 187, Von Ribbentrop stated: "The declaration which Italy was going to make to the Soviet Union ought not to be phrased in such a way as to permit the Soviet Government to infer that the guarantees would not apply as regards to Russia. Rather, we considered it essential to let the Soviet Government know in appropriate form that Italy as well as Germany, in view of the vital interests which both countries had in Rumania, would not allow any encroachment upon the territory of the Rumanian state within its present boundaries."

[189] The Von Ribbentrop memorandum, after recalling that if Italy had become part of the Danube Commission, it was due solely to Germany's efforts and that therefore there was no need for Italy to be excessively accommodating to the U.S.S.R. on this matter, added, "We are determined on our part to insist not only upon completely equal participation of Germany, Italy, Rumania and Russia in the international supervision of the maritime Danube but will insist also that in the organization to be established for the practical implementation of the program, Rumania, on whose national territory the organization would carry out its program, must naturally have the lead. We have also promised this to General Antonescu."

[190] The Von Ribbentrop memorandum put particular emphasis on this point: "The development of the military situation in Albania makes the military intervention by Germany in the Balkans probable. Consequently, the relationship of the Axis Powers to Bulgaria and especially to Turkey comes now to the forefront of attention. . . . If Italy now were to make any concrete promises to the Soviet Government concerning the Straits at Turkey's expense, this would surely become known to Turkey and might decisively influence her attitude in the coming months."

items had not been emphasized in the Ciano letter to Alfieri, refrained from immediately taking a position, reserving the right, however, to do so at a later date when the Fascist government had transmitted the text of the proposals it planned to submit to Moscow.[191] Thus, although the German reply was incomplete, it achieved the aim, already expressed by Von Ribbentrop to Ciano, of delaying the negotiations still further.

The Berlin memorandum did not evoke any particular reaction in Rome.[192] After the Berchtesgaden meeting, its tone was no longer taken seriously. At this point, Palazzo Chigi could have begun to prepare replies to the questions raised by Molotov and not mentioned in the Wilhelmstrasse note, and then submitted them to Berlin for approval. This alternative does not appear to have been considered by Ciano, who, either to avoid any further delay or because the question never entered his mind, immediately telegraphed the three German formulas to Rosso, affirming that they represented "the Italian point of view on the Rumanian, Danubian, and Straits questions." The Ambassador was instructed to inform Molotov of this fact in the name of the Italian Foreign Minister. Furthermore, Rosso was informed that these formulas had been "agreed upon personally" by Ciano and Von Ribbentrop. Ciano "believed that he had thus replied in principle to the questions raised by Molotov and waited to learn the latter's observations and eventual further developments in the negotiations."[193]

With the instructions sent on January 24 to the Italian Ambassador in Moscow, the Italo-Soviet conversations were about to enter a new and decisive phase.

9

Rosso received Ciano's telegram on Saturday morning, January 25, and immediately asked to be received at the Kremlin. Molotov promised to reply to this request on Monday[194] and did, indeed, receive the Am-

[191] In his memorandum, Von Ribbentrop, after emphasizing the need "for close coordination of German and Italian policy toward the Soviet Government" indulged himself in the following series of affirmations, which are distinguished for their falsity: "I always in the past secured *the agreement of Count Ciano and the Duce himself regarding all moves undertaken* by the German side *in relation to the Soviet Government*. It is obvious that the questions now raised in the Italo-Russian conversations are inseparably connected with the ideas which were developed by us *in agreement with the Italian Government* for M. Molotov during his visit to Berlin." (Italics added.)

[192] Ciano made no comment on this in his diary, and the same may be said for Simoni.

[193] Ciano to Rosso, telegram, January 24, 1941, No. 32. Copy of this telegram was dispatched to the Ambassador in Berlin on the same day via courier telegram No. 2763/PR.

[194] Rosso to Ciano, telegram, January 26, 1941, No. 62.

bassador on January 27. Rosso summarized this important ninety-minute colloquy in a dispatch which was promptly telegraphed to Rome and read as follows:

I opened the conversation by informing Molotov, in your name, of the statements outlined in your telegram No. 32 relative to the three issues: Rumania, Danube, the Straits.

Except for some minor transpositions and for some slight variations in form—made necessary by the translation into Russian—I transmitted the text exactly as I received it.

Molotov allowed me to make my entire statement without interrupting me, asking only that the interpreter translate very slowly and very clearly so that his secretary could transcribe the statements in their entirety. He then commented and asked questions on each of the three issues in turn.

Regarding the Italo-German guarantee to Rumania, Molotov made it clear that the Soviet government was extremely interested because the U.S.S.R. borders Rumania and, therefore, "the problem is of major concern to her."

He then returned to the questions already elaborated in the conversation of December 30, 1940, and repeated that Italy and Germany had not acted in these circumstances as the Soviet government had the right to expect. He added a new motive for recrimination: while in the Tripartite Pact the signatory powers saw the need to insert a clause referring to the U.S.S.R., the latter had been completely ignored in the matter of the guarantee to Rumania.

He also added, "This sort of action could not then, nor can it today, satisfy the Moscow government."

However, Molotov concluded his observations on this problem by stating that my exposition of the Italian position "was clear and that he had fully understood it."

Turning to the problem of the Danube, Molotov stated that he was taking note of the Italian government's statement that it desired to collaborate with the other delegations at the Bucharest conference to find an acceptable and satisfactory solution for all powers concerned. In a lightly ironical vein, he added that the Soviet government will look forward to the implementation of the Italian position in the hope that our delegate will show greater objectivity than he has heretofore in his systematic and exclusive support of the Rumanian proposals, without regard for the Soviet position.

He concluded his comments on this point by noting that there was need to go into further detail; actual practice would indicate whether the problem will be resolved.

On the Straits Question, Molotov, after reflecting for an instant, started to speak slowly, weighing his words carefully.

He stated, "This is a much more complex problem than the two discussed previously, and I reserve the right to study the Italian declaration, which must be examined in detail."

He then asked me whether he had clearly understood the Italian position, i.e., that the Italian government agreed that the free navigation of the Straits was to be limited to naval vessels of the powers bordering the Black Sea.

I replied by repeating the statement and emphasizing the passage "it would, for example, agree that," etc., etc.

Molotov then raised a second question: "Does the Italian government already know whether Turkey will accept or is in accord with the Italian point of view on the matter of the revision of the Straits Convention?"

I replied that I had no information on the subject. However, I did not believe that the Italian government had queried the Turkish government on the matter because it had no reason to do so.

I pointed out that the Straits Question had been raised by Molotov himself during the course of our conversations and that it had been posed only from the point of view of Soviet interests, that is, those of Soviet security in the Black Sea. Therefore, this was a question which he himself had raised only as a "Soviet problem." It was thus not up to the Italian government to take the initiative to ascertain the Turkish attitude on the matter.

I also made it clear to Molotov that the Italian government had already taken a positive step on this matter by declaring that it favored a revision of the Straits Convention to the advantage of the U.S.S.R. and, more important, that it would be able to support what had always been a traditional postulate of Russian foreign policy, i.e., prohibiting transit of the Straits by naval vessels of powers not bordering the Black Sea.

I reminded him that at the Montreux Conference England had bitterly resisted the Soviet thesis and had insisted on free passage through the Straits of the naval vessels of any nation at war. The Turkish position at Montreux had been rather equivocal. Italy had not taken part in that conference and, therefore, had no occasion to take sides at that time. Today, Italy was stating to the U.S.S.R. that in general it favored the thesis of the U.S.S.R. and that Molotov should recognize that this already represented an important demonstration of goodwill and friendship on our part.

Molotov promptly agreed, recognizing that my statement had a "positive content" and that the attitude of the Italian government on the Straits matter was "new," "important," and "very interesting." He fully appreciated all aspects of the Italian gesture.

Nevertheless, Molotov added, the reservation contained in the last part of the Italian declaration, which stated that "the details of the revision must, of course, be resolved in future negotiations with Turkey," in effect makes Italian consent contingent on Turkish consent. This was the reason why it was so important to know the Turkish intentions.

I interrupted at this point to note that I was in agreement with him on the importance of knowing Turkey's views on the subject. Since Turkey controlled the territory on both shores of the Straits and, therefore, effectively controlled the use of the Straits, she was one of the parties directly concerned with the question. It was for precisely this reason that the Italian government, in replying to the question posed by Molotov, could do no less than take into account the existing situation and, accordingly, mention the need to negotiate with Turkey. I also repeated that it was not up to Italy to take the initiative in the matter.

Molotov then turned the discussion to the Balkan problems. He stated that "the German government has informed us that it intended to send its troops, now concentrated in Rumania, southward across Bulgaria, in the event that England extended its military operations to Greece. Turkey is England's ally and is also tied to Greece by an assistance pact. If and when the German troops do march toward Greece, in all probability Turkey will enter the conflict. This would mean the extension of the war to the Straits and to the Black Sea area. England has already established air and submarine bases on the island of Lemnos, that is, at the entrance to the Straits, which means that the security of the Black Sea and therefore of the U.S.S.R. becomes directly involved. *In view of this possibility, it is of vital interest to the U.S.S.R. to know what Italy's thinking would be in such a situation.* How does Rome regard the position of the Turks?"

I replied that I had no official information on the subject and that therefore I could express only my personal opinion. I restricted my comments to noting that it was natural for Italy to presuppose that Turkey would not go to war against the Axis powers. Therefore, it was logical to keep in mind the need for Turkish participation in any revision of the Straits Convention.

I did recognize that in the present situation it was impossible to completely reject the opposite hypothesis advanced by Molotov, that is, Turkey's entrance into the war. In fact, rumors were rife both pro and con. Personally, I had the feeling that, since neither Italy nor Germany had any intention of damaging Turkey's interests, the latter would continue to remain neutral.

I then asked whether the Soviet government, on the other hand, possessed any information which would indicate that Turkey would enter the war.

Molotov replied that he had no *positive* data but that he was nevertheless convinced that a German military action in the Balkans would inevitably bring Turkey into the war on the side of England and Greece.

For this reason, he added, the discussion of an eventual revision of the Straits Convention in concert with the Turkish government would only have a theoretical and academic value. "The situation is moving rapidly and events may be precipitated. Therefore, the hypothetical question I have raised can, from one moment to another, become an immediate reality. The question is precisely the following: *What would Italy's position be regarding the problem of the Straits in the event that Turkey, willingly or unwillingly, becomes involved in the conflict?*"

I said that I could not reply in the name of the Italian government and that I could only refer to Rome what he had told me.

However, in the interest of enabling me to explain clearly to my government the situation as viewed by Moscow, I, in turn, requested certain clarifications.

He, Molotov, had affirmed that with the entrance of Turkey into the war the conflict would inevitably be extended to the Straits and to the Black Sea, thus raising the problem of the Soviet Union's security.

Could he tell me what possible foreseeable developments, as he saw them, would provoke an extension of the war to the Black Sea and thus raise the question of the Soviet Union's security? This was of interest to me in transmitting his thoughts on the matter to Rome.

To this direct question, designed to reveal something of Soviet intentions, Molotov replied evasively. He repeated again that the passage of German troops across Bulgaria, even if provoked (and here he added, in a slightly ironical tone, "as the Germans foresee") by the British intention of expanding their belligerent activity to Greece, would bring Turkey into the war. The British bases on Lemnos indicate that, in this event, military action would be extended (he immediately caught himself and said "could be extended") to the Black Sea as well, which would imply a serious threat to Soviet security.

Molotov concluded by saying that he clearly recognized that he could not "expect" that the Italian government would inform him of its precise thoughts and intentions. However, he would be extremely interested in knowing them, and for this reason he asked me to present this new problem to you for comment.

As for himself, he would refer the statements I made in Your Excellency's name to his colleagues in the government (Stalin), and together they would study them to determine whether they required further clarification. In that event, he would ask me to see him again. Otherwise, he would wait to learn the Italian government's views on the problem raised during the present conversation.

I summarize my impressions below.

On the questions of the Rumanian guarantees and of navigation on the Danube, Molotov revealed that he considered the matters closed, at least for the time being. While repeating his recriminations, he did, in fact, indicate his appreciation for our explanations regarding the first question, and he did state that he took note of our views regarding the second one.

As was foreseeable, he instead sought to probe the matter of the Straits in great detail; evidently this is today the most pressing and important question for the U.S.S.R.

In my view, it is obvious that Moscow intends to exploit possible military developments in the Balkan peninsula in order to resolve the question (of the Straits) to its own advantage.

In effect, Molotov sought to tell us that at this very moment, which may be the eve of Turkey's entrance into the war on the side of England, it is completely useless to talk of mutually agreeable " revision" of the Montreux Convention, which would imply, at the very least, Turkish consent. Therefore, it is important to consider another solution, which could be a military one.

His next move was to ask what position Italy intends to take on the problem of the Straits in the event of Turkey's entrance into the war. This question, in all likelihood, meant: "Are you Axis powers ready to come to an agreement with me to resolve the question among ourselves? Are you disposed to recognize as justified and to support my demand to participate effectively and directly in the control of the Straits, with Soviet garrisons, for example, stationed on the European shore of that passageway which is so vital to the security of the Black Sea and of the U.S.S.R.?"

In my opinion, this was the real significance of the statements made and the questions asked by Molotov.

To his question regarding the Italian attitude in the event of Turkey's entrance into the conflict, it would have been easy for me to reply that the day on which this took place the Axis powers would have the right to take whatever action a belligerent has the freedom to take against an adversary at war. With this, from a purely formal point of view, the reply would have been logical and complete.

I took great pains to avoid doing so, it being very clear that my interlocutor might have been encouraged to press the conversation on this point even further, and might have raised other questions of a more precise nature or presented proposals which the Italian government might not find convenient to discuss at this particular time.

Therefore, I maintained an attitude of reserve, limiting myself to resisting Molotov's tendency to become too inquisitive and asking him, in turn, albeit indirectly, what the Soviet Union's real intentions and plans were. As I foresaw, Molotov evaded my question and insisted, instead, on the one he himself posed in order to learn the views and intentions of the Italian government.

Having faithfully reproduced the essentials of the conversation with the President of the Council of Peoples' Commissars and emphasized what I believe was the real intent of his words, I have fulfilled my obligation and now await instructions from Your Excellency as to the direction you may wish to give these negotiations.

Immediately after the conversation of December 30, I expressed the opinion that the Soviet government was sincerely interested in reaching a political understanding with Italy but that it would not settle for a vague accord lacking positive and concrete substance.

Today I reassert this opinion. However, I ask myself whether it would not be possible to give Molotov a reply to his question on the revision of the Straits Convention, in view of our statement on the problem, without definitely committing ourselves to a future course of action (which I realize must be subordinated to general policy problems of major importance), and yet which would succeed in giving him the feeling of our goodwill and collaboration, thus opening the way for useful commercial negotiations.[195]

There remains little to add to Rosso's observations. As always, he had devoted his best efforts to the conversations and was anxious that they not fail. Molotov's attitude on the first two problems (Rumania and the Danube) appeared to be more conciliatory than what might have been predicted and evidently supported the position taken on the matter by the Wilhelmstrasse. Moreover, the Soviet Foreign Minister had refrained from noting that Ciano's reply was far from complete and had not returned to the question of recognizing Soviet interests in the Balkans and in Asia. Molotov may have employed this particular approach because it was related to the fact that the Straits Question could become a "live" issue at any moment and that therein lay the importance of promptly determining the position of the Fascist government on it.

For this reason Molotov introduced a new element into the discussion: the possible intervention in the war by Turkey. Although this prospect had already been suggested to Berlin by Moscow as a likely consequence of military action by the Wehrmacht in the Straits area,[196] the hypothesis advanced by Molotov at this time was not identical to that advanced by

---

[195] Rosso to Ciano, telegrams, January 27, 1941, Nos. 67 and 68, and report, January 28, 1941, No. 328-123. The text given above is the more complete of the two and is taken from the report. The italics appear in the original. Rosso informed Von Schulenburg of this colloquy. Von Schulenburg to Von Ribbentrop, telegram, January 29, 1941, G.D., Series D, XI, Doc. 727.

[196] Von Weizsäcker to Von Ribbentrop, memorandum, January 17, 1941, ibid., Doc. 668.

him to Von Schulenburg. On this issue particular significance was apparently attached to the British military presence on the island of Lemnos, a fact repeatedly referred to by Molotov. However, regardless of the difficulty Rosso encountered in seeking to uncover Molotov's ultimate aims— he had quickly evaded Rosso's question—the latter's opinion that a formula might be found to answer Molotov to his satisfaction so that they might proceed toward concluding the desired commercial agreement was, in practice, impossible to realize.

Mussolini, who had taken over the active direction of the Foreign Ministry in Ciano's absence on military duty, reacted favorably to the information transmitted by the Italian Ambassador to Moscow. On January 29 the Duce transmitted to Berlin the Rosso summary of his colloquy with Molotov in its entirety and added the following:

Inform the German government of the following:

Regarding Rumania, Molotov has maintained his position, albeit recognizing that the clarifications "were clear and understandable," and evidently there is no reason to discuss this further.

For the Danube, too, we can limit ourselves to what has been agreed to by Rosso, except for arriving at an Italo-German agreement on the instructions to be given to the German and Italian delegates to the conference when it reopens. In any case, Silenzi[197] has always acted in concert with his German colleague.

The Straits. Naturally, this is by far the most important question and one to which Molotov has requested an answer, a reply which might well be in our interest to give. Molotov desires to know Italy's position in the event that Turkey, willingly or unwillingly, becomes involved in the war.

In order to reply to Molotov it would be necessary to know the Soviet point of view regarding the Straits problem. To date, Molotov has asked whether Italy "*understood the interest of the U.S.S.R. in the Straits* in relation to the problem of Soviet security in the Black Sea," and we have made it known that "we would view sympathetically a revision of the Straits Convention in favor of the U.S.S.R.: for example, *transit granted only to naval vessels* of the states bordering the Black Sea." However, we do not know exactly what the Russian point of view is on the matter.

We could request the necessary clarifications and, meanwhile, reply to Molotov by enlarging and further detailing what has already been told him, namely, that (1) if Turkey should enter the war against Italy, there would evidently be a good reason for accepting the Soviet point of view on the Straits (the Soviet view is understood to be no more than what has already been communicated to us); (2) if Turkey remains neutral or nonbelligerent, the Soviet point of view could become the subject of discussion; (3) in any event, given the present Turkish attitude, Italy is disposed to consider or discuss the Straits Question, giving priority to Soviet interests.[198]

[197] Italian delegate to the Bucharest Conference on the Danube.
[198] Mussolini to Cosmelli, telegram, January 29, 1941, No. 21R. The italics appear in the original.

If the formula personally developed for the Straits by Mussolini[199] revealed a willingness to go a long way toward satisfying Soviet aspirations, it was, at the same time, highly confusing and, in its final portion, departed from the position taken by the Wilhelmstrasse without any real reason for doing so. Aside from the fact that there was a certain contradiction between admitting that the precise Soviet views were not known and proposing to seek further clarification from Molotov, on the one hand, and deciding to proceed to assume, without further ado, serious obligations in a reply to Molotov, on the other, the three points were not, in fact, very clear.

The first point contemplated the hypothesis of Turkish intervention in the war and anticipated the automatic acceptance of the Russian claims within the limits previously established in Rosso's report from Moscow. Mussolini probably meant that the desired revision of the Montreux Convention would be imposed on the Ankara government by the victorious Axis powers. The use of the adverb "evidently" a priori excluded the idea of taking advantage of an eventual conflict with Turkey to impose a unilateral solution by the Axis on the matter of navigation of the Straits.

The second point referred to the current situation: Turkish neutrality or nonbelligerence. Given this hypothesis, the Soviet viewpoint could become a subject for discussion. Discussion with whom? With the U.S.S.R.? But this was already taking place, so that the future conditional was out of place. With Turkey? Here too the future conditional was not in order because Rosso, as suggested by the Wilhelmstrasse, had already been instructed to communicate to Moscow—and Moscow had accepted—the stipulation that Ankara's consent to a peaceful revision of the Montreux Convention was regarded as necessary. Therefore, either the correct wording should have been "will form the subject for discussion with Turkey" or Turkey's consent was not deemed necessary. In the latter case, apart from representing an astonishing Italian about-face, there would have been no reason whatsoever for distinguishing between the first and second points.

Finally, apart from the role of Turkey, Mussolini affirmed the Italian intention of giving priority to Soviet interests. Here too, aside from its usefulness in dictating a pro-Russian and anti-Turkish state of mind, Mussolini's third point, insofar as the Moscow negotiations were concerned, was completely redundant in that the recognition of the priority of Soviet interests had already emerged in the direct and uncomplicated statements

---

[199] A marginal note in the original reads as follows: "The concluding portion of the attached telegram was dictated by the Duce who wished to re-read it and to personally sign it."

communicated to Molotov and in the absence of any conversations with Ankara regarding the Straits. In effect, if Mussolini had limited himself to replying to the precise question posed by the Soviet Minister of Foreign Affairs by indicating that, in the event of Turkish intervention in the war (against the Axis), Italy would be disposed to ignore the matter of Ankara's consent to a revision of the Montreux Convention, he would have achieved greater clarity, satisfied the U.S.S.R., and avoided increasing German ill-feeling.

The Italian Chargé d'Affaires in Berlin on February 1 carried out his instructions and promptly reported to Rome as follows:

I transmitted the communication to Secretary of State Von Weizsäcker, who listened with careful attention. He thanked me and will refer it immediately to Von Ribbentrop.

With reference to the three hypotheses postulated in the last part of the telegram regarding the Straits in relation to the Turkish attitude, I report that I was asked, in confidence, what I thought Turkish reaction would be to the passage of German troops across Bulgaria. I replied that I was in no position to provide a knowledgeable, informative opinion. When asked for my personal impression, I limited myself to observing that from what I had learned from reading the dispatches of our representatives, the situation, despite any number of opinions, appeared to be very uncertain. The Secretary of State probably summarized German thinking on the matter by unofficially and confidentially informing me that if we proceed with caution it will not be impossible to keep Turkey out of the conflict. I seemed to gather that our formulation of the three points, at first glance, appeared to him to be based on too pessimistic a view of the Turkish attitude or, at least for the moment, on too condescending a position toward Moscow. In his view, this would seem to prejudge the Turkish attitude and, perhaps, reflected the concern ("a solution at the expense of Turkey could weigh heavily on relations with the latter") already expressed on January 22 last, referred to in my telegram No. 93. Of course, the above, while I await an official reply, must be regarded as a confidential personal impression.[200]

[200] Cosmelli to Mussolini, telegram, February 1, 1941, No. 133. On this colloquy, see also Von Weizsäcker, memorandum, February 1, 1941, *G.D.*, Series D, XII, Doc. 5, in which the Secretary of State, in addition to noting that the portion concerning the Straits revealed "a considerable lack of clarity," affirmed that "the Italian suggestions certainly go further toward meeting the Russian desires than has been agreed upon with the Italian Government." It is worth noting how the attitude assumed by Von Weizsäcker on that occasion, unofficial and therefore spontaneous, is in complete contradiction with what he wrote in his memoirs (Von Weizsäcker, *Erinnerungen*, p. 307), where he affirmed that, early in 1941, he had taken a position against Von Papen's proposals designed to support a pro-Turkish policy. The passage in question reads as follows: "In reply to this I wrote that, if we had to make a choice in the East—at the moment there was no need for this—Turkey would have to take second place: this seems to me to be our painful duty, regardless of the sympathy we could have for our former ally. We had to regard Russia as more important."

Thus the first reaction from the Wilhelmstrasse was negative, and this should be related both to Germany's persistent tendency to maintain a rigid position vis-à-vis the Soviet Union and to the German diplomatic activity under way in Ankara to ensure Turkey's neutrality when the Wehrmacht moved across Bulgaria to attack Greece.

The Germans were less pessimistic regarding the prospects of success in the attempt to ensure Turkish neutrality because of reports received in Berlin from Von Papen, in which he recommended great caution and suggested a series of measures to be taken (including a personal letter from Hitler to the President of Turkey guaranteeing the inviolability of Turkish territory) to calm Turkish apprehensions.[201] The initiative and the optimism of the German Ambassador to Ankara had some effect in Berlin. Yet at first, despite the fact that he promptly implemented the suggestions made by Von Papen, Hitler was not completely convinced regarding Ankara's reactions,[202] It appears highly probable that, in view of the attack contemplated against the Soviet Union, the idea of strengthening German-Turkish ties appealed to him. Such an assumption makes it easy to understand his determination to avoid any action that would facilitate Turkey's entrance into the war against the Axis powers and thereby compromise his dream of conquering Russia, a dream which was coming ever closer to realization.

The Wilhelmstrasse's reply to the Italian communication transmitted by Cosmelli was delayed for a short time. On February 3 the Italian Chargé d'Affaires in Berlin was called to the Wilhelmstrasse and was informed by Von Weizsäcker that Von Ribbentrop desired to make a detailed study of Mussolini's message and that, therefore, the German official reply would be postponed for a brief time. Since the Nazi Foreign Minister regarded the communication from Mussolini as being much more than a mere informative note—as, in effect, a consultation—it was presumed by the German government that until its official reply was forthcoming no further negotiations with the Russians would take place. Cosmelli assured Von Weizsäcker that he would immediately transmit the message to Rome, stressing that it would be necessary to answer Molotov's questions without delay.[203]

Palazzo Chigi bowed to Von Ribbentrop's request and informed Rosso

---

[201] Von Papen, *Memoirs*, p. 471; Von Weizsäcker, *Erinnerungen*, p. 307.

[202] In a letter dated February 5, 1941, Hitler wrote to Mussolini: "The aggravating thing is . . . the uncertain attitude of Turkey which forces us in any case to provide many more troops than would otherwise be necessary (I hope as regards Russia that she will make no further difficulties)." Hitler to Mussolini, letter, February 5, 1941, *G.D.*, Series D, XII, Doc. 17.

[203] Cosmelli to Mussolini, telegram, February 3, 1941, No. 142.

and Cosmelli that negotiations would not proceed until a response from Berlin had been received.[204]

On February 6 Cosmelli met with the German Foreign Minister and reported to Rome as follows:

Von Ribbentrop thanks Your Excellency for your courteous communication regarding the conversation between Rosso and Molotov and notes with great satisfaction that these talks have been set on the course agreed upon between Your Excellency and him at Berchtesgaden. However, in the present circumstances he cannot help but be somewhat concerned with the reply we are thinking of giving Molotov on the Straits matter and in response to the question raised by the latter. We should, as a matter of fact, expect certain leaks, and, if Turkey were to learn something of Italy's intentions on the Straits Question, this would probably have an unfavorable effect on forthcoming events. Therefore, he begs Your Excellency to again examine the problem to determine whether it is absolutely necessary at this moment to give Moscow further explanations. Moreover, Molotov himself stated that he did not expect an immediate reply. Therefore, it should be possible to postpone the reply for a time or at least to wait until Molotov himself raises the question again.

If, on the other hand, we believe it imperative to reply immediately, Minister Von Ribbentrop would appreciate it if Your Excellency would again consult with him before doing so.[205]

Here again, as in the telegram from Berlin of February 1, one is struck by the marked difference between the nature of the reporting from the Italian Embassy in Moscow and that from Berlin, news from Berlin, the capital of the allied country, being much less detailed, even hurried and circumspect, devoid of personal impressions and, therefore, of much less help in facilitating an understanding of the thinking and of the intentions of the ally on specific matters as well as in providing a detailed examination of the basic issues yet to be negotiated. Evidently, Von Ribbentrop, still uncertain about Turkey's attitude, was trying to gain time in order to learn what position Ankara would adopt.

In any case, the argument advanced by Berlin to justify a policy of delay for Italy in dealing with Moscow—that is, possible indiscretions by the Soviets—was inconsistent. If the Kremlin, in fact, desired to reveal Axis intentions toward Turkey to Ankara, it would hardly have had to fall back on Rosso's communications. It could have revealed the proposals concerning the Straits advanced by Von Ribbentrop to Molotov on November 13, 1940.[206] Furthermore, it was impossible to see just what in-

[204] Mussolini to Rosso and Mussolini to Cosmelli, telegrams, February 8, 1941, Nos. 41 and 165.

[205] Cosmelli to Mussolini, telegram, February 6, 1941, No. 163; Von Weizsäcker, memorandum, February 6, 1941, *G.D.*, Series D, XII, Doc. 25.

[206] Cf. Hilger, memorandum, November 18, 1940, *G.D.*, Series D, XI, Doc. 329. See also the related proposal for an accord, *ibid.*, Doc. 309.

terest the Soviet Union could have in such a move because it would have revealed its own intentions toward the Straits. In effect, if the Axis agreed to this, Moscow would have been the sole beneficiary.[207] However, Von Ribbentrop's basic position of intransigence toward the U.S.S.R., evident since the previous November, must have been behind the stand now taken by him on the matter of the Italian negotiations with Moscow. On the whole, his reaction to the Moscow negotiations was not entirely negative but seemed, nevertheless, to reveal a certain amount of German perplexity on the matter.

Undoubtedly, Mussolini believed that his ally was stalling, and though he intended to give these arguments due consideration, he apparently regarded the talks with Moscow as important and was anxious not to permit them to drop. In any event, he allowed a few days to pass before taking a decision, and on February 14, upon his return from Bordighera, where it appeared that the possibility of Franco's entering the war was becoming increasingly remote, Mussolini telegraphed to Berlin as follows:

I have also re-examined the problem in the light of the sound observations made by Von Ribbentrop. Undoubtedly, taking too clear a position on the Straits Question—which most certainly could become known to Ankara—would have an unfavorable effect in Turkey, and I agree with Von Ribbentrop that this should be avoided, particularly in the light of forthcoming events.

However, one must keep in mind the course of the negotiations which date back to last June, as well as the more recent ones, and I do not believe that Molotov's question can be conveniently ignored. In effect, therefore, it would be best if Rosso made a reply, naturally without saying anything new or assuming any new obligations.

The reply could be more or less the following:

"The communication already made concerning the Straits refers to the situation as it presently exists and is part of an overall friendly approach to the U.S.S.R. It represents an unmistakable manifestation of goodwill toward the Soviet Union and a desire to collaborate. A recognition of these facts appears also to be evident in Molotov's own observations. Molotov's question, on the other hand, refers to a situation which does not actually exist, and, therefore, no factual data currently exists upon which to base a concrete reply. If such a hypothesis should be verified, however, we will examine it with that same spirit of comprehension and desire to collaborate that we earnestly hope will characterize our relations with the U.S.S.R."

Ask for Von Ribbentrop's comment on this and telegraph a reply.[208]

In reality, given the acceptance without discussion of Von Ribbentrop's

---

[207] The accuracy of this statement is confirmed by the facts. The revelation of the content of Molotov's requests was made by Hitler in his speech of June 22, but, despite this fact, Moscow preferred to remain silent on the matter.

[208] Mussolini to Cosmelli, telegram, February 14, 1941, No. 187; Von Weizsäcker, memorandum, February 15, 1941, G.D., Series D, XII, Doc. 57.

observations, the formula advanced by Mussolini, at first glance, appears to have been well-calculated, even though it was hardly an ideal way in which to conclude the Moscow negotiations on a positive note. However, upon careful examination, the idea of anticipating a general policy position based on a hypothesis which could only be that of a Turkish intervention in the war against the Axis contradicted the premises assumed: Soviet indiscretions and the need to avoid assuming new obligations which might cloud the relations with Ankara. Moreover, the situation was made even more difficult by the fact that, despite the contradiction, the new premise was not likely to satisfy Molotov.

Once again, it was a question of a superficial treatment of the problem. Even given the desire to remain within the confines of the limited consultations with the Germans, it was necessary, at the very least, to bring up for discussion without any reservations whatsoever the matter of the presumed Soviet indiscretions. It is true that Mussolini had no knowledge of a written German statement for an accord on the Straits, which had already been presented to the Soviets, but he was at least aware of the general policy lines of the proposals which Hitler and Von Ribbentrop intended to present to Molotov during the Berlin meeting. These proposals, even if presented orally, did not differ materially from those which Rosso was supposed to have been instructed to present orally to Moscow. However, it was not necessary to know all of this. It would have been sufficient only to ask oneself *cui prodest?* to see the flimsiness of the Nazi Foreign Minister's arguments when he implied indiscretions by Moscow. Indeed, a tradition of maximum reserve characterized Soviet diplomacy.

The key issue lay elsewhere. It was a matter of finally asking Berlin a question which would reach the heart of the problem: what were the Reich's real intentions toward the U.S.S.R.? Rosso and Molotov had given Rome a reasonably efficient instrument with which to come to grips with Berlin on this fundamental issue, which might well determine the outcome of the conflict. Perhaps because of the aura of invincibility with which the victories of the Wehrmacht had surrounded the might of the Reich, or because Italy's failures in Greece and in Africa had shaken its faith in its own power, Rome did not grasp the opportunity that had presented itself and, in so doing, surrendered to Berlin its freedom of action in the field of foreign policy.

As was predictable, Mussolini's proposal did not displease the Wilhelmstrasse, which, with unusual speed, gave it its blessing. On February 17 the Chargé d'Affaires in Berlin telegraphed to Rome: "Von Ribbentrop has just now requested that you be informed that he concurs that Rosso reply to Molotov without saying anything new or assuming new obligations. He has no other observations to make on the matter, not even on the tenor of the statement as proposed by us."[209]

Evidently, it was the desire of the Nazi Foreign Minister to place the emphasis on the promise not to assume any new obligations or to say anything new, rather than on Mussolini's formula, which went beyond what Rosso had actually outlined to Molotov in the January 27 conversations. Accordingly, three days later the Duce authorized Rosso, "without assuming obligations or saying anything new, to reply to the *new* question raised by Molotov" in the terms indicated by Berlin. Mussolini added, for the benefit of the Ambassador, that everything had been agreed upon with Von Ribbentrop.[210] With Mussolini's instructions to Rosso of February 20, the Italo-Soviet negotiations entered their last phase.

10

The Italian Ambassador to Moscow was received at the Kremlin on the afternoon of February 24. He immediately reported his conversation with Molotov to Rome, as follows:

Limiting myself to the instructions given to me in your telegram No. 59, I spoke to the President of the Council in approximately these terms:
"In referring to my government on the conversation I had with you on January 20 last, I naturally did not fail to submit to Rome the question which you then raised, when you expressed a desire to know what Italy's position would be regarding the problem of the Straits in the event that Turkey became involved in the conflict, that is, that Turkey entered the war against Italy and Germany and on the side of England.
I have now received a telegram signed by Mussolini instructing me to reply to you with the following declaration:
When, during our conversation of December 30, 1940, you asked, "Does Italy understand the Soviet interest in the Straits in relation to the matter of Soviet security in the Black Sea?" the Italian government gave you an implicitly affirmative reply, in that it declared that it would be ready to support a revision of the Straits Convention so that the freedom of navigation of the Straits would be reserved exclusively to the naval vessels of the countries bordering the Black Sea. With this statement the Italian government demonstrated that it was ready to collaborate in seeking a revision of the rules governing the use of the Straits which would work to the advantage of Soviet security in the Black Sea.
With this statement the Duce desired to give you, and in fact gave you, indisputable proof of his goodwill in conceding to the Soviet *desiderata*, thereby demonstrating his sincere desire to develop political collaboration between our two countries. You at that time recognized the importance of the Italian declaration and indicated your deep interest in it.
Of course, in giving you this reply the Italian government had based its

[209] Cosmelli to Mussolini, telegram, February 17, 1941, No. 209.
[210] Mussolini to Rosso, telegram, February 20, 1941, No. 59.

reasoning on the existing situation, that is, on the fact that Turkey was not involved in the war on the side of England against the Axis powers.

Your second question, on the other hand, was based on the premise that Turkey did enter the war against us. This is an eventuality which not only has not come to pass but is one which Italy believes and desires will not come to pass. In these circumstances, you must recognize that it is not easy to take a precise and positive position on a purely hypothetical situation which is, at least, very doubtful and the developments of which we cannot foresee because they may be determined by events beyond our control. Therefore, the Italian government does not see how it can give a precise and specific reply to your question at this time.

However, the Duce has instructed me to state that in the event that the hypothesis which you described—that is, Turkey's entrance into the war— becomes a fact, the Italian government would examine the new situation which this development would create in the same spirit of comprehension of Soviet interests which it demonstrated in its earlier declaration on the Straits Question and in the desire to create the necessary solid bases for that collaboration which Italy desires to establish in its relations with the U.S.S.R."

Having made the above statement in the name of the Italian government, I added some personal observations.

For example, I said that I supposed that Molotov would find our declaration satisfactory because it clearly indicated that Italy could be trusted to be always well disposed to take into account Soviet interests, interests whose existence had already been implicitly recognized by us in the declaration I had made to him during our earlier conversation on the Straits issue.

Anticipating his probable observations, I invited him to consider that, in the present situation, when no one could foretell what new course the war in the eastern Mediterranean basin might take (and a new development might even be determined by factors beyond our control), what I had communicated to him was the most the Italian government could say for the moment. However, he should recognize that I had told him something interesting and important.

Having listened to me with a rather noncommittal expression, Molotov said, "In your reply to my question there is something which is not very clear and which requires reflection." Then he was silent, almost as though he wished to limit his comments to this alone.

I then noted that I believed that I had expressed myself in sufficiently clear terms, but that if some point required further elucidation, I was prepared to provide it. I also added that if our reply was not more specific or more precise, I had indicated that it was not possible for us to make it otherwise on a question based wholly on a purely hypothetical situation which no one could possibly say would come to pass and, if it did, under what circumstances, with what aspects, and with what developments.

Molotov replied to this with a rather cryptic statement: "You already know the point of view of the Soviet government." He then admitted that he understood very clearly what I had said, but then added that, notwithstanding this fact, he was forced to repeat that "the reply was not clear and that he preferred to reflect on it."

I realized that Molotov did not intend to enter into any discussion with me and I therefore did not insist that he clarify his rather laconic statements.

When I took my leave, Molotov made no reference to future talks, and, on my part I did not believe it opportune to bring up the subject.

The impression I gained during my colloquy with Molotov yesterday is that he is no longer particularly interested in pursuing our conversations because he no longer has any hope that these can lead to the concrete and positive solution which the U.S.S.R. hopes to impose on the Straits matter. It seems to me reasonable to believe that at the present, when here in Moscow we have the feeling that important military developments in the Balkans are imminent (events which, according to Molotov's predictions, will inevitably bring Turkey into the war), the Soviet government sees greater prospects of fulfilling its ambitions via a lightning exploitation of any favorable situations which may appear in the near future than through discussions which continue to be restricted to somewhat academic generalities.

The Italian offer to support the traditional Soviet thesis on the Straits (prohibiting passage to ships of war of nations other than those bordering the Black Sea) is unquestionably a manifestation of goodwill and should be so considered by the Kremlin leaders, and if this offer could have been made some months ago (during our conversations of last June, for example) it would have probably been considered by this government as a positive and important contribution to the policy of Italo-Soviet collaboration. Instead, I have the impression that in the new situation created by recent events (particularly the concentration of German troops in Rumania, presumably poised to move southward), the Italian position on the Straits Question is now being regarded as a gesture, friendly, to be sure, but of little practical value.

This is the interpretation I am inclined to give to Molotov's attitude. However, I am not excluding the possibility that this attitude may be explained by the current uncertainties—by the varied unknown factors which suggest to these leaders that they should await for events to unfold before deciding whether they should insist on an accord on the Straits.

Perhaps even a third hypothesis should not be excluded, and this one is related to Germany. Without possessing specific information on the question, I have had the feeling here that the German government considers it neither convenient nor a matter of urgency to conclude the negotiations at this moment on the Straits. If this assumption of mine is correct, it is likely that Moscow is aware of the German view and that, therefore, it is useless for her to seek to modify a directive which she is fully aware is common to the policy of both the Axis powers.

My conversations with Molotov seem, therefore, destined to be inactive for a period, and this time it will be the result of silence on the part of the Soviets.

It is understood, of course, that I will make no move to reopen these talks unless I receive instructions on this matter from Your Excellency.[211]

Rosso's comments apparently evaluated Molotov's attitude rather accurately. On the eve of Bulgaria's adhesion to the Tripartite Pact (March 10, 1941) and of the Italian crisis in the Balkans (ultimately

[211] Rosso to Mussolini, telegram, February 24, 1941, No. 107, and Rosso, report, February 25, 1941, No. 607/214. The text reproduced here is the much more complete one from the report.

concluded by the Wehrmacht's occupation of Yugoslavia and Greece), together with the fact that the Wilhelmstrasse had abandoned talks with
Moscow on the proposed four-power pact, the Kremlin decided to put
aside its less urgent problem of expansion for the moment in order to
devote its energies to concluding a new defensive arrangement that would
provide certain guarantees, such as those represented by the accords with
Belgrade of April 5, 1941, and with Tokyo of April 13, 1941. Berlin's
failure to reply to the Soviet proposals of November 25, 1940,[212] terminated the phase of the negotiations which had begun with Molotov's trip
to Berlin, and the conversations with Rome, closely linked to the Moscow-
Berlin talks, lost any real significance.

Moscow's reply to Rosso was immediately transmitted to Berlin,[213] and
on March 1 the Italian Chargé d'Affaires in Berlin reported to Rome the
reaction of the Wilhelmstrasse as follows:

Today I informed the Wilhelmstrasse as instructed. The Secretary of State
asked whether I believed that the conversations had therefore reached a stalemate. I replied that I considered it hardly likely that they could be reopened,
at least for the moment. He added that the present situation obviously made
the exchange of views on the Straits Question hardly feasible.

He indicated his conviction that, under the circumstances, Russia, while not
likely to be pleased by the developments in the Balkans, will, at the most, present a protest or publish a new denial. As Your Excellency probably knows,
within the past twenty-four hours two pontoon bridges have been constructed
on the Danube, and the movement of German troops southward from the
Dobruja has begun. He also confirmed that the movements will be slower and
more gradual.

The latest information concerning Turkey is clearly reassuring, and it is
believed that she will adapt to the situation. I was told that Germany has formally informed Angora [sic] that the Nazis intend to respect Turkish territorial
sovereignty. This communication could also have had a determining effect.

There is general satisfaction for the diplomatic success achieved, which
would be an even greater triumph if Greece surrenders without fighting.[214]

On this note the Italo-Soviet conversations for a political understanding
definitely came to an end.[215]

---

[212] Molotov's last inquiry to Von Schulenburg occurred on January 17, 1941.
Von Schulenburg to Von Ribbentrop, telegram, January 17, 1941, G.D., Series D,
XI, Doc. 669. Von Ribbentrop's failure to reply apparently convinced Moscow of
the Reich's negative attitude. Von Ribbentrop to Von Weizsäcker, telegram, January 21, 1941, ibid., Doc. 681.

[213] Anfuso to Cosmelli, courier telegram, No. 669204.

[214] Cosmelli to Mussolini, telegram, March 1, 1941, No. 296.

[215] The negotiations for a trade pact continued laboriously and inconclusively. On
March 19 Rosso transmitted to Vice Commissar Lozovsky seven lists of proposals
prepared by the Fascist government. Early in May, just as the tension between Ber-

11

In concluding this detailed reconstruction of the failure of the Rome-Moscow negotiations for a political entente during the World War II, it may serve some useful purpose to supplement the observations made during the course of the narrative by an attempt to evaluate the negotiations in their entirety. Once the principal phases of the negotiations have been identified, it will be possible to refer to the positions adopted, directly or indirectly, by the three powers (Germany, Italy, and the U.S.S.R.) in each separate phase, thereby providing a technico-diplomatic and historico-scientific basis for the investigation.

The major phases of the Italo-Soviet negotiations were five. The first began on August 23, 1940, and terminated with Italy's entrance into the war; the second ran from June, 1940, to the conclusion of the Vienna Arbitrage; the third, from August, 1940 to Molotov's journey to Berlin; the fourth took place in November and December, 1940; and the fifth was represented by the renewal of the conversations between Italy and the U.S.S.R. beginning on February 24, 1941.

During the first phase, Germany was the power most clearly interested in an Italo-Soviet rapprochement aimed at eliminating one of the most dangerous disharmonies existing in Axis foreign policy. Under this pressure, Rome's first reactions were very circumspect; that is, Rome was clearly negative and became increasingly cool to the prospects of a rapprochement as the Finnish crisis mounted. Italy shifted her position radically only after her entrance into the war on the side of the Reich. Even at that early date there existed a difference in viewpoint between Mussolini and Ciano on the matter. Mussolini tended to accept the suggestions of his German ally more readily; Ciano sought instead to resist the German maneuver and to offset it, while continuing to distrust Moscow. The Kremlin at first did not regard Von Ribbentrop's suggestion for an improvement of relations with Italy with any particular disfavor, which might have strengthened the German hand in the ultimate analysis. Later the Kremlin became openly hostile to the Fascist government, and the

---

lin and Moscow was reaching its climax, Mikoyan told Rosso that the proposals were, in general, satisfactory as a basis for discussion and that he would be pleased to receive an Italian delegation authorized to negotiate. On that occasion, Mikoyan indicated a number of changes to be introduced into the proposals regarding quantities, in effect reducing the amount of raw materials to be delivered and the number of products requested. On May 23, in a meeting presided over by Riccardi, the Italian requests were defined and the delegates for the Moscow trade mission were named. Despite the pressure applied by Mussolini to hasten the negotiations (evidently he was still unaware of Hitler's intentions), these, too, resulted in failure. Ciano, *Diario*, II, p. 36.

Soviets finally returned to the position of favoring an improvement of relations with Italy, although they left the initiative up to the Italians. Essentially, this phase reflected the degrees of success of the military operations in the west, the development of the Finnish crisis, and the reaction to the collapse of France. Nevertheless, during the period of Italian nonbelligerence, continuity of policy was exclusively German, since Germany was the only one of the three powers embroiled in the conflict, and relations between Rome and Moscow were strained, without reaching the breaking point; the two governments maintained positions of watchful waiting.

The second phase began with Molotov's friendly overtures to Rosso in the first colloquy after the latter's return to Moscow. The warmth of Molotov's reception induced Mussolini (prior to France's request for an armistice), suddenly, and without consulting Berlin, to take the initiative for a negotiation which he probably conceived as a rapprochement in only a general sense, but yet sufficiently positive to allow the Fascist government greater freedom of maneuver in the area of foreign policy. The immediate, precise character of Molotov's postulation of the negotiations caught Mussolini unprepared. Ciano certainly did not facilitate matters and, already thinking of the attack on Greece and the breakup of Yugoslavia and sensing a cooling in Nazi-Soviet relations, did nothing to help develop this embryonic plan. When Ciano, for reasons which were largely economic, sought to reopen the talks with Moscow, he met with resistance from Berlin and thus dropped the last real prospect for concluding an entente with the U.S.S.R. On the other hand, Russia, preoccupied by the temporary military hegemony of Germany and knowing that the Rumanian problem was about to become critical, viewed with favor an agreement with Italy which would, in accord with the Axis, at one and the same time safeguard Russian interests in the Balkans and strengthen the Soviet position vis-à-vis Berlin. As for Germany, her military successes led her to reject the idea of any further European concessions to Moscow and whetted her appetite for expansion into the Balkans as well. Under these conditions, an Italo-Soviet rapprochement no longer attracted Berlin, for the same reasons that it appealed to Moscow. In conclusion, during the period between the Italian entrance into the war and the Rumanian crisis, only one power, the U.S.S.R., was effectively and consistently in favor of an understanding between Moscow and Rome. The Fascist government took the initiative in seeking the accord, at a time when it had no clear idea of its significance, but then retreated from this position, ultimately adopting the negative stand of the Nazis without, however, seeking a thorough understanding of the motivations for it.

The third phase was apparently strongly influenced by the Greek crisis.

The key power in this phase was Germany, which intended to resolve the entire Balkan question on its terms and sought to purchase Soviet acquiescence in this solution by offering to make concessions to Russia in Asia. The U.S.S.R. was not entirely opposed to the idea and indicated that it could be a subject for study, while Italy, further weakened by military failures in Greece and Africa, accepted Hitler's projects simply by climbing on the Nazi bandwagon. During this period the problem of an Italo-Soviet rapprochement became a matter of secondary importance in both Berlin and Moscow. Only the Fascist government retained a strong interest in the subject, although Rome immediately agreed to postpone any further action on it until after the conclusion of the proposed four-power pact.

The fourth phase was one of preparation for the U.S.S.R., of growing intransigence and watchful waiting for Germany, and of dismay for Italy. The Kremlin launched a search for premises on which to reopen the conversations with Rome in an effort to overcome the obstacles encountered by the Soviets during the Berlin talks, to clarify the real position of the Axis, and to avoid the possibility of being cut off from participating in the imminent solution of the Balkan crisis. Germany, disappointed and irritated by the failure to realize her goal of creating the four-power pact, avoided informing her ally of the details of the Nazi-Soviet talks and remained anchored to her policy of opposition to any further concessions to the U.S.S.R. in Europe, though not definitely and totally abandoning all idea of achieving an understanding by increasing the pressure on Moscow. Germany did not even consider using an Italo-Soviet rapprochement to arrive at a clear understanding of ultimate Soviet aims. As for the Fascist government, it was simply being dragged along in the wake of events determined by Berlin. Italy agreed to the Balkan projects as outlined by Berlin, took note of the growing anti-Soviet tendencies of the Wilhelmstrasse, and avoided asking for detailed information on the exchange of views between Hitler and Molotov. Rome was pleased by the indications of goodwill and understanding emanating from the Narkomindiel, without seeking to probe the real reasons for this attitude. During this period of deadly contest between Berlin and Moscow, Rome remained passive. The idea of an Italo-Soviet understanding seemed to be alive only among the Soviets.

In the fifth phase, primarily for reasons of growing economic urgency, Palazzo Chigi was anxious to talk with Moscow again. Despite the experience of the summer of 1940, the decision was preceded by an ambiguous consultation with Berlin. Faced with the immediate and increased Soviet demands, the Fascist government was disposed to accept them, but, rejecting the prospect of a thorough examination and confrontation with its Axis partner on the matter of foreign policy, Rome, instead chose to adopt the restrictive formulas suggested by the Wilhelmstrasse, formulas which were regarded as being inadequate to meet the needs of the Kremlin. In turn, the U.S.S.R. initially appeared to be in favor of a broadly based entente with Italy, which represented a substantial step beyond the Berlin talks and also served as an indirect reply to the Germans, who had failed to respond to the Soviet counter-proposal of November 25, 1941. However, when Moscow recognized the more modest limits which Palazzo Venezia imposed on an understanding, it concluded that nothing useful could be gained by continuing the negotiations, particularly since military developments in the Balkans and German behavior directly and indirectly made the Soviet leaders believe that it was time to put aside, at least temporarily, those aspects of the accords which would aid the U.S.S.R. in realizing its long-term goals, and to give total attention to the more urgent matter of defensive agreements. Insofar as Germany was concerned, its position on the contemplated Italo-Soviet rapprochement was substantially negative. Faced with Rome's insistence, Berlin appeared willing to agree to a limited accord, but nothing more. During this last period, the initiative appeared to be Italian, but it was a weak effort, insufficient to overcome Berlin's resistance. At first, Moscow accepted the approach with satisfaction, but when it fully realized the extent of Mussolini's inability to respond freely and fully to its proposals, the Kremlin decided that Berlin's role in the situation was now clear and that the best course for Russia was to drop the entire matter of negotiations with Rome.

In this rough game of conflicting interests, the diplomatic actions of Mussolini and Ciano were based on a superficial, incomplete, and limited vision of the problems involved. Thus, notwithstanding the apparent Italian initiative in the matter, the real direction of the negotiations was allowed to pass alternately to Germany and Russia, both of which could act with much greater freedom.

The Italian Ambassador to Moscow again demonstrated his unusual professional ability. He went to great lengths to present to Rome continually—within the limitations of the information available to him—the exact tenor of the local situation. He was often faced with the multiple difficulties, frequently aggravated by both Ciano's and Mussolini's indifference, of filling in the serious lacunae all too often present in the instructions received from Rome and of forcing his own government to make promptly those decisions which were vital. He did not conceal the fact that he favored an accord with Moscow, and he worked diligently to prevent the collapse of the negotiations. While he fully understood all the ramifications of the German aspect of the negotiations, he did not always sufficiently emphasize them, even though, in the final analysis, this particular problem, and the entire matter of Axis policy toward the U.S.S.R., was the primary concern of Rome and not of the Embassy in Moscow. In contrast with Rosso's passionate involvement and concern, the Italian Embassy in Berlin adopted a passive attitude toward the negotiations even when Germany was directly involved and at no time contributed toward a better delineation of the pertinent issues or assisted in surmounting the obstacles.

In contrast, Soviet diplomacy was consistently coherent, clear, and tenacious of purpose. The Kremlin always remained in control of the negotiations, though it remains to be seen whether or not it chose the wisest course in determining these to be of minor importance in comparison with the negotiations with the Japanese.

Finally, Von Ribbentrop's diplomatic actions revealed his heavy hand and his susceptibility to the Wehrmacht's military successes. This pride played a determining role in the final negative result of the negotiation. Undoubtedly, this resulted in a German victory, but it may be ascribed principally to the intrinsic difficulties of reaching an accord, to the subjective weakness of the proposals, and to Italian military weakness. On this point, it is interesting to note (although the postulates of the problem are only partially the same) the parallel which might be established between the negotiations carried on almost simultaneously with the U.S.S.R. by the governments of Rome and Tokyo. Both sets of negotiations had been prompted by friendly pressures from Berlin. With the change in German plans, both were blocked by Berlin just as they were about to be concluded. Yet Von Ribbentrop's negative pressure, applied almost simultaneously and in identical terms to both the Italians and the Japanese, produced different results. Japan went ahead and signed the treaty of April 13, 1941, and remained neutral during the Nazi-Soviet conflict, while Italy did not conclude the proposed accord with Moscow and immediately joined the Reich in the attack on Russia.[216]

[216] Of course, any speculation as to what the Fascist government's policy might have been at a time so close to the eventual conclusion of an Italo-Soviet political pact—which Moscow did not desire with the same intensity as that with Japan—enters the realm of the imagination. Nevertheless, it appears likely that the political weight of the nonaggression treaty of 1933, which did not deter Mussolini from his decision, but which the Fascist government at one time thought necessary to bring up to date, was inferior to the new enlarged and more pertinent treaty just signed by the Soviets and Japanese. In any event, in June, not only did Berlin fail to exert any pressure on Rome to intervene, but the German Embassy in Moscow, on the very eve of the attack on Russia, considered the Italian intervention so unlikely that on June 20, Von Schulenburg asked Rosso to look after his personal affairs after the outbreak of the war. Rosso to Ciano, telegram, June 20, 1941, No. 278.

At this point it might be worth while to evaluate, from the point of view of each of the three interested powers, the arguments for and against the conclusion of the Italo-Soviet accord. Insofar as the Axis Powers are concerned, arguments in favor of the accord are found in Rosso's communications, which also report Von Schulenburg's considerations on the subject; arguments against are to be found in Von Ribbentrop's memoranda. On the other hand, there is an almost total lack of official information on the manner in which the Soviet government viewed the pros and cons of an accord with Italy, and only conjectures have been advanced as to its thinking on the matter. In any case, even if this important lacuna were ignored, an evaluation of the Soviet position would be a purely political one and, therefore, outside the scope of this investigation.

Despite these reservations, an observation may be made which, in the final analysis, is linked to a factor repeatedly suggested in the preceding pages. Hitler's instructions to Von Ribbentrop in August, 1939, when he believed, or at least hoped, that the Polish campaign was an end in itself, recognized the presence of the Soviet Union in Finland, in southeastern Europe, and in the Straits.[217] Yet slightly more than a year later, in the Berlin conference of November, 1940, when, despite the smashing victories over the French and their continental allies, the war continued and spread because of stubborn British resistance, Hitler's views were altered. The war aims of all of the belligerents had changed; they had enlarged. Now Hitler no longer wanted the U.S.S.R. to continue to expand in Finland and in the Danube-Balkan Basin, or to establish itself in the Straits. Instead, Slavic dynamism was to be directed elsewhere, toward India, thereby helping Berlin (since this would have been the inevitable result) to achieve an uncontested domination of Europe. What Russia could never have accepted of her own volition she was helped to reject by the development of events.

Was it possible, in November, 1940, before Axis relations with Russia worsened dramatically, to return to the positions of August, 1939? Could there have been a compromise? How? With what consequences? These questions have far-reaching implications, and their answers might well involve much earlier relations between Russia and the West.

Neither Mussolini nor Ciano nor the Italian Ambassadors to Berlin and Moscow—to the extent that they were concerned—nor the appropriate offices in Rome really studied this serious problem (at least, thus far no such evidence has been discovered), either its general implications or its specifically Italian effects, either before November, 1940, or after. In 1943,

[217] Von Ribbentrop, memorandum, June 24, 1940, G.D., Series D, X, Doc. 10.

in a situation already compromised, Mussolini wholeheartedly supported an accord with the U.S.S.R. at any price,[218] but in Florence in October, 1940, he had accepted Hitler's proposal for a four-power pact designed to eliminate Russia from Europe.

It is true that the political negotiations of the Fascist government with the Kremlin (aside from Mussolini's first impulsive move) were aimed at satisfying immediate economic needs, but even with these limitations, it was virtually impossible for them to proceed and to achieve positive and satisfactory results without a basic agreement with Berlin. A move to achieve this agreement was never seriously undertaken by the Italians, either in the interest of the overall policy of the two Axis Powers or in the specific interest of the negotiations. Thus, the negotiations never amounted to more than a series of delays and multiple cases of negligence.

In essence, then, insofar as Italy's action is directly concerned, it may be said that, to the imbalance between the two allies in strength, with as a consequence the will and interests of the Italian ally reduced to minor importance, one must add the sketchiness of Italian acquaintance with the problem and the disorganized handling of the negotiations. These weaknesses surfaced at precisely those points where only by serious study and highly developed organizational skill can the weaker power offset its difficulties and impose its point of view.

From an exclusively historical viewpoint, it may be noted that the proposed Italo-Soviet understanding appeared destined to have a number of points in common with the famous Racconigi Agreements of 1909 with Tsarist Russia; it may also be recalled that at one particular moment, Soviet Russia did admit, albeit non-specifically, that Italian interests were

---

[218] Walter Hagen, *Die Geheime Front* (Linz: Nibelungen, 1950), p. 439. Hagen is particularly well informed and draws his information from qualified sources and from his own personal recollections. He writes as follows:

It appears that Mussolini and Ciano were not of the same opinion regarding the opportuneness of concluding a separate peace with one of the adversaries. Ciano was of the opinion that a compromise should be sought with the West and the war against Russia continued until bolshevism was destroyed. Mussolini tended instead toward seeking an accommodation with the Soviet Union and continuing the war against the West. Ciano was coldly calculating and surpassed Mussolini in correctly evaluating foreign policy. He was of the opinion that the German expansionist drive should be given free rein toward the east, where Germany could remain involved for an undetermined time so that the future Italian domination in the Mediterranean would not be compromised. By his very nature, Ciano was a man oriented toward the West, while Mussolini, according to Ciano, was preoccupied with England and the United States. His dearest wish was to see the Western Powers forced to capitulate. For him the defeat of France and England was the necessary prerequisite for the enlargement of the Fascist empire in North Africa.

pre-eminent in the Mediterranean. While this had also been admitted previously by the Germans, it had not been contained or proposed in any agreement before this time.

Finally, to conclude the observation made at the beginning of this investigation, the Italian documents illustrate a facet of the policies of Moscow, Rome, and Berlin that has remained in the shadows, despite the publication of the material taken from the archives of the Wilhelmstrasse, which cover a period during which Germany and the U.S.S.R. had ceased to discuss the problem of Russian claims. However, it will be possible to reconstruct this page of the diplomatic history of World War II definitively only after the Soviet sources become accessible.

IV.

RESUMPTION OF DIPLOMATIC RELATIONS BETWEEN ITALY AND THE SOVIET UNION DURING WORLD WAR II

Summary: 1. Premise. 2. Delusions of the Badoglio government concerning Anglo-American treatment after the armistice. 3. Stalin's resentment of the exclusion of the Soviet Union from the Italian negotiations. English-American-Soviet discussions leading to the creation of a politico-military inter-allied commission. 4. The Moscow and Teheran conferences. Solutions given to the problems of the Consultative Commission for Italian Affairs and the distribution of the Italian fleet as spoils of war. 5. New Italian misunderstanding and resentment over the weakening of the Cunningham-De Courten naval accord, the isolation of the Badoglio government enforced by the English and Americans, the Allied refusal to allow an Italian political representative to be attached to the Liaison Commission headquartered in Algiers, and the exclusion of Italian representation on the consultative commission. 6. The first Vishinsky-Prunas meeting, January 8, 1944, in Salerno. 7. The second Vishinsky-Prunas meeting in Salerno, January 10, 1944. 8. Waiting for Moscow's decisions on Prunas' proposals. The United States, Great Britain, and Soviet Union accord to fill the gap in Italian naval tonnage caused by the Teheran Conference promise to Stalin of a portion of the Italian fleet by a temporary transfer of Anglo-American naval units to the Italian fleet on a loan basis. President Roosevelt's press conference of March 3 and its possible ultimate effects. 9. The Bogomolov note of March 4 to Badoglio indicating agreement with the Italian initiative to reopen direct diplomatic relations between the two countries and outlining the procedure planned by the Soviet Union to realize this goal. The official request for the re-establishment of direct diplomatic relations made by Badoglio on March 6 and Bogomolov's reply of March 11. 10. Prunas' frank conversations with Reber and Caccia to inform them of the accord reached by the Italians with the Soviets and to suggest that London and Washington abandon the rigid position adopted by the western allies during and after the armistice. The selection of Minister Quaroni as Italy's political envoy to Moscow communicated to Soviet Minister Goryarkin. 11. The negative reaction of the English and Americans to the Italo-Soviet initiative reflected in their order prohibiting the Italian government from establishing diplomatic relations with other countries and their refusal to accede to Badoglio's request that Italy be granted the status of an ally. Soviet satisfaction with the selection of Quaroni and Stalin's reply to the Badoglio message. 12. Persistence of English and American distrust. The beginning of Quaroni's mission in Moscow. Badoglio's instructions of May 29. First Molotov-Quaroni colloquy, June 5. 13. Conclusions.

* An earlier version of this chapter appeared in Comunità Internazionale, I (1962).

1

On March 14, 1944, an official communiqué from the office of the Italian Prime Minister announced: "In response to the wishes officially expressed at an earlier date by Italy, the government of the U.S.S.R. and the Royal Italian government have agreed to establish direct diplomatic relations between the two countries. In conformity with that decision both governments will proceed without delay to an exchange of duly qualified representatives according to established diplomatic practices."

The renewal of diplomatic relations between Salerno and Moscow after a break of approximately three years following the declaration of war, so recklessly decided and in such singular circumstances,[1] aroused the deepest astonishment everywhere. This announcement, greeted with satisfaction and hope in the Kingdom of the South, was at the time regarded as a major achievement of Italian diplomacy and constituted the most significant achievement of the Badoglio government between the Armistice proclamation and the liberation of Rome. Moreover, since this aspect of Italian foreign policy remains virtually unknown and unappreciated despite the extremely difficult conditions under which it took place, a closer view of these developments is appropriate. The re-establishment of direct diplomatic relations between Italy and the Soviet Union was to trigger a series of reactions in London and Washington, not only vis-à-vis the Badoglio government but also vis-à-vis the U.S.S.R. How did the Italian government arrive at this decision? What were the immediate effects of the action? More than a quarter of a century has passed since this memorable event, and it is time to reconstruct its origins, to the extent that the available material permits, while awaiting the publication of further documentation which, added to what appeared after the war, will ultimately reveal the full details.

2

In order to understand the reasons which prompted the Badoglio government to take the initiative mentioned in the official communiqué of March 14, and those which induced the Soviet Union to accept it with

[1] The highly unusual procedure chosen by Count Ciano of presenting the Italian declaration of war on the Soviet Union in Rome rather than in Moscow also had the effect of placing Ambassador Rosso—unaware of his government's intentions—in the awkward position of learning of the event from a radio news broadcast, in precisely the same way in which the Soviet government first learned of the Italian action. For a time, therefore, the Italian Ambassador to Moscow was placed in an equivocal situation without precedent in diplomatic history. On this point, see Mario Toscano, "L'intervento in guerra dell'Italia contro l'Unione Sovietica nel giugno 1941 visto dalla nostra ambasciata a Mosca," *Nuova Antologia* (March–April, 1962).

dispatch, one must return to the conclusion of the Armistice and to the events immediately following its signature, events which, for various reasons, had given rise to misunderstandings in Moscow and bitterness in the Kingdom of the South.

When the Armistice of Cassibile was signed, the Badoglio government rested all of its hopes on the promemorial appended to the conditions presented in Lisbon in General Eisenhower's name by General Bedell Smith to General Castellano—a promemorial commonly known as the "Quebec Document."[2] In this document it was noted, among other things, that "these terms do not visualize the active assistance of Italy in fighting the Germans. The extent to which the terms will be modified in favor of Italy will depend on how far the Italian government and people do, in fact, aid the United Nations against Germany during the remainder of the war."[3]

On September 21, 1943, two weeks after General Eisenhower's announcement that the armistice with Italy had been signed, King Victor Emmanuel III addressed himself directly to President Roosevelt and to King George VI, calling their attention to the need for hastening the expulsion of the Germans from Italy; for restoring Italian administration in those territories already liberated; for improving the exchange rate between the lira and the dollar and the pound sterling; for returning the Italian government to Rome; for reconstructing the country politically by restoring parliamentary government; and for bringing into being Italo-American-British military collaboration.[4] It was evident that behind this

---

[2] On the origins of this document, see Winston S. Churchill, *The Second World War*, V: *Closing the Ring* (London, Cassell: 1952), pp. 88–89; Robert E. Sherwood, *Roosevelt and Hopkins* (New York: Harper, 1948), pp. 742–46; *Correspondence between the Chairman of the Council of Ministers of the U.S.S.R. and the President of the U.S.A. and the Prime Minister of Great Britain during the Great Patriotic War of 1941–1945* (Moscow: Foreign Languages Publishing House, 1957), I, pp. 144–47; II, pp. 79, 82, 84–85; hereafter cited as *Correspondence U.S.S.R.*; Herbert Feis, *Churchill, Roosevelt, and Stalin, the War They Waged and the Peace They Sought* (Princeton: Princeton University Press, 1957), pp. 100–164; Llewellyn Woodward, *British Foreign Policy in the Second World War* (London: Her Majesty's Stationery Office, 1962), pp. 228–29; Giuseppe Castellano, *Come firmai l'armistizio di Cassibile* (Milan: Mondadori, 1945), pp. 105–14; Giuseppe Castellano, *La guerra continua* (Milan: Rizzoli, 1963), pp. 62–74.

[3] Aide-memoire to accompany armistice conditions presented by General Eisenhower to the Italian Commander-in-Chief, reproduced in Ministero degli Affari Esteri, *Documenti relativi ai rapporti tra l'Italia e le Nazioni Unite (luglio-novembre, 1943)* (Rome: Tipografia Riservata del Ministero degli Affari Esteri, 1945), pp. 23–25; hereafter cited as *Italia e le Nazioni Unite*.

[4] The letters were received by Eisenhower on September 23, 1943, and transmitted on the same day to King George and to President Roosevelt. For the text, see *Foreign Relations of the United States. Diplomatic Papers, 1943* (Washington, D.C.: U.S. Government Printing Office, 1964), II, pp. 374–75; hereafter cited as

appeal there lay the hope of a quick transformation of the nature of the existing political agreement.

This hope was undoubtedly premature. Too little time had passed since the termination of hostilities, and the memory of Fascist aggression was too recent for the past to be so quickly forgotten. In Washington, where the mistrust of Victor Emmanuel and Badoglio was then even more deep-seated than in London,[5] President Roosevelt limited his reply to a declaration of his agreement about the necessity of taking joint action to liberate the Italian territory still under German occupation and to a promise to consider carefully the other requests made by the Italian sovereign.[6] In London, despite the fact that Churchill had indicated his desire to apply a policy of understanding toward the Italian monarchy and the Badoglio government, George VI, in his reply to Victor Emmanuel, made it clear that while Great Britain was willing to have de facto relations with the Badoglio government on questions stemming from the implementation of the armistice terms and the elimination of the Germans from Italian territory, the British government did not consider the Badoglio regime as an allied government. Moreover, any provisional accords reached between the two governments would in no way limit the right of the Italian people to choose any form of democratic government they preferred at the termination of the conflict.[7]

This was the first dash of cold water thrown on the hopes expressed by the monarchy and the Badoglio government. Others were soon to follow. On September 29 Marshal Badoglio was obliged to sign the more encompassing armistice of Malta,[8] which markedly worsened the Italian position. These more detailed terms had been especially requested by Churchill in order to avoid constant discussions with the Badoglio government and to clarify the relations between the United Nations and Italy.[9] Just how little both King Victor Emmanuel and Badoglio understood the

---

Foreign Relations, 1943. See also Castellano, *La guerra continua,* p. 175; Mario Toscano, *Dal 25 luglio all'8 settembre: Nuove rivelazioni sugli armistizi tra l'Italia e le Nazioni Unite* (Florence: LeMonnier, 1966), pp. 88–89.

[5] Feis, *Churchill, Roosevelt, and Stalin,* pp. 100–164; *The Memoirs of Cordell Hull* (New York: Macmillan, 1948), II, p. 1550.

[6] For the text of the letter, see Roosevelt's telegram to Eisenhower of September 30, 1943, in *Foreign Relations, 1943,* II, pp. 379–80.

[7] This portion of King George VI's letter did no more than repeat, in a terse and abbreviated form, the substance of a message from Churchill to Roosevelt of September 21, 1943. The text of this message can be found in Churchill, *Closing the Ring,* pp. 167–68, and in *Foreign Relations, 1943,* II, pp. 372–73. The text of King George VI's letter appears in Castellano, *La guerra continua,* pp. 227–29.

[8] *The United States and Italy, 1936–1946: A Documentary Record* (Washington, D.C.: U.S. Government Printing Office, 1946), pp. 55–64.

[9] Cf. Churchill, *Closing the Ring,* pp. 168, 171; *Correspondence U.S.S.R.,* I, p. 164.

exact nature of the situation at that time is made even clearer by the fact that, at Malta, Badoglio felt obliged to express the King's reservations to General Eisenhower's request for an immediate declaration of war by Italy against Germany and, instead of greeting with pleasure the Allied request to include Count Sforza in his government, Badoglio—always in the King's name—asked that Count Dino Grandi be permitted to return to Italy so that he could be named Foreign Minister.[10]

On September 30 General Castellano reported from Algiers the news that an inter-allied commission for the Mediterranean was about to be created. Badoglio replied on October 3, instructing him to sound out the Allies on the prospects for an eventual Italian membership in it. In the event that a condition for membership on the commission were an Italian declaration of war against Germany, this would serve to help overcome Victor Emmanuel's resistance.[11] However, these instructions were not carried out because Castellano notified Badoglio on October 9 that the projected commission was still in the embryonic stage and that the nature of its role had yet to be determined.

The declaration of war against Germany occurred on October 13, and on the same day the governments of Great Britain, the United States, and the Soviet Union recognized Italy's co-belligerence.[12] This was certainly a step forward but, as we shall see, immediately afterwards new shocks were to deeply embitter the Italian government.

3

At this point, the state of mind of the Soviet leaders regarding the Italian situation becomes pertinent. At the conclusion of the Quebec Conference, Roosevelt and Churchill transmitted to Stalin the text of the de-

---

[10] The Italian minutes of the Malta meeting are reported in their entirety in Toscano, *Dal 25 luglio all'8 settembre*, pp. 108–18. The texts reported in Agostino Degli Espinosa, *Il Regno del Sud (8 settembre 1943–4 giugno 1944)* (Rome: Migliaresi, 1946), pp. 87–88, and in Ruggero Zangrandi, *1943: 25 luglio–8 settembre* (Milan: Feltrinelli, 1964), pp. 963–64, are incomplete. The revision presented by Marshal Badoglio (*L'Italia nella seconda guerra mondiale* [Milan: Mondadori, 1946], p. 148) is incorrect, particularly his reference to the question of the Italian declaration of war against Germany: "Afterward there was a sort of a conference in which General Eisenhower immediately raised the question of our declaration of war against Germany. I replied that it was my intention to take this step as soon as possible." The request to allow Count Grandi to enter the government was firmly rejected by Roosevelt in a message to Churchill on October 2, 1943 (Cf. Churchill, *Closing the Ring*, p. 176). For an overall evaluation of the Malta meeting, see Toscano, *Dal 25 luglio all'8 settembre*, pp. 118–26.

[11] Cf. Castellano, *La guerra continua*, p. 177. At that time General Castellano was Chief of Mission for the Italian government at the Allied Command Headquarters in Algiers.

[12] On this question, see Toscano, *Dal 25 luglio all'8 settembre*, pp. 126–34, and the sources cited therein.

mands they proposed to make to the emissaries of the Badoglio government,[13] thus completing the preliminary information on the matter transmitted earlier to Moscow by both the State Department and the British Foreign Office.[14] Stalin replied on August 22, 1943, affirming that the Soviet
government had not been kept adequately informed of the negotiations
with Italy and proposing the creation of an Anglo-American-Russian
politico-military commission to handle those problems related to negotiations with the governments that had severed their ties with Germany. Up
to that moment the United States and Great Britain had been reaching
accords between themselves, and the Soviet Union had been informed of
the resulting agreements only as a passive third party. The commission
proposed by the Soviet government was to be constituted immediately and
to be temporarily quartered in Sicily.[15] Two days later, Stalin, in a new
message to Roosevelt and Churchill, while approving the instructions sent
to Eisenhower containing the armistice conditions for Italy, repeated, "Still,
I consider the information received so far insufficient for judging the steps
that the Allies should take in the negotiations with Italy. This circumstance confirms the necessity of Soviet participation in reaching a decision
in the course of the negotiations. I consider it timely, therefore, to set up
the military-political commission representing the three countries, of which
I wrote to you on August 22.[16]

The position taken by the Soviet Union, even though it was initially
suggested by an idea advanced in London in July, aroused dissatisfaction
in Quebec.[17] Nevertheless, on August 29, Churchill and Roosevelt assured
Stalin that they were examining his proposals and that they were convinced that it would be possible to develop satisfactory plans for the creation of the proposed tripartite commission.[18] Churchill went a step further
by suggesting the inclusion of representatives of the French Committee

[13] See *Correspondence U.S.S.R.*, I, pp. 144–47; II, pp. 79–82. A reading of the
entire text of the message sent by Churchill and Roosevelt to Stalin on August 19,
1943, makes it possible to correct the inexact statement appearing in Feis, *Churchill,
Roosevelt, and Stalin*, p. 173, according to which Stalin had not been informed of
the promise made to the Italians to re-examine the armistice conditions in terms of
the Italian contribution to the war effort against Germany. This inaccuracy stems
from the fact that, prior to the publication of Stalin's correspondence with Churchill
and Roosevelt, the Hopkins papers and Churchill's memoirs contained only the
initial portion of the August 19 message, and, moreover, the wording was slightly
different from that appearing in the version published in Moscow.

[14] On this point, see Toscano, *Dal 25 luglio all'8 settembre*, pp. 50–55; Feis,
Churchill, Roosevelt, and Stalin, pp. 166–69, 170–74.

[15] *Correspondence U.S.S.R.*, I, p. 149; II, p. 84.

[16] *Ibid.*, I, p. 150; II, pp. 85–86.

[17] Feis, *Churchill, Roosevelt, and Stalin*, p. 172.

[18] *Correspondence U.S.S.R.*, I, p. 151; II, p. 87.

of National Liberation and received immediate Soviet agreement on this point.[19]

On September 5, Churchill telegraphed his views on the matter to Stalin. The British Prime Minister suggested that, in the event an official commission were created, the members of such a commission should be political representatives and each should refer directly to his own government. The commission could not limit, substitute, or replace the rights enjoyed by the interested powers; it could request the help of military experts. It would be kept informed of political and military developments which could have an effect on its labors, and it in turn, would keep the governments involved informed on local developments. It could present joint recommendations, but it would not have the power to take definitive decisions, and it would not seek a role of any kind in the military functions of the Allied High Command. Churchill voiced no objections to quartering the commission in Sicily but suggested that either Algeria or Tunisia would be more satisfactory. Some attention, he said, might be given to the participation of the Greeks and Yugoslavs in addition to the French, by developing a procedure for consultation on those matters that concerned them directly. Initially, the proposed commission should limit itself only to the Italian question. When other problems arose, experience would indicate which was the proper organ to best coordinate the views and plans of the Allies. Roosevelt, on the other hand, thought that it would be sufficient to attach a Soviet officer to Eisenhower's General Staff. As for the proposed scheduling of a conference of the three Allied foreign ministers in Moscow, this idea advanced by the President of the United States might resolve the question for the moment. In any event, the British government was eager to know Stalin's point of view.[20]

If the attention which Churchill gave from the beginning to the limitation of the competence of the proposed commission revealed a desire to prevent the Soviets from assuming a major role in Anglo-American policy for Italy, this concern was even greater in Washington, where General Marshall echoed Eisenhower's anxiety over possible interference in his policy toward the Badoglio government. If, in assuming this position of exclusiveness, the Anglo-American military command succeeded in limiting Moscow's voice in Italian affairs, it also set a precedent that ultimately

[19] *Ibid.*, I, p. 152. This proposal was probably the result of the reaction of the French National Committee of Liberation in Algiers to negotiations with Italy without French participation. On the question, see Charles de Gaulle, *Mémoirs de guerre*, II: *L'Unité 1942–1944* (Paris: Plon, 1956), pp. 527–28.

[20] *Correspondence U.S.S.R.*, I, pp. 152, 153–54. This portion of the Churchill-Stalin-Roosevelt correspondence was published after the appearance of Feis's volume and therefore could not have been utilized by him.

worked to the disadvantage of Washington and London: when Bulgaria, Rumania, Hungary, and Finland capitulated, the Red Army was able to act in those countries with an almost entirely free hand.

In his proposals of September 6, with reference to the meetings of the commission to resolve the questions with the Italians, President Roosevelt asked Stalin whether the Soviet government would send a Soviet officer to be attached to Eisenhower's General Staff. He would join the Americans and British already at work on the Italian problem. The American President had no objection to the inclusion of a French officer on the commission but regarded as unreasonable any French participation in the discussions of the problems relative to the military occupation of Italy because the Italians would find such a presence offensive. The problem of a conference with the Greeks and Yugoslavs could be discussed at a later date.[21]

Stalin replied to both Churchill and to Roosevelt on September 8. In his view, the most urgent question was that of the politico-military commission. He had assumed, on the basis of the earlier messages, that the problem had been settled immediately and in a positive manner; instead, despite their urgency, they remained unresolved. The issue was not one of working out this or that detail, which could be done without difficulty. As for attaching a Soviet officer to Eisenhower's staff, Stalin asserted that this would not in any way substitute for the commission, which should have been functioning at this moment but which, in fact, did not yet exist. If Roosevelt had any doubts, he went on, the participation of a French representative on the commission could be postponed to some future time.[22]

The position taken by Stalin could not have been more explicit, but notwithstanding this fact for various reasons the creation of the commission was further delayed. Churchill replied to the Stalin note on September 10, indicating his approval of the immediate establishment of a three-power politico-military commission to be quartered either in Sicily or Algeria. A French representative would participate as a fourth member. The British government nominated Harold Macmillan as its representative. He was to retain his post as British delegate on Eisenhower's General Staff in Algeria. Great Britain would not nominate a military representative, but Macmillan would be assisted by a qualified general staff officer. According to Churchill, the functions of the commission were to receive detailed information on present and future relations with the Italian government or with any other enemy government which, in the future, found itself in an analogous position. To examine these questions the repre-

[21] *Ibid.*, II, p. 89.
[22] *Ibid.*, I, p. 157; II, p. 90.

sentatives themselves would fix the frequency of their meetings. They would maintain permanent contact with their respective governments and could render advice and counsel both collectively and individually. They would receive directives on general policy lines, but they would also be encouraged to take the initiative. This would not in any sense minimize or limit the ultimate and definitive responsibility of the three governments concerned, it being inadmissible that the commission would make a decision and take steps to realize it on its own.[23]

The following day Roosevelt also approved the creation of the commission and proposed Algeria as headquarters and September 21 as the date for the first meeting. A detailed picture of present and future negotiations would be furnished, but the members of the commission would not have unlimited powers; until such time as decisions were definitely approved, authorization would have to be requested from their respective governments. French participation was approved. It was considered important that the commission operate with absolute secrecy.[24] The next day Stalin replied, nominating Vishinsky, Vice President of the Council and Under Secretary for Foreign Affairs, as his representative; Ambassador Bogomolov was designated as alternate. A group of political and military experts were to accompany them. A date between September 25 and 30 was suggested for initiating the work of the commission. No objection was raised to housing the commission in Algeria until such time as it was convenient to transfer it to Sicily or to some other locality in Italy. Stalin regarded the considerations advanced by Churchill on the functions of the commission as sound but believed that after a time, taking advantage of the experience gained in actual operation, these functions could be defined both with regard to Italy and other countries.[25]

This apparent accord concealed profound differences in points of view regarding the duties and functions of the proposed commission. According to the Soviet government, the commission was to direct and coordinate the activity of all of the military organs and of all of the Allied civil authorities operating in enemy territory on questions of the armistice and as a control commission on the application of the armistice itself. Thus, on this interpretation, the commission could also issue, from time to time, instructions and directives to the Italian government and, under similar situations, to the governments of the other Axis countries, since it was understood that all of the questions of military operations would be re-

[23] *Ibid.*, I, pp. 159–60.
[24] *Ibid.*, II, p. 92.
[25] *Ibid.*, I, pp. 162–63; II, p. 93.

ferred to the Allied commanders-in-chief.[26] This concept was in perfect harmony with the Soviet practice of placing military operations under constant political surveillance, but its acceptance would have meant granting Moscow an important role in the formulation of Anglo-American policy for Italy. Even if this constituted a precedent for future conduct in the territories of Germany's other allies when they capitulated to the Red Army, neither London nor Washington was disposed, at that time, to grant the commission the right to give orders to the military Commander-in-Chief or to replace the control commission provided for in Article 37 of the detailed armistice terms.[27] This position was to have grave long-range consequences for the English and Americans, and its short-range result was the creation of delusions and resentment in Moscow.

It is true that the British Foreign Office had suggested to the State Department on September 25 that the Soviet Union be granted a more important role in the Armistice Control Commission and that the State Department was not adverse to the proposal, but the War Department opposed it, and, for the moment, the idea was put aside. However, Vishinsky's long illness forced the postponement of the first meeting of the proposed commission until November 24, a situation which facilitated further discussions.

4

The work of the Moscow conference of the foreign ministers of the three Allied powers from October 19 to November 2 gave Molotov the opportunity to emphasize the Kremlin's desire to be better informed on Italian developments and to participate actively in the formation of Allied policy for the peninsula. The question of the composition and competence of the proposed consultative commission was once again debated and was resolved by limiting the work of this commission to the handling of Italian problems and by an agreement to create another consultative commission for European affairs to be located in London. Furthermore, it was also agreed to maintain the autonomy of the military command and to limit the powers of the consultative commission for Italy to recommendations in

[26] *Ibid.*, II, p. 290, n. 37. These viewpoints are outlined in a Molotov note to the American Embassy in Moscow, October 3, 1943 (see also Feis, *Churchill, Roosevelt, and Stalin*, pp. 184–85).

[27] In a note dated September 25, 1943, to the American Embassy in Moscow, Molotov expressed the opinion that the creation of the politico-military commission had rendered the existence of the Control Commission null and void (see Feis, *Churchill, Roosevelt, and Stalin*, p. 184).

matters of general policy.[28] After animated discussions the insertion of the following paragraph in the final communiqué of the conference was approved:

The Conference also agreed to establish an Advisory Council for matters relating to Italy, to be composed in the first instance of representatives of their three governments and of the French Committee of National Liberation. Provision is made for the addition to this council of representatives of Greece and Yugoslavia in view of their special interests arising out of the aggressions of Fascist Italy upon their territory during the present war. The Council will deal with day-to-day questions, other than military operations, and will make recommendations designed to coordinate Allied policy with regard to Italy.[29]

The same communiqué also contained a tripartite declaration listing seven principles which should govern the policy of the three governments toward Italy.[30] These principles were proposed by Molotov in the October 22 session and, with some amendments, were accepted by Eden and Cordell Hull. During this session Molotov also advanced a proposal designed to obtain the immediate transfer to the Soviet Union of one Italian battleship, one cruiser, eight destroyers, four submarines, and forty thousand tons of Italian merchant shipping.[31] Eden evidently did not regard this request with disfavor, and he observed that it would be impossible to assure peace in the Mediterranean if the Italian fleet remained intact.[32] Roosevelt, on the other hand, cabled Hull that he was disposed to concede the provisional transfer of the Italian ships to the U.S.S.R., but suggested that a definite decision be postponed to a later date in order to avoid negative repercussions on the Italian war effort;[33] Churchill too, preoccupied by the predictable reactions of the Italian navy, proposed that the subject be discussed at the scheduled conference at Teheran.[34] The obvious Soviet dissatisfaction[35] prompted Roosevelt to propose a formula which, while remanding every final decision to the peace conference, recognized that one-third of the Italian fleet was to be used by the Soviet

---

[28] Matters concerning Italy were discussed primarily during the course of the fourth, fifth, eleventh, and twelfth sessions. See *Foreign Relations, 1943*, I, pp. 604ff., 617ff., 662ff., 679ff. See also Hull, *Memoirs*, II, pp. 1283–84; Feis, *Churchill, Roosevelt, and Stalin*, pp. 186–87.

[29] *The United States and Italy, 1936–1946*, p. 73. On the negative French reaction, see De Gaulle, *Mémoirs de guerre*, II, pp. 191–92, 596.

[30] *Foreign Relations, 1943*, I, pp. 758–59.

[31] *Ibid.*, pp. 612–13.

[32] *Ibid.*, p. 613.

[33] *Ibid.*, p. 643; Hull, *Memoirs*, pp. 1301–2.

[34] Churchill, *Closing the Ring*, pp. 262–63.

[35] *Foreign Relations, 1943*, I, pp. 669, 672.

Union.[36] In any case, in the final secret protocol of the Moscow Conference, dated November 1, note was taken of the Soviet request; it was affirmed that neither Eden nor Hull had raised any objections but that they had reserved the right to make a final reply to the request at a later date.[37]

During the Teheran Conference, at the session of December 1, when requested by Molotov to clarify his position, Roosevelt said that the Italian ships should be employed by the three countries in the common cause until the end of the war, at which time a final division of the fleet could be arranged based on claims and on possession. Churchill asked when the Soviet Union would be ready to receive the Italian ships, and it was agreed that the transfer would take place toward the end of January, 1944.[38] At the Moscow Conference, therefore, the foundation had been laid for a more active political role for the Soviet Union in Italy, but at the same time the request relative to the Italian fleet could have introduced a disturbing element into the three-power relationship if it had not been tempered by a number of provisional technical accords.

5

News of the deliberations of the conference of foreign ministers in Moscow reached the Badoglio government first via the regular radio newscasts, and the Marshal was forced to write to General Joyce on November 8, requesting the text of the final conference communiqué. At that time the situation within the Italian government was rather critical. As early as October 17, General Taylor had informed the Italian government that the United States, Great Britain and the Soviet Union had agreed to permit a number of revisions in the terms of the detailed armistice,[39] but, at the same time, a request was presented to introduce into the Cunningham-De Courten accord of September 23,[40] which regulated the use of the Italian fleet, a clause that seriously jeopardized the Italian naval

[36] *Ibid.*, pp. 683, 685, 687, 695. See also *The Foreign Relations of the United States. Diplomatic Papers. The Conference at Cairo and Teheran, 1943* (Washington, D.C.: U.S. Government Printing Office, 1961), pp. 127–29; hereafter cited as *Foreign Relations, Teheran.*

[37] *Foreign Relations, 1943,* I, p. 751; Churchill, *Closing the Ring,* pp. 347–48; Sherwood, *Roosevelt and Hopkins,* p. 797.

[38] *Foreign Relations, Teheran,* p. 597.

[39] The text of General Taylor's letter to Badoglio of October 17, 1943, is found in *Italia e le Nazioni Unite,* p. 44. Regarding the Anglo-Russian-American negotiations for the revision of the armistice, see *Correspondence U.S.S.R.,* II, pp. 95–97; Feis, *Churchill, Roosevelt, and Stalin,* p. 180.

[40] *The United States and Italy, 1936–1946,* pp. 53–55.

position.[41] The precise origins of this supplementary request are not at all clear. The fact that it would permit the transfer of units of the Italian fleet to the Soviet Union could, at first glance, suggest that it was linked to Molotov's request for portions of the Italian naval force, but this request was officially formulated for the first time at the October 22 session of the Moscow Conference and, therefore, apparently after the presentation of the proposed revision of the Cunningham-De Courten accord.[42]

Badoglio resisted this arrangement as long as possible, but, faced with the alternative of a return to the conditions imposed by the detailed armistice of September 29, in the end ordered Admiral De Courten to sign the damaging amendment. The signatures were actually affixed to the new document on November 17.[43] The Marshal then addressed a direct appeal to both President Roosevelt and Winston Churchill, strongly denouncing the request as gravely damaging to an understanding freely agreed upon after the signing of the armistice and as one which negatively affected the most efficient remaining Italian military instrument for participation in the war against Germany.[44] This episode created deep bitterness among those who had deluded themselves that they could, in a short time, earn the right to return to the Allied camp. This delusion would have been immeasurably greater had the Italian government known the details of the decisions on principle concerning the Italian fleet that had been reached at the conferences of Moscow and Teheran. In any event, neither Churchill nor Roosevelt replied to Badoglio's appeal.

[41] It read as follows: "It is understood and agreed that the terms of the present accord concerning the immediate employment and disposition of Italian naval and merchant vessels do not alter the right of the United Nations to take whatever measures they deem necessary with respect to all or part of the Italian vessels. Their decisions on this matter will be transmitted to the Italian government from time to time." Moreover, the last sentence of the last paragraph was amended as follows: "They will be manned to the extent that it is possible to do so by crews provided by the Italian Navy Ministry, and they will fly the Italian flag." See *Italia e le Nazioni Unite*, p. 82.

[42] This assumes that Badoglio's statement that the two documents concerning the revision of the armistice were presented to him simultaneously is correct. In fact, General Taylor's note to Badoglio of October 17 announces the imminent transmittal of the amendments to the detailed armistice, but not those to the naval accord. Moreover, the first critical comments regarding the requested revision of the De Courten-Cunningham Naval Accord made by Badoglio to MacFarlane date only from November 9. Is it possible that he waited that long to formulate them? Finally, the repeated inaccuracies in Badoglio's memoirs, which will be noted, create considerable doubt regarding his assertions.

[43] On that occasion Admiral De Courten protested to Badoglio in writing. For the text, see *Italia e le Nazioni Unite*, p. 84.

[44] The letter in question is dated November 20, 1943. For the text, see *Foreign Relations, 1943*, II, pp. 393–95; Badoglio, *L'Italia nella seconda guerra mondiale*, pp. 153–55.

Meanwhile, the consultative commission for Italy was about to begin its deliberations in Algiers,[45] while awaiting the transfer of its activities to the peninsula. This circumstance induced Badoglio, on November 26, to ask the president of the Allied Control Commission for authorization to attach Mr. Dino Philipson to the Italian military mission which had been accredited to General Eisenhower's headquarters in Algiers. This authorization was intended to permit the Italian government political contact with the members of the consultative commission for Italy. This request was immediately denied (on December 1) by General Joyce on the pretext that only military personnel could be attached to the Italian mission in Algiers. Badoglio replied on December 2 with the observation that the text of the armistice spoke only of "Italian representation" without specifying that this should be exclusively military. The Allied refusal constituted another restrictive interpretation of the clauses of an armistice which, as a whole, was already severely restrictive. The total segregation from the outside world to which the Italian government was subjected not only was extremely prejudicial to Italy, but gave the Allies no appreciable advantage. Italian diplomats in neutral countries and the millions of Italians who lived abroad were disoriented and perplexed. The Fascist regime of northern Italy was given, in effect, a completely free hand abroad by the quarantine imposed on the Badoglio government by the Allies. Since the latter, without reason, was not allowed to look after its varied interests abroad, these were progressively damaged by the inattention. Any action permitting Italy to emerge from its forcible isolation would have contributed to the common interest of all.

Misunderstanding and isolation thus characterized the attitudes of the men responsible for Italian policy at this time. A third factor, humiliation, was to be introduced at the imminent meeting in Brindisi, the seat of the Badoglio government, of the consultative commission for Italy without the participation of the Italians.[46] This sentiment, prevalent among Italian

[45] The Soviet representative, Vishinsky, on November 23 made several significant statements to De Gaulle outlining the principles which would guide him during his activities on this mission. See De Gaulle, *Mémoirs de guerre*, II, pp. 603–4. In his view, the commission had a twofold objective. Its immediate aim was to implement the terms of the armistice, but this was to be done in a democratic manner designed to bring Italy into the war against Germany, while at the same time aiding Italy to chart a course toward a peaceful future. In so doing it was important to examine the political currents dividing the Italian people and to assist in establishing a government that would be fully representative in the true democratic sense.

[46] As has been noted, the idea of calling a meeting of the Consultative Commission on Italian soil was repeatedly advanced by Stalin in his correspondence with Roosevelt and Churchill and promptly proposed again by Vishinsky in his colloquy with De Gaulle on November 23. In all probability, the Brindisi meeting took place

political leaders, was expressed by Badoglio in a second letter to General Joyce dated December 2, in which authorization was requested to permit the participation of an Italian member in the deliberations of the commission under any guise whatsoever, even that of a simple observer.

Badoglio's request did not elicit an immediate reply because the members of the commission remained in Brindisi only for a few days and then moved to Palermo and to Naples. According to information gathered on December 6 by the Secretary-General of the Foreign Ministry, Prunas, the meeting in Brindisi was convoked primarily to give the Soviets the feeling that Russia was now directly involved in Mediterranean affairs in general and Italian affairs in particular, areas from which, up to the time of the Moscow conference, it had been systematically excluded. The Italian request to participate in the work of the consultative commission would have probably been considered at the next commission meeting, scheduled for Palermo, and it appeared that neither the Soviet nor the French delegate, Massigli (with whom Prunas had the occasion to speak on December 6), would have raised any objections.

The news of the English and American recognition of the Soviet Union's role in Italy had a certain effect on Prunas. He immediately sought a meeting with Vishinsky, who informed him that he would be most pleased to see him upon his return to Brindisi, adding that he certainly would have sought such an encounter if the request of the Secretary-General of the Italian Foreign Ministry had not preceded his own. In informing Badoglio of Vishinsky's reply, Prunas observed that such a meeting would be their first official contact with the Soviets,[47] a contact which,

---

at the request of Vishinsky, who was obviously anxious to learn more about the Badoglio government on the scene before engaging in any conversations with its members.

[47] This assertion contradicts the view expressed by Raimondo Luraghi ("Sui rapporti diplomatici tra l'Italia e l'Unione Sovietica agli inizi dell' anno 1944," *Il Movimento di liberazione in Italia*, LII–LIII [July–December, 1958], p. 116) that Prunas had met earlier, toward the end of October, 1943, with Ambassador Bogomolov in Algiers, at which time the Russian referred to the possibility of re-establishing direct diplomatic relations between Italy and the Soviet Union. It is evident, however, that it was during Vishinsky's visit to Brindisi, when he met with the Socialist professor Guido Pazzi, that, of his own volition, he suggested the possibility of reopening direct diplomatic contact. Apparently, it was this information that induced Prunas, during his meetings with Vishinsky at Naples on January 8 and at Salerno on January 10, 1944, to propose the idea of renewing direct diplomatic relations between Italy and the U.S.S.R. Professor Pazzi had been Undersecretary of Information in the Badoglio government for only one day (November 25, 1943): his tenure was brought to an abrupt end by the fact that his statements to the press regarding his plans to establish contacts with the Allies in the name of the Socialist Party had provoked a very negative reaction in official government circles. On this episode, see Degli Espinosa, *Il Regno del Sud*, pp. 201–3.

up to that very moment, had been discouraged by the English and Americans but which he intended to develop further, either for the obvious importance it commanded or for the prospects which it undoubtedly offered of increasing the possibility of Italian activity, at that time tightly contained within the military and bureaucratic barriers imposed by the English and Americans.

On December 14 Eisenhower gave instructions to reply in the negative to Badoglio's request for authorization to permit Italian participation in the work of the consultative commission.[48] It is not at all certain that these instructions were carried out, but, in any event, on December 22 Badoglio instructed General Castellano in Algiers to seek to interest General Bedell Smith, Eisenhower's Chief of Staff, in the Italian case and to learn whether or not there was any truth to the rumor emanating from French sources in Brindisi that the Soviet Union had also been granted the right to participate as a member of the Allied Control Commission created by the armistice. Finally, on December 30, Prunas was informed unofficially by the English and Americans that an Italian representative would be allowed to speak to the Commission at the session to be convened in Naples on January 7, 1944.[49] At the same time the British diplomats Reber and Caccia told Prunas that up to that time the primary Soviet concern expressed within the commission was that the purging of Fascist influences in Italy would proceed effectively. According to the two diplomats, in essence, the Soviet Union apparently feared that the actions taken in the territory occupied by the Allied troops and in those areas gradually occupied were designed to leave intact and to favor those bourgeois and capitalist structures which were opposed to Soviet theory and practice.

There is no doubt that this was a discreet warning to the Badoglio government not to succumb to the temptation to do Moscow's bidding. However, this action was offset by a conversation which took place in Cagliari on January 4 between General Magli and Vishinsky, during the course of which the Soviet statesman affirmed that his government intended to see that Italy emerged free, strong, and independent because this outcome was in Europe's best interests.

The situation on the eve of the first official direct Italo-Soviet contact was characterized by (1) Italy's disappointment over its failure to improve its position rapidly within the framework of the United Nations; (2) a constant search for a way to break out of the isolation imposed on the Badoglio government by the English and Americans; (3) Soviet dissatisfaction with the initial Allied decision to exclude the U.S.S.R. from direct

[48] Cf. *Foreign Relations, 1943*, II, pp. 437–38.
[49] Cf. *ibid.*, p. 441.

participation in the settlement of the Italian questions and its desire to regain lost time by thoroughly exploiting every opportunity offered by the dual participation it now enjoyed in the Consultative Commission for Italy and in the Allied Armistice Control Commission (membership for the Soviets was agreed to toward the middle of January). In addition, it appears that one of Moscow's major concerns at that time was also the problem of involving the Italians more actively in the war against the Germans. Many of the actions contemplated by the Kremlin were inspired by this goal.[50]

6

The first Prunas-Vishinsky meeting occurred in Naples on January 8. The Soviet delegate received the Secretary-General of the Italian Foreign Ministry in his hotel room without fanfare and most cordially. He gave the impression of being a man who was quiet, serious, and thoughtful. He frequently reiterated that his opinions on Italian matters could not be expected to be precise because they had been developed very recently and should be accepted only on that basis, but that he desired to become better informed and to further his understanding and impressions. He noted that he had seen very nearly all of liberated Italy and that he had contacted many Italians, among them Count Sforza and Benedetto Croce.[51] Prunas responded that the Badoglio government had been anxious to establish official contacts with the Soviet government immediately after the armistice but that until now it had been impeded largely because of and, to some extent, by the English and Americans. He referred to an old telegram in which instructions were given to the Italian Ambassador to Ankara to arrange contacts with his Soviet colleague immediately. This telegram had never been delivered.[52] Vishinsky noted the fact with interest. Prunas then went on to state that the Italian government was fully cognizant of the enormous contribution the Soviets had made to the war

[50] A lucid and detailed exposition of these positions appears in an article in *Izvestia*, March 30, 1944, reproduced in its entirety by Degli Espinosa in *Il Regno del Sud*, pp. 317–20.

[51] There is no reference in Croce's diary to such a meeting having taken place on January 7, 1944. There is a reference there to the meeting of January 11. See Benedetto Croce, *Quando l'Italia era tagliata in due* (Bari: Laterza, 1948), p. 60. However, the fact that such conversations with the opponents of the Badoglio government (to say nothing of the one with Professor Pazzi mentioned above) had preceded the one with Prunas is significant and is to be linked to Vishinsky's statements to De Gaulle regarding his proposal to give Italy a truly representative government.

[52] To correct this situation, Prunas sent one of his closest associates to Portugal to arrange to have new instructions transmitted to the Italian representatives in Ankara and in Lisbon. This action was just being initiated.

effort and of the impressive and admirable effort of the Soviet people. He had no doubt that Russia was, and in the future would become even more, a determining and dominant element in European war and postwar policy. He was ready to take note of this circumstance realistically and to draw, equally realistically, as soon as possible, all of the necessary conclusions. He begged Vishinsky to communicate these observations, which he was making officially and in the name of the Badoglio government, to Moscow. Vishinsky, evidently pleased, gave him his assurances.

Prunas then added that it would be Italy's goal and desire to arrange the means for direct communication with the Soviet government, which was at present totally impossible for the Badoglio government. Prunas regarded as absurd the fact that the Italian government should be forced to continue to communicate with Moscow through the admittedly courteous but uncertain good offices of the English and Americans. Vishinsky learned with interest and some surprise that a telegram from Brindisi to Moscow sent through Anglo-American channels required up to thirty days for transmittal. The Soviet delegate assured Prunas that he would look into the problem and take the necessary steps to improve the situation. It was superfluous to emphasize—aside from the formal implications—the importance that a permanent and regularized direct contact with the Soviet government would have for Italy. It would constitute a further breach in the wall of isolation imposed on Italy by the Allied Control Commission, and a more important one than that already opened with the French Committee of National Liberation.[53]

The two diplomats then turned to a detailed examination of the Italian situation, which Prunas described as that of a country badly shaken by the war and politically, economically, and spiritually in a critical state which the Allied occupation tended to aggravate rather than alleviate. Vishinsky indicated his understanding of the situation. He believed that every people was, at least in part, responsible for the nature of its government but that the Italians had paid a very heavy price for the errors and the faults of the regime which they had supported for twenty years. Moreover, he did not have the impression that the battle against fascism was being carried on with sufficient vigor or that the Italian government was sufficiently representative of public opinion. He also appeared to be firmly convinced that the Allied occupation and control was not only ex-

[53] As has been noted, Prunas met briefly with Massigli in Brindisi on December 6, 1943, and on that occasion there was a reference to the opportunity to arrange for direct Italo-French contact, in view of the presence of a French diplomat, De Panafieu, in the peninsula and of the Italian military mission in Algiers under General Castellano.

tremely severe but that it was, above all, amateurish and thus capable of aggravating rather than improving the situation. Vishinsky then repeated with great vigor and certainty that the present phase was only temporary and transitory; that is, it was destined to be replaced by more responsible and stable controls and that outside intervention and interference would become less burdensome. In his judgment, this improvement could be greatly facilitated and hastened by increasing the tempo of the struggle against fascism or by progressively widening the basis of the government, or both. Vishinsky added, in the certainty of correctly interpreting the thoughts and plans of his government on the matter, that the Soviet Union was convinced that Italy would be reborn and that it was moving, after experiencing the gravest of trials, toward a future characterized by freedom and independence.

Prunas insisted that it was untrue that the struggle against fascism was not being vigorously prosecuted. The battle was being waged with all of the energy possible under the circumstances, which were what they were and not subject to change. Anti-Fascist activity could be carried on in two ways. The imagination of the masses could be captured, but this would be superficial and without long-lasting beneficial effects. Another much more serious, although much less spectacular, method was designed to destroy the evil at its roots. What was required was an effective combination of both approaches. By applying only the first of the two, anti-Fascist activity would be reduced to a simple man hunt and to emptying of the political prisons, only to fill them again. The second approach consisted of ascertaining the causes of the disease and treating them directly. The Italians, a highly civilized and cultured people, were also poor and proletarian. They had to be brought to life. It was necessary to resolve this problem with equity and justice. This was the only radical, effective anti-Fascist cure known to him, Prunas said. The first approach was only a method of repression and punishment, an approach that was absolutely necessary, but which was in itself also totally insufficient. The government, too, should conduct its own anti-Fascist struggle, since this issue was extremely real to it, along these same lines and with the same directives. Were the Soviets to support the Italian cause within the Allied councils toward this end, they would be making a major contribution to the whole concept of purification and of peace. Russia was disinterested, according to Prunas. It had no problems of space or of resources. Italy faced these problems in their gravest forms, and the decision to peg the exchange for the lira at four hundred to one certainly did not help to resolve them. Since Prunas expressed himself with great emotion, Vishinsky took pains to assure him that Italy could count on Soviet support even in this sense, that is, that of disinterested assistance in resolving the Italian problem with equity and justice.

At this point in the conversation the Italian diplomat called Vishinsky's attention to several particularly urgent questions. Regarding the Italian prisoners in Russia, he stated that it would be a very great comfort to be given the exact number being held, a list of their names, and some indication of their condition. Moreover, such information would greatly aid the propaganda effort in northern Italy, home of the majority of the families of these prisoners, who for such a long time had been totally without any news of their loved ones. Prunas added that negotiations were under way with the English and Americans for an agreement on the employment and utilization of prisoners of war. The Badoglio government would gladly negotiate the same kind of an agreement with the Soviets. Prunas also called Vishinsky's attention to the fact that all Italians had sincerely and thoroughly deprecated the intervention in Russia. It was unanimously agreed that the troops of the ARMIR (Italian Army in Russia) had acted humanely. A great many officers and soldiers had returned to Italy indignant at the atrocities they had seen committed by the German troops in Russia, which had contributed to widening the gulf between Italy and Germany. Vishinsky agreed that although a number of Italian units had also committed atrocities against the people in occupied Russian territory, their conduct was generally much more humane than that of the Germans. In any event, he assured Prunas that he would not fail to cable his government immediately and would support the request made of him, promising to have a reply for the Italian diplomat when he returned to Italy.

Prunas then asked Vishinsky, in the name of the Badoglio government, whether the Soviet government would assume direct care and protection of Italian interests, buildings, and possessions in the Soviet Union which were, at that moment, entrusted to the Japanese. In all likelihood, the Tokyo government would reply that it had received the request for care and protection of Italian interests and holdings in Russia from the Fascist government, which was still recognized by the Japanese as the sole and legitimate Italian government, and would consequently decline the request. In any event, it would be an excellent occasion for the Soviet Union to indicate to Japan that it recognized the King's government as the sole and legitimate one and was acting accordingly. Without question, this would have the effect of lowering Fascist prestige. Vishinsky assured the Italian representative that, notwithstanding the delicacy of current Soviet-Japanese relations, he would certainly transmit the Italian request to his government and would inform the Italians as soon as possible of the Soviet decision, which he had reason to believe would be favorable.

Prunas then took the opportunity to describe to Vishinsky the miserable living conditions of Italian embassy and consular employees interned in Tokyo and Shanghai and begged him to seek further information on the matter. Of course, he added, the Italian government would be extremely grateful if the Soviet government, in addition to assuming this mission of a purely informative nature, would agree to use its good offices to convince the Japanese to alleviate the inhuman conditions imposed on the Italian government employees. Vishinsky believed that Moscow would also agree to this request, which, while it would help the Italian internees, would at the same time entrust the de facto protection of Italian interests in the Far East to the Russians. This would constitute a concrete and cordial renewal of relations between Italy and the Soviet Union.

The Secretary-General of the Foreign Office also informed the Soviet diplomat that as soon as the Badoglio government received Togliatti's request for repatriation it immediately gave instructions to the Ambassador in Ankara to inform his Soviet colleague that there would be no objection or difficulty and that, moreover, in the absence of its own facilities, it had asked the Allied authorities to help in the journey.

Prunas reported his impression that, everything considered, this first official contact with the Soviet government, a contact which, for obvious reasons, had clearly defined limits, had gone very well. He had found Vishinsky, on the whole, receptive, anxious to form his own opinion of the situation, and extremely cautious in expressing himself regarding the English and Americans. He touched upon such subjects as propaganda, proselytizing, doctrine, and pragmatism only with great prudence, almost as though he were anxious to avoid annoying or aggravating the English and Americans, rather than the Italians. He appeared to be well-disposed toward Italy and, therefore, to be cultivated with great care. According to Prunas, once the anti-Fascist premises advanced by Vishinsky were satisfied and the government given a wider democratic base—principles which were laid down at the Moscow conference and to which the Soviet delegate returned insistently—the Italian government could surely find aid and support in him. Prunas pointed out that his personal position both in Algiers within the Consultative Commission and probably also in Moscow, where for many years he was Molotov's closest collaborator, was, in all likelihood, extremely strong. At the termination of the colloquy the Soviet statesman asked the Italian diplomat to feel free to visit him frequently during his next sojourn in Italy, and Prunas in turn asked Vishinsky to appeal directly to him for all of the news, information, and clarification he might require.

This was the substance of the Vishinsky-Prunas conversation of January 8 and the first impressions reported by the Secretary-General of the

Foreign Office on that occasion. In view of our earlier attempts to reconstruct the psychological position of the two countries, their attitudes need
no further comment. The conversation adhered perfectly to the premises
which had evolved during the weeks between the opening of the negotiations for an armistice and the end of 1943; that is, Italian bitterness over
the isolation imposed on the Badoglio government and Soviet resentment
over the secondary role reserved for Moscow in treating the affairs of Italy.
If Prunas became very emotional in presenting his case, Vishinsky, for his
part, did his best to encourage him to expect a great deal. As evident from
his comments, Prunas was obviously very favorably impressed, even to the
point of abandoning his usual professional caution. At the same time,
Vishinsky could not have remained unmoved by the arguments that were
presented, particularly by the tone in which this was done.

Obviously informed of the ideas that the Soviet delegate had expressed
to Professor Guido Pazzi, Undersecretary in the Italian Ministry of Information, Prunas promptly opened the discussion on the theme of a
direct Italo-Soviet contact, without, however, specifying the nature of the
contact he had in mind. His defense of what he believed to be the best
method for combating fascism reflected his concern over the necessity for
answering the criticisms advanced earlier by the Soviet diplomat of the
steps taken by the Badoglio regime, but in this first colloquy he does not
appear to have grasped the full significance of Vishinsky's criticism of the
democratic base of the Badoglio government as too narrow. His proposal
for the employment and utilization of the Italian prisoners of war in
Russia was effectively presented, but apparently did not particularly move
the Soviet delegate; if it had, Vishinsky would not at that time have
referred to his own primary anxiety over increasing Italy's role in the war
against Germany. While Prunas' request for information concerning the
Italian prisoners in Russia reflected a desire common throughout the
peninsula, the ideas he presented regarding the protection of Italian interests in the Soviet Union and in the Far East were extremely interesting.
However, for a long time to come no further mention was made of these
matters, nor does it appear that Moscow gave them more than passing
consideration.

7

Two days later Vishinsky again requested Prunas to meet with him in
Salerno for further talks. Vishinsky opened the conversation by stating he
had re-examined the proposal for a renewal of direct contacts between
Italy and the Soviet Union during the night. He noted that, technically
speaking, the re-establishment of this contact would certainly be justified

in that it would do no more than place the Soviet Union in the position enjoyed by the British and the Americans; that is, it would provide parity for the three major allies. The political problem was much more complicated because of the serious direct and indirect effects it would have on both the internal Italian situation and the relations between the Soviet Union and Great Britain and the United States.

Prunas then observed that undoubtedly such an undertaking would have to be accompanied by a change in the attitude of the Italian Communist Party, which, at that moment, was violently opposed to the government. In his opinion, such a position led up a blind alley, and it would be advantageous to correct this aspect of the Italian internal situation. Moreover, a change in attitude on the part of the Italian Communist Party would have a decisive effect on the attitudes of the other five parties as well, leading, in all likelihood, to the creation of a government with a broader democratic base, the common objective. The Italian diplomat did not ignore the fact that, from an international point of view, a renewal of Italo-Soviet diplomatic relations most assuredly could not be realized through a solution agreed upon by the Soviet Union, Great Britain, and the United States. In his view it was necessary, therefore, that it be brought about by Moscow at an opportune moment via a secret bilateral undertaking. For obvious reasons the Badoglio government would have to give the overt impression of being almost forced into the situation. Once their immediate surprise and distrust had subsided, the Allies would most certainly accept it, since they had no means with which to oppose it. Prunas also believed that such a gesture from the Soviets might well provoke a similar gesture from the British and Americans. Therefore, it was possible that at one and the same time two critical problems—the Italian internal situation and the intolerable armistice conditions—could be resolved, and more acceptable and constructive positions could be taken in both areas, which was in the interest of all parties. The Secretary-General of the Italian Foreign Office regarded as superfluous emphasizing the enormous impetus such an undertaking would give to Soviet influence in Italy, providing Russia with all those advantages which the British and Americans, maintaining their rigid positions on the armistice, could never attain. Prunas pressed this point and developed it in great detail.

Vishinsky listened to the arguments advanced by the Italian with obvious interest and said that he would give the matter further thought. He indicated that, as a matter of fact, he had sought the second meeting in order to get the Italian view on an eventual *modus procedendi*. He would soon return to Moscow and in the Soviet capital would be in a position to study and develop concrete solutions; there he would have the advice and counsel of many competent, intelligent Italian Communists.

Prunas had the clear impression that Vishinsky definitely intended to take action, but he could predict neither the time nor the procedure to be employed. The reference to the Italian Communists in Moscow might, perhaps, be a clue. In his opinion, however, it was imperative that the matter be treated with the utmost secrecy.

Undoubtedly the second Vishinsky-Prunas meeting, despite the fact that it was the direct consequence of the first encounter, surpassed it in importance. During its course the Italian diplomat revealed his own thoughts even more clearly than he had earlier. His principal objective remained, as always, that of breaking the isolation imposed by the armistice terms and then attempting to set off a chain reaction which might also lead to the reopening of direct diplomatic relations between Italy and Washington and Italy and London. Convinced that his objective was unattainable in any other way, he did not hesitate to negotiate secretly with the Soviet Union for recognition and renewal of normal diplomatic relations without the knowledge of the occupying powers.[54] His conviction resulted from the disappointments experienced during the initial phases of the application of the armistice terms and the failure of attempts to assure Italy a more favorable position within the framework of the United Nations. Prunas was convinced that a frank and open four-power approach to the problem would abort any positive action, and he was equally certain that the refusal to grant Italy the status of an ally was solely the result of the ill-will and rancor nourished by the English and Americans. While there is much that is true in this evaluation, it is not completely valid.[55] In any event, Prunas' state of mind was such that, having tried one approach without the slightest success, he preferred trying an entirely new route to attempting the old one again. He had no doubt that Allied surprise and distrust at the renewal of normal Italo-Soviet relations would recede and that, despite the fact that only their armies remained in southern Italy,

[54] The preoccupation with maintaining the secrecy of the negotiations with Moscow was so great that Prunas did not even mention them to his colleagues in the Foreign Office at the time. He assembled them in Salerno later to ask each of them individually for his opinion regarding the opportunity of re-establishing direct diplomatic relations with Moscow, but he did so only after March 4, 1944—that is, when he already knew that Moscow favored the idea. On that occasion, all the Italian diplomats, with just one exception, favored the proposal.

[55] Feis (*Churchill, Roosevelt, and Stalin*, p. 178) notes that on two occasions Stalin expressed doubts concerning the advisability of modifying the conditions imposed by the Italian armistice even in the modest sense proposed by the British and Americans on October 17, 1943. These assertions, however, are not supported by precise documentation.

the projected undertaking would assure a Soviet influence in Italy strong enough to make it impossible for the English and Americans to maintain their very rigid positions on the armistice. This interpretation, on which he placed so much stress, was, in part, in contradiction to what he envisioned for the Soviets when he predicted a similar gesture coming from Washington and London. On the other hand, the suggestions and conclusions of Prunas contradict the statement in Badoglio's memoirs that "the substance of that colloquy [with Vishinsky] was immediately transmitted by me to General Joyce."[56] Finally, we must note the correctness of Prunas' predictions regarding the positive results that a change in the Italian Communist Party's attitude regarding the Badoglio government might have had on resolving the problem of widening its political base. Unknowingly, Prunas touched upon a theme of very great interest to Vishinsky.

Not even on that occasion was the problem of expanding Italy's role in the war against Germany openly discussed. The degree of Vishinsky's concurrence in the idea of a renewal of direct Italo-Soviet diplomatic relations—all the more significant because in the first meeting the Italian diplomat refrained from entering into particulars—did not surprise Prunas at all, either because he was aware of what had transpired in the Vishinsky-Pazzi talks in Brindisi or because he was completely convinced that he had won over his Soviet counterpart. Obviously, it is difficult today to understand the conditions and the degree of isolation in which Italian diplomats labored; contrariwise, it is difficult to avoid reasoning on the basis of ex post facto knowledge and complete or almost complete information. Given the candor displayed by Prunas and his frank arguments, we may well ask ourselves who would have been able to avoid succumbing to the attraction of an argument which had all the appearance of irrefutable logic. The most important problem for the Italians at that time was to escape from what appeared to be a blind alley.

8

The following day Badoglio was admitted to a part of the session of the Consultative Commission for Italy in Naples,[57] during the course of which

---

[56] Badoglio, *L'Italia nella seconda guerra mondiale*, p. 164.

[57] On this point Badoglio, in his recollections (*ibid.*, p. 163), is wrong on two counts when he writes, "General Joyce begged me to join him in journeying to Naples to participate in the first session of that commission." In fact, as has been pointed out, it was Badoglio who repeatedly and insistently asked to be invited to the meeting. Second, the session in Naples was not the first but the fifth, as is noted in the official communiqué published in the newspapers on January 13, 1944. These rather flagrant inaccuracies arouse even greater suspicion regarding the exact date indicated by Badoglio as the moment when the Allies requested the amendments to the Cunningham-De Courten Naval Accord.

he made a lengthy statement concerning the objectives of the actions taken by his government, an exposition which appeared to create a favorable impression upon the delegates present.[58] The comments in the Allied camp garnered by functionaries of the Italian Foreign Ministry indicated that, beginning with Vishinsky, everyone had been favorably impressed by the frankness, the loyalty, and the moral tone of the words pronounced by the Italian at the opening of the session. According to these comments the question of Italian participation in the work of the Consultative Commission would have been temporarily resolved de facto. The specific problems raised by the Marshal would be given careful consideration, and every effort would be made to ameliorate the situation. The meeting between Badoglio and the commission, it was reported, had been a success for the Prime Minister.

In reality, these reports were overly optimistic. They consistently ignored the unwavering, intransigent opposition of the French delegate, who, a few days later, presented a note to the commission demanding the immediate abdication of King Victor Emmanuel and the dismissal of Badoglio.[59] Moreover, assertions that the problem of Italian participation in the work of the commission could have been resolved de facto and that the problems raised by Badoglio would be seriously considered and every effort made to ameliorate the situation had no factual basis whatever.[60]

After this promising beginning, nothing of consequence occurred for several weeks. On January 26, 1944, it was learned in Brindisi that General Solodovnik had been appointed to represent the Soviet Union on the Allied Control Commission. According to General Castellano, who reported from Algiers on January 30, Solodovnik received favorably the idea that an Italian should go to Moscow to discuss post-armistice Italy, its needs and just aspirations, and promised to speak to Vishinsky on the matter. This was another interesting confirmation that the Soviets were at that time carefully considering the question of opening direct official contact with Italy. On February 14 Prunas learned from British sources of

---

[58] This positive evaluation was also confirmed in substance by the report on the meeting transmitted to Hull by Ambassador Reinhardt. See Foreign Relations, 1944 (Washington, D.C.: U.S. Government Printing Office, 1962), III, pp. 999–1002.

[59] Ibid., pp. 1005–6. The note was presented at the January 24 meeting of the Consultative Commission and, at the same time, to the governments of London, Moscow, and Washington through the offices of the French Committee of National Liberation, but it aroused negative reactions everywhere. The Italian government became aware of this action approximately two months after the event (see p. 316).

[60] According to Reinhardt, the members of the commission lost no time in making it clear to Badoglio that the invitation extended to him was under no circumstances to be interpreted as an invitation to participate in the work of that body on a regular basis. See Foreign Relations, 1944, III, p. 1000.

Vishinsky's departure for Moscow without plans to return either to Algiers or Italy. Macmillan was in London and Murphy in Washington, evidence that a period of inactivity was under way as far as the commission was concerned. Prunas regretted Vishinsky's recall because he considered the Soviet diplomat's activity in Italy to be wise and well-balanced. On February 19 information from Algiers indicated that the commission on the previous day had held its seventh meeting, attended for the first time by participating representatives from Greece and Yugoslavia. Ambassador Bogomolov had taken Vishinsky's place. These facts induced Badoglio to request once again, on February 26, that Italy be assured a permanent position as a participant.[61]

Meanwhile, unknown to the Italian government, the problem of transferring the naval units promised at Teheran to the Soviet Union had been the object of extensive negotiations among the United States, Great Britain, and the U.S.S.R. The episode is worth recalling because of its perhaps not entirely unintentional connection with the problem of the renewal of diplomatic relations between Italy and the Soviet Union.

On December 20, 1943, the American Ambassador to the Soviet Union, Averell Harriman, anticipating a request by Molotov for details on the action taken by the United States to implement the obligation assumed at Teheran, cabled to the American President for information.[62] Roosevelt replied immediately that it was his intention to transfer to the Soviet Union one-third of the Italian fleet.[63] On December 23, Harriman pointed out that at Teheran no mention had been made of one-third of the Italian fleet, but rather of the transfer before February 1, 1944, of those naval units requested by Molotov during the Moscow conference.[64] The same observation was made to Roosevelt by the British Ambassador to Washington, Lord Halifax, at Eden's request.[65] Roosevelt then requested Harriman to provide him with the details, based on the minutes of the Teheran conference. Harriman examined the texts in question and confirmed that the obligation assumed involved one battleship, one cruiser, eight destroyers, and four submarines.[66]

At this point Roosevelt began to meet with resistance from within his own General Staff. On January 9 he cabled Churchill for his opinion. The President intended to keep the promise made at Teheran and to avoid arousing resentment and suspicion in Moscow. The revision of the

[61] On this point, see *ibid.*, pp. 1042–43.
[62] *Foreign Relations, Teheran*, p. 852.
[63] *Ibid.*, pp. 852–53.
[64] *Ibid.*, pp. 856–57.
[65] *Ibid.*, p. 857.
[66] *Ibid.*, p. 862.

Cunningham-De Courten Naval Accord granted the Allies the right to dispose of the Italian fleet as they saw fit, but the American high command feared that the Italians might react by sinking their own ships— ships which were considered vitally important for the projected opening of the second front in France. Roosevelt asked whether this was a matter to be discussed with Stalin. An Anglo-American understanding appeared to be indispensable, but the promises made at Teheran certainly had to be kept.[67] Churchill replied to Roosevelt on January 16 in a long message. He concurred with the opinion of the American General Staff concerning the dangers inherent in antagonizing the Italians, but he was prepared to approach Badoglio secretly, if Roosevelt insisted. However, Churchill suggested another possibility: an offer to lend Stalin an equivalent number of Allied naval vessels until such time as the transfer of the Italian ships could be effected without endangering military operations.[68] Roosevelt chose this second alternative and on January 23, joined by the British Prime Minister, he approached Stalin on the matter.[69]

Stalin replied on January 29. After indicating some surprise that there was further discussion of the question, which had been resolved at Teheran, and that in all this time no mention of the decision had been made to the Italians, he accepted the British-American offer on condition that the number and types of craft correspond to what had been requested during the Moscow conference.[70] It is not impossible that Stalin's conciliatory position was also connected with the decision he was about to make regarding the Prunas proposal, transmitted to him by Vishinsky upon his return to Moscow. On the other hand, Churchill cabled Stalin on January 24 to call his attention to the unfavorable repercussions in Great Britain produced by the repeated attacks on the British-American administration in Italy appearing in the journal *Voina i raboci klass* (*The War and the Working Class*). In his view, the proper place for such remonstrances was in the meetings of the Consultative Commission for Italy, which would avoid making public whatever discord existed among the Allied powers.[71] In any event, the question of substituting British and American naval units for Italian ones was ultimately settled through a

[67] Churchill, *Closing the Ring*, pp. 402–3; *Foreign Relations, Teheran*, p. 866.
[68] Churchill, *Closing the Ring*, pp. 404–5; *Foreign Relations, Teheran*, p. 871.
[69] *Correspondence U.S.S.R.*, I, pp. 186–88; II, pp. 115–17.
[70] *Ibid.*, I, pp. 190–91; II, pp. 117–18; Churchill, *Closing the Ring*, pp. 405–6; *Foreign Relations, Teheran*, pp. 873–74.
[71] *Correspondence U.S.S.R.*, I, pp. 189, 192. Stalin replied on January 29, 1944, that the magazine in question was a labor union publication and that the government could not assume responsibility for its articles. Furthermore, he added, the fundamental principle on which the strengthening of ties with the Allies was based did not exclude, but rather presupposed, friendly criticism.

series of brief exchanges among the three statesmen regarding the operational efficiency of the British and American ships offered in loan.[72]

This entire episode, albeit interesting, would not be of any particular relevance to this inquiry if, on March 3, during a press conference, President Roosevelt had not mentioned the fact that there existed the possibility of transferring one-third of the Italian fleet or an equal number of British-American warships to the Soviet Union to aid that country in its war effort.[73] This promptly provoked an immediate reaction from Churchill[74] and great concern in Italy.[75] The protests of the Badoglio government[76] were finally satisfied by a joint British-American declaration on March 10, which stated that at Teheran the most effective way of employing the Italian fleet against the common enemy had been discussed, along with the quota of the fleet due the Soviet Union. The United States and Great Britain would provide for Moscow's needs by lending the Russians the necessary craft from their own fleets. For the moment there were no plans to transfer Italian naval vessels to the Soviet Union.[77]

What prompted these indiscretions by Roosevelt during his press conference of March 3? The President was perfectly well aware of what the psychological reaction would be among Italians, since it was he who had mentioned the danger inherent in the projected transfer of portions of the Italian fleet, and he chose, from the two alternatives suggested by the British Prime Minister, that which was the most onerous for the British and Americans but which avoided offending the Italians. Moreover, at that date the question had been, to all intents and purposes, resolved with Stalin. In a telegram to Churchill on March 3, Roosevelt affirmed that his statements to the newsmen had been made in reply to the insistent questions raised at the press conference.[78] This insistence was insufficient reason for such an indiscretion. The President of the United States was no neophyte at this game, and it would not have been difficult for him to avoid answering questions whose intention was suspect. Why did the newsmen choose this time to pose a question which would more logically have been raised either at the time of the armistice or at either the Moscow or the Teheran conferences? Somewhere there must have been a leak, and it could hardly be accidental. Washington may have known that the very

[72] *Ibid.*, I, pp. 197–98, 206–9, 210–11; II, pp. 118–19, 125–26, 129–30, 131.
[73] The Reuter telegram version, as well as Roosevelt's own version of his declarations, may be found in *Foreign Relations, Teheran*, pp. 875–76.
[74] *Ibid.*, pp. 876–78.
[75] Cf. Degli Espinosa, *Il Regno del Sud*, pp. 300–1.
[76] *Ibid.*
[77] *Ibid.*, pp. 301–3.
[78] *Foreign Relations, Teheran*, p. 876.

next day, March 4, Ambassador Bogomolov was to transmit to Badoglio Moscow's reply to the proposal made by Prunas to Vishinsky on January 10, or this statement may simply have been intended as a general warning to the Italians not to approach the Soviets on their own. There is no evidence to formulate a precise answer, but the fact remains that the coincidence was indeed singular.[79] However, it may be more apparent than real. It is entirely possible that Roosevelt intended his remarks to put the Italians on their guard against the Soviets, and that the Kremlin reacted by immediately taking a step toward renewing diplomatic relations with Italy on the basis of a decision in principle reached earlier. There is much that is logical about this hypothesis, but there is no evidence to favor it over the others.

9

On March 4, therefore, Bogomolov asked to be received by Badoglio. He observed that in a colloquy between Ambassador Vishinsky and Minister Prunas on January 11[80] the latter had expressed the desire of the Italian government to have direct contacts with the Soviet government and to renew regular diplomatic relations. In reply to this request the Soviet government had instructed Bogomolov to inform the Italian government that Moscow was ready to renew official diplomatic relations with Italy. Specifically, Russia was willing to send a representative to the Italian government without ambassadorial status. This representative would not present the usual credentials but simply those of an "official representative." Similarly, Russia would be disposed to receive an official Italian representative. Both representatives would be granted full diplomatic privileges and immunities. The Soviet government urged the Italian government to request such an arrangement officially; an acceptance along the lines outlined above would be forthcoming immediately.

---

[79] A highly responsible Italian diplomat whom I questioned on the matter reported that he had learned, many years after the fact, that the American intelligence service had hidden a microphone in Badoglio's office. This would, of course, have permitted Washington to know of the Italian move. It is difficult, obviously, to render an objective judgment on such an interpretation. The Vishinsky-Prunas colloquies were held elsewhere, and the Soviet communiqué indicating Moscow's acceptance of the Italian proposal was transmitted only the day after Roosevelt's press conference. One may ask whether Bogomolov's request for an audience was made earlier and whether it offered the opportunity for an exchange of ideas between Badoglio and Prunas, or whether the Americans possessed some information about the Vishinsky and Solodovnik proposals.

[80] The difference of one day in dating the second Vishinsky-Prunas colloquy is probably because Moscow used the date on which the Soviet minutes of the conversation were drafted.

Ambassador Bogomolov added that the Soviet initiative was an indication of the true measure of Russian feelings and, consequently, of general policy toward Italy, and that this fact should be appreciated by the Italian government. Marshal Badoglio asked the Ambassador to thank his government for the communication, which would be received with profound satisfaction by the Italian government as well as by the Italian public which would surely appreciate its enormous importance and significance. The requested note would be sent as soon as possible. Badoglio then repeated the question asked earlier of Vishinsky by Prunas regarding the status of the Italian prisoners of war in Russia and the possibility of receiving detailed and exact information concerning them. Bogomolov reassured the Marshal on this point.[81]

Immediately after this colloquy Badoglio wrote a note to Prunas asking him to give serious thought to the selection of a representative of the highest competence to send to Moscow. The fact that Italy was about to enjoy the privilege of sending a plenipotentiary to the Soviet Union was in itself a major accomplishment, but anyone not highly qualified would do more damage than good in that crucial post. The official Italian note to Bogomolov was sent on March 6. It affirmed that the preceding January the Italians had indicated to Ambassador Vishinsky their desire to have more effective and direct contacts with the Soviet government and to establish more normal and regular diplomatic relations. In response to the Soviet communication of March 4, Marshal Badoglio noted that he was confirming that request and added that the Italian government sincerely hoped that normal relations between the two countries could be promptly established, thereby opening a new and fruitful period of peace and collaboration between Italy and the Soviet Union, inspired by those sentiments of friendship and reciprocal respect which up until very recent times had always characterized Italo-Russian relations.[82]

---

[81] In recalling the episode, Badoglio (*L'Italia nella seconda guerra mondiale*) is once again inexact in that he maintains that Bogomolov referred to a colloquy which took place in Naples between the head of the Italian government and Vishinsky. The Ambassador referred only to the Vishinsky-Prunas meeting and to the date of that encounter. This alteration of the facts also led Luraghi ("Sui rapporti diplomatici," p. 117) to an erroneous conclusion. Moreover, Luraghi also refers to an exchange of ambassadors, while it consisted only of official representatives. In Italian diplomatic circles at Salerno the story at the time circulated that Bogomolov's entry into Badoglio's office caught the Marshal by surprise while reading a mystery story, which he quickly put away in a desk drawer. This circumstance would seem to exclude the hypothesis that an audience had been requested earlier, as well as a conclusion regarding the possible objective of the Soviet action.

[82] Badoglio, *L'Italia nella seconda guerra mondiale*, pp. 173–74; Luraghi, "Sui rapporti diplomatici," p. 117. It was precisely the question of drafting this document that induced Prunas to assemble all of the Italian diplomats at Salerno in

With this note the Italian government quickly and unhesitatingly accepted the Soviet choice of procedure in renewing direct diplomatic relations. In his second meeting with Vishinsky, Prunas suggested that Moscow should make what would appear to be an autonomous decision, a decision which the Badoglio government would give the impression of being "forced to accept" for "obvious reasons." This line of conduct would have been wholly dishonest and undignified, an expression of real weakness, and a clumsy attempt to be cunning. Moscow, which had been informed orally by Vishinsky (who was very circumspect in his judgments of Allied policies) in a manner reflecting his concern for the eventual repercussions such a maneuver might have on Russia's relations with London and Washington, chose not to accept the procedure suggested by the Badoglio government. If the Italian government truly desired to open direct diplomatic relations between the two countries, it should at least have had the courage to assume responsibility publicly for such an initiative. It must be added that while at that time the significance of the statements made by President Roosevelt during his press conference were not entirely clear, the Italian government did not hesitate to request the renewal of diplomatic relations formally.

On March 5 Prunas met with Bogomolov. During the course of the conversation the Secretary-General of the Italian Foreign Ministry emphasized the surprise of all of the Italian people at Roosevelt's totally unexpected statements to the press, statements which were completely different in tone and spirit from those made by Churchill in his speech to the House of Commons.[83] Having received only fragmentary and unconfirmed reports on the matter via the radio newscasts, the Italian government immediately requested clarification of the matter, reserving the right to take whatever action it considered necessary. Prunas expressed the hope that

---

order to obtain their individual opinions on the advisability of taking the initiative to open negotiations with Moscow for a re-establishment of diplomatic relations at this time. The participants at this convocation were unaware of the content of the Vishinsky-Prunas conversations of January 8 and 10, 1944. It is likely that the Secretary-General of the Italian Foreign Ministry took this particular course for three reasons. First, contrary to his original proposal, the Badoglio government should have assumed the responsibility for the initiative. Second, the Roosevelt press conference cast a shadow over the Soviet aims, and, at that particular moment, exactly how the question of the Italian fleet would be resolved remained unknown. Third, one should not exclude the possibility that Prunas, banking on the Allies' eventually learning of the Italian activity through a leak, believed that it would serve to convince them that Moscow's decision had come as a complete surprise to the Italians.

[83] These statements were made on February 22, 1944. For the text, see Degli Espinosa, *Il Regno del Sud*, pp. 283–84.

the reports by the news agencies were not accurate. A breakup of the Italian fleet such as the news agencies suggested would unquestionably have meant the end of the Italian military effort against Germany, a government crisis, and chaos throughout the country. Prunas then added that initially the Badoglio government had no objection in principle to the collaboration of a part of the Italian navy with the Soviet fleet on the terms and conditions under which it gave its cooperation and loyalty to the British and American fleet. A bilateral accord between the two general staffs would be sufficient, with the consent of the other two allies, of course.

Bogomolov replied that he was not sufficiently informed on the matter to render either an opinion or a decision but that he would, in his own name, promptly cable to Moscow the views expressed by Prunas. He then urged that the Italian government lose no time in submitting the official note which Bogomolov had requested Badoglio to present concerning the renewal of diplomatic relations between the two countries. The Soviet Ambassador laid great stress on the mutual advantages to be gained from the re-establishment of normal diplomatic exchanges, which would undoubtedly give both parties greater autonomy and freedom of action.

On this occasion, Prunas reported, Bogomolov—who was much more reticent than Vishinsky and, all in all, much more the bureaucrat than the statesman—was obviously very suspicious and distrustful of the British and Americans. Prunas was convinced that Bogomolov was speaking the truth when he said that he knew nothing of the proposed disposition of the Italian fleet.[84] Moreover, the Soviet delegate was of the opinion that the negotiations referred to by Roosevelt must have been motivated by the Soviet interest in participating in all matters concerning western Europe and the Mediterranean, areas which the British and Americans obviously considered to be outside its interest and competence, rather than by any anti-Italian objectives. If this view is considered correct, Prunas added, the Italian proposals for discussions and direct bilateral accords, within the overall picture of an imminent renewal of relations with Moscow, could undoubtedly help in allowing the question to be examined on an entirely different and more acceptable level; that is, it was just possible that the Roosevelt statements, the manner in which they were made, and

[84] This interpretation appears to be entirely reasonable, and one may suppose that Vishinsky too, at the time of his conversations with Prunas, knew nothing of the decisions taken at Teheran. On the other hand, it is much more difficult to imagine that the then Vice-Minister of the Soviet Foreign Office, who had arrived in Algiers only at the end of November, 1943, was unaware, regardless of how indisposed he may have been during the Moscow Foreign Ministers Conference, of the fact that on October 22 Molotov had presented a formal request for part of the Italian fleet.

their timing[85] could have been motivated by a desire to block an Italo-Soviet rapprochement or any attempt by Russia to increase its influence in the Mediterranean. In the almost complete vacuum in which the Italian government was forced to exist, as far as news and direct information were concerned, such suspicions could only be hypothetical, but no more so than explanations of Roosevelt's declarations as motivated by internal electoral considerations (in effect, the acceptance of the Fiorello La Guardia thesis of greater leniency to win the Italian-American vote) or as reflecting a difference of opinion between Roosevelt and Churchill regarding Italian internal affairs.

Aside from the suspicion voiced by the Italian diplomat that Roosevelt's statements might be designed to sabotage the Italo-Soviet rapprochement (a suspicion which did not affect in the slightest his optimism regarding the possibility of effectively utilizing the renewal of diplomatic relations with Russia as an instrument to help Italy), the suggestion made for an Italo-Soviet naval collaboration is very interesting. Evidently this idea, which was cabled to Moscow by Bogomolov, was not seriously considered by Stalin nor was it communicated to the British and Americans. At that time Prunas did not consider, even momentarily, the questions of whether the Soviet approach might have been motivated by Roosevelt's revelations at the press conference, or whether Bogomolov might be trying to represent a request by Stalin for a portion of the Italian fleet as the simple expression of the Russian desire not to be cut out of the Mediterranean and western Europe. In reality, this request was based on the Soviet desire to intensify the war effort against Germany, a step the Russians considered vital and to which the Italian contribution was regarded as inadequate. Furthermore, Prunas did not ask himself then whether, in addition to its desire to establish its presence in the Mediterranean, Moscow might not have other specific objectives, such as facilitating the formation of an Italian government that would be representative of all of the anti-Fascist forces for the purpose of stimulating the Italian war effort. This lapse on Prunas' part is rather astonishing in view of the fact that the whole question of a change in the Italian Communist Party's policy toward the Badoglio government had been discussed during the second Prunas-Vi-

[85] According to Prunas, Roosevelt made these statements on exactly the same day and at precisely the same time as Bogomolov's overture to Badoglio. In reality, even allowing for the six hours' difference in time between Washington and Salerno, Roosevelt's press conference took place earlier. As a matter of fact, the Reuters dispatch on the Roosevelt statements which aroused so much emotion reached London by 5:30 P.M. London time on March 3, as is clear from the second telegram on the question sent by Churchill to Roosevelt the same day. See *Foreign Relations, Teheran*, pp. 873–74.

shinsky meeting. Moreover, Prunas did not properly evaluate the significance of Moscow's insisting on a formal Italian request for the renewal
of diplomatic relations which markedly modified Prunas' original proposal.

Bogomolov's official reply to the Badoglio letter of March 6 was sent
on March 11. It simply indicated that the Soviet government, having examined the formal Italian request of March 6 regarding the establishment
of direct diplomatic relations between the two governments, agreed to the
exchange of representatives who were to be accorded the usual diplomatic
status.

Earlier, however, on March 7, Ambassador Bogomolov requested an audience with Badoglio, in which he asked the Italian government's permission to establish, in an area to be determined, between Bari and Brindisi,
a Soviet air base of modest dimensions. This base was to maintain the
contacts between the Russians and Marshal Tito's Partisan forces. Badoglio
replied that he was pleased to consent to this request and would aid in
facilitating its realization, adding that two Italian divisions were fighting
with Tito against the common enemy. The Ambassador emphasized the
fact that the Soviet government had made it a point to consult with the
Italian government in order to win its approval on the matter in advance,
rather than to approach the Allied command directly on the question,
which it certainly could have done. Bogomolov thanked the Italian government for the prompt acceptance of its request and promised to inform
Moscow immediately.

10

On March 8, at the direction of Marshal Badoglio,[86] Prunas informed
the American representative on the Allied Control Commission, Samuel
Reber, of the imminent renewal of diplomatic relations between Italy and
the Soviet Union. The Italian diplomat emphasized that it was Marshal
Badoglio's strong wish that the American government be informed without
delay of the action in order to eliminate the possibility of any doubt arising
as to Italy's complete loyalty to the United States. Prunas explained that
some time earlier the Italians had expressed their desire to normalize their
relations with the Soviet Union to Vishinsky. Italy was attempting to do
so with all of the United Nations, he said, which was a reflection of a

[86] Badoglio, *L'Italia nella seconda guerra mondiale*, p. 174. Once again Badoglio's
recollection is incorrect. He affirms that he sent Prunas to confer with General
MacFarlane, Chief of the Allied Control Commission, while the fact is that Prunas
spoke only with Reber, the American diplomat attached to the commission. Moreover, he insists that he based his approach on an earlier communication sent to
General Joyce in Naples in January. This he could not have done, since no such
communication was made.

deliberated policy to reduce tension and promote peace, a policy which Italy hoped to follow with each nation. The Secretary-General of the Foreign Ministry added that the sudden Soviet decision to renew diplomatic relations with the Badoglio government represented an obvious and a not insignificant success of that policy. Moreover, it would be received as such not only by public opinion in the portion of Italy already liberated but also in central and northern Italy, still under Nazi-Fascist occupation. Soviet prestige, already firmly entrenched as a result of its military victories, could not help but be further strengthened. The Italian government therefore hoped that the United States and Great Britain would also decide to break down the rigid barriers imposed by the armistice conditions, which had prevented and would continue to prevent the Anglo-Saxon powers from instituting any truly reconstructive policy. Prunas noted that the Soviet action had removed these barriers insofar as the Soviet Union was concerned, thus giving the Moscow government greater freedom of action and a greater prospect of exerting its influence in western Europe, realities which it would be absurd to ignore or challenge either in meaning or significance.

Reber asked Prunas to thank the Marshal warmly for the information and added that the Americans had never doubted the absolute loyalty toward the United States of both the Italian head of state and the Italian Foreign Minister. The information transmitted was simply a further confirmation of that attitude and, as such, would be sincerely appreciated by the president of the Allied Control Commission. The American diplomat then asked whether Prunas felt that he could also inform his British colleague, Caccia, about the matter. The Secretary-General of the Foreign Ministry made it clear that he had called on him, Reber, expressly to inform him of the Italo-Soviet action, but that since he had raised the question of informing the British, he could do nothing else but consent. It was therefore agreed that Reber would immediately inform General MacFarlane in Badoglio's name.

Prunas then told Reber of the Soviet request for an air base between Brindisi and Taranto to aid in Moscow's contacts with Marshal Tito. The American was already aware of that request; in fact, Ambassador Bogomolov had approached General MacFarlane with the same request and had been told that the final decision on the matter would have to come from General Wilson, in his capacity as Commander of the Allied forces. In confidence, Reber added that the British and Americans were carefully scrutinizing Soviet initiatives in this sector.

Prunas received the impression that the information he had given to the American had been sincerely appreciated, and he had no doubt that it would be equally well received by the British. During the course of the colloquy the existing mistrust between the Soviets and the Allies came to the surface. Prunas insisted that the adoption of a more liberal and farsighted policy by the United States and Great Britain would serve to block the progressive growth of Soviet influence. This view was promptly communicated to both Washington and London. The simple announcement of the renewal of Italo-Soviet diplomatic relations seemed to give the Badoglio government some room for maneuver in the diplomatic game.

At the time of his first communication with the British and Americans regarding the imminent Italo-Soviet action, Prunas apparently exposed his entire hand. In no way did he hide the fact that the initiative for the renewal of diplomatic relations came from the Italians and that it dated back to the time of Vishinsky's visit to the peninsula. However, this version is contradicted by the account presented by Reber. According to him, Prunas not only failed to mention his previous exchanges of views with Vishinsky but also attributed the initiative to Bogomolov, almost as though the move had been an entirely unexpected one which the Italian government was hardly in a position to reject.[87] Of the two versions, Reber's seems to be the more accurate. The British and Americans did continue to believe that the Soviets were the first to propose the re-establishment of relations between Italy and the Soviet Union, and this belief further intensified the suspicions of the Allies concerning Soviet plans in Italy.[88]

On March 14 the Italian press reported the official communiqué of the Italian Prime Minister containing the announcement of the understandings reached with Moscow.[89] At the same time, Marshal Badoglio cabled

[87] Cf. *Foreign Relations, 1944*, III, pp. 1038–39.

[88] On this entire matter see *ibid.*, pp. 1039–42; Harold Macmillan, *The Blast of War, 1939–1945* (London: Macmillan, 1967), pp. 483–84.

[89] On March 13 Bogomolov informed Reinhardt of the imminent exchange of representatives between the Italian and Soviet governments (*Foreign Relations, 1944*, III, pp. 1044–45). It should be noted that, at the moment of publishing the communiqué, the Italians explained to General MacFarlane that the initial phrase of the communiqué, which suggested that the initiative for the exchange came from the Italian government, had been inserted at the request of the Soviets and referred "to the general expression of Italian desire for closer relations with the Allied Powers, a general request made in December to all members of the Advisory Council when on their trip to Italy." *Ibid.*, p. 1048. This interpretation was accepted as valid by General MacFarlane, to the extent that when asked to protest to Badoglio on March 16 concerning the action taken by the Italian government (*ibid.*, p. 1057), he replied that he could not carry out this request, since the initiative for the exchange of representatives had come from the Soviet government and that the Italian government "had immediately informed him of the proposal advanced by Moscow." *Ibid.*, p. 1060. The episode is worth noting since it both demonstrates that the Allied authorities continued to ignore the previous contacts between Prunas and Vishinsky and confirms the absence of veracity—at least on this point—in the Prunas version of his colloquy with Reber.

Stalin that the Italians, fully cognizant of the imposing and victorious Soviet military effort, were more than ever convinced of the necessity to restore Italo-Russian relations to their traditionally fruitful and friendly plane, a plane that had been temporarily and tragically abandoned by that regime which the two governments were now joined in a struggle to destroy. The first comments in the British press were entirely negative.[90] Despite the fact that Badoglio was to some extent surprised by these reactions, he promptly proceeded with the selection of Italy's official repre-

[90] Degli Espinosa, *Il Regno del Sud*, pp. 309–12, contains the essential excerpts. The question also provoked a sharp exchange among London, Moscow, and Washington. On March 13 the British Ambassador to Moscow made it clear to Vishinsky that if the other powers followed the Soviet example and renewed diplomatic relations with Italy, the Consultative Commission would have lost all semblance of authority and that, moreover, the Soviet decision was incompatible with Italy's position, since Italy was still formally at war with the United Nations. *Foreign Relations, 1944*, III, p. 1046. Similar action was taken the same day by Averell Harriman, the American Ambassador in Moscow. Vishinsky, in his reply to Harriman, emphasized that the initiative had come from Prunas and noted that the action taken did not imply a formal renewal of diplomatic relations but rather a simple de facto contact which would not interfere with the work of the Consultative Commission. *Ibid.*, p. 1046–48. Harriman returned to the argument the next day in a memorandum to Vishinsky. He focused his protest primarily on the fact that the Soviets had failed to consult the other Allies on the matter (*ibid.*, pp. 1050–51), and in his report to Cordell Hull he emphasized the necessity of making clear to the Soviets once and for all that the procedure adopted by Moscow was not to be tolerated and could lead to the most serious consequences on a much wider scale. *Ibid.*, pp. 1051, 1055–56. It may have been because of pressure from Harriman that Hull reacted most energetically to the issue, both in his colloquy with the Soviet Ambassador to Washington, Gromyko, and in charging Harriman to make clear to Molotov that the problem of political responsibility toward Italy was the concern of the Allied Commander-in-Chief and that no accord between the Italian government and another government could alter this responsibility. *Ibid.*, p. 1061. Moreover, Harriman was directed to call Molotov's attention to the fact that the Moscow Accords had been designed to coordinate the action of the Allies and to avoid "the seeking by individual members of the Allied nations of special advantage or influence through bilateral arrangements with the Italian government." *Ibid.*, p. 1057–59. The Soviets replied to the British memorandum of March 13 that the decision to reopen direct relations with the Italian government was deemed necessary in order to protect Soviet interests in Italy and to modify the unequal position of the U.S.S.R. in its relations with the Italian authorities in comparison with that enjoyed by the American and British governments. *Ibid.*, pp. 1062–65. In a letter of March 25 to Harriman, Molotov denied that the re-establishment of relations between the Soviet Union and Italy was a matter which fell within the competence of the Consultative Commission, the Allied Control Commission, or even the Commander-in-Chief of the Anglo-American forces in Italy, since it had no bearing on military operations. However, Molotov added that he was disposed to examine the question further through normal diplomatic channels. *Ibid.*, pp. 1078–79; see also Hull, *Memoirs*, pp. 1449, 1463, 1556–59; Churchill, *Closing the Ring*, pp. 446–47; Feis, *Churchill, Roosevelt, and Stalin*, pp. 326–28.

sentative to the Soviet Union, and his choice was Pietro Quaroni, at the time Minister to Kabul.[91]

On March 20 at Naples Prunas met the Soviet Minister, Goryarkin. The latter asked what reactions were noted among the British and Americans when they were informed of the renewal of Italo-Soviet diplomatic relations. The Secretary-General of the Italian Foreign Ministry forthrightly reported that he had the impression that they were unhappy and disappointed. He added that the Allied Control Commission had requested further information from the Italians and that the details demanded would be furnished without delay in clear and simple terms.

Prunas went on to explain that Badoglio had decided to choose the future representative to Moscow from the ranks of career officers rather than from politicians or others. A candidate not a career diplomat would have to undergo a relatively long period of apprenticeship and could be tempted to formulate personal policy, which might not be advisable in view of the delicacy of the situation. The career officer, instead, offered a greater guarantee of obedience to government orders, of technical know-how, and of professionalism. The Italian then asked whether the Soviets were prepared to receive the nomination. Goryarkin unhesitatingly replied in the affirmative, and Prunas went on to name the Italian Minister to Kabul as the government choice for the Moscow post, describing him as an able and clear-thinking officer. All available information on Minister Pietro Quaroni was requested by the Soviet representative and was promptly furnished by the Italians. Minister Goryarkin noted the fact that Quaroni's wife was Russian and the possibility that he could quickly reach Moscow from Kabul without having to ask the Allies for visas, authorizations, or navicerts, as would otherwise be necessary. In spite of these considerations, however, Prunas took pains to emphasize that the delicacy of the Italian situation in general and of the diplomatic service in particular limited the choice, and that the nomination of Minister Quaroni had been made purely and entirely on the supposition that among those qualified and available he would be the most acceptable to Moscow. The Italian government was, of course, willing to nominate another candidate in the event that the Soviet government had objections, since it was the goal that the nominee be fully acceptable to the Soviets.

[91] According to the then Undersecretary to the Prime Minister, Dino Philipson, the primary reason for this choice was the fact that Kabul was the capital closest to the Soviet Union and could be reached directly. In reality, the Italian Foreign Ministry supported the choice because Quaroni was one of Italy's most astute diplomats, he knew Russian, he had an ideal background, and he was an expert on Soviet affairs, having previously served in the Italian Embassy in Moscow.

On the same day, March 20, Prunas met in a long secret session with Reber and Caccia to discuss the nature of the Soviet initiative. Prunas immediately sought to re-emphasize Italy's loyalty to the Allies, asking that London and Washington be so informed once again. In effect, he stated that the Badoglio government intended, as one might expect, to bring its relations with each of the forty-four United Nations to a level of friendship and collaboration. The Italian request to normalize its relations with the most powerful nation militarily, the Soviet Union, was clearly a part of that overall plan. How would it have been possible to act otherwise toward Moscow, Prunas asked, and how would it have been possible for Badoglio to reply otherwise to so human and generous a gesture from the Soviets? Certainly not by declining to renew diplomatic relations with the U.S.S.R. and proposing to remain chained to the armistice conditions. Moreover, the Italians had requested an alliance with Britain and the United States, which was obviously a far more important matter than the re-establishment of a normal diplomatic contact.[92]

Prunas then insisted that the Soviet gesture was certainly not an isolated one. Rather, it revealed the nature of an entire program, of which it was merely a first step; there would undoubtedly be further developments. Certainly the governments of Washington and London would do well to take note of these and to concern themselves with them. The Soviets had not identified themselves with the armistice. They had no occupation troops in Italy and were completely uninvolved in the daily and increasingly grave conflicts and incidents brought on by the occupation. Insofar as the Italians were concerned, the Soviets automatically acquired a greater autonomy of action and stood on a much more fertile and solid ground than any of the others. According to the Italian diplomat, the United States and Great Britain could effectively reply to the Russian move only by placing themselves in the position that had promptly and realistically been chosen by the Soviet Union. If, on the other hand, Great Britain and the United States persisted in remaining trapped within the confines of the armistice and the Control Commission arrangements—that is, unwavering in their illiberal and unintelligent insistence on unconditional surrender and on exerting a paralyzing, suffocating control of the country's activity—every possibility of a constructive policy and of concrete action would be eliminated, and, more important, Soviet influence would enormously increase and multiply. Prunas dwelt at length on this point, calling the attention

[92] Regarding Badoglio's request and Roosevelt's negative reply of February 21, 1944, see Cordell Hull, *Memoirs*, II, pp. 1554–55; *Foreign Relations, 1944*, III, pp. 1011–12, 1031. The request for an alliance actually concerned all of the United Nations and not only the British and Americans.

of his listeners to it again and again. He asked that, for a moment, the British and Americans place themselves in the position of the Italians and imagine what their reply would have been to an approach by Bogomolov designed to conclude advantageous accords or understandings. Would they, in all honesty, have rejected this approach?

At this point Reber and Caccia asked how, in Prunas' opinion, their governments could reply realistically to the Soviet move. Given the premise, indicated much earlier by Badoglio, that the route toward the conclusion of an alliance would be by far the best, Prunas went on to add that, at least in the initial stages it would be absolutely indispensable to change the nature of the relations between Italy and the British and Americans from those based on the armistice. He pointed out that of the ten clauses of the armistice of September 3, 1943, nine were no longer applicable, since the terms had been executed. As for the forty-eight clauses of the armistice of September 29, 1943, twenty-four were no longer applicable, either because it was materially impossible to implement them or because they had been replaced by other accords (such as the Cunningham-De Courten agreement, transfer of provincial administrations to the Italians, etc.). Thus, it would be necessary to scrap those two documents— to his mind they reflected anything but honorably on the British and Americans—and to replace them with a new one, more liberal and more humane, which, while fully safeguarding the overriding military rights of the Allied armies, would describe the de facto co-belligerency as co-belligerency, and not as surrender, and would define more realistically the position of the new Italy after six months of loyal and complete collaboration. Moreover, such a document would do no more than recognize in fact an existing situation, and recognize in a word—"co-belligerency"—a fact already accepted by public opinion in the Allied countries. Such a step would not create an entirely new or novel situation, the type which usually arouses opposition and conflict.

Prunas reported that he believed that his exposition of the Italian position had a strong effect on both Reber and Caccia. Both men assured him that they would immediately refer the conversation to their respective governments, stressing the explanations and clarification of the Italian attitude, the eventual probable developments of Soviet policy in Italy, and the means and methods by which Anglo-American policy could be given a new character that would allow for greater freedom of action and increased effectiveness.

Once again, therefore, in his conversation with the two diplomats Prunas came to grips with the crucial issue in the Italian situation without equivocation. In this second colloquy with Caccia and Reber, conducted with almost complete frankness,[93] the Secretary-General of the Foreign Ministry sought to develop and bring to a successful conclusion the diplomatic maneuver which he had conceived at the very beginning of his tenure. It consisted of utilizing the renewal of relations with Moscow as a point of departure to obtain a revision of the armistice terms. The arguments presented were certainly worthy of consideration, even if they were unduly optimistic in evaluating the immediate developments in Soviet as well as Anglo-American policy toward Italy. What really impressed Reber and Caccia was Prunas' reference to possible Soviet proposals for accords and understandings with Italy. According to their versions of the colloquy, Prunas was very precise on this point: he not only made it clear that the Soviets intended to exploit the advantageous position they had gained to extend their influence in Italy but also described the form that the Soviet proposals would probably take—that is, the offer of a treaty not dissimilar to that concluded on December 12, 1943, between Czechoslovakia and the U.S.S.R., which, by the nature of its content, appeared to be exceptionally binding.[94] It is completely understandable, therefore, that, faced with such a prospect, the British and American reaction was extremely strong.[95]

11

Commander Ellery W. Stone, vice president of the commission, in a colloquy with Prunas on March 23, 1944, officially informed the Italian government that Moscow's example would not be followed either by Washington or London.[96] The explanation offered for the American position was as follows: Great Britain, for geographic as well as politico-military reasons, tended to offer very little resistance to Soviet pressure. A typical example would be the position taken by Churchill vis-à-vis the Soviets on both the Polish and Yugoslav issues. Given this British tendency to give in to Soviet demands, as soon as regular direct diplomatic relations were adopted and Allied policy toward Italy would no longer be conducted through the ponderous and bureaucratic machinery of the Al-

[93] Obviously Prunas had not emphasized the fact that the initiative for proposing a renewal of diplomatic relations with the Soviets had been Italian, but this was only a venial sin in the overall picture.

[94] *Foreign Relations, 1944*, III, p. 1069.

[95] Cf. Macmillan, *The Blast of War*, p. 484.

[96] However, on March 17 Hull, during a press conference, declared that the decision to exchange diplomatic representatives had been taken by the Italian and Soviet governments without prior consultation with Washington and that, in any event, the United States would continue to contact the Italian government through the Allied Control Commission, *Foreign Relations, 1944*, III, pp. 1061–62. Analogous declarations were made by Eden in the House of Commons on March 22, 1944. *Ibid.*, pp. 1072–73.

lied Control Commission, it would then cease to be uniform and would be divided in at least two ways: there would be the policy of the United States on the one hand and that of the Soviet Union, dragging Great Britain along, on the other. These developments would be to the disadvantage of the Americans and, in the final analysis, to Italy's disadvantage as well.[97] This rather singular viewpoint did not correctly reflect Churchill's attitude toward the Badoglio government. In any event, as a result of his numerous colloquies with Reber and Caccia, Prunas gained the impression that a major policy split was developing between London and Washington. The Americans were convinced, he thought, that the renewal of diplomatic relations between Italy and the Soviet Union was caused by the intransigence demonstrated by the British government toward Italy, and that this fact was sufficient motivation for the Americans to follow a policy of greater generosity toward the Italians. These conflicts between Washington and London, according to Prunas, in effect worked to strengthen Italy's position.

On March 25 Bogomolov informed Marshal Badoglio that the Soviet government would be pleased to accept Minister Quaroni as Italian representative to Moscow. At the same time he told Badoglio that the Soviet choice to represent the U.S.S.R. in Italy was Counselor of the First Class Kostylev, whose promotion to the rank of Minister was imminent. Either because it was in their interest to hasten the appointments or because it gave them the opportunity to express an approval which might not have been requested, the Italians had previously indicated their acceptance of any nominee the Soviets cared to send. Kostylev therefore immediately assumed his office and read a telegram from Stalin to Badoglio in which the Soviet leader expressed his appreciation for the good wishes Badoglio had expressed to him when normal relations were resumed.[98]

The understanding between Moscow and Salerno had been brought into existence and perfected. In the meantime, the prospects of an Italo-Soviet treaty modeled on the one concluded between the Soviet Union and Czechoslovakia in December, 1943, triggered the expected American and British reactions. Instructions were sent from London to Macmillan to inform Bogomolov that the Italian government did not have the right to

[97] Several of these concepts may be found in a dispatch from Hull to Murphy of May 16, 1944. Hull, *Memoirs*, II, 1559.

[98] Once again Badoglio in his recollections (*L'Italia nella seconda guerra mondiale*, p. 174) makes an incorrect assertion. He says that when Bogomolov announced the name of Kostylev as Soviet representative to the Italian government, he, Badoglio, promised to name the Italian representative later. On this colloquy see also the later statements made by Badoglio, Reber, and Macmillan in *Foreign Relations, 1944*, III, p. 1081.

conclude accords with any power, allied or neutral, without the authorization of the Supreme Allied Commander, such authorization to be requested via the offices of the Allied Control Commission, and that, beyond the specific rights established in the armistice agreements, the commander of the occupation forces had the general right, for reasons of military security, to oversee the relations of the Italian government with all other governments. The British position was transmitted to Washington on March 24,[99] and on the same day Hull sent analogous instructions to Ambassador Reinhardt in Algiers,[100] while General Sir Frank Noel Mason MacFarlane was charged with informing Marshal Badoglio of the position taken by the Allies. He did so the following day, just before the start of Badoglio's interview with Bogomolov.[101]

Badoglio replied to General MacFarlane's communication with a letter of protest on March 29.[102] Two days earlier the Italian Prime Minister had met with Macmillan, who informed him that the British public was inclined to consider the treatment accorded Italy by the Allies as too generous. The stark memories of the war and of 236,000 British dead and wounded in the Mediterranean were still vivid. Churchill was among the leaders advocating a more liberal policy for the Italians. The British ruling classes, too, despite the recent events, considered the reconstruction of the old Italo-British friendship to be necessary. But, as a democracy, it was impossible for the British government to ignore public opinion; it could only guide and direct it, and this could be done only very slowly. Other states, the autocratic and authoritarian ones, could move more rapidly and radically. But friendships sanctioned by decrees and not by the will of the people, said Macmillan, were fragile and uncertain. The tree of renewed

[99] Ibid., pp. 1076–77.

[100] Ibid., p. 1077. On the same day Hull informed Harriman of the news received from Prunas regarding the possible developments in Italo-Soviet relations and instructed Harriman to make it clear to Molotov that, as long as the military operations against Germany lasted, the American government expected that "any further developments in the relations of the U.S.S.R. with Italy will be referred to the Advisory Council of Italy for consideration and appropriate action." Ibid., p. 1074. Vishinsky, in his meeting with Harriman of March 27, repeatedly denied the rumors of new Italo-Soviet accords. Ibid., pp. 1079–80.

[101] Ibid., pp. 1080–81. This episode is also recalled incorrectly by Badoglio (L'Italia nella seconda guerra mondiale, p. 175), insofar as both the date and the content of the Allied communication are concerned. A marginal note written by the Marshal on the document from MacFarlane informed Prunas that, according to the statements made by Macmillan, the step taken by the Allies concerned the future and not the past; therefore, the accord with Moscow remained valid.

[102] The more important passages of this letter are published in Badoglio, ibid., pp. 175–77. However, the author leaves the impression that this was a record of an immediate reply given orally, which was not the case.

Anglo-Italian friendship would be sounder, stronger, and more deep-rooted if time were allowed for it to grow.[103]

This declaration may have had its merits, but it did not meet Italian expectations. They were left instead, with a bitter feeling toward the British, which did not augur well for the immediate future.

On March 29 Prunas again met with Bogomolov. He informed the Russian of the steps taken by MacFarlane and Macmillan to ascertain the exact nature of the Italo-Soviet discussions which had led to the renewal of direct diplomatic relations and to block any further Italian initiatives vis-à-vis the Soviets, as well as other neutral or Allied powers. In addition, he permitted the Soviet diplomat to read General MacFarlane's memorandum of March 25. Prunas added that he had been informed that the Americans would take steps in Moscow to bring the Soviets back into the framework of the armistice terms and to convince them generally to observe, insofar as Italy and the Mediterranean were concerned, those limitations and conditions London, Washington, and Moscow had agreed upon. Prunas then succinctly described his meeting with Macmillan and gave the reasons why the Italians regarded the action taken by the British and Americans to put an end to Italy's initiatives in foreign policy as a purely arbitrary one which seriously aggravated the already extremely harsh armistice conditions.

Bogomolov, after saying that it would be advantageous to the Italians to collaborate with the British and Americans—with which Prunas promptly agreed—firmly declared that the existing direct relations between Italy and the Soviet Union, regardless of what the Allies thought about them, would remain precisely as they were. Prunas then asked when and if Bogomolov would consider it opportune to release a communiqué announcing the nomination of the official representatives to each of the two countries, a communication eagerly awaited by the Italian public. The Soviet diplomat asked that any such publication be delayed until instructions from Moscow, which had already been requested, arrived. A similar delay was requested in order to work out the details of communication with Quaroni—who was totally ignorant of the plan—and to put the accord into effect. At this point Prunas had the impression that the fissure created in the Allied coalition by the Italo-Soviet entente was destined to remain, despite the efforts of the British and Americans. In his judgment, it was likely that, after the initial reaction, the British government would be induced to recognize, with its habitual realism and spirit of compromise, the new

[103] Ibid., p. 189. Another conversation along the same lines but in greater detail took place between Prunas and Macmillan in Salerno on April 5, 1944.

situation created by this breach in the Allied façade, to abandon all attempts to force a return to the *status quo ante*, and to seek to neutralize the effects of the entente by adopting measures substantially parallel to those taken by the Soviets, albeit formally and apparently much more orthodox in nature. The United States would be drawn into taking similar action.

Prunas's optimism thus persisted, but Macmillan had spoken the truth when he had affirmed that London was not yet ready to re-examine its Italian policy. This became clear a few days later. Ambassador Bogomolov, on the other hand, expressed to Badoglio on March 29 the Soviet desire to aid the Yugoslav partisans by all possible means and asked that the Italian government permit, in those areas of Italy already liberated, an appeal to be made to all Slavs residing in Italy to volunteer for service with the Partisans in Yugoslavia. Badoglio, while promising to study the Soviet request, immediately noted the difficulties such an appeal would create for those Italians of Slavic origin serving in the Italian armed forces. On April 2 Kostylev reported to Badoglio that Marshal Tito had stated that Slavic soldiers in the Italian army were treated like slaves. This assertion was protested by Badoglio in a written memorandum to Kostylev the following day. The Italian government was prepared to accept an Anglo-American-Soviet commission of inquiry to ascertain that in the Italian armed forces there were only citizens of the Kingdom of Italy. The Slavic refugees were in Allied hands. As for the Italian citizens of Slavic origin serving in the armed forces, the law prohibited their being sent as volunteers to serve in a foreign army.[104] On the other hand, the Italian government readily complied with Kostylev's requests that Soviet war bulletins be published in their entirety in the *Corriere* and that the published commentaries note that the Russian people considered the natural political frontiers of the Soviet Union to be those achieved in 1939.

The realistic attitude of the Italian Communist Party had paved the way for a widening of the political base of the Badoglio government immediately after the Italo-Soviet accords[105] and on April 3, the eve of the date they were to become effective,[106] prompted the Marshal, referring to Roosevelt's letter of February 21 in which Italy's request for an alliance

[104] *Ibid.*, pp. 178–80.

[105] For details concerning this episode see Degli Espinosa, *Il Regno del Sud*, pp. 317–39; Croce, *Quando l'Italia era tagliata in due*, pp. 98–120; Badoglio, *L'Italia nella seconda guerra mondiale*, pp. 194–200. Togliatti arrived in Naples on March 28, 1944. After the Prunas-Vishinsky colloquy, the United States and Great Britain announced that they had no objection to his return to Italy. Hull, *Memoirs*, II, p. 1553.

[106] The event occurred on April 22, 1944.

was rejected "until the government of Italy can also include the articulate political group of anti-fascist liberal element,"[107] to write again to the American President reiterating the request.[108] This request was examined jointly by the British and Americans, and on April 20 London informed Washington of its opposition to granting Italy the status of ally. According to the British Foreign Office, while the position of co-belligerent assured Italy better treatment than would normally be accorded to a defeated power, Italy should not forget that it was a defeated enemy power and should not seek to claim the privileges of an ally. The greater the concessions made at this time, the more difficult it would be to impose on Italy, after the liberation of its entire territory, those sanctions which the Allies would determine at the end of the conflict. London also proposed to obtain Moscow's agreement with this point of view.[109] The only concession made was that of sending two diplomats to Italy with the rank of ambassadors, Sir Noel Charles for Great Britain[110] and Alexander Kirk for the United States,[111] but without reciprocity.

Roosevelt replied to Badoglio on April 30 in a very courteous letter which, in effect, offered no change in the situation.[112] The phase of diplomacy immediately following the announcement of the renewal of direct diplomatic relations between Italy and the Soviet Union thus came to a close without substantive positive results for Italy as far as British and American policy was concerned.

12

The suspicion with which London and Washington continued to view the Badoglio government's relations with Moscow was apparent once again in a meeting between Caccia and an official of the Italian Foreign Ministry on April 21 in Salerno. On that occasion the British diplomat insisted on knowing the exact details of the process by which Quaroni was informed of the decision to transfer him to Moscow and how he received his instructions. Caccia was told that when Kostylev was given Quaroni's name as the Italian government's choice for its official representative in Moscow, the Russian offered to communicate the news to Quaroni in Kabul. Caccia noted that it was highly unusual for an Italian diplomat to so receive his instructions without the possibility of checking on their

---

[107] Hull, *Memoirs*, II, pp. 1554–55; Badoglio, *L'Italia nella seconda guerra mondiale*, p. 188; *Foreign Relations, 1944*, III, p. 1031.

[108] *Foreign Relations, 1944*, III, p. 1087.

[109] *Ibid.*, p. 1105; Hull, *Memoirs*, II, p. 1559.

[110] Churchill, *Closing the Ring*, p. 616.

[111] Feis, *Churchill, Roosevelt, and Stalin*, p. 328.

[112] *Foreign Relations, 1944*, III, p. 1106.

accuracy. The Italian official replied that, unfortunately, the Badoglio government had no means of communicating directly with its representatives abroad and that, therefore, no graceful way could be found to refuse the Soviet offer. Moreover, he added, all Italian Chiefs of Mission abroad were substantially in the same situation—that of having to receive their instructions from the Italian Foreign Ministry through the good offices of Allied diplomatic missions abroad. Furthermore, in Quaroni's case, it was possible for him to check on the communication he had received by listening to Radio London, which had reported his transfer.

It was obvious that the British questions were prompted by a desire to learn whether any instructions were given to Quaroni relative to his new post and, if so, their exact nature. As a matter of fact, Quaroni had not yet received any detailed or precise instructions from Italy and had departed for his new post in Moscow armed only with broad general directives, a fact which was later confirmed by the First Secretary of the Italian Legation in Kabul, Anzilotti.[113]

On May 9 Prunas informed Kostylev of Badoglio's conviction, expressed earlier to Ambassadors Charles and Kirk, that the problem of the armistice must be re-examined as soon as possible after the creation of the new government.[114] Minister Togliatti also resolved to speak in the same vein to Bogomolov, urging that he take whatever action he might deem opportune within the Consultative Commission. Kostylev replied that of course the government of the U.S.S.R. was favorable to the Italian position.

In the meantime Quaroni arrived in Moscow. On May 29 Badoglio

---

[113] In Kabul, Quaroni did not receive Radio London transmissions, but he did listen to Radio Delhi, which did not report the news. He actually learned of his transfer from the Fascist radio in Berlin, which asserted that "Badoglio was sending Moscow's man to Moscow." Badoglio's note to Quaroni, transmitted to him by the Soviets, stated simply, "Your Excellency has been named Italian representative to Moscow. I need not emphasize the importance of the mission entrusted to you." The first real instructions to Quaroni from his government were carried to Moscow in August, 1944, by the then Legation Secretary, Gerolamo Messeri, who arrived in the Soviet capital only after an adventurous journey. Quaroni never for a moment doubted the authenticity of the telegram delivered to him in Kabul by the Soviet legation. For some time he had been accustomed to receiving the infrequent communications from Badoglio through the British. It appeared very logical to him that a telegram of that nature could not be sent through the British agencies. All telegrams and the pouch from and to Moscow were always sent via the Soviets. With the entrance of the Red Army into Rumania and Bulgaria, this means of communication ceased. Despite the understandings reached at Salerno between the Italian and Soviet governments, Quaroni lived in Moscow for a long time before he received funds of any kind. This was therefore a very difficult period for him materially as well.

[114] Badoglio, *L'Italia nella seconda guerra mondiale*, pp. 210–11.

cabled his first instructions to him. He urged Quaroni, in beginning his mission, to convey to Stalin a cordial greeting from the democratic Italian government. He noted that the impetus and drive of the Soviet nation were the object of profound and sincere admiration in Italy. He expressed his belief that, united in the common conflict against the Germans and Fascism, Italy and the U.S.S.R. would be able to establish their relations on bases of mutual understanding and fruitful collaboration. Italy pledged a democratically active and reconstructive policy and presumed that the Italian state would soon regain its autonomy and its sovereignty. Italy, fully cognizant of what the U.S.S.R. had already contributed, was profoundly grateful to Stalin for the aid given under the most difficult circumstances and for what it would be able to do in the future.

Quaroni immediately replied that upon the advice of the Peoples' Commissariat for Foreign Affairs he had transmitted the greetings of the Italian government to Stalin by mail instead of insisting on a personal interview at that time. In general, insofar as his mission was concerned, Quaroni believed the wisest course of action was to leave up to the Soviets the decision as to when his mission was to begin formally. Given the circumstances, he thought that it would be preferable to take a modest approach rather than insist on protocol in a purely formal matter.

Quaroni was received by Molotov for the first time on June 5. In replying to the Italian diplomat's communication, the Soviet Commissar stated that Italy's future was entirely in the hands of the Italian government, which would have to demonstrate that it was able to rally the resurgent forces of the nation against the Germans and their ally, Mussolini. In commenting on the explanations offered by Quaroni, Molotov stated that he was fully aware of all of the difficulties of the situation faced by the Italian government, particularly those stemming from the occupation authorities but repeated that it was imperative that the Italian government demonstrate its will to act positively.

Quaroni reported that he had the impression that the Soviets believed that the Italians could do more in the area of military collaboration with the Allies. The Soviet government desired to see all available forces concentrated in order to deal a decisive blow to Germany and to hasten the end of the war. The Soviet Union, in its relations with Italy, had taken the lead in promoting a policy that would end the paralysis in which Italy found itself, but, in return, it was expected that Italy would reply with deeds and not words. If the Italian government demonstrated its serious intention to work toward this goal, it could count on the friendly support of the Soviet government vis-à-vis the other Allies in an attempt to correct the conditions which could interfere with the actions of the Italian government, but, for the moment, Moscow was disposed to consider only the principal question at issue.

During the course of the conversation, Molotov repeatedly emphasized that, in its relations with Italy, the Soviet government was obliged and desired to proceed only in full accord with its Allies.[115]

The position taken by the Peoples' Commissar for Foreign Affairs might have somewhat dampened Italian aspirations, but it was fully comprehensible. While he was conferring with Quaroni, the Anglo-American invasion forces were moving into position to launch their invasion of Normandy, which began a few hours later. The opening of the second front marked the turning point in the war: it was the fulfillment of a solemn promise made by Roosevelt and Churchill to Stalin. At that moment, the solidarity among the three Allies reached its apex. Every effort was directed toward dealing Germany a mortal blow. If Italy continued to be paralyzed by the limitations imposed by the armistice, that was a matter of purely secondary importance. The recent past had put the Italian government in a position where declarations of good intentions were no longer sufficient. This was the stark reality, the direct consequence of faults which could be remedied only by military, not by politico-diplomatic, action. Even though it was not particularly advantageous to others to facilitate these acts of redemption, it remained, nevertheless, the only way left open to Italy.

13

There is little to add by way of comment in concluding this investigation. The facts emerging from the detailed reconstruction of the events, are, in themselves, sufficiently eloquent. The Italian initiative to re-establish direct diplomatic relations with Moscow emerged from the bitterness of the Badoglio government over its failure in several attempts to convince Washington and London to annul the armistice terms and to accept Italy as an ally. In the mind of Prunas, Soviet acceptance of the proposal made to Vishinsky, in addition to ameliorating Italo-Soviet relations and recognizing the new politico-military situation brought into being by the Red Army, was to pave the way for a basic modification of the armistice conditions.

The reasons for Moscow's positive reply to the Italian request are to be found in Soviet discontent over its spectator's role in Italian affairs imposed by Washington and London and in the Soviet desire to ensure that

[115] On this colloquy, see Pietro Quaroni, *Il mondo di un'ambasciatore* (Milan: Ferro, 1966), pp. 169–73.

in the affairs of the peninsula it would play a part equal to that of London and Washington. The observations recorded in the Soviet memorandum of March 19[116] are not only clear on this point but, in all probability, honestly express the Soviet position. Moreover, the Soviet Union, regarding Italian participation in the war against Germany as entirely inadequate, had set about to create a new situation in the peninsula which would have removed a majority of the obstacles preventing action by the government by favoring an enlargement of the base of the Italian government so as to include all of the anti-Fascist parties. Quaroni commented on this matter in succeeding weeks, in a series of lucid reports, explaining not only the reasons for the Soviet decision but also the military factors involved, factors which, after the opening of the second front in Europe, tempered Moscow's interest in the Italian front.

On the other hand, from the psychological viewpoint, the general lines laid down by Badoglio, posing the question of Italy's participation in the war in terms of give and take, had done much to cool the Soviet interest in championing the Italian cause. Vishinsky had gained the impression that the Italians were burning with a desire to fight the Germans. Instead of organizing mass demonstrations which would have forced the British and Americans to retreat from their position of intransigence, however, Badoglio limited his activity to argument via the chancelleries. The only measurable effect of the entire diplomatic undertaking was the affirmation of the principle of a Soviet presence in the Mediterranean and in Italy.

Prunas's maneuver as an Italian diplomatic achievement was unsuccessful. In fact, it aroused suspicion and resentment in both Washington and London and provoked an even more rigid application of the armistice terms. In addition, the U.S. State Department, which had at first reacted favorably to the requests made by Badoglio on December 27, 1943, to permit Italy's adherence to the principles of the Atlantic Charter, ceased to press the Italian case on this point in London.[117] Roosevelt himself, in his letter to Badoglio of February 21 (drafted by the State Department), put off acceptance of the Italian request for recognition of its status as a full-fledged ally until such time as the Italian government included representatives of all anti-Fascist parties.[118] However, when this requirement was fully met, he joined the British Foreign Office in declaring, on

[116] See n. 90.

[117] Hull, *Memoirs*, II, p. 1559. In a memorial to Hull of March 31, 1944, the British Ambassador, Lord Halifax, emphasized that it would be perilous to embark on a course which could create the impression of assuming an obligation to preserve Italian territory intact. See also *Foreign Relations, 1944*, III, pp. 1084–87.

[118] *Foreign Relations, 1944*, III, p. 1031.

April 29, that there was no intention of granting to Italy the status of an Allied power.[119]

Insofar as the internal problem was concerned, opening the door to Moscow paved the way for the realization of the program outlined by Prunas in his second colloquy with Vishinsky regarding the possibility of the Italian Communist Party's abandoning its opposition to the Badoglio government. It was almost exclusively because of this reversal of position that finally, on April 22, it became possible to forge the first national coalition government in Italy. If, at that moment, every political calculation had been subordinated to the need to concentrate all of the nation's energies on the military effort, this would have been in itself a major accomplishment but, unfortunately, this was not the case.

It was Molotov who, in his first conversation with Quaroni on June 5 and in language much stronger in tone than that used by Roosevelt in his letter of April 30 to Badoglio,[120] called Italy's attention to some disagreeable realities. Italy could not gain the new place she sought in the family of free nations through shrewd political calculations or extraordinary cleverness alone. It was necessary that she act, on her own initiative, with blood and sweat, as, in a dramatic moment in the history of his own country, Churchill had outlined England's course and destiny to his fellow citizens. There was no diplomacy, no matter how astute, that could replace those elements of character, of will, and of courage which constitute the ultimate measure of every nation in moments of crisis.

[119] *Ibid.*, p. 1106.

[120] On that occasion, among other things, the President of the United States said:

May I meanwhile speak again with that frankness which my countrymen and yours prefer? Now that Italy has moved in the direction of truly democratic government, public opinion in the United States is watching earnestly for clear evidence that the Italian people are sincerely and passionately resolved to drive the invader from their soil and contribute to that common victory which Italy's defection under Fascism rendered so much costlier. I know that all Italian patriots share the feeling of the peoples of the United Nations and it is for the Italians themselves to prove that they do not seek spurious rehabilitation through external acts but Italy's national and international regeneration through their own courageous efforts. Every sign that Italy has truly shouldered the burden of her responsibilities and has aligned herself in deed and spirit with those who fight for the triumph of humanity will, I am sure, be received with genuine sympathy by the peoples of all the United Nations.

Foreign Relations, 1944, III, p. 1106.

V.

RESUMPTION OF DIPLOMATIC RELATIONS BETWEEN FRANCE AND ITALY DURING WORLD WAR II

Summary: 1. Premise. 2. The first meeting between Prunas and Massigli at Brindisi, December 6, 1943. 3. The second Prunas-Massigli meeting at Ravello, January 12, 1944. First comments from General Castellano on the French attitude toward General Badoglio. The Prunas-Panafieu conversations of April 7 and 14. Their influence on Italian actions. 4. Badoglio's declaration of June 6 nullifying the armistice of Villa Incisa and the June 22 statement by the Bonomi Cabinet denouncing the Fascist claims and the aggression of 1940 and 1941. 5. The reaction of the Bonomi government to the nomination of Colonel Petit as governor of the island of Elba and Prunas' approach to Kirk on the question of the condition of the Italian prisoners of war in French hands. The provisional government in Algiers' denunciation of the conventions of 1896 relative to Tunisia and the expulsion of 4,500 members of the Italian community from the Regency. 6. The De Gaulle-Prunas meeting in Naples on July 1. 7. Analyses of the declarations by the head of the French provisional government and by the Secretary-General of the Italian Foreign Ministry. 8. The Bonomi letter to De Gaulle of July 6, and the Prunas-Couve de Murville and Bonomi-Couve de Murville meetings of July 7 and 18. 9. Gradual increase in French intransigence following liberation of the continental territory and the first indications of a change in Prunas' views in the face of the growing resistance in Paris. The fragmentary nature of the Prunas-Couve de Murville negotiations of August–October. First evidence of French territorial claims against Italy. The Zoppi proposal of November 8 for an exchange of letters between Bonomi and De Gaulle. 10. The status of Franco-Italian talks at the time De Gasperi assumed the Foreign Ministry portfolio on December 15. De Gasperi's telegram to Bidault and the statements of the French Foreign Minister to the Sunday Times. The Zoppi memorial of December 20. 11. The December 28 communiqué of the French radio in Rome on the status of the Franco-Italian conversations. The problem of the treatment of Partisans who had retreated into France and the Da Re proposal for the creation of an Italian military unit in France drawn from these disbanded elements. The official French proposals of January 18, 1945, for the liquidation of the Tunisian question and the renewal of diplomatic relations. De Gasperi's initial reactions. The expulsion of the Italians from Tunisia and the De Gaulle press conference of January 25. 12. The Prunas memorial of January 26, substantially favorable

* An earlier version of this chapter appeared as "La ripresa delle relazioni diplomatiche fra L'Italia e la Francia nel corso della seconda guerra mondiale" in Storia e Politica, IV (1962), pp. 523–604. Where no other reference is given, the documentation is contained in the unpublished archives of the Italian Foreign Ministry.

to the acceptance of the French demands with only two exceptions. The Italian Council of Ministers' acceptance of the recommendations of the Secretary-General of the Foreign Ministry and the De Gasperi-Couve de Murville colloquy of January 31. 13. The De Gasperi letter to Couve de Murville of February 1 and the conversation on the same day between Prunas and Couve de Murville. The acceptance by the Paris government of the Italian counterproposals. The Franco-Italian exchange of notes of February 28 concerning the liquidation of the Tunisian question and the renewal of diplomatic and consular relations between the two countries. Bonomi's letter to De Gaulle of February 10 and De Gaulle's reply of February 23. The official communiqué given to the press on March 2. 14. Conclusion.

1

The events leading up to the renewal of diplomatic relations between Italy and the Soviet Union during the course of World War II[1] are not only of historical interest but also of political importance. The same may be said of the similar negotiations with General De Gaulle. The negotiations with the French began in December, 1943, that is, prior to the initiation of the Italo-Soviet talks, and continued long after the negotiations with the U.S.S.R. were concluded in March, 1944. They finally ended in February, 1945, at a time when, with the return of the government to Rome, the period of the "Kingdom of the South" had come to an end and Alcide de Gasperi had become Foreign Minister in the Bonomi Cabinet.

The essence of these events is worth recording today for a variety of reasons. First, France was the first country with whom Italy sought to renew diplomatic relations following the armistice. This fact becomes very significant when related to successive developments in relations between Rome and Paris. Second, the negotiation in question is linked to the decision adopted on June 4, 1944, by the Badoglio government during its last cabinet meeting denouncing the armistice of Villa Incisa of June 24, 1940. Third, this reconstruction of the events will permit further understanding of why, among the many questions awaiting solution at the peace conference, the Italians chose to resolve only the Tunisian one, via a simple exchange of notes with the French government. Fourth, it will be possible to examine several of the principal political guidelines which, after the Allied landing in France, De Gaulle hoped to adopt for his future course of action. Several of these guidelines were relatively short-lived because of unexpected developments in Europe and the emergence of the Cold War between East and West, but some of them help to explain a number of the French

[1] See pp. 253–304.

chief of state's later attitudes and may be considered to be the basis for them. Finally, a comparison between the terse version of his first declarations to an Italian diplomatic representative in General De Gaulle's memoirs with the interpretations Palazzo Chigi gave to his words constitutes a politically and historically exciting exercise, on the basis of which it is possible to suggest certain hypotheses that, although logical and consistent, are not yet established as accurate.

2

The first Italo-French official diplomatic meeting occurred on December 6, 1943, in Brindisi, the seat of the Badoglio government, between René Massigli, Commissioner for Foreign Affairs of the French National Committee of Liberation of Algiers, and Minister Renato Prunas. At that time, the De Gaulle government had the full recognition of the Soviet Union and only limited recognition by the British and Americans. The Badoglio government had not yet taken a position on the matter, while the Algiers Committee considered Italo-French relations to be within the framework of the armistices of September, 1943.

During the Fascist period, Ambassador Massigli had been a chief participant in the violent arguments between Paris and Rome concerning the failure of the naval accord of 1930 and played a major role in formulating the Anglo-French-Turkish alliance of 1939. He was perhaps not an ideal choice to set Italo-French relations on the new course the situation demanded (the same might well be said for Prunas, who had been Chargé d'Affaires in Paris in 1937 and 1938), but the colloquy nevertheless took place, apparently in an atmosphere of mutual understanding and goodwill.

The key issues may be summarized as follows. Prunas began by noting that it was in the common interest of both powers to open a new era of collaboration and understanding. The first thing necessary was to establish a friendly atmosphere between the two countries. The wounds in all sectors of the French public resulting from the aggression of 1940 had been deep and were still not healed. Therefore, the task would have to be carried on slowly and patiently and with considerable caution by both parties. Massigli recognized, said Prunas, that the Italian military occupation of French territory had been, on the whole, very humane. Undoubtedly, this was a positive factor. The statements made by General De Gaulle and immediately echoed by Marshal Badoglio were certainly a first step along the road. Prunas pointed out to Massigli the political significance of a decree issued a short time before regarding the confiscation of the anti-French publications appearing in the liberated portion of Italy and the meaning of several unofficial articles appearing the preceding week in the press of the Kingdom of the South. Massigli was aware of them and was pleased by their content. Prunas suggested that it would be opportune for the French press to give them prominent space and comment favorably on them, a roughly parallel action.

The Algiers Committee of Liberation resented, as did the Badoglio government, the fact that the Allies forced them to exist in isolation. Prunas agreed with Massigli to arrange for direct Italo-French contact. A French diplomat (De Panafieu), already in Italy in a military capacity, could be retained there for a short period in a civilian one. General Castellano's military mission—accredited to Allied General Headquarters according to the armistice terms—could, in turn, maintain the necessary contacts in Algiers. These, for the moment, were to be the initial steps. The matter was regarded as important because it might become the first breach in the Great Wall of China built by the British and Americans. Of course, the matter would have to be kept confidential, for some time at least.

After noting that he was speaking unofficially and advancing only a personal opinion, Prunas told Massigli that a genuine international solution to the problem of the development of the territory and resources of Africa would most certainly find the Italian government fully cooperative. Prunas repeated the condition that it be a truly international effort. If this solution were not forthcoming, it would perhaps be necessary for the French and Italians to resolve their controversies on a bilateral basis. In any event, it was possible to reach a mutually satisfactory solution quickly. Massigli then referred to the Tunisian conventions, which, in his judgment, would have to be regarded as abrogated. Prunas noted that the Italian problem (with respect to Tunisia), even with due consideration for the intemperate acts, the nationalistic and imperialistic excesses, which he did not hesitate to call "malignant cancers," continued to be very difficult to solve but had to be settled fairly. Resolving the problem only in terms of emigration would have been adopting the role of slave traders and would plant in Europe and in the world the seeds of a fatal conflict.

Subsequently, Prunas asked Massigli to let him know in what way the Badoglio government, in his judgment, might be useful to the Committee in Algiers. The French diplomat assured Prunas that as the occasion arose he would certainly inform him. Prunas then called Massigli's attention to two precise issues: the condition of the sixty thousand Italian prisoners in North Africa and the situation in Corsica. Regarding the first point, Massigli promised to use his influence and proposed to raise the question at a meeting of the Consultative Commission for Italy. As for the second point, he referred to the possibility of entrusting the Swiss with the protection of Italian interests in Corsica, to which Prunas replied that he would have preferred a de facto understanding between the governments of Brindisi and Algiers without recourse to third parties.

In summarizing this colloquy in his report to Badoglio, Prunas noted that it was not possible and, perhaps, unwise, to press a first contact much beyond what had been said. The Italian and French situation at that moment would hardly permit more detailed plans and projects. However, both sides had explicitly admitted the existence of a desire for a rapprochement and understanding on the bases of their common misadventures and their common hopes for a rebirth. Prunas reported the clear impression that Massigli viewed with skepticism the enormous bureaucratic-military machine created by the British and Americans in Europe. However, he viewed the victory of the democracies as a certainty, given the enormous superiority in materiel, a superiority which permitted a very large margin of waste and amateurism without danger. Massigli did not believe that the Soviet Union was interested in the Bolshevization of Europe. In his judgment, Bolshevism would be absorbed by a militant, nationalistic Slavism whose nature and needs were entirely different. Judging from the Italian experience, he hoped the war would not be carried to metropolitan France, where, as in Italy, the military techniques of the British and Americans would bring, along with the German ones, suffering, mourning, and infinite destruction. Moreover, he was certain that if Germany did not collapse before this time, the second front would be opened in the spring of 1944. The French would have an army of four hundred thousand men at their disposal.

A brief courtesy call on Marshal Badoglio by Massigli immediately following the meeting, according to Prunas, helped greatly in emphasizing the desire for an understanding and the unqualified sincerity of the Italian desire to do what was necessary to establish a link with France in order to rebuild the close rapport based on the concept of "Latin sister-states," a concept which, in recent years, had disappeared.

Undoubtedly, the idea of escaping from the straitjacket of isolation which the British and Americans had imposed on the Badoglio government immediately after the armistice by beginning with a French rapprochement was an excellent one. However, because the Algiers Committee found itself in a weak position, the overture could have assumed a much broader scope from the beginning. A confidential and prudent approach avoided risks and unknowns, but, by the same token, it could not produce significant results. Certainly the psychological difficulties to be overcome on both sides were enormous, but one almost has the impression that the Italians lacked the necessary desire to push forward resolutely. The establishment of direct contacts between the two governments would have constituted a first small step, actually more one of form than of substance. In reality, at that moment, Algiers still regarded the Badoglio government with suspicion. It was considered unrepresentative of Italy, and Victor Emmanuel III was regarded in the same light, as co-responsible for the aggression of 1940. These circumstances constituted a further grave obstacle to the proposed rapprochement between the two countries.[2] General De Gaulle had expressed himself in these terms a few days before, on November 23, in conversation with the Soviet representative on the Consultative Commission for Italy, Vishinsky,[3] and, as will be noted below, much time elapsed before this suspicion would be overcome. In response to the general considerations advanced by Prunas, Massigli promptly replied that the Tunisian question was one of the most painfully

[2] See De Gaulle, *Mémoirs de guerre*, II, pp. 193–94.

[3] His comments appear in *ibid.*, pp. 603–4, as follows:

M. Vishinsky mentioned that he will represent his government on the commission for the Mediterranean. The latter will be called Consultative Commission for Italy.

M. Vishinsky stated that it is imperative that the Commission go to Italy as soon as possible. It has a two-fold objective. The immediate one is the application of the armistice clauses. This should be done in a democratic manner, however, so as to ensure Italy's participation in the war against Germany and to lead the country toward peaceful goals. Therefore, it will be necessary to examine the various political currents dividing the Italian people in order to assist in the creation of an Italian government that truly merits the title of government.

General De Gaulle replied by defining our Italian policy.

Despite the difficulties and disappointments which have befallen France, to his mind fundamental hostilities between the two peoples do not exist. However, for a long time there have been anti-French tendencies in Italy which have been the cause for serious antagonisms. They became acute during Crispi's time and then lessened in intensity in the face of the German threat. They reappeared after World War I, even before the triumph of Fascism in Italy, and were accentuated under Mussolini, who saw in the hatred for France the trampoline from which to launch his country on a policy of war and conquest. And finally, the war between France and Italy broke out, under the circumstances which all of us know. However, in the final analysis, this antagonism was due less to a deep-rooted hostility than to an erroneous policy adopted by Italy which has led her to disaster.

For the future, General De Gaulle does not believe it necessary to crush Italy. On the contrary, it is necessary to support and defend those who will set the scene for a firm understanding. This is the reason why it is important for us to see a popular government established in Italy. But Marshal Badoglio's government is not the government of Italy. We can tolerate it as a matter of passing necessity, but, in our view, it is not a government which should last for long in Italy.

M. Vishinsky noted his agreement.

On the same day, November 23, Massigli, in accepting the invitation extended to the French Committee of Liberation to send a representative to the Consultative Commission for Italy, emphasized that this acceptance did not imply any obligations whatsoever on the part of the French toward the Badoglio government. See *Foreign Relations, 1943*, II, p. 430.

difficult to resolve.[4] The French focused their pressure on this particular point to the extent of insisting on the radical solution to this problem as a condition sine qua non for a renewal of diplomatic relations between the two countries.

Badoglio was unaware that in October General De Gaulle, in a conversation with Count Sforza during the latter's stopover in Algiers on his way back to Italy, had outlined the French territorial claims against Italy thus: "Abrogate the privileges enjoyed by Italian citizens in Tunisia; return the cantons of Briga and Tenda, which, although French, had been turned over to Italy after the plebiscite of 1860, to France; modify the frontier affecting the Larche peaks, Mont Genevre, Mont Cenis, and the Little St. Bernard to eliminate troublesome border lines; insist that Val d'Aosta be given the right to be what it is, i.e., French in mentality; demand certain reparations, particularly in naval and merchant vessels. These are the very limited but very precise advantages which I decided to ensure to France."[5] As for the colonies, De Gaulle considered remaining in the Fezzan.[6]

Although the surprising precision with which the head of the Free French anticipated what were to become the exact conditions of the peace treaty of 1947 suggests that this proposal was reviewed at a later time, the fact remains that the plan served to clarify the views of General De Gaulle and those of his collaborators regarding the conditions the French would insist upon for re-establishing a basis for friendship with Italy.

The Prunas-Massigli conversation is also important in that it permits a better comprehension of the state of mind and the political position of the two diplomats. Both revealed their obvious dissatisfaction with British and American controls, and Prunas took considerable satisfaction in reporting Massigli's views on the matter. The latter, perhaps because of a psychological reaction against the position assumed by London and Washington toward the French National Committee of Liberation in Algiers, and perhaps also influenced by General De Gaulle's views, revealed a basic optimism in his thinking regarding the evolution of future Soviet policy. There is no record of any comment on the subject by the Italian diplomat, but it may be that Massigli's words encouraged Prunas in the overture toward Moscow which he was to make a short time later. In

---

[4] It is interesting to note in this context that, immediately after the announcement of the armistice with Italy (the French Committee of Liberation had not been informed of the negotiations of this armistice), Massigli expressed the fear that it included "a political deal possibly involving Tunisia." Cf. *Foreign Relations, 1943*, II, p. 363.

[5] De Gaulle, *Mémoirs de guerre*, II, p. 192.

[6] *Ibid.*, p. 193.

describing Italy's postwar problems, Prunas reflected concepts which were about to become obsolete, but Massigli's views were not markedly different. Insofar as the two other items were concerned (the prisoner of war and Corsica questions), the French diplomat was not, of course, very encouraging, and this, perhaps, should have been sufficient warning against excessive optimism.

3

After the official Prunas-Massigli initial contact, a month passed before the conversations were reopened. The occasion prompting the renewal of the talks was the meeting of the Consultative Commission for Italy in Naples on January 11, 1944, during the course of which Marshal Badoglio was allowed to participate in order to make several programmatic statements.[7] Massigli asked to confer with Prunas again, and the meeting between the two men took place the following day at Ravello.

Massigli opened the conversation by affirming that he was completely convinced that the British-American control over Italy was extremely rigid, which was bad in itself but, even worse, was inefficient. He praised Badoglio's clarity and firmness and stated that he was pleased by his statements to the French Committee of National Liberation.[8]

Subsequently, the two diplomats took note of and reconfirmed the common interest of France and Italy in arriving at a policy of cooperation and understanding. Massigli was of the opinion that something concrete could be realized immediately, particularly in the economic field. Prunas reminded him that a preliminary meeting for an exchange of views on this subject had already taken place and had also been attended by the undersecretaries Jung and Corbino. The Italians had no objections to continuing and to further developing these talks. Of course, above all else, it was necessary to arrange at least a minimum amount of transportation, which, for the moment, neither Italy nor France had available. During the next few days the two parties examined the problem to see whether the Allies might be approached on the matter with any hope for success. Certainly it would be most useful if the small amount of foreign trade which was possible could be revived.

---

[7] On this point see *Foreign Relations, 1944*, III, pp. 1000–1.

[8] The statement made by Badoglio on that occasion was as follows: "The Italian government is particularly pleased to see that, seated beside representatives of the great and friendly British Empire and the North American republic, there are also the representatives of the Soviet Union, which has given the world an admirable example of national solidarity and military virtue under the guidance of a leader who has always been equal to the occasion, and of the French Committee of Liberation, whose patriotic tenacity is a stimulating example for all."

The two diplomats then re-examined the question of direct contact between the Gaullist elements and the Brindisi government, a question raised during their first encounter. It was agreed that counselor de Panafieu would remain in Italy representing the Algiers Committee and General Castellano, or someone in his place, would represent Italy at Algiers. For the moment this would be no more than a de facto representation, without official status. But it would open a useful door without delay or outside interference as soon as circumstances permitted. In concluding the meeting Prunas, in Badoglio's name as well as his own, urged Massigli to continue working within the Consultative Commission (of which, as Commissioner for Foreign Affairs, he was President) on Italy's behalf, which Massigli promised to do.

Thus, the second Prunas-Massigli meeting did not indicate any further political progress; rather, as will be noted below, there was a real setback. Both parties reiterated their intention to bring about a policy of collaboration and understanding between the two countries, but the conversation was limited to generalities and nothing precise was formulated. Massigli carefully avoided revealing his own and General De Gaulle's thinking on the Badoglio government, and the reference to the Tunisian question, which had been touched upon at Brindisi earlier, was not even mentioned.[9] Massigli was increasingly anxious to avoid touching upon any issues which, from his point of view, might have prejudiced an effective clarification of Italo-French relations. These issues included the formal condemnation of Fascist aggression and Mussolini's claims against France. Nevertheless, the desire to create a permanent de facto contact between the two governments was reiterated, and consideration was again given the possibility, albeit remote, of economic exchanges between the Kingdom of the South and French North Africa. Prunas must have experienced at that time a feeling of impotence so overwhelming that he refrained from raising the subject of the treatment of Italian prisoners of war, the matter of protection of Italian interests in Corsica, and the solution to the African problems at the end of hostilities, issues which had been raised at Brindisi earlier. It is true, of course, that on January 8 and 10 the Secretary-General of the Italian Foreign Ministry met with Vishinsky, who seemed to lend a sympathetic ear to Prunas' pleas in defense of Italian interests and his arguments in favor of removing the barriers which had, in effect, isolated

[9] It should be noted that it was during this precise period that the hostility of the French Committee of Liberation toward Italy was arousing concern in Washington and London, where it was beginning to be thought that it might have been a mistake to allow the French a determining voice in Italian affairs. Cf. *Foreign Relations, 1944*, II, p. 1004.

the Kingdom of the South from the rest of the world and re-establishing Italo-Soviet relations on a friendly basis.[10] However, despite Prunas' optimism regarding the Kremlin's reception of the logic of his arguments, it is difficult to understand why he desired to surrender his second card prematurely, in this game. To be sure the French card was, at least for the moment, much less significant than the Soviet one, but, at the same time, it was much less dangerous and of greater direct concern to Italian foreign policy. Therefore, the hypothesis that Prunas was momentarily discouraged regarding the possibility of succeeding in promptly restoring a climate of real comprehension between France and Italy is probably the closest to the truth.

Direct dialogue between the Badoglio government and the Algiers committee remained interrupted for three more months. During that period two events of particular importance occurred in the Kingdom of the South: the Kremlin's decision, on March 4, 1944, to renew diplomatic relations with Italy on the basis of the proposal made by Prunas to Vishinsky,[11] and the reconstitution of the Badoglio government on April 22 to include the participation of all of the anti-Fascist parties.

General Castellano reported from Algiers on March 15 the reasons for the silence of the French Committee of National Liberation during the period immediately following the two meetings between Prunas and Massigli. During the course of a friendly conversation between Castellano and a high official in the Gaullist Foreign Ministry, a man very close to Massigli, he was told that the French believed that the Badoglio government lacked a sufficiently broad base and did not include in its roster men representative of Italian public opinion. At the same time, the Italian government was blamed for not having officially renounced the famous Fascist claims against France. Castellano was of the opinion that the first of the two accusations really reflected the writings and speeches of the British and Americans rather than a basic French conviction and that, therefore, it had no real meaning to the French except as a plausible explanation for their conduct. He believed that the second accusation was the true determinant of the state of affairs and that a clarification of the sort desired by the French would produce a positive effect.

Unfortunately, General Castellano underestimated the importance of the questions of principle which prevented De Gaulle, whose program conflicted with that of General Pétain and who had disapproved British-

[10] For details of this conversation see pp. 269–77.

[11] The event was not well received by the French Committee of Liberation in Algiers, which feared that the action would strengthen Italy's political position. Cf. *Foreign Relations, 1944*, III, p. 1052; Macmillan, *The Blast of War*, p. 483.

American dealings with Admiral Darlan, from viewing favorably any government combination led by the same Marshal Badoglio who had been the Chief of the General Staff at the time of the Fascist attack against France in June, 1940. De Gaulle had expressed himself in unmistakably clear terms on this point in the above-mentioned conversation with Vishinsky in Algiers on November 23, 1943. Furthermore, the clarification of the Italian position vis-à-vis the French was not as simple a matter as Castellano implied. While a public renunciation of the Fascist claims was an indispensable premise, it alone was insufficient to resolve the situation. Much more was required, and this was to become clear on the day on which, *in extremis*, the Badoglio government decided to make this gesture.[12]

A colloquy at Salerno on April 7, 1944, between Prunas and De Panafieu confused the thinking of the Italian government leaders even more. During these conversations Prunas learned that just two days earlier Washington and London had decided to grant General Eisenhower full power to negotiate with and to recognize any French government he chose, with the exception of the Vichy government, at the time of the Allied landings in France. No assurances were given to Algiers. The news had created extreme concern among the members of the French National Liberation Committee. De Panafieu informed the Secretary General of the Italian Foreign Ministry, in words almost disdainful, of the Allied action. Meanwhile, General De Gaulle took all civil and military powers into his own hands and drew a step closer to Moscow by appointing two Communists to the Committee of Liberation. For these reasons Prunas concluded that within a short time the French in Algiers would make a friendly approach to Italy. A proposal in this sense, according to what was learned by an Italian diplomat, was to be suggested by Massigli to De Gaulle. In commenting on this news, Prunas noted that, given the scarcity of accurate information in possession of the Italian government, it was not possible to determine accurately the extent and degree of the Committee of Liberation's authority in continental France. In his judgment, therefore, every Italian approach to the Committee of Liberation should be subordinated, insofar as possible, to a realistic evaluation of the situation, i.e., the position of De Gaulle and Gaullism in a liberated France.

At that moment the Secretary-General of the Italian Foreign Ministry could not have predicted the effect his conversations with De Panafieu would have on Italo-French relations, but today it is clearly evident that it had a strong negative influence on the Badoglio government and, in the

---

[12] Another indication of the French reservations regarding Badoglio appeared in a report in the *New York Times*, February 4, 1944, reprinted in Italy by *Azione* only on April 5.

final analysis, the time lost was very costly. With the best of intentions, in venting his anger over the Washington-London decision the French diplomat made two extremely dangerous statements to Prunas. He revealed the weakness of the Committee in Algiers with respect to London and Washington, and he gave the impression that De Gaulle was about to take a spontaneous step toward rapprochement with Italy.

This was all the Italian government needed to increase its bewilderment. If the Americans and the British, who possessed highly accurate information on the situation in continental France, had granted such sweeping authority to General Eisenhower, how could the Badoglio government lend further credence to the strength of the Committee of Liberation in Algiers? Since it was easier to wait than to pay the price of reconciliation with France, it is easy to understand the position taken by Prunas, while not approving it. Could the price that Paris would ask be presumed to be any less than that asked by Algiers? If anything, it would be more. On the other hand, the landing in North Africa, engineered with the cooperation of Admiral Darlan, should have provided the necessary caution about the theoretically unassailable logic working in favor of France's "foremost resistant."[13] This point was understood neither by Badoglio nor by Prunas. Instead of playing the Algerian card as a trump at the most opportune moment, Salerno avoided taking any action until the situation developed to Italy's disadvantage.

On April 15 Prunas again met with De Panafieu, who confided that Massigli, the preceding January, had presented a statement to the Consultative Commission for Italy substantially in opposition to Badoglio, describing him as another Pétain, someone to guard against. However, De Panafieu added that Guerin, French replacement for Massigli on the Consultative Commission for Italy, on April 10 asked his colleagues on the Committee to regard the Massigli statement on Badoglio as having been invalidated by events.[14] Consequently, Prunas inferred that the French prejudices against Badoglio had largely disappeared and had been replaced by a more realistic view favorable to the current Italian situation. The truth was, according to General De Gaulle's memoirs, that on Jan-

---

[13] Moreover, Commander Ellery W. Stone, then Vice President of the Allied Control Commission, on April 13 explained to First Secretary Roberti how the opportunistic political and military criteria which at one time had induced the government of the United States to send an Ambassador to the Vichy regime and to reach an agreement with Admiral Darlan for the invasion of North Africa had been violently criticized by the American public, and how this public outcry had made it impossible for Washington to act otherwise concerning King Victor Emmanuel.

[14] However, this cannot be confirmed by State Department documents presently available.

uary 22 the French National Liberation Committee, in a note addressed to Washington, London, and Moscow, had proposed that the "throne and government in Italy be swept clean."[15]

While De Panafieu's confidential comments made no mention of the French opposition to Victor Emmanuel III, they did give the false impression that the reservations regarding Badoglio had been overcome. Yet Salerno should not have ignored the fact that, when De Gaulle came to Italy in March and again in May to inspect French troops, he refused to meet with Prince Humbert and with Marshal Badoglio, "not recognizing that the father of the prince continued to wear the crown and that the Marshal was still in the government."[16]

However, neither General Castellano's report nor De Gaulle's attitude —due in part to De Panafieu's unfortunate comments of April 7—served to alert Badoglio or his immediate collaborators. Perhaps nursing the illusion that when the new Italian government had been created the major reasons for France's suspicion would be overcome, they failed to take any effective action. The reasons for this inertia have already been noted. Yet even if Prunas was deluded initially by Massigli's statements in Brindisi, there was no reason for him to ignore the warnings regarding the state of mind in Algiers.

It was the French representative on the Consultative Commission for Italy who provided, in the course of a conversation with Prunas on May 4 in Naples, a partial clarification of the situation. The delegate from Algiers explicitly stated that a declaration from Marshal Badoglio, made on some appropriate occasion, would undoubtedly be very useful in clearing away the heavy clouds hanging over the relations between the two countries. In such a statement it would only be necessary to emphasize clearly the fact that Fascist foreign policy was most certainly not the one which the new Italy intended to pursue toward France and, furthermore, that the new policy was in sharp contrast with that of the previous regime. In effect, it would be a public denouncement of Fascist claims to Savoy, Corsica, Nice, and Tunisia.[17]

[15] De Gaulle, *Mémoirs de guerre*, II, p. 194. The note was presented on January 24, 1944, to the three Allied governments and on the following day by Massigli to the Consultative Commission. *Foreign Relations, 1944*, III, pp. 1005–6. According to Harold Macmillan (*The Blast of War*, p. 478), the note also demanded that Italian naval and merchant vessels, along with other materiel, be ceded to France in compensation for the 1940 attack. However, a similar request had already been made by Massigli on September 17, 1943. Cf. *Foreign Relations, 1943*, II, p. 366.

[16] De Gaulle, *Mémoirs de guerre*, II, p. 194.

[17] Notwithstanding this opening, the attitude of the French Committee of Liberation continued to be one of open hostility to the Italians. On May 20, when Bogomolov presented to the members of the Consultative Commission a resolution concern-

This report of this conversation, transmitted by Prunas to Badoglio, was not accompanied by a favorable comment or by a suggestion for action. The rape of the women of the Ciociaria several weeks later by Moroccan troops under the command of General Juin certainly contributed nothing toward clearing the atmosphere.[18] This, then was the status of Franco-Italian affairs on the eve of the Allied entrance into Rome.

4

On June 4, 1944, Prunas informed Marshal Badoglio that he had learned that General Juin was completing the plans for a ceremony at Villa Incisa, where the armistice with France was signed in 1940. It was likely that, in the name of the French provisional government, the armistice would be declared null and void and its terms cancelled as a result of the victories by the French armies, the ceremony to be performed in the place where the government of Marshal Pétain had been forced to accept the dictates of Mussolini.

It was equally well known that the Algiers government had persistently attempted to play a role in determining the armistice imposed on the Italians by the British and Americans in September, 1943, and, as a result of its efforts, had obtained the right to participate in the Consultative Commission for Italy. Thus, the Algiers government had continued its attempt to nullify the 1940 armistice between France and Italy, while seeking to weld Italy to that of 1943.[19] According to Prunas, this situation explained

---

ing the purging of Fascists from government, in which he expressed satisfaction that the Badoglio government had added representatives of the anti-Fascist parties to its ranks, and made reference to the participation of Italian forces side by side with the Allies in the war against Germany, the French representative, Couve de Murville, rejected the proposal because he had no intention of approving either the Badoglio government or Italy's co-belligerent status. *Foreign Relations, 1944*, III, pp. 1115–16, 1122.

[18] On June 2, 1944, De Panafieu left the front and went to Salerno expressly for the purpose of informing Prunas that "General Juin had been particularly sorry to learn of the grave incidents provoked by the Moroccan troops at the expense of a number of Italian civilians. He wishes it to be known that extremely severe orders have been issued to prevent any recurrence of these incidents and that the most rigorous sanctions have been imposed. In fact, a number of the most violent and dangerous offenders have been executed on the spot without even a summary trial." According to Prunas, the gravity of the incidents demanded that the communication be made in writing, that is, in a more official and binding form. However, De Panafieu, who had been advised of the atrocities perpetrated by the Moroccan troops, assured Prunas that, from the information available to him, in recent days no further incidents had occurred and that the people in the liberated villages had greeted the French enthusiastically.

[19] It should be recalled that on September 17, 1943, the French Committee of Liberation formally claimed the right to participate "in any armistice settlement with Italy" and emphasized, in a note addressed to the British and American representa-

the natural and understandable reluctance of the Italians to declare the armistice of Villa Incisa to be null and void. However, a ceremony by the French at Villa Incisa would, in all likelihood, have forced the Badoglio government to accept the nullification of the armistice, thus placing the Italian government in the position of having again been defeated, or so it would seem, at the very time when Rome was being liberated without the direct participation of the Italians.

Prunas therefore suggested that Badoglio, taking advantage of the imminent meeting of the Council of Ministers, request that urgent consideration be given to a unilateral Italian declaration that the armistice of 1940 was null and void. This would reduce the impending ceremony at Villa Incisa to a simple commemorative rite, not a *diktat* imposed by the force of arms. In Prunas' judgment, such an initiative would be the logical consequence of a foreign policy that was publicly known.[20] Furthermore, it was to be hoped that such an act might make some useful contribution to a clarification of Franco-Italian relations, continually aggravated by French treatment of the Italian prisoners of war, the abuses suffered by the Italian community in Tunisia, the constant anti-Italian incidents in Corsica, and the conduct of the Moroccan troops on the Italian front. It was obvious, of course, that nothing was to be expected in return for such a gesture. Instead of telegraphing De Gaulle, the Italian action could be formalized in a brief communiqué stating that the Council of Ministers, examining Italian foreign policy at the request of the President of the Council, had decided to proclaim, as a logical consequence of its previous declarations, the nullification of the armistice of 1940 as a gesture of solidarity with the French on the eve of the invasion of the Continent.

In this position taken by Prunas, one point is perplexing: why, up to that moment, was the Badoglio government reluctant to denounce the armistice of June 24, 1940? The short armistice of September 3, 1943, had specified that Great Britain and the United States of America were acting "in the interest of the United Nations," and the long armistice of September 29 stated that on the basis of the terms of the Armistice of Cassibile "hostilities were suspended between Italy and the United Nations on certain terms of a military nature." The Consultative Commission for Italy had been instituted following the armistice of 1943 and included the representative of the French Committee of Liberation of Algiers among

tives, that "in the Committee's opinion, one of the first consequences of the Italian capitulation should be a formal declaration on the part of Italy that the Armistice of 1940 is considered null and void." *Foreign Relations, 1943*, II, pp. 365–66.

[20] This refers to the statement by the Badoglio government of May 23, 1944, in which, among other observations, the war against France and other countries was condemned.

its members, so that it would be highly unrealistic to think that the cessation of hostilities between France and Italy could still be governed by the Armistice of Villa Incisa of 1940 and not by the armistice of 1943. Furthermore, in the event that the Italian government did accept this thesis, it would be reasonable to ask why it was not proposed that the declaration denouncing the armistice of 1940 be accompanied by a statement that the Cassibile instrument was held to be valid with regard to the French as well. Otherwise, Frenchmen and Italians would still find themselves in a state of war. If such a thesis, at the proper time, were advanced by the French, it would have surprised no one. That the Italian side failed to see the danger of the argument presented seems surprising indeed.

Prunas completely ignored the position taken by the Algiers Committee both at the time of the short and at the time of the long armistices of 1943 and in the matter of the creation of the Consultative Commission for Italy. Upon being informed of the armistice with Italy, De Gaulle and Massigli had protested violently because they had not been adequately informed of the negotiations.[21] The question was raised again in the days immediately following,[22] and on this issue the French Committee of Liberation, on September 9, 1943, published a statement emphasizing the reasons which "demanded French participation in any convention concerning Italy."[23]

A note to the United States and to Great Britain on September 17[24] reiterated this position, but it was only on September 27—that is, on the eve of the Malta meeting—that Massigli was given the text of the long armistice. Massigli protested at having been presented again with a fait accompli,[25] but the protest was ignored.

The Algiers Committee was equally incensed by the fact that the Foreign Ministers Conference in Moscow had discussed the Italian question without including the French in the talks[26] and that the inclusion of representatives of the Committee of Liberation in the Consultative Commission for Italy had not been contemplated from the beginning.[27]

[21] See *Foreign Relations, 1943*, II, pp. 361–62, and De Gaulle, *Mémoirs de guerre*, II, pp. 524–26, where Massigli's account of his colloquy with Macmillan and Murphy of September 9, 1943, is recorded.

[22] Cf. *Foreign Relations, 1943*, II, pp. 365–66; De Gaulle, *Mémoirs de guerre*, II, pp. 526–27, 528–29.

[23] For the text, see De Gaulle, *Mémoirs de guerre*, pp. 527–28; see also *Foreign Relations, 1943*, II, pp. 361–62.

[24] The text is in De Gaulle, *Mémoirs de guerre*, II, pp. 590–91. Cf. *Foreign Relations, 1943*, II, pp. 365–66.

[25] De Gaulle, *Mémoirs de guerre*, II, pp. 190–91, 592–93.

[26] *Ibid.*, p. 191. To Cordell Hull, during the latter's stopover en route to Moscow, De Gaulle explicitly stated that it was necessary that "we, together with you and on an equal footing, should decide what will happen to Italy."

[27] *Ibid.*, pp. 191–92, 596. See also *Foreign Relations, 1943*, II, p. 421.

The proposed Italian maneuver would have put the Badoglio government in an extremely delicate situation, and it would have been prudent to avoid weakening the Italian position vis-à-vis the French Committee of Liberation by openly favoring the Anglo-American thesis, i.e., that the armistices of Cassibile and Malta also bound Algiers as well. It should also be noted that Prunas preferred a public declaration by the Badoglio Cabinet to a telegram to the Algiers Committee directly on this thorny issue. In a sense, this choice was the logical consequence of a policy line maintained until now toward the Committee, presided over by General De Gaulle, and of the fact that there was no time for negotiations. These facts notwithstanding, it certainly could not be considered a demonstration of sympathy toward the leader of the Free French.

On June 6, 1944, an official communiqué was issued, as follows:

> The Council of Ministers met last night at 2200 hours and examined various matters affecting internal and foreign policy. The Council of Ministers, in last night's meeting, basing its decision on its previously announced statements on foreign policy, unanimously decided to declare the Armistice of Villa Incisa, signed by the plenipotentiaries of Marshal Pétain and Mussolini, to be null and void. With this declaration voiding the armistice with France, the Council of Ministers seeks to emphasize, via this particularly significant gesture on the very day of the liberation of Rome and on the eve of the attack against Fortress Europe, the solidarity of the Italian nation with the French state, secure in the knowledge that it conveys the sentiments of all of the Italians who pay homage to the valor of France's sons fighting on the Italian front.

Despite the best intentions, the formula selected by the Italian government for a unilateral declaration, prompted by the urgency of a situation which had foolishly been allowed to deteriorate despite warnings, was open to serious question. The nullifying declaration presupposed the validity of the Armistice of Villa Incisa, but if the instrument of 1940 had been regarded as valid up to that moment, this also signified that the Italians did not consider the armistice of 1943 to affect Italo-French relations. How, then, was it possible to execute the ceasefire declared in June, 1940? The ambiguous situation resulting from the failure of the Badoglio government to take a position on the question of extending the armistice of 1943 to include France complicated rather than simplified relations between the two countries. Nonetheless, it must be noted that the proposed French ceremony at Villa Incisa took place as scheduled.[28]

[28] "Moreover, General Dody, commanding this division, some days later in a ceremony designed to formally expunge from the record the Franco-Italian Armistice imposed on France in 1940, ordered our colors to be raised at Olgiata in front of the Villa Incisa, where this Armistice had been signed." Maréchal Juin, *Mémoirs: Alger, Tunis, Rome* (Paris: Fayard, 1959), I, p. 329.

If the last formal act of the Badoglio government involved the denunciation of the Armistice of Villa Incisa, the first act of the new Bonomi
Cabinet, which took office on June 22, 1944, consisted of a declaration
condemning Italy's intervention in the war, along with the Fascist claims.
Included in the text of this declaration was the following:

The Council of Ministers, in its first meeting, notes that it, based on its
political origins, represents the great majority of the Italians who in 1940 were
already opposed to Fascist domination and against Italy's intervention in the
war on the side of Hitler's Germany. Therefore, as its first act, the Council
affirms that only Fascism is responsible for Italy's adherence to the tripartite
pact and for Italy's entrance into the war and that, therefore, the breaking of
the ties to those who were not the allies of Italy but the allies of Fascism is no
more than the legitimate consequence of the political upheaval which has
occurred whereby the nation, no longer subjected to the most oppressive of
police systems, was able to take control of events and freely decide its own
destiny. Therefore, the Council denounces the so-called Fascist claims against
the honor and integrity of other nations and condemns Fascist aggression
against France, Greece, Yugoslavia, and Russia, aggressions which have shat-
tered the noblest of Italian traditions so firmly implanted at Solferino, Domoks,
and later on all of the battlefields of the great war of 1915–1918.

By this act, albeit tardily, the Italians met a number of the French demands, but the road to be traveled before a real improvement could be
achieved was a long and rocky one.

5

A number of events developed the next week which tended to worsen
Franco-Italian relations. With the intention of emphasizing the importance
of the French military contribution to the struggle against the Germans,
De Gaulle nominated Colonel Petit as Governor of the island of Elba.
Prunas met with De Panafieu on June 24 to discuss the matter. He pointed
out that the nomination would surely have an adverse effect on the Italian
public, which would interpret it as evidence of French participation in the
Allied control of Italy. This most assuredly would be a negative factor in
the whole process of improving relations between the two countries, which
was a matter of vital interest to both governments.

De Panafieu agreed with Prunas but assured him that the gesture had
been made primarily to convince the Anglo-Americans that France had
made and was continuing to make heavy sacrifices in the Italian campaign
and, therefore, was entitled to greater consideration than had been accorded her. The colloquy closed with Prunas' recommendation that this
nomination be regarded as merely an affirmation of principle, which would
be, therefore, provisional in nature.

Three days later, after many fruitless attempts to get the Algiers Committee to improve the treatment of Italian prisoners of war in North Africa, the Italian Foreign Minister presented the American Ambassador, Kirk, with a promemorial calling attention to the delicate question.

The document noted that there were approximately forty thousand troops under the control of the Algiers Committee of Liberation. Only a minority of these had been captured by the French. The vast majority were transferred to French authority by the British and American commands, although it was a known fact that such transfers from power to power were prohibited by international conventions.

Until a short time before the promemorial was presented, the conditions of the prisoners of war in French Africa were very nearly intolerable. This information had been confirmed by all of the sources available to the Italian government. In fact, intervention in the matter had been requested of the International Red Cross, the protecting power (Switzerland), the Allied Control Commission, and the American consular authorities. Unofficially, the Algiers Liberation Committee had also been requested to investigate. All of these pressures produced some improvement, but it was small and erratic. In general, the treatment of the prisoners remained highly unsatisfactory.

The Italian government desired that the prisoners, whose labor was vitally important to the French, become a means for a rapprochement between Italy and France rather than a source of conflict. To this end, the Italians would have preferred, from the beginning, to treat with the French directly. However, the document continued, since the results of direct contacts with the French Committee of Liberation up to that time were negligible and since it was impossible to remain indifferent to the sufferings of tens of thousands of fellow Italians, any pressure that could be applied by the Americans to alleviate this situation would be welcome.

Undoubtedly, the problem was important from a purely humane point of view, but the fact that the Italian government felt it necessary to appeal to the Americans to intervene indicates a complete lack of faith that the question could be resolved on a bilateral basis; that is, a conviction that there would be no immediate improvement in the relations between the French and the Italians. On the other hand, it was highly unlikely that problems such as these could be resolved through the intervention of third parties.

The next day, June 28, in the official gazette of the French Republic, published in Algiers, the provisional government, dated June 22, announced that all conditions stipulated in the three Italo-French conventions of September 28, 1896, or in internal regulations emanating from an application of the terms of these conventions were regarded as null and void as of June 10, 1940, the day Italy entered the war against France.

The news was telegraphed to Rome by the Italian Consul General in Tangiers, Berio, and constituted further evidence of the disintegration of Franco-Italian relations. The declaration of war of June 10, 1940, did permit France to take this position, but, aside from the complex legal aspects of the question (theoretically, the abrogation of the conventions of 1896 should have returned the situation to the status quo ante, an even more favorable one for the Italians because it was based on the agreements existing between Italy and the Tunisian regime prior to establishment of the French protectorate in the region), the fact remained that this decision was taken by the French government not during the period of hostilities between the two countries but after the Armistice of Villa Incisa had been denounced and at a time when the Italians were seeking to create a new atmosphere of friendship between the two countries. Evidently, the Algiers Committee had decided to put an end to the problem immediately and definitely.

This decision became even more obvious when, a short time later, De Panafieu informed Prunas that his government had interned about 1,600 Italian heads of families, all of them residents of Tunisia. The Committee of Liberation of Algiers proposed to repatriate approximately 1,000 of these persons and to permit the rest to return to ordinary Tunisian civilian life. The total number to be repatriated (including their families) was about 4,500, out of the approximately 100,000 persons comprising the Italian community in Tunisia. Of course, the expulsion, from the French point of view, had been prompted by Fascist activity in particular and by anti-French activity in general.

According to Prunas, it was obvious that the plan was to expel the leadership of the Italian community and keep only those persons regarded as necessary to the economy of the country. What remained was a mass of Italians, deprived of most of their leaders, and therefore amorphous and amenable, easily handled and absorbed.

During the course of his conversation with Prunas on this subject, De Panafieu stressed the fact that the Tunisian question, a problem about which every Frenchman was intransigent, would be moved toward a de facto solution as a result of the measures planned, which would automatically eliminate its inherent threat to the relations between the two countries. Undoubtedly, this would represent a very grave sacrifice for Italy, but it would serve, more than anything else, to help improve relations between the two countries by lessening that sense of hostility and rancor against the Italians that still permeated all of France. De Panafieu added that, insofar as the possessions of the expellees were concerned, the authorities would make every effort to arrive at a negotiated, equitable solution. While waiting for these solutions, the Italians in question were in concentration camps, and the longer they were away from their interests, the greater the risk of their being seriously compromised.

However painful the Algiers decision, it was the epilogue to the disastrous failure of the Fascist adventure. The French measures were not only an understandable type of retaliation but also a legitimate defense for the future. This retaliation had not occurred earlier because the period of hostilities had been so brief and because the Armistice of Villa Incisa had prevented it. The denunciation of the 1940 armistice by the Italians without any reference to the armistice of 1943 had given the Committee of Liberation in Algiers the opportunity to make up for lost time. This was another negative result of the tardy and foolish decision made by the Badoglio government. Evidently, when the Allies landed in France and the Italian government returned to Rome, the abrogation of the conventions of 1896 was regarded by De Gaulle as the key factor in resolving the Tunisian question. Now the Bonomi government was brought face to face with the French position and had to make its choice. It should be remembered that, up to that moment, the French were still searching for a de facto solution and had not yet requested formal accords. However, everything indicated that sooner or later the French would ask for formal action. In examining the total picture, one wonders if it would not have been the wisest course to make a virtue of necessity by proposing a formal solution which would liquidate the question once and for all, in exchange for a new and amicable period in Franco-Italian relations. This end was reached ultimately, but only after a long and involved negotiation and an exchange of views at the highest levels permitted the Italians to evaluate the situation more realistically.

6

On the morning of July 1[29] the French representative on the Consultative Commission for Italy, Couve de Murville, informed Prunas that General De Gaulle would be passing through Naples that afternoon and had asked to see him at French headquarters. Prunas appeared at the appointed hour. At the gates of the General's villa a company of sharpshooters was

[29] Although the memoirs of General De Gaulle (II, p. 232) give the impression that he met with Prunas before June 30, the day of his colloquy in Rome with Pius XII, the account of the Italian diplomat, bearing the date July 1, refers, in a note, to De Gaulle's impressions of his visit to the Pontiff, which indicates that the Naples conversation took place on July 1.

drawn up, and along the access road to the villa itself other sharpshooters were stationed at intervals. Prunas reported his impression that the General sought to emphasize protocol, as if fearing that otherwise his role as leader of France would not be accepted. He employed the somewhat artificial airs and tone of a head of state granting an audience. He spoke slowly, as if to show his visitor that each word was carefully pondered, with a definite weight and particular responsibilities. However, Prunas did not believe that De Gaulle exuded that magnetism and physical bearing which normally emanates from men accustomed to command. Instead, he had a quasi-mystical air about him as though he had lived for a long time with a dream which, perhaps even with a certain surprise, he had seen grow, bloom, develop, and become generally accepted. He gave the impression that he regarded himself as something of a man of destiny, guided by his star. In his report to Bonomi, Prunas emphasized these impressions without being ironical or drawing any arbitrary parallels, but simply providing an objective picture of the atmosphere in which the talks took place. It is also probable that he reported these details because, unaware that De Gaulle had met with Count Sforza in Algiers in October, 1943, he regarded his meeting with the General as the first conversation between an Italian diplomat and the probable representative of the new France.

De Gaulle spoke simply, and his expressions were basic and reassuring. His greeting was extremely courteous, and he opened the talks by referring to the years that Prunas had spent in Paris just prior to the war as Chargé d'Affaires and commented appreciatively on Prunas' activities.

At De Gaulle's request, Prunas summarized the current Italian situation. He emphasized the harshness of the armistice, the errors of the Allied military government, the burdens of the occupation, the impossibility of foreign administration of a nation with as ancient a civilization as Italy's, the constant and systematic interference, often organizationally destructive and humiliating, of the Allied controls. Prunas painted a grim picture. He believed that De Gaulle was interested in the subject and that he fully agreed with the analysis presented because it struck at the heart of a major French concern. Repeatedly, and with bitterness and disdain, the General said, "Nous connaissons déjà tout cela à Alger, nous en avons fait et nous en faisons l'expérience nous-mêmes."

De Gaulle then asked whether Prunas would enlighten him as to Bonomi's views of French affairs. Prunas took the occasion to refer to the three specific declarations made by the Italian government, the two made by the Badoglio government and the third, which solemnly confirmed the preceding ones, made by the Bonomi cabinet. Specifically, they were categorical condemnation of Fascist aggression, the declaration nullifying the

1940 armistice, and categorical repudiation of the so-called Fascist claims. Prunas then emphasized that there was not the slightest shadow of a doubt that not only Bonomi but all of the members of the government, in absolute sincerity, sought an amelioration of relations with France and the establishment of a solid collaboration on a firm base. He added that no real or fundamental difference of views separated them. He also emphasized that even the Tunisian question (which was not a Fascist territorial claim but an old Franco-Italian problem) could be quickly solved by negotiation if it could be included in the larger framework of the overall relations between the two countries.

The General replied that he had read the declarations with great interest. He believed that it was imperative to re-establish Franco-Italian solidarity as soon as possible. He knew that there were no deep-rooted reasons for conflict. He pointed out that the conventions of 1896 regarding Tunisia had been denounced and were therefore dead letters insofar as the provisional French government was concerned. Meanwhile, he concurred with Prunas that a solution which would be acceptable to both sides could be quickly achieved. Since this was a first exploratory conversation and not a negotiation, Prunas chose not to mention that the simple denunciation of the conventions of 1896 would automatically bring back into force those earlier treaties which guaranteed Italy an even more favorable position than under the conventions. De Gaulle then continued to reaffirm vigorously that France had no territorial claims to press against Italy. Moreover, Italy's territorial integrity was a positive factor in French policy. He desired to respect it and to see it respected. Therefore, he had no doubts that the two countries would follow a course of friendship in the very near future.

The General then summarized his European policy. Of course, France would have to rebuild herself and take her proper place among the world's powers. He repeatedly stated that it was his firm intention that this rebirth should come within a framework of order and discipline. He repeated "Je dis, dans l'ordre et dans la discipline" in a tone that indicated that, if necessary, he had the will and the strength to impose it. He conceived not a federation, which was a complex idea arousing certain suspicions and fears, perhaps justified, but a grouping of Latin countries: France, Italy, Spain, and then Belgium and other countries which would gain strength from the group. Naturally, each country, within the framework of the group, would preserve its complete autonomy and sovereignty. Before all else, economic agreements would have to be reached, followed by general cultural accords and, perhaps, security pacts. Under no circumstances should Russia be allowed to become isolated in Europe or to have the sensation of being so. Its political and military weight would be enormous. According to the General, the evolution of the Soviet Union toward forms of coexistence other than those usually attributed to her was evident. Insofar as he was concerned, De Gaulle had already informed Moscow that he was ready to conclude a hard and fast Franco-Russian alliance. He did not know to what extent the British would favor or would choose to participate in the grouping he had in mind. In any event, it was important to work toward its realization.

There remained, of course, the German problem. There was no doubt, said De Gaulle, that any artificial or forced solutions would be sterile and transitory. A nation of eighty million people could not be destroyed. There was only one Beneš, who could conceive the removal of an entire population, for example, the two million Sudetes from Czechoslovakia.[30] Unquestionably, the German people were destined to suffer a great deal and to nurse deep rancor. These were the seeds of discontent and dangerous rebellious tendencies. It would be necessary to take these into consideration and prepare accordingly. At this point, Prunas commented on what every Italian had always regarded as a fundamental error of Mussolini, i.e., binding Italy to Germany, which had led to the present situation. Prunas also noted that the armistice and the Italian declaration of war against Germany would, at least for a generation, make the Italians, in German eyes, "guilty of the most treasonable act in history." The Italian and German peoples would remain separated by an abyss, in contrast to 1919, when common discontent created a bridge between two peoples who had always been adversaries. Therefore, this was another basis for an understanding with France which had not existed before and upon which it would be possible to build.

At this point, De Gaulle asked Prunas his views of Austria. The Italian diplomat, speaking unofficially and personally, replied that he believed that Italy would have to support Austrian independence, as it had always done down to the *Anschluss*. Of course, the natural frontier was and should remain the Brenner Pass, and Austria should perhaps be given a greater area, at the expense of southern Germany. The twenty thousand Germans in the Alto Adige (the General was not aware of the number and obviously believed it to be exaggerated), would constitute no particular threat to an ethnically compact state such as Italy.

In conclusion, De Gaulle asked Prunas to tell Bonomi that he proposed to keep an authorized representative at Palazzo Farnese, in the person of Couve de Murville, with whom it would be possible to discuss and ne-

[30] This conversation with Beneš occurred on January 2, 1944, in Algiers, and its content is recalled by De Gaulle in his memoirs (II, pp. 203–5).

gotiate directly without outside interventions. The General emphasized that the contacts should be direct and secret without the intervention of third parties: "Vous comprenez, entre vous et nous." Prunas then reminded him that, at the time of the renewal of relations with the Soviet Union, the Allies prohibited Italy from negotiating any future agreements with other powers or with the United Nations.[31] The recollection made both men chuckle with satisfaction. In dismissing Prunas, De Gaulle asked that he convey his greetings to Bonomi, in whose integrity and ability he had complete confidence.

In his report Prunas pointed out that, in order to arrive at an exact evaluation of the significance of this exceedingly important conversation, it must be recalled that it was the fruit of long months of labor, talks with Massigli, and frequent meetings with De Panafieu. Throughout these months it had been his constant conviction that an overture for a renewal of relations would have a much stronger impact and be of far greater significance if it came from the French, particularly from De Gaulle, than from the Italians. If the Italians made the gesture, it would be the natural step of the offender seeking to placate the injured party; if the French made the gesture it would be the injured party, recognizing the offender's change of heart and the change in circumstances, who recognized the need and the reciprocal advantages to be gained by the reconciliation. From this premise stemmed his course of action and the particular importance he attributed to the De Gaulle interview. Of course, on the part of the Italians, it had been necessary to prepare the ground for such an undertaking, both by insisting on the three above-mentioned Italian declarations and by contacting Algiers directly each day regarding matters of purely Italo-French concern, that is, avoiding, as far as possible, the intervention of third parties, particularly that of the Allied Control Commission and the Allied High Command.

In any case, Prunas had no doubts that De Gaulle seriously intended to arrive at an Italo-French understanding. This was in part because of the obvious consideration that western Europe, sandwiched between Slavs and Anglo-Saxons, must, if it hoped to survive, decide to act as a bloc, and in part because of De Gaulle's conviction that France would easily regain her position as a great power—which she hoped to assume—if she were supported by the rest of the Latin states of Europe. Other considerations were a disinterested sense of a common race, culture, way of life, and a desire to salvage them and to lead in their rebirth.

Naturally, according to Prunas, this was an extremely important open-

---

[31] See pp. 294–304.

ing, albeit a vague one, which would have to be developed in detail in succeeding contacts and negotiations. Couve de Murville's presence at Palazzo Farnese would make these contacts possible. However, the fact must not be ignored that the Quai d'Orsay, in its usual fashion, would attempt to make difficulties by imposing its habitual bargaining formulas and a priori opposition. Prunas added that at this point De Gaulle seemed to have placed himself on a higher and, therefore, a more constructive level politically and morally. He had not uttered a word of recrimination about the past or a phrase which suggested "stab in the back" or any similar concept, although such a comment might not have been entirely unjustified. Prunas went on to say that, after referring to the very grave errors Mussolini had made, De Gaulle observed: "Mussolini etait certainement un grand homme et même un très grand homme. Peut-être n'avait-il pas l'instrument nécessaire à sa politique." These words certainly lacked objectivity and were recalled by Prunas only because to him they seemed to lack that rancor which continued to characterize French public opinion toward Italy, at least in French Africa.

The Italian diplomat noted that De Gaulle often and openly indicated his own rancor toward Great Britain and the United States. It was obvious that his association with the Anglo-Saxon world for the past five years had not been particularly easy, nor was it then so. This was further common ground on which the two countries could draw together without necessarily specifying details. For example, Prunas suggested the possibility of eventually using the Italian military mission in Algiers to establish a contact paralleling that of Palazzo Farnese in Rome, but De Gaulle firmly rejected this, observing that he regarded with extreme disfavor not the Italian officers in Algiers, but any mission which even gave the appearance of being under Allied control.

In concluding his report, Prunas noted that none of the ideas expressed by the General, either regarding specific relations with Italy or relations in Europe in general, seemed to be unacceptable to Rome. In fact, although the necessary details would have to be worked out, the ideas themselves seemed to be perfectly acceptable. All in all, according to Prunas, the conversation that day seemed to open the door for an improvement in Italo-French relations in the best possible manner and by the person best qualified to do so for France. In the situation in which the French provisional government found itself at that time, it was not possible for General De Gaulle to go any further or to be more conciliatory.

In a supplement to his report, drafted the same day, July 1, Prunas added the following details on his conversation with the French General: De Gaulle described with unconcealed emotion the reception that the people of Rome had accorded both him and the French troops.[32] In Prunas' opinion, this contact with the Italians had fixed in De Gaulle's mind the idea of moving ahead without further delay on the matter of rapprochement with Italy. De Gaulle spoke of the Pope with great respect and expressed his satisfaction with his visit to the Vatican.[33] He found Pius XII well informed on French affairs, acutely interested in everything concerning the future rebirth of France, and particularly responsive and positive to the possibility of an effective rapprochement between France and Italy.

The General also believed that the English would block an Italo-French understanding, seeking to multiply rather than to reduce the differences between the two countries. He asked Prunas if he had any evidence that the British had already launched this operation. The Italian diplomat replied that, in fact, the British as well as the Americans never failed to allude to the supposed violent opposition of the French every time an effort was made to ameliorate the armistice conditions for Italy.

7

The De Gaulle-Prunas conversation merits careful scrutiny not only because the entire Italian diplomatic action of that period was to be based on it, but, also, as has been demonstrated earlier, because it helps in understanding the General's later attitudes and provides a basis for evaluating his memoirs. It is necessary to divide this analysis into four parts, the first, De Gaulle's declarations regarding Italy; the second, his views on Europe's political problems in general; the third, the historical version of this encounter written by the General himself; and the fourth, a consideration of Prunas' comments.

From Prunas' extremely accurate and minutely detailed summary account is it clear that the position taken by De Gaulle on the specific problem of Franco-Italian relations was singularly generous and farsighted. Despite some minor details which should not obscure the overall view, it reflected the man's nature, revealed even more clearly later in historical perspective. A typical example was his policy of rapprochement with Germany.

In effect, De Gaulle not only stated his desire to satisfy his country's requirement for the total liquidation of the Tunisian question but also said

[32] On these receptions, see De Gaulle, *Mémoirs de guerre*, II, pp. 194, 234.

[33] On the content of the colloquy with Pius XII on June 30, see *ibid.*, pp. 232–34. According to Marshal Juin (*Mémoirs*, I, p. 237), De Gaulle wrote a personal letter to Pius XII earlier, which De Panafieu took to the Vatican on the eve of the entrance of the Allied troops into the Eternal City, while German troops were still present.

unequivocally that France had no territorial claims of any kind to make against Italy. Italy's territorial integrity, moreover, would become an integral part of his policy; he desired to respect Italy and to have her respected.

This attitude was certainly uncommon, but did Prunas' account accurately represent the General's words and thoughts? Reference has already been made to the private conversation between De Gaulle and Sforza in October, 1943, in which the French general presented his demands. The singular precision with which he anticipated the clauses of the 1947 peace treaty has been mentioned; in any event, this would have been an a priori agreement designed to reduce French demands and not to increase them. The position taken by the Algiers Committee at the conclusion of the armistices of Cassibile and Malta, the creation of the Consultative Commission for Italy, and the De Gaulle statements to Vishinsky and to Cordell Hull appeared to be inspired not only by resentment at the failure to grant France a role in the formation of Allied policy commensurate with her position but also by certain reservations regarding Italy, not only those specifically concerned with Victor Emmanuel and the Badoglio government.[34]

On the other hand, in the often-mentioned Sforza conversation, De Gaulle is reported to have said that "considering the fact that Yugoslavia had joined the Allies and considering the efforts that the troops of General Mihajlovic and of Tito had never ceased to make, it was clear that Italy would not be able to retain her prewar holdings on the eastern Adriatic shore. However, we are ready to help her retain Trieste."[35] Moreover, the General added, "As to your colonies, if Cyrenaica, where the English hope to remain, is lost to you, and the Fezzan, if we decide to remain there, in return we hope that you will be able to remain in Somalia, Eritrea, and Tripolitania as well. For the latter you will undoubtedly have to find a workable formula for integrating with the local populations; for the former, in exchange for the rights which will be accorded you, you will have to recognize the sovereignty of the Negus."[36]

In view of this position,[37] the interpretation of the words relating to the territorial integrity of Italy may take on a meaning other than a purely

[34] The following phrase used by De Gaulle is typical: "Some days later, Badoglio is to declare war against the Reich with the joint approval of Great Britain, America, and Russia, but without our being consulted." Mémoirs de guerre, II, p. 191.

[35] Ibid., p. 193.

[36] Ibid.

[37] This is summarized in the following sentence: "I mentioned to Count Sforza that our views were very much alike on this crucial point, but that after what had happened, a reconciliation with Italy could not be made entirely gratuitous, although it was our plan to be as lenient as possible." Ibid., II, p. 192.

literal one, and it may be that, in De Gaulle's mind, there was no real contradiction. Perhaps he intended his words to refer to a general principle and did not include amputations of territories in the territorial modifications he had in mind. However, for those who were completely ignorant of all of this, it was natural that only the literal sense of the words counted. It will be recalled that De Gaulle, having first championed certain territorial demands, dropped them during the Naples meeting and then returned to his original position.[38]

Once this fundamental point has been clarified, the rest of De Gaulle's statements concerning Italy and the reconstruction of a basis for friendship between the two countries all appear to have been inspired by a wish for conciliation and to reflect, in substance, the ideas expressed eight months earlier to Count Sforza. Evidently, the presence of Victor Emmanuel on the throne and of Badoglio at the head of the Italian government was a decisive factor in preventing the enunciation of these views, but it still remains noteworthy that the General chose to make his policy declarations to Prunas rather than to the new President of the Council, Bonomi. De Gaulle regarded this meeting as of particular importance; he referred to it in his memoirs and commented on it to Ambassador Quaroni when he met the latter for the first time in Moscow in December of that same year. As to his statement on Mussolini, it is only mildly surprising. It is the typical statement of a foreigner who was looking at Italian internal affairs from the outside, and it is essentially the sort of statement which Churchill made to De Gasperi in June, 1953, and to Scelba in February, 1955.

General De Gaulle's comments regarding the political future of Europe were no less important. He intended to construct French action initially on a grouping of the Latin states, but the most striking point is the insistence on the need to preserve each state's complete autonomy and sovereignty. It was the exact position De Gaulle took later, in the negotiations for a European political union; it was a concept that had been long maturing and was not likely to be modified. While the position of France toward Spain did not reflect the General's statement, his reference to his proposal for an alliance with the Soviet Union indicates that the decision which was to culminate in the Treaty of Moscow, signed in December, 1944, had been germinating for a very long period. It is true that De Panafieu's confidential statements to Prunas on April 7, 1944, revealed that Algiers was considering such a proposal and that on December 6, 1943, Massigli

---

[38] This view is supported with convincing arguments by Aldus, "Le rettifiche apportate alla frontiera italo-francese con il trattato di pace del 1947 nelle Memorie di guerra del generale de Gaulle," *Rivista di studi politici internazionali*, IV (1962).

had given Prunas a very optimistic interpretation of the policy that the Soviet Union could conduct in Europe, but these were the words of minor personalities. This time it was the chief of the Free French in person who had made the statement. His observations on the question of whether and to what extent—then unknown to him—the British would participate in the European grouping he had in mind were prophetic.

In this European arrangement he had very clear views on priorities and needs; economic accords were first, while the military question appeared last on his agenda and was rather ill-defined. The General's ideas on Germany were surprisingly realistic and certainly did not contradict his later thinking. The only discordant note concerned the impossibility of the transfer of populations on a vast scale, which he later fully supported. No less interesting was his question regarding Austria and his surprise at the figures given for the German minority in the Alto Adige. As for his unconcealed resentment of London and Washington, it was entirely comprehensible because the humiliations he had suffered at their hands were fresh in his mind. This memory was to be so decisive in shaping his thinking that perhaps even during the Fifth Republic it was the key to understanding his attitudes.

On the Naples meeting, De Gaulle's memoirs contain only the following brief note: "Brief stopover at Naples, where Couve de Murville presented Mr. Prunas, Secretary-General of the Italian Foreign Ministry. This important official brought the greetings of his government, established at Salerno. I ask him to inform Mr. Bonomi of my desire to establish direct relations with him through Couve de Murville. The President of the Council replied in writing that he accepted my proposal with pleasure."[39]

The fact that the only detail of this entire conversation mentioned by the General was the task entrusted to Couve de Murville is perplexing, particularly when the same volume contains an unusually detailed account of the colloquy with Sforza in October, 1943. Yet, the above-cited letter from Bonomi, which will be discussed later, and a report from Couve de Murville on a conversation with Prunas on July 7, both of which are reproduced in their entirety in an appendix to his memoirs, could have refreshed his memory, at least concerning the proposed grouping of the Latin states of Europe even if he chose, at that time, to make no mention of the Naples colloquy of July 1. While the General's version does not contradict that presented by Prunas, it does give the impression of focusing on one relatively minor point. Why? Many hypotheses can be advanced, but perhaps the most logical is that De Gaulle chose not to dwell on expressions he had uttered in a moment of abandon and which, after he had

[39] De Gaulle, *Mémoirs de guerre*, II, p. 232.

returned to his more reserved position, perhaps at the urging of his advisers, seemed difficult to maintain. In support of this view, the influence exerted on the General by his reception in Rome, as Prunas noted, and by the words of Pius XII on Italy must have been decisive in creating an emotional state of mind which prompted him to make very generous dispositions. Furthermore, it must be remembered that both France and Italy were currently occupied by the enemy and that the political and military situation was to change gradually in favor of the Paris government. The General's version of the colloquy seems to imply that it came about at the request of the Italian government and took on the character of a mere courtesy visit to bring the greetings of the Bonomi Cabinet to the leader of the Free French. It must be concluded that De Gaulle's account is not as truthful as that given by Prunas. It should be recalled once more that this was not a meeting on a governmental level but one, as the General emphasizes, with an "important official."

Prunas' statements and comments must be understood within the framework of the situation at that time. Such statements, for example, as those referring to Italo-German relations and to Anglo-Saxon policies may today appear strange, but they reflected a fairly widespread belief. Even the references to the legal consequences of the revocation of the conventions of 1896 were purely formal and were made at a time when very few people realized that the age of imperialism was moving toward its end. The Italian diplomat did not express surprise that the General did not ask to meet with Bonomi (in Rome De Gaulle did spend considerable time with Pius XII). During his previous visits to the peninsula, moreover, he had rejected every suggestion that he meet with Badoglio and the Prince of Piedmont. On the other hand, Prunas overestimated the importance of his conversations with Massigli and the belated declarations of the Badoglio government. Moreover, he asserted at the time that his entire action had been inspired by the conviction that the initiative for improving relations would be much more fruitful if it first came from the French rather than the Italians. This admission, made at a time when events seemed to support his view, casts considerable light on the Prunas policy during the entire period preceding the liberation of Rome and on the value he placed on the encounter with De Gaulle.

The Italian diplomat did not fail to recognize the nobility and the generosity of De Gaulle's words, although he did not ignore the fact that the Quai d'Orsay would have some reservations about De Gaulle's gestures. He did not repeat to De Gaulle the declaration he had made to Vishinsky in January regarding the role of the Soviet Union, and, without the usual professional caution of the diplomat, he accepted the General's words without hesitation. The assurances De Gaulle gave Prunas on that day to the effect that Italian territorial integrity should be preserved guided the Secretary-General of the Italian Foreign Ministry in advising Italian statesmen on the action Palazzo Chigi should take toward Paris, even when it was reasonably clear that De Gaulle's assurances had lost much of their meaning or, at least, should be interpreted in a very restricted sense. A number of his comments on De Gaulle's personality seem to be extraordinarily accurate; others were far less so.

In any case, it should be remembered that the Prunas account of the Naples meeting with De Gaulle constituted, for a long period, the basis for the Rome government's policy toward France, and a long time elapsed before an Italian minister again met with the leader of the new France. The general nature of the conversation,[40] which persuaded Prunas not to raise the Tunisian question in detail, also concealed the significance of the Couve de Murville mission at Palazzo Farnese. The principle of reciprocity—accepted in the understanding with the Soviet Union in March, 1944—was not defined, and it appeared that the Algiers Committee of Liberation sought instead to imitate London and Washington, where it was decided in the spring of 1944 to confer on Sir Noel Charles and on Kirk the rank of Ambassador without accepting an Italian representative in those capitals. Stalin, on the other hand, promptly declared his acceptance of the exchange of diplomatic representatives. In effect, then, this development marked a step backward when compared with the understanding Algiers reached many months earlier accepting the Castellano military mission as the vehicle for Italian contacts. For psychological reasons Prunas approved De Gaulle's anti-British and anti-American stand, and this placed him in the position of seconding the General's view regarding the opposition of the two countries to the realization of a real Franco-Italian rapprochement. Prunas had apparently forgotten the note he sent a few days earlier regarding the treatment of the Italian prisoners of war held by the French in North Africa and the memorial presented to Badoglio to anticipate any French initiative regarding the Armistice of Villa Incisa. It could not really be said that the Algiers Committee had adopted a more liberal attitude than the British and Americans insofar as the Consultative Commission and the armistice of 1943 were concerned. However, at this point Prunas was propelled more than anything else by the desire to assure the Rome government greater freedom of action to-

---

[40] It is interesting to note that Prunas went into detail only on the question of the Brenner Pass and the German minority in the South Tyrol. His personal views regarding an eventual enlargement of Austria at the expense of southern Germany should also be noted.

ward London and Washington by playing the French card for all it was worth, just as the Soviet one had been played.

8

Prunas' summary account of the meeting with De Gaulle created a very favorable reaction in Rome, prompting Bonomi, as President of the Council and Minister of Foreign Affairs, to address the following letter to General De Gaulle:

Minister Prunas has reported in detail your conversation with him in Naples, along with your kind expressions toward me, which were deeply appreciated. I wish to say forthwith that your plan to have in Rome, at the Farnese Palace, in the person of Mr. Couve de Murville, a representative of the Provisional French government with whom it will be possible, without the intervention of third parties, to undertake conversations on present and future Italo-French relations seems to me to be an excellent one from every point of view, and as such has my complete support. Surely it will be possible, at the appropriate time, to have a comparable Italian representative near you. I desire, also, to confirm what Minister Prunas has already told you: that is, that an amelioration of relations between France and Italy and the re-establishment of their old friendship are among the fundamental goals my government seeks to achieve. And I am delighted that you share my profound conviction on this point. There is no doubt in my mind that the Latin peoples of Europe must support each other in the storm which threatens to overwhelm them and which they will certainly overcome if—and I am certain that they will—they have the resolution and the capacity to stand and to be born again. I take this occasion, General, to reciprocate the good wishes you extended to me and to my government and especially to express my feelings of deep and abiding solidarity for your success in the military operation which will undoubtedly lead to the liberation of France, so nobly represented by you. Accept my sincerest regards.[41]

The acceptance of the De Gaulle proposal could not have been more complete. It is interesting that Bonomi also took the occasion to refer discreetly to the need for the accreditation of an Italian representative to the French Provisional Government at a propitious time and to comment on the General's idea of an entente of the Latin powers of Europe. On the other hand, it should also be noted that Bonomi's letter did not say a word about the Tunisian problem. The prudence of Palazzo Chigi was not inferior to that of the Quai d'Orsay. In actuality, the emphasis on general references to an amelioration of Franco-Italian relations and to a rapport among Latin countries involuntarily placed the accent on the proposal to establish a French representative in Rome at Palazzo Farnese, which is precisely what De Gaulle stated in his memoirs.

[41] *Ibid.*, pp. 653–54.

The letter of the President of the Council of Ministers was handed to Couve de Murville in Naples on July 7. Both minutes are available on this meeting. According to Prunas, the French diplomat was very much pleased by Bonomi's letter. Prunas and Couve de Murville agreed that once the government was transferred to Rome, it would be appropriate to examine the Tunisian question immediately in order to identify the basic points and the possibilities of solution. Prunas emphasized that it would be expedient, in the meantime, for the French to assure a progressive improvement in the treatment of Italian war prisoners and civilian internees in North Africa and to take the necessary action to prevent the recurrence of incidents in Corsica, as well as to bring about a modification of the language used by the French press in North Africa, which was not in harmony with the concepts expressed by General De Gaulle. Prunas also insisted that the French cease their efforts to insert themselves in either the armistice structure of 1943 or in the Control Commission. He was assured that, with De Panafieu's imminent departure, every French effort in these areas would definitely cease.

The overture toward resolving the Tunisian question was timely, as was the reference to the treatment of the prisoners and civilian internees and the prevention of further incidents in Corsica. It was not entirely necessary, however, to insist on a modification of the tone of the French press at a time when the situation was anything but regular and normal. The request to abandon all attempts to participate in the administration of the armistice terms and in the Control Commission was not necessarily politic. After denouncing the armistice of 1940, it was dangerous to risk everything on the willingness of the French in Algiers to forget the Italian declaration of war in 1940. Keeping France out of the armistice structure of 1943 paved the way for an automatic return to a state of belligerency between the two countries. Prunas should have had sufficient experience with the Cartesian logic of the French mind to foresee this eventuality. On the other hand, if he had such complete faith in the generosity of De Gaulle that he cast all caution to the winds, why did he seek to block the admission of De Gaulle's representatives to the armistice administrative structure, where they could make their presumably liberal voices heard in an atmosphere which he had described as oppressive? Clearly, there is an inadvertent contradiction here. From a psychological and formal point of view, how could the French provisional government—which was in an extremely weak position at that time and therefore extremely sensitive to the matter of prestige—have agreed to forget the aggression of 1940 by renouncing as well any claim to participate in the armistice terms of 1943?

The summary account of this meeting telegraphed by Couve de Murville to Algiers on July 8, read as follows:

Yesterday I met with the Secretary General of the Italian Foreign Ministry. The conversation centered primarily on the repercussions of General De Gaulle's recent trip to Italy.

(1) From an overall point of view, the declaration made by the General in Rome to the newspapermen made a strong impression, not only for its allusion to a Franco-Italian rapprochement, but for the sentiments expressed with reference to the Eternal City, cradle of Latin civilization and the seat of the Catholic Church. This impression was widely reflected in the city's newspapers. It is particularly prevalent in Vatican circles.

(2) The President of the Council of Ministers has been extremely moved by the General's words in the colloquy with Prunas. First of all, he is particularly grateful that the General said nothing regarding the past, which is condemned by everyone. He is especially pleased by what he regards as a gesture toward his government and toward Italy. He is in complete accord with the program for an entente between the Latin countries of Europe and regards it in Italy's interest for France to resume her role as a great power as soon as possible. According to Bonomi, nothing separates France from Italy; there remains only the Tunisian problem. He is ready to discuss it, and Prunas asked me whether we could begin discussion on this matter as soon as the government is established in Rome. I replied that I did not believe there would be any objection, since the point of departure is the disappearance of all Italian privileges in Tunisia. On the other hand, Prunas himself goes further, and does not hesitate to say that a general formula of understanding and reciprocal aid in the postwar period could be found. I refrained from accepting this proposal. In any event, it is clear that the Italians are very pleased to be able to add another card to a diplomatic game which has become more complex since the Soviets agreed to direct relations with Salerno. In the spirit expressed above, Bonomi saw fit to address a letter to General De Gaulle to thank him for what he had said to Prunas, to accept his offer for direct Franco-Italian contacts through my office, and to affirm his hope for a strengthening of Franco-Italian relations in the future.[42]

It is interesting to note how, in Couve de Murville's telegram, the public statements made to the press in Rome by De Gaulle are given the same importance as the statements given in private to Prunas. To Prunas' pointed reference that only the Tunisian question remained to be resolved, Couve de Murville offered no qualification or reservation, but he did note that this was an Italian idea. Couve de Murville's silence with reference to Prunas' offer for a postwar understanding (there is no trace of this in the Italian account) indicates a certain coolness toward Italy which he emphasized when he reported his colloquies to Algiers, while his comment on the Italian state of mind is certainly not inspired by any particular

42 *Ibid.*, pp. 654–55.

sympathy. Bonomi's reference in his letter to the possibility of accrediting an Italian representative to the French provisional government was not even mentioned, while note was taken of Prunas' reference to Italian support of the plan for an entente among the Latin powers in Europe. Couve de Murville said nothing about the treatment of prisoners of war, civilian internees, the press, the Corsican incidents, or the armistice. This was the first indication, still unknown to the Italians, that things would not be as simple as they had imagined.

On July 18 at the residence of the Undersecretary for Foreign Affairs, Visconti Venosta, Bonomi met Couve de Murville for the first time. On that occasion the ideas expressed by General De Gaulle and Bonomi some days earlier were confirmed. An agreement was reached that the proposals be given practical application as soon as possible. Bonomi urged that, in the meantime, the French should make every effort to improve the situation of the prisoners of war in North Africa, the civilian internees, and the Italians in Corsica, and to alter the attitude of the French press, which continued to be hostile and bitter toward Italy.

Couve de Murville emphasized that the Tunisian question, which was the only real point of friction between the two countries, had been resolved, insofar as the French provisional government was concerned, by the declared expiration of the conventions of 1896. However, he was in agreement that this unilateral decision of the French could be advantageously replaced by a negotiated bilateral accord. He pointed out, however, that any discussion on this point should acknowledge that the old conventions on Tunisia were to be considered null and void. Since he was leaving the next day for Algiers and returning to Rome a few days later, it was agreed that he should discuss the question with his government, in the following manner. The advisability of promptly engaging in direct conversations on the Tunisian question to ascertain the real significance of the new atmosphere created by the fact that Italy no longer had political aspirations in that region, a fact which changed the nature of the problem and simplified its solution, was to be explored. The Italian community in Tunisia was unusual, in the sense that it could not be absorbed by a French or other foreign group (largest non-Tunisian element, distinctive institutions with deep roots). Therefore, the conversations would be aimed at exploring the possibilities of formalizing the rather unique situation of that community by some specific agreements. Any future Italian sacrifices in Tunisia should be offset by concessions in the area of general relations between the two countries. These sacrifices should lay the groundwork for some form of general understanding between France and Italy, which, in turn, should establish the outlines for the Latin union mentioned in the French and Italian plans.

It was also agreed that the French and Italians would simultaneously inform the British and Americans that direct conversations had already begun between the French and Italians on particular aspects of their relations. This would be done as soon as Couve de Murville returned from Algiers and received instructions from his government on the matter. This action was planned to dispel the suspicions that would inevitably have developed over the long silence on the matter.

According to the version of this conversation prepared by Prunas, the impression was that General De Gaulle's suggestions concerning the reconstruction of Italo-French relations on a friendly basis could be put into effect without any great difficulty. In reality, the obstacles to be overcome proved much greater than anticipated.

9

On August 6 Prunas met again with Couve de Murville, after the latter's return to Rome from Algiers. The French diplomat stated that he was awaiting instructions from Massigli, who was expected to return from London within a matter of days. As for current matters of lesser importance, in reply to the request made by Prunas, Couve de Murville suggested that the Director of Political Affairs for the Italian Foreign Ministry could contact immediately the Secretaries at Palazzo Farnese, Beaumarchais, Fouché, and Vial. Couve de Murville added that he had discussed the Italian theses in detail at Algiers. However, one unknown element remained; this was public opinion in metropolitan France, where the possibility that strong opposition existed would in some way hamper approaches to the goal both governments hoped to reach.

On the other hand, in Algiers there was no indication of any change in the view that the conventions of 1896 were null and void, although it was recognized that a bilateral agreement on the matter would be more suitable than a unilateral act based on force. Couve de Murville also explained the ideas advanced by Prunas, such as the possibility of negotiating a new convention on the Tunisian issue, inclusion of the specific question of the Italian community in Tunisia in the larger one of the reconstructive activity of Italians in France in the postwar period, and, finally, offsetting the Italian sacrifices in Tunisia by a concrete Franco-Italian understanding. These several ideas were being examined by the provisional French government, and Couve de Murville reserved the right to inform Palazzo Chigi of the time when the Franco-Italian contacts could be simultaneously announced to the Allies.

What was the significance of these delaying tactics? On July 15 (the news reached Rome only on August 23) the Gaullist newspaper in Algiers, *Derniers nouvelles*, published an article entitled "Our Claims against Italy," signed by Roche, in which it was pointed out that, at the termination of the war, France's frontier with Italy would have to be re-examined. This was another warning which might have been heeded. However, much greater concern should have been aroused by Couve de Murville's statement regarding the unknown quantity represented by the public of metropolitan France. This element would have been a limited factor in any negotiation between Salerno and Algiers in 1943. However, on the eve of the liberation of Paris it should have been given much greater consideration, and it was not difficult to foresee that, for a whole series of psychological reasons, its effect would be negative.

During the latter half of August, Prunas frequently met with Couve de Murville. In reporting these conversations on August 25, Prunas noted that Couve de Murville had received official authorization from Algiers to negotiate with the Italian government on a solution to the Tunisian question but that, by all appearances, he had received only very general instructions regarding directives, procedures for practical approaches to the issue, and the criteria to be established. Couve de Murville's personal opinion was that the Italian government should declare in writing that it took note of the action of the French provisional government in declaring the conventions of 1896 null and void. The French would then reply with a written declaration of their own, in which the French provisional government would agree to a predetermined date for discussing and reaching agreement with Rome on the guarantees to be given to the Italian community in Tunisia in place of the now defunct conventions.

Prunas told Couve de Murville that his idea was unacceptable to Visconti Venosta because, above all, it did nothing more than postpone the discussion which both parties were anxious to undertake in order to re-move the one existing obstacle between them. Therefore, the Rome government chose to insist that (a) negotiations be undertaken immediately for a new convention restricted to Tunisia, in which both the sacrifices made by the Italians and the guarantees to be given to the Italian community would be defined, and (b) the Tunisian question be linked to the general question of Italo-French relations, using it as a launching platform to bring into being as soon as possible that Italo-French rapprochement planned by both General De Gaulle and Bonomi. Prunas' personal view was that they should agree to proceed, if and when a solution was found to the Tunisian question, to a reciprocal declaration of goodwill, in which, for example, both parties would accept the obligation to support each other for the rapid recovery of Italy's autonomy and sovereignty on the one hand, and for France's re-entrance into the great power ranks, an aspiration of all Frenchmen, on the other.

The talks had thus reached something of an impasse on this point, but the subject would be approached in future conversations. Couve de Murville was to leave for Algiers toward the end of August, would report on the Italian viewpoint, and would return with instructions and directives to proceed toward a solution. Meanwhile, Palazzo Chigi proposed to continue to insist on an improvement in the conditions of the prisoners of war, the civilian internees, and the Italians in Corsica.[43]

The contrasting viewpoints emerging from these conversations were both comprehensible. If the change in the Tunisian situation was to be France's only claim against Italy, Palazzo Chigi's failure to accept the fait accompli without further delay must have been frustrating to the Algiers committee. Moreover, neither Couve de Murville nor the Algiers provisional government had, as yet, committed itself on the proposed declaration of mutual support, by which they evidently believed Italy stood to gain far more than France at that time. This was the period, too, of De Gaulle's triumphal entry into Paris,[44] and it appeared that the liberation of the entire Continent would be only a matter of a few weeks. Even if De Gaulle's views on future Italo-French relations were valid, they would

[43] The question of the conduct of the Moroccan troops in Italy (Marshal Juin makes no mention of this whatsoever in his memoirs) offered the Undersecretary for Foreign Affairs, Visconti Venosta, the opportunity on August 5 to ask the Holy See to intervene in the matter in any way it would consider opportune. The Italian Chargé d'Affaires, Babuscio Rizzo, referred to the Italian government's strong desire to arrive at a general clarification of its relations with France, to his hope that the presence of French troops in Italy might help produce a rapprochement rather than friction and conflict, and to the related fact that, precisely in view of these considerations, the atrocities must be severely punished and action taken to prevent their recurrence. The Holy See, in Visconti Venosta's judgment, could eventually approach the problem not merely from a purely humane standpoint, which was certainly appropriate to the Church, but also from this point of view. Babuscio Rizzo carried out his instructions on August 7; he transmitted a promemorial on the matter to Monsignor Giovanni Battista Montini, Adjunct Papal Secretary of State and conferred with Monsignor Domenico Tardini, Adjunct Papal Secretary of State. He was told that the policy of rapprochement with France had the strongest approval and sympathy of the office of the Secretary of State but that it was recognized that grave obstacles existed. In any event, the Holy See would not fail to help Italy.

It is also interesting to note that on August 5 Visconti Venosta telegraphed Quaroni in Moscow to tell him to inform Molotov that Italy intended to participate in the creation of a stable peace on the Continent and would work toward this end, particularly toward re-establishing cordial relations with France and Yugoslavia. Rome was fully confident that the Soviet Union would help to realize this policy of peace in the Adriatic. Quaroni replied that he had been repeatedly told in Moscow that the Soviets viewed with pleasure the constant improvement in Italian relations with France. However, Moscow made no mention whatsoever of Italo-Yugoslav relations.

[44] On that occasion Bonomi telegraphed to De Gaulle as follows: "At the moment the liberating troops are entering Paris, the Ministers of free Italy unite with you and assure you that our people share with yours joy and deepest emotion." In turn, the mayor of Rome, Doria Pamphili, sent the governor of Paris, General Koenig, the following telegram: "Rome sends to the people of France its fraternal greeting at this hour of the liberation of Paris, which marks a further great step toward the liberation of Europe."

be applicable at a later date, when the Rome government had regained its complete sovereignty.

On the other hand, while Rome accepted De Gaulle's words in their literal sense, they had also been given a significance that probably went beyond the intention of the speaker, since he may have been looking toward a distant future. Rome intended to proceed cautiously before assuming the responsibility for liquidating a problem which historically antedated Fascism by many years. In the final analysis, if it were not possible to arrive at even a rudimentary political understanding with France, Italy might as well wait for the determinations to be made by the peace treaty.

This state of affairs was to exist for some time,[45] in part because of the inevitable initial disorganization in the transfer of the French provisional government to Paris, which, incidentally, also hindered the dispatch of new instructions to Couve de Murville.

The appointment of the Christian Democrat Bidault to the post of Minister for Foreign Affairs raised Rome's hope for a productive supporting action by Pius XII to induce the Quai d'Orsay to accept the Palazzo Chigi point of view. Meanwhile, on September 18, Prunas suggested to Visconti Venosta that the Holy See be acquainted with the details of the discussions then under way with the French. The point should be made to the Holy See that the sacrifices Italy would be called upon to make in Tunisia should be offset by a general and fundamental Italo-French rapprochement. The Holy See could support the action taken by Palazzo Chigi by urging that the new accords to be reached on Tunisia be accompanied by a first and concrete step toward an effective Italo-French rapprochement. However, toward the end of September, the representatives of the National Committee of Liberation in Turin informed the Italian Legation in Berne that a delicate situation was developing in the Val d'Aosta, where it appeared that French elements were seeking to es-

[45] In another note on September 1 Prunas summarized the results of the conversations under way as follows: (1) The French could see no difficulty in negotiating for a new convention to replace that of 1896. However, in the French view, it would have to be an ordinary convention which would take into account only the special nature and particular characteristics of the Italian community in Tunisia. All of the privileges previously enjoyed by the Italians would have to be abolished. (2) The Italians, of course, were ready to negotiate a new convention which guaranteed the unquestionable special situation of the Italians in Tunisia. (3) The Italians also insisted that the delineation of the Tunisian question, in addition to settling the only serious element of conflict between Italy and France, also be utilized to provide the basis for a later comprehensive Franco-Italian understanding. It was obvious that if Palazzo Chigi could, for example, have achieved at the same time a joint declaration of mutual goodwill which would lay the cornerstone for such an understanding, it would most certainly help to justify in the eyes of the Italian public the sacrifices to be made in Tunisia. The question was, for the moment, closed at this point, to be touched upon again later by Couve de Murville in Paris.

tablish a movement in support of annexation to France. At the same time it was also asserted that French troops were seeking to reach the valley via the Bard gorge. From that moment, therefore, Rome began to consider the possibility of other French territorial claims against Italy. In order to prevent a repetition of the unfortunate incidents which occurred on the island of Elba and the inevitable unfavorable repercussions they would have on the Italian resistance movement, Palazzo Chigi, on September 27, decided to interest the Allied Control Commission in ensuring that the Val d'Aosta be occupied by forces of the American Seventh Army, which, it appeared, were in the vicinity of the Alpine passes. In fact, the Commission had already been informed of the situation in a telegram from the American Minister to Berne, Harrison, as early as September 22.

During the month of October there was no further progress in the discussion between the two governments on the Tunisian question.[46] Early in November the French government proposed that direct relations between Paris and Rome be established, with the nomination of Couve de Murville as Ambassador to Rome. There would, however, be no reciprocity. Insofar as the Tunisian question was concerned, the earlier offers were repeated. In Prunas' judgment, these suggestions were unacceptable. Instead of clarifying Italo-French relations, as had been stressed by both governments, they would becloud them even more. A solution of this kind, at a time when all other countries were re-establishing normal relations with Italy, would have been an insulting and certainly humiliating discrimination. Rome was disposed to begin discussions on Tunisia imme-

[46] On October 10, following the Churchill-Roosevelt understanding on Italy, which culminated in the declaration of September 26 (for this text see *The United States and Italy, 1936–1946*, pp. 88–89), Sir Noel Charles informed Bonomi of Great Britain's decision to re-establish diplomatic relations with Italy and of the limits and conditions of this renewal. On October 25 the Soviet Union decided to re-establish full diplomatic relations with Italy by nominating an ambassador extraordinary with plenipotentiary powers, and asked that Kostylev be approved for this post. On October 26 Roosevelt announced his decision to submit Kirk's name to the Senate for confirmation as United States Ambassador to Italy. The official communiqué noted that this decision had been taken after consultation with the other American republics and with the governments of London and Moscow. See *The United States and Italy, 1936–1946*, p. 93. These actions were quickly imitated by almost all the members of the United Nations, and by November 5, 1944, the Undersecretary for Foreign Affairs, Visconti Venosta, asked the Italian Chargé d'Affaires at the Vatican, Babuscio Rizzo, to point out that only France, Yugoslavia, Czechoslovakia, Greece, Poland, Belgium, and Holland maintained unilateral de facto relations with Italy in the sense that they were represented in Rome in various ways without similar Italian representation at their seats of government. Consequently, Visconti Venosta hoped that the Holy See would intervene in a friendly way with a number of the Catholic governments to urge this action, which was now long overdue. Such an intervention might serve to overcome the remaining resistance and prod the stubborn and the difficult. The office of the Secretary of State of the Vatican reacted favorably to this request.

diately, not on the basis of the conventions of 1896, but only to establish a fundamentally liberal agreement. At the time that this obligation was assumed, consular representation was to be immediately effected. The signing of a new convention on Tunisia should coincide with (a) the re-establishment of normal diplomatic relations between France and Italy, and (b) agreement by the French (which might take the form of an un-publicized exchange of letters between De Gaulle and Bonomi) that claims against Italy had been liquidated and that, since the only reason for friction between the two countries had been eliminated, France and Italy would not hinder each other in their efforts to regain their normal positions in Europe and the world and, indeed, would aid each other in every endeavor directed toward this end.

In view of France's clear resistance, Prunas began to shift his position slightly. He accepted Couve de Murville's suggestion that the negotiations on Tunisia be divided into two parts. In assuming the obligation to ne-gotiate a convention formalizing the new situation in Tunisia, no demand for a simultaneous renewal of diplomatic relations was to be made, nor was there to be any insistence on mutual support for each other's goals in Europe and the world. Only after the conclusion of the convention on Tunisia would steps be taken to renew full diplomatic relations and to exchange letters. These letters, according to Prunas, would not contain any reference to mutual support but would simply promise not to hinder each other. In return, for the first time, appeared an explicit request to consider the accounts between the two countries to be definitely settled. This ac-tion was prompted by repeated hints of further French territorial claims against Italy.

On the basis of this new postulation of the issue, Minister Zoppi, Di-rector General for Political Affairs, on November 8, 1944, prepared a draft text of the desired De Gaulle-Bonomi letters in which Italy formally repeated her earlier condemnation of the Fascist policy of aggression, abandoned the Fascist claims, and recognized the nullification of the armistice of June 24, 1940. In turn, France, in the exact wording used by De Gaulle, declared that she had no claims to make against Italy and that she intended to respect and to ensure respect for Italy's territorial in-tegrity.[47]

---

[47] The text of the Zoppi proposal was as follows:

The French and Italian governments note with mutual satisfaction that, since the resolution of the problems concerning the Italian communities in Tunisia, there are no longer any serious bases for discord or conflict between France and Italy.

On this occasion the Italian government is happy to confirm the solemn declara-

10

This formula met the resistance of the Quai d'Orsay. The French General Staff was bringing pressure for a number of frontier adjustments, and there did not appear to be any particular urgency about bringing into existence the political understanding outlined by De Gaulle in Naples. However, France had not remained intransigent in its position. She was disposed to take some very minor steps forward, but nothing comparable to what was desired by Rome. Couve de Murville and Prunas met frequently, but the only concessions wrested from Paris, with the greatest difficulty, concerned the renewal of diplomatic relations.

On December 15, when De Gasperi took over the reins of the Italian Foreign Office, the status of the conversations with the French was as follows: (1) The Paris government considered the conventions of 1896 to have been abrogated and therefore null and void. However, it was prepared to seek a bilateral accord on the solution rather than impose one unilaterally and by force; that is, France was prepared to negotiate a consular convention for Tunisia which formally recognized the status quo in that country. However, this convention was to be based simply on common law; it would be a formal recognition of the new situation. Absolutely no consideration would be given to any special structure, nature, or character of the Italian community in Tunisia. (2) Negotiating a new convention would involve a long delay. In order to reduce this delay, France for the time being would request merely a written commitment to negotiate a convention in the near future based on common law and, in

---

tions which it made earlier condemning Fascist policies of aggression, rejecting the so-called Fascist claims, and recognizing the nullification of the armistice of June 24, 1940. In turn, the French government is pleased to announce that it has no claim to make against Italy, that it intends to respect it and see that its territorial integrity is respected.

The governments of France and Italy are convinced that upon these fundamental bases it will be possible to re-establish between the two countries the climate of cordial collaboration and friendly solidarity which they regard as essential for their reciprocal interests and for the peace of Europe.

The two governments agree to support each other, during and after the war, in order that both France and Italy may regain their proper positions.

Talks will begin between the two countries as soon as possible in order to conclude without delay economic, commercial, cultural, and emigration agreements— and those aimed at establishing the new Franco-Italian collaboration on an increasingly solid basis.

As is obvious, the Zoppi proposal differed somewhat from Prunas' views regarding the request for reciprocal support, which Zoppi still maintained, and regarding the introduction of the obligation to conclude economic, cultural, and emigration agreements promptly.

consequence, recognizing the nullification of the conventions of 1896. As soon as France possessed this written commitment from Italy, she would put forth no obstacles to an immediate renewal of diplomatic and consular relations between France and Italy, along the lines used by London if necessary, that is, through personal representatives with the rank of Ambassador but without credentials. Italy could immediately open consulates in France, at Paris, Marseille, Toulouse, and Nancy.

Palazzo Chigi's viewpoint, in contrast, was as follows: Italy should be paid a price for sacrificing the conventions of 1896, with the consequent loss of privileges and guarantees which these conventions assured to the Italian community. By the French proposal, the price was French consent to a renewal of diplomatic relations. Rome hoped instead to include at least a first step toward an Italo-French rapprochement and hoped that Paris would agree that, after the accord on Tunisia was reached, it would consider all reasons for conflict with Italy eliminated and consequently all claims against Italy liquidated, thus clearing the way for a progressive economic, political, and cultural rapprochement.

In effect, if the Quai d'Orsay had re-examined its own position in the matter of renewing diplomatic relations and had accepted the bilateral nature of these to the same extent as had Moscow, London, and Washington, Palazzo Chigi, in turn, had consented to a thorough review of its own position. The proposed convention on Tunisia would be based simply on the common law, and the political entente would be regarded only as desirable. The sole point on which Palazzo Chigi remained firm was that explicitly introduced in the last phase of the negotiation: a precise statement by France indicating that all claims against Italy were considered liquidated.

This was a much more realistic position than the earlier one, which had been formulated at a time when the echo of De Gaulle's statements in Naples had given the Italians illusions concerning the future rapport with France. Once Rome realized that France was reluctant to move quickly toward the indicated goal of renewed political friendship and was put on guard by persistent rumors of territorial claims against Italy, Italian diplomats turned to the idea of immediately abandoning the concept of give and take between the two governments. This had been a plausible but, unfortunately, an entirely illusory aspiration. In a moment of emotional generosity De Gaulle had temporarily abandoned those claims which he had outlined to Count Sforza in October, 1943. When that moment passed, with the period of weakness of the Algiers Committee overcome, the provisional government established in Paris, virtually all of metropolitan France liberated, and the factor of a French public which had had direct experience of Italian military occupation introduced into the dialogue, it was difficult to suppose that the Fascist aggression of 1940 could be forgotten by simply substituting a new convention for Tunisia based on common law for the abrogated conventions of 1896. Although at first glance it may seem rather strange, this hope was all the more difficult to maintain when it is recalled that the initial idea advanced by De Gaulle for a prompt political understanding had been temporarily put aside. One could be very generous toward a state formally recognized as a friend, but not toward a state regarded as only a potential one.

In assuming the direction of the Italian Foreign Ministry, De Gasperi, on December 16, sent Bidault a warm telegram in which he asserted that all of Italy admired France's rebirth and her rapid return to the rank of a great power, a guarantee for stability and order in Europe and in the world. He was especially anxious to reassure his French colleague regarding his deep faith in the future of Franco-Italian relations, asserting that, with goodwill, every difference between the two countries could be resolved and a degree of collaboration between them could be established which would be beneficial to both countries and contribute much to the peace of Europe. De Gasperi then declared that he was particularly pleased that this great task of rapprochement could be made easier by the ideals and concepts of life that he shared with the director of France's foreign policy.[48] In reality, this program was becoming increasingly cumbersome. During this same period, on the occasion of Churchill's visit to Paris, Bidault had granted the Sunday *Times* an interview, in which his only reference to Italy was as follows: "It is essential that our friends realize that France will regain her position of importance and, as a result, will have to participate in making all major decisions. Our trust, for example, cannot be increased in the event that, without consulting us, Italy is granted the status of quasi-ally."

As on the occasion of the armistices of 1943, the Foreign Ministers Conference in Moscow, and the constitution of the Consultative Commission for Italy, the question arises of whether the provisional French government was fighting only on the matter of principle in seeking to participate in the decisions regarding Italy, or whether France opposed the decisions themselves. De Gaulle's words had clarified this point, but there had been no immediate implementation of them. For these reasons, Palazzo Chigi's concern continued to grow. It was revealed in a study drafted on December 20 by the Director-General for Political Affairs, Minister Zoppi. He

[48] As is noted below, Bidault replied to this message on February 19, 1945, affirming that he had just received it.

introduced his observations by noting that, on the basis of an examination of all of the information which had come from the French, it had to be concluded that Paris tended to view the settlement of the Tunisian problem as a preliminary condition to the normalization of diplomatic relations between the two countries. The question of the Tunisian statutes had not been raised by the Italians; instead, it had been the French who declared that these statutes had been abrogated and had accompanied this declaration with authoritative indications that this abrogation was to be considered definite and irrevocable. At one point it was implied that it would be possible to substitute for the conventions of 1896 a consular convention that would give some consideration to the special character of the Italian community in Tunisia. These conciliatory overtures were later abandoned. The French refused to regard the Italian proposals, presented unofficially, as a basis for a possible discussion and declared that they regarded the question as resolved.

On the other hand, the French did not feel completely at ease with their unilateral denunciation of the conventions and desired to ensure themselves against the possibility that the question might be raised again later. In Rome in the past it had always been maintained that the abrogation of the conventions of 1896 would imply a return to the conventions signed between the Italian states and Tunisia, guaranteeing the Italians capitulation rights in the Regency. While insistence on this thesis would have encountered the unyielding hostility of the French and, for obvious reasons, would have had no chance of consideration, it was to be recognized that on a legal plane it would be possible to challenge the right of the French to impose French citizenship on the Italians in Tunisia. As a matter of fact, French rights in Tunisia were only those of a protecting power and did not imply the privilege of legally imposing French citizenship on foreign residents, albeit of several generations' standing, in the Beylik. The granting of citizenship to foreigners was generally recognized as a typical function of a state exercising its full sovereignty and, therefore, could not be imposed in a territory defined as a protectorate. The question had already been the subject of conflict between Paris and London in 1923, and the Permanent International Court of Justice, at the request of the British government, rendered an opinion which affirmed the international character of the problem and supported the thesis described above. It was probably French awareness of the possibility that Italy might use this argument that prompted France to seek the Italian government's signature on an act which would recognize the irrevocable abrogation of the Tunisian statutes by substituting a consular convention formalizing the new situation.

At this point it was pointed out that the Tunisian statutes had been vigorously defended by every Italian government since they were set up in 1896; every government prior to the advent of Fascism had been supported by the public and Parliament on this issue. This condition had to be considered in any decision to accept or reject the formal proposal advanced by Paris at this exceptional time in the internal history of the country and in the current parliamentary situation. It was true that Italy had lost the war, and Italy's ability to protect her rights and interests at the international level in 1944 was therefore far less than it had been at any time between 1896 and 1939. However, with every passing day, the most disastrous period in Italy's recent history receded further into the past, and it was not to be excluded that as the war progressed and international competition increased, possibilities and situations might emerge which would permit Italy to improve her diplomatic position. Apparently the French had also considered this possibility, in addition to the legal argument described above; otherwise, there would be no way of explaining the pressure exerted by the Quai d'Orsay on Palazzo Chigi to recognize the fait accompli in Tunisia and to accept immediately conditions which, by any definition, properly belonged in a peace treaty. The Allies, in matters involving their specific interests, had made no similar requests of any kind.

Of course, the matter would have been entirely different if the sacrifice requested by the French could have been offset by a suitable concession elsewhere. This concession would have had to be something tangible, and not merely a symbolic concession such as a formal declaration, the renewal of diplomatic relations along the restricted lines described above. The statements made by the French representative before the U.N.R.R.A. council, the measures taken with regard to the Italians in France and in the French colonies and protectorates, the treatment of Italian prisoners of war and internees, the attitude of the French toward the dislocated troops of the Fourth Army, who were considered to be prisoners of war even though many of them had fought with the *maquis*, the treatment accorded the patriots of northern Italy who were forced to cross the border into France, the reservations the French indicated as to the extent of the damage done by Italian troops, and the references to territorial and colonial claims against Italy were all symptoms of a state of mind which did not appear likely to be drastically changed by any formal indication by Rome that Italy was abandoning one hundred thousand Italians in Tunisia to their own fate.

Zoppi continued his observations by noting that an accord formally obligating the French would therefore have to be reached at the same time that the Italians consented to the French demands concerning Tunisia. In such an accord, if the French agreed to a complete normalization of relations, a clear concession could be acquired from them. This would provide that the Italians living in France and in territories under French control could normalize their economic lives, that the necessary measures would be taken to repatriate Italian soldiers and partisans, and that France would renounce further claims against Italy. This approach to the problem would reflect the view so often expressed by leading Frenchmen, that is, there would be no other political issue to be resolved between the two countries once the Tunisian problem was settled. At the same time, it would be wise to seek to negotiate a regular convention covering the French colonies and protectorates, similar to the one concluded between France and Italy in 1930 but containing additional guarantees and concessions which would take into account the exigencies of colonial life, so that Italian emigrants or those desiring to emigrate to French colonies and protectorates would have a sense of security and faith in the future.

Once these elements of conflict were eliminated, it also would be possible, while developing the accords, to examine ways and means of collaborating on a political plane for mutual advantage and of contributing to the pacification and reconstruction of Europe. Zoppi was of the opinion that, in the event that such negotiations were undertaken with the French, the governments of London, Washington, and Moscow should be promptly informed, in order to avoid giving the impression that both France and Italy were seeking to establish a policy that might be in conflict with the interests of the major Allied powers. Such an impression, under current conditions, would do incalculable damage to Rome.

In developing his position in this study, the Director-General of Political Affairs for the Ministry of Foreign Affairs made several observations which focused on the key unknown factor: was there justification for the liquidation of the Tunisian question before a future peace conference? Immediately after the De Gaulle-Prunas meeting in Naples on July 1 there was no doubt of it; six months later the reservations threatened to become overwhelming. This was the heart of the matter. The legal arguments had been established. It was reasonable to presume that Italy could markedly improve her diplomatic position before the conclusion of a peace conference in which, to be realistic, she would be given a treaty containing clauses which would be much more severe than the simple acceptance of the abrogation of the Tunisian conventions. In all likelihood, no thought would be given to stipulating a convention establishing equality before the law, and the Bey would act in accord with the wishes of Paris. Moreover, the Tunisian question would not be the only one considered at a peace treaty negotiation. Even without allowing for other French claims, the Brenner Pass problem remained to be resolved, along with that of the Adriatic frontier, the colonial, and the reparations questions. Liquidating the Tunisian issue bilaterally with France could mean widening the circle of powers favorably disposed toward Italy.

The question was, therefore, essentially a political one, involving political responsibilities. The same historical argument relating to the position assumed by the pre-Fascist Italian governments regarding the Tunisian question had merit precisely for this reason; otherwise, it could have been easily refuted. It was specifically because the Tunisian question had kept Paris and Rome apart since the nineteenth century that the French government, as Couve de Murville told Prunas at Salerno on July 7, regarded "the point of departure [for the establishment of Franco-Italian friendship] is the elimination of all Italian privileges in Tunisia."[49] And De Gaulle, in his conversation with Count Sforza in Algiers in October, 1943, had used approximately the same words, saying that it was necessary to "liquidate the Italian rights of appeal and privileges in Tunisia"[50] and indicating that this was the major issue in Franco-Italian relations. The General alluded to this on November 23, 1943, when he said to Vishinsky, "However, anti-French tendencies have existed in Italy for a long time, and they have been the cause of serious misunderstandings. This tendency, which had emerged as a dominant factor with Crispi, was dissipated by the German threat. It appeared again after the close of World War I and even before the emergence of Fascism."[51]

According to Zoppi, the question of the Tunisian statutes was not raised by the Italians but by the French, who declared them to be null and void. This was only formally true. Aside from the political abuse of these statutes by the Rome government, immediately after the declaration of war in June, 1940, Palazzo Chigi drafted plans for substituting an Italian protectorate over Tunisia for the French one. Wartime developments prevented the Italians from presenting the French with a formal demand on this matter, but Paris was fully aware of the existence of these proposals, and the French sought to guarantee that any such dangers in the future would be eliminated by abrogating the accords of 1896.

It was clear that Paris was interested in seeing the negotiations materialize. Otherwise, such a policy would have been merely a gratuitous gesture which could hardly be expected from any government, let alone from one that had been based on the desire to defend the national inter-

---

[49] De Gaulle, *Mémoirs de guerre*, II, p. 654.
[50] *Ibid.*, p. 192.
[51] *Ibid.*, p. 604.

ests at all costs. But on what bases could a reasonable equilibrium be achieved? Zoppi had prepared a rather detailed list of demands. A number of these did not appear to be absolutely indispensable, while others related to conditions of a peace already achieved, rather than to an armistice period. Current prospects were thus even less clear.

Nevertheless, the demand that all claims be totally liquidated remained. Would a written and categorical obligation be necessary, or would a verbal statement suffice? Would it be possible to take a calculated risk or not? Would it be possible to totally ignore public opinion in metropolitan France, which, when De Gaulle spoke to Prunas in Naples, was still under German control even if, at the time, it could not be clearly determined? Though it may seem paradoxical, one cannot help wondering whether it would not have been preferable to examine the question further, to learn immediately what other claims Paris had in mind, and to satisfy these on some basis infinitely preferable to what Italy would have to accept at the peace conference, while in the process insuring a political entente with France. The time for a purely political choice was approaching. In this choice the Secretary-General of Palazzo Chigi was in a better position than the Director-General for Political Affairs and the Foreign Minister. The Prime Minister and the Bonomi government were to decide in favor of the position of the Secretary-General.

11

On December 28, 1944, the French radio in Rome made a significant announcement. Referring to a release the previous day by a news agency regarding the renewal of Italo-French diplomatic relations, the radio broadcast made it clear that such a statement was premature and that it was also premature to affirm that negotiations on the issue had taken a favorable turn, as, up to that moment, no unofficial preliminary contact with the Rome government had taken place since the earlier one was interrupted by the ministerial crisis. Moreover, the broadcast went on, it was incorrect to state that the Tunisian statutes figured among the subjects under discussion. In fact, the Tunisian conventions of 1896 had been nullified by the Italian declaration of war on June 10, 1940. This state of affairs had been confirmed formally on June 22, 1944, by an ordinance of the provisional government of the French Republic. Thus there was no room for discussion apart from that concerning future regular conventions. Insofar as the territorial questions were concerned, it was clear that they had not been raised during the course of the conversations on the re-establishment of Franco-Italian diplomatic relations and that they would not be examined until the peace treaty provided the means of negotiation.

This was a particularly rigid position, and the implications regarding the French policy toward Italy was somewhat alarming for those who continued to believe that all accounts could be squared by the simple liquidation of the Tunisian problem. Further, it was made unmistakably clear that territorial questions remained to be resolved. The text of the communiqué was officially brought to Prunas' attention in a letter from Couve de Murville dated December 30. The letter emphasized what had been explained in the broadcast originating from the French radio station in Rome and corrected several statements appearing in the press in the name of the Italian government regarding Franco-Italian relations. The French diplomat noted that two days earlier he had stated his reservations regarding the press conference to be held by Dr. Rossini and further affirmed that, for the conversations to be successful, it was imperative to avoid all publicity.

In replying to this letter, Prunas noted that the need for a Franco-Italian rapprochement was so clearly felt throughout the country that it was deemed wise to give it some public support. He then added that the press statements themselves only expressed a desire for peace and goodwill and, therefore, should be in no way prejudicial. However, De Gasperi immediately suggested to Bonomi that, in the future, all publicity which might be counter-productive be avoided.

Another unfortunate episode occurred shortly thereafter. On January 9, 1945, in the hope of preventing their recurrence, Prunas called Couve de Murville's attention to instances in which Piedmontese partisans who had been forced to cross over into France during the course of operations against the Germans had been disarmed and put into concentration camps. During the winter and spring of 1944 a promising collaboration had developed between the Italian partisans and the French *maquis*, but after the liberation of France the treatment accorded the Italians by local French authorities was often far different. Many partisans were in fact given the alternative of enrolling in the French Foreign Legion, being placed in concentration camps, or being assigned to forced labor units. This information caused considerable shock and if it had become public knowledge could have had serious repercussions on the morale of the patriots. Therefore, it was in the common interest for the local authorities, who were probably acting at their own discretion and ignoring the cordial cooperation that had existed earlier between French and Italian patriots, to be given instructions to aid the Italians who were forced to cross the border and who indicated their desire to continue the struggle against the Germans by helping them, in the common interest, to rearm and re-equip themselves. The wounded and the sick were to be assisted and hospitalized. The expenses incurred for their treatment were to be paid by the Italian government.[52]

On January 18 Couve de Murville consigned to De Gasperi a proposal for an exchange of notes between the two governments, approved by the French Council of Ministers only after a long and acrimonious discussion and, therefore, in his view, not easily subject to amendment. As soon as he received the Italian reply, which he hoped would be affirmative, he would leave for Paris to formalize the exchange of diplomatic delegations based on the British model and to arrange for the opening of three consular offices, in Paris, Marseille, and Toulouse. De Gasperi immediately observed that, if the new accord could not go into effect until after the ratification of the peace treaty, the Tunisian question would remain alive and

[52] It should be recalled here that on December 31, 1944, De Gasperi wrote to Bonomi, to the Minister of War, and to the Chief of the General Staff suggesting that it would not be wise to discourage the attempt being made by a certain Da Re to establish in France, with the help of the Paris government, a large military unit made up of internees and displaced elements of the Fourth Army, although it was an uncertain and incomplete project. Moreover, De Gasperi felt it to be politically opportune, at that stage of development, that Da Re be authorized to report to French military organizations, whose goodwill he was interpreting as follows: (a) there was not nor could there be any objection on Italy's part that Italian soldiers and internees in France be utilized, under given conditions, in Italian military units and under Italian command in the common effort and that, furthermore, this was Italy's goal and major interest; (b) given this premise, it would be necessary, however, that the project be preceded by a detailed and friendly exchange of views between representatives of the French and Italian general staffs. For such purposes, the Italian representatives would be ready to travel, with proper authorization, to any locale which might be named.

In his reply to De Gasperi on January 3, 1945, the Chief of the Italian General Staff, Marshal Messe, saw no difficulty arising from authorizing Da Re to inform the French military authorities of the Italian acceptance in principle of the proposal to organize an Italian military unit in France under Italian command made up of displaced Italian soldiers and internees in France. However, Messe considered it preferable that Da Re, on such a mission, represent the Italian government and not the General Staff as such. In any event, this preliminary contact would in no way compromise the complete freedom of the Italian representatives in any eventual further negotiations between the two general staffs, during the course of which, and only then, would it be possible to determine the seriousness and the feasibility of the proposal. Marshal Messe doubted that the French had the resources to arm, equip, and maintain an Italian military unit composed of tens of thousands of men. Furthermore, it was imperative that careful consideration be given to the enormous difficulties involved in transforming, in a brief time span, such a heterogeneous mass of persons into an army unit without resources sufficient to provide a basic sense of well-being and confidence in the unit's strength and capabilities. In addition, it was necessary that careful thought be given to learning, a priori, the Allies' view of the matter, since they particularly cherished their control over the conduct of the war.

unresolved for a dangerously indefinite period. Couve de Murville assured De Gasperi that, as a matter of fact, as soon as the diplomatic delegations became operative, the work of finding equitable solutions to a number of questions regarding the Italians in both France and Tunisia (workers, military, internees) could be begun. However, De Gasperi postponed his reply until he could examine the notes further. Couve de Murville mentioned that it would be in the best interests of all concerned if the press said little of the proceedings, and, above all, that statements in the press not be based on inaccurate information. Although earlier he had made some reference to a revision of the Fezzan frontier, on this occasion Couve de Murville denied that France had any aspirations to Italian territory.

After nearly six months of exchanges following the liberation of Rome, the negotiation was now entering its final and official phase. While Palazzo Chigi was proceeding with the careful study of the French proposals, two events occurred which influenced the attitude of the Rome government. On January 23 the Political Department of Berne (Switzerland was protecting Italian interests) informed Rome that the French authorities in Tunisia had decided to proceed with the expulsion of Italian citizens arrested and interned there after May 1, 1943; 1,200 decrees of expulsion had been released. The people involved were not to be transferred to Algeria, as had been originally planned, but, for the moment, were to be allowed to go free or to accept internment in concentration camps. If this situation were allowed to continue for any length of time, the resources of the exiles and of their families would be exhausted. Only prompt repatriation could save them from destitution. Moreover, other groups of Italians in Tunisia had indicated their desire to return to Italy.

On January 25 General De Gaulle, during the course of a press conference, spoke at length about Italy. Among other things, he said that it was necessary to look toward the future and that he believed that sooner or later Italy and France would have cordial relations and would cooperate in the interest of humanity, especially in the Mediterranean basin. Temporarily, however, some questions remained to be resolved. He hoped to be able to resolve them with the Bonomi government, in which he had great faith. This government had done its very best in extremely difficult circumstances both internal and external, to bring Italy into the war and to re-establish good relations with those who were, or should be under normal circumstances, Italy's friends. De Gaulle regarded these efforts by the Bonomi government as well-intentioned, and for this reason he hoped to reach a cordial and practical accord with the new Italy as soon as possible. When this had been done, it would be very easy to re-establish normal diplomatic relations.[53] This reassertion of the positive, albeit limited, proposals advanced by De Gaulle and the confirmation of the fact that there should be no illusions regarding the destiny of the Italian community in Tunisia were to prompt the Bonomi government to proceed further toward an accord with Paris.

12

On January 26 Prunas handed De Gasperi a detailed memorial on the proposals presented by Couve de Murville on January 18. This document, while it contained some reservations on matters of detail designed to open the way for reasonable counter-proposals, in general favored the acceptance of the French offers. Prunas insisted that circumstances clearly impelled a

[53] The complete text of the statements by General De Gaulle relative to Italy was transmitted by Couve de Murville to Prunas on January 29, 1945, and read as follows:

Question: Do you envisage a recognition of the Italian government?

Reply: We have good reason to complain about what Italy has done to France. It is a painful chapter in the history of these two Latin peoples, a matter to be truly deplored. But we are looking toward the future and we believe that, sooner or later, France and Italy are destined to meet again in cordial rapport and to cooperate for the good of humanity, particularly in the Mediterranean basin. However, at present, there are some matters to be settled. We hope that we will be able to settle these matters with the Bonomi government, for which we have the highest regard. This government, under extremely difficult conditions both internally and externally, is doing its best to bring Italy into the war in order to place it at the side of those who are or should normally be its friends in good standing. We regard the steps taken by the Bonomi government to be favorable to what we aim to accomplish; that is to say, sooner or later we hope to arrive at a cordial working arrangement with the new Italy. At that time it will be a simple matter to establish normal diplomatic relations with this new Italy.

Question: There is the problem of the Italians in Tunisia.

Reply: The convention signed between France and Italy in 1896 on this subject is abrogated. No such convention now exists, since Italy, in making war against France, destroyed all such conventions. Therefore, the problem no longer exists. We can only hope that the Italian government of its own accord recognizes that this convention no longer exists.

Question: News dispatches announce that Italy has been able to mobilize a fairly large number of military classes against Germany.

Reply: We are pleased, of course, but I must add that we are envious of the Italians, who, it seems, were able to obtain the necessary equipment.

Question: Can you throw some light on this subject?

Reply: I have little light to cast on this matter. Moreover, it is a subject to be approached with care. It is imperative to say nothing against the just pride of those Italians who are taking up arms against the enemy. But, having said that, I can see no cause for comparison between the position of France and the French military force with Italy or the Italian army. I say it again, without seeking to injure the pride of the Italians—of those Italians who are fighting the enemy in the areas he occupies. We know that they are making great efforts and achieving useful results.

cancellation of what the French continued to interpret as an "Italian lien against Tunisia." In other words, it was perfectly logical to expect that the chickens released by the declaration of war in June, 1940, were now coming home to roost. An accounting would be painful, to be sure, but it was useless and prejudicial to seek to avoid it. Moreover, it should also be remembered that France had denounced the conventions of 1896 as early as September, 1918, and from that time forward they had been tacitly renewed only quarterly by the French. Furthermore, it should be recalled that the problem had definitely been compromised by the Fascist government in the Mussolini-Laval accords of January, 1935, which, although they had not been ratified, nevertheless had an unmistakably clear significance. They provided that the convention of 1896 and its various annexes were to remain in effect until March 28, 1945, and that after that date, albeit gradually, steps would be taken toward equality of status and elimination of privileges for the Italians. Any attempt to avoid such a settlement would have meant a hostile and enemy France at this extremely delicate and critical period in Italy's national and international life, at a time when France was obviously moving toward a progressive and presumably rapid recovery of her status as a great power. Surrounded by open or veiled hostility, without friendly support at the international level, with the country literally torn apart, a central authority that was still fragile, and enormous problems of survival to resolve, Prunas concluded that Italy held virtually no trumps to play in any game of resistance to the French demands.

The Secretary-General of Palazzo Chigi went on to note that the Tunisian question had not been created by Fascist territorial claims, but had long been a source of conflict between France and Italy, in which many of Italy's positions were and continued to be based on a firm legal and factual foundation. It was wise to keep clearly in mind exactly what Italy's sacrifice would entail. As a victorious power, France could seek to impose a recognition of the abrogation of the Tunisian conventions in the subsequent peace treaty. Instead, she preferred to achieve the same ends via the stipulation of an agreement indicating consensus, such as in the exchange of letters on the matter. Paris applied pressure on Rome toward this end by insisting that this agreement was the sine qua non to a renewal of diplomatic and consular relations. Such an agreement would have gained for France these advantages: (a) formal Italian recognition of the abrogation of the conventions of 1896; (b) elimination, via the proposed formula,[54] of all legal arguments for the defense of Italian privileges; (c)

---

[54] "Now no written agreement determines the status of the Italians."

the achievement of an unquestioned political-diplomatic success. On the other hand, it was imperative to recognize the status to which the Italians had in fact been reduced in Tunisia. Almost all of the property they held had been confiscated. Professional people, with very few exceptions, were no longer able to carry on their activities (a number of physicians had their clinical, sanitary, and radiological instruments sequestered). Almost all the Italian merchants had been deprived of their licenses. Offices occupied by Italians had been requisitioned on a major scale. Italians of draft age were placed in forced labor battalions. Almost two thousand Italians, largely from the affluent and the professional classes, were interned in two concentration camps located in southern Tunisia and subjected to extremely harsh treatment. A consortium was created to take over the large and small agricultural holdings which the Italians, by one means or another, had been forced to cede. Five hundred other Italians, on a basis entirely unknown to Palazzo Chigi, had been declared "enemies of the state" and were subjected to very drastic treatment, including proscription and confiscation of their possessions.

These policies, and the methods with which they were applied, drove most of the Italians in Tunisia to ruin. By one means or another they lost their livelihoods and their property, as well as that of their fathers, and were transformed into a class of dispossessed. The sale of the small land-holdings of Italians reduced their proprietors to the ranks of day laborers. These were the same colonists who, out of nothing, had created Tunisia's prosperity.

The Italians had to submit because there was no doubt that the cancellation of the Italian lien against Tunisia was the premise for any rapprochement between France and Italy. Consequently, Prunas advised that it was necessary to accept the French proposal for an exchange of letters, for high moral reasons above all else—that is, to atone for Fascist aggression, and to do so without any substantial modification of the French terms. Insofar as the matter of aggression was concerned, it was imperative that any formal statement indicating that the conventions of 1896 had been nullified by the declaration of war be avoided. Any such declaration would have been tantamount to recognizing a very controversial point in international law, thereby creating a very dangerous precedent, not only in relation to the other conventions in effect between France and Italy prior to June 10, 1940, but also in relation to other states. It would have been sufficient to take note of the ordinance issued by the provisional French government on June 22, 1944, and to state that the conventions cited therein no longer governed the Italians in Tunisia. By so doing, the question of whether the convention of 1896 did or did not include the

Mancini protocol of 1884 regarding consular jurisdiction would remain to be determined, since the implication of the proposed French note affirming that currently there was no convention in effect regarding the Italians in Tunisia would also be ignored.[55]

Another concern referred to the clause in the French proposal whereby the new agreement on Tunisia would be signed only after the peace treaties terminated the hostilities. It was not yet known whether peace treaties, in the traditional sense, would be drafted or whether new formulas might be devised. Moreover, the proposal raised the threat of new sacrifices to achieve peace. Meanwhile, it was suggested that the accord considered for Tunisia become effective on a date agreed upon by both parties.

Prunas then proceeded to review the evolution of the negotiation and the structure given to it by Palazzo Chigi. The French had agreed only to a proposal for a new convention on Tunisia based solely on general principles of international law, to come into effect after the conclusion of the peace treaties. On the other hand, they had no intention of giving any assurances in writing that, once the Tunisian question was settled, all other claims against Italy might generally be considered to be resolved. In Prunas' judgment it was unlikely that the French would compromise on the demand that the convention to be negotiated conform only to general principles of international law. Given this state of affairs, he suggested that Italy insist that, once the exchange of letters had been effected, a provisional arrangement be worked out which would protect the Italians during the period when no convention of any kind would be in effect and that the measures presently in effect against the Italians in France and in North Africa be revoked, permitting the people, in the case of Tunisia, to repossess their properties and renew their professional and business activities. This should be done, first, to give the Italians in Tunisia the necessary protection; second, to bow to Italian public opinion on the Tunisian question; and, finally, to avoid the intrusion of dangerous anti-French sentiments into Italian life which would awaken ancient antagonisms and conflicts that should be eliminated.

In the event that it was absolutely impossible to include even the most general assurances in the proposed exchange of letters, it would be necessary for Bonomi to address a personal letter immediately to De Gaulle in

[55] The formula proposed by Prunas was as follows: "The Italian government has taken note of the ordinance issued by the provisional government of the French Republic on June 22, 1944. In recognizing that the written agreements cited in the above-mentioned ordinance now no longer determine the status of the Italians living in Tunisia," etc.

which, while reaffirming the good faith with which the destruction of
Italy's position in Tunisia had been accepted, he would repeat as cer-
tainties the following points: (a) measures damaging to the Italians would
cease; (b) the new convention would be inspired by just criteria of protection and respect for the work of the Italians in Tunisia, and in France
the work of Italians would generally be legally protected; (c) once the
Tunisian question was resolved, Italo-French relations would be considered
definitely clarified and the two countries launched on the road toward the
economic, cultural, and political collaboration which was in their mutual
interest.

This thoughtful, courageous, and realistic position assumed by the
Secretary-General of Palazzo Chigi was well worth considering. In it,
every attempt at rhetoric and demagogy had been rejected. Doubtless it
had cost a man as proud as Prunas pain to use some of these phrases, but
his sense of responsibility and duty prevailed. It would have been much
easier for him to have left the responsibility to the leaders of government
and to have limited himself to a simple exposition of the facts, but he
chose not to barricade himself behind a purely formal statement of position and sought to involve himself directly in a historical document.

His thesis was promptly accepted by De Gasperi and approved by the
Bonomi cabinet. De Gasperi received Couve de Murville on the afternoon
of January 31. He opened the conversation by warmly proclaiming friendship for and loyalty to France and noted that the day before he had made
it clear that he would exert every effort to improve and stabilize Italian
relations with France; he added that he fully appreciated the value of
De Gaulle's statements to the press. Couve's reaction was one of cautious
attention. Then De Gasperi turned to the proposed modification of the
French text: the nullification of the conventions of 1896 as a result of the
declaration of war and the framework within which a new convention
could be drafted. Couve objected to the first modification because it was
an established norm in international relations. De Gasperi insisted, but
Couve replied that it would be poorly received in Paris, and added that he
would not care to present the proposed modification, fearing that it would
lead to a complete rupture. De Gasperi concluded his argument by reiterating that it was a matter of juridical scruple and a protective measure to
prevent damage by third parties. He then sought to demonstrate the substantial similarity between the two suggested formulas. Couve replied that
the French formula was to be regarded as definitive. De Gasperi replied
that the Italian amendment was a proposal but not a condition.

As for the second modification, the debate was long and bitter. Couve,
without explicitly referring to the armistice condition, insisted that the

French formula reflected the legal situation. De Gasperi replied by asking why it was necessary to bind themselves to decisions made by third parties: Italy was suggesting only that once the accord was reached it should also be put into effect. He explained that there was a psychological reason for this suggestion as well; that is, it would give the Italians who had been left without protection at least the hope that it would be possible to replace the old statute with a new one quickly, even though the new one would be based simply on general principles of international law. De Gasperi repeatedly insisted on this point. Couve resisted but then gradually gave ground (the Italian Foreign Minister cited the opinion of Count Sforza, whose pro-French articles could hardly be questioned by the French) and finally stated that the condition seemed to him to be acceptable on condition that the last phrase (appeal to French fairness) be omitted. He recognized that the Italians should be required to demonstrate regret for their role in the war, but he urged them to do so fully. After repeated explanations, De Gasperi dropped the matter, saying that the same thought was expressed in Bonomi's letter. This discussion led to another. Couve considered it necessary that the list of the exceptional measures taken against the Italians in Tunisia be omitted, and it was finally agreed that the list would be replaced by a general statement. It was agreed that the next day De Gasperi would formalize the results of the conversation and would transmit them to Couve de Murville with the understanding that the Italian government was disposed to accept the French text apart from its time limit. Couve expressed his agreement and his willingness to communicate these results to Paris.

On the whole, the bitter debate produced positive results.[56] It is true that De Gasperi did not succeed in getting Couve to accept the first of his two amendments, but its value was largely theoretical. As a matter of fact, only at the moment of the conclusion of the peace treaties would it be known which of the prewar conventions the former enemy states wished to continue in effect, and the mere fact that nothing was said in the accord on Tunisia of the abrogation of the conventions because of the declaration of war would not prevent them from nullifying any number of them. Insofar as the Mancini protocol of 1884 was concerned, who could really believe that it was possible to resurrect consular jurisdiction in Tunisia? It was also noteworthy that, notwithstanding Prunas' suggestions,

[56] In a marginal note to the summary account of the conversation, De Gasperi observed that Couve was courteous and often expressed his comprehension of the difficulty of the situation, but was cold and inflexible. De Gasperi spoke to him of the exiled and of the interned. He replied that they were Fascists. However, he agreed that if the accord were not concluded, their lot would be even worse.

the Bonomi cabinet immediately fell back on the idea of a personal letter from the Prime Minister to De Gasperi. This was a realistic act.[57]

13

On February 1 Prunas delivered to Couve de Murville the official Italian reply previously announced by De Gasperi. In this letter the reasons which had induced the Bonomi government to suggest the amendments to the text of the exchange of notes proposed by the Quai d'Orsay were reiterated. De Gasperi then hastened to announce that, after the conversation of the previous day and a new consultation with Bonomi and with the ministers directly concerned, in order to give further proof of its goodwill and loyalty, the Italian government, responding to the urgent requests made by Couve, was disposed to proceed without further delay to sign the texts proposed by the French; that is, it would not insist further on the modifications and addenda examined the previous day, with the exception, as had been agreed, of fixing by mutual accord the date when the new agreement would go into effect. However, De Gasperi asked that in informing his government of the Italian decision Couve also bring Paris up to date, even if only for informative purposes, on the nature and substance of his proposal of the previous day, and particularly on the matter of a rapid and progressive normalization of the situation for the Italians in the Regency. De Gasperi again made it clear that this proposal was designed exclusively to facilitate his task, not an easy one in the face of Italian public opinion, and, at the same time, to emphasize in a very special way the need to avoid every possible reflection of discontent and resentment that could further disturb the relations between the two countries, which this decision sought to launch on the road toward marked improvement.

In presenting De Gasperi's letter to Couve, Prunas once again made it clear that the Italian gesture in renouncing the conventions of 1896 should be interpreted by the French as an act of absolute loyalty, made with

[57] On the same day Massigli (then Ambassador to London) paid a return visit to the Italian Embassy and conferred with Carandini for over an hour. In contrast to the first visit to his Italian colleague, during this extremely cordial conversation, Massigli stressed the necessity of re-establishing reciprocal trust and affirmed that, insofar as the French were concerned, no serious resentment existed. He revealed complete comprehension of the Italian problems. He also indicated his interest in reopening diplomatic relations and asked Carandini if he knew of any reason for this inexplicable delay. With nothing precise to say, the Italian diplomat replied in equally expansive and general terms and noted that it was the common view in Italy that discussions of differences in viewpoint on any problem with the French should be subordinated to the matter of re-establishing the traditional friendship.

complete awareness of the extent of the sacrifices it involved, but without reservations or hesitations. He explained that the proposed modifications were inspired exclusively by a desire to facilitate the government's task and to place the Italian community in Tunisia immediately in a condition which would tend to strengthen Italo-French relations rather than weakening them.

Couve de Murville replied that he fully appreciated the Italian situation and the gesture of the Bonomi government. De Gasperi's statements on the previous day, based on complete loyalty, had fully informed him on the matter. He confirmed his belief that a new phase in Franco-Italian relations was about to begin which would undoubtedly evolve into a friendship which was the aim and the interest of both parties. He would immediately telegraph the Italian decision to Paris along with the motivations behind it, which had been described for him orally and in writing by De Gasperi.

Couve would be leaving for Paris within a week to learn the terms for the exchange of representatives and for the opening of the consulates, which, at first, would be limited to three, with that number subject to immediate increase. Prunas added that if, instead of the exchange of letters, a joint communiqué summarizing the accord reached were released, the Italian government would have no objections. The French diplomat replied that he would discuss the matter in Paris and would convey the French reply upon his return. During this colloquy Couve appeared not only satisfied by the accord but fully aware of its significance and of the implications given it by the Italians.

On February 6 Prunas apprised the American and British ambassadors of the status of the conversations with the French and commented on the significance of the exchange of letters on Tunisia and the resulting renewal of diplomatic and consular relations between Paris and Rome. Both Sir Noel Charles and Kirk indicated complete comprehension.

On February 9 Couve de Murville informed De Gasperi that his government was in accord on the exchange of letters, including the modification proposed by Italy relative to the effective date of the new convention. He added that the frank and clear words written him by De Gasperi had created an excellent impression in Paris. He planned to leave immediately for the French capital to effect the exchange of letters and of diplomatic and consular representatives. He would suggest to the Quai d'Orsay, which had asked that this last exchange be confirmed by another letter containing the various declarations made by Italy concerning France, that it be a simple one modeled on that sent to Palazzo Chigi earlier by Sir

Noel Charles.[58] Moreover, he suggested that, instead of letters, a joint communiqué should be published at an appropriate time.

With this prompt French acquiescence, the essentials of the negotiation between Paris and Rome were concluded. On February 10 Prime Minister Bonomi provided Dr. Russo, who was about to leave for Paris, with an impressive message for the Italians living in France. The same day Bonomi addressed his personal letter to De Gaulle.

In his opening words Bonomi noted that since the accord on Tunisia had been reached and the renewal of diplomatic and consular relations was imminent, it was an appropriate time for him to renew his contact with De Gaulle, which he had looked forward to with great anticipation for some time. It was with profound conviction that both he and his government had made a decision directly affecting tens of thousands of Italians who for generations had collaborated in creating the prosperity of Tunisia and who would honestly and loyally continue to collaborate toward this end in the future. In accepting without reservations the end of the conventions of 1896, which for half a century had governed the Italian community in Tunisia, the Bonomi government clearly intended and desired, as indicated in its previous declarations, to liquidate a recent past which the Italian people sincerely deplored, to clear the ground of the only obstacle to good relations between the two countries, to pave the way for that faithful collaboration which was a fundamental prerequisite for Italy's rebirth and mutual interest, and generally to create a new situation between France and Italy. Bonomi wrote that he placed great faith in those efforts undertaken to normalize relations and to eliminate the war measures, and that he was confident that De Gaulle would take those steps which he would consider necessary, in the spirit of French fairness and French tradition, with regard to Italian citizens and interests both in metropolitan France and throughout the empire, which would hasten the realization of these goals. Bonomi recalled with pleasure the words addressed to him indirectly by De Gaulle the previous July in Naples immediately after the liberation of Rome at a time when he, under extremely difficult conditions, as De Gaulle well knew, assumed the reins of government. Those fine and humane words regarding Latin solidarity and hope would provide the solid foundation, once the differ-

[58] The letter in question was dated October 10 and announced the decision of the London government to re-establish relations on an unconventional basis, in view of the unusual circumstances. The Rome government was invited to propose the name of its representative to London. Bonomi replied on October 12, and on October 13 Visconti Venosta listed the four basic points on which the exchange of representatives between the two countries could take place. On October 25 the British Ambassador in Rome issued a communiqué on the accord that had been reached.

ences over the Tunisian question were eliminated, for the rebirth of an understanding between the two peoples. Through successive economic, emigration, cultural, and security agreements, this understanding should and must become ever closer and more cordial. The single serious conflict had been swept away, and, on the eve of the resumption of relations, Bonomi desired to reaffirm now, as he had earlier, his complete agreement and full cooperation with De Gaulle's position. He expressed his sincere hope that the Italian representative in Paris and the French representative in Rome would be able to work with patience and determination toward that goal. In closing, Bonomi begged De Gaulle to accept his sincerest compliments for his admirable work in governing France and bringing her again to that great power status so justly due her, which every Italian viewed without suspicion or concern.

On February 23 De Gaulle replied to this impressive letter, which contained the statements that had been seen earlier in Rome as first steps toward a formal accord.[59] The General declared that he was touched by the letter that he had received at the conclusion of the conversations regarding the status of Italian citizens in Tunisia and the imminent renewal of direct relations between the two countries. The French government appreciated the spirit with which the Italian government and Prime Minister Bonomi had accepted without reservations the abrogation of the conventions of 1896. This was a good omen for future relations between the two countries. In an atmosphere of trust it would now be possible to examine those problems raised by proximity and the possibilities offered by the common spirit and civilization of the two countries. The settlement of the Tunisian issue was a first step. In time, mutual goodwill should make it possible to overcome other problems, since De Gaulle believed, then as now, that France and Italy were destined to find themselves again in cordial rapport and fully cooperating for the welfare of Europe and the

[59] Four days earlier Bidault replied to the message sent to him by De Gasperi when the latter assumed the reins of the Ministry for Foreign Affairs on November 15, 1944. In that telegram the head of the Quai d'Orsay noted that he had only just received the letter from the Italian Foreign Minister. He apologized for the delay, which did not represent his sentiments, and he shared De Gasperi's faith in the future of Italo-French relations, a faith shared by the French people, who hoped that the disharmony between the two countries and the painful memories produced by the regime which the Italians were in the process of eliminating would be forgotten. This reciprocal faith was, moreover, strengthened by the progress made, after De Gasperi's message, toward understanding and rapprochement. No one was more pleased than he, said Bidault, satisfied as he was that the spiritual agreement mentioned by De Gasperi could do no less than support the efforts of the two governments to arrive at a reconciliation designed to serve at the same time the interests of the two countries and the high principles which motivated both peoples.

world. He observed with approval the work undertaken by Bonomi under the most difficult conditions for the reconstruction of Italy. Bonomi was to know that De Gaulle wished him every success.

With this promising exchange of letters between the two heads of state the long and difficult negotiations which led to the liquidation of the Tunisian question and to the renewal of Franco-Italian diplomatic relations during the course of World War II came to an end.

The result was the following letter of February 28 from De Gasperi to Couve de Murville:

Will you be kind enough to bring the following communication to the attention of the French government:

"The provisional government of the French Republic has expressly stated, in its ordinance of June 22, 1944, that the three conventions of September 28, 1896, relative to the jurisdictional rights of the Italians living in Tunisia have been nullified by the Italian declaration of war against France on June 10, 1940.

The Italian government, like the French government, realizing that these conventions have in effect ceased to exist, recognizes that no convention of any kind now governs the Italians residing in the Regency. The Italian government also hopes that the government of France will be disposed to negotiate a regulatory convention based on the general principles of international law for the purpose of defining the conditions of residence and work of the Italians in Tunisia."

Couve began his reply by quoting verbatim the above communication. He then went on:

At the request of my government I have the honor of noting the receipt of this communication. The French government has taken note of the desire expressed by the Italian government and is disposed to proceed, together with the competent Italian authorities, with preliminary exchanges of views for the purpose of defining, on the basis of the general principles of international law, the conditions of residence and work of the Italians residing in Tunisia. The resulting accord will be signed by the two governments on a date to be agreed upon by them.

Couve de Murville also transmitted the following communication to De Gasperi:

I have the honor of calling your attention to the following communication which my government has instructed me to transmit to the Italian government:

"The provisional government of the French Republic has decided to reestablish direct relations with the Italian government. To this end it has named M. Couve de Murville its delegate to the Consultative Committee for Italian Affairs, as its representative to the Italian government with the rank of ambassador.

The provisional government of the French Republic is disposed to receive a representative of the Italian government under the same conditions.

It is also in agreement with the plan to send Italian consular officers to Paris, Toulouse, and Marseille, whose competencies will be determined later."

The Italian Foreign Minister replied:

I have the honor of noting the receipt of your note of this date, in which Your Excellency informs me that the provisional government of the French Republic has decided to re-establish direct relations with the Italian government and, for this purpose, has designated Your Excellency as its representative, with the rank of ambassador.

You add that the provisional government of the French Republic is disposed to receive, under the same conditions, a representative of the Italian government and agrees to the dispatch of Italian consular officers to Paris, Marseille, and Toulouse.

The Royal Government is extremely pleased by the re-establishment of direct relations between the two countries and hopes that it will produce fruitful results in the interest of both countries as well as that of Europe.

At the same time De Gasperi sent the following personal note to Couve de Murville:

I am particularly pleased to add this brief postscript to the official letter I sent to you today, intended to express our pleasure in learning of your nomination as representative of France to the Royal Government. It is a nomination which we all receive with great satisfaction because there is no one better qualified to fulfill the requirements of this post, which demands a high level of human understanding and political intelligence.

Therefore, I congratulate you most warmly, in the certainty that I can count on your cordial and influential friendship in the effort to arrive at a goal which is very dear to both of us.

The communiqué released by the two governments to the press on March 2, 1945, read as follows:

The Italian and French governments have agreed to re-establish direct relations, in addition to sending Italian consular officers to Paris, Toulouse, and Marseille. Couve de Murville has been designated as French representative to the Italian government, with the rank of ambassador. The Italian government will nominate its representative with the same rank. The Italian and French governments have also exchanged letters, in which the Italian government recognizes the nullification of the conventions of 1896 governing the Italians in Tunisia. The French government is prepared to negotiate a new regulatory convention based on the general principles of international law.

14

In conclusion, some observations may be appropriate. The Franco-Italian negotiations passed through four distinct phases. The first of these began with the Prunas-Massigli meeting of December 6, 1943, and terminated with the reorganization of the Badoglio government on April 22, 1944. The second started on this date and ended with the liberation of Rome. The third spanned the period between the De Gaulle-Prunas meeting in Naples on July 1, 1944, and the presentation of the first official proposals by the French government on January 18, 1945. The actual negotiations represented the fourth phase.

During the first phase, Algerian prejudice against Victor Emmanuel and Badoglio dominated the situation, but, at the same time, neither in Brindisi nor in Salerno was there a clear idea of the real dimensions of the problem. It is true that the Badoglio government made its first overtures to the French Committee of National Liberation after the armistice, but it is equally true that these overtures were not followed up with gestures and formal decisions which would have constituted the basis of a rapprochement between the two countries. At this point it may be objected that, even if Badoglio had immediately and publicly condemned the 1940 aggression, denounced the Fascist territorial claims, and denounced the Armistice of Villa Incisa, these acts still would not have been enough to precipitate a dialogue with Algiers.

This objection is valid, particularly when it is recalled that De Gaulle, until he returned to Paris, abstained from concluding any formal political agreement. He did not do so with the Soviet Union, with whom he had earlier decided he would seek an accord, and there was even greater reason for him not to do so with Italy, which at that time, could not give him support of any kind, not even in the diplomatic area. However, this does not justify the fact that Badoglio, who was unaware that De Gaulle disliked him, refrained from making the necessary preliminary gestures. The reasons for his attitude were essentially three: Italy was not prepared to face the fundamental question; there was uncertainty as to the real role the French National Committee of Liberation in Algiers would play in metropolitan France once the territory had been liberated by the Allies; and Prunas was convinced that it would be preferable to let France take the real initiative for a reconciliation between the two countries in order to ensure its permanency. However, it should also be pointed out that in this first fruitless Italo-French contact Massigli immediately indicated that the Tunisian question was the key issue to be resolved on a preliminary basis. The reply he received at that time revealed the persistence of serious misconceptions in Italian government circles.

During the second phase conspicuous progress was made by the Badoglio government, and a number of serious obstacles were cleared away by a series of public declarations. Aside from the tardiness of the denunciation of the aggression of 1940 and of the Fascist claims, the method chosen to denounce the Armistice of Villa Incisa was unwise. Based on the determination to prevent the ceremony which the French intended to observe immediately after their entrance into Rome (and which, in any case, they did observe), the denunciation failed to become linked to the armistice of 1943. This silence was to work in favor of the French thesis that there was no instrument which could govern the cessation of hostilities between the two countries. A situation was created the price of which was paid by the Italians living in France and by the partisans obliged by military operations to cross over into French territory. This situation also offered the Algiers Committee a formal basis for denouncing the Tunisian conventions of 1896. In addition, De Gaulle refused to meet with either Badoglio or with the Crown Prince.

The third phase opened with the first statement by the Bonomi government and the De Gaulle-Prunas meeting. For the Italians, it was a time of great hopes. Some were based on words spoken by the French leader in a moment of euphoria; others, equally excessive, included the possibility of negotiating a new convention for the Italians in Tunisia which would not be based simply on the general principles of international law. In Rome it was sincerely believed not only that accounts with France could be settled definitely by the simple substitution of another convention (a special one at that) for that of 1896, but that it would also be possible to conclude a political entente immediately with the Quai d'Orsay.

Instead it was in this very period that the French position on the Tunisian question became clear and rigid, while the effect of the liberation of the metropolitan territory complicated the psychological situation by exaggerating the values of the resistance, by initiating the participation in the government of those elements which had suffered most as a consequence of Fascist aggression, and by favoring the formulation of territorial claims on the frontier between the two countries.

One might ask whether the Bonomi government might not have been able to effect an understanding with the Algiers Committee on the bases desired. With the Paris provisional government this was no longer possible. A number of hypotheses may be advanced as to the meaning of De Gaulle's words in Naples on July 1, 1944, and they have been, but once the French tasted the sweetness of their recaptured sovereignty and the situation in the peninsula remained static, the political basis of the problem had changed. Rome was slow in fully realizing this, however, and the initial French proposals aroused negative reactions.

During the fourth phase the work of clarification was slowly accomplished. This slowness is comprehensible and should be respected for the sense of responsibility it inspired among the Italian leaders. The idea of an immediate entente with Paris had to be abandoned. All hope of being able to win French agreement to an understanding that, with the liquidation of the Tunisian question, all claims against Italy would be satisfied was lost. At the same time, the first symptoms of French territorial claims were emerging in clearer form, and the idea of a new regulatory convention for the Italians in Tunisia based on the special characteristics of the Italian community had to be abandoned. The resistance of Palazzo Chigi was tenacious but not unduly obstinate because of Prunas' realism and the wisdom of De Gasperi, Bonomi, and the members of his cabinet. An attempt was made not only to assume, on behalf of the nation, what amounts to historic responsibility, but also to anticipate the work of a future peace conference by seeking to resolve one of the problems created by the war. The sense of duty and the determination to pave the way for the reconstruction of Franco-Italian friendship prevailed over demagogy and the fear of unpopularity.

As for the French, they decided to choose an approach which, although less generous than that of almost complete forgiveness implied by De Gaulle, was not excessively harsh. Certain positions taken by Paris might appear to be rigid, but they were not unjust; moreover, given the state of public opinion then prevailing beyond the Alps, they were responsible and not demagogic.

The liquidation of the Tunisian question and the renewal of diplomatic relations between Rome and Paris in February, 1945, did not, as was hoped by the Bonomi cabinet, settle all of the war accounts. Even more difficult negotiations of a territorial, military, economic, and cultural nature were to follow. That was another painful chapter, but there is no doubt that the decisions taken in February, 1945, were those that made possible, within the span of a very few years, the tripartite declaration on Trieste of 1948, the customs union accord, the entrance of Italy into the Atlantic Pact, and the Council of Europe. All of these accomplishments were sponsored by France. At the end of this road exists the European Economic Community, along with a solidly established friendship between France and Italy.

VI.

ITALIAN SOUNDINGS TO ABANDON THE CONFLICT PRIOR TO MUSSOLINI'S FALL

Summary: 1. Premise. 2. Soundings requested by the Fascist government. The first soundings authorized by Ciano in Lisbon immediately after the Anglo-American landings in North Africa. Eden's totally negative official reaction. The Fransoni-Pangal contact never entirely interrupted. 3. The second sounding authorized by the Fascist government. Bastianini, after meeting Cardinal Maglione, succeeds in wresting authorization from Mussolini on July 18 to sound out the English on disassociating Italy from Germany. The instructions given to Fransoni and Fummi. The completely negative reply to the request to save Mussolini given Fransoni in Lisbon by the British, which reached Rome only after the fall of Fascism. 4. Approaches made without the knowledge of the Fascist government. Negotiations undertaken in Geneva by Consul Marieni in December, 1942, upon instructions from the Duke of Aosta, which dragged on until July 25, 1943. The end of the negotiations. 5. The Lisbon negotiation undertaken at the personal initiative of the Princess of Piedmont. 6. Badoglio's soundings in Geneva in January, 1943, and the decision of the British government to ignore them. 7. Conclusion.

1

The publication of the American diplomatic documents relating to Italian events in 1943[1] has provided new and more precise information on Italian soundings, before the fall of Mussolini, to ascertain the conditions under which it would have been possible for Italy to withdraw from World War II. Prior to this important publication only fragmentary materials on several of these probes were available from the Italian side, particularly in Badoglio's[2] and Bastianini's memoirs.[3] From Allied sources it was possible to obtain only general data, as in a note in the volume of the official British history of World War II written by Professor Woodward.[4]

---

* This article first appeared as "Sondaggi Italiani per uscire dal conflitto prima della caduta di Mussolini," *Clio* (April, 1965).

[1] *Foreign Relations, 1943,* II.

[2] Badoglio, *L'Italia nella seconda guerra mondiale.*

[3] Giuseppe Bastianini, *Uomini, cose, fatti. Memorie di un ambasciatore* (Milan: Vitagliano, 1959).

[4] "Italian approaches had been made to the British Government in December 1942. The Foreign Office was willing to listen to them, but did not think any successful revolt against fascist control likely until the military situation had become more unfavourable to the Italians. Mr. Eden informed the United States and Soviet Governments of these approaches." Woodward, *British Foreign Policy in the Second World War,* p. 225, n. 1.

Greater light needs to be cast on this entire question, and in all likelihood much more time will pass before it will be possible to complete an exhaustive inquiry into the attempts to find and establish top-secret contacts exclusively with British representatives and not with those of the United States. The reason for this may have been sheer coincidence, although perhaps the explanation is that Rome, before the armistice, did not understand that the key to the politico-military situation lay in Washington and not in London and that it was the United States and not Great Britain which had some understanding of the Italian case. These attempts must be divided into two major categories: those undertaken in the name of the Fascist government and those made without any knowledge of that government.

These brief notes will begin with the revelations contained in the volume of American documents.[5] The new sources of information which were courteously made available to me have permitted a partial reconstruction of these soundings by filling certain gaps and by correcting a number of inaccuracies emerging from the documents. The conclusions drawn may be of value because they help to explain why the *coup d'état* of July 25, 1943, was solely an internal affair with no connection with the British and Americans. On the other hand, they also highlight the rigidity of the British position toward Italy with regard to both Fascists and anti-Fascists. Therefore, if Rome did not understand either before or after July 25, that the harsh formula of unconditional surrender was applicable to everyone, it does not follow that evidence of this fact had not promptly reached the Italian capital. In the event that this inquiry stimulates other investigations or makes new sources available,[6] it will have been further justified.

[5] For the new data provided by this material, see Mario Toscano, "Nuove rivelazioni sugli armistizi del 1943 fra le Nazioni Unite e l'Italia," *Nuova Antologia* (September–October, 1964); and "Altre rivelazioni sull'Armistizio di Malta e sulla dichiarazione di cobelligeranza italiana," *Nuova Antologia*, November–December, 1964.

[6] It must be made clear that if my research has revealed that neither the Archives of the Foreign Office in London nor those of the Department of State in Washington contain diplomatic documents of major significance on this problem other than those found in the above-mentioned *Foreign Relations* volume, the possibility remains that important material may exist elsewhere. The fact that the bulk of the material concerning Italian soundings to abandon the conflict prior to the fall of Mussolini is not to be found at the Foreign Office leads to the supposition that this material was initially deposited in the archives of the British Prime Minister's office and in those of the Intelligence Service, access to which is much more difficult than to the archives of the Foreign Office, although the archives of the Intelligence Service have since eliminated many of their holdings. As for the apparent lacunae in the archives of the Department of State, the most reasonable hypothesis is a very simple one: in all probability London did not communicate to Washington all of its contacts with Italian emissaries prior to July 25, maintaining silence on those which

2

The first more or less official approaches made to the British in the name of the Fascist government came toward the end of November, 1942. Palazzo Chigi became receptive to the idea of contacting the British government indirectly immediately after the Allied landings in North Africa but before the Casablanca Conference, at which Churchill and Roosevelt reached an agreement on the famous "unconditional surrender" formula.

In the opening paragraph of a letter from the British Foreign Minister, Eden, to his American counterpart, Cordell Hull, dated December 18, 1942, the following words appear:

I feel that the United States Government should know that we have received in recent weeks certain "peace feelers" from Italians outside of Italy. They are as follows:
(1) The Italian Legation at Lisbon have used a Rumanian intermediary to show His Majesty's Embassy and the Polish Embassy at Lisbon their interest in a separate peace.
We have decided not to pursue this "feeler," since the Italians in Lisbon are servants of the present regime, and to maintain contact with them could only serve to throw suspicion on our declarations that we are out to destroy Fascism.[7]

After reading this excerpt I approached Ambassador Fransoni, at that time the Italian Minister to Lisbon, directly. He was an honest official and far from being the "servant of the regime" claimed by Eden. From him I learned other details regarding the episode. These details complete and modify to a considerable degree the British version. The events apparently developed as follows.

Fransoni was in Rome at the time of the Allied landings in North Africa, landings which he had repeatedly stressed in his dispatches were imminent, based on information which had reached him from Freetown. Rome failed to devote the necessary attention to these reports, which are contained in the telegrams and reports of the Minister in Lisbon and are preserved in the Historical Archives of the Italian Foreign Ministry. As Ciano noted in his diary,[8] the Italian Foreign Minister received him at

---

seemed to be the least promising. However, the somewhat singular fact remains that the Secretary of State, Cordell Hull, who on December 23, 1942, approved Mr. Eden's suggestion that the negotiations initiated in Geneva by the Duke of Aosta be pursued further (*Foreign Relations, 1943*, II, p. 317), failed to request further information on these negotiations, which continued until Mussolini's fall.

[7] *Foreign Relations, 1943*, II, p. 315.
[8] Hugh Gibson, ed., *The Ciano Diaries (1939–1943)* (New York: Doubleday, 1945), p. 537.

Palazzo Chigi on November 1, that is, one week before the landings. During the course of the conversation with Ciano, Fransoni reported British plans to strike at Italy's metropolitan territory in the near future, at a time when the ratio of Allied.to Italian forces had reached ten to one. This information came from the British Legation, whose Chief of Mission was Sir Ronald Campbell. He had served as Counsellor in Paris while Fransoni was serving in the same capacity in the Italian Embassy in the French capital, and a friendly rapport had developed between the two. The information had been reported to Fransoni—who, after the outbreak of war, had had no direct, personal contact with Campbell—by a mutual friend, a Rumanian national, Jon Pangal, one-time intimate of Take Jonescu, Deputy Undersecretary for Foreign Affairs, friend of Italy, and Rumanian Minister to Lisbon. Jonescu later fell from grace after the abdication of King Carol, whom he helped escape from Spain to Portugal.[9]

As soon as he learned of the landing in North Africa, Fransoni hastened to his post by car through Italy and France and by plane from Spain to Lisbon. There he gathered a great deal more important but discouraging information and returned to Rome shortly afterwards to report in person to Ciano. There is no mention of this second meeting in Ciano's diary, probably for good reason. In fact, it was during the course of this conversation that Fransoni, after again referring to the British plans, asked Ciano whether any hope remained for an Axis military victory. Receiving a negative reply, he then asked for authorization to sound out the British for the purpose of learning what London's intentions would be in the event that Italy asked for a separate peace. Undoubtedly, given the upheaval in the military situation, time was running out, but this was the last moment in which a move of this nature might bear fruit. Ciano gave his authorization that such soundings be made, but it was clear that this was hardly based on careful political preparation; for that matter, he did not even have Mussolini's tacit consent for such an undertaking.

Upon returning to Lisbon, Fransoni resorted to Pangal's good offices but was unable to arrange serious soundings. Contrary to Eden's above-noted letter to Cordell Hull and the American Secretary of State's concurrence, dated December 23, in the decision to ignore the Italian overtures made

[9] In 1948 Pangal was deprived of his Rumanian citizenship by the Communist regime in Bucharest. In his memoirs, Renato Bova Scoppa (*Colloqui con due dittatori* [Rome: Ruffolo, 1949], p. 35) recalls having learned from Pangal as early as January 9, 1941, of the first references to British plans for a landing in North Africa, which he transmitted to Rome. Moreover, it should be recalled that Ronald Campbell had returned to France as British Ambassador in 1940 and in this guise was present at the conversations between Churchill and Reynaud which preceded the decision of the Bordeaux government to ask the Germans for an armistice.

in Lisbon,[10] Ambassador Fransoni stated to me that the Italo-Rumanian-British contact arranged by him was never entirely interrupted or broken and that it was because of this fact that Bastianini turned to Fransoni in an attempt to establish a link to Campbell in July, 1943. By this time Fransoni had returned to Rome permanently and had been replaced in Lisbon by Renato Prunas.

While this undertaking by Fransoni is not correctly recalled in the otherwise excellent volume by Deakin[11] and is noted only in passing by Woodward,[12] it should be pointed out that a summary account of the affair does exist in a volume which, while difficult to evaluate, contains a series of remarkably accurate accounts of important episodes.[13] However, there was no connection between the overture made by the Italian Minister to Lisbon and the action taken in the Portuguese capital in the name of the Princess of Piedmont, a fact which was not entirely clear to me until I had the opportunity to speak to the protagonists in the two episodes.

In any event, Fransoni's soundings, taken at a very difficult moment but when such efforts still might have been productive—that is to say, prior to the Casablanca Conference and before Italy proper had been invaded by German divisions—was not supported by sufficient political strength. Because it was the result of an evaluation of a political and military situation which had not yet reached its nadir, Ciano did not feel that he should do more than tacitly consent to a simple sounding. At that moment, much

---

[10] *Foreign Relations, 1943*, II, p. 317.

[11] F. W. Deakin, *The Brutal Friendship. Mussolini, Hitler and the Fall of Italian Fascism* (London: Weidenfeld and Nicolson, 1962), p. 395. Deakin writes: "There had been inconclusive contacts with British agents in Lisbon at the end of 1942, which had been severed on Ciano's instructions." In reality, as has been demonstrated, the undertaking had been approved by Ciano, and in any case, according to Eden's version, it was interrupted by the Foreign Office in agreement with the State Department. Fransoni maintains, instead, that the contact was never entirely broken off. No reference to this event is to be found in either the volume by Maxime Mourin (*Les tentatives de paix dans la seconde guerre mondiale* [Paris: Payot, 1949]) or in the third volume of Eden's memoirs (Anthony Eden, *The Reckoning* [London: Cassell, 1965]).

[12] *British Foreign Policy in the Second World War*, p. 225, n. 1.

[13] I was only able to read the Spanish translation of this work (Condesa de Listowell, *Guerra segreta* [Barcelona: Editorial Ahr, 1953], pp. 162–93). The title of the English edition is *Crusader in the Secret War*. In addition, the volume contains numerous other references to the rapport existing between Pangal and the British Intelligence Services (pp. 97, 131) and on the contacts with the Italian Legation prior to the Allied landing in North Africa (pp. 151–61). It is affirmed that Fransoni returned from Rome for the first time on November 18, 1942 (p. 161) and that after his second trip, Ciano's instructions were mentioned on December 14 (p. 162). It was confirmed that the contacts through Pangal were never broken off (pp. 164–81).

more was required. To break down British resistance in London, a concrete request for a separate peace was needed. Moreover, in this case, the
choice of making contact with the English rather than with the Americans
was imposed by Pangal's connections and was not the result of a specific
decision. In addition, it should be emphasized that when in July, 1943,
Fransoni was requested to draft a written summary of the sounding he
made in Lisbon,[14] this request did not mean that Ciano's initial tacit authorization and consent had received confirmation elsewhere. According to
Bastianini's version,[15] the steps taken by Pangal the year before were presented as having been requested by the British. This was certainly not
the case: formally at least, London broke off the contact without seeking
to develop it further. Finally, it should be emphasized that, if one accepts
the version advanced by Victor Emmanuel III in his letter of June 1, 1944,
to the Duke of Acquarone, in which he claimed to have "definitely decided
to bring the Fascist regime to an end and to dismiss Mussolini as head of
state" as early as January, 1943,[16] then the soundings taken by Fransoni in
Lisbon occurred near the end of the period in which the Fascist government still enjoyed the support of the Crown. The extent of this support is
shown by Victor Emmanuel's rejection, a short time earlier, of the possibility of utilizing the encouragement offered by Sir Samuel Hoare through
the Vatican. This sounding was brought to the attention of the King by
the Princess of Piedmont and tended to establish the bases for negotiating
Italy's abandonment of the conflict.

3

Information is much more plentiful regarding what was apparently the
Fascist government's second and last attempt to contact the British government on the eve of Mussolini's fall. This undertaking was formulated
on July 18 and supported by the then Undersecretary for Foreign Affairs,
Bastianini, who recalls the event in his memoirs as follows:

The following morning I went to Mussolini and told him that the time had
come for us to take the initiative because we could no longer delude ourselves
regarding the enemy's intentions and we could not bank on support from our

14 As might well be imagined, there is no trace of this highly confidential summary—compiled only in July, 1943, at Bastianini's instructions, since Ciano had
ordered that it should be reported only orally—in the archives of the Foreign Ministry. However, Fransoni told me that the drafting of this document was an extremely difficult affair and that he had to rewrite it because it was determined that
greater emphasis should be placed on the fact that a precedent existed, along with
the possibility of arranging a contact which would never be broken off.
15 Bastianini, Uomini, cose, fatti, p. 118.
16 Gianfranco Bianchi, 25 luglio: crollo d'un regime (Milan: Mursia, 1963), pp.
285–86.

ally adequate to our enormous needs. I told him that since we were reduced to this condition, that is, that we were now a handicap to the Germans, it would be in the latter's interest for us to disassociate ourselves from them. We cannot wait for Hitler to tell us so *apertis verbis*, nor could he, on the other hand, condemn us for doing so. Bismarck did so in 1866 as a victor, concluding an armistice with the Austrians at the very moment that Garibaldi, from Bezzecca, was advancing on Trent and Cadorna and was marching on Trieste from the Isonzo. That move by Bismarck cost us six hundred thousand dead in the 1915–18 war. Nations have their sacred rights, which cannot be suspended for any reasons. I was in a position to assure [Mussolini] that, on the other side of the Tiber, there was a willingness to come to our aid, and I supposed that such a step by us would not be rejected a priori by the enemy: first, because the prospect of undertaking a new military campaign in Italy, climbing from the toe of the peninsula only to arrive sorely tried at the Alpine bastion, was not an appealing one to any general staff; second, because we would be able to offer not only our own abandonment of the conflict but also that of Hungary and Rumania, thus giving the Germans the opportunity to block Russia's access to the Danube, adding a plausible incentive to a new and undeniable fact. Mussolini listened to me with rapt attention, staring directly into my eyes; I said to him, "Give me a free hand and do not ask me a thing until I am ready to report to you. You will be completely unaware of the steps I will take, and I will not tell you what they will be because, in the event that they should be discovered by Von Ribbentrop, you will be able to assert truthfully that you know nothing about them. In that event, you could fully satisfy the demands of our ally by dismissing me as a meddler; however, it is not impossible that he, too, may reap some advantage from this action!"

Mussolini did not remove his eyes from my face and said not a word;[17] I lost no time in taking my leave and rushed toward the elevator for fear that he might have second thoughts. I returned to the Ministry, and he did not attempt to reach me by telephone for the rest of the day. Early the next morning I called Fummi to my home and asked him to leave for London on the first plane departing for Lisbon. He accepted the mission, fully aware of the difficulties involved, and promptly went to claim his passport from Cardinal Maglione. I directed the Minister Plenipotentiary, Fransoni, to leave immediately for Lisbon, to apprise Prunas of my plans, if possible, to put him in contact with those individuals who, a year earlier, had approached him in the Portuguese capital and proposed conversations on behalf of the British, and to attempt to accept their earlier overture at this time. I telegraphed to Paulucci in Madrid and directed him to come to Rome immediately. Cardinal Maglione informed me that, from what he had been able to learn, neither Washington nor London had given any consideration to creating a phantom Italian government and that, insofar as the bombing of Italian cities was concerned, we should be under no illusions that it would be mitigated.[18]

---

[17] It should be noted that on this occasion Mussolini did no more than revert to the position he had taken some time earlier in his talks with Acerbo, who told him that it was imperative to sound out the Allies in order to abandon the conflict and that he intended to go to Switzerland. More details will become available when Giacomo Acerbo's memoirs are published in the near future.

[18] Bastianini, *Uomini, cose, fatti*, pp. 115–18.

The most charitable analysis of Bastianini's version is that, while motivated by the best of intentions, it reveals a singular lack of realism in
evaluating the political and military situation. The Casablanca formula of
unconditional surrender had become the prime theme of Anglo-American
propaganda, and after the landing in Sicily had been accomplished, to
conceive that Great Britain would agree not only to negotiate with
Mussolini but to save him so that he might persuade Hitler to retreat from
the peninsula in two stages signified that, though Bastianini had been
Ambassador to London, he had not the slightest understanding of the
British mentality. This was the country that, in 1918, had continued to
fight for weeks against the Germans after William II had accepted Wilson's Fourteen Points because she had no intention of negotiating with
the Kaiser, who had already been totally removed from the negotiations
as a symbol of evil—a symbol created by war propaganda machines which
were much less ferocious than those in operation during World War II.
Furthermore, although Bastianini was in no position to know it, British
and American interest in the military conquest of Italy was at a low level.
The major efforts were directed toward the opening of the second front in
France. Only very limited amounts of equipment and supplies were assigned to operations in the peninsula; moreover, both London and Washington intended to reduce these operations even further.[19]

Aside from the fact that in the passage cited above there is no indication
of the nature of the instructions given to Fransoni based on the desire to
save Mussolini at all costs, Bastianini's exposition might be reasonable had
it represented a series of *ad personam* arguments to persuade Mussolini to
accept the undertaking and not his own thoughts. Instead, for various reasons one is led to the conclusion that Bastianini told his chief exactly what
was on his own mind.

In the first place, the summary which Bastianini wrote of the colloquy
which he had the previous night with Cardinal Secretary of State Maglione,[20] while certainly inspired by a sincere patriotism, reveals such a

[19] Regarding the thinking of the Allies at that time, see Toscano, "Nuove rivelazioni."

[20] Bastianini, *Uomini, cose, fatti,* pp. 115–17:

   At night, accompanied by Babuscio-Rizzo, I went to the Vatican. The Cardinal
welcomed us in his apartment, greeting us with a smile tinged with sadness. I
wasted no time in such amenities as recalling our first encounter in Berne in the
summer of 1924, our conversation on that day during an official dinner, and the
instant mutual respect which gave our conversation a frank and cordial tone from
beginning to end. Nineteen years have passed since that day, and he looks the
same; surely I must appear changed to him. We enter his study, which was
tapestried in red damask and enveloped in silence. No sound except the splashing
of a fountain in the courtyard reaches us. We look into each other's eyes for a

marked degree of naïveté that even its author ultimately recognized it as such. Even if one assumes that in speaking directly to Mussolini Bastianini might have considered it expedient to avoid being brutally frank, in talking with Maglione this consideration was certainly less pressing. The look in Cardinal Maglione's eyes should have put Bastianini on his guard, for

---

brief moment without uttering a word, but he is an expert in reading human souls and rests his hand on mine in a paternal gesture. I thank him for having consented to see me at this hour, and he brushes my thanks aside. I beg him to help me, he promises that he will, and I then ask him for three things. Would he grant my request for a passport from the Holy See for a person who could, at any moment, leave for London. I seek to forestall his objections by noting that the person in question is well regarded in Vatican circles and universally respected and that he also represents American financial interests in Europe; I name the banker Fummi as the person I would ask to undertake this mission. The Cardinal replies that he believes he can grant my request. The other two requests are much more delicate: I ask whether the Vatican could, in some way, approach the Allies for the purpose of reducing the cruelty of the aerial bombings of our cities, which occur without any regard whatsoever for targets; I would also like to know something of what the Allied political objectives are with respect to Italy and, specifically, whether they plan to create a provisional government for Italy abroad made up of exiles. The Cardinal is not aware of any plan to establish such a government abroad, but he promises to seek further information on this point.

This observation allowed us to see the Italian situation more clearly. It became evident that the Vatican foresees changes in the near future insofar as Italy is concerned, no eventuality is excluded, and the Holy See is prepared for the worst. I referred to the grave dangers which would develop from a prostrated Italy in the hands of a coalition of Communists, Anti-Papists, and Protestants. The Cardinal raised his eyes to heaven, pointed to an ivory crucifix, whose rigid arms extend above his well-ordered desk, and said, "Yes, we are in God's hands, all of us, and surely, as we are speaking in this room, many Italian souls are rising to join Him from the smoking ruins of our undefended cities." This thought left me speechless, and the Cardinal whispered, "You have faith; intensify it because faith moves mountains." I told him that those of us who served a civilized ideal also had faith in the fatherland of this earth and faced the terrible prospect that a great dream about to be realized had disappeared. Jesus Christ, too, loved his fatherland and wept at the atrocious fate reserved for Jerusalem. Our poor cities which the aerial bombings are reducing to ashes are not so many Sodoms and Gomorrahs. The enemies' cities hold unenviable records in this matter of immorality, which say a great deal about the right which the enemy arrogates to himself to teach us public and private morality. Certainly we have our faults, but are they above reproach? The Cardinal replied, "All have faults and commit errors and God knows it." I added that to cut out the infection from the sound flesh was a worthy act, but to seek to prevent and to reduce evil was a Christian act. The Cardinal replied, "I appreciate your effort, and I will do everything that I can to support your action. Count on my complete understanding and be assured that the Holy Father, to whom I will report this conversation immediately, is fully disposed to help you." I begged him to express my appreciation to the Holy Father, and finally I asked whether he could obtain permission for Fummi to enter England in the guise of an administrator of the Vatican's holdings. The Cardinal believed this to be possible.

I have no need to dwell further on my intention to entrust Fummi with the

the prelate knew better than anyone else that neither London nor Washington was disposed to reduce the bombings in Italy and had even refused to spare Rome itself.[21]

In the second place, the singular assertions in later chapters of Bastianini's memoirs, a full sixteen years after the event, concerning the dilatory British attitude confirm the fact that the former Undersecretary of State for Foreign Affairs in the last Mussolini Cabinet did not understand the realities of the times. He wrote as follows:

> If the conspirators had already had direct contacts with the enemy, and even to this day we are not certain of that, it is a fact that at that moment Fummi was in Lisbon awaiting British permission to proceed to London, and that on July 25 he was still waiting for this permission. It cannot be anything but strange that the Allies failed to show any interest in this attempt to approach them, an approach which might have made it possible to resolve, without doubt advantageously, the problem which was currently vexing them, that is, which plan to adopt in order to launch the invasion of the Continent with a minimum of risk. We know that it was during those very days that Churchill and Roosevelt were engaged in violent debate, the former supporting a plan for an invasion of the Balkans to be launched after the occupation of Sicily, the latter seeking other approaches in order to avoid raising obstacles to Stalin's plan to occupy at least eastern Europe.
> Whether the Allies were in no hurry to meet the Italian emissary, who was persona grata to them, because they already knew that Badoglio would offer them unconditional surrender as soon as possible will probably remain an unanswered question for a long time to come.[22]

Aside from the inaccuracies regarding the struggle between Roosevelt and Churchill over the opening of the second front, which was supposed

---

task of sounding out directly the possibility of negotiating the withdrawal of Italy, Hungary, and Rumania from the war. The Cardinal expressed doubt that the British and Americans would be willing to negotiate with a member of the Fascist regime, given their repeated statements and the character of their alliance. I replied that first of all it was a question of Italy and of avoiding having her fall into a situation which the British and Americans could hardly desire because it could be of no possible advantage to them and would only cause a great deal of concern. Fummi would certainly be in a position to explain that a "Russified" Italy would mean the end in continental Europe and that an invading army would surely not relish fighting its way up the entire length of the boot to the Po. I studied the Cardinal's face as he looked at me with paternal eyes, and he clearly believed that I was deluding myself. What more could I say to him? We talked for over an hour without either of us baring our soul to the other, separated by a wall which we would have known how to topple only at the foot of an altar. I took leave of the Cardinal, who escorted me to the staircase of his apartment; he placed his hand on my head, and I bid him farewell.

[21] For details on the action taken by the Holy See, see *Foreign Relations, 1943,* II, pp. 910–29.
[22] *Uomini, cose, fatti,* p. 123.

to take place at that time,[23] it is difficult to understand what Bastianini really meant by the "strangeness" of the attitude of the British government. The English had before them not a plenipotentiary armed with proper credentials but a person who, while acceptable to them since he was not a Fascist (that is, he was opposed to that government of which Bastianini was a part) and was carrying a Vatican passport, nevertheless came with no precise, realistic, or binding proposals. This circumstance also explains why the overture conceived by Bastianini (which was made at the same time as an approach in the name of the Princess of Piedmont) is not mentioned in the American collection of diplomatic documents. In all probability, the Foreign Office did not attribute much importance to the Bastianini initiative, especially in view of the fact that the Fascist government had fallen in the meantime and was no longer a factor. As for the insinuations regarding Badoglio's plans, it should be recalled that the soundings made in Switzerland prior to July 25, 1943, had been rejected by London from the very beginning. After the fall of Fascism and the creation of the Badoglio Cabinet, the armistice negotiations dragged out for a time, with very damaging results for Italy because not even Marshal Badoglio could resign himself to the idea that the British and Americans were determined to negotiate only on the basis of unconditional surrender.

The Bastianini account should also be corrected in its reference to the Fransoni mission. Fransoni left for Lisbon on July 19 (the day of the bombing of Rome and by sheer coincidence—unknown to him—on the same plane as the Princess of Piedmont's envoy), after an hour's delay at the airport because Palazzo Chigi had failed to issue the proper instructions to the airport officials. This mistake led to a detailed interrogation of the Italian diplomat in which an S.S. officer took part. Things were going very badly for Fransoni, and he was finally saved only by a quick-witted police official, who pretended to arrest him and then helped him onto the plane. Once in Madrid, Fransoni changed planes and proceeded to Lisbon, not so much to inform Prunas of Bastianini's intentions as to convince Pangal to act.[24] As emphasized above, in addition to what Bastianini reported of his conversation with Mussolini, Fransoni was primarily charged with asking that the Fascist head of state be spared.

[23] On this point see Trumbull Higgins, *Winston Churchill and the Second Front (1940–1943)* (New York: Oxford University Press, 1957); and Feis, *Churchill, Roosevelt, and Stalin, the War They Waged and the Peace They Sought.*

[24] Listowell, *Guerra segreta*, p. 183, correctly dates the Fransoni-Pangal meeting as July 22, 1943. The presence in Lisbon of an Italian agent was made known to the Germans from Madrid. Deakin, *The Brutal Friendship*, p. 393. However, it is not clear whether Fransoni or Fummi was meant. It was impossible for the information to have referred to the Princess of Piedmont's representative, Emo Capodilista.

Despite Bastianini's account in his memoirs, the British reply was immediate: no promise was made to safeguard Mussolini, and permission for Fransoni to proceed to London was given only if he possessed valid credentials.[25] Fransoni left immediately for Madrid, where he stopped for lunch at the Italian Embassy, and then proceeded by car toward Rome via Paris; before crossing the Franco-Spanish frontier he learned of the fall of Mussolini. The event did not surprise him too much because, on the eve of his departure from Rome, he had heard that General Ambrosio was making preparations to "do something." After a stopover in Paris,

[25] Copies of the following messages exchanged through Pangal, acting as intermediary, were made available to the author from Ambassador Fransoni's personal archives:

1. A British telegram to Pangal during the night of July 22, 1943: "Meeting possible if substantive summary of basic views can be provided first. Absolute discretion. Secrecy. Warmest thanks."

2. A telegram from Fransoni to Pangal during the night of July 22, 1943: "An exchange of views between persons of goodwill on the present situation and the possible development of the political and military points of view is in the common interest. Absolute discretion and secrecy guaranteed."

3. A British telegram to Pangal:

Whom do you represent? If it is Mussolini, it is impossible. One may recognize that Mussolini is Italian, a great patriot, etc., and that he may maintain his post until such time as an accord is reached to transfer this power. To whom will it be transferred? The military, high officials, financiers, industrialists. Mention several names . . . generals excluded, not compromised by Fascist connections, royal family, etc. How do you assess the action? We are not asking whether they can resist, where and for how long. We know that Mussolini has aged greatly, that he has lost a great deal of weight; we are not asking for such details. No military information. If Fransoni is part of the group which will assume power, we can reiterate the promise of an eventual trip to London for him. Now the moment has passed for attempts to learn the nature of conditions in detail in order to decide. It is merely a question of deciding whether or not one wishes to abandon the conflict; and it is not from Fransoni that we seek an answer.

4. A British telegram received by Pangal on July 23, 1943, at 6 p.m.: "For your guidance and strictly personal to Signor Fransoni. The communication of July 22, 5 p.m., was insufficient to make a decision on the trip. Fransoni still has a minimum of forty-eight hours in his favor. Thanks to Fransoni if he sends his impressions. Warmest thanks."

5. Pangal's telegram to the British of July 24, 1943:

While Fransoni has not been sent here officially, he does represent a widespread preference in Italy, on the part of those who are not die-hards, for seeking, in the present situation, some honorable solution other than that of the force of arms. Given this atmosphere, Fransoni reasoned that an encounter with Campbell would make it possible to determine how to achieve his desired objective. This is the reason why common agreement on certain fundamental principles would most certainly contribute to a rapid solution to the question. A meeting would have the objective, not of probing the ground, but of finding, together, the most effective action. Even if the meeting—not possible then—cannot take place in time, Fransoni is appreciative of the courtesy shown to him in these circumstances.

Fransoni returned to Rome. Bastianini was no longer at Palazzo Chigi awaiting the reply of the English, which was made promptly but which is not found in his memoirs.

On the other hand, if it is true that Fummi, who initiated his contact with the English after those of Emo Capodilista and Fransoni, was still in Lisbon on July 25, waiting to be transported to London, it is also true—and this information is also not mentioned in Bastianini's memoirs—that he subsequently reached the British capital. At that point, with the fall of the Fascist government, Fummi's mandate no longer had any real meaning, and his contacts could add nothing to the negotiation undertaken first by Guariglia with Lanza d'Ajeta and with Berio, and later by Ambrosio with Castellano and Zanussi.

Many years before Bastianini published his memoirs, Attilio Tamaro published the text of the note transmitted to Cardinal Maglione during the evening of July 17.[26] This was the note in which Bastianini outlined the first phase of the initiative he had planned for the purpose of contact-

[26] Attilio Tamaro, *Due anni di storia (1943–1945)* (Rome: Tosi, 1948), I, pp. 70–71:

1. The military positions as they are today suggest that the war may be prolonged for an indefinite period. As a matter of fact, the German forces are extremely powerful, and any shortening of their lines only helps to concentrate their military resources. However, the fact that today the war is focused on Italy and that each day she suffers sacrifices and destruction of her riches and art treasures dictates a careful examination of her position within the framework of war.

2. Rumors have reached us concerning initiatives which the Pope would not be unwilling to undertake if he were assured beforehand of Italy's and Germany's agreement (see the Russo file).

3. Italy can take no initiative on her own for moral reasons, such as having to defend the national honor, nor can she do so for material reasons, since any unilateral attempt to disassociate herself from Germany would automatically transform the nation into a battlefield.

4. In the event that the military situation in Italy should worsen, the only person capable of convincing Hitler that he should withdraw German troops from Italian soil would be the Duce. Thus it is imperative that the British and Americans refrain from demanding the immediate dismissal of the Duce, this because it is in their own obvious interest. In fact, the Germans would first retreat to the Po, where the British and Americans would have to meet them, and then to the Brenner Pass. An approach to Hitler by Mussolini could mean that the British and Americans would not have to face the Germans twice on our soil.

5. Italy has its own special position in the Danubian-Balkan region, which her opponents should recognize.

6. Therefore, in the meantime, it is imperative that the British and Americans avoid establishing a provisional government composed of exiles. This would mean civil war in Italy and unending suffering, which the Church will certainly seek to prevent.

7. A pejorative difference has been noted between the wording of the texts of Churchill's and Roosevelt's messages as transmitted via radio and as printed in the leaflets dropped by planes on Rome.

ing the English. This document is especially interesting in that it reveals Bastianini's great concern that the Allies would create a provisional Italian government abroad made up of exiles, while it also sets down the outlines on which he hoped to base his negotiations with them. The first concern proved to be without foundation, and the proposed negotiations aroused no interest in London and Washington.

Bastianini's mission to take Italy out of the war, which is treated in greater detail by Deakin,[27] had developed during Mussolini's meetings with the Hungarian Prime Minister, Kallay, early in April in Rome and with the Rumanian Foreign Minister, Antonescu, at Rocca delle Caminate[28] on July 1, 1943[29] (both men had come to Italy to seek a way to abandon the conflict). The meetings permitted the Italians to speak in the name of these Danubian states as well. They were the result of a series of pressures on Mussolini by the military[30] and diplomats[31] to convince him to speak plainly to Hitler. This time, in contrast to what had occurred toward the end of 1942, the attempt to break the link with Germany had adequate backing from forces in the government, but it developed too late. The military situation had gone from grave to catastrophic, and the Fascist regime fell before Palazzo Chigi received London's reply to the overture made by Bastianini.

4

The soundings made by the Italians prior to July 25, 1943, without the knowledge of the Fascist government, may be divided into two categories: those undertaken by the royal family and those initiated by anti-Fascist elements of the military. There are two soundings undertaken by the royal family about which information is available. The first occurred in Geneva at the request of the Duke of Aosta with the consent of the Prince of Piedmont and of King Victor Emmanuel; the second took place in Lisbon at the personal initiative of Princess Maria José of Piedmont. The letter

[27] The Brutal Friendship, pp. 393–95.

[28] Nicholas Kallay, Hungarian Premier (New York: Columbia University Press, 1954), pp. 144–78; Bastianini, Uomini, cose, fatti, pp. 90–91; Deakin, The Brutal Friendship, pp. 257–58.

[29] Bova Scoppa, Colloqui con due dittatori, pp. 112–31; Bastianini, Uomini, cose, fatti, pp. 113–14; Deakin, The Brutal Friendship, pp. 306–15; Barbul, Memorial Antonescu (Paris: Éditions de la Couronne, 1950), p. 202.

[30] Castellano, Come firmai l'armistizio di Cassibile, passim; Castellano, La guerra continua, pp. 9–41; Deakin, The Brutal Friendship, pp. 279–87.

[31] Bastianini, Uomini, cose, fatti, passim; Alfieri, Due dittatori di fronte, pp. 286–301; Bova Scoppa, Colloqui con due dittatori, pp. 96–112; Zangrandi, 1943: 25 luglio–8 settembre, pp. 82–86.

of December 18, 1942, from Eden to Cordell Hull, mentioned above, commented on the Geneva overture as follows:

The Italian Consul General at Geneva is anxious to establish a channel of communication between His Majesty's Government and the Duke of Aosta (formerly Duke of Spoleto). The Duke is represented as being prepared, in return for certain guarantees from us, to lead an armed uprising against Mussolini and the Fascist regime. He is said to be confident that he can count on the support of the Italian Navy and certain elements of the Bersaglieri, although he could not depend on the Army, and the Italian Air Force is stated to be definitely Fascist.

The Guarantees required would [be?]

(a) RAF support to deal with the Germans and Italian Air Force;

(b) an agreed landing by British and United States troops, on the understanding that they should land as Allies to assist in the overthrow of the regime and not as troops to conquer and occupy Italy;

(c) no demands to be made to hand over the Italian Fleet;

(d) preservation of the monarchy in Italy;

(e) guarantees along these lines to be given in the name of all of the Allied countries.

Our view is that this approach is probably genuine, but we are not greatly impressed by the possibilities of making anything of it. It is clear for instance that we would find a hostile air force, no support from the army with the exception of the Bersaglieri (i.e., at most about 27,000 men), and probably no active cooperation from the navy. Point (b) moreover stipulates an "agreed landing" which at best presents complicated problems of coordination and timing and at worst may be nothing better than a trap.

Nevertheless the prize to be won if we can hasten an Italian collapse is so great that we have decided that it is worthwhile keeping this line of communication open. The Duke of Aosta has undertaken to discuss his plan with the Prince of Piedmont and to inform our intermediary of the result.[32]

Before reporting the results of the research undertaken to delve into the information contained in this second excerpt from Eden's important letter, a few general remarks about this part of the document may be useful. In the first place, it seems to reveal a certain evolution in the British position. On November 30, 1942, Eden, in a telegram to Lord Halifax, British Ambassador to Washington,[33] supported the thesis that the best way in which to hasten the collapse of Italy was to emphasize her desperate military situation and the determination of the United Nations to prosecute the war with maximum vigor. There was nothing to be gained in making direct or indirect appeals to sentiment and to history in order to overthrow

[32] *Foreign Relations, 1943*, II, pp. 315–16.

[33] For the text, see *ibid.*, pp. 314–15. This position had been inspired by a note from Churchill of November 25, 1942, reproduced in Churchill, *Closing the Ring*, pp. 50–51.

the regime until such time as it was possible to support a dissident movement or a leader who would be able to defy the existing government. Such
movements or leaders were nonexistent at that time. In this letter the
British Foreign Minister is no longer ready to exclude these possibilities
a priori and has decided to keep the channel to Geneva open. In the second place, it is worth noting that London clearly distinguished between
Italy's Consul General in Geneva, Luigi Cortese, identified as the spokesman for the Duke of Aosta, and the members of the Italian legation in
Lisbon, erroneously regarded, as has been noted, as "servants of the
regime." Third, the importance attributed by the Foreign Office to Italy's
collapse merits attention because London did not always hold this view,
and, moreover, it contradicts previous British positions on the issue. Fourth,
it is interesting to note that a number of the conditions formulated on
this occasion by the Duke of Aosta, a typical one being that of an agreed-
upon landing, to a certain degree parallel ideas advanced by the Italians
during the course of the official negotiations for the armistice with the
representatives of the Badoglio government. Last, it is certain that the
Aosta overture was not taken without the knowledge of the King. While
it is a factor that must logically be considered, particularly in relation to
the *coup d'état* of July 25, it was entirely ignored, although the possibility
should not be excluded that the result of such a sounding may have ultimately had some influence on Victor Emmanuel's final choice, in the sense
of separating the internal action to remove Mussolini from the international move to influence the stipulation of the armistice.

My investigations of this episode bore fruit when I was able to establish that it was the Adjunct Consul in Geneva, Alessandro Marieni,
who acted, not the Consul General, Cortese. The latter was only vaguely
aware of the general outlines of what was being undertaken, and he remained apart from the negotiation. Marieni was well-known to the Duke
of Aosta. He had been the Duke's secretary during the latter's mission to
Iran in the spring of 1938 and had been an official witness at his wedding.
When Marieni was sent to Geneva as Adjunct Consul in the spring of
1942, he took advantage of a brief stopover in Rome to call at the Quirinale
to pay his respects to the Duke. The conversation was deeply pessimistic
regarding Italy's military position in the war, which the Duke knew very
well, particularly from the air and naval point of view, since he was the
commandant of the navy's assault craft. He stated that Italy should leave
the conflict as soon as possible—primarily in order to separate her own
responsibility from that of the Germans, whose atrocities were being
brought to light in increasing numbers—by finding a way to negotiate
with the British and Americans so that the armistice and peace conditions

would not be excessively hard; that is, such conditions should take into consideration the value of an Italian initiative to shorten the war. In taking his leave, Marieni promised to keep the Duke informed of the possibility of eventually making contact with the British and Americans that he would meet in Geneva.

After he had been at his new post for some time, with the help of the journalist Dr. Giacomo Cicconardi, a Geneva correspondent for several Italian newspapers, today a high official in the Common Market, Marieni was able to meet a colonel on the British General Staff, Victor Farrell, on detached service in Geneva with the title of Adjunct Consul for Great Britain. Cicconardi knew Farrell well, and Marieni was able to meet Farrell several times in Cicconardi's home. Between trips to Italy to report to the Duke of Aosta, with whom, through the cooperation of the latter's Aide-de-Camp, Commander Mazzucchetti, he had developed a code based on conventional phrases which would permit them to communicate even via telegraph, Marieni maintained virtually uninterrupted contact.

At that time the Duke of Aosta's command was at Lerici, and he told Marieni that he was acting with the full consent of the Prince of Piedmont, who agreed that finding a way out of the critical situation which had befallen the country was a matter of the greatest urgency and that it was necessary to sound out the intentions of the Allies. The Duke evidently reported regularly to the Prince on his contacts with Marieni, who believed that even the King was also kept informed.

An oral statement on this point was transmitted to me from Cascais, which seems to confirm this hypothesis. According to Marieni, the English requested as a first condition—perhaps also in order to obtain some assurance of good faith on the part of the Italians—that a Prince of the House of Savoy move to Sardinia and there establish a free government ready to cooperate with the Allies and move against the Germans. At the time the scheme was attractive because it might have made it possible to avoid excessively heavy peace terms, but it was not a simple matter to execute successfully because it required the assistance of the very sizable military force which garrisoned the island in addition to the armed assistance of the Allies.

While the American documentary collection contains only the favorable response of Cordell Hull on December 23, 1942, to Eden's suggestion that the line of communication to the Duke of Aosta be kept open, albeit with the reservation that a common policy toward Italian leaders disposed to cross over to the United Nations camp must be defined,[34] the negotiations

[34] *Foreign Relations, 1943*, II, p. 317.

on the shores of Lake Leman continued inconclusively until the creation of the Badoglio government. According to the recent version of Marieni, the initial soundings revealed the following: (1) the Americans left dealings with the Italians exclusively to the British, as Italy was regarded as within the British sphere of political influence; and (2) the Allies hoped for the overthrow of the Fascist regime by the Italians themselves, who would enter the war against the German forces in the peninsula as soon as possible, and where feasible, in the Mediterranean theaters of war. Briefly, it was desired that an Italian Gaullist movement be created with the establishment of a free government in some part of Italy. It was in this way that the island of Sardinia came into the picture: since it was an island, it would lend itself to the purpose. There a prince of the House of Savoy could establish himself and nominate a new government.

Marieni then received instructions to reply that this proposal could be taken into consideration but that in order to move toward realizing it it was necessary for Italy to know the consequences of such an overturn of fronts and alliances. The Duke of Aosta requested to know (1) what Italy could expect in the way of better treatment at the war's end, as it would have been extremely difficult to persuade military units to take an entirely new position and overthrow a regime while in a state of war unless there were real assurances that this act would improve the country's position at the peace table; and (2) what air and sea support the Allied forces could provide for an Italian action such as that proposed.

At this point the negotiations entered an extremely delicate phase, and Marieni noted a remarkable lack of understanding of the Italian situation, a confusion of ideas, and an absolute incapacity to modify pre-established plans in order to take advantage of the new possibilities which were being offered to shorten the conflict. Marieni attributed this attitude to the usual disparity between the views of the civil and the military authorities, the over-all effort, in his opinion, being further complicated at times by the unrealistic picture of the situation which the Italian exiles must have painted for this same multiplicity of authorities, thereby increasing their tendency to attempt to ensure an even tighter control of the future Italy.

The British never responded in clear and precise terms to these Italian requests for information. Instead, they were evasive and delayed their replies. They offered nothing tangible in the way of naval and air support for an eventual anti-Fascist and anti-German revolt by a part of the Italian armed forces. The invariable British attitude was, "Do something, and then we'll see." In addition, the British failed to give even minimal assurances as to the treatment Italy might expect in the future if the Duke of Aosta were able to overthrow the Fascist regime along with the German alliance.

It appeared almost as though someone on the British side preferred to see the negotiations fail so that Italy would emerge from the war completely destroyed and at the mercy of the victors, who could then do as they saw fit. In a word, it seemed as though the decision to impose unconditional surrender had already been reached. Of course, this attitude did nothing to facilitate the Duke of Aosta's task and made it extremely difficult for him to win the support of significant numbers of the armed forces. A great deal of time was lost in this way.

Marieni's observations are in substantial agreement with the American diplomatic documents regarding the policy, determined by Great Britain and accepted by Washington, toward Italy prior to the fall of the Fascist government. The surprise and chagrin experienced by the Italian negotiator in Geneva and by those who had sent him must have been great, but the Italian effort conflicted with an insurmountable political and military reality, and there was nothing to do but note this fact.

Even if the data provided above do not substantially alter the view of the Duke of Aosta's negotiations in Geneva, they are important in that they support the idea that this overture had a marked influence on Victor Emmanuel's "doing something" himself, only to learn after the *coup d'état* that there was no alternative to unconditional surrender.

5

The Princess of Piedmont's overture, in addition to being entirely personal and autonomous, was the last in a long series of attempts to alleviate, insofar as possible, the human misery resulting from Italy's intervention in the war and to take Italy out of the war in the best possible way. In serving as Inspector General of the Red Cross Maria José acquired firsthand knowledge from the wounded and their families of the real feeling of the country, as contrasted with the "official" thinking. In addition she had frequent contacts with such exponents of anti-Fascism as Benedetto Croce, Umberto Zanotti Bianco, Guido Gonella, Carlo Antoni, Ivanoe Bonomi,[35] and many others, whom she met as discreetly as necessary.

The sufferings of the people prompted her to launch several undertakings designed to reduce the tempo of the bombing in Italy. Her meetings with the then Monsignor Montini of the Vatican Secretariat of State, meetings

[35] See also Zangrandi, *1943: 25 luglio–8 settembre,* pp. 71–72, n. 25; Bianchi, *25 Luglio,* pp. 132, 155, 267, 268, 287, 365, 366, 393, 637, 762; Ivanoe Bonomi, *Diario di un'anno (2 giugno 1943–10 giugno 1944)* (Milan: Garzanti, 1947), pp. 9–10.

which undoubtedly encouraged the repeated, although vain, appeals of the Holy See to London and Washington—appeals which are amply documented in the American collection of diplomatic documents[36]—represented one such undertaking. For the purpose of further dramatizing the humanitarian nature of these appeals, Maria José did not hesitate to contact, albeit indirectly, the British Minister to the Vatican, Osborne.

On the other hand, the conversations she had with representatives of the opposition made the Princess of Piedmont fully aware of the real alternatives that the political situation offered, being either the *loser* or the *lost*. These conversations, together with the understandably violent but human pressures reaching her from the military hospitals, prompted Maria José to break through the screen of protocol which surrounded her and to express her real thoughts, which echoed those of the majority of Italians.

During the summer of 1942 the Princess of Piedmont met with Marshal Badoglio in the Val D'Aosta. While he spoke of the eventuality of a *coup d'état*, at the same time, because of the current strategic position, he revealed his concern regarding Germany and his conviction that the united front had to be maintained.[37] On October 3, 1942, that is, before El Alamein and the fall of Stalingrad, the Princess of Piedmont learned from the Vatican that the British Ambassador to Madrid, Sir Samuel Hoare, had stated that if Italy would abandon the conflict she would be accorded special consideration (reference was made to postwar economic assistance) and the Italian contribution to the cause of the democracies would be fully taken into account.

To date there is no evidence of the real political effect of this declaration. In all likelihood, it was a statement reflecting only Hoare's personal view, made confidentially to the apostolic Nuncio to Madrid, rather than an overture officially sanctioned by the Foreign Office. Even if the statement reflected only Hoare's own thoughts, however, it was of great interest and mirrored the military situation of the moment. The fact that Hoare makes no reference to this episode in his memoirs[38] is not conclusive. The British Ambassador to Madrid repeatedly manifested his sympathy for Italy, both as Foreign Minister and in the way he reported the content of his colloquy with General Castellano to Churchill,[39] which was a decisive

[36] *Foreign Relations, 1943,* II, pp. 910–37.

[37] In recalling the meeting, Badoglio affirms that the Princess pressed him to take drastic action. Badoglio, *L'Italia nella seconda guerra mondiale,* p. 62.

[38] *Ambassador on Special Mission* (London: Collis, 1946).

[39] *Ibid.,* pp. 213–14; Churchill, *Closing the Ring,* p. 92; Castellano, *Come firmai l'armistizio di Cassibile,* pp. 92–95.

factor in the decision reached by Churchill and Roosevelt to approve the
famous Quebec document providing for a revision of the armistice terms
for Italy on the basis of the Italian contribution to the struggle against
Germany.

Maria José immediately communicated this crucial information to the
Duke of Acquarone, Minister of the Royal House. The reply, which one
must assume was only in part the Duke's, was totally negative; the Vatican
was not an acceptable intermediary in a situation of this nature. Evidently
the Lateran Pact of 1929 had not completely cancelled Porta Pia, but at
the same time, at the Quirinale Victor Emmanuel had probably not yet
lost all faith in Germany's military prospects. In any event, he preferred
another means of approach.

It was at this point that the Princess of Piedmont, whose efforts to act
as a simple intermediary in creating a situation which could then be
developed directly or indirectly by the King had been rejected, turned her
thoughts to a personal and autonomous undertaking. She was encouraged
to think along these lines by the people she saw frequently, among them
Professor Guido Gonella, who was acting on De Gasperi's instructions, and
the outcome of military operations left no doubt as to the seriousness of
the situation and the necessity for action. It was at that time, perhaps also
because of a suggestion made by the banker Raffaele Mattioli, that Maria
José's attention began to turn toward Salazar as an intermediary to learn
under what conditions Italy might abandon the conflict.

At first glance the choice of Salazar offered notable advantages. He was
a Catholic statesman with a long-standing friendship for Italy and the
head of a neutral state. At the same time he was tied to Britain by a
centuries-old alliance. More particularly, President Salazar had taken a
position favoring a union of the Latin countries, and this plan had long
been appealing to the Princess of Piedmont.[40] Everything considered, no
other choice could have offered greater advantages.

Maria José met repeatedly with the Portuguese Ambassador to the Holy
See, Antonio Pacheco, who fully understood her views. The first sounding in Lisbon dated from these meetings and was designed to determine
whether President Salazar would agree to receive an emissary from the
Princess of Piedmont and to assume the role that was being requested of
him on behalf of Italy.

Notwithstanding the warnings he received to report to Lisbon only via
courier, Pacheco telegraphed a summary of his conversations with the

---

[40] For Salazar's political thoughts on this matter, see Bova Scoppa, *Colloqui con
due dittatori*, pp. 9, 17–20.

Princess of Piedmont. These telegrams were decoded by the Military Intelligence Service, and one day, in the office of the family physician, Maria José was asked by General Ambrosio, Chief of the General Staff, what the tangible results of her meetings with Pacheco had been. The Princess was momentarily stunned but then admitted that she had had these meetings. She gained the impression that General Ambrosio was not at all displeased by the episode. Maria José later saw Pacheco again and made it clear that his codes were no longer secure, a fact which shocked the diplomat.

In any event, in June, 1943, Salazar's positive reply arrived. Once it was known that Salazar was willing to act, it became a question of how best to utilize his services. After very careful consideration, Giuliana Benzoni, sister of an anti-Fascist diplomat who later fought with the resistance forces, suggested to Maria José that Alvise Emo Capodilista be asked to approach Salazar. The choice would arouse no suspicion because Capodilista had family interests in Portugal which had taken him to that country during the war, and he was in a position, with the aid of his sister-in-law, the Marquesa Olga de Cadaval, to reach Salazar without delay.

On July 17, the day of the Bastianini-Maglione meeting, Emo Capodilista, who had been invited to dinner along with Professor Gonella, had his first meeting with the Princess of Piedmont at the Quirinale. In the course of the dinner, Maria José, without going into the background of the undertaking, explained to Capodilista the terms of the mission. The proposals to be presented to the Allies were as follows: (1) Cessation of hostilities by both sides and a termination of the bombings of Italian cities; (2) retention by the Italian armed forces of their equipment in order to defend themselves against the inevitable German reaction; (3) support of these forces; (4) placement of the navy, an efficient and autonomous armed force, under the authority of the Allied High Command for possible operations in other theaters; (5) retention of the monarchy.

The Princess of Piedmont's overture had many points in common with the objectives of the negotiations which were being undertaken in Geneva by Alessandro Marieni in the name of the Duke of Aosta, in particular insistence upon the necessity of Anglo-American assistance to counter the expected German reaction, the role foreseen for the navy in collaborating with the United Nations on honorable terms, and some assurance of support for the monarchy. In all likelihood, these analogies sprang from a similar evaluation of the situation and were purely accidental. At that time, Maria José was unaware of the sounding being made in Geneva by her cousin; she learned of it only much later. The overture was well stated but had the disadvantage of coming after the decision on unconditional surrender had been reached at Casablanca and of containing only oblique references to the political and military strength lying behind the overture. Doubts were thus created in London and Washington about the real significance of the approach. Naturally, the mere fact that the Princess of Piedmont was openly assuming responsibility for the overture should have led to the conclusion that the King's wishes were identical to those of his daughter-in-law and that, for obvious reasons of security and prudence, he had permitted the initiative to be made in this manner. During the course of the meeting on July 17, it was agreed that Maria José would give Capodilista a simple letter of introduction to Salazar, which would be sufficient to accredit the Italian emissary.

On the following day, July 18, Capodilista returned to the Quirinale and met with Maria José and Professor Gonella. On this occasion he received the letter of introduction to the Portuguese head of state, along with a gift of a gold pencil which had belonged to the Princess of Piedmont's grandmother, whose name she bore (Maria José de Braganza, whom Salazar had known personally), and was given his final instructions. On July 19 he boarded the same plane which was to transport Fransoni as far as Madrid. (As mentioned above, each was unaware of the mission of the other, and half an hour after their departure the first bombing of Rome occurred.)

Capodilista's journey to Lisbon was without incident, and during the same evening he met with Marquesa Olga de Cadaval. He told his sister-in-law no more than was necessary, but he described the seriousness of the Italian situation and pointed out the need for a meeting with Salazar to ask his intervention in favor of Italy. The Marquesa de Cadaval immediately arranged for the meeting with Salazar in the latter's office on July 21. The circumstance that he was his sister-in-law's house guest and not living in a hotel prevented the various intelligence services from drawing any conclusions as to the purpose of his visit to Lisbon. Thus absolute silence surrounded the action in Lisbon, and not even the extremely well-informed author of *Crusader in the Secret War* mentions the episode, although this work does refer to Fransoni's mission.

The meeting between Capodilista and President Salazar could not have been more cordial. Salazar expressed his satisfaction at having been chosen for the task and stated that he was pleased to be of some service to Italy in this dramatic situation. At the same time, he recalled that he had always supported the idea of close cooperation among the Latin nations to offset the influence in Europe of the Germanic and Slavic blocs. Salazar did not hesitate to admit that in the past he had drawn from Mussolini's experiences a number of guidelines for his own governmental policies and, far from taking advantage of the difficulties in which Italy found herself to criticize or to assume an attitude of superiority, he expressed a real sense of understanding and friendship. Salazar concluded the audience with the promise that he would meet that very day with the British Ambassador, Ronald Campbell, in order that the latter might become Salazar's emissary to Churchill for the Italian requests. Salazar's choice of the British rather than the American Ambassador was not the result of any suggestion from the Italian emissary but rather because President Salazar was a close personal friend of Campbell. In this situation it was a matter of coincidence rather than choice. Unfortunately, this accident once again prevented the Italian overtures from being presented to the Americans rather than to the British. It should also be emphasized that the Portuguese head of state immediately accepted Capodilista's credentials and did not concern himself with the extent of the political and military force behind Maria José's proposal. Undoubtedly, this was due in part to Salazar's immediate sympathy and kind disposition toward Italy, as well as to the previous approaches made to the Portuguese President through Antonio Pacheco, which simplified matters a great deal.

On the following day, July 22, Salazar again called Capodilista to his office to ask for further details on the Italian proposal in order to transmit them to the British Ambassador, who had requested them. These clarifications concerned only the five points mentioned in the Italian overture, and Salazar's query was, in effect, a request for their confirmation. At that time the Portuguese President informed Capodilista that the Italian proposals would be immediately transmitted to Prime Minister Churchill, who was, he said, at that moment in Ottawa conferring with President Roosevelt at a conference of the Allies. This last statement is perplexing. On July 22 Churchill was still in London, where he remained until August 4. At that time he boarded the Queen Mary, which anchored off the Canadian coast on August 9.[41] For what reason was Ambassador Campbell instructed to give Salazar false information? If it was simply a matter of the security of the Prime Minister's journey, why did Campbell report that Churchill and Roosevelt were in Ottawa? (The conference was planned for Quebec and did, in fact, take place there.) This was a strange method of procedure—to announce in advance, on the very eve of Churchill's departure, a meeting which should have remained secret for some time. However, the possibility should not be excluded that by announcing that the journey had been made it was believed that the element of danger was reduced. The statement may have been designed to create the impression

[41] Churchill, *Closing the Ring*, pp. 62, 72.

of great faith in Salazar while simultaneously giving the impression of a close understanding between Great Britain and the United States insofar as any requests from Italy were concerned. These are questions which, on the basis of the present publication of diplomatic documents, cannot be answered.

Four days later, on July 26, Capodilista was again called to see Salazar. Again at the request of Ambassador Campbell, Salazar desired to know whether the Italian proposals were to be considered valid even after the collapse of the Fascist regime. The Italian emissary replied affirmatively, emphasizing that his mandate had been given by the Royal House and not by the Mussolini government. The question and the answer were certainly understandable, even if Campbell's request revealed more than anything else his hostility and bureaucratic mind. It should not be forgotten that only a few days earlier he had received Fransoni's overture through Pangal and that he had already transmitted London's reply. Fransoni's action, apart from the fact that it was extremely general, differed from Salazar's on one point: his request that Mussolini be saved at all costs. In the five points listed by the Princess of Piedmont no mention was made of Mussolini, and assurances were requested regarding the monarchy. Therefore, the two soundings could not be confused.

After this request for clarification, Capodilista waited for eight days.[42]

---

[42] It was on July 29, 1943, that the following message was transmitted by General Eisenhower to the Italian people (*The Times* [London], July 30):

We commend the Italian people and the House of Savoy on ridding themselves of Mussolini, the man who involved them in war as the tool of Hitler and brought them to the verge of disaster. The greatest obstacle which divided the Italian people from the United Nations has been removed by the Italians themselves. The only remaining obstacle on the road to peace is the German aggressor, who is still on Italian soil.

You want peace; you can have peace immediately, and peace under the honourable conditions which our governments have already offered you. We are coming as liberators. Your part is to cease immediately any assistance to the German military forces in your country. If you do this, we will rid you of the Germans and deliver you from the horrors of war.

As you have already seen in Sicily, our occupation will be mild and beneficent. Your men will return to their normal life and to their productive avocations, and, provided all British and allied prisoners now in your hands are restored safely to us, and not taken away to Germany, the hundreds of thousands of Italian prisoners captured by us in Tunisia and Sicily will return to the countless Italian homes who long for them.

The ancient liberties and traditions of your country will be restored.

However, it should not be overlooked that the day before, July 28, 1943, Roosevelt, in a radio speech, affirmed that "our terms to Italy are still the same as our terms to Germany and Japan—unconditional surrender." *The United States and Italy, 1936–1946* (Washington: U.S. Government Printing Office, 1946), p. 45.

Finally, on August 3 he met Salazar for the last time. Salazar, with visible annoyance, stated that Churchill had replied negatively to his overture.[43] The Allies refused to consider any proposal made by the Italians; they would meet only with a person properly qualified and empowered to offer unconditional surrender. The communication given to the Portuguese head of state by Campbell seems to have been in perfect harmony with succeeding events and with the experiences of the Badoglio government, and there were no surprises as far as its content was concerned. In fact, when compared with the response given to Fransoni a week earlier, one finds the same request for a precise mandate for the negotiators. As for the rest of it, it had the single merit of greater sincerity: Fransoni had been told only that there was no need to talk of Mussolini's safety and that, once he had returned to Lisbon with a written mandate, he would be transported to London.

There is no record of any consultation between Churchill and Roosevelt with regard to this Italian overture in Churchill's memoirs or in the American diplomatic documents. Further research at the State Department indicates that there is no material of British origin on this particular point which has been withheld from publication for fear of subjecting President Salazar to criticism. It cannot be said with complete certainty that consultations between London and Washington on this matter did not occur. On the other hand, there is no doubt that if they had, the results would have been no different.

In dismissing Capodilista, President Salazar gave him a letter for the Princess of Piedmont in which, understandably, he made no mention of his contacts with Campbell but limited himself to referring to his position favoring a union of the Latin nations. Maria José's envoy left immediately for Rome. On August 5 he was received at the Quirinale by the Princess, to whom he reported the outcome of his mission. She asked him to draft a written summary of the events, which he gave to her the following day. This permitted her to inform the Minister of the Royal House, the Duke of Acquarone, and General Ambrosio, Chief of the General Staff, of the outcome of this sounding.

General Ambrosio replied with an expression of appreciation for the effort and then informed the Foreign Minister, Guariglia, of the results of the overture, which is mentioned in the latter's memoirs.[44] The Duke of Acquarone expressed his reservations about the choice of a Portuguese

---

[43] In his meetings Salazar never once mentioned Roosevelt or Eden, perhaps in order to emphasize implicitly that it was a matter of direct relations between heads of state.

[44] Raffaele Guariglia, *Ricordi* (Naples: E.S.I., 1950), p. 573, writes: "The Princess of Piedmont took the initiative some time before July 25 by confidentially ap-

intermediary and about Portugal as the appropriate site for the sounding, yet a short time later Portugal was selected both for the soundings made by D'Ajeta and by Castellano, although without the good offices of Salazar.

On August 6 Victor Emmanuel met with his daughter-in-law at Villa Savoia, and, after talking to her about her indiscriminate circle of acquaintances and about her meetings, he asked her, because of them and for reasons of security as well, to leave the following day with her four children for Sant'Anna di Valdieri. She left within twenty-four hours from the suburban train station at Settebagni, the only one which had escaped damage from aerial bombings. Only later, at the suggestion of her lady-in-waiting, Guendalina Spalletti, did she leave Sant'Anna di Valdieri for the Sarre castle in the Val D'Aosta, a move which enabled her to escape the tragic fate which befell her sister-in-law, Mafalda. She arrived in Switzerland on September 9, after having taken leave of the wounded soldiers in the D'Aosta military hospital, fleeing just in time to avoid being captured by the Germans.

This episode casts much light on the personality, tenacity, and independence of the Princess, as well as demonstrating her absolute certainty that she was working in the best interests of her country. Its additional interest lies primarily in the fact that Maria José's initiative made it possible for the Italians to learn immediately after the *coup d'état* of July 25 the precise conditions laid down by the Allies for an armistice with Italy. They learned of the determination in Washington and London to impose terms of unconditional surrender.[45] Unfortunately, this knowledge did not dispel the illusions existing in both diplomatic and military circles in Rome regarding the possibility of negotiating with the Allies in order to abandon

---

pealing to a number of Portuguese officials to effect some soundings in Lisbon in order to learn what the Allied attitude would be toward Italy in the event that the latter abandoned the war."

[45] Another written official confirmation was received on August 13, 1943, when the British Consul General in Tangiers handed his Italian colleague, Berio, the following document:

The message that follows has been sent by the Governments of Great Britain and the United States:

It is imperative that Marshal Badoglio realize that we cannot negotiate but demand unconditional surrender. This means that the Italian Government should place itself in the hands of the two Allied Governments who will then make their terms known. These terms will provide honorable conditions. Call Mr. Berio's attention to the fact that the two heads of state have already manifested their desire that Italy occupy a respected position in the new Europe just as soon as the conflict is brought to an end and that General Eisenhower has already announced that the Italian prisoners in Tunisia and Sicily will be released.

Alberto Berio, *Missione segreta (Tangeri, agosto, 1943)* (Milan: Dall'Oglio, 1947), p. 73.

the conflict under more favorable conditions. On the other hand, news of the surrender terms aroused the Italian public, which was completely unprepared to face the reality of the situation and which believed that, with the collapse of the regime, all its responsibility for participating in the war against the democracies would also disappear. Consequently, another month was lost while, on the peninsula, the ruins from bombings increased, as did the German divisions sent by Hitler. If these circumstances made the choice left to the Badoglio government even more painful, they did not substantially modify it.

6

In order to complete the outline of the soundings effected prior to July 25 without the knowledge of the Fascist government, it is necessary to include that made by Marshal Badoglio in Geneva, indicated in a letter which the British Foreign Minister sent on February 1, 1943, to the American Chargé d'Affaires in London. The letter reads as follows:

I wrote to you on the 17th December last to inform you of certain peace feelers which we had received from Italy. There has now been a further approach of which I think the United States Government might wish to hear.

One of our representatives in Switzerland learned through an intermediary that Marshal Badoglio is willing at the right moment to take over and establish a military government in Italy. He is in touch with Marshal Caviglia who would assist him in this project. Marshal Badoglio suggested that he should send an emissary, General Pesenti, to Cyrenaica to discuss coordinated action from outside and inside Italy aimed at the overthrow of the Fascist regime. Marshal Badoglio did not ask for any assurances regarding the future but only that General Pesenti should hold these discussions with us and that he should be given facilities for recruiting a force from among the Italian residents abroad and prisoners of war.

The proposal has been carefully considered but it is felt that the advantages likely to be derived from it are not sufficient to outweigh the disadvantages and the risks involved. There is clearly a serious danger that General Pesenti's journey and the object of it might become known and the fact that we were treating with the Italian Army leaders might be misunderstood. It was also considered that any force which General Pesenti might raise would be of little or no military value. The main disadvantage which we foresaw was that if General Pesenti came out of Italy, negotiations with him could not continue without some undertakings being entered into on our side—and we do not consider it advisable at this stage to commit ourselves to the support of any individual Italian without considerably more information regarding the degree of support which he could command inside Italy.

In these circumstances we have decided not make any response for the time being to Marshal Badoglio and Marshal Caviglia.

I am sending a similar letter to Monsieur Maisky.[46]

[46] *Foreign Relations, 1943*, II, pp. 320–21.

Eden's letter takes on singular importance in reconstructing the internal events leading to the *coup d'état* of July 25 and the external events preceding the armistice. From the internal point of view, two points seem to be especially relevant: first, the time, January, 1943, of Badoglio's first contacts with the English; second, the link between Badoglio and Caviglia. In his memoirs, in which inaccuracies are common,[47] Badoglio wrote as follows: "Through the intervention of trusted intermediaries, I was able to contact English officials in Switzerland, but they were unable to bring about any tangible results, and the only accomplishment was that the English government was informed that I was seeking every way possible to reach agreement with it."[48] From the context, it appears that this contact occurred in June and not in January, 1943. In any event, Badoglio makes no reference to Caviglia or Pesenti. Another new piece of information is the fact that, at that time, Badoglio as well as the Duke of Aosta was thinking of acting in concert with the English to overthrow Mussolini and not simply of a *coup d'état* engineered internally. In contrast to the overture made by the Duke of Aosta, the question remains of whether or not the Badoglio sounding was effected with the King's knowledge.

From the external point of view, the British decision to ignore the Italian overture, while it fits into the framework of the general negative attitude announced by Eden on January 14,[49] does not appear to take seriously the statement made at the same time that only a military leader such as Badoglio would be able to overthrow Mussolini at the opportune moment. The impression is that the Foreign Office and the British General Staff acted within a preconceived rigid framework, while the arguments used to reject the proposal for General Pesenti's journey are indeed perplexing. In the event that the contact became known, what would London have risked? As for refusing to assume obligations to Italians committed to the plot, one cannot help but ask what dangers these obligations could have created. On the other hand, without a direct contact it would have been impossible for Great Britain to evaluate Badoglio's real chances for success. This episode may have had some effect on the purely internal form of the *coup d'état* of July 25. The fact that Badoglio asked for no guarantees before beginning the talks in Cyrenaica was of no importance. Obviously, this matter would have been discussed during the course of the negotiation proper. Moreover, it is apparent that Washington and Moscow were to be presented with a *fait accompli*. Perhaps Churchill's prolonged absence

---

[47] See pp. 277–304 *passim*.
[48] Badoglio, *L'Italia nella seconda guerra mondiale*, p. 63.
[49] *Foreign Relations, 1943*, II, pp. 318–20.

from London during those weeks was not completely unrelated to the negative decision, which aroused no particular reaction in Washington.

Limiting the discussion to Badoglio's initiative, it is entirely understandable that, after El Alamein and the fall of Stalingrad, Marshal Badoglio, if he had not completely reversed himself, had drastically modified his position regarding the Germans from that in the summer of 1942 when he met with the Princess of Piedmont. In the Geneva contacts Badoglio in effect reiterated the proposal he had already advanced to Maria José to bring about a *coup d'état*, but he did not explicitly state that he intended to move against the Germans. Yet, in asking that his efforts be coordinated with those of London and that he be authorized to recruit a force to overthrow the regime from among Italian prisoners of war and Italian residents abroad, he was taking a real step in that direction. What continues to be perplexing, however, is the assertion regarding the link between Badoglio and Caviglia. While no further information regarding Marshal Badoglio's activities has been brought to light despite many requests to the competent British authorities, some statements I made during the National Congress for the History of the Resistance Movement held in Rome on October 23 and 24, 1964,[50] elicited several corrections from Mrs. Bianca Ceva regarding General Pesenti, who is mentioned in Eden's letter as the emissary Badoglio intended to send to Cyrenaica to "discuss coordinated action from outside and inside of Italy aimed at the overthrow of the Fascist regime." Mrs. Ceva's statement follows:

I desire to offer only a very brief clarification on one point mentioned by Professor Toscano in his address. He cited an American document in which reference is made to the accords reached between Marshal Badoglio and Marshal Caviglia, a matter which may leave us perplexed.

It appears that in January, 1943, Marshal Badoglio, directly or through a third party, planned to have General Pesenti—a Genoese general noted for his anti-Fascism—transferred clandestinely to Cyrenaica for the purpose of creating a sort of a representative of the army outside of the country; I hesitate to state that he was to be something akin to a De Gaulle, but that appears to have been the idea.

The episode also seems to require clarification because the document in question is very ambiguous. I am intervening in this debate for a very simple reason: I was personally involved in that episode and I can offer my direct testimony.

As a matter of fact, the event per se did take place, but, from what I clearly recall of the last days of January and the first days of February, 1943, I do not believe that it has been reported accurately. It was the work of a group of

[50] See "Atti del Convegno Nazionale sulla Resistenza" (meeting held in Rome at the Palazzo Valentini), October 23–24, 1964, *Rassegna del Lazio*, 12th year, special edition, 1965, pp. 24–28.

Milanese anti-Fascists, and the most active person in that group, who constantly traveled to and from Switzerland, was a friend of ours whose name I will not mention at this time because I would like to acquire a more complete and exact account of the affair from him.

In any event, matters developed as follows: negotiations had taken place with MacCaffery, the Allied representative in Switzerland, where it was agreed to transfer General Pesenti, for clandestine accords. I do not recall that it was decided to transfer him to Cyrenaica; my recollection is rather that he was to be transferred to Switzerland. From there he would probably have passed over into Allied territory, probably to England. Everything was ready, and I was in contact with the air officer from the military air field near Milan, who was ready to attempt this dangerous operation to carry General Pesenti across the frontier. The officer would then seek sanctuary in Switzerland. At a certain point I was warned that the military authorities had greatly reduced the fuel allowance for each aircraft and had cut off further refueling for this officer. He was not, however, directly interfered with. Of course, when I became aware of this I was alarmed for a moment, fearing that things were going badly. A few days later our Milanese friend, who had been the *deus ex machina* of the whole plot, was arrested by the Military Intelligence Service in a Rome hotel. Without any explanation for his arrest, without being interrogated by the police, he was immediately sent off to the *confine* in Basilicata. At this point we realized that the risk we had run was serious, and we awaited an even greater reaction.

Evidently the Military Intelligence Service had received some warning and immediately made several arrests, thereby disrupting the plot. General Pesenti was, therefore, not able to cross the frontier.

Now I wish to recall a detail which may cause some smiles, but it is important in order to indicate the sometimes romantic framework of certain undertakings. A day or so before the date established for the flight, I learned that General Pesenti planned to leave with nothing but a volume of Pascal's *Pensées* in his pocket. This was the way in which one of our generals thought he could accomplish such an undertaking. However, the history of the event remains to be written.

I do not challenge the assertion contained in the American document: it is what it is, and we know how it came into being, but I have some doubt as to the interpretation of the rapprochement between Badoglio and Caviglia. It is exceedingly strange. Above all, I claim for the clandestine organization and for the anti-Fascist organization of Milan the sponsorship of this undertaking, which might have been important: in any event, from a spiritual point of view it had its significance from the moment of the intervention of no less a personage than Blaise Pascal.[51]

This is all that is known to date on this episode, and I have called to the attention of scholars Eden's letter to Mathews of February 1, 1943. It is not much, but it does substantially confirm the Badoglio overture, even though a great deal of uncertainty remains. However, it appears certain

---

[51] *Ibid.*, pp. 69–70.

VII.

SPECIFIC PROBLEMS IN THE HISTORY OF WORLD WAR II

Summary: 1. *Premise.* 2. *The influence of the intelligence services on the important political decisions which led to the outbreak of World War II.* 3. *Sorge's activities in Tokyo and the work of a Soviet agent in Rome, which permitted Stalin to receive crucial information on Hitler's intentions and on the position of the British government at the moment that he made his decision in favor of an understanding with Germany.* 4. *The effect on Hitler of the British documents concerning the Nazi regime and Eden's proposals, transmitted to the German Chancellor by Mussolini.* 5. *The information gathered by the Italian Intelligence Service and Mussolini's policies toward Great Britain and Greece.* 6. *The decoding by the Germans of Colonel Beck's last instructions to the Polish Ambassador to Berlin and the problems that this raised. How London learned of Mussolini's decision not to enter the war and of the content of the planned German proposals to Poland.* 7. *The democracies and the information gathered by the intelligence services. Conclusion.*

1

The "specific problems" to which the scholar's attention is called concern the influence which the work of intelligence services had on several important political decisions taken before and during World War II. The problem of the role of the intelligence service is not new. In the years preceding 1914 there were several significant episodes of the same nature. For example, aside from the work of the famous "Black Cabinet" in St. Petersburg, which decoded the majority of the telegrams sent and received by the diplomatic corps accredited to the Tsarist government, a very serious crisis developed in Franco-Italian relations toward the close of 1913, when the French were able to decode the telegraphic correspondence of the Italian Embassy in Paris and learned the details of several articles of the Triple Alliance and of the existence of an Austro-German-Italian naval convention.

---

* Originally presented as a paper to the Ninth International Congress for the Historical Sciences meeting in Paris in 1950, this chapter was later published as an article entitled "Problemi particolari della storia della seconda guerra mondiale," *Rivista di studi politici internazionali*, III (1950). When these pages were first wrtten the problem had not yet been given proper consideration by scholars. In recent years, perhaps in part because of this paper, historians have paid increasing attention to this theme. Recent publications in the field are mentioned in the footnotes in order to bring the discussion up to date.

406

The second example suggests that the possession of this type of secret information is not always advantageous to its owner. This assertion may at first be surprising, but it can be justified by the fact, sufficiently clear in itself, that no matter how well informed one may be about one's adversary, one cannot expect to know everything about him, and decisions are made on the basis of knowledge so limited that errors are almost inevitable. In the 1913 episode, in November of that year, the responsible leaders of the Quai d'Orsay were so astonished to learn that the Triple Alliance also covered contingencies in the Mediterranean that the French dropped the negotiations then under way in Rome aimed at an accord that would assure the maintenance of the status quo in the Mediterranean. This happened at the very moment when the Italian Foreign Ministry was on the verge of modifying its international position. The reaction of the Quai d'Orsay officials was even more unfortunate because, on the basis of the few sentences which had been decoded, they had erroneously jumped to the conclusion that the arrangements for the Triple Alliance to cover contingencies in the Mediterranean had come into existence only during the negotiations for the most recent renewal of the alliance (when, in fact, they dated from the 1887 renewal). In addition, on that occasion, the Quai d'Orsay believed, a naval convention had been signed between Italy and the Central Powers (when in fact, it was signed in August, 1913, to offset the Franco-Russian naval convention and the concentration of the French fleet in the Mediterranean). These developments appeared to be extremely serious because, in December, 1912, Italy had formally assured France that the alliance had been renewed without alteration. Thus the erroneous interpretation of the information gathered by the French intelligence services led to the conclusion that the Italians had lied in a very crude way and induced the Quai d'Orsay to regard the proposals made by Rome as untrustworthy.[1] This confirms the fact that the work of the intelligence service can have negative effects—on the judgment of statesmen—which are frequently more significant than its positive value. This work is, however, of great importance to the historian, who can find

[1] On this question, see the recent publication by Gianluca Andrè, L'Italia e il Mediterraneo alla vigilia della prima guerra mondiale: I tentativi di intesa mediterranea (1911–1914) (Milan: Giuffrè, 1967). It should also be pointed out that the decoding of the Italian telegraphic correspondence by the French intelligence services continued beyond this period. Immediately after the presentation to the Italian Parliament of the Green Book relating to the negotiations with Austria-Hungary (May 20, 1915), the Quai d'Orsay was in a position to prepare an unusually precise resumé of Italian foreign policy. Reference was made to the instructions sent to the Italian Ambassador to London, Imperiali, on February 3, 1915, and the resumé . . . contained the later telegram of March 3 instructing Imperiali to begin negotiations with the British government.

in it the roots of a great many important decisions. However, it should also be pointed out that from the evidence available it does not appear that the activities of the intelligence services have influenced any government's decision to declare a war, with perhaps the notable exception of the episode related to the famous Zimmermann telegram.[2]

2

One case in which information gathered by intelligence services is believed to have played an important role is the negotiations leading up to the conclusion of the Soviet-German Pact of August 23, 1939. The subject has been studied in detail on the basis of the rich German documentation, but there are still aspects which are not entirely clear because it is impossible to consult the Soviet sources. To be specific, it is not yet possible to reconstruct accurately the process by which Moscow arrived at the decision to sign the accord with Berlin, rejecting the offers made at the same time by the western powers to sign an anti-Nazi alliance.

At this point a brief digression may be worthwhile. On the basis of the documents contained in the Historical Archives of the Italian Foreign Ministry, I was able to analyze the German decision in the summer of 1938 to begin negotiations for the conclusion of an Italo-Japanese-German military alliance, an alliance which had been urged for several months in various Japanese military circles.[3] The negotiations began only in January, 1939, when Mussolini's earlier reservations vanished. However, contrary to the predictions of Von Ribbentrop, who was counting on a rapid decision, a serious difficulty arose during the course of the highly secret talks between Tokyo and Berlin. Japan was willing to assume military obligations only against the Soviet Union, while Germany was particularly interested in an alliance that would be valid as an instrument to neutralize France, Great Britain, and the United States. As the weeks went by, the divergent points of view became even more irreconcilable. Finally, rather than abandon the idea completely, the Nazi government not only settled for an alliance with Italy alone, which served its purposes only in a very limited way, but also ran the serious risk of dangerously compromising its own relations with the Empire of the Rising Sun at an extremely critical time.

---

[2] On this episode, recently reconstructed in detail, see Barbara W. Tuchmann, *The Zimmermann Telegram* (London: Constable, 1959). See also David Kahn, *The Codebreakers: The Story of Secret Writing* (London: Weidenfeld and Nicolson, 1966), p. 266 *et seq.*, which was written after the declassification of important material in January, 1965.

[3] Toscano, *The Origins of the Pact of Steel.*

3

At this point an unusual Soviet intelligence operation provided Moscow with significant information on Nazi-Japanese relations, along with other material. On February 10, 1949, the headquarters of the American Command in the Far East published a report on the Sorge case.[4] As a result of the occupation of Tokyo the Americans had acquired data concerning the most important case of espionage (in favor of the Soviet Union) uncovered in Japan during the course of World War II. Those involved were Richard Sorge, a press attaché and influential member of the staff of the German Embassy in Tokyo, and Ozaki Hozumi, unofficial adviser to the Konoye Cabinet and consultant to the South Manchurian Railway Company. Sorge, a close friend of General Eugen Ott, one-time military attaché and later German Ambassador to Tokyo, was well informed concerning the most delicate secrets of the German Embassy. Ozaki Hozumi's position within the Konoye Cabinet was no less important, as he was authorized to examine the most important state papers. Moreover, a long friendship tied him to Ushiba Tomohiko and Kishi Michizo, two private secretaries to Prince Konoye. Sorge and Ozaki Hozumi were arrested in October, 1941, and executed in November, 1944. Their confessions and the summaries of the messages they sent to Moscow make it possible to reconstruct the messages transmitted by them. Those concerning the negotiations for an Italo-Japanese-German military alliance[5] merit careful scrutiny because this information placed Moscow in a position to judge the sincerity of Hitler's assurances when he declared that he had no aggressive intentions toward the U.S.S.R. and that his interests lay elsewhere.

At the same time it was learned from the former Soviet Embassy Counsellor in Rome, Helfand, that the person who opened the safe each day at the British Embassy in Italy photographed all of the documents it contained and gave one copy to the Russians and one to the Italian intelligence service. In this way Stalin learned from a telegram sent by Lord Halifax to the British Embassy in Berlin and then transmitted to Rome by Ambassador Henderson that, while London was negotiating with Moscow, the British would have preferred an agreement with Germany. Of course, it is not possible to determine the influence of this information on the final Soviet decision. The least that can be said is that, given a question as difficult as that of choosing among offers presented simultaneously by London, Berlin, and Paris, exact knowledge of the true objectives of

[4] National Military Establishment, Department of the Army, *Sorge Spy Ring: A Case Study in International Espionage in the Far East.*
[5] *Ibid.,* p. 41.

Nazi policy and the lack of British enthusiasm for an entente with Moscow could not but be a factor of singular importance.[6]

The fact that the documents contained in the British Embassy safe in Rome were regularly photographed and brought to the attention of the Soviet Embassy Counsellor must have had other effects as well, not all of which can be determined. For example, it was by this means that the Kremlin learned, on the occasion of Chamberlain's visit to Rome in January, 1939, that Mussolini ignored Chamberlain's reference to the eventuality that German dynamism might point toward the east. Without touching on the particulars of that episode,[7] it will suffice to note that the Soviet government was so favorably impressed by Mussolini's conduct that it modified its attitude toward the Fascist government. At the time, that sudden change in policy was surprising, but in the light of these later revelations the explanation is quite clear.

4

A second episode involving the work of the intelligence services is linked to the origins of the Rome-Berlin Axis. For the purpose of clarity it is necessary to review the psychological situation facing the two dictators. The time was the fall of 1936, following the conquest of Ethiopia and the occupation of the demilitarized zone of the Rhineland. Mussolini was visibly concerned with the specter of isolation. During the period of the sanctions, Germany's attitude was somewhat ambiguous, and doors were opened in several directions. Even after the beginning of the Spanish Civil War had reduced Mussolini's chances of an accord with the democracies, the Wilhelmstrasse continued to pursue a relatively prudent policy. Evidently, Hitler had not yet abandoned the hope of realizing the portion of his program outlined in *Mein Kampf* related to the conclusion of a political accord with Great Britain. Von Ribbentrop, recently appointed ambassador to Britain, was working feverishly toward this end, while engaging in a personal power struggle with Von Neurath.

At this point the intelligence services played their role. On September 3, 1936, the Italian Ambassador to London, Dino Grandi, had succeeded in

---

[6] This important consequence of the information sent by Sorge has not been adequately emphasized by many historians who have reconstructed the story of the famous spy, while some (for example, Charles A. Willoughby, *Shanghai Conspiracy: The Sorge Spy Ring* [New York: Dutton, 1952], p. 104) have completely reversed the positions of Tokyo and Berlin, attributing to the Japanese government the intention to conclude an alliance directed against the United States and Great Britain. The episode is reported correctly in F. W. Deakin and G. R. Storry, *The Case of Richard Sorge* (London: Chatto and Windus, 1966), pp. 220–21. See also Kahn, *The Codebreakers*, pp. 654–57.

[7] For greater detail see pp. 48–123.

obtaining a dossier containing thirty-two documents gathered by Eden for confidential examination by members of the Cabinet. The collection was entitled "The German Peril." The documents were no less than a selection of the most important reports from the British Ambassador to Berlin, Sir Eric Philipps, from the spring of 1933 to January, 1936, in which the programs and activities of the Nazi regime were detailed and severely criticized. The collection contained an introduction drafted by Eden in which, after demonstrating how "Hitler's foreign policy might be synthesized as the destruction of the order established by the peace treaties and the restoration of Germany to her dominant position in Europe," he concluded that it was vitally important to hasten the completion of Great Britain's rearmament and to seek in the meantime a *modus vivendi* with Nazi Germany. Of course, Mussolini immediately made plans to bring this material to Hitler's attention. As early as September 23, 1936, in a colloquy with Minister Frank, he referred to the matter, adding that when Von Ribbentrop had seen the dossier he would be enlightened "on what could be the results of his missions: England intends to *ménager* Germany only in order to gain time to complete her rearmament."[8]

Count Ciano was charged with the mission, and after meeting with Von Neurath in Berlin on October 21, he asked his German colleague to arrange a visit for him to Berchtesgaden to present the dossier to the Führer personally. Von Neurath replied that he was "very pleased that these documents would reach the Führer, who could then abandon without regrets those remaining illusions created for him by Von Ribbentrop, according to whom England desired to conduct a policy of friendship and collaboration with Germany."[9]

The meeting at Berchtesgaden took place on October 24. The episode of interest to us was recalled in the minutes of the meeting drafted immediately afterward by Ciano.

At this point, as the Duce's special envoy, I presented the document in question to Hitler. Hitler read Eden's circular and Philipps' telegram, in which the British ambassador described the German government as composed of dangerous adventurers. Hitler was deeply impressed and, after a moment of silence, reacted violently. In the judgment of the English there are two countries in the world ruled by adventurers: Germany and Italy. But England, too, was governed by incompetents. Hitler was excited by the two documents. He then stated that to counter the entente existing between the democracies another

---

[8] Ciano, *L'Europa verso la catastrofe* (Milan: Mondadori, 1948), pp. 78–79. There is no reference to this in the very brief summary drafted by Hans Frank (*Documents on German Foreign Policy 1918–1945*, Series C, V, Doc. 533).

[9] Ciano, *L'Europa verso la catastrofe*, p. 88. The corresponding German minutes do not contain an explicit reference to the question.

must be created, guided by our two countries. But we must not limit ourselves to a passive attitude. We must assume an active role. We must move to the attack.[10]

Hitler's reaction immediately went beyond the limits set by the weak understanding on a few points solemnized a few days earlier in Berlin in a pact initialed by Ciano and Von Neurath. Thus, the Rome-Berlin Axis, which Mussolini, basing his speech on the notes provided by Ciano, was to announce to the world from Milan on the following November 1, was born. Even without exaggerating the importance of the episode, it must be noted that it (a) increased the significance of the Italo-German meeting; (b) assisted Von Neurath's efforts to sabotage Von Ribbentrop's plans; and (c) hastened the development of Hitler's anti-British thinking.

5

The Berchtesgaden episode is also interesting because it explains certain psychological impulses behind Mussolini's foreign policy. In fact, a large part of this policy must be related, directly or indirectly, to the interceptions and decoding of the intelligence service. The diplomatic documents which the intelligence service regularly transmitted to Palazzo Venezia were the ones which the Duce read most avidly. He underlined certain passages and added abundant marginal notes. The influence of these letters on Mussolini's thinking was incalculable. If a few articles in the foreign press—such as, for example, those commenting on Von Ribbentrop's visit to Milan in May, 1939—could produce a strong reaction in the Duce's mind, to the point where they may be considered among the major factors contributing to his decision to hasten the conclusion of the military alliance with Germany,[11] what can be said about his reaction to reading secret official foreign documents?

The fact, for example, that for a certain period of time the British Ambassador's safe was opened and its contents photographed is essential for a comprehension of some of the Duce's attitudes toward England—at times audacious, at other times, resentful, and at still others inflexible. What weight in Palazzo Venezia's decision to undertake the Ethiopian campaign must be assigned to Mussolini's reading of the famous Maffey secret report, which, with limited reservations regarding Lake Tana, concluded that the Fascist program of expansion in East Africa was compatible with British imperial interests? No one can say exactly, but the fact that, at a given moment, Palazzo Venezia issued the rash order to

[10] *Ibid.*, p. 94. The German minutes of this colloquy have not been found.
[11] Toscano, *Origins of the Pact of Steel*, pp. 305, 321.

have the Maffey report published in Paris—an act which risked compromising the entire operation of the Italian intelligence service—indicates the resentment caused by the British Cabinet's condemnation of an Italian action taken in part on the strength of the conclusions reached by a commission of British experts.

The publication of the Maffey report did not put the British Intelligence Service on the track, and the work of the Italian service continued undisturbed. In any event, Palazzo Venezia's policy throughout the Ethiopian campaign was largely based on these interceptions, which revealed the conflicts existing in the democratic camp and British military unpreparedness. Regarding the latter, certain arrogant statements made by Mussolini to the British Ambassador to Rome, Sir Eric Drummond, on the day that Drummond went to Palazzo Venezia to announce the arrival of the Home Fleet in the Mediterranean, were based on an intercepted dispatch from the Fleet Admiral to the Admiralty in London, which noted the difficult situation with respect to the crews and the dangerously low munitions supply.[12] The collapse of the Anglo-Italian Gentlemen's Agreement signed on January 2, 1937, must also be traced to Mussolini's desire to spite the British because he had read the anti-Italian instructions that Eden dispatched after the conclusion of the agreement to the various British legations in the Balkan capitals—particularly to Belgrade. They were designed to block Italian policy initiatives toward an understanding with Yugoslavia. Such instructions regularly appeared on Mussolini's desk. Similarly, Mussolini's decision to attack Greece had its origin in the period of Italy's nonbelligerence, when the Duce learned that King George of Greece, whom he thought he had won over during the course of a recent colloquy in Rome, had been highly critical of him in London. On the other hand, it should also be noted that the Italian intelligence service obtained no information regarding the Soviet Union or Nazi Germany. (In the latter case, it was the result of Mussolini's decision to prohibit Italian intelligence service activity.)

Upon close examination, from a psychological point of view, what happened was not at all surprising. Not only is the possibility of free discussion of political problems, such as exists in the democratic camp, lacking in dictatorships, but dictators are served by officials who, even when motivated by the best of intentions, tend to blur the edges of adverse situations. For this reason such leaders are especially likely to give major

[12] It appears that this dispatch deliberately struck a particularly alarmist note in order to force the government to grant further funds to put the navy in a position to face the Japanese threat in the Far East, which was a permanent concern of the British Admiralty.

importance to news reaching them via the intelligence services, but, at the same time, when they do not have perfect control of their emotions they tend to be excessively impressed by the "novelty" of the adversaries' evaluations. Moreover, one should not forget that dictatorships draw a good portion of their internal strength from the secret services. Why not attribute at least the same weight to the external intelligence effort? In any event, Mussolini's reactions were generally impulsive and based on personal resentment. He was often incapable of action of any kind in a political maneuver which gave evidence in its early stages of being doomed to failure.

From the historical point of view this intelligence activity poses two types of problems, both extremely difficult to solve. In the first place, the material in question is rarely archived and is generally excluded from the official documentary publications. But even granted the highly improbable hypothesis that a historian might succeed in seeing such documents or learning of their content (the examples cited above became known to the United Nations only after the occupation of Rome and Tokyo, and, for obvious reasons, only their general outlines were made public; no further mention was made of them), it is almost never possible to ascertain the exact time at which the dictator read them. Thus it is almost impossible to determine accurately how much of the dictator's attitude reflects his reaction to the information gathered by the intelligence services and how much represents a spontaneous and completely subjective decision.

In this respect the materials in the Fascist archives are typical. There are many traces of intelligence activity, which are confirmed by the personal recollections of many of the surviving important functionaries of the period, but they are incomplete and fragmentary. Therefore, the Italian experience, highly instructive and admonitory from a general point of view, seems to be at the same time extremely disconcerting for the student of such a complex and tormented period.

6

The memoirs of Birger Dahlerus, the Swedish industrialist who traveled, at Goering's request, during the critical weeks of August, 1939, between London and Berlin to meet with the leading personalities in an attempt to find a solution to the current political problems, mention an episode related to the German intelligence activity that is of considerable historical interest.

On August 31, shortly after 1 P.M., in his own home, Goering was discussing the situation with Dahlerus when he received an envelope containing the decoded copy of a telegram sent by Beck to the Polish Ambassador, Lipski, at 12:40 P.M., which arrived in Berlin at 12:45 P.M. Goering became greatly agitated upon reading it. The text was as follows:

Request a meeting and state as follows:
Last night the Polish Government received from the British Government a report of an exchange of views between the German and British Governments regarding the possibility of an agreement being reached directly between the German and Polish governments.
The Polish government will consider the British government's proposal and will make a formal reply to the British government within a few hours (*not to the German government*).
The following special and secret message is addressed to the Ambassador:
Do not under any circumstances enter into any factual discussions; if the German government makes any verbal or written proposals, you are to reply that you have no authority whatever to receive or discuss such proposals and that you are only in a position to deliver the above message from your government and that you must await further instructions.[13]

Even if one can rule out the possibility that the decoding of this message could have influenced the order to attack Poland—the order was issued at 12:40 P.M.,[14] that is to say, at the same time as the dispatch of the telegram from Warsaw—the episode raises a series of questions. It should be noted, first, that evidently the Germans had the Polish code. Did knowing the secret directives of Warsaw's policy have some effect in Berlin? Second, the text of the same telegram was published in the Polish White Book. However, there are differences between this text and that given to Dahlerus by Goering immediately after he had read it and shown several hours later to Henderson. The version in the Polish White Book reads as follows:

I am in receipt of your report and beg you, M. l'Ambassadeur, to request an audience with the Foreign Minister of the Reich or the Secretary of State, and inform them as follows:
Tonight the British government informed the Polish government about its discussion with the German government regarding the possibility of direct negotiations between the German and Polish governments.
The Polish government considers the British government proposal in a favourable spirit and a formal reply will be given to this government within a few hours at the latest.[15]

[13] Birger Dahlerus, *The Last Attempt* (London: Hutchinson, 1948), p. 106 et seq.

[14] *Trial of the Major War Criminals before the International Military Tribunal* (Nuremberg: 1949), XXXIV, Doc. 126-C, p. 456.

[15] *Official Documents Concerning Polish-German and Polish-Soviet Relations, 1933–1939*, published by authority of the Polish government (London: Hutchinson, 1940), Doc. 110.

The discrepancies between the two texts are immediately evident. If the Polish version is the correct one, it would have to be concluded that we are in the presence of a German maneuver to detach Britain from Poland. This appears to have been Ambassador Henderson's initial impression. However, this hypothesis is not borne out in the postwar literature, since the action taken by Ambassador Lipski on the afternoon of August 31 confirmed the German version, which was also confirmed by other passages in the British Blue Book.[16] The decoding work of the German intelligence service thus permits the identification of a not unimportant omission from the Polish White Book.[17]

If Beck's telegram did not affect the decision to issue the attack order to the Wehrmacht, is it possible to be equally certain that it had no effect on the order being carried out? As is known, the earlier order of August 23 fixed the date for the attack as August 26, but this order was revoked during the evening of August 25, following the news of the signing of the Anglo-Polish accord and Mussolini's decision not to intervene immediately in the conflict. A second postponement was highly unlikely, but, in any event, Beck's instructions must have discouraged any serious attempt to initiate one.

When Goering recovered from the shock of reading the letter, he told Dahlerus that, contrary to what he had believed up to that moment, it was finally proved that it would not be Von Ribbentrop's fault if the ne-

---

[16] *Documents Concerning German-Polish Relations and the Outbreak of Hostilities between Great Britain and Germany on September 3, 1939* (London: Her Majesty's Stationery Office, 1940), Docs. 96 and 100. These have now been reprinted in *Documents on British Foreign Policy*, 3rd series, VII, Docs. 608 and 632.

[17] The text of the above-cited telegram has been reprinted in Waclaw Jedrzejewicz, *Diplomat in Berlin 1933–1939: Papers and Memories of Josef Lipski, Ambassador of Poland* (New York: Columbia University Press, 1968), p. 572, and reads as follows:

   With reference to your reports, please request an interview with the Minister of Foreign Affairs or the Secretary of State, and inform him as follows:
   Last night the Polish government was informed by the British government of an exchange of views with the Reich government as to the possibility of direct understanding between the Polish and German governments.
   The Polish government is favourably considering the British government's suggestion and will make them a formal reply on the subject in the next few hours at the latest.
   End of declaration for the Ministry of Foreign Affairs. Next passage for the Ambassador's information.
   Please do not engage in any concrete discussions, and if the Germans put forward any concrete demands, say you are not authorized to accept or discuss them and will have to ask your government for further instructions.

A note to the document adds that "the Ambassador was also informed that the word 'understanding' was meant in the sense 'communicating with each other' and should, therefore, be translated as *Verständigung* and not as *Vereinbarung*."

gotiations with the Poles could not take place.[18] Dahlerus' memoirs make it possible to determine the source (Goering) through which Great Britain learned of Mussolini's decision not to intervene. (Because of Von Ribbentrop's suspicion that Ciano was responsible for this information leak, the Fascist later paid with his life in Verona for an action he did not take.) Henderson acquired the text of the German proposals to Poland, which Von Ribbentrop permitted him to glance at and on which he was able to report immediately in detail to London.

7

There is nothing in the experiences of the democracies analogous to the role of intelligence information in the totalitarian states. This may not be entirely the result of the fact that materials from the victors are less abundant. However, one cannot help being puzzled by what is already known of the events preceding Munich, Pearl Harbor, and Yalta. We know that London was aware of the plot of the German generals directed by the chief of the General Staff, Beck, to overthrow Hitler if he embarked on a war against Czechoslovakia; we know that Washington was promptly informed of the Japanese political and military directives on the eve of the attack of December 7, 1941, and of the Japanese Emperor's decision to bring to a rapid conclusion a war considered lost.[19] In these cases, was the failure to act on the information simply the result of lack of coordination between the various services, or did it reveal a tendency to be influenced by external factors, previously discussed, either publicly or in parliamentary debate, before the government made its decisions as to course of action? This is another question which should be added to those raised above, which are primarily intended to focus attention on a number of "specific problems" which seem worthy of particular consideration by future historians of the origins of World War II.

[18] Dahlerus, *The Last Attempt*, p. 106.

[19] What was the influence on Washington of the fact that the American decoding service was able to intercept the instructions sent by Tokyo to the Japanese Ambassador in Moscow to utilize the good offices of the Soviet government to bring about a cessation of hostilities in the Pacific? At present an accurate reply would be difficult. However, the impression does exist that one of the arguments employed to defend the dropping of the atomic bomb on Hiroshima is not entirely valid. It has been claimed that this decision was taken without knowledge of Japan's intention to cease resistance and was motivated by the desire to avoid the extremely high loss of lives which a landing in the Japanese islands would have involved. On the decodings, see Walter Miller, ed., *The Forrestal Diaries* (New York: The Viking Press, 1951), pp. 74–77; Robert J. C. Butow, *Japan's Decision To Surrender* (Stanford, Calif.: Stanford University Press, 1954), pp. 129–31; Herbert Feis, *The Atomic Bomb and the End of World War II* (Princeton, N.J.: Princeton University Press, 1966), pp. 67, 77, and 80–81; Kahn, *The Codebreakers*, p. 610.

088573